D1240692

572A $4.95

THE
THEOLOGY
OF THE
OLDER
TESTAMENT

THE THEOLOGY OF THE OLDER TESTAMENT

J. BARTON PAYNE

ZONDERVAN PUBLISHING HOUSE
GRAND RAPIDS   MICHIGAN

103707

THE THEOLOGY OF THE OLDER TESTAMENT
Copyright 1962 by
Zondervan Publishing House
Grand Rapids, Michigan

Second printing 1969
Third printing   1971

Library of Congress Catalog Card No. 62-13172

Printed in the United States of America

This volume is gratefully dedicated to
PROFESSOR JOHN MURRAY
orthodox scholar, Biblical theologian, and Christian
gentleman, who first introduced the writer to the
thrill of true Biblical theology and in conversation
with whom, at Westminster Seminary in the fall of
1948, was suggested an organization of Old Testament theology around the theme of the testament.

Preface

For the last ten years, in his teaching to seminary classes the great truths of the theology of the Old Testament, the writer has attempted to compensate for the lack of an adequate textbook of evangelical character by providing increasing amounts of supplementary material for his students. At the same time he has found it more and more essential to alter the arrangement of the subject matter, away from that found in existing textbooks to one that more nearly corresponds to the historical sequence and redemptive character of Biblical theology. Finally, in 1956, the writer had come to a point where he found it necessary to produce a completely independent syllabus of mimeographed lecture outlines. These outlines were sufficiently well received that he has felt encouraged to expand and convert them into the present book form.

The thesis of the following study is that God actively directs human history for the purpose of redeeming men to Himself. Objectively, He has accomplished our redemption once and for all by sending His Son Jesus Christ to die on the cross for man's sin. Subjectively, however, He mediates this salvation to mankind through the instrument of His covenant or, to use a more accurate term, His testament. It is the divine "last will" by which He bequeaths to His own people an inheritance of reconciliation to Himself, as they on their part fulfill its conditions of faith and obedience. Since there is only one saving death of Christ, it follows that there is only one testament. Chronologically considered, however, the testament possesses both an older aspect and a newer aspect. The difference between these two rests upon the historical question of whether the death of the Savior is still being anticipated or has become a matter of commemoration. The theology of the older testament thus describes the way of salvation and its conceptual implications, as God was pleased to reveal these facts during the ages prior to the coming of Christ. Since the record, however, of these revelations is preserved only in the Old Testament, and since the Old Testament on its part has as its all-embracing purpose the practical proclamation of God's plan of redemption (rather than the theoretical presentation of a system of doctrine), the theology of the older testament becomes in fact the theology of the Old Testament.

In approaching the Old Testament, the writer has made two assumptions: 1) that this book is the equivalent of God's words; and 2) that its teachings are binding upon Christian faith and practice.

The only exceptions to this latter assumption might relate to certain of the Old Testament ceremonies and to a few of the specific applications of its moral principles that concern ancient Near Eastern society (e.g., inheritance laws). The former assumption marks it as evangelical and distinguishes it from theological liberalism; the latter marks it as traditionally orthodox and distinguishes it from modern dispensationalism.

The study is intended as a guide and a textbook for Bible students. Accompanying each of its topics, there have been suggested approximately two chapters of relevant Bible reading and about forty pages of basic collateral work. A number of the footnotes are then designed to correlate the statements of the text with the positions that are presented in the collateral reading. The most frequent reference is made to Geerhardus Vos' excellent work, *Biblical Theology* (Grand Rapids: 1948). Vos, however, is somewhat incomplete and was outdated before it first came to be published. The purpose of the present book is therefore to make an inclusive survey of the teachings of the Old Testament, with numerous Scriptural references to be used as guides for further study. Biblical citations are generally taken from the American Standard Version of 1901, which is our most accurate English translation, though direct appeal is made to the Hebrew wherever required. References to contemporary literature have been kept to a minimum. The presuppositions that lie behind much of the liberal writing in the field forbid serious consideration by evangelical students of either its methodology or its conclusions. Suggestions for diversified further reading are, however, given at the end of each topic, with annotations as to the character of each of the articles cited. These works have been selected as representative of various theological positions, and they include also certain specialized studies on points of particular interest or importance. Books that cover the entire range of Old Testament theology are not singled out in the suggestions for each particular topic, for a complete, annotated list of English works is given at the close of the book. Reference should therefore also be made to these for further information on any given point.

Grateful acknowledgment is hereby made to Abingdon Press; Alec R. Allenson, Inc.; The Asbury Seminarian; Columbia University Press; Concordia Publishing House; Wm. B. Eerdmans Publishing Co.; The Evangelical Theological Society; Harper and Brothers; The Liturgical Press; Loizeaux Brothers, Inc.; The Macmillan Co.; Meridian Books, Inc.; Moody Press; New Brunswick Theological Seminary; The New Catholic Encyclopedia; Oxford University Press, Inc.; The Philosophical Library Publisher; The Presbyterian and Reformed Publishing Co.; St. Anthony Guild Press; Student Christian Movement Press, Ltd.; The Tyndale Press; The University of Chicago Press; Westminster Press; The Westminster Theological Journal; W. A.

Wilde Co.; and Yale University Press for the privilege of making quotations from their respective publications.

Many people today fail to appreciate the relevance of the theology of the older testament. Actually, however, its truths contain the permanent solutions to the greatest questions of human life, for "the grass withereth, the flower fadeth; but the word of our God shall stand forever" (Isa. 40:8). It is the writer's prayer that the one who reads the following synthesis may be led to follow the teaching of the Word with his whole mind and with his whole heart; for by so doing he will find guidance for daily life, hope for the future, and eternal salvation in Jesus Christ our Lord.

J. BARTON PAYNE

Wheaton College Graduate School of Theology
December, 1961

Contents

Contents

V. The Effectuation: Grace

VI. The Conditions: Commitment

VII. The Inheritance: Reconciliation

Appendices

CONTENTS

CONTENTS

Guide to the Pronunciation of Biblical Hebrew

Hebrew words, as they appear in the text, are written in transliteration in such a way as most closely, and yet most simply, to represent their English phonetic equivalents. These then appear alphabetically, with their Hebrew equivalents, in Index A.

Attention is directed to the following.

a — the "a" in mat	ai — might
ā — father	dh — the "th" in this
e — met	g — get
ē — mate	th — thin
i — mit	' (between consonants) — a reduced vowel, as
ī — machine	the "a" in barometer, "b'rometer"
o — ought	' (between vowels) — a break, as between the
ō — mote	two "o"s in cooperate, "co'operate"
u — put	
ū — rūle	

All Hebrew words are accented on the last syllable, unless otherwise noted, as *zéra*.

THE THEOLOGY OF THE OLDER TESTAMENT

Part I. The Communication of God's Will: Special Revelation

"Yahweh came from Sinai, and rose from Seir unto them. . . . He came from the ten thousands of holy ones: at His right hand was a fiery law for them" (Deuteronomy 33:2).

1. The Nature of Biblical Theology*

God directs human history. He created man to glorify Himself by doing His will. He continues to uphold and to govern all things by His providence. From the very beginning, moreover, He has employed special means to acquaint men with His sovereign design. Initially, God revealed His purposes for men's lives through direct communication, or by means of dreams or visions. In the course of history, He furnished men with a written record of His will for them, commencing with Moses and the "fiery law" from Sinai. Such facts are presupposed in a valid Biblical theology; and it is only upon such a basis that the aimlessness, uncertainty, and sin of the modern man can be resolved into a life of meaning and hope.

A. PRESUPPOSITIONS. Specifically, a Biblical theology that is true and real, that represents the Bible in a way consistent with its own teaching, has the following seven foundational assumptions.

1) *The historical existence of religion.* Men of every period have recognized sets of values for human living. This phenomenon is observable in all cultures, whatever may be one's individual evaluation of the religions concerned.

2) *The normativeness, or personally binding quality of religion,* as opposed to skepticism. This refers to the fact that a man must make a personal commitment to his set of values; he cannot restrict himself an impartial description of them.[1] Micah 6:8, for example, assumes both the reality of a known "good" and the necessity for

---

*BIBLE READING: I Kings 18; Hosea 11

Collateral Reading: Geerhardus Vos, Biblical Theology (Grand Rapids: Wm. B. Eerdmans Publishing Co., 1948), pp. 11-27.
Gustav F. Oehler, *Theology of the Old Testament.* Translated by George E. Day (Grand Rapids: Zondervan Publishing House, c. 1883), pp. 1-21.

---

[1]The objective vs. subjective religion of Geerhardus Vos, *Biblical Theology* (Grand Rapids: Wm. B. Eerdmans Publishing Co., 1948), p. 11.

15

human conformity to it. This sort of positiveness is satisfying and is preferable to an irresolution that is "ever learning and never able to come to the knowledge of the truth" (II Tim. 3:7). Even communism presents an appeal of faith and requirements which is more attractive to men than a barren skepticism.

3) *The existence of deity as ultimate truth*, as opposed to naturalistic atheism. The highest value must be a personal God (Gen. 1:1). Even ethical standards cannot substitute for deity. "Modernists" may assert that there is no heresy except in conduct,[2] but ethical truths prove incapable of motivating the very conduct that they stress. It is their reference to the Supreme Being that makes standards compulsive.

4) *The knowableness of divine truth*, as opposed to agnosticism. This does not assume that men can totally comprehend God (cf. Job 11:7b; Ps. 139:6; Rom. 11:33); but it does insist that God can truthfully communicate His will to men (e.g., I Kings 18:1). This may include propositional truths about Himself. Belief in the legitimacy of such communication stands in marked contrast to the theory of neo-orthodoxy, which limits God's contacts with men to "existential" encounters of personalities and which denies the possibility of the communication of factual knowledge. This latter view is thus but a specialized form of agnosticism. It is, moreover, inconsistent with the doctrinal truths it seeks to uphold. Creation, for example, demonstrates that the infinite can be and is in relationship with the finite; and, even as He created, God should be able to communicate, really though incompletely. Also, the continuing existence of God's image in man (Gen. 9:6) demonstrates a point of contact of God with man, so that God's absolute truths may be meaningful to him even with his limited perception (I Cor. 13:12).

5) *The fact of revelation*, as opposed to deism. By this we mean that God graciously makes Himself known to man (Rom. 1:19). Both because of the originally limited nature of man and because of the subsequently devastating effects of sin upon his mind (Eph. 4:17-19), man cannot hope to find out God by his own searching (Job 11:7a).

6) *The limitation of effective revelation to Scripture*, as opposed to rationalistic liberalism, Romanism, mysticism, and the cults. There is, confessedly, a general revelation of God, available to all in nature, history, and the heart (Ps. 19:1; Rom. 1:20). Man's sinfulness, however, has blinded him to it (Rom. 1:21, 28). It is only when God's Holy Spirit illumines a man through the special revelation of the Scrip-

---

[2]See J. Gresham Machen, *Christianity and Liberalism* (Grand Rapids: Wm. B. Eerdmans Publishing Co., 1946), pp. 19-21, 31. In James 1:27, "Pure religion and undefiled is this, to visit the fatherless," etc., the word for religion, *threskeia*, relates not to the essence of religion, but to the external forms of devotion. Ultimately, "as a man thinketh in his heart so is he" (Prov. 4:23; 23:7).

tures that the general revelation becomes meaningful for him (Ps. 19:7; 119:18).[3]

7) *The identification of the whole of Scripture with revelation,* as opposed to views of partial inspiration. All Scripture is God's words, and therefore without error in the inspired autographs (Acts 24:14). Neo-orthodoxy, as it works out in practice, indeed seeks to "pick and choose" among the teachings of the Word. But the will of God must be sovereign: only the mind that is yielded to receive the truths of Scripture as found in Scripture can sympathetically experience Christ's power to meet man's needs through Scripture (John 5:47).

The studies in this book will be based on these seven successive assumptions. Scripture itself, without so much as attempting proof, assumes them throughout.[4]

B. DEFINITION. Biblical theology may be defined as *the Biblical history of divine redemption.*

First, Biblical theology is *historical.* It deals with objective affairs and ideas, through a long succession of time periods. To take a major example, the nation of Israel was a) first raised up (Hos. 11:3) and then b) punished (v. 6). Chronology is therefore the organizing factor of Biblical theology. The ever-present and important question is, "When does any given event or concept appear?" In this connection it must be remembered that the point of occurrence may precede the composition of the Biblical books in which an event is related. For example, that which is related in Genesis 3:15 dates to Adam, not to the time of Moses who recorded it. The interpretation of an occurrence, however, may appear with its writing rather than with the event described. For example, the awareness of Satan as indicated in I Chronicles 21:1 dates to Ezra (?) who recorded it, not to David who held the census. Biblical theology is thus built on a time framework.

Second, Biblical theology is *divine;* i.e., it deals with divinity. The basic truth in Biblical theology is the reality of God, actively communicating His will in history (Ex. 20:1; I Kings 18:24, 39). It was because He had really freed the Hebrews from Egypt, and because He had answered Elijah with real fire, that Israel knew that "Yahweh[5] He is God!"

Arising from the divine character of Biblical theology are four corollary matters. 1) Biblical theology relates primarily to God. The Sinaitic testament, for example, was fundamentally God's binding

---

[3]Cf. Westminster Confession, I:1; John Calvin, *Institutes of the Christian Religion,* I:IV, VI. (Trans. by John Allen; 7th American ed.; Philadelphia: Presbyterian Board of Christian Education, [n.d.]).

[4]The latter three assumptions receive detailed Biblical description and are considered further under topics 3 and 4, Revelation and Inspiration.

[5]The very name Yahweh indicates His active presence, see topic 11. Note Gustav Oehler's excellent insistence upon Biblical religion as fact, not simply doctrine, *Theology of the Old Testament* (Grand Rapids: Zondervan Publishing House, c. 1883), pp. 6, 9-10, 13.

Himself to save Israel (Ex. 6:7; 19:4), though the fact that He confronted Israel with His law assumes certain effects that relate secondarily to man. 2) Since God both acts and thinks, Biblical theology is concerned with both a) the doings of God, active revelation (revealing), and then as a result b) His truths, static revelation [knowledge revealed] (cf. II Peter 1:16). The term "revelation" in both instances, of course, implies manward effects as well. For example, God's testament on Sinai resulted actively in things done for men: on earth Israel was granted possession of Canaan, and in eternity true Israelites inherit heaven's bliss. It also resulted statically in certain truths being revealed to men — e.g., the necessity of life-blood (Christ's) for reconciliation with God, and the illegitimacy of false witness.[6] 3) Since there is but one God, it follows that Biblical theology is an internally consistent unity, recorded under the guidance of one Spirit. 4) God has, however, spoken at different times in different ways (Heb. 1:1). As a result Biblical theology exhibits variety. It is a cumulative knowledge of the many facets of the living God. But because of the unity of Biblical theology, this variation never means theological replacement, correction, or self-contradiction (I Peter 1:10, 11). Instead, it means variety, supplementation, and clarification.

Third, Biblical theology is *redemptive*. Even now, current events furnish a clear demonstration of man's lost condition. But God is concerned about mankind's desperate plight. He is eager to come to man's rescue: "How shall I give thee up!" (Hos. 11:8). His purpose in history is to bring men back to Himself through Jesus Christ (II Cor. 5:19); and, historically, God's revelation has appeared only in conjunction with God's redemption.

To this, another four corollaries appear. 1) Since redemption at all times has been in Christ (John 14:6), Scripture presents but one plan of salvation. This is the most important single feature of the general unity of Biblical theology. 2) Since God's redemptive acts were progressive, preparing the way for Christ who should come in the fulness of time (Gal. 4:4), the accompanying truths that were revealed show in most cases a progressive development. That is, God graciously unfolded both His redemption and His revelation in ways corresponding to man's capacities to receive them (cf. Acts 17:30).[7] The variety of Biblical theology is therefore that of an organic interrelationship, which results in a growing appreciation of God's re-

---

[6]It is noteworthy that the static truth depends upon the active deed. Without the historical reality of the event, the principles drawn therefrom would have no proof and no real value. If the Israelites, in the above example, do not attain heaven, then not only is there no support for the doctrine of redemption through the blood (of Christ), but the doctrine itself is also seen to be false. Compare E. J. Young's insistence that if we are not studying genuinely divine revelations, then we are not studying theology — *The Study of Old Testament Theology Today* (London: J. Clarke, 1958), pp. 29-31.
[7]Cf. *Ibid.*, pp. 36, 37.

demptive plan. 3) Since redemption reaches its climax in Christ (Heb. 1:2), it is Christ who becomes the focal point of both the Old and New Testaments (Acts 10:43). Thus, when Judaism seeks to make the Old Testament an end in itself, it misses Christ who is its center, and therefore fails to grasp its true meaning (II Cor. 3:14-16). 4) Since men today need this same redemption that God has revealed in Scripture, Biblical theology constitutes an eminently practical guide to a God-blessed life of faith and practice.[8]

Fourth, Biblical theology derives its knowledge of the will of God from *the Bible*. It claims but one source of information: Scripture, the sixty-six canonical books of the Old and New Testaments. As the prophet Daniel put it, "I understood by the books" (9:2). The importance of this limitation lies in the fact that Scripture is the equivalent of special revelation. It is true that God historically used various means of special revelation — the Bible was itself one of these means. But the Bible is now the only extant record of the others.[9] Biblical theology is therefore equivalent to the history of special revelation.[10] The justification for this limiting of revelation to Scripture lies in the correlation that exists between revelation and redemption. God's concern is redemptive, and only with the historical unfolding of redemption has He seen fit to grant specific revelations. Redemption, moreover, is fully accomplished in Christ (Col. 2:10), the One who constitutes the ultimate exhibition of God (John 1:14). As a consequence, special revelation is completed for the present; and no Biblical theology is to be sought beyond the New Testament. Though its truths are reaffirmed today whenever a believer accepts Christ, there is no new revelational content.[11] Spirits that now speak to men may be recognized as of God, and not Satan, by their testimony to the historical Jesus as revealed in Scripture (I John 5:1, 2). Only with Christ's second coming to finish the application of redemption may corresponding revelations be anticipated.

C. Related Studies. Theological study as a whole divides itself into four major theological disciplines. These are: exegetical theology (the study of the Bible), historical theology (church history, missions), systematic theology (dogmatics, philosophy of religion), and practical theology (homiletics, Christian education etc.). Each division of these disciplines, in turn, has subdivisions. For example, under systematic

---

[8]See especially topic 29, Redeemed Life.
[9]Much of the apocrypha, the pseudepigrapha, and the writings of the Qumran community arose, indeed, in the historical period between the Testaments. But because of their non-inspired character, they cannot serve as sources for true Biblical theology. Roman Catholic authors are accustomed to disregard this distinction.
[10]Vos, *op. cit.*, p. 23.
[11]Compare Vos's distinction between objective-central redemption and subjective-individual redemption, *ibid.*, p. 14.

theology, dogmatics divides itself into theology,[12] Christology, eschatology, etc.

Biblical theology finds its place as a specific subdivision under
exegetical theology. The field of exegetical theology as a whole may
be analyzed as follows:

1) Background—the historical appreciation of the Bible
    Biblical geography   Biblical archaeology
    Ancient Near Eastern history   Religions of the Near East

2) Content—the textual appreciation of the Bible
    Hebrew, Aramaic, and Greek grammar   Related languages
    Hermeneutics (principles of Biblical interpretation)
    Exegesis (surveys, book studies, special passages)

3) Publication—the literary appreciation of the Bible
    General introduction: textual (lower) criticism; canonics
    Special introduction: higher criticism

4) Truth—the revelational appreciation of the Bible
    Biblical apologetics   Biblical theology

Each of the other exegetical subdivisions provides prerequisites
that are necessary for the construction of a valid Biblical theology.
The background studies make meaningful the life situations in which
God revealed Himself to His people. History was the medium of
divine revelation. Furthermore, it is our historical knowledge of the
religions of the pagans who surrounded Israel that serves to explain
certain terms or forms that God chose to use in His own true religion.
The very names of God in Biblical Hebrew, which is a Canaanitish
language, illustrate this point. Again, the errors of the pagan religions
serve both to underline the contrasting excellencies of the faith of the
saints[13] and to explain why similar superstitions came to arise among
the apostate in Israel. Scripture often describes such apostasy,
though only to condemn it (I Kings 18:26-28).

Concerning Biblical content, it is clear that a careful exegesis of
the text of Scripture, in its original languages and by sound hermeneutical principles, must precede the reformulation of its ideas in Biblical
theology. This, in turn, assumes the practice of sound textual criticism,
to reconstruct as closely as possible the readings of the original,
inspired manuscripts. It also presupposes the determination of the
canon, designating which books are the ones from God.[14]

Biblical theology is also greatly dependent upon higher criticism,
for it is the date critically assigned to a given Biblical writing that

[12]Note that "theology" may refer to religious study generally, or to the major
division of systematics, or to its subdivision on the specific doctrine of God.
[13]G. Ernest Wright, *The Old Testament Against Its Environment*, (Chicago: H.
Regnery Co., 1951).
[14]See J. B. Payne, *An Outline of Hebrew History* (Grand Rapids: Baker Book
House, 1954) for the Old Testament canon and the higher-critical placement of
its books.

helps determine the chronological position of its ideas.[15] This is the factor that renders relatively useless much of the modern writing in Biblical theology for one who believes the Bible. If, for example, the book of Leviticus is dated, not in the time of Moses, as Scripture states, but centuries or even a millennium later, as the liberal higher critics propose, then the chronology of revelation is thrown into chaos. In fact, the very existence of revelation as historical reality ceases. This in turn illustrates why Biblical apologetics is so significant; for it demonstrates the plausibility of the assertions of Scripture,[16] on the acceptance of which Biblical theology must be constructed. Built, as it is then, upon these prerequisite studies, Biblical theology stands as the crown of the discipline of exegetical theology.

Regarded from another angle, Biblical theology is the mid-point in a series of three theological studies which deal with the nature of religion: the history of the religion of Israel, Biblical theology, and systematic theology. At the same time it must be carefully distinguished from both of the others.

On the one hand there is the history of the religion of Israel, which belongs to the background division of exegetical theology. The study of Israel's religion may be considered along with that of the other religions of the Near East. It asks, "What did Israel believe?" It concerns human ideas. But although some of Israel's leaders were truly taught of God, even the best of them failed to grasp all that God had revealed (Dan. 12:8; I Peter 1:10, 11), and many of the common people were worse than the surrounding heathen (Jer. 2:11). Biblical theology, in contrast, belongs to the revelational division of exegetical theology. It asks, "What did God reveal?" To a great extent this may have been, at a given point in Israel's history, identical with the religious beliefs of Israel's spiritual leaders at that time. There is, however, a significant difference. Biblical theology consists of the sum total of God's ideas that had been revealed up to any given point. This eliminates all false human concepts (I John 1:5). It also adds truths, some of which may have been undiscoverable (Gen. 1) or even incomprehensible to the contemporary human insight (Dan. 12:8). For messages may be verbally revealed and recorded before being fully appreciated. "Revelation" must not be confused with a man's perhaps delayed understanding.

On the other hand, there is systematic theology, which builds upon exegetical theology, but which exists as a separate theological

---

[15]The reverse is also true: it is the theology that constitutes the prime factor in determining the placement of undated books, such as Job. Similarly, theology may serve to correct the exegesis of particular verses in the light of the teaching of the whole of Scripture and, above all, of Christ.
[16]Not that rational arguments "prove" Scripture: Scripture can only be accepted upon the authority of Christ, see p. 508. But apologetics does show the inconsistency of unbelief and confirms the believer in his God-given faith.

discipline. Systematic theology concerns timeless knowledge, without
direct reference to the circumstances of its communication. It asks,
"What is true of God?" It contains the same facts as Biblical theology,
for good systematic theology is Biblical! But it arranges them in a
topical synthesis, rather than in the order of their revelation as Biblical
theology does.

To demonstrate the difference between these three methods, we
may take the latter part of Psalm 2:7, "Yahweh said unto Me, 'Thou
art My Son; this day have I begotten Thee.'" The history of the
religion of Israel approaches this verse from a man-centered viewpoint. It is concerned with what these words may suggest concerning
the religious beliefs and the culture of the Hebrews and of the pagans
that surrounded them.

Antisupernaturalistic scholars restrict matters still further. They
regard this quotation from Psalm 2 as stating a concept which must
have evolved *naturally* in human thought, without reference to a
possible supernatural communication of ideas from God. One comes
almost to expect that when it was written it meant something entirely
different from what it subsequently has been interpreted to mean.
The following explanation of "Thou art My Son" is then typical of the
antisupernaturalistic history-of-religion method:

> The king was the appointed representative and agent of
> Yahweh. As such he was called Yahweh's son. In Psalm 2 (prob-
> ably the coronation ode of a king of Judah) the ruler is hailed as
> having just become God's son: . . . the "begetting" must mean
> adoption. . . . (This presupposes that these psalms were not
> originally meant to refer to the future Messiah.)[17]

Such reasoning, of course, refuses to consider the repeated teaching of
the New Testament that Psalm 2:7 does specifically describe the
Messiah. Acts 13:33, Hebrews 1:5 and 5:5, however, make it clear
that God, who knows the end from the beginning, had Christ in
mind when He had David write this Psalm, and that there were
those in the history of Israel who accepted this at face value. But the
antisupernaturalistic history-of-religion approach rules out God's mind.
It "presupposes" that what was "originally meant" must be limited to
the mind of the human author, or, more exactly, to the *antisupernaturalistic* reconstruction of what *might* have been in the mind of the
human author. In the history of Near Eastern religion, men's belief
in the adoption of kings by gods, or even in the deity of the kings,
was a common phenomenon. This same interpretation is therefore
assigned to Scripture and offered as the one valid explanation for
Psalm 2:7.

This methodology which is employed in the study of the history
of religions does incorporate one of the features of Biblical theology,

---

[17]Millar Burrows, *An Outline of Biblical Theology* (Philadelphia: The Westminster Press, 1946), p. 99.

namely that of its historical character. But it rejects the other three features: that Biblical theology is divine, redemptive, and Biblical. Moreover, even as valid Biblical theology may not incorporate from history what is untrue, so historical analogy must not be allowed to eliminate from Biblical theology the supernatural, or even the contemporaneously incomprehensible. Many of our so-called "Biblical theologies," by their very definition of the subject, tend to limit themselves to histories of religion. For example, Hermann Schultz asserts: "The question is . . . simply what form did religion take during the various stages of religious life in Israel up to the close of the apostolic period,"[18] and A. B. Davidson defines the subject as merely "the historical and genetic presentation of the religion of the Old Testament."[19] Much that is in these books is worthwhile and stimulating. But when they claim the right to reduce Biblical teachings to the level of contemporary concepts, humanly evolved and fallacious in nature, at such points they cease to contribute to Biblical theology. In the specific case, therefore, of Psalm 2:7, when it is discussed in the pages that follow,[20] scant notice will be granted to the "adoption of the king" theory, or to similar attempts that would restrict God's words to the category of human religious formulations.

True Biblical theology, by contrast, takes Psalm 2:7 at its face value and accepts it as a valid statement of God addressed to, and descriptive of, His Son, the Messiah. The following quotation serves to exemplify the methodology:

> In Psalm 2:7 the Messiah (the very word appears in v. 2) declares that Yahweh has said to Him, "You are my son, today I have begotten you." . . . The words, "You are my son," occur nowhere in the Old Testament in the sense of adoption. Only in Ps. 2:7 do we find the expression that God begot, or gave birth to a specific person. The Messiah accordingly is the Son of God in a most unique way.[21]

The method, then, of Biblical theology is concerned with what God reveals. It seeks to make an accurate synthesis of the information that God really made known at the time of the Psalm's composition. But more than this, Biblical theology does not, and should not, attempt. In the case, therefore, of Psalm 2:7, when the verse is considered below, its contributions are discussed within the topic, "The Messiah's Deity." But such ultimate truths as the Trinity, or the two natures of Christ, or Christ's status as eternally begotten of the Father do not there appear. These latter doctrines belong rather to the conclusions of systematic theology, the discipline which synthesizes the

---

[18]*Old Testament Theology.* Trans. by J. A. Paterson (2nd English ed.; Edinburgh: T. & T. Clark, 1898), I:2.
[19]*The Theology of the Old Testament* (Edinburgh: T. & T. Clark, 1925), p. 6.
[20]See below, pp. 261, 262.
[21]Paul Heinisch, *Theology of the Old Testament* (Trans. by William G. Heidt (Collegeville, Minnesota: The Order of St. Benedict, Inc., c. 1955), p. 347.

truths that concern God, whether revealed at the time of Psalm 2 or not.

Systematics, however, rightly asserts the doctrines of the Trinity and of the natures and status of Christ. It states them, moreover, not simply as what is true of God, but also as the explanation for the form of the words that God used to communicate His will in Psalm 2. A paragraph of Berkhof's systematics thus makes the following combination of doctrine and of Scriptural reference: "The eternal generation of the Son, Psalm 2:7 . . . [but it also adds] John 1:18."[22] The two references, together with others, produce the doctrine. Systematics thus accepts the features of the divine, the redemptive, and the Biblical character of Biblical theology. But by synthesizing revelations of diverse historical origin it no longer seeks to preserve the chronological framework of the latter discipline. Both methods must be employed with care and with understanding. Systematics must be on guard against using the Davidic verse without the Johannic proof text in accompaniment. Biblical theology, in turn, must guard itself against reading back into the Davidic revelation more than God had actually revealed at that time. Much was unknown, such as the pre-existence of Christ. But what was known, such as His unique, divine Sonship, was true and was precious. It was the·means for David's salvation; and it is still today the vital message of the God who confronts men with the requirement to "kiss the Son," or to "perish from the way" (v. 12).

For Further Reading:

Bernard Ramm, *The Pattern of Authority.* Grand Rapids: Wm. B. Eerdmans Publishing Co., 1957. A summary of the evangelical presuppositions of revelation and knowledge.

Robert C. Dentan, *Preface to Old Testament Theology.* New Haven: Yale University Press, 1950. Part II. A Neo-orthodox approach to the nature of Biblical theology.

Francis L. Patton, "Theological Encyclopaedia," *Princeton Theological Review,* 2:1 (Jan., 1904), 110-136. His stimulating inaugural address on the interrelationship of the theological disciplines.

---

[22]Louis Berkhof, *Textual Aid to Systematic Theology* (Grand Rapids: Wm. B. Eerdmans Publishing Co., 1942), p. 72.

2. The History of Old Testament Biblical Theology*

A. PREPARATIONS. The Old Testament was appreciated by its contemporaries as a revelation from God, and it was used by its own later writers as a theological source book (Ps. 78; Jer. 26:18; Ezra 7:10; Neh. 8:1-8). Jesus Christ regularly spoke from it as the basis and description of His own teaching and work (Matt. 5:17; Luke 4:17-21; 24:27). The apostolic circle, including the New Testament writers, studied it as prophetic of the Savior (Acts 3:24). They stressed the truth of God's previous activity in Israel's history (Acts 7; 13:16-41) and drew from the Old Testament much of their preaching to the New Testament church (Acts 2:16, 25; Matt. 1:22). There is no record, however, of Biblical theology as an organized study. Judaism developed methods of literal Bible study, but its insights became perverted by the legalistic casuistry of the Pharisees. Jewish traditions made void the original word of God (Mark 7:13). Later this legalism degenerated even further into a "letterism" and into a stress upon Biblical numerics, known as Cabbalism, and into the self-righteous theology of the Talmud. The Jews, by rejecting the redemption which is in Christ Jesus, cut themselves off from the true understanding of God's revelation.

The early patristic Church, with its sense of the historical accomplishment of salvation, gave promise of developing a true Biblical theology. Its first author of note was Irenaeus (about A.D. 180), the pupil of Polycarp who had been the pupil of the apostle John himself. Irenaeus not only laid the foundations for the theology of the Church, he also wrote as an essentially Biblical theologian. In particular, he emphasized the unity that is found within God's progressive revelation. He asserted:

> After this fashion also did a presbyter, a disciple of the apostles, reason with respect to the two testaments, proving that both were truly from one and the same God. . . . For all these do not contain or imply an opposition to and an overturning of the

---

* BIBLE READING: Psalm 14; Proverbs 2:1-9; 3:13-35; Obadiah 1-4

Collateral Reading: Charles T. Fritsch, "New Trends in Old Testament Theology," *Bibliotheca Sacra.* 103:411 (July-Sept., 1946), pp. 293-305.
Norman W. Porteous, "Old Testament Theology," in H. H. Rowley, *The Old Testament and Modern Study* (Oxford: Clarendon Press, 1951), pp. 311-344.

[precepts] of the past . . . but a fulfilling and an extension of them.[1]

Augustine in his *City of God*, Books 15-17 (about A.D. 425), went further and proceeded to analyze Old Testament revelation on the basis of five historical periods. But the patristic Church had also inherited from Alexandrian Judaism an allegorical method of interpreting the Old Testament. Such allegorizing was carried to extremes by Origen in the third century; and, with the eventual triumph of the allegorical method, theology came to be divorced from the literal history of Israel. Then, with the replacement of Biblical authority by that of ecclesiastical tradition under medieval Roman Catholicism, Biblical theology was condemned to abeyance for over one thousand years.

The Protestant Reformation in the sixteenth century re-established two principles that were prerequisites to the development of Biblical theology. The first was the principle of "the analogy of Scripture." It denied the right of the Church, the pope, or any other human agency to establish the interpretation of Scripture. Interpretation, according to this principle, can come only from other Scriptures; that is, it is the Lord who must give the true wisdom of Himself (Prov. 2:6). The second was the principle of "the literal sense." This, in turn, eliminated the allegorizing that had dominated the Middle Ages; and it made possible a revival of interest in the truly historical development of revelation. Exegesis now came into its own, based upon the original languages of Scripture. The commentaries and Biblically oriented theology of John Calvin set an all-time standard, with permanent relevance. But the conflict with Roman sacerdotalism led the reformers into an understandable emphasis upon the final results of theology, rather than upon its historically earlier stages. They tended, accordingly, to seek the details of New Testament doctrine in the Old.[2]

It was over a century later that John Cocceius (1603-1669) made the first serious advance since Augustine in relating theology to God's historical activity. Best known for his "federal theology," he sought to develop a Biblical approach to doctrine, as opposed to the then preva-

[1]*Against Heresies*, IV:13, 1; 32:1, Alexander Roberts and James Donaldson, eds., *The Ante-Nicene Fathers* (New York: The Christian Literature Co., 1896), Vol. I. See the writer's study in the Evangelical Theological Society volume, *Inspiration and Interpretation*, John F. Walvoord, ed. (Grand Rapids: Wm. B. Eerdmans Publishing Co., 1957), chap. 1.
[2]Note that the reformation belief in the doctrinal unity of the Testaments, far from excluding a proper appreciation of the true meaning of the Old Testament, as claimed by Charles T. Fritsch, "New Trends in Old Testament Theology," *Bibliotheca Sacra*. 103:411 (July-Sept., 1946), p. 294, is actually the only basis for grasping the real meaning of Scripture. Calvin's understanding of the "covenant" is particularly significant in this regard; cf. John Murray, *The Covenant of Grace* (London: Tyndale Press, 1953), pp. 3, 4. Some of the reformers, however, did assume from the harmony of the Testaments an unwarranted completeness of revelation in the Old.

lent dogmatic approach. Furthermore, by organizing his thought around God's successively revealed covenants, he indeed grasped Scripture's own key to the progress of divine revelation. Cocceius stressed two major covenants: 1) the covenant of works, with Adam in his innocency, and 2) the covenant of grace, concerning God's redemptive activity with fallen man. The latter he organized into three dispensations: before the law, the law, and the Gospel. But despite his basic insight, the actual exegesis of Cocceius was often arbitrary and was characterized by an excessive use of typology. Throughout the seventeenth and eighteenth centuries God's historical revelation was overshadowed by the dogmatic systems of the orthodox, the antisupernaturalistic denials of the rationalists, and the exclusive devotionalism of the pietists. Johann Bengel, indeed, attempted to relate practical piety to salvation as experienced in history.[3] Bengel stressed the progressive stages in revelation in his *Ordo Temporum*, 1741; but he exerted little permanent influence.

B. NINETEENTH CENTURY OLD TESTAMENT THEOLOGY. Biblical theology, as a distinct discipline, is new — less than 200 years old. Its birth is marked down at the inaugural oration (in 1787) of John Philip Gabler, "Concerning the Correct Distinction Between Biblical and Dogmatic Theology." Gabler described Biblical theology as "the religious ideas of Scripture as an historical fact, so as to distinguish the different times and subjects, and so also the different stages in the development of these ideas." This distinction of course required the separation of Old Testament from New Testament theology. The first theology of the Old Testament was then that of Lorenz Bauer in 1796. Gabler's motivation, however, for a distinct Biblical theology sprang from his own rationalistic distrust of the supernatural. He refused to equate the thought of the Old Testament writers with true theology, nor would he accept supernaturalistic interpretations for the historical phenomena exhibited by Scripture. Bible-believing scholars were therefore slow to recognize the possibilities that lay in the employment of progressive revelation, to confirm rather than to explain away the supernatural. It was E. W. Hengstenberg who first demonstrated the value of Old Testament theology in his monumental *Christology of the Old Testament*, published in 1829-35 and revised in 1854-57.[4] Liberal writers have indeed criticized Hengstenberg's work as a reading of New Testament Christology back into the Old Testament. At most points, however, his exegesis is careful and represents the revelations that God actually made. The presuppositions of disbelievers simply prohibit them from acknowledging such revelations as historic!

---

[3]Cf. his position as the first modern premillennial scholar.
[4]English translation by Theod. Meyer and James Martin; reprinted, Grand Rapids: Kregel Publications, 1956, 4 vols.

Hengstenberg's *History of the Kingdom of God under the Old Testament* was published posthumously in 1869-71.[5]

Other significant works to appear in this field were Hävernick's incomplete lectures on Old Testament theology, 1848; Kurtz's *History of the Old Covenant*, 1853-58;[6] and Auberlen's *Divine Revelation*, 1864.[7] Hävernick's work was revised in 1863 by Hermann Schultz; and then in 1869 appeared Schultz's own significant *Old Testament Theology*.[8] This two-volume work is a thorough study that traces the thought of the Old Testament, first chronologically and then topically. It exhibits a general reliability, though parts do show a tendency to question the divine normativeness of Old Testament religion. The last important work to come from the Continent was Gustav Oehler's *Old Testament Theology*, 1873-74.[9] This study is still one of the two most adequate, complete treatments of the subject. Only at scattered points, such as on the theory of sacrifice, or on life after death, does Oehler fail to do justice to the divine character of the Biblical record. An abridgement of his work was published by R. F. Weidner under the title *Biblical Theology of the Old Testament* in Chicago in 1886. Four works from Britain are to be noted. W. L. Alexander's *System of Biblical Theology* (1888) covered both the Old and New Testaments, but it is more systematic than Biblical. W. H. Bennett produced *The Theology of the Old Testament* (London: Hodder and Stoughton, 1896), a handbook that made broad concessions to radical criticism. In first place stands A. B. Davidson's *The Theology of the Old Testament*, a study that was edited from Davidson's papers by S. D. F. Salmond and published posthumously in Edinburgh, 1904. It has probably had more influence than any other book in English on the subject. Though it claims to accept the destructive higher criticism of the Old Testament, Geerhardus Vos remarked:

> Dr. Davidson's views in regard to the content of the truth of the Old Testament were substantially worked out in a period previous to his aligning himself with the modern hypothesis. Afterward the critical conclusions were superimposed, but they did not have time materially to reshape the body of doctrinal convictions.[10]

[5]English translator not named; Edinburgh: T. & T. Clark, 1872, 2 vols.

[6]English translation, Vol. I, by Alfred Edersheim, vols. II-III, by James Martin; Philadelphia: Lindsay & Blakeston, 1859.

[7]English translation by Rev. A. B. Paton; Edinburgh: T. & T. Clark, 1867. Auberlen is characterized by a careful premillennialism.

[8]Second English edition, translated by J. A. Paterson; Edinburgh: T. & T. Clark, 1898, 2 vols.

[9]Translated by George E. Day; Grand Rapids: Zondervan Publishing House, c. 1883.

[10]"Reviews of Recent Literature," *Princeton Theological Review*, 4:1 (Jan., 1906), pp. 115-120; and cf. the comments by Proteous, "Old Testament Theology," in H. H. Rowley, *The Old Testament and Modern Study* (Oxford: Clarendon Press, 1951), p. 314.

In the same year, and British in origin though published in New York, appeared C. F. Burney's *Outlines of Old Testament Theology*, a survey which is more consistently liberal in outlook. The first American work was a small volume by Robert V. Foster of Tennessee, entitled *Old Testament Studies, an Outline of Old Testament Theology* (New York: 5, 1890). The book was evangelical, though brief, "badly written and poorly printed."[11]

C. HISTORICISM. Davidson's *Theology* marked the practical end of valid Biblical theology in Britain. Belief in God's communication had been overshadowed by a rising cloud of historicism. The "historicists," as a school of interpretation, limited Scripture to a history of religion: the Bible became a product of human, evolutionary development, and not of supernatural revelation. Gabler himself had set up Biblical theology as a counterpoise against the supernaturalism of dogmatic theology. Historicism then proceeded to adapt New Testament theology to its own ends by creating the well-known contrast between the simple "religion of Jesus" and the invalid "accretions" of Paulinism. In reference to the Old Testament, even Lorenz Bauer's initial Old Testament theology of 1796 set a fatal pattern; for it evaluated certain aspects of Old Testament thought as but "the weaker philosophy of the Hebrews."[12] G. P. C. Kaiser's "Biblical theology," 1813-21, was specifically written for those

> . . . who, refusing to believe that any one Church is in sole possession of salvation, are learning to find out and appreciate the honest worshipper of the Divine in every age and clime, whose religion is neither Judaism, Christianity, Mohammedanism, nor Paganism, but religious Universalism, Catholicism, in the true sense of the word, what our theologians call perfectible Christianity.[13]

The demonic element, therefore, in historicism was not its stress upon the historical, for Christianity itself must be historical if it is to be true. Nor was it historicism's emphasis upon the comparative history of the various Near Eastern religions, for God's people had constantly to recognize and to resist such pagan inroads. The evil lay in the historicist's underlying assumption that God did not really communicate His will, that only what could be explained upon a theory of religious evolution might be considered historical, and that Biblical truths must stand trial before the bar of human rationalism. Thus, like the Edomites of old, "the pride of their heart deceived them" (Obad. 3).

But pride is appealing, and historicism came increasingly to dominate Biblical scholarship. It arose first in Germany and penetrated subsequently into the English speaking world. Its advocates included

---

[11]Robert C. Dentan, *Preface to Old Testament Theology* (New Haven: Yale University Press, 1950), p. 32.
[12]Oehler, *op. cit.*, p. 34.
[13]Schultz, *op. cit.*, I:83.

scholars like the moderate De Wette, 1813; Vatke, who in 1835 applied Hegelian philosophy to Scripture; and Von Cölln, whose classic Biblical theology appeared in the following year. In 1869 Kuenen introduced the Graf-Wellhausen concept, which claimed for the prophets a position prior, historically, to that of the Pentateuchal priestly legislation; and in 1880 Hitzig denied special revelation altogether. Then came such historicists as Kayser, Piepenbring,[14] and Reuss, 1886; Smend, 1893; Budde, 1900; Marti, 1907; and Kautzsch, 1911. Later works in English included H. P. Smith, *The Religion of Israel* (New York: Charles Scribner's Sons, 1914); J. P. Peters, *The Religion of the Hebrews* (Boston: Ginn & Co., 1914); H. T. Fowler, *The Origin and Growth of the Hebrew Religion* (Chicago: University of Chicago Press, 1917); and G. A. Barton, *The Religion of Israel* (New York: 1919). There were a host of others.

The very names of these books indicate the historicism of their contents. Others employed the term "theology" in their titles or have been sometimes classified as Biblical theologies; but they would hardly suggest themselves to be studies of a historically true revelation. These latter include Ewald's *Old and New Testament Theology*, 1871-76,[15] four volumes that are more of a philosophy than a theology; Duff's *Old Testament Theology* (1891), which is simply another history of religion; H. Wheeler Robinson's *The Religious Ideas of the Old Testament* (London: Duckworth, 1913); and Albert C. Knudson's *The Religious Teaching of the Old Testament* (New York: The Abingdon Press, 1918). Among the leading recent representatives of historicism in English are W. O. E. Oesterley and T. H. Robinson's *Hebrew Religion: Its Origin and Development* (2nd edition; New York: The Macmillan Co., 1937), a thorough work that seeks to trace the evolution of the Old Testament religion from animism, fetishism, etc., up through polytheism, to monotheism. Harry Emerson Fosdick's *A Guide to Understanding the Bible: the Development of Ideas within the Old and New Testaments* (New York: Harper and Brothers, 1938) has popularized such evolutionary religious concepts for the liberal layman. Theophile J. Meek, in his *Hebrew Origins* (Revised edition; New York: Harper and Brothers, 1950), propounds such blasphemous theories as the "origin" of Yahweh as a Kenite god. Finally Charles H. Patterson's *The Philosophy of the Old Testament* (New York: The Ronald Press Co., c. 1953) presents an unoriginal and outdated history of religion by an antitheistic philosopher, while Robert H. Pfeiffer's posthumous *Religion in the Old Testament* (edited by C. J. Formen; New York: Harper and Brothers, 1961) epitomizes the most extreme conclusions of liberal criticism.

---

[14]*Theology of the Old Testament*. Trans. by H. G. Mitchell (New York: Thomas Y. Crowell, 1893).
[15]English translation by T. Goadby; Edinburgh: T. & T. Clark, 1888.

In sharp reaction against godless historicism, there arose in nineteenth century Europe the two movements of German *Heilsgeschichte* and Plymouth Brethren dispensationalism. Each contained a measure of truth, but each suffered under serious defects as well. In Erlangen, Germany, J. C. K. Hofmann, whose writings commenced in the year 1841, founded the school of *Heilsgeschichte*, or "Sacred History." Hofmann's interpretation emphasized the truth of God's redemptive activity in history; and it laid stress upon the organic and progressive development of salvation, experienced throughout the Old Testament. The focal point of "Sacred History" was seen in the person of Christ, first in His incarnate ministry, but also in His yet future millennial rule.[16] This Christ-honoring approach of *Heilsgeschichte* was welcome indeed. But Hofmann then allowed his emphasis upon sacred events to practically exclude the corollary doctrine of God's written revelation, which is so necessary if men are to comprehend what God has done. Furthermore, because the word had become overshadowed by the event, Hofmann was willing to accept, to some extent, historicism's destructive criticism of Scripture.

A number of able theologians were influenced by the Erlangen school. For example, the Old Testament scholar Franz Delitzsch (d. 1890) is considered a product of *Heilsgeschichte* theology. Its last consistent exponent at Erlangen, however, was Philip Bachmann, who died in 1931, and *Heilsgeschichte* has ceased to exist as a distinct movement. It is represented today chiefly by Otto Piper of Princeton (cf. his *God in History*, New York: The Macmillan Co., 1939). Piper maintains the reality of the supernatural in history, but he rejects the verbal inspiration of the Bible.[17] Indirectly, however, the theory of *Heilsgeschichte* continues to exert considerable influence. It has become the theological dynamic for a number of critical scholars who, in recent years, have set out in quest for something more satisfying than barren historicism. A typical example is seen in G. Ernest Wright's pamphlet, *God Who Acts*.[18] By and large, the attempt of *Heilsgeschichte* to preserve sacred events while minimizing the sacred record has been assimilated into the general movement of neo-orthodoxy.

At about the same time as Hofmann, there arose in England the movement of Plymouth Brethren dispensationalism. The real founder of Brethren theology was John N. Darby (1800-82), the author of five volumes entitled *Synopsis of the Books of the Bible* (New York: Loizeaux Brothers, 1942). Brethrenism commenced as a protest against the liberalism and the apathy toward eschatology that characterized

---

[16]Cf. Christian Preus' article, "The Contemporary Relevance of von Hofmann's Hermeneutical Principles," *Interpretations*, IV:3 (July, 1950), 311-321.
[17]Cf. Bernard Ramm's discussion in the revised edition of his *Protestant Biblical Interpretation* (Boston: W. A. Wilde, Co., 1956), pp. 79-83.
[18]*Studies in Biblical Theology*, No. 8 (Chicago: H. Regnery, 1944).

the Church of England of those days. The movement grew and eventually rejected as apostate the whole concept of church organization and of the ordained ministry. It distinguished sharply between the true, Pauline Church and the "professing" church, which was associated with Peter and the Hebrew Christians. This distinction, in turn, seriously affected the Brethren in their study of Old Testament theology, because the very thought of connections between Christians and organized Israel had become abhorrent. The Church was wholly divorced from Israel: either Israel past, which included the Old Testament and the New Testament up to Palm Sunday, or Israel future, which included the Old Testament predictions of the future earthly kingdom. This divorce, however, sacrificed the unity, both of Scripture and of the very plan of salvation. The Lord's Prayer could not be used in church, because it belonged to Israel's "dispensation." But the liberal-mythological concept of an Old Testament *hades* could be unhesitatingly adopted, because what happened to dead Israelites was a matter distinct from the fate of Christians at their death.

Plymouth Brethren dispensationalism has been widely popularized, particularly through the notes of the *Scofield Reference Bible;*[19] but until recently it has been without serious scholarly support. Meanwhile, however, the dark night of an antisupernaturalistic historicism was settling over the Church. For almost half a century following the posthumous appearance of Oehler's work in 1873, Protestant Germany failed to produce a single Biblical theology. One might well have wondered, in the inspired words of David, "if there were any that did understand, that did seek after God" (Ps. 14:2).

D. NEO-ORTHODOXY. All was not well, however, in Germany. A perverted historicism had eliminated God from history. But the insufficiency of the man-made religion with which it left its followers was made all too clear by the disillusionment that followed upon Germany's defeat in World War I. Something would have to be found for bewildered mankind that would ring with a clearer note of authority than had the hypotheses of evolutionary naturalism. But, instead of a consistent Biblical Christianity, what has risen to fill the gap is the half-faith, variously described as "neo-supernaturalism," "crisis theology," or "Barthianism." Its most common designation, however, is "neo-orthodoxy." Neo-orthodoxy appeared officially with the publication of Karl Barth's commentary on Romans in 1919, the year, significantly, that followed the European armistice.

Both Barth and Emil Brunner, the two leading neo-orthodox spokesmen, recognize their intellectual debt to the subjectivism of certain pietistic leaders of the preceding century and particularly to

---

[19]Cf. Oswald T. Allis, *Prophecy and the Church* (Philadelphia: The Presbyterian and Reformed Publishing Co., 1945), pp. 7-15.

the religious philosopher, Kierkegaard.[20] The proper appreciation of neo-orthodoxy's approach to Biblical theology must, therefore, begin with an understanding of certain Kierkegaardian, or "existential," philosophical and theological tenets; for these constitute the key to the movement as a whole. Kierkegaard had concluded, "Subjectivity is truth," and subjectivism has indeed become the foundation stone for neo-orthodoxy and for the philosophies of extentialism in general. Existentialists, the non-Christian as well as the Christian, are alike committed to belief in the autonomous freedom of human personality[21]—that is, man's own feelings and mystical experiences have become for them the final measure of truth. Kierkegaard was extreme in his individualism: he refused to be bound by rational laws or other standards, and he considered any commitment to norms that were external to himself to be a denial of true "existence."[22]

Karl Barth was responsible for bringing this kind of subjectivism into its present prominent position within theological thought. On the one hand, he sharply condemned liberal Protestantism, with its evolutionary historicism. Liberalism, he charged, had denied the reality of the transcendent God and had substituted a barren rationalism. But at the same time, he attacked traditional orthodoxy even more bitterly. Orthodoxy, he observed, has unswervingly insisted that the Bible is God's objective word to man. Existentialism, however, was committed to the position that God, the ultimate reality, could be known only in certain subjective encounters of personalities. He was "wholly other," and it was unthinkable that His words could ever serve as objects for human analysis. Barth insisted that the Bible *was* not the Word of God; it could only *"become* the Word of God." By this he meant that as it was read, the Bible might become the medium for an existential event, the encounter of the living God with a man.[23]

---

[20]Brunner spoke for both Barth and himself: "For the best which we had when we started we were indebted, humanly speaking, to . . . Pietism . . . and Kierkegaard, in conflict against a false Objectivism," *The Divine-Human Encounter.* Trans. by A. W. Loos (Philadelphia: The Westminster Press, c. 1943), pp. 39-40. Used by permission.

[21]J. M. Spier, *Christianity and Existentialism.* Trans. by David H. Freeman (Philadelphia: Presbyterian and Reformed Publishing Co., c. 1953), pp. 5, 6.

[22]*Ibid.,* p. 8; cf. p. 9, "Temporal man is confronted by God and stands before Him in despair and faith; and this *is to exist.*"

[23]Karl Barth, *The Doctrine of the Word of God.* Trans. by G. T. Thompson (New York: Charles Scribner's Sons, 1936), pp. 124-125. Even in his later modifications, Barth still restricts the real "Word" of God to the area of subjective encounter: "Christian faith is the meeting with this 'Immanuel,' the meeting with Jesus Christ and in Him with the living Word of God. In calling Holy Scripture the Word of God (and we so call it, because it is so), we mean by it Holy Scripture as the witness of the prophets and the apostles to this one Word of God, to Jesus," *Dogmatics in Outline.* Trans. by G. T. Thompson (New York: Philosophical Library, 1949), p. 17. Evangelicals, of course, recognize the need for a personal meeting with the "Word," Jesus Christ; without it orthodoxy would be dead. But He is not the only Word. The true believer insists on the objective written Word of God as well, for the facts of Scripture form the prerequisite to

Barth thus limited divine revelation to personal experiences; it could not include objective communications of God's will, capable of being grasped by men.

Negatively, then, Barth opposed both the liberals and the conservatives. As Van Til has summarized his position, "All theologians who claim in any sense to possess the truth are thrown on the theological scrapheap."[24] Yet, positively, Barth and his followers in neo-orthodoxy have usurped certain appealing features from both of these other groups. From the liberals they have taken over the liberty (so satisfying to the human ego!) of denying the supernatural events and teachings of Scripture, whenever they have felt such a course to be advantageous. The neo-orthodox have thus accepted the same destructive Biblical criticism that characterized the older liberalism.[25] Historical reliability, after all, becomes a matter of secondary significance when religion is defined in terms of personal experiences, rather than in terms of objective facts. From Bible-believing evangelicals, however, they have taken over the proclamation of such gospel affirmations as seem needful to the present plight of mankind. The neo-orthodox have thus insisted upon the great doctrines of the sovereignty of God, the sinfulness of man, and the need for redemption through faith in Jesus Christ. They rightly understood that only such preaching as stressed these doctrines could fill the religious void that had become so obvious in Germany in 1919 and in the years that followed.

The situation that produced Karl Barth in theology led to similar results in the Biblical field. In 1921 Rudolf Kittel, himself a historicist, wrote concerning Old Testament studies, "The foundation is failing for the building and there is no plumb-line."[26] Historicism, that is, had proved unable to meet the human needs. The very next year, indeed, witnessed the publishing of a theology of the Old Testament by Eduard König, the first of its kind since Oehler's. The book consisted of a conservatively oriented survey of Israel's history, followed by an explanatory synthesis (more systematic than historical) of the dominating ideas. Otto Eissfeldt's study followed in 1926. Eissfeldt

---

any acceptable personal meeting with God. The Bible must not be limited to a "witness" to the living God; it must itself be God's real words, as Jesus Himself claimed it to be.

[24]Cornelius Van Til, *The New Modernism* (Philadelphia: The Presbyterian and Reformed Publishing Co., 1946), p. 1.

[25]"We owe a profound debt of gratitude to the historical criticism that has made it quite impossible to maintain . . . this mistaken faith in the Bible," Emil Brunner, *Revelation and Reason.* Trans. by Olive Wyon (Philadelphia: The Westminster Press, c. 1946), p. 168. Used by permission. Cf. Van Til's evaluation in B. B. Warfield, *The Inspiration and Authority of the Bible* (Philadelphia: The Presbyterian and Reformed Publishing Co., 1948), pp. 59-66.

[26]Fritsch, *op. cit.,* p. 297. Cf. T. W. Manson's chapter in C. W. Dugmore, ed. *The Interpretation of the Bible* (London: Dulwich College, 1944), which is significantly entitled "The Failure of Liberalism."

categorically denied the possibility of any real activity of God in history, just as had the historicists. At the same time, however, he tried to maintain a theology that was "real" in the existential sense, but subjective and totally distinct from history.[27]

In the ten years following Eissfeldt, there did appear in Germany three major works of genuine Old Testament theology. No one of their writers was willing to accept the whole of the Old Testament as God's truth, but each did find within it certain teachings that were considered divinely significant. The most important was Walther Eichrodt's three-volume work, *Theologie des alten Testaments* (Leipzig: J. C. Hinrichs, 1933-39). The theme around which his book centers is that of the reality of God's covenant with Israel; that, as we would say, our redemption comes about as an inheritance, through a death (Christ's). Eichrodt himself is not committed to this "testamentary" concept; but, particularly in his first volume, he does show real insight into the function of the covenant as the unifying element in divine revelation. He views it, and rightly so, as the great historical relationship between God and man, on the basis of which all the rest of Old Testament theology unfolds. This insight constituted a major step forward in appreciating the truth that Cocceius had been the first to recognize. It will be further elaborated in this present study. Ernst Sellin's two-volume work, *Alttestamentliche Theologie auf Religionsgeschichtlicher Grundlage* (Leipzig: Quelle and Meyer, 1933) commences, as indicated by its title, as a history of religion. But it then moves on to accept as true theology such teachings as Sellin feels to be fulfilled in the Gospel. Its particular stress is upon the holiness of God. Ludwig Kohler's *Theologie des alten Testaments* (Tubingen: Mohr, 1936)[28] seeks to bring unity out of the variety of the Old Testament by focusing on the thought of God as Lord. The full works of Eichrodt and Sellin have not yet appeared in English;[29] but the theological effect of these three men has been revolutionary.[30]

German neo-orthodoxy recognized man's need for the Word of God, for a Bible that possessed divine authority beyond the uncertainties of human philosophy, and for a Christ who could save from the frustrations of human relativism. Thus Otto Procksch, who was

[27]Cf. Millar Burrows, *What Mean These Stones?* (New Haven: American Schools of Oriental Research, 1941; copyright 1956 by Millar Burrows; Living Age Books Edition copyright 1957 by Meridian Books; reprinted by permission of the author and Meridian Books), "Religious truth is one thing; historical fact is another. Neither necessarily presupposes or accompanies the other," p. 4, a position that leaves religion unreal and man, who is in history, unhelped.
[28]English translation by A. S. Todd; Philadelphia: Westminster Press, 1957.
[29]Except for Eichrodt's brief *Man in the Old Testament (Studies in Bible Theology)*, No. 4, trans. by K. and R. Gregor Smith (Chicago: H. Regnery, 1951) and Vol. I of *Theology of the Old Testament*, trans. by J. A. Baker (Philadelphia: Westminster Press, 1961).
[30]Cf. John Lowe's essay, "The Recovery of the Theological Interpretation of the Bible," in Dugmore, *op. cit.*, final chapter.

closely associated with Eichrodt, insisted upon the unity of the
Testaments (1950); and both T. C. Vriezen (1949)[31] of Holland and
Edmond Jacob (1955)[32] of France maintain that the Old Testament
is to be understood only from its fulfillment in Jesus Christ. Some
recent studies, such as *The Witness of the Old Testament to Christ*
by Karl Barth's disciple, Wilhelm Vischer,[33] appear almost as the
work of Bible believers. Some of the above writers, moreover, are
not technically neo-orthodox in the sense of being committed to
Barth's existential epistemology. All, however, support his crusade
against the optimistic rationalism of the older historicism. Eichrodt,
for example, reviewed Fosdick's *Guide to the Understanding of the
Bible* as a relic of antiquated thinking.[34] But what is more significant,
these writers have, with Barth and Brunner, continued to cling to the
destructive higher criticism that identified Wellhausen and his followers. They reserve the right to reject any and all of the supernaturalistic elements of the Old Testament that they consider to be rationally untenable. Further, they not only question the divine nature of
much of Scripture; they even demand the total abandonment of the
reformation principle of "the analogy of Scripture." Only so may one
construct "Biblical theology in the modern sense!"[35] Thus, it is
maintained, one can be as intellectually self-determining as the rankest
liberal and yet preach salvation with all the authority of a Bible-
believer. The combination, however, is an unstable one. It appears as
a temporary accommodation, created by unique historical pressures.
That is, had there been no World War I, followed within a generation
by a World War II, self-determining man would doubtless have had
no such appreciation of his need for salvation and for authority. More
fundamentally, to reject the principle of the analogy of Scripture is to
reject the truth of the uniformly divine character of Scripture and to

[31]*An Outline of Old Testament Theology*. Trans. by S. Neuijen (Newton, Mass.:
Charles T. Branford Co., 1958).
[32]*Theology of the Old Testament*. Trans. by A. W. Heathcote and P. J. Allcock
(New York: Harper & Brothers, 1958).
[33]English translation by A. B. Crabtree from 3rd German ed.; London: Lutterworth Press, 1949, Vol. I. It is interesting how Vischer has been criticized by
other neo-orthodox writers for "allegorizing" and "not taking historical criticism
seriously," Porteous, *op. cit.*, pp. 337-340.
[34]*Journal of Biblical Literature* 65:2 (1946), pp. 205-217.
[35]Dentan, *op. cit.*, p. 6. For one of the most dismal examples of the neo-orthodox
attempt to combine destructive criticism with some degree of revelational validity,
note *The Interpreter's Bible* (Nashville: Abingdon-Cokesbury, 1951-1957), 12
vols. From the first tier of critical notes, the second homiletical tier struggles
desperately (and despairingly) to recover preaching values. Compare Vriezen's
effort to affirm the revelation of God in Jesus Christ, while at the same time treating the Old Testament "in a scholarly [rationalistic] fashion," and granting it
authority only "when it shares in the truth revealed in [Vriezen's evaluation of]
Jesus Christ," for he insists that "There are lines in the Old Testament that lead
to Judaism and may draw the reader away from Christ," *op. cit.*, pp. 9, 87, 98.
The truth of the Old Testament is thus limited to what Vriezen chooses to accept
after its "confrontation with the New Testament," p. 124.

introduce elements of human error. These elements then combine to produce but another history of human religion. At length, even those elements which are still claimed to be divine exist so only upon the basis of human selection. A faith of this sort is, in essence, idolatry: the worship of that which man himself has devised. It is not God-given theology.

But, however inconsistent the neo-orthodox mixture of authoritarianism and rationalism may be, the idea of "having your cake and eating it, too" has shown a sensational theological sales appeal in the mid-twentieth century. Neo-orthodoxy has swept the scene. In Scandinavia the stress has been upon the cultic origin of much of the Old Testament and upon God's working through ancient Hebrew sociology. An outstanding work is Pedersen's *Israel, Its Life and Culture*, 1926-40,[36] the method of which has been carried forward by the recent German theology of Gerhard Von Rad (1957). Out of a different background, but voicing an even stronger reaction against Wellhausenism, has come the Israeli scholar, Yehezkel Kaufman. His *Religion of Israel* (trans. by Moshe Greenberg; Chicago: Univ. of Chicago Press, 1960) views the Old Testament as dominated by a popular monotheism instituted by Moses, though its procedures are still those of negative criticism. In England the leading spirit in the neo-orthodox movement has been H. H. Rowley. His pioneering work, *The Relevance of the Bible* (1941), pointed the way of the new trend by its very title. Britain was soon flooded by a host of brief, neo-orthodox studies. Among the more significant of these are the works of Rowley, A. G. Hebert, Christopher B. North, G. E. Phillips, W. J. T. Phythian-Adams, Alan Richardson, Norman H. Snaith, and H. F. D. Sparks.[37] To date the only publication approaching a complete survey has been Rowley's *The Faith of Israel* (Philadelphia: Westminster Press, 1956).

In America, too, neo-orthodoxy has rapidly caught fire. In the January 1943 issue of the *Journal of Religion*, there appeared an article by J. D. Smart entitled, "The Death and Rebirth of Old Testament Theology." The next year G. Ernest Wright published *The Challenge of Israel's Faith* (Chicago: University of Chicago Press, 1944). Similar works have followed by Wright, John Bright, Robert C. Dentan, L. Hodgson, and Paul Minear. Three full works have appeared. *An Outline of Biblical Theology* (Philadelphia: Westminster Press, c. 1946) by Millar Burrows is a sketchy treatment that includes the New Testament. It is liberal to the extent that one wonders whether it should properly be called a theology at all. Its own remarkably candid admissions about authority furnish ample data for this

---

[36]English translation, Vol. I, by Mrs. Aslaug Moller (London: Oxford University Press, 1926), Vol. II by Annie I. Fausboll (London: Oxford University Press, 1940).

[37]Cf. Fritsch, *op. cit.*, pp. 299-302.

criticism. Otto Baab's *The Theology of the Old Testament* (New York: Abingdon-Cokesbury Press, c. 1949),[38] is a more solid study that frankly recognizes the failure of historicism. Yet, by clinging to the destructive criticism of Scripture, Baab fails to provide conclusions of a much more satisfying nature. Its deficiency is apparent from its coverage of the testament, or covenant, in just slightly over two pages. The latest to be published in America is by the New Zealander, George A. F. Knight, *A Christian Theology of the Old Testament* (Richmond, Va.: John Knox Press, 1959). Its Christ-centered approach constitutes Knight's work the most evangelically acceptable of the three. But still there remains within Old Testament Scripture much which the author sees fit to reject as non-authentic historically or as sub-Christian theologically.

In addition to these books, attention should be drawn to two journals and to a booklet series. The journal *Theology Today*, published at Princeton Seminary, has become the world mouthpiece of neo-orthodox theology. It contains occasional articles on Biblical subjects. The journal *Interpretation*, published at Union Seminary, Virginia, concentrates upon Biblical theology and has made available a number of significant articles. It is, however, devoted to the propagation of the neo-orthodox approach to Scripture and of its accompanying theological conclusions. *Studies in Biblical Theology* consists of a series of monographs on both Old and New Testament subjects and includes English translations of a number of German neo-orthodox studies. It is published jointly in London and Chicago, with H. H. Rowley and G. Ernest Wright as the Old Testament editors. In the decade since its inception in 1950, it has already released some thirty titles of interest. Neo-orthodoxy, in the space of but a few years, has thus dethroned historicism and acquired from it most of the professorial chairs in America's leading seminaries. These include such formerly liberal institutions as Union in New York and McCormick in Chicago. It has, however, also acquired the control in such formerly conservative seminaries as Princeton and Southern Baptist in Louisville. Neo-orthodoxy is dangerous. It exerts a strong appeal as it proclaims with a holy enthusiasm its "discoveries" — the covenant, salvation by faith, the election of Israel, and so on—doctrines which have been the heritage of evangelicalism from the start!

E. TWENTIETH CENTURY CONSERVATISM. Theologians who believe the Bible have received little recognition, other than scorn, from those who have arrogated to themselves the right to judge and reject it. As Rowley frankly admits,

---

[38]A development of the theories he expressed in his article, "Old Testament Theology: Its Possibility and Methodology," in Harold R. Willoughby, editor, *The Study of the Bible Today and Tomorrow* (Chicago: University of Chicago Press, c. 1947).

THE HISTORY OF OLD TESTAMENT BIBLICAL THEOLOGY

There were conservative writers who stood outside the general body of critical scholars and who rejected most of their conclusions, but they did not seriously affect the position. For while many of them had considerable learning . . . their work had little influence amongst scientific scholars who were concerned only with the evidence, and the conclusions to which it might naturally lead.[39]

Jeremiah 9:23, 24, however, suggests an alternative to the equation of the term "scientific" with rationalistic interpretation!

In the early twentieth century, England produced a few conservative works, such as R. B. Girdlestone's brief but comprehensive survey, *Old Testament Theology and Modern Ideas* (London: Longman's, 1909). But the center of gravity for evangelical scholarship shifted across the Atlantic to America. For the first quarter of the century the stronghold of orthodoxy lay in Princeton Theological Seminary, New Jersey. There the standard for consecrated Old Testament study that had been set by the publications of William Henry Green in the 1890's was maintained by men such as John D. Davis, Geerhardus Vos, and Robert Dick Wilson. B. B. Warfield served also in Biblical theology prior to his assuming Princeton's chair of systematics. The *Princeton Theological Review* was their chief outlet for major articles and reviews, until its discontinuance at the more liberal reorganization of the seminary in 1929. At the neighboring Reformed Seminary in New Brunswick, John Howard Raven[40] published *The History of the Religion of Israel* (New Brunswick, N. J.: New Brunswick Theological Seminary, 1933). This volume, despite its title, is a genuine Biblical theology. It commences, for example, with a serious discussion of the revelations that God granted to Adam. Raven's work, however, is not complete. It extends chronologically only to the reign of Manasseh, in which period Raven placed the Book of Job. But it does present a generally satisfactory picture of just those earlier periods that have been the most distorted by disbelieving historicism and neo-orthodoxy. The finest single work presently available on Old Testament theology is Geerhardus Vos' *Biblical Theology* (Grand Rapids: Wm. B. Eerdmans Publishing Co., 1948). The manuscript was compiled by Vos' son from his father's classroom syllabi and lecture notes a number of years after the latter's retirement. It covers the major themes of Old Testament theology but not the full range of

---

[39]*Op. cit.*, p. xv. For example, Wilhelm Moller, "a most capable and able defender of the faith" (Edward J. Young, "The Old Testament," in Carl F. H. Henry, ed., *Contemporary Evangelical Thought*, Great Neck, N.Y.: Channel Press, 1957, p. 17), has had his *Biblical Theology of the Old Testament* (1938) marked down by a neo-orthodox writer as "an eccentric work, notable chiefly for its advocacy of the doctrine of 'verbal inspiration' and its complete rejection of critical methods" (Dentan, *Preface to Old Testament Theology*, p. 37). Cf. also Herbert F. Hahn, *Old Testament in Modern Research* (Philadelphia: Muhlenberg Press, 1954), p. 23.
[40]Best known for his *Old Testament Introduction* (New York: Fleming H. Revell, c. 1906), which for forty years was the standard conservative text in English.

doctrines. It breaks off, moreover, rather abruptly near the beginning
of Christ's incarnate ministry. Still, Vos' volume exhibits masterful
exegesis and theological insight. Repeated reference will be made to it
in the pages that follow.

The Princeton position has been perpetuated by Westminster
Theological Seminary, Philadelphia. Of Westminster's Old Testament
representatives, Oswald T. Allis has been the guiding genius.[41] He is
best known for his works on higher criticism, but his contributions to
Biblical theology include his anti-dispensational study, *Prophecy and
the Church* (Philadelphia: The Presbyterian and Reformed Publishing
Co., 1945). Edward J. Young is the leading evangelical Old Testament
scholar in America today. He also is known for his studies in introduction and criticism, but his theological interest appears in works of his
such as *My Servants the Prophets* (Grand Rapids: Wm. B. Eerdmans
Publishing Co., 1952), *Studies in Isaiah* (Grand Rapids: Wm. B. Eerdmans Publishing Co., 1954), and *The Study of Old Testament Theology Today* (London: James Clark & Co., Ltd., 1958). Outstanding as
a Biblical theologian in both the Old and New Testaments is John
Murray. The acuteness of Murray's Bible-centered reasoning is witnessed by several recent works: *The Covenant of Grace* (London:
Tyndale Press, 1953); *Redemption, Accomplished and Applied* (Grand
Rapids: Wm. B. Eerdmans Publishing Co., 1955); *Principles of Conduct* (Grand Rapids: Wm. B. Eerdmans Publishing Co., 1957), and
The Imputation of Adam's Sin (Grand Rapids: Wm. B. Eerdmans
Publishing Co., 1959). In addition, *The Westminster Theological Jour-
nal* has included a number of significant articles on the Old Testament.
Baptist conservatism is apparently on the wane. It has, however, pro-
duced J. Washington Watts' two volumes entitled *A Survey of Old
Testament Teaching* (Nashville: Broadman Press, c. 1947). The work
consists of book-by-book outlines.

Dispensationalism has attracted a large popular following in
America. It has, moreover, received serious scholarly leadership in
recent years from the Dallas Theological Seminary, Texas. Dallas has
assumed the publication of *Bibliotheca Sacra,* a quarterly journal of
long standing, which has become an important source for Bible-believing studies. Significant dispensational works in Biblical theology include
Merrill F. Unger's *Biblical Demonology* (Wheaton, Ill.: Van Kampen
Press, 1952), Charles L. Feinberg's *Premillennialism or Amillennialism?*
(Revised edition; Wheaton, Ill.: Van Kampen Press, 1954), and Charles
C. Ryrie's *The Basis of the Premillennial Faith* (New York: Loizeaux
Brothers, 1953). These very titles indicate dispensationalism's characteristically eschatological emphasis, though many would question
their identification of premillennialism with what is peculiarly Darby-
ite interpretation.

---

[41]See the tribute to Allis by Edward J. Young, *op. cit.,* pp. 20-23.

Finally, the last ten years have been marked by a strong revival of American evangelical scholarship, particularly in the independent and in the smaller conservative, denominational institutions. From Gordon Divinity School (Massachusetts) has come *The Gordon Review* with important general articles. It was Gordon, moreover, that led in the founding in 1949 of the Evangelical Theological Society. By holding firmly to the inerrancy of the Biblical autographs, the "E.T.S." has proved a rallying point for Bible-believing scholars of various backgrounds. The publication of its quarterly *Bulletin, Annual Papers*, and *Monograph Series* has made available important studies in Biblical theology.

In England a similar evangelical revival is represented by the Tyndale Fellowship, with an Australian branch organized in 1956. Finished books on Old Testament theology have yet to appear. But the quality of work represented, for example, by the introductory articles in *The New Bible Commentary*, Francis Davidson, A. M. Stibbs and E. F. Kevan, eds. (Grand Rapids: Wm. B. Eerdmans Publishing Co., 1953), gives promise of future productivity.

On the Continent, neo-orthodoxy has all but destroyed what historicism may have left of Bible-believing scholarship. The only real exception is the Old Testament theology of Wilhelm and Hans Möller (1938), who were converted from Wellhausenism to a full acceptance of verbal plenary inspiration. With the decline, however, of evangelical Protestantism, certain valuable studies in Old Testament theology have arisen out of continental Roman Catholicism. In 1893 the encyclical letter of Leo XIII served to arouse Romanist leaders to the necessity for their more active study and defense of Scripture. Papal Christianity could not longer ignore the attacks of the "higher critics":

> They deny that there is any such thing as revelation or inspiration . . . they see, instead, only the forgeries and the falsehoods of men; they set down the Scripture narratives as stupid fables and lying stories. . . . And it is deplorable to see these attacks growing every day more numerous and severe. . . . For all the books which the Church receives as sacred and canonical are written wholly and entirely, with all their parts, at the dictation of the Holy Spirit; and so far is it from being possible that any error can coexist with inspiration, that inspiration not only is essentially incompatible with error, but excludes and rejects it as absolutely and necessarily as it is impossible that God Himself, the supreme Truth, can utter that which is not true.[42]

In 1901-02 Leo went on to establish the Pontifical Biblical Commission. The function of the Commission was to secure the observance of Leo's decree and to publish specific decisions on matters of Biblical orthodoxy. It proceeded, in the years that followed, to issue a series of directives defending, for example, the Pentateuch as substantially and integrally the work of Moses, and Isaiah as the unified work of the

[42]Paul Heinisch, *Theology of the Old Testament*, pp. 385, 395-396.

prophet of that name. It also sought to stimulate Biblical research. Shortly thereafter Roman Catholicism did enter the field of Old Testament theology and produced Michael Hetzenauer's *Theologia Biblica,* Vol. I, *Vetus Testamentum* (1908), which is an excellent conservative study.

But even with papal decrees and Biblical Commission decisions to the contrary, the poison of destructive higher criticism has slowly infiltrated Romanism. Despite a general conservativism,[43] an increasing number of Romanist scholars have exhibited typically Jesuit casuistry in evading the decisions of their own Commission. J. Coppens, for example, has explained relative to the integrity of Isaiah:

> The Commission is satisfied with asserting . . . that the arguments of the critics are not compelling. . . . Such an answer does not at all imply . . . that the brief for a Deutero-Isaias is untenable. On the contrary, it implies that the theory does not lack a certain degree of probability[!]. . . . Yet it should not be proclaimed a certain and definitely accepted opinion.[44]

In practice, however, Coppens, who is by no means alone, assumes without question the critical verdict that the latter part of the "prophecy" is in fact Deutero-Isaiah, a non-authentic, exilic forgery. He flatly rejects Christ's authority on critical matters,[45] and his practical disregard of Leo's papal infallibility is evident.[46] Even the Biblical Commission itself has repudiated its own former directives:

> According to pronouncements made in 1955 . . . these are now, in the altered circumstances of today, of binding force only in matters which, directly or indirectly, treat of faith or morals.[47]

---

[43]Cf. Robert H. Pfeiffer's comment that "Roman Catholic scholars generally defend the traditional theory (of the exilic authenticity of Daniel)," *Introduction to the Old Testament* (New York: Harper & Brothers, c. 1941), p. 755.

[44]*The Old Testament and the Critics.* Trans. by Edward A. Ryan and Edward W. Tribbs (Paterson, New Jersey: St. Anthony Guild Press, 1942), p. 149.

[45]*Ibid.,* p. 155. Cf. John L. McKenzie's conclusion, "Fundamentalism has been losing ground in Catholic interpretation of the Bible," *The Two-Edged Sword: An Interpretation of the Old Testament* (Milwaukee: Bruce Publishing Co., 1956), p. 105.

[46]In theory, of course, papal infallibility is maintained; and a large, though decreasing, number of Romanist scholars still take Leo's words on inspiration seriously. For example, James H. Cobb, "Current Trends in Catholic Biblical Research," in Harold R. Willoughby, ed., *The Study of the Bible Today and Tomorrow,* states, "The Catholic scholar . . . begins with Scripture and tradition, the total deposit of the faith, as, and only as, this is officially interpreted by the living *magisterium* of the church. Thus he adheres to its dogmatic theology and to the special rulings of its constituted authorities. . . . Among other things, Catholics reject the Graf-Wellhausen theory of the composition of the Pentateuch and all its varients. They reject the theory of a Second and Third Isaiah. The book, they hold, was the work of the pre-Exilic Judean prophet," pp. 117, 119. A summary of divergent views within Romanism, together with the decisions of the Commission may be found in John E. Steinmueller's *A Companion to Scripture Studies* (New York: J. F. Wagner, 1941-1943), 3 vols.

[47]Edmund F. Sutcliffe, "Bible," in Vincent C. Hopkins, ed., *The Catholic Encyclopedia* (New York: Robert Appleton Company, c. 1950-   ), Supplement II, Vol. XVIII.

In the case of the Pentateuch a recent decision even states:

> No doubt exists about the Pentateuch having been composed with the use of sources, written or oral, or about the increase of Mosaic laws due to the conditions of later times.[48]

Little wonder, then, that Romanist monographs in the area of Old Testament theology have shown increasingly liberal tendencies. Sutcliffe's recent study on the future life, for example, does not hesitate to attribute to the faith of Israel the same superstitions that characterized Near Eastern religion in general.[49] Romanism's latest complete theology, Paul Heinisch's *Theology of the Old Testament* (1940),[50] makes correspondingly broad concessions to a mythological interpretation of the Old Testament's cosmology and eschatology. Among its defects are a failure to maintain careful chronological distinctions, its constant references to the Apocrypha, and its occasional deviation into such Romanist distinctives as Mariolatry. Heinisch's work is nevertheless sound on such basic matters as the Messiah and His atonement. It is a gold mine of Biblical truth, and it towers far above the contemporary works of Protestant neo-orthodoxy. Along with Oehler, it stands as one of the two best, complete, Old Testament theologies.

Finally, from post World War II Germany have come Erich Sauer's outline studies, *The Dawn of World Redemption*[51] and *From Eternity to Eternity*.[52] The treatment is somewhat superficial (Sauer loves to list things in sevens) and mildly dispensational. But the author finds the key to history in the saving work of Jesus Christ and is himself thoroughly yielded to the truth of God's words. And we must remember that for the writing of theology, this stands first in the eyes of Him who "scorneth the scorners but giveth grace unto the lowly" (Prov. 3:34).

For Further Reading:

Edward J. Young, *The Study of Old Testament Theology Today*. London: James Clark & Co., 1958. A penetrating analysis of the deficiencies of neo-orthodox Biblical theology by today's foremost evangelical Old Testament scholar.

H. F. Hahn, *The Old Testament in Modern Research*. Philadelphia: Muhlenberg Press, c. 1954. Chap. VII gives a recent survey of Old Testament theology from the neo-orthodox viewpoint.

Robert C. Dentan, *Preface to Old Testament Theology*. New Haven: Yale University Press, 1950. Part I. A survey of the history of Old Testament theology as a theological discipline. Note also his concluding bibliography.

---

[48]*Loc. cit.* Coppens concedes, "One must be willing to interpret liberally the information given in the Bible on the authenticity of the inspired writings," *op. cit.,* 129.

[49]*The Old Testament and the Future Life* (2nd ed.; Westminster, Md.: The Newman Bookshop, 1947).

[50]Translated by William G. Heidt (Collegeville, Minn.: Liturgical Press, c. 1955).

[51]English Translation by G. H. Lang (London: Paternoster Press, 1951; Grand Rapids, Wm. B. Eerdmans Publishing Co., 1952).

[52]English translation by G. H. Lang (Grand Rapids: Wm. B. Eerdmans Publishing Co., 1954). This last volume surveys God's purpose in the total sweep of history. Together with his New Testament outline entitled *The Triumph of the Crucified*, the set forms Sauer's trilogy on the history of salvation.

3. Revelation*

That God communicated His will to men like Isaiah and Jeremiah is one of the basic assumptions of Biblical theology.[1] Scripture, moreover, provides considerable information on the way in which God communicated with them. As an introduction, therefore, to the study of the content of God's special revelation, this topic and the following one will describe the mode of the divine communication and of its preservation. They survey, in other words, the Bible's own teachings about itself as a product of revelation and of inspiration.

God's revelations have come to men from the very first (Gen. 1:28). With the passage of time, however, they have come in different ways (Heb. 1:1). Gabler's original stress lay upon distinguishing "the developing stages in the historical fact." The following ten periods are, therefore, proposed as the historical stages through which Old Testament revelation developed.[2]

A. THE PRIMEVAL PERIOD, up to the time of Abraham. This period includes both the revelations that God granted prior to man's fall and those that follow it. The former may be said to have set the stage for redemption, while the latter possess a redemptive significance that has continued without abatement to the present. These revelations are contained primarily in Genesis 1—11:26. Revelation during this first period was on a simple, person-to-person basis. God met men almost as if He were another man (Gen. 3:8). The content of God's verbal revelations related to God's plans and actions: His earliest recorded words to man concerned the covenant of works that He had set up in Eden; and His next, the redemptive testament that followed upon man's fall. These, in turn, became the basis for all subsequent revelations of Himself (cf. topics 5-8). Knowledge about God is thus not an end in itself. It becomes effective only as it produces an active response on the part of its hearers. An obvious example is God's telling Noah to enter the ark (Gen. 7:7)![3] But at the

---

*BIBLE READING: Isaiah 6; Jeremiah 15:15-21

Collateral Reading: Vos, *Biblical Theology,* pp. 82-85, 120-22, 209-15, 230-52.
  Millar Burrows, *An Outline of Biblical Theology* (Philadelphia: Westminster Press, c. 1946), pp. 1-16.

[1]See above, p. 2.
[2]Some writers, as Oehler and Vos, recognize only two Old Testament periods, the Mosaic and the prophetic. This, however, seems to minimize the uniqueness of Eden, of Abraham, of the post-exilic days, etc. Liberals, of course, differ completely on the relative position of the Pentateuch, of the wisdom literature, and of other critical portions of Scripture.
[3]Cf. Burrows, *Outline of Biblical Theology,* Sec. 5, pp. 10-13.

same time God's actions were both preceded by, and then explained
by, His verbal communications (Amos 3:7). The Flood offers a case in
point. God granted a revelation through an act in nature, namely, the
rainbow; but God's action would have been meaningless without His
special explanation first (Gen. 9:12-17).

   B. THE PATRIARCHAL PERIOD, Abraham to the birth of Moses,
2166-1527 B.C.[4] The primary Biblical source extends from Genesis 11:27
to the end of the book, with some supplementation from the descriptions of Job. Revelation in this period is no longer as casual as before.
It is, moreover, restricted to God's chosen recipients, the patriarchs,
and to those associated with them. Where nature is used for revelation, as in Genesis 15:5, the needed, accompanying explanation is given
only to the chosen. The most characteristic form of revelation in this
period is that of the theophany, a visible appearance of God (Gen.
12:7 and thereafter). The nature of most of the theophanies is not
described. Their reality, however, is indicated by the consistent
patriarchal erection of altars in connection with these experiences.[5]
To the patriarchs, "God's word" is first specifically said to have come
(15:1). This phrase may occasionally have reference to God's impersonal activity (Ps. 147:18), but with the patriarchs it refers to His
personal communication (147:19). Two other forms are mentioned as
well. The vision (Gen. 15:1) involves a recipient who is awake but
who becomes transported beyond his material environment (through
cf. v. 12). In such a vision God may either reveal Himself directly or
in a symbol, for example, that of the burning, portable oven (v. 17).
The dream (28:12) involves a recipient who is asleep and therefore
more passive. Dreams are thus suitable for the immature (28:12;
37:5) or for the heathen (20:3; 40:5). Sometimes dreams are belittled
as "chaff," (Jer. 23:28) or as due to worries (Eccl. 5:3); but in this
period many served as true revelations of God (Job. 33:15, 16).

   The Old Testament identifies three classes of human media for
divine revelation—that of the prophet, the priest, and the wise man
(Jer. 18:18). All three are introduced in the patriarchal period. The
term "prophet" appears first in Genesis 20:7 (cf. Ps. 105:15), signifying
a man who knows God (18:22). The prophet does not yet, however,
function as a teacher. The priest, Melchizedek, is distinguished by his
power to grant God's blessing (14:18, 19). Lastly, the wise are made

---

[4]For a discussion of chronology, see the writer's *An Outline of Hebrew History*,
pp. 34-36, 122-124.
[5]Vos claims certain exceptions, *Biblical Theology*, p. 83, but see below, p. 360
Philosophers have objected that the limitation of such real revelations to but a few
chosen patriarchs reflects on the impartiality and justice of God. The objection,
however, lacks validity, because it overlooks the fact of human sinfulness and
assumes that God must be under some obligation to deal with all men in the same
way. But surely God has the right to bestow His grace as He pleases. Cf. Carl F.
H. Henry, *The Protestant Dilemma* (Grand Rapids: Wm. B. Eerdmans Publishing
Co., 1949), p. 50.

up of the more important, older men who sat in the gate (19:1; 23:10); but no mention is yet made of their possessing any special word from God. See below under periods D, C, and F, where each class respectively gained prominence in Israel. To some of the patriarchs God granted special revelations of a predictive character when they were near death (49:1, 2; cf. 27:4; 50:24; Deut. 33:1).

C. THE MOSAIC PERIOD, 1527-1406 B.C. The sources for this period include the last four books of the Pentateuch and Psalm 90 by Moses. But they also include such of the third person explanatory data of Genesis as stems from the time of Moses. The quoted speeches, of course, express facts that were known earlier by the patriarchs themselves. The first two chapters of Genesis, with their description of God's work in creation (see topic 10-B below), are thus Mosaic revelations. One might expect that creation would, in itself, reveal God's power and His goodness, even as man's creation in the image of God would reveal His personal nature (Ps. 148:7-13; cf. Rom. 1:20). But men, by their own sin, have hardened themselves against the truth of God that is found in creation (Jer. 2:5; cf. Rom. 1:28). As a result, the general revelation has become ineffective. What was known, men have perverted to idolatry and to demonism (Deut. 32:17; Rom. 1:23). Thus, for all practical purposes, God's ways are hidden until He reveals them to His own through His special law (Deut. 29:29; See below, period E).

More significant than creation for the knowledge of God were His providential acts, especially in His freeing Israel from Egypt. These acts included many outright miracles, revelations of "His mighty hand and outstretched arm" (Deut. 4:34). But the greatest single manifestation of God was His spectacular appearance upon Mt. Sinai in the spring of 1446 B.C. for the adoption of Israel as His people (Ex. 19:16-19). The heart of the Old Testament faith was this: "Yahweh came from Sinai, and rose from Seir unto them" (Deut. 33:2).[6] From Sinai, God spoke to Israel. The method resembled that of His earlier contact with Hagar (Gen. 21:17): there was an audible voice but no visible form (Deut. 4:12). In post-Old Testament times such a phenomenon was called bath qōl, "daughter of a voice." It was the sort of event that the Pharisees seemed to have had in mind when they demanded of Christ a "sign from heaven" (Mark 8:11).

There are four specific theophanic media that appear in the Mosaic period, all of which may be summarized under the phrase, God's "glory," Hebrew, kāvōdh. The literal meaning of kāvōdh is "heaviness," from which comes the idea of honor. A man of kāvōdh carries "weight" in the eyes of his fellows (Gen. 45:13). God's kāvōdh is,

---

[6]The reference to "Seir" perhaps indicates that the storm which accompanied His appearance advanced to Sinai from Seir (Edom) in the east (cf. Judg. 5:4; Hab. 3:3).

therefore, the visible extension of His divine perfection. In the first place, God's glory is equated with a supernatural pillar of cloud and fire (Ex. 24:16). This pillar originally led and protected Israel in the Exodus (13:21, 22; 14:19; 16:7, 10). It appeared on Sinai (24:16). At the dedication of the Mosaic Tabernacle, it filled the Holy of Holies and came particularly to rest between the cherubim on the cover of the ark (25:22; 40:34-38). Eventually, it entered Solomon's Temple (I Kings 8:11).[7] In post-Old Testament times the theophanic cloud (or, technically, the divine presence which caused it) came to be called the sh'khînā, which means God's "dwelling" with His people (Ex. 25:8).[8] The glory cloud is associated with Christ's first coming and with His second coming as well (Matt. 17:5; Acts 1:9; Rev. 1:7; 14:14). God acted in fire from His "glory" (Lev. 9:23-24; 10:2; cf. 16:2), and the "shekinah" was representative of His glory in heaven (I Kings 8:30, 39).

Secondly, God's glory is equated with His pānîm, His "face" (Ex. 33:18-20). This glory, too, was a true theophany, for it is said that when God appeared at the Exodus, He brought Israel out of Egypt by His pānîm (v. 14; Deut. 4:37). In one sense, no man can really see God's face (His presence) and live (Ex. 33:20). But the *manifestation* of His face could be survived (Gen. 32:20). In Ex. 33:23 this is called God's "back."[9] Still, Israel feared such divine manifestations; and as a result, Moses was petitioned to act as the people's mediator (Ex. 20:19-21). The two other theophanic media subsumed under the concept of "glory" were God's "name" and His "Angel." These will be considered in more detail in topics 11 and 13-A respectively. All four media, however, appear in association—the cloud and the Angel (Ex. 14:19); the cloud and the name (I Kings 8:29); and the face and the name (Num. 6:25-27). All equaled God's presence.

The outstanding human medium for God's revelation in this period was Moses himself. He was a prophet (Deut. 18:18; Hos. 12:13), but he was more than a prophet. Prophets received dreams and visions, but Moses was granted theophanies of a unique sort (Num. 12:6-8). God spoke with Moses face to face (Deut. 34:10).[10]

---

[7]See the discussion by R. E. Hough, *The Ministry of the Glory Cloud* (New York: Philosophical Library, 1955).

[8]*Shākhan* means "to dwell." Compare the name of the Tabernacle, *mishkhān*, the "place of (His) dwelling," topic 26-C.

[9]Cf. Edmond Jacobs interesting, though destructively critical, discussion of "face," *The Theology of the Old Testament*, pp. 77-79. Robert Girdlestone equates the manifestation of God's face in Exodus 33:23 with an appearance of His "name," *Old Testament Theology and Modern Ideas* (London: Longmans, Green and Co., 1909), p. 67.

[10]This factor is of basic importance for appreciating the three divisions of the Old Testament canon. The unique position of the Pentateuch (its first division) follows from the unique position of its author, Moses, as a recipient of divine revelation. Indeed, it is the status of the human authors that constitutes the one tenable explanation for the three-fold division. See William Henry Green, *General Introduction to the Old Testament: the Canon* (New York: Charles Scribner's Sons, 1898), chapters IV-VI.

The greatest of these revelations took place on Mt. Sinai when God spoke to Moses the words of the testament, the instrument of divine grace that brought salvation to Israel (Ex. 34:27).

Moses' brother Aaron, however, along with their sister Miriam, also received communications of God's will (Num. 12:2). This fact, in turn, marked the founding of the priestly class as one of the three official groups through which divine revelations came to be received.[11] The priests were those who would "enquire" of Yahweh for the guidance of the people (Num. 27:21). They were also the official teachers of the law (Lev. 10:11). These duties fell naturally to them, because it was the priests who·exercised the ministry before the divine presence that was over the ark (Judge 20:27, 28). Specifically, they were to seek God "by judgment of the Urim" (Num. 27:21). This latter term refers to the *ūrīm* and *thummīm*, which were put in the breastplate of judgment that was worn by the high priest (Ex. 28:30). The Hebrew words mean, respectively, "lights" and "perfections"; and the thought that suggests itself is that of the precious stones of the breastplate (vv. 17-21), which Aaron bore over his heart (v. 29). "The judgment of the Urim" would thus signify the personal revelations that God granted to the one who wore the high priestly breastplate. In such a way God would answer the official questions that were brought in before the cloud of His presence. Those who question the reality of such supernatural communications generally consider the *ūrīm* and *thummīm* to have been some kind of dice, a sort of sacred lottery.[12] It is true, of course, that lots were known to Israel at this time as a means of making property distributions (Num. 26:55, 56). But dice-casting as a regular means of divine guidance smacks of magic in a way that is unworthy of God's Word. I Samuel 28:6, moreover, lists urim in a category that is between dreams and prophets. It suggests that urim is simply another form of God's personal revelation, namely, that which is mediated through priests (cf. Deut. 33:8, 10).

In the Mosaic period, prophecy appears only sporadically (Num. 11:25) (see section D that follows), though Jeremiah 7:25 notes that God began to send prophets from the time of the Exodus onward. Attempts to gain divine revelations through spiritism (Lev. 19:26; 20:27) or through astrology (Deut. 17:3) are expressly forbidden and are later condemned as spurious (Isa. 47:13-14). God's people are to seek Him through the true medium of prophecy (Deut. 18:15). A series of revelations of an unusual nature were those granted through Balaam at the Plains of Moab in the spring of 1406 B.C. Balaam was dominated by greed, was an advocate of idolatry, and died in battle fighting

---

[11]The nature and ceremonial function of the priests is considered in Topic 27-A; but, as a medium of revelation, they must be noted here as well.
[12]Burrows, *op. cit.* pp. 35, 275.

against God's people (Num. 31:8, 16; II Peter 2:15; Jude 11). Yet he had his eyes opened by God (Num. 24:4) and was constrained to speak His word of blessing on Israel (22:18).

D. THE PERIOD OF CONSOLIDATION. This was the time of Israel's slow establishment in Canaan, from Joshua through Saul, 1406-1010 B.C. The sources consist primarily of Joshua and Judges, to which should be added such parts of Ruth and I Samuel as were revealed at the time that the events described were going on. Other parts of Ruth and I Samuel seem to have been revealed only later, at the time the books were written, which was in the Davidic (E) and the disruption (F) periods respectively. The four centuries between Moses and David were, until near their close, times of comparatively little revelation (I Sam. 3:1), except for the official priestly oracles (23:9-12). This scarcity may well have been due to the frequent apostasies of Israel, who kept turning to idols or to spiritists (cf. 28:3). God did, however, raise up Joshua and certain priests, judges, and Nazarites (see topic 29-E) as "charismatic" leaders to deliver Israel. Such men — and women — were specially filled by the *charism,* or gift, God's Holy Spirit (Judg. 6:34), whose personal activity comes to the fore in this period. But the most significant feature of the consolidation period lies in the development of Biblical prophecy into its second major stage, namely, the rise of the prophets into an organized class for regular use by God.

The function of prophecy within Old Testament revelation had been first defined in Deut. 18. There, shortly before his death, Moses had predicted that God would raise up a Prophet, unto whom Israel was to hearken (v. 15). This expectation attained its fulfillment in Jesus Christ, the One who ministered as a Prophet, as well as a Priest and a King.[13] But, since it was the same Spirit of Christ who spoke through the Old Testament prophets (I Peter 1:11), the whole prophetic movement must also be included in the thought of Deuteronomy 18. The prophets, as Moses expressed it, were to be "like unto himself." That is, they would supplement the Word of God that had, so far, been revealed through his own mediation. The attempt, therefore, that is made by liberalism to place prophecy in opposition to the law, or even anterior to it, runs counter to the testimony of Scripture itself. Biblical prophecy was based upon, and was a development out of, the law (Isa. 8:20; Dan. 9:11). God's revelation to Moses was, in fact, qualitatively superior to that granted to the prophets (Num. 12:7); and no subsequent prophet became Moses' equal (Deut. 34:10). Yet new situations would arise that would demand new applications of the Mosaic legislation. As E. J. Young has pointed out:

---

[13]Acts 3:22; 7:37; and see below, pp. 280-282.

After the entrance into Canaan [God's elect] would need
more detailed instructions as to the way in which the Lord
would have him walk.[14]

It is significant, in this regard, that Amos 2:10, 11 describes the
historical appearance of the prophets as a logical sequel to the three
previous actions that God had taken on Israel's behalf, namely, the
deliverance from Egypt, the forty years of guidance in the wilderness,
and the bestowal of the Promised Land. Specifically, the inhabitants
of Canaan had become addicted to the oracles of spiritists; and it was
the need to counteract this evil influence that occasioned the rise of
regular prophecy (Deut. 18:14, 15). It should be further noted that
prophecy first came into prominence in the years that followed the
first battle of Ebenezer in about 1090 B.C. Because of this defeat, the
Philistines captured the ark, destroyed the central sanctuary of Shiloh,
and brought about the death of the high priest Eli. Thus, it was when
the established institutions of Israel were in abeyance that God raised
up Samuel the prophet to re-establish and to confirm the faith once
delivered through Moses. Similarly, throughout the nation's history,
the prophets fulfilled the role of guardians of the theocracy. They
not simply supplemented the work of the king and of the priests; the
degree, indeed, of their activity seems to have been directly proportionate to the degree of the apostasy of the others! They ceased,
then, with the enthronement of God's written revelation under Ezra.

The origin of prophecy, as already indicated, lies therefore in
God's gracious concern for the welfare of His own in their times of
crisis. "I raised up of your sons for prophets" (Amos 2:11). Liberalism,
however, has exhausted itself by trying to account for the phenomenon
of Biblical prophecy as a natural development out of the environ-
mental situation of Canaanite or Near Eastern religion. Pedersen, for
example, has sought to explain prophecy as stemming from primitive
soothsaying or divination;[15] Meek has reduced the movement's beginnings to those of a nationalistic Hebrew reaction against the Philistine oppressions of the eleventh century;[16] and Hölscher has traced
its origin to psychological frenzy, such as was exhibited by the
prophets of Baal in the royal courts of Canaan.[17] But when one ex-
amines the contemporary "prophesyings" that are found in the pagan
cultures surrounding Israel, he is impressed anew by the supernatural
uniqueness of Biblical prophecy.[18] The consistent conviction of the

---

[14]*My Servants the Prophets* (Grand Rapids: Wm. B. Eerdmans Co., 1952), p. 20.
Cf. p. 54 on the subordinate position of the prophets.
[15]Johannes Pedersen, *Israel, Its Life and Culture* (Trans. by Annie I. Fausboll;
London: Oxford University Press, 1940), II:III.
[16]Theophile Meek, *Hebrew Origins* (Revised edition; New York: Harper & Brothers, 1950), p. 156.
[17]Cf. Young's careful analysis of various representatives of this widely held position, *op. cit.*, Ch. IX.
[18]*Ibid.*, pp. 193-205.

prophets themselves was that "the Lord hath spoken this word" (Isa. 24:3); and their conviction has yet to receive an adequate explanation, other than that God actually did communicate His will to these men.[19]

Daniel defines the prophets as "God's servants, which spake in His name" (9:6). The priest, in contrast, served primarily as a speaker on men's behalf to God; but the prophet was the spokesman of God to men (Ex. 7:1, 2). As Jeremiah later observed (15:19), he was one who ministered "as God's mouth." In the early days a prophet was called in Hebrew a rō'e or a hōze (I Sam. 9:9). Both terms mean "one who sees," a "seer," and are descriptive of God's mode of revelation to the prophet prior to the latter's transmission of the message. (Num. 24:4; Isa. 30:10). The more common name, however, came to be nāvī, "prophet." The term nāvī is uncertain in its etymology, but it comes most likely from the root meaning "to announce."[20] This title, therefore, describes the prophet's activity, subsequent to his receiving the message from God. Similarly, his message is styled a massā (Num. 24:3), from the root meaning "to lift up (the voice)." Massā is thus frequently translated "burden" (a load lifted up). The word may, however, leave an incorrect impression, for the proclamation was not necessarily "burdensome"!

Even as God's overall purpose in history is the redemption of mankind, so the message of prophecy climaxes in its foretelling[21] of Jesus Christ (Rev. 19:10; Deut. 18:18) who should come to provide for man's redemption (I Cor. 1:30). But prophecy also seeks to stimulate an immediate holiness in the lives of its contemporary hearers. God, accordingly, made the prophets foretellers in certain non-Messianic areas as well (cf. I Sam. 9:6, 20). His purpose in granting such predictions was not simply to prevent the people's turning to pagan diviners (Deut. 18:14, 15) but also, through the promises and the threats, to encourage their right conduct in daily life. For the same reason, He made the prophets "forth-tellers," direct preachers of righteousness (I Sam. 15:22). Thus the prophets would include preaching (though it was unwanted!) with their oracles (I Kings 14:3, 7-16).

[19]Cf. Vos, op. cit., pp. 231-32, "The earnestness would stand in inverse ratio to the consciousness of the preacher, that he had to resort to pretence. The prophets would, no doubt, have discovered sooner than modern preachers seem to be able to do, that every such mental reservation broke the force of their enthusiasm."
[20]So the latest studies, as Ludwig Kohler, Lexicon in Veteris Testamenti Libros (Leiden: E. J. Brill, 1953), p. 588b, though cf. Vos, op. cit., pp. 209, 210.
[21]It is of course recognized that the prophets were not limited to "foretelling." Prophecy contains, quantitatively, more moral preaching than it does prediction. This, however, hardly justifies the older liberal position, which came to deny the reality of prediction altogether; cf. Charles H. Patterson, The Philosophy of the Old Testament (New York: The Ronald Press Co., 1953), pp. 142-43, 528. Modern neo-orthodoxy exhibits a renewed appreciation for the predictive elements within prophecy; cf. H. H. Rowley, The Relevance of Apocalyptic (2nd edition; London: Lutterworth Press, 1952), pp. 13, 35.

They might even refuse oracles to those whose lives were faithless (Ezek. 14:3).

The means by which God communicated His will was to bring the prophet under the personal influence of His Holy Spirit, who then conveyed to them "the word of God." On occasion a prophet might become practically another man (I Sam. 10:6-9). Sometimes this overshadowing came about involuntarily, by God's direct intervention (19:20); at others, the prophet might prepare himself (e.g. by freeing his mind from mundane affairs through the use of music, 10:5; II Kings 3:15). It is noteworthy that the later Davidic singers were classed as "prophets" and "seers" (I Chron. 25:1, 2, 5). With this may also be compared the prophetic receptivity that is associated with the sound of flowing rivers (Ezek. 1:3; Dan. 10:4). Studies in comparative religion have emphasized the frenzy that characterized certain pagan prophets (I Kings 18:26, 28; cf. Hos. 9:7). Similarly, worldly Israelites sometimes called the true prophet a "mad fellow" (II Kings 9:11); and Saul in his demon-possessed ravings is said to have "prophesied" (I Sam. 18:10). These observations, however, fail to justify the liberal criticism that early Hebrew prophecy was no more than ecstatic emotionalism.[22] The frenzied Saul of I Samuel 18, for example, is a far cry from the Spirit-possessed leader described in chapter 10. Though the early prophets undoubtedly preached energetically (19:24), it is significant that only Saul is said to have fallen down naked and overcome before Samuel. This, moreover, was by a special act of God. The superstitions of divination have likewise nothing to do with true prophetic methods.[23]

Like the judge, the prophet was raised up of God (Deut. 18:15; Amos 2:11). No further qualification was necessary. Prophets could be women, as Miriam (Ex. 15:20; Num. 12:2) or Deborah (Judg. 4:4). The founder of organized prophetism, however, was Samuel. His call as a boy (I Sam. 3:4-14) serves as a classic example of the objective nature of God's communication. "The word of God" was a real, person to person conversation (v. 10; cf. Isa. 6:8).[24] After his own judgeship, however, Samuel proceeded, not only to anoint a king, but also to secure for prophecy the responsibility that it henceforth exercised— that of acting as a divine check upon the monarchy and its officers (I Sam. 16:1; cf. 22:5). Furthermore, Samuel established the schools of the prophets, perhaps as Spirit-filled leaders gathered around him in

---

[22]Criticism in which even evangelicals have occasionally joined, cf. Raven, *The History of the Religion of Israel* (New Brunswick: New Brunswick Theological Seminary, 1933), p. 189; but see Vos, *op. cit.*, pp. 221-224.

[23]See Young's able discussion, *op. cit.*, pp. 25, 26.

[24]Evangelicals, such as J. G. S. S. Thomson, are thus careful to include within "the word of God" the objective element of "knowledge given," on the basis of which may be attained the ultimate goal of "existential fellowship," *The Old Testament View of Revelation* (Grand Rapids: Wm. B. Eerdmans Publishing Co., 1960), pp. 14, 9.

the absence of a central sanctuary. These "schools" became permanent organizations of prophets who lived (19:20) or traveled (10:5) together. See further under period F. Aubrey Johnson, together with certain representatives of recent Scandinavian neo-orthodoxy, has advanced the contention that the prophets existed as official representatives of Israel's cult and sanctuaries.[25] It should be noted that this theory is, in itself, a healthy reaction against the older liberalism that had placed the prophets in opposition to the rituals, the types, and the atonement practices of the Mosaic legislation. The prophets could, after all, serve as God's spokesmen for the requiring of blood sacrifices (II Sam. 24:18, 19). There is no evidence, however, of their regular, personal employment at the altar. E. J. Young has concluded:

> There was indeed some connection between the prophets and the place of sacrifice. What this connection was, however, we for our part are unable to say. We are unable to follow Johnson in his contention that the prophets were cultic specialists.[26]

E. THE DAVIDIC PERIOD, the forty years of the reign of David, 1010-970 B.C. These four decades mark a distinct period and a high point in God's historic revelation. Its sources consist primarily of the Psalms that were composed by David and his associates (see topic 4 that follows). Also to be included are such statements in II Samuel and I Chronicles as were revealed at the time of the events described. The communication of God's will comes to a particular focus in the life and poetry of the king himself. David was "the man after Yahweh's own heart" (I Sam. 13:14), the words of whose tongue were those of God's own Spirit (II Sam. 23:2). During David's reign various prophets were also active in writing (I Chron. 29:29); but their works, presumably, did not carry the seal of divine inspiration.

It is in the writings of King David that the distinction between general and special revelation first comes to conscious expression. Psalm 19 speaks in verses 1-6 of the heavens declaring the glory of God, but goes on in verses 7-11 to describe the more perfect testimony of Yahweh in the specific revelation that is His law. The former, general revelation, is addressed to all (v. 4); and it may be conveyed through various media. God may be seen in nature (vv. 1, 2), "the work of Thy fingers" (Ps. 8:3; cf. Isa. 40:22). Again, He speaks to man through his own constitution, which is made but "a little lower than the angels" (Ps. 8:5). Man, that is, should know of God from what he himself is and from what he feels from within himself. A true analogy exists between the creature and the Creator:

> He that planted the ear, shall He not hear?
> He that formed the eye, shall He not see? (Ps. 94:9).

Finally, there is a knowledge of God to be had from His providential dealings with mankind in history (Ps. 8:6-9). As Psalm 94 proceeds to

---

[25] *The Cultic Prophet in Ancient Israel* (Cardiff, Wales: University of Wales, 1944).
[26] *Op. cit.*, p. 103.

ask, "He that chastiseth the nations, shall He not correct?" (v. 10). Special revelation, in contrast, is directed to specified recipients; and even then discernment is not to be expected among the unregenerate (Ps. 69:22, 23; cf. Rom. 11:7-11). It is, however, addressed to sinners for their redemption (Ps. 19:11, 12); and for those who are converted through the precepts of Yahweh, "in keeping them there is great reward."

David thus made it clear that a genuine knowledge of God is to be had through general revelation (v. 2). Compare Isa. 40:21, 26, "Hath it not been told you from the beginning? Have ye not understood from the foundations of the earth? Lift up your eyes on high, and see!" But at the same time general revelation is an acted revelation and not a verbal one. "There is no speech nor language; their voice is not heard" (Ps. 19:3). General revelation cannot save, or provide an effective knowledge of God, or even furnish a basis for religion. The heathen confess, "Thou art a God that hidest Thyself" (Isa. 45:15); no one perceives His word (Jer. 23:18). The fact of the matter is, the heathen are dismayed at the signs of the heavens (10:2); "Every man is become brutish" (v. 14). David explains that the nations, in their wickedness, have "forgotten" the revelations for which they are held responsible (Ps. 9:17). They have, moreover, perverted the truth of God into the futilities of idolatry itself (Isa. 41:28, 29; Rom. 1:21-23). Thus, for all practical purposes, God in His general revelation remains concealed (cf. Prov. 25:2). As Calvin put it,

> Notwithstanding the clear representations given by God in the mirror of His works, both of Himself and His everlasting dominion, such is our stupidity, that, always inattentive to these obvious testimonies, we derive no advantage from them.[27]

But, when guided by special revelations, such as Psalm 19 itself, the Christian may be restored to an appreciation of the unspoken word. We may be as thrilled, as was David, with the heavens that declare the glory of God and the firmament that showeth His handiwork (v. 1).

F. THE DISRUPTION PERIOD. This revelational unit embraces the Hebrew decline under Solomon and the period of the divided kingdoms up to the appearance of the inspired, writing prophets. It covered the two centuries 970-760 B.C. The sources for the period consist primarily of the Song of Solomon; Psalm 72, by Solomon; Psalm 45, which was written for him; and the wisdom literature. This last consists of the wisdom writings, both of Solomon himself (Ps. 127, Proverbs, and Ecclesiastes) and of the writer of the book of Job. The book of Job seems to have taken its place as a part of God's revelation to Israel at this point, even though the man Job had lived in Edom

---

[27]*Institutes of the Christian Religion*, I, V, XI, I:73.

centuries before.[28] Other sources include the theological explanations of the writer of the books of I and II Samuel, which were composed near the commencement of this period, and such revelations as accompanied the events that are described in I Kings and in the earlier portions of II Kings and II Chronicles.

Under Solomon, the "wise men" (Prov. 1:6; 24:23) first rose to prominence as the last of the three major classes that God historically used to communicate His revelation. These three classes were: the priests, with the law; the prophets, with the vision and the word; and the wise, with counsel (Jer. 18:18; Ezek. 7:26). Concerning their respective functions, it might be said that the priest guided the repentant to the way of forgiveness in the law; that the prophet had presumably already roused the sinner to the point of his repentance; but that the wise man had counseled him not to do the wrong thing in the first place! Israel as a whole was to have been "a wise and understanding people" (Deut. 4:6), though they proved to be just the opposite (32:6). Over the years the elders who sat in the city gates developed a store of proverbial wisdom (cf. I Sam. 24:13). There arose also certain particularly noted wise men, as Ethan and Heman, the Ezrahites (of the clan of Zerah in the tribe of Judah, I Kings 4:31). Wise women, too, exercised influence' (II Sam. 14:2-20; 20:16-22). But the wisest man of all history was Solomon himself, whose understanding was given of God (I Kings 3:12; 4:29-34).

The Hebrew word for wise, $hākhām$, exhibits the developing connotations of cautious, careful, skillful, and finally wise.[29] The noun $hokhmā$, "wisdom," may thus indicate simply skillfulness, ability in applied knowledge (Prov. 20:18; 24:3-6). But it is not limited to such externalities. $Hokhmā$ is more primarily concerned with that which lies within a man: "Keep your heart with all diligence, for out of it are the issues of life" (4:23). Wisdom, therefore, emphasizes practical morality. It describes the conduct that God Himself desires. The wise man, therefore, is righteous (9:9; 10:31); and wisdom is the opposite of wickedness (10:23). The characteristic form of wisdom literature is the $māshāl$. Originally meaning any comparison, the $māshāl$ developed into the Biblical proverb, which may be defined as a pointed statement of self-evident moral truth. Correspondingly, the wisdom literature as a whole is ethical in character and not primarily doctrinal, ritualistic, historical, or even philosophical.

The wisdom books are universalistic in outlook. They appeal to all (Prov. 1:20) and they cover a bewildering array of subjects. Their illustrations are frequently drawn from nature, which is the concern of men everywhere (I Kings 4:33; Prov. 30:24-28); and their teachings

---

[28]See Edward J. Young, *An Introduction to the Old Testament* (Grand Rapids: Wm. B. Eerdmans Co., 1949), pp. 309-313.
[29]Kohler, *op. cit.*, p. 297.

are generally divorced from Hebrew national life and ceremony (with but few exceptions, as Prov. 3:9). The Proverbs are timeless, separated from the limitations of localization. With the book of Psalms, Proverbs is among the most individualistic of the Old Testament revelations. It stresses personal retribution and reward (cf. Prov. 6:1-5; 25:17). Never, however, does it degenerate into a self-calculating attitude, as claimed by liberalism, or into the coldly aristocratic approach of the book of Ecclesiasticus in the Apocrypha. Biblical wisdom puts spiritual ends ahead of wealth and success (11:4; 15:16). The ultimate basis for morality can be found only in reverence and faith: "The fear of Yahweh is the beginning of wisdom" (1:7).[30] Wisdom, therefore, embraces all that is best in life (3:16-18) and reveals God's answers to such great problems as retribution and theodicy (Job), or the purpose of life (Ecclesiastes). Israel's wise men drew their conclusions from observation and reflection (Job 8:10; 12:3; Prov. 2:1; Eccl. 12:9) rather than from direct revelations of the sort that God granted to the priests and the prophets. Nevertheless, they spoke absolute truth (Prov. 22:21). Their words came to them from God Himself (2:6; cf. 16:20; Job 4:12, 13; 32:8), who was the one great Shepherd, even of Solomon in all his glory (Eccl. 12:11).[31]

During the period of disruption, and specifically in the reign of Ahab (874-853 B.C.), Biblical prophecy entered its third major stage: that of the reforming prophets—Elijah, Micaiah, and Elisha. The distinguishing feature of the preceding stage had been the establishment under Samuel of regular prophetic organization. But with organization had come the danger of external forms without the true presence of God's Spirit. In actuality, Israel had, by Ahab's time, become plagued with false prophets. These, in turn, fell into three major categories. There were Jezebel's outrightly pagan prophets, who served Baal and Asherah (I Kings 18:19); there were the hypocritical charlatans of Ahab's court (22:6, 7), prophets for pay, a disgrace to the name of the Lord (Micah 3:11; cf. Amos 7:12); and there were sincere prophets, who were well-meaning but still revelationless, and hence mistaken (I Kings 13:11-18). The false prophets came eventually to predominate, so that Amos objected to being classified with the regular prophets at all (Amos 7:14). But even from the first, God had revealed certain tests for distinguishing the true prophets from the false. These tests

---

[30]Parallel, then, to the gradations within wisdom, are the corresponding types of "fools": the *pethi*, "simple," who is neutral or misled and reclaimable (Prov. 19:25; 21:11); the *k'sil*, who opposes truth and morals, but only because of thoughtlessness or a lack of understanding, and not necessarily because of perversity (17:24); and the *lēs* (known earlier as the *nāvāl*, "Nabal," (I Samuel 25:25), the "mocker," who is willful and hopeless, because his resistance to the wise simply manifests his more deep-seated opposition to God. (Prov. 9:8; Ps. 14:1, 2). Cf. Knight, *A Christian Theology of the Old Testament* (Richmond, Va.: John Knox Press, 1959), pp. 260-261.
[31]Cf. the corresponding belittling in the Biblical wisdom literature of human sources for understanding (Job 11:7; Prov. 3:5; Eccl. 8:16, 17).

were three: 1) their ability to perform miracles (Ex. 4:6), and 2) the fulfillment of their predictions (Deut. 18:21, 22). But either of these first two tests might not apply to some true prophets and yet might appear true for some false prophets. The most important test, then, was 3) the conformity of their message to God's word as it was already known (Deut. 13:1-3; Isa. 8:20). Thus, God taught Elijah that the "still small voice" of His word was more significant than the storm wind, the earthquake, and the fire of His catastrophic manifestations in nature (I Kings 19:11, 12). God, moreover, had not forsaken His word. But as the influence of the false prophets grew, God raised up His crusading reformers who overthrew Baal, or who anointed the kings who would. Elisha thus even directed the royal succession in neighboring Damascus (II Kings 8:13; cf. I Kings 19:15).

Under Elisha the "schools" of the prophets also became more prominent. Three such schools are specifically noted in his days (II Kings 2:3; 2:5; 4:38), organized into groups of fifties (2:7, 16) or even hundreds (4:43). Such organizations appear less frequently in the more godly southern kingdom of Judah, but even there they could arise in times of persecution (Isa. 8:16). The members were styled the "sons of the prophets." These men of God could either maintain a married home life (II Kings 4:1) or live in special communities (4:38). Elijah was noted for the austerity of his dress and life (II Kings 1:8; cf. Isa. 20:2; Zech. 13:4; and John the Baptist, Matt. 3:4). The "sons of the prophets" were respected by the people (II Kings 4:8) but mocked by the worldly leaders (9:11) and by the paid court prophets (Jer. 29:26) who claimed God's Spirit as their own (I Kings 22:24). Occasionally they suffered martyrdom at the hands of the godless kings they reproved (II Chron. 24:20-22; Jer. 26:23). Although Vos distinguishes the prophets of the schools by their inability to perform miracles,[32] and although their chronicles were probably not inspired (cf. II Chron. 20:34), these men and their leaders yet communicated God's will in history. The people gathered regularly to hear them in Sabbath services (II Kings 4:23) and they could even receive the Mosaic offerings (4:42) in default of legitimate worship in northern Israel.

G. THE PERIOD OF THE EIGHTH CENTURY PROPHETS. More exactly, this designation refers to the time of the first prophets who wrote down their messages and whose books constitute inspired Scripture. The group consists of Isaiah[33] and the first six minor prophets: Hosea,

---

[32]*Op. cit.* p. 219.

[33]The writer assumes the authenticity of chapters 40-66 as dating from the victory over Sennacherib in 701 B.C. The references in particular to a Jewish captivity have relevance to this time, cf. Raymond P. Dougherty, "Sennacherib and the Walled Cities of Judah," *Journal of Biblical Literature* 49 (1930), 160-171. The final chapters of Isaiah then extend down into the early years of the apostate Manasseh.

Joel,[34] Amos, Obadiah, Jonah, and Micah (about 760-690 B.C.). Certain data from II Kings and II Chronicles, which was revealed contemporaneously with the events described, is also included in the sources for this period. Here begins the fourth and final stage of Old Testament prophecy, in which God directed His ministers not simply in speaking but also in writing His redemptive message. They became the "watchmen" of Israel (Isa. 58:1; Mic. 7:4; cf. Jer. 6:17; Ezek. 3:17) in a day when the more official watchmen were "dumb dogs," fast asleep (Isa. 56:10-12). Isaiah, for example, radiated a zealous monotheism: he denied the existence of any legitimate knowledge of God among the surrounding pagans (Isa. 41:22-24; 43:9; 44:7), and he therefore called upon Israel to return to the true God and to His previously revealed words (8:20). For, contrary to the liberal position which dates the prophets as prior to the law, these men presented themselves not as innovators or as religious pioneers, but, if the Bible's own statements are to be granted validity, as reformers calling Israel back to her former faith.[35]

Isaiah and his associates were conscious mediators of special revelation. They recognized that God's words would be effective (55:11), for punishment (9:8; cf. Jer. 5:14 and 23:29, "like a fire" and "like a hammer"), for deliverance (cf. Ps. 107:20), or for controlling the whole world. Especially would this be the case as these words would some day be spoken by the Messiah (Isa. 11:4; cf. Ps. 147:20; 119:25). By God's words, the prophets predicted the future (Amos 5:27; Obad. 19; Isa. 41:25, 26; 42:9; and so on through chapters 43-48). They appealed, in fact, to the predictions as a major proof of their inspiration (Isa. 48:3).[36] An outstanding example of prophetic foretelling, which ranks second only to the anonymous prophecy of the work and name of Josiah some 309 years in advance (I Kings 13:2; II Kings 23:10), is Isaiah's prediction, by name, of Cyrus, one century

[34]Dating Joel and Obadiah at about 735 B.C., Payne, *An Outline of Hebrew History*, pp. 135-136; and cf. John D. Davis, *A Dictionary of the Bible* (4th revised edition; Grand Rapids: Baker Book House, 1953), pp. 398-399, 548-549.
[35]Cf. Vos, *op. cit.*, pp. 224-229. It may, therefore, seem in the following studies, which emphasize the first appearances of God's revelations, that these prophets are neglected. If so, it is only because the great truths they enunciated were often repetitions of what had been revealed previously through Moses, David, and others.
[36]See above, pp. 51, 52. At the same time, it becomes necessary to maintain exact limits on the extent of Biblical predictions. We must be careful not to find prophecies where none were originally intended. These include: 1) Symbols. Moses and Joshua may have been symbols to their people (Deut. 34:10), but they were not typical predictions of Christ (cf. Deut. 18:15). 2) General statements, Zech. 1:3 and Mark 4:24, for example, are timeless in their reference. 3) Statements of immediate intention, such as Zech. 8:10-15 (especially v. 15). But if the immediate action does not lie in the power of the speaker, then the statement is predictive (Jonah 1:12). Commands, as Gen. 1:3, are not predictive if violated (Zech. 8:19).

and a half before his appearance (Isa. 44:28; 45:1).[37] The word of God, His special revelation, stands forever (40:8)![38] These prophets guided kings; they were, like Elijah and Elisha before them, "the chariots and horsemen of Israel" (II Kings 13:14; cf. 2:12); and, for lost men today, they yet mediate God's peace, assurance, and power.

The vocation of the prophets was no human calling (Amos 7:14). God ordained them, even before birth (Jer. 1:5). They had no alternative but to speak the word that He gave to them (Amos 3:8), though voluntary obedience characterized them as well (Isa. 6:8, 9). Their dominating conviction was that God had communicated to them an all-important message that they must relay to their fellow men (Joel 1:1; Mic. 1:1, etc.). The verbal nature of these revelations achieves its final significance in reference to the books that the men then wrote. It will, therefore, be considered further in the following topic on in-

---

[37]For a detailed study vindicating the authenticity of this prediction, see O. T. Allis, "The Transcendence of Jehovah, God of Israel," Princeton Theological Seminary, *Biblical and Theological Studies* (Princeton: 1912), pp. 579-634. Prophecy, however, must not be understood as history "written in advance." Note the symbolism and the generalizations that mark even such detailed predictions as Daniel 11:2-39 (v. 40 ff. seems to refer to events still future today).

[38]The following may be considered among the basic principles for the interpretation of Biblical predictions. Their neglect causes most of the differences in modern evangelicalism's prophetic interpretations.

Necessary fulfillment. If a prophet is true, his word will come to pass (Deut. 13:2). 1) God is true; and, despite liberalism's denials, His words cannot fail (Zech. 1:6). 2) Since God's purpose in predictive prophecy is moral reformation (Ezek. 33:11), some threats may be postponed by repentance (I Kings 21:29; Mic. 3:12; cf. Jer. 26:19). 3) Some prophecies, moreover, are completely conditional (Jonah 3:4; II Kings 20:1-5); but such are limited to those of near application, and with conditions capable of satisfaction by the prophet's contemporaries. Cf. Jer. 18:7-10 and Joel 2:1 where the prophet warned of a locust plague, but where Judah turned to god (vv. 12-17), so that Yahweh became "jealous for his land and had pity on his people" (v. 18) and averted it. For the limiting principles in reference to conditionalness, see L. Berkhof, *Principles of Biblical Interpretation* (Grand Rapids: Wm. B. Eerdmans Publishing Co., 1950), p. 150.

Single fulfillment. Meaning in Scriptural passages is not manifold but one, and therefore the expectation of further fulfillment beyond the one true accomplishment is unwarranted. Further, more than one meaning means no meaning! Cf. II Samuel 7:12-14, each part of which refers to either Solomon or Christ, but all of which cannot refer to both. See Bernard Ramm, *Protestant Biblical Interpretation,* pp. 88-89; and, for a more detailed treatment, J. B. Payne, "So-Called Dual Fulfillment in Messianic Psalms," Evangelical Theological Society, *1953 Papers,* pp. 62-71. 1) There may, however, appear in one context a series of successive prophecies (cf. Zechariah 9:1-10). 2) Or one term may be used differently in different places (Amos 5:20, Zech. 14:1). 3) "Prophetic telescoping" may connect two events which are widely separated in fulfillment (Amos 7:9; Isa. 61:1-2 [cf. Luke 4:18, 19]; Obad. 21).

Interpretation by analogy. God wrote the whole Bible and directs all history, so harmony must exist between the Old Testament prophecies and the history they predict. 1) Since prophecy is given in relation to historical situations, its accomplishment is preferably to be sought at the nearest subsequent point of adequate fulfillment. 2) The Holy Spirit is as equally responsible for the New Testament as for the Old; hence New Testament explanations of fulfillment are determinative for meanings (as Isa. 7:14).

On the subject of typology (acted prophecy), see below, pp. 355-360.

spiration. Amos was aware, however, that after his time the prophetic phenomenon would cease for northern Israel (Amos 8:12).

H. THE LATER PROPHETIC PERIOD extends down to the fall of Jerusalem to the forces of Babylon in 586 B.C. It includes the ministries of the seventh century minor prophets—Nahum, Zephaniah, and Habakkuk, in that order—the great prophecies of Jeremiah; and, again, such of the data of II Kings and II Chronicles as was contemporaneously revealed. This period differs from the preceding in that it was restricted to southern Judah, Samaria having fallen. It also is marked by a series of distinct doctrinal developments, such as the climactic enunciation of the new testament (Jer. 31:31-34). In reference to the mode of special revelation, the fellowship of Jeremiah with God serves as the highest single example of the objectivity and yet of the personal nature of the way in which God communicated with the prophets. The descriptions given by Jeremiah of his own reactions are among the most intimate recorded in the Old Testament. The prophet even felt free to accuse God of giving him false words (15:18), though their truth was ultimately vindicated (ch. 52). During this period, dreams were treated as a mark of lying prophecy (Jer. 23:25). Jeremiah, it should be said, also suffered more at the hands of various false prophets than any other recorded servant of God (28:15; 29:21, 31).

I. THE EXILIC PERIOD, the time of the fall and the deportations of Judah. The actual dates of this period overlap for some twenty years with those of the one that preceded it, for the full seventy years of the captivity extend from 605-538 B.C. The subject matter, however, is distinct, for it commences with Daniel and the first deportation[39] and moves on into the prophecies of Ezekiel to the Jews of the second (597 B.C.) deportation. The situation is exilic, even though chronologically prior to the destruction of Jerusalem in 586. Subsequent sources include Jeremiah's Lamentations, the revelations that were given through the exilic author of Kings, and certain psalms, such as the famous 137th. It was in this period, shortly after the deportation in 597 B.C., that Ezekiel had his vision of the departure of the *sh'khīnā*, the cloud of God's presence from the temple (Ezek. 10:18). As Isaiah (59:2) had prophesied long before, sin had caused a separation between God and His people. But still, God revealed His power in such miraculous deliverances as are recorded in Daniel 3 and 6. During the exile, prophecy decreased greatly (Ps. 74 [exilic]:9; Lam. 2:9). The very destruction, however, of Israel's political and religious institutions constituted an active revelation of the nature and will of God (Lam. 1:12). Far away in Babylon, moreover, the dream form reap-

---

[39]The historical veracity of the Biblical references to the Babylonian campaign of 605 B.C. has received confirmation from the new Nebuchadrezzar texts, published in 1956. Cf. J. B. Payne, "The Uneasy Conscience of Modern Liberal Exegesis," *Bulletin of the Evangelical Theological Society* 1:1 (Winter, 1958), pp. 14-18.

peared as an instrument of God's revelation. The medium of the dream characterized certain revelations that God granted to pagan men (Dan. 2:1; 4:5); but it was employed in the case of Daniel as well, perhaps that he might the more effectively minister to the pagans who were concerned (7:1). Ezekiel received divine revelation through visions (Ezek. 1:1). He also experienced the new form of "rapture," by which the prophet, in a vision, was carried to distant scenes to observe and to learn (8:3; 11:1). Ezekiel's methods of transmitting God's revelation were often similarly dramatic, as he emphasized his messages by symbolic actions of various sorts (3:1; 4:1; 37:16). Such spectacular, and almost bizarre, symbolism is found also in the verbal prophecies of Daniel, and it serves as a mark of apocalyptic literature.[40] The apocalypse is thus a specialized form of prediction, though without difference in its essential nature from the more normal predictive prophecies of Scripture.[41] Examples of the apocalyptic form had appeared before, particularly in Joel and Isaiah; but it reached its

---

[40]The Apocalyptic literature differs from the rest of Biblical prophecy in certain features of its content as well as of form. Its background was one of world distress. As a result, 1) its basic purpose becomes one of comfort and of encouragement (cf. Rev. 14:12; contrast Hos. 4:1, but note also Isa. 40:1). 2) Apocalyptic lays stress on divine determinism (Dan. 4:35). 3) It exhibits a greater dualism: angels and the Messiah vs. Satan and the Antichrist. 4) There is less on present moral reform (but Dan. 9:4-19; Rev. 2-3). 5) It has a universal orientation (Rev. 20:8). 6) It is marked by a division of time into periods; for example, the "Seventy weeks." 7) It stresses divine intervention by cataclysm: hope lies in invasion from the higher world. 8) There is little mention of judgment on God's people (as compared with Amos 5:18). These differences, however, are only matters of degree. The supernaturalistic climax to human history that characterizes apocalyptic is an essential element in the prophetic world view as well. Similarly, the inspired apocalypses exhibit a degree of present optimism and a prophetic ethic that stands in marked contrast to the disappearance of these elements from post-canonical Jewish apocalyptic. The difference between true prophecy and true apocalyptic is thus one of emphasis. Moreover, even this difference serves to provide a full revelation of the kingdom of God which, as taught by Jesus, possesses both a present reality and a future consummation. Cf. George E. Ladd, "Why Not Prophetic-apocalyptic?" *Journal of Biblical Literature*, 76:3 (Sept. 1957), pp. 192-200.

[41]Thus Milton S. Terry concludes, "The hermeneutical principles to be observed in the interpretation of apocalyptics are, in the main the same as those which apply to all predictive prophecy," *Biblical Hermeneutics* (Revised ed.; New York: Phillips and Hunt, 1890), p. 340. Liberalism, it is true, has insisted upon numerous distinctions between prophecy and apocalyptic, both in respect to form and content. The former include such matters as pseudonymity (that the name of Daniel, for example, was falsely attached to a much later book), esoteric character (that an ancient authorship was supported by tales of the book's having been hidden from the public), artificial claims to inspiration, pseudo-ecstasy (particularly in the receiving of the visions), and a tendency to "play with numbers." The latter include the apocalyptist's pessimistic treatment of history, their belief that history would climax in their own day, and their addiction to mythology (angels fighting with dragons, etc.); cf. H. H. Rowley, *The Relevance of Apocalyptic*. But though such distinctions were often true of the non-inspired apocalypses that flourished in the intertestamental period (as II Esdras in the Apocrypha, or I and II Enoch in the Pseudepigrapha), they cannot fairly be applied to Biblical literature. The "special interpretation" that liberalism demands for apocalyptic consists chiefly of new reasons for not believing Scriptural truth! Cf.

greatest expression in the exilic revelations that came through Daniel. Zechariah's work in the next period also exhibits apocalyptic features.

J. THE POST-EXILIC PERIOD, from the decree of Cyrus, 538 B.C., authorizing the return of the exiled Jews to Palestine, to the completion and close of the Old Testament canon, shortly after 423 B.C.[42] This revelational period includes the historical books of Ezra, Nehemiah, and Esther, and such of the contents of Chronicles as were first revealed through its post-exilic author, probably Ezra. Other sources to be considered are the writings of the 6th and 5th century minor prophets, respectively Haggai and Zechariah, and then Malachi; and a certain few, final anonymous psalms, such as 146-150.[43] The postexilic period marked the termination of God's pre-Christian redemptive activity in special revelation. The priests had no more *ūrīm* (Ezra 2:63) but were admonished to teach the already-revealed law (Mal. 2:7), which embodied God's infallible, spoken "word" (Ps. 105:42; 130:5). Their duties, moreover, became increasingly restricted to the performance of temple ceremonials, as even this teaching function was assumed in intertestamental times by the scribes (cf. Ezra 7:6, 10) and by the rabbis and Pharisees in the synagogues. Prophecy was known to be about at its end (Zech. 13:5). Though its mode of communication to the previous prophets, through God's Spirit (Zech. 7:12), was clarified, no further prophecy was expected. It ceased with Malachi in the 5th century. (Cf. the matter-of-fact witness to its cessation that is found in the Apocrypha, I Maccabees 9:27.) Only the coming of Elijah (Mal. 4:5; that is, John the Baptist, Matt. 11:14) to herald the appearance of the Messiah (Mal. 3:1) would break God's silence which extended for over 400 years. The kind of revelations that God granted through the Old Testament cannot, therefore, be described as "natural." He does not work in this way today; and such methods of communication could not be expected to continue until there should arise some new development in historical redemption. For Israel's restoration to Palestine did not finish redemption. God Himself would yet come to earth, when the setting was fully prepared (Gal. 4:4), to give His life as a ransom for many (Mark 10:45). But in that period there would be no *sh'khinā* and no ark (Jer. 3:16); the Word would become flesh and tabernacle among us (John 1:14).

For Further Reading:

   Louis Berkhof, *Introductory Volume to Systematic Theology.* Grand Rapids: Wm. B. Eerdmans Publishing Co., 1932. Pp. 116-143 provide an excellent survey, though from the systematic point of view, of the nature of revelation.

---

the more evangelically oriented, but equally invalid distinctions argued by H. L. Ellison, *Ezekiel: the Man and His Message* (Grand Rapids: Wm. B. Eerdmans Publishing Co., 1956), pp. 104-105.

[42]Payne, *Hebrew History*, pp. 169-172.

[43]Note for example 147:2, 13, which apparently refers to the work of Nehemiah in 444 B.C.

Edward J. Young, *My Servants the Prophets.* Grand Rapids: Wm. B. Eerd-mans Publishing Co., 1952. An evangelical study on the nature of prophecy.
John Davison, *Discourses on Prophecy.* Oxford: James Parker and Co., 1870. Discourses III-VI cover the structure of prophecy in its several periods.
James G. S. S. Thomson, *The Old Testament View of Revelation.* Grand Rapids: Wm. B. Eerdmans Publishing Co., 1960. A recent evangelical work, recog-nizing the positive elements in neo-orthodoxy's stress on revelation as "en-counter." Chs. 1-4 discuss the nature of O.T. revelation, its media, and "the word of God."

4. Inspiration*

Revelation makes truth known, but inspiration provides for its infallible recording. The Bible is the result of this latter activity on the part of God. It preserves the record of revelation, and its preeminent feature is that of its divinely guaranteed truthfulness. Scripture, how-ever, is at the same time the historical source for our data on the nature, mode, and extent of inspiration itself.

No mention is made of inspired writing in the first two periods of Old Testament revelation. Its history commences rather with the Mosaic period.

A. THE LAW OF MOSES. Exodus 17:14 records God's first com-mand to write down an event that is a part of Scripture. It is true that inspiration is not here asserted for what Moses wrote, but the verse does claim to contain a direct quotation of God's words. Also, this writing by Moses was to be inserted, according to the Hebrew Maso-retic pointing, *bas-sêfer,* "in *the* book." It was to become a part, pre-sumably, of some historical record already composed. What this record was is not stated, but it may well have consisted of the whole Penta-teuch up to this point of Exodus 17. Even the historical narratives of Genesis, moreover, present themselves as an authoritative standard for divinely-approved conduct (Gen. 39:9).

When Israel reached Sinai, Yahweh "came from the ten thousands of holy ones"; but also, "at His right hand was a fiery law for them" (Deut. 33:2). The translation of *ēsh-dāth* as "fiery law" is subject to some uncertainty, but this historic rendering may claim the support of the analogy of the New Testament. Calvin long ago observed:

"It is probable that both Paul and Stephen derived from this passage their statement that the Law was 'ordained by Angels in the hand of a mediator' (Gal. 3:19; Acts 7:53).

---

*BIBLE READING: Jeremiah 36; Ezra 7

Collateral Reading: R. Laird Harris, *Inspiration and Canonicity of the Bible* Grand Rapids: Zondervan Publishing House, c. 1957), pp. 45-50, 61-71. Burrows, *An Outline of Biblical Theology,* pp. 16-53.

As to its significance, the great Reformer goes on to state:

> "The Law is placed at *His right hand* . . . for He did not merely show Himself as king, but also made known how He would preside over them. . . . It designates all the doctrine whereby God's dominion is maintained."[1]

God is specifically stated to have put the Decalogue, the moral standard of His testament, into writing. Its two tables consisted of words written by God's own hand (Ex. 24:12; 31:18; 32:16; 34:28; Deut. 9:10; 10:4). The rest of the Exodus legislation, the "Book of the Testament," was written down by Moses (34:27); but it still presents itself as the direct quotation of God's words (cf. Lev. 1:1, 2 and the rest of the legal codes). God, that is, not only acted in history; He then left with His people an objective record and explanation of His actions. Furthermore, since the record itself is God's words, it also automatically becomes revelation.

As Moses continued to publish the sections of the Pentateuch, it is significant that his own written words (as Deut. 17:14-20) appear with the same canonically binding authority as do God's. They were to be read before the people, even the children, every seven years (Deut. 31:10-13; cf. Neh. 8:18). They were diligently to be taught (Deut. 6:6-9), especially by the priests (Lev. 10:11; Deut. 17:18). The whole book of the law (the Pentateuch through Deut. 30?) was to be preserved beside the ark (31:26);[2] and the commandments of the book were to be neither added to nor diminished (Deut. 4:2; 12:32). Moses' work thus came to be called simply the "law of God" (Neh. 8:18). Though the process of inspiration is not yet described,[3] the end product consists of a book that is the equivalent of God's own composition. It is true that the coming of a new testament in some post-exilic day is vaguely hinted (Deut. 30:6); but the possession of the older, objective law continued to be a central feature of Israel's faith, her unique privilege among the nations (4:8; Rom. 3:2).

At the outset of Joshua's ministry, God charged him to be subject to the law of Moses (Josh. 1:8). Later, after his conquest of central Palestine, Joshua publicly reaffirmed the divine authority of this law. Moses, prior to his death, had given instruction that the law be recorded on plastered stones that should be raised up on Mount Ebal (Deut. 27:4-8); and this Joshua proceeded to do (Josh. 8:32-35). Just how much of the Pentateuch, however, Joshua actually inscribed on

---

[1]*Commentaries on the Four Last Books of Moses Arranged in the Form of a Harmony* (Grand Rapids: Wm. B. Eerdmans Publishing Co., 1950), IV:381.

[2]The authenticity of such preservation is confirmed by analogous practice in the case of Hittite "suzerainty covenants," George E. Mendenhall, "Covenant Forms in Israelite Tradition," *The Biblical Archaeologist* 17 (1954), pp. 60, 64-65.

[3]Ex. 4:12, on God's instructing Moses on what to speak, refers to Moses' oral communications with Pharaoh, not to his composing Scripture. Num. 16:28, however (cf. 24:13), does show negatively a conscious denial of his own mind as the source for his teachings in general.

the stones is not certain, since by "all the words of this law" (Deut. 27:8) Moses may have meant simply his second address on the Plains of Moab (Deut. 5-30). At his death in about 1395 B.C., Joshua is recorded as writing some of his own words as a designed addition in "the book of the law of God" (Josh. 24:26). Compare the similar activity by Samuel almost three and a half centuries later (I Sam. 10:25). It may well have been by such a process that Joshua also added Deut. 34, concerning the death of Moses, to the Pentateuch. The book of Joshua was produced by one of his contemporaries as is shown by the use of the pronoun "we" (Josh. 5:1) in the narrative. It could hardly have been done by Joshua himself (cf. 24:31). This book, as well as Judges, seems to have been composed by certain unknown prophets[4] during the period of consolidation. The details, however, are not given. The important thing is that as rapidly as these inspired works were written they were added to what had already been received as God's word.

B. DAVID AND SOLOMON. David equated the law of Moses with "the charge of Yahweh" (I Kings 2:3; cf. Ps. 78:5, 6); but he became himself also a medium for God's inspired words. The plans of the temple he was "made to understand in writing from the hand of Yahweh" (I Chron. 28:19). It is in this context that the source of inspiration is for the first time indicated as being God's Spirit (v. 12). David's chief literary contribution lay in the form of poetry. From early years he had displayed talent with the harp (I Sam. 16:18); and his contacts with Samuel (19:18; cf. v. 20) may have trained him in receptivity, through music, to the revelations of the Spirit. David became "the sweet psalmist of Israel" (II Sam. 23:1). He knew himself on occasion to have had God's words on his tongue, so that the Spirit spoke by him (v. 2). He was a true prophet (Acts 2:30), though at times he may have been unconscious of this fact as he wrote. His was no "dictation" inspiration; his personal emotions conveyed God's words from a Spirit-filled heart. The titles of the Psalms indicate that David composed seventy-three out of the collection of one hundred fifty.[5] These titles, moreover, appear in the oldest manuscripts as authentic, and they are confirmed in the New Testament as true evidences of Davidic authorship.[6] David is known from Scriptural analogy to have written five others: Psalms 2, 95, 96, 105, and 106,[7] and he is probably responsible for many more. Other psalms, though

[4]Though the authors remain anonymous, their moral, prophetic approach to history is obvious (Josh. 21:43-45; Judg. 2:11-15).

[5]Cf. Ps. 18 as a particularly clear example of the meaning of David's name in the titles. Liberal writers uniformly deny their authenticity; but for their vindication, see Robert Dick Wilson, "The Readings of the Psalms," *Princeton Theological Review*, 24:1, 3 (Jan. and July, 1926), 1-37, 353-395.

[6]Ps. 16; Acts 2:25; Ps. 32; Rom. 4:6; Ps. 69; Acts 1:16 and Rom. 11:9; and Ps. 110; Luke 20:42 and Acts 2:24.

[7]Ps. 2 from Acts 4:25; 95 from Heb. 4:7; and the others from I Chron. 16.

not by David (cf. Ps. 90, the oldest, by Moses), were composed by his contemporaries and were doubtless produced under his stimulation. This group includes most of the twelve that bear the name of Asaph, whom David appointed as his chief musician (I Chron. 16:37); ten by the Korahite singers; two by Solomon; and one each by the wise men Heman and Ethan. Three of those, however, that are identified by the title "Asaph" may be of later composition, written by the course of singers that bore Asaph's name (cf. Ezra 3:10).[8] In the study of the development of revelation that follows, those psalms that claim David or his friends as authors will be recognized as belonging historically to his generation. Psalms that are without indication of their historical origin will be treated without reference to their chronological position, or simply as originating in the latest period.

Solomon minimized books (Eccl. 12:12), but not his own, which he prized as coming from God (v. 11). The "word" of the wise was thus treated as of equal authority with the *miswā*, "the commandment" of the law.[9] The very term *māshāl* (proverb), from its previously noted root meaning of a "comparison," comes to identify not only a maxim or a parable, but also a specifically infallible dictum of God, as compared with a changeable opinion of sinful man. *Māshāl* may thus mean an "authoritative statement" (Job 27:1; 29:1; cf. 28:28). Shortly after Solomon's death some anonymous prophet[10] compiled I and II Samuel as a historical supplement to the growing canon. In the years that followed, evil kings would neglect the written word, but the righteous ones stressed its authority. A noteworthy example of the latter is Jehoshaphat's traveling officers, who "taught in Judah having the book of the law of Yahweh with them" (II Chron. 17:9). The "testimony" given little Joash at his coronation (II Kings 11:12) may have been a copy of God's law book (cf. Deut. 17:18, 19 and similar stipulations; see below, p. 322).

C. THE PROPHETS. The eighth century prophetic period and the later prophetic period that follows it are the most significant for the Old Testament doctrine of its own inspiration. The writing prophets give details of their actual experiences with God, and these details apply to their recording of the revelations as well as to their receiving of them. In the first place, what they wrote is expressly denied to be their own ideas. Men, of themselves, could not acquire God's word by seeking (Amos 8:12; Ezek. 7:26); His thoughts were higher than theirs (Isa. 55:8, 9). Their own feelings and personalities (Isa. 6:5), or their contemporary environments (v. 1, cf. Ezek. 24:18), might help to explain the particular words that they used; for "the spirits of the

---

[8]Ps. 83 fits II Chron. 20:14 and Jahaziel of Asaph; Ps. 74 and 79 seem to be right after the fall of Jerusalem in 586 B.C.

[9]Cf. Edmond Jacob, *Theology of the Old Testament,* p. 132.

[10]Perhaps Ahimaaz, son of Zadok, for II Sam. 17:17 ff. (cf. 18:19) imply an eyewitness. Note also the prophetic emphasis as in 12:7-10.

prophets are subject to the prophets" (I Cor. 14:32). But their basic experience was neither natural, nor did it come from themselves. They reacted emotionally, and with surprise even, to what they saw or heard (Isa. 21:3, 4; cf. I Pet. 1:10). They were fundamentally men that "had God's Spirit" (Hos. 9:7), being "full of power by the Spirit of Yahweh" (Mic. 3:8). Isaiah 48:16 may be understood in two ways: "Yahweh hath sent me, and His Spirit." But whether "Spirit" be subject or object, the objective reality of the Spirit is clear.

The Spirit used different means to convey His message to the prophets. Sometimes they "saw" it (Isa. 2:1), sometimes in a vision (Amos 7:7; 8:1). At other times they "heard" it audibly (Isa. 21:10); "for the mouth of Yahweh hath spoken it" (1:20; 58:14). Again, it came to them inaudibly, or at least so quietly as to register in the prophets' ears alone (5:9; 22:14; 28:22); it was no more than "a sound of gentle stillness" (I Kings 19:12). But the result was that their words were, at the same time, God's words. Amos, for example, spoke and then wrote, in the first person, as if he were God (3:1); and Isaiah referred to his own book, which he had just written, as "the book of Yahweh" (34:16). The prophets' purpose in writing was that "the word" which the Spirit had conveyed to them might be preserved (8:16; Hab. 2:2, 3)[11] "for the time to come for ever and ever" (Isa. 30:8). Their books, moreover, were accepted as God's words and were included in the developing canon of Scripture as rapidly as they were written. Joel 2:32, for example, quoted Obadiah 17, with the identification, "as Yahweh hath said." Isaiah 2:2-4 seems to cite Micah 4:2-4 as the equivalent of a vision from God Himself, and an entire block of Isaiah's work (chapters 36-39) came to be included in II Kings (18:13; 18:17-20; 19). Hezekiah recognized that the psalms of David and of Asaph were divinely authoritative (II Chron. 29:30); and his men copied out and added to the book of Proverbs a number of additional chapters that were appreciated as fully inspired with the rest (Prov. 25:1).

The evidence from the later (seventh century) prophetic period confirms the conclusions stated above. Jeremiah, like his predecessors, disclaimed his own mind as the source of his information. In fact, what distinguished the false prophets was that they spoke "out of their own heart" (Jer. 23:16, 30; Ezek. 13:2). Jeremiah had to pray to God for information (Jer. 32:16; 42:4); sometimes he and his colleagues had to wait for answers (42:7; Hab. 2:1); and their own ideas are expressly distinguished from what they finally wrote (Hab. 2:1, 2). Sometimes God actually compelled them to speak and to write what was contrary to their own judgment and wishes (Jer. 17:16; 20:7, 9;

[11]Cf J. G. S. S. Thomson's stress on the abiding, objective character of "the Word of God" in written form, so that it "did not perish when those who spoke and wrote it perished . . . the Word of the Lord written, corresponded to its Author," *The Old Testament View of Revelation*, p. 78.

cf. 1:6). Therefore, there were times when, in a very literal sense, Yahweh "put His words in his mouth" (1:9) and then commanded, "Write thee all the words that I have spoken unto thee in a book" (30:2; 36:2). Jeremiah 36 goes on to furnish the most complete Biblical description of the production of a part of one of its own books: v. 2, God's words to the prophet; v. 4, the prophet's dictation of these words to a scribe; v. 4, the scribe's writing them in a book (scroll form); and v. 32, their reproduction, because in this case the king had burned the original copy.

But divine dictation is not the normal method of Biblical inscripturization. Even in those sections of Jeremiah that are singled out above, God used the prophet's own thought forms and vocabulary. After all, Jeremiah's whole personality had been made up in accordance with God's predeterminate counsel (1:5)![12] The result is thus an organic rather than a mechanical mode of inspiration. The chapters that the prophets wrote seem also to constitute summaries, rather than complete reproductions of God's revelations. To the books that ensued, however, God "signed His name," accepting full responsibility for them as equal to His own words and completely authoritative. The Lord could say: "And I will bring upon that land all My words which I have prophesied against it, even all that is written in this book, which Jeremiah hath prophesied against all the nations" (25:13). Only the coming of God's new testament, which would be written on men's hearts (31:31-33), could transcend the glory of the written record thus given.

Jeremiah twice validated the inspiration of eighth century prophets. Jeremiah 26:18 quotes the written content of Micah 3:12 as being God's own prophecy; and 49:14-19 quotes from Obadiah as tidings of Yahweh. Most of the kings of this period were corrupt. Josiah, however, not only recognized the concept of inspiration, but he is distinguished by his zeal for God's book (II Kings 23:25). Scripture had fallen into oblivion under Manasseh, but in the temple repairs of 621 B.C. the high priest uncovered a copy of the law of Moses (22:8). Judging from the reforms that Josiah then undertook, the scroll must have included Deuteronomy and, from its description as "the book of the testament" (23:2), Exodus. The recovered manuscript may have been the official copy of the Pentateuch laid up beside the ark (Deut. 31:26; cf. II Chron. 35:3). But the priests corrupted the law (Jer. 8:8), even while relying on the externality of possessing it (18:18). The fulfillment of Moses' inspired curses could no longer be delayed (Deut. 28:36, 37).

D. THE CLOSE OF THE CANON. During the exilic period that followed, the growing canon of Scripture received testimony as to the

---

[12]See Gordon H. Clark, "Verbal Inspiration: Yesterday and Today," *The Southern Presbyterian Journal* (Sept. 12, 1956), p. 7.

reality, both of its primary divine authorship, and of its human secondary authorship. Daniel was not an official prophet; so his book is not included in the prophetic part of the Old Testament Hebrew canon. Yet Daniel possessed the prophetic gift of God's Spirit (Dan. 4:8; Matt. 24:15), and his writings exhibit a correspondingly superhuman origin. He admitted that he was not able to understand his own recorded visions (8:15; 12:8; ch. Zech. 4:4, 13). Their meanings had rather to be "revealed" (10:1), and by a source so external to himself that he was physically overcome in the process (10:8, 9).[13] He was, however, no mere passive recording device, for he described his own sensations during the experience (vv. 10, 11). It was he, moreover, who personally wrote the book, though as God commanded it (12:4). The only example of a purely mechanical divine writing is that of the hand at Belshazzar's feast (5:5) which stands unique, except for the fiery law of the Decalogue.

During this same exilic period, an unnamed prophet produced the final compilation of I and II Kings.[14] His parallel usage of "law"[15] and "prophecy" in II Kings 17:13 demonstrates the identical authoritativeness of these two major divisions of Old Testament literature. Degrees of Biblical inspiration are of course impossible; for guaranteed truthfulness, which is the ultimate characteristic of God's books, either exists or it does not. With the exile's relative lack of direct revelation, moreover, there arose an increased study of God's written revelations in the past. Men "understood by the books" (Dan. 9:2), a tendency which became more pronounced as the Old Testament canon neared its completion.

After the return from exile, the priestly author of Chronicles, presumably Ezra, described the Pentateuch as, literally, "The book of the law of Yahweh, by the hand of Moses" (II Chron. 34:14). The phrase well conveys the balance of the divine and the human that constitutes the Biblical definition of inspiration. It was during these years that the production of the concluding historical and prophetic books was directed by God's Spirit (cf. topic 3-J). Scripture could not, obviously, record the closing of its own canon; but non-inspired tradition assigns this activity, with likelihood, to Ezra and Nehemiah.[16] Ezra, though a priest, was preeminently the *sōfēr*, or scribe (Ezra 7:6). The literal meaning of *sōfēr* is "enumerator," and the term develops in connotation from "mustering officer" (Judges 5:14) to

---

[13]At other points also, God's objective revealing-activity produced physical reactions, either tiring (Dan. 8:27) or strengthening (Isa. 8:11).
[14]Indications of its prophetic character are seen in its moralizing upon history (II Kings 17:7-23) and its consistent evaluations of rulers' conduct (15:3, 9, etc.).
[15]The Hebrew term *tōrā* meant originally simply "instruction." But by the exilic period phrases such as that in this 13th verse, "the *tōrā* which I commanded your fathers," seem to have specific reference to the Mosaic Pentateuch, the law *par excellence*.
[16]The Apocryphal writings, II Esdras 14:45 and II Maccabees 2:13.

"scribe" (II Sam. 8:17) or "secretary" (Jer. 45:2). But the literary interest of the Biblical scribe centered on one inspired Book: "Ezra had set his heart to seek the law of Yahweh, and to do it, and to teach in Israel statutes and ordinances" (Ezra 7:10). The essence of Ezra's commission lay in his enforcement of the Mosaic law (v. 14), even upon the surrounding Gentiles (v. 25). In 444 B.C. accordingly, after the rebuilding of the walls of Jerusalem, he and Nehemiah and the Levites read the law, explained it, and re-established it as it had not been since the days of Moses himself (Neh. 8). The Book dominated religion (Ezra 3:2; Mal. 4:4); and the faithful would exclaim, "Oh how love I Thy law! It is my meditation all the day" (Ps. 119:97). This could be, and later was, perverted into Pharisaism. But the truth remains that the Book is the one record of God's redemptive activity in history, as the Spirit later wrote through Paul:

> Now I make known unto you, brethren, the gospel . . . by which ye are saved, if ye hold fast the word. . . . For I delivered unto you first of all that which also I received: that Christ died for our sins according to the Scriptures; and that He was buried; and that He hath been raised on the third day according to the Scriptures (I Cor. 15:1-4).

See below, Appendix A, "The Basis for Believing in Inspiration."

For Further Reading:

Westminster Theological Seminary, *The Infallible Word.* Philadelphia: Presbyterian Guardian, 1946. A faculty symposium relating the evangelical doctrine of inspiration to the various areas of theological study today.

Alan Richardson, W. Schweitzer, *et al, Biblical Authority for Today.* Philadelphia: Westminster Press, 1951. A World Council symposium, predominantly liberal.

H. H. Rowley, *The Authority of the Bible.* Birmingham: 1950. A standard Neo-orthodox attempt to get back to Biblical authority without submitting to it.

Part II. The Relationship: The Testament

"Behold the days come, saith Yahweh, that I will make a new testament with the house of Israel, and with the house of Judah: not according to the testament that I made with their fathers" (Jer. 31:31, 32).

5. The Organizing Principle of Biblical Theology*

A. THE CONTENT OF SPECIAL REVELATION. Recognizing that God has communicated with man in history (Part I preceding), one must go on to ask, "With what?" It is in answer to this question that the basic inadequacy of neo-orthodoxy becomes apparent. Its leaders have stressed the reality of God's encounter with sinful man,[1] and their writings have thus furnished contemporary theology with a welcome reaction against the practical godlessness of the old "modernism." But at the same time, neo-orthodoxy has failed to reckon with the objective content of this event, the communication of which Scripture teaches to have been the very purpose of God's revelation. In contrast, the premise of existentialism in general and of Barth's belief in the discontinuity of God and man in particular is that God cannot become an observable object in the "encounter." He can exist only as an experienced subject who confronts man, so that man is mystically overwhelmed by the divine Presence.[2] As John Baillie has summarized the neo-orthodox position:

> What is revealed to us is not a body of information concerning various things of which we might otherwise be ignorant . . . it is not information about God that is revealed, but very God Himself.[3]

But while appreciating the value of this stress on God's living presence, one cannot but feel that at heart the "new modernism" is worse

---

*BIBLE READING: Exodus 24; Jeremiah 31:18-34

Collateral Reading: Wilhelm Vischer, *The Witness of the Old Testament to Christ.* Translated by A. B. Crabtree (London: Lutterworth Press, 1949), 1:7-34. Charles C. Ryrie, *The Basis of the Premillennial Faith* (New York: Loizeaux Brothers, 1953), pp. 105-125.

[1]For example, Emil Brunner, *The Divine-Human Encounter.*
[2]E.g., Barth, *The Doctrine of the Word of God.* Needless to say, Barth's principle, which amounts to agnosticism, is not consistently maintained.
[3]*The Idea of Revelation in Recent Thought* (New York: Columbia University Press, 1956), p. 28.

71

than the old; for the old at least presented men with certain objective values to be possessed.[4] Neo-orthodoxy, on the contrary, refuses to recognize the objectivity that is involved in God's meeting with man, or to ask in a realistic way, "encounter, with what?"

The Old Testament gives two basic answers to the question of the content of special revelation. 1) God comes to man with redemption. This was, in pre-Christian times, a redemption that had not yet been historically accomplished. Meanwhile, however, its benefits were graciously offered to those who would accept the terms that God laid down for a restored harmony with Himself. For example, when God encountered Israel at Mt. Sinai, He prescribed through Moses certain offerings of blood (Ex. 24:5). These, in turn, signified Israel's redemption, a redemption made possible by means of a life sacrificed to God for the propitiation of His wrath against the people.[5] The result was that the elders, as representatives of the nation, were able to ascend the mountain and sit down at a fellowship meal with God; and this they did without, as would otherwise have been the case, His laying His hands in holy wrath upon them (Ex. 24:11; cf. 19:12). They had come into a state of reconciliation with God. The ultimate accomplishment of this redemption took place when Jesus Christ shed His divine blood on Calvary's cross. His death provided the ransom that rendered satisfaction in full for the sins of all those whose names have been written in the Lamb's Book of Life from the foundation of the world (Rev. 13:8).[6] Finally, in the individual application of salvation, it is the living person of Christ who yet confronts sinful man for reconciliation with God (Rev. 3:20; II Cor. 5:20),[7] even as it was He who spoke redemption through the Old Testament prophets (I Peter 1:11). This is the "scarlet cord" that binds together the Biblical revelation and constitutes its very heart: God and sinners reconciled! He is theirs, and they are His. It was true for Abraham (Gen. 17:7); it was

---

[4]Cornelius Van Til, *The New Modernism*, p. 1, thus observes that neo-orthodoxy opposes liberal Protestantism, Romanism, and traditional orthodoxy, all three. Its antagonism, he explains, is due to the fact the other three hold at least this one thing in common: they all maintain the concept of "the *beati possidentes*, blessed possessors," that is, they assume "the possibility and actuality of a direct revelation of God to man in history and experience."

[5]See below, p. 251. Knight (neo-orthodox) indeed recognizes redemption as the central theme of the Old Testament but would minimize its objective aspects, such as the very propositions of the testament, *A Christian Theology of the Old Testament*, p. 9.

[6]Yet Emil Brunner, the neo-orthodox leader, in effect denies the necessity of the whole historical incarnation of Christ. His real stress lies upon Christ as contemporaneous with the believer.

[7]It is this real truth of the personal encounter of Christ with men that Brunner champions, though one-sidedly, to the exclusion of objective revelation, cf. *op. cit.*, p. 139.

true for Moses (Ex. 20:1); and it continues so, right on through to the end (Rev. 21:3).[8]

2) The Old Testament further teaches that God comes to man with truth. Revelation is not only a form of communication, it is also the propositional content communicated (Cf. John 3:34; 16:12). Neo-orthodoxy may indeed limit revelation to the existential meeting of personalities; but the Bible goes on to describe objective facts and propositional truths, some of them of a most earthy quality (e.g. the "lost asses" of I Sam. 9:20; cf. 10:22!).

Scripture, however, preeminently identifies the content of God's revelation with one fact that combines in itself the two general categories of redemption and truth. It is this: that God has placed before man the terms of the arrangement by which He mediates His redemption — "Mine ordinances which, if a man do, he shall live in them" (Lev. 18:5; cf. I Cor. 6:9, 10). These terms, moreover, are summed up in the "testament,"[9] the legal instrument established by God, through which men may be brought into reconciliation with Himself (Gen. 17:7). When it is put into writing, the "book of the testament" becomes the objective source for man's religious hope (Ex. 24:7). The testament concept is, therefore, not only one of many possible organizing principles for Biblical revelation; the communication of its features constitutes *the* historical event of God's saving encounter with men. As E. J. Young has put it, "The subject matter with which Old Testament theology is concerned *is* that covenant which God has made with man for the purpose of man's salvation."[10] To this supreme revelation all other facts of Biblical theology appear as corollaries. The very incompleteness of Scripture in respect to certain doctrines appears to be due to their incidental relationship to the testament.

B. THE UNITY OF THE TESTAMENT. Salvation becomes possible only through God's gracious activity. It rests upon His resolve to have mercy upon men (Jer. 31:21; Eph. 2:8, 9). With the exception of the brief period before the Fall, all men have stood, and do stand, guilty and unable to effect reconciliation with God (Ps. 51:5; Rom. 5:8, 18). Hope lies only in God: "Turn Thou me, and I shall be turned" (Jer. 31:18). Salvation, moreover, objectively considered, comes about only

[8]Herein lies the underlying failure of dispensationalism. For by its stress upon dispensational distinctions it surrenders the unity of redemption as the organizing principle of revelation. A leading dispensationalist makes a significant admission when (as though defending Calvin's emphasis upon the sovereignty of God) he criticizes an opponent for maintaining that "the kingdom of God is the unfolding of the plan of redemption rather than the sovereignty of God," John F. Walvoord, "A Review of 'Crucial Questions About the Kingdom of God,'" *Bibliotheca Sacra*, 110:437 (Jan. 1953), p. 3.

[9]For the preferability of the translation "testament" to "covenant," see topic 6.

[10]*The Study of Old Testament Theology Today*, p. 61; cf. Vriezens conclusion that in the God of the covenant we have the essence of Israel's faith, *An Outline of Old Testament Theology*, p. 30. Note also John Murray, *The Covenant of Grace*, pp. 4, 27, 31.

through a man's identification with the righteous life, substitutionary death, and resurrection of Jesus Christ (Col. 1:27; Matt. 3:15; I Pet. 2:24; Phil. 3:21; John 14:6). This applies equally to the saved of all ages, to those of the Old as well as of the New Testament (Heb. 11:40). Israel stood quite literally under the blood (Ex. 24:8; Heb. 9:19); and the effectiveness of the blood lay not in bulls and goats (Heb. 10:4) but in its anticipation of the offering of the body of Jesus Christ once for all (v. 12).[11]

In consequence, salvation, subjectively considered, is at all periods appropriated by faith alone (Gen. 15:6; Deut. 6:4, 5; Col. 2:5; Heb. 11:6 ff.), though a man's faith is, of course, demonstrated by his works (Gen. 17:1; Deut. 6:6; Col. 2:6, 7).[12] Hence there is basically only one testament. It was this arrangement upon which the various patriarchs trusted (II Kings 13:23; I Chron. 16:16, 17), as did Israel at Sinai, *along with them* (Lev. 26:42, 45). In Asa's day, "they entered into *the* testament" (II Chron. 15:12). The Asaphite singers of the exile prayed God to "have respect unto the testament" (Ps. 74:20); and it is impossible to tell which of the testamental revelations may have been intended! Josiah's rediscovered law book, which probably included the whole Pentateuch, is called simply "the book of the testament" (II Kings 23:2), Ultimately, Matthew 26:28 records the words of our Lord Jesus Christ, who said, "This is My blood of *the* testament,[13] which is shed for many for the remission of sins."

C. THE DEVELOPMENT OF THE TESTAMENTAL RELATIONSHIP. There exists, however, within the basic unity of the testamental relationship a real historical development. The primary gradation lies between the older[14] and the newer testaments, as is marked by the very division of the Bible into "Old Testament" and "New Testament." These two adjectives, moreover, correspond to the organization and even to the terminology that Scripture imposes upon itself. Jeremiah, for example, recognized that he was living under a testamental relationship which God had established with the fathers of Israel of old (Jer. 31:32); but he also looked forward to a new testa-

---

[11]Note Wilhelm Vischer's fundamental grasp of the coming of Jesus as the realization point of the Old Testament's teachings, *The Witness of the Old Testament to Christ*. Trans. by A. B. Crabtree (London: Lutterworth Press, 1949), I:11, with which the reconstructions of liberal scholarship stand in marked contrast. I:28-29.
[12]Compare the seriously fallacious distinction of dispensationalism: "As a dispensation, grace begins with the death and resurrection of Christ. The point of testing is no longer legal obedience as the condition of salvation, but the acceptance or rejection of Christ, with good works as a fruit of salvation," C. I. Scofield, editor, *The Holy Bible* (New edition; New York: Oxford University Press, c. 1917), p. 1115; contrast Vischer, *op. cit.*, p. 20.
[13]"New" is not in the better manuscripts, though from I Cor. 11:25 it is known that Christ did use the term.
[14]So throughout this study "older" will be used for God's former saving arrangement, both to emphasize its essential unity with the "newer" and also to distinguish it from the "Old," capitalized, the first 39 inspired books of the canon.

ment that God would yet reveal. Already in Moses' day, less than forty years after God's thundering from Sinai (which constituted the most significant revelation of the older testament), Moses' prophecy in Deuteronomy 30:6 anticipates a time of a more internal redemptive working of God in the heart. Similarly, Jeremiah 3:16 foresees a relationship in which the ark, the most sacred object of the older testament, would lose its entire function. What is more, it would not even be missed or remembered! The New Testament speaks explicitly of pre-Christians as having lived under the "first" testament (Heb. 9:15, 18) and of the reading of the "old" testament (II Cor. 3:14). But it states that now Christ has also become the Mediator of a better "second" testament (Heb. 8:6, 7), and it identifies His apostles as ministers of a "new" testament (II Cor. 3:6). Believing Christians are indeed reckoned to be the heirs of the promises of the older testament (Gal. 3:29), and the old ceremonies are appreciated as foreshadowing what Christ would do in the newer (Col. 2:16, 17). But there is still a factor of distinction that marks these eras as two major dispensations or administrations within redemptive history — the older, mediated salvation by anticipatory faith in redemption yet to come (Heb. 8:5); and the newer, by commemorative faith in redemption once for all accomplished (Heb. 9:12; 10:10).

The validity of this structure into which the Bible organizes its own development has been attacked from two directions. The one attack, the liberal, need only be mentioned in passing. Antisupernaturalists, as might be expected, refuse to admit the reality of salvation through Christ in the Old Testament. They do concede that Christ and His apostles taught this view; they just do not believe it![15] The other attack, the dispensational, is more serious because it seeks on Biblical grounds to disprove the truth of the one testament in its two stages of growth.[16] The root of the problem lies in the Plymouth Brethren doctrine of the discontinuity of the church. By their presuppositions, dispensationalists are thus forced to the denial, not simply of the New Testament Church as the culmination of Hebrew history, but of its very mention within the pages of the Old Testament.[17] The most extensive discussion centers around Jeremiah's prediction of the new testament (31:31-34) and its application in Hebrews 8:6-10:22 to the Church.[18] It is understandable, moreover,

---

[15]Cf. W. T. Davison's cautious recognition, "The evangelists and apostles held a view of the Psalter, which they so often quoted, that cannot be defended; if, neither by way of prophecy nor of type, is Christ contemplated in the Psalms at all," James Hastings, editor, A Dictionary of the Bible (New York: Charles Scribner's Sons, 1927), IV:160.

[16]Cf. Charles C. Ryrie, The Basis of the Premillennial Faith (New York: Loizeaux Brothers, 1953).

[17]Cf. above, pp. 31, 32, 40. The Church is styled a "mystery" which is defined as being totally outside the scope of Old Testament thought.

[18]An indication of the basic character of this passage is that Heb. 8:8-12 constitutes the longest single Old Testament quotation to be found in the New.

why dispensational leaders should attempt to escape the force of the Hebrews passage; for it is one of Scripture's clearest presentations on the organic, testamental development of Israel into the Church. The argument centers generally on two points.

1) Dispensational writers stress the fact that the predicted new testament is to be made "with the house of Israel and with the house of Judah" (Jer. 31:31; Heb. 8:8) and claim, therefore, that it cannot be fulfilled in the Church.[19] This assertion, however, begs the question by assuming the very lack of identity between Israel and the Church that is under investigation. Furthermore, the New Testament teaching on this subject is hardly mistakable. Christ's ministry was to Israel and Judah (Matt. 10:6). Elect Jews did receive the Gospel and were the ones who made up His church (Matt. 18:17), thus continuing as God's people (Rom. 11:5). Faithless Jews ceased to constitute true Israel and were cut off (Rom. 9:6), becoming instead the very synagogue of Satan (Rev. 2:9). But then the Church expanded; and, just as in the cases of proselytes down through the preceding centuries, Gentiles continued to be ingrafted into Israel (Rom. 11:17). They became joint citizens in Israel and heirs under the testament (Eph. 2:12, 13; cf. Phil. 3:3), "the Israel of God" (Gal. 6:16).[20] It is true that at certain points in the New Testament "Israel" is applied to the unbelieving portion of the Jewish nation, particularly with references to their conversion at the Lord's second coming (Rom. 11:25-27). But this in no way affects the status of the Church as the true Israel. Far from indicating any future distinction, Scripture expressly guarantees that the standing of the believing Gentiles is to continue without change (11:22); it is the converted Jews, rather, that join the Church and who will thus be reingrafted into Israel (vv. 23, 24). "And so all Israel [even those once obdurate] shall be saved" (v. 26).[21]

2) Dispensational writers also claim that the Epistle to the Hebrews quotes Jeremiah's new testament as descriptive, not of God's present relationship with the Church, but of His future relationship with Israel. This claim, however, is difficult to support. Ryrie, for example, concedes:

> One cannot deny that the Church receives similar blessings to those of the new covenant with Israel. . . . Regeneration, indwelling of the Holy Spirit, teaching of the Holy Spirit, and forgiveness of sins, which are the four important blessings promised to Israel in Jeremiah 31:31-34, are all promised to those who believe on Christ in this age.[22]

---

[19]Ryrie, op. cit., pp. 108-110.
[20]Taking the conjunction kai as "even upon the Israel of God." To translate it "and," as if a distinct group of Hebrew Christians were contemplated, would oppose the anti-Judaistic thrust of the epistle as a whole.
[21]See below, page 485, footnote.
[22]Ryrie, op. cit., pp. 117-118.

It is even admitted that the "better testament" of which Christ is the Mediator and which supersedes the older testament of Moses (Heb. 8:6) refers to the Church. But still this better testament, so they contend, must be sharply distinguished from the "second testament," which is the new testament with Israel and which is described in the verse that follows (Heb. 8:7).[23] The explanation of the passage put forward by dispensationalists is this: Jeremiah's quotation is introduced in Hebrews 8, not, as might be expected, to prove that the superseding of the older testament had been predicted by the prophet and that it is now accomplished in the new testament of the Church. They contend that Jeremiah's statement is quoted to prove that since, in the millennium, there will be a superseding of the older testament by the new testament which will then be made with the nation of Israel, so now, by analogy, it is not impossible to think of a superseding of the old by the better testament of the Church.

This interpretation by dispensationalism suffers, at the outset, from the inherent unlikelihood of such unelaborated subtlety of thought. It results, moreover, in a weakened argument for the epistle. Its readers were being confronted with the temptation of lapsing back into Mosaic ceremonialism. To explain that Jeremiah predicted that in the millennium ceremonialism would be replaced by a more spiritual form of worship would be hardly as convincing as to quote the prophet to prove its replacement now! There appear, finally, at least three major contextual objections to the distinctions that are drawn by dispensationalism. (a) Hebrews 8:13 states that it is by means of Jeremiah's new testament that God makes the first testament old. Yet the period of Moses' first testament was limited to the pre-Christian era (9:8). Furthermore, as dispensationalists admit, the passage "goes on to show in Hebrews 9 how the Christian order superseded the sacraments of the Mosaic covenant"[24] (9:11). It follows, therefore, that the Christian order must itself be Jeremiah's new testament. (b) In 9:14 the purging of "your" (contemporary New Testament church) consciences is the equivalent to the forgiveness promised by the new testament in 8:12; and this forgiveness is accomplished through Christ's death as He mediates the new testament (9:15). Ryrie concedes that the new testament of 9:15 was established by Christ's death;[25] but since he is obligated to maintain the new testament of 8:12 as one that is distinct from the Church, he is forced to the conclusion that there must be two "new testaments" in Hebrews, the future one in chapter 8 and the present one in chapter 9.[26] As if further to complicate dispensational exegesis, (c) Hebrews 10:16, 17 again quotes Jeremiah's new testament. So this also must be claimed

[23]Ibid., pp. 120-121.
[24]Ibid., p. 121.
[25]Ibid., p. 117.
[26]Loc. cit.

to be the future new testament.[27] Yet because of the remission of sins
that will result from this "future" new testament, the writer says to the
Church, "Having therefore, brethren, boldness . . ."! (v. 19). The conclusion to be drawn from these contexts is clear. The testament is one;
but it has two major stages: the older, represented by Moses; and the
newer, predicted by Jeremiah and mediated by Christ to the Church,
the Israel of God. Within the framework, moreover, of these two major
dispensations, there may be identified a number of sub-dispensations,
a progression of testaments (plural) (Rom. 9:4), as developed in
topics 7 and 8 that follow.

For Further Reading:

Alan Richardson, "Instrument of God," *Interpretation,* 3:3 (July, 1949), 273-285;
and Paul E. Brown, "The Basis for Hope," *Ibid.,* 9:1 (Jan. 1955), 35-40.
Two neo-orthodox articles, the former on the unity of the Biblical doctrine
of salvation, and the latter on the place of the covenant in formulating a
Biblical philosophy of history.

James F. Rand, "Old Testament Fellowship with God," *Bibliotheca Sacra,*
108:430-109:435 (April 1951-Sept. 1952); and John F. Walvoord, "The New
Covenant with Israel," *Ibid.,* 110:439 (July, 1953), 193-205. Two dispensational articles on the relationship of the testament, Israel, and the Church.

6. The Nature of the Testament*

A. B'RĪTH. The Hebrew word which has been translated "testament" is *b'rith.* The verbal root that is postulated to lie behind this
noun is *baraya,* but there is disagreement as to its etymological meaning. Frequently *baraya* has been related to the Akkadian *barû,* "to
fetter," from which comes the noun *birîtu,* a fetter.[1] Köhler, on his
part, gives the meaning of the root as "to eat bread with, to keep the
community of a meal with." From this etymology, the noun *b'rith*
would mean a "sharing of a meal;" and then, a "relation or connection
(effected by the sharing of a meal);" and finally, an "alliance, mutual
obligation, or arrangement."[2] Both of these etymologies favor the

---

*BIBLE READING: Genesis 8:20-9:17; Deuteronomy 7

Collateral Reading: Vos, *Biblical Theology,* pp. 28-43, 66, 67.
Young, Edward J., *The Study of Old Testament Theology Today* (London:
James Clark & Co. Ltd., 1958), pp. 61-78.

---

[27]*Ibid.,* pp. 121-122.
[1]Brown, Driver, and Briggs, *A Hebrew and English Lexicon of the Old Testament* (Oxford: The Clarendon Press, 1939), p. 136.
[2]*Lexicon in Veteris Testamenti Libros,* p. 152; though in his *Old Testament Theology* (Trans. by A. S. Todd; Philadelphia: The Westminster Press, 1957), he
departs from the concept of pure mutuality to the extent of recognizing *b'rith* as
an arrangement between two unequal parties, a "table fellowship, which a healthy
person offers to a sick person," p. 62.

concept of "covenant," a mutually binding agreement. On the other hand, contract laws of the Hittites stem not from the concept of parity but from that of the "suzerainty covenant." In this situation, a vassal enters into an oath of loyalty and trust toward his king and the king's dynastic successors, out of gratitude for royal favors that have already been received. The benefits derived, moreover, gain their legal force with the death of the suzerain. As Merdith Kline summarizes it,

> From the viewpoint of the subject people a treaty guaranteeing the suzerain's dynastic succession is an expression of their covenantal relation to their over-lord; but from the viewpoint of the royal son(s) of the suzerain the arrangement is testamentary . . . it is not in force while the testator lives.[3]

Thus Gesenius-Buhl derives b'rîth from the root baraya as it is used in I Sam. 17:8, meaning "to decide" or "allot to."[4] These etymologies point toward the giving of an inheritance and favor the meaning "testament." Basically, however, the solution to the meaning of the word b'rîth is to be sought, not in its original derivation, or even in its significance as found in the pagan cultures that surrounded Israel. It is only in the transformed usage of the term as it appears in God's own historical revelation that its ultimate import is disclosed.

B. The Old Testament Usage. In the Old Testament, b'rîth means in general a legally binding obligation. Vos' claim that it was, in addition, the sanction of a religious ceremony that made an obligation into a b'rîth[5] seems open to question. Many of the humanly devised b'rîths of the Old Testament contain no suggestion that a religious sanction was essential, though such may have been present; and there are decrees of God, which necessarily have religious sanction but which are not b'rîths. The b'rîth seems rather to be simply an obligation, the particular nature of which is to be determined, as Berkhof has observed, on no other basis "but simply on the parties concerned."[6]

Three distinct usages of b'rîth appear in the Old Testament. 1) When the parties concerned either have conceded, or are willing to

---

[3]"Dynastic Covenant," *The Westminster Theological Journal*, 23 (1960), p. 13, making particular reference to Esarhaddon's Nimrud treaty. Cf. George E. Mendenhall, *Law and Covenant in Israel and the Ancient Near East* (Pittsburgh: Biblical Colloquiam, 1955), a reprinting of two articles in *The Biblical Archaeologist*, May and September, 1954), and E. J. Young, *The Study of Old Testament Theology Today*, p. 62.
[4]*Hebräisches und aramäisches handwörterbuch über das Alte Testament* (Leipzig: C. W. Vogel, 1915). Cf. Vos' discussion in which he derives b'rîth from the root meaning "to cut," hence, "to determine or define a law or ordinance," *Biblical Theology, op. cit.*, p. 277. For further discussion and bibliography see Gerhard Kittel, *Theologisches Wörterbuch zum Neuen Testament* (Stuttgart: W. Kohlhammer, 1950), under diatithēmi, II: 106-127.
[5]*Op. cit.*, pp. 32, 277.
[6]*Systematic Theology* (Grand Rapids: William B. Eerdmans Publishing Co., 1941), p. 262.

concede, to each other a generally equal standing, the *b'rīth* is a true, dipleuric (two-sided) covenant. The respective benefits and obligations may be mutually determined; or, as is more generally the case, one party takes the initiative and comes to terms with the other. But the net result is still a "partnership," an agreement voluntarily accepted by both parties.[7] Such covenants could involve individuals (Ps. 55:20) as David and Jonathan (I Sam. 18:3, 4), or groups, as Joshua and the Gibeonites (Josh. 9:15), or whole nations, as Edom and its confederates (Obad. 7). The marriage agreement is a *b'rīth* (Mal. 2:14). Making a *b'rīth* could involve bargaining (I Sam. 11:1), or simply concession to the vanquished (I Kings 20:34). The Old Testament contains some unusual, figurative *b'rīths*: with one's own eye, against lust (Job 31:1); with the stones, so as to live in harmony with nature (5:23; cf. 41:4 on leviathan—the crocodile—with whom no such covenant can be made); or even with death, to avoid it (Isa. 28:15, 18). A covenant was binding for as long a period as had been agreed upon, the phrase "a covenant of salt" (Num. 18:19) indicating this character of permanent preservation. A man gave his hand as a specific pledge of fidelity (Ezek. 17:18). The phrase *kārath b'rīth*, "to cut a covenant," seems to come from symbolized action by which the parties concerned passed through the divided corpses of animals. It implied a threat of similar dismemberment for the one who violated the agreement (Jer. 34:18-20). Still, the pagan nations broke their covenants, both with each other (Amos 1:9) and with Israel (Isa. 33:8), and faithless Hebrews were not beyond the practice either (Ezek. 17:15, 16)!

Men are not, however, on an equal standing with God. Scripture contains no reference to God's entering into a covenant with Israel.[8] Therefore *b'rīth* in this dipleuric sense can concern Him only in the following ways. (a) Men may invoke God as a witness to their own covenant agreements. Phrases, therefore, such as are found in I Samuel 20:8, "to bring thy servant into a covenant of Yahweh with thee," or in Ezekiel 17:19, "God's covenant that he hath broken," are actually identical in thought with phrases such as "a covenant before Yahweh" (I Sam. 23:18; cf. II Sam. 5:3; I Chron. 11:3). Indeed, it was for this purpose of calling God to witness that covenant oaths seem frequently to have been made in the house of Yahweh (II Kings 11:4; II Chron. 23:3; Jer. 34:15). On this same basis today, marriages are usually solemnized in churches. But as a result, the minister who goes through the Christian marriage service for an unbelieving couple may find himself guilty of sacrilege; for marriage is "the covenant of her God"

---

[7]Cf. Köhler, *Old Testament Theology*, p. 62.
[8]The clause in Ps. 50:5 which describes the saints as "Those that have made a covenant with me" reads literally, "Those that have cut (entered) my covenant," that is, "the covenant already established by me." Compare Moffatt's rendering, "Who pledged their troth to me."

(Prov. 2:17) and is a mockery if Christ is not truly invoked as the God of the couple involved. (b) Men may make a covenant among themselves to perform God's service (II Chron. 23:1)[9] or to maintain His standards (Jer. 34:8, 10). Israel, for example, was to observe the Sabbath "for a perpetual covenant" (Ex. 31:16). As an exactly opposite example, Psalm 83:5 speaks of a *b'rith* against God, that is, a league of Israel's enemies against God's people.

2) When the parties concerned are not equal, the *b'rith* becomes a disposition, imposed by the superior party (Ezek. 17:13, 14). Hence, there appears on the one hand the terms "to establish," or "to command," a given *b'rith*; and on the other, "to obey" or "to transgress" it (Josh. 23:16). *B'rith* used in such a connotation becomes a synonym for *hōq*, "statute." Scripture often employs *b'rith* in this sense to describe the legal relationships that exist between God the Lord and man the servant. Although there may at times appear certain mutually binding conditions so that we call the resultant arrangement a "covenant," these conditions do not represent the essence of the *b'rith*. It is still a sovereignly imposed, monopleuric injunction. Obligation, without review by the human party, characterized God's relation with Adam and Eve in the Garden of Eden, the "Thus saith the Lord" of Mt. Sinai, and the acts of the God of Dan. 4:35 who "doeth according to His will . . . among the inhabitants of the earth." Hence, God chooses the word *b'rith*, the available term for a legally binding instrument, to describe what is His sovereign pleasure.

3) When the parties concerned are God in His grace and man in his sin, on whose behalf God acts, the *b'rith* becomes God's self-imposed obligation for the deliverance of sinners. It becomes an instrument of inheritance for effectuating God's elective love (Deut. 7:6-8; Ps. 89:3, 4). Through it, He accomplishes the gracious promise that is found from Genesis to Revelation, "I will be their God; they shall be My people." John Murray thus defines this third divine *b'rith* as "a sovereign administration of grace and promise. It is not 'compact' or 'contract' or 'agreement' that provides the constitutive or governing idea but that of 'dispensation' in the sense of disposition."[10] It was, of course, understood that this reconciliation between God and man was not a matter of automatic inheritance. Though essentially monergistic, effectuated by "one worker," (God, not man and god), the *b'rith* required that men qualify. Specifically, God's holiness demanded a removal of sin. This removal, in turn, came about by atonement, the

---

[9]This is the case in II Kings 23:3 (cf. II Chron. 34:31), where Judah made a covenant to confirm the words of the testament that were written in the book. Cf. II Chron. 29:10, "It is in my heart to make *a* (not *the*) covenant with Yahweh, that his fierce anger may turn away from us"; or Jer. 34:13, 14, *a* covenant (not *the* testament) to release bond servants on the seventh year; or Ezra 10:3.
[10]*The Covenant of Grace*, p. 31; cf. pp. 10-12, 14-16.

covering of sin's guilt.[11] Atonement, then, demanded blood sacrifice, a substitutionary surrender of life (Lev. 17:11). Furthermore, only God or His representative could make such atonement (Ex. 15:13).[12] As Genesis 15:17, 18 dramatically puts it, God committed Himself to the threat of self-dismemberment. Is, therefore, the *b'rīth* a testament, the last will of the dying God bequeathing an inheritance of righteousness to Israel? The Old Testament does not so declare, and for two reasons. (a) Though the analogy of Hittite kings, guaranteeing protection to those vassals who remained faithful to their successors, was evidently familiar to Moses, the concept of a personal will remained relatively foreign to Hebrew thought until the days of the Herods.[13] (b) The fact that God's only Son would constitute the sufficient, sacrifical ransom was not yet clearly revealed. That, to satisfy God, God's Son must die so that men might inherit His divine life and be with God was incomprehensible under the Old Testament. Its knowledge was far too seminal, both of the Trinity and the incarnation, and of the crucifixion followed by the resurrection. But neither does the Old Testament deny to *b'rīth* the possibility of this testamentary interpretation, for actually all of its essential factors are present. The Old Testament simply assigns to God's legally binding, monergistic declaration of redemption the title *b'rīth;* but for the elucidation of the precise, divinely-intended meaning of *b'rīth*, one must then turn to the New Testament.

C. THE NEW TESTAMENT EXPLANATION.[14] In the New Testament the Greek word that represents *b'rīth* is *diathēkē*. The primary meaning of *diathēkē* is a "disposition of property by will."[15] Philo goes so far as to associate this with God Himself: "God will leave to the sinless and blameless an inheritance *kata diathēkēs* (by the terms of a will)."[16] But there is a secondary usage from Aristophanes (427 B.C.) onward in which the word means a "convention, or arrangement

---

[11]See below, topics 19 and 27.
[12]Cf. A. B. Davidson, *The Theology of the Old Testament,* p. 321.
[13]Flavius Josephus, *Antiquities,* 17:3, 2; *The Jewish War,* 2:2, 3; in *The Life and Works of Flavius Josephus* (Philadelphia: John C. Winston Co., 1936).
[14]To employ the analogy of Scripture in this way is not, as previously noted, to impose upon the Old Testament ideas that are foreign to it. One Spirit wrote both halves of the Book. The testamental concept lay behind much of the Old Testament ritual; indeed, without the typical anticipation of the testament, the Mosaic ceremonies would be little more than meaningless magic. Biblical theology studies what God actually revealed, not just contemporary understandings; and what may have been foreign to early Hebrew thought was not foreign to God the Holy Spirit, omnisciently active in verbal inspiration. Vos seems to have missed this important distinction when he categorically states that *b'rīth* in the Bible never means "testament," while basing his conclusion on the fact that the idea of testament was unknown to the ancient Hebrews, *op. cit.,* p. 32.
[15]Henry George Liddell and Robert Scott, *A Greek-English Lexicon* (8th edition; Oxford: The Clarendon Press, 1901), p. 346.
[16]*De nom. mut.,* 6.

between two parties, a covenant; and so in later writers."[17] Thus in the Septuagint, the pre-Christian Greek translation of the Old Testament, *diathēkē* is employed to translate *b'rīth* throughout;[18] and this includes not simply the divine *b'rīth* but also the human *b'rīths*, which are clearly not testaments, but covenants. The Greek translators, however, seem deliberately to have avoided representing *b'rīth* by the word *sunthēkē*, which is the ordinary term for a compact or mutual agreement. *Sunthēkē* means literally a thing "put together" and its connotations of legal equality rendered it inappropriate for application to the revealed will of the sovereign God. *Diathēkē*, a thing "put through" was thus assigned to *b'rīth* and was then used for all occurrences of the Hebrew word, even when it described a human agreement. *Diathēkē* had become a comprehensive term. On the basis, therefore, of lexicography, one cannot decide either for "testament" or for "covenant," though the former is indeed the more normal meaning. Again, it is the Biblical context that must be determinative.

Within the context of the New Testament the most crucial passage is Hebrews 9:15-22, and especially verses 16 and 17. Verse 16 reads, "For where a *diathēkē* is, there must of necessity be brought the death of him that made it." This strongly indicates a last will.[19] The next verse is decisive: "For a *diathēkē* is of force where there hath been a death: for it doth never avail while he that made it liveth."[20] As Dean Alford states:

> "It is quite vain to deny the testamentary sense of *diathēkē* in this verse. . . . I believe it will be found that we must at all hazards accept the meaning of testament here, as being the only one which will in any way meet the plain requirement of the verse."[21]

But what is involved in Alford's "all hazards"? First, the fact

---

[17]Liddell and Scott, *loc. cit.*
[18]Except for two doubtful passages (Deut. 9:15; I Kings 11:11). At eight other points in the Septuagint *diathēkē* translates words other than *b'rīth*, including in Zech. 11:4 *ahawā*, "brotherhood," again clearly not testament but covenant. In Isa. 28:15 it is used in parallelism with *sunthēkē*.
[19]Marcus Dods, Hatch, Moulton, Westcott, and a few others have argued that the "death" meant the self-imprecation of dismemberment for nonfulfillment, which was "brought out" by the ratifying ceremonies of a covenant. But this is unlikely, for it is not the threat of death but the death itself that is brought out or adduced. Furthermore, the threat of death does not seem always to have been a necessary element in covenant thought, cf. David and Jonathan.
[20]B. F. Westcott has argued: "Probably the fundamental idea was that so far as this special arrangement was concerned they had no longer will or life. The arrangement was final and unchangeable," *The Epistle to the Hebrews* (London: Macmillan and Co., 1889), p. 301. But his argument is unconvincing. It is not "they," both parties, only "he," one party, who is concerned; and he, the maker, is not will-less, but dead.
[21]*The Greek Testament* (5th edition; London: Rivingtons, 1874-1875), IV: 173-174. The Revised Version agrees, for here, though only here, is *diathēkē* translated "testament."

that the same term, *diathēkē,* appears twice in Hebrews 9:15, the verse preceding, and is implied in v. 18, which follows. Verse 15 reads:

"And for this cause He [Christ] is the mediator of a new *diathēkē,* that a death having taken place for the redemption of the transgressions that were under the first *diathēkē,* they that have been called may receive the promise of the eternal inheritance."[22]

In this passage one again notes the presence of death. There is also the use of the term *klēronomia,* inheritance; and the whole statement is closely associated with what follows in v. 16: "For, where a testament is . . ." etc. One must conclude that "testament" is the meaning of *diathēkē* in v. 15 as well as in vv. 16 and 17. Verse 18, moreover, reads, "Wherefore even the first (*diathēkē*) hath not been dedicated without blood." This reference to *diathēkē* must also be rendered in accordance with the context, and particularly with the prior mention of the "first" *diathēkē* in v. 15. It cannot, therefore, be translated "covenant," but must be, as in the Authorized Version, "testament." Such a conclusion is required, not only for the sake of consistency, but also for the understanding of the argument of the passage. Meredith Kline has suggested that the explanation for Hebrews 9 must lie in the Hittite-type dynastic treaty, particularly as reflected in Moses' "last will and bequeath" to Joshua (Deut. 33-34), Christ being both the dying representative of God (Moses) and at the same time, together with His redeemed brethren, the resurrected inheritor of universal dominion (Joshua).[23] The point of reference is a testament; for, Dods has asserted:

To adduce the fact that in the case of wills the death of the testator is the condition of validity, is, of course, no proof at all that a death is necessary to make a covenant valid.[24]

Throughout Hebrews 9, *diathēkē* means testament, and thus both the old and the new *diathēkēs* are testaments.

Proceeding further, one finds that in the rest of the New Testament the *diathēkē* passages fall into two groups: those referring to

---

[22]The Revised Version and most scholars translate "covenant" (though the RV margin has "testament"), claiming "Amphiboly, or two-fold use, by which the writer of Heb. in ix. 16 sq. substitutes for the meaning *covenant . . .* that of testament," Joseph H. Thayer, *A Greek-English Lexicon of the New Testament* (Corrected edition; New York: American Book Company, c. 1889), p. 137.

[23]Kline, *op. cit.,* p. 14 (see below, pp. 102-104).

[24]W. Robertson Nicoll, ed., *The Expositor's Greek Testament* (Grand Rapids: William B. Eerdmans Publishing Co., [n.d.]), IV; 336. For a liberal such as Peake, it is possible to say, "The ambiguity of the word covered for the author, as also for the Greek commentators, the logical hiatus" *Hebrews* (*The Century Bible*; Edinburgh: T. C. and E. C. Jack, [n.d], p. 188; but for an evangelical, who holds that God is the primary author of Heb. 9, any interpretation which necessitates the lumping of the Almighty with Greek commentators in need of extenuation for logical hiatuses is inconceivable.

God's Old Testament *b'rīth,* and those referring to the new *diathēkē*
of Jesus Christ.[25] The latter passages include such verses as Matthew
26:28, "This is My blood of the *diathēkē,* which is poured out for
many unto remission of sins";[26] and to all such references A. R. Fausset's summary applies:

> These requisites of a testament occur — 1. A testator; 2. Heir;
> 3. Goods; 4. The Testator's death; 5. The fact of the death
> brought forward; 6. Witnesses; 7. A seal, the sacrament of the
> Lord's supper, the sign of His blood. . . . The heir is ordinarily
> the successor of him who dies and so ceases to have possession.
> But Christ comes to life again, and is Himself (including all that
> He had), in the power of His now endless life, His people's in-
> heritance.[27]

In the light of Hebrews 9, where the blood of Christ is noted as
specifically testamentary, there seems to be no more plausible translation than "testament."

Among the New Testament passages that refer to the Old Testament *b'rīth,* the following are particularly significant. Luke 1:72
equates God's remembering this holy *diathēkē* with His raising up in
the house of His servant David a horn of salvation, namely Jesus, who
should save His people from their sins. In Galatians 3:17 the promise
of the *diathēkē,* which was confirmed beforehand by God and which
the law could not annul, is an inheritance of which one must become
an heir by becoming Christ's; and thereby he becomes automatically
Abraham's seed as well. In Ephesians 2:12, to be a stranger from the
*diathēkē*s of promise is equivalent to being separated from Christ,
though now ye are "made nigh by the blood of Christ," thus becoming fellow citizens. Such a legal instrument is a testament. The
conclusion is this: Wherever *diathēkē* occurs in the New Testament,
it means just one thing, "testament."[28]

D. THE SIGNIFICANCE OF B'RĪTH. In the light of the New Testament explanation, the true significance of *b'rīth* in the Old Testament
becomes clear. Its three previously noted connotations will be taken
in reverse order.

3) The meaning of *b'rīth* as God's redemptive instrument for
effecting the reconciliation of men with Himself must be "testament."

---

[25]The lone reference to a human disposition (Gal. 3:15) should probably be
rendered "testament" or "will" as in the Revised Standard Version (cf. Murray,
op. cit., p. 30), but is too uncertain in its significance to carry real weight.
[26]Cf. Vos' admission, *op. cit.,* p. 35, "There are passages . . . for instance those
recording the institution of the Lord's supper, where a further return to 'testament'
may seem advisable."
[27]Jamieson, Fausset, and Brown, *A Commentary, Critical, Experimental and Practical on the Old and New Testaments* (Philadelphia: [n.d.]), VI:556
[28]As in Jerome's Vulgate. It is significant that in the two New Testament passages
where the concept of "covenant" is required and where "testament" would be
impossible, namely Luke 22:5 and Rom. 1:31, *diathēkē* does not appear, but
rather forms that are allied to *sunthēkē.*

This may be demonstrated both by analogy and by the nature of the *b'rīth* itself. For the former, since Hebrews 9:15 reads, "He is the mediator of a new testament"; then, by analogy v. 18 must read, "Wherefore even the first *testament* hath not been dedicated without blood." The old, that is, must be in the same category as the new. For the latter, Franz Delitzsch has remarked concerning the inherent nature of God's instrument:

> The old *B'rīth* was . . . a testamentary disposition, insofar as God bound Himself by promise to bestow, on Israel continuing faithful, an 'eternal inheritance.' . . . Being thus a testament, it is also not without such a death as a testament requires, albeit an inadequate foreshadowing of the death of the true *diathemenos* [testator].[29]

As Hebrews 9:15 states, Christ "is the mediator of a new testament, a death having taken place for the redemption of the transgressions that were under the first testament." In other words, no man — and this includes all those from Adam to John the Baptist — "cometh unto the Father" but by Jesus Christ (cf. John 14:6) and by faith in Him crucified (cf. Gal. 3:26). This faith in His death, it must be confessed, was anticipatory and veiled; but even from the first it was known that for the serpent's head to be crushed, the heel of the seed of woman would have to be bruised (Gen. 3:15).

2) For *b'rīth* as God's statute, sovereignly and graciously imposed on man, "testament" again appears as the best translation. This, moreover, follows as a natural development from the concept of *b'rīth* as a redemptive bequeath. A last-will carries requirements: An heir may break his testamental obligation, but by so doing he forfeits his inheritance. So, though the testament is truly a bestowal, it is, as Delitzsch noted, a bestowal "on Israel continuing faithful." Here apply such verses as Leviticus 24:8, where the preparation of the presence-bread, "shewbread," is styled a perpetual *b'rīth*. At first glance the use of *b'rīth* in this context might seem to be simply the equivalent of "statute." But the *b'rīth* was more: the "shewbread," in this case, stood as a symbol of God's graciously redeeming presence; so that to make provision for it was to carry out an ordinance that contributed to man's participation in divine salvation. Minor as it was, it expressed Israel's faith in the gracious Testator. "To keep His *b'rīth*" means, therefore, "to satisfy His testament" in its conditions for inheritance. Similar in nature are II Kings 11:17, "He executed *the* testament [not a covenant] that they should be Yahweh's people," and II Chronicles 15:12, which speaks of entering into *the* testament. Indeed, all of God's sovereignly imposed *b'rīths* are "testaments," re-

---

[29]*Commentary on the Epistle to the Hebrews* (Edinburgh: 1871), II:110. Cf. J. Massie's final definition of the testaments as "the documents containing the attested promises of blessings willed by God and bequeathed to us in Christ," James Hastings, editor, *A Dictionary of the Bible*, IV:721.

quirements for redemption that He graciously reveals to His own, so as to enable their reconciliation to Himself.

There are but three exceptions — two minor passages and one major situation. The former are these: Jeremiah 33:20, 25 refer to God's covenanted "ordering of day and night," which is spoken of as a *b'rīth;* and Zechariah 11:10 refers to God's "breaking his *b'rīth* which He had made with all the peoples." The contextually suggested meaning is that while God used to order world history in favor of Israel (cf. Deut. 32:8), now He has freed all peoples from this "covenant" obligation.[30] The latter situation concerns God's preredemptive arrangement with Adam. Scripture refers to it as a *b'rīth* (Hos. 6:7), and it is not inaptly styled the "covenant" of works. For though Eden exhibits no partnership of equals and no voluntary mutual agreement was reached prior to God's sovereign disposition, there yet existed a certain balance of obligations and benefits that were equally binding upon the two parties concerned. But never again has history witnessed such a situation, with the exception of the life of the man Christ Jesus, who was the representative last Adam and who fulfilled all righteousness (I Cor. 15:45). In all other passages the *b'rīth* of God with man is a last will or testament.

(1) For *b'rīth* as a dipleuric arrangement between parties of equal standing, entering voluntarily into a mutual obligation, the translation would have to be "covenant" rather than "testament." But, as already noted, for God's instruments with men, which is the primary concern of Biblical theology, not one such case exists in Scripture. Certain of the Psalms do refer to the covenant of redemption between God the Father and Christ the Son, under which the latter would undertake redemption for mankind.[31] But the actual term *b'rīth* is not employed, nor are the contracting parties God and men.

E. THE FEATURES OF THE B'RĪTH. On the basis of Hebrews 9, "testament" may be defined as a "legal disposition by which qualified heirs are bequeathed an inheritance through the death of the testator." Five major aspects to the testamental arrangement appear: *the testator,* who gives and is styled "the mediator" (Heb. 9:15); *the heirs,* who receive and are also referred to as "the called" (9:15); *the method of effectuation,* namely, by a gracious bequeath that is executed upon the death of the testator (9:16); *the conditions,* by which the heir qualifies for the gift, for as Hebrews 9:28 puts it, the testament is "to them that wait for Him" (cf. its being "commanded," 9:20); and *the inheritance* which is given, namely, "eternal salvation" (9:15, 28). These five testamentary aspects constitute the outline for the remainder of this study, Parts III to VII. Since, however, the

---

[30]C. F. Keil and Franz Delitzch, *Biblical Commentary on the Old Testament, The Twelve Minor Prophets* (Edinburgh: T. and T. Clark, 1889), II:366.
[31]See below, p. 275.

revelation that came from God concerning each of these aspects was historically mediated, it becomes necessary first to establish a perspective and gain an appreciation for the historical development of the testament as a whole. This we will try to do through topics 7 and 8 that follow. But such a historical survey is itself rendered understandable as the following basic features within the five major aspects of the testament are recognized and appreciated.

The Testator is God the Son (Heb. 9:15), the divine *Logos*, or "Word" (John 1:1), who communicates God's will. By the means of His incarnation by the Holy Spirit in the womb of the Virgin Mary (Luke 1:35), the *Logos* was joined to a human nature. Thus there appeared in history the divine-human Messiah, who had been predicted so long before by David (Ps. 2:7; 110:1). He is changeless in His perfection (Heb. 13:8). There is none other name than His given among men for salvation (Acts 4:12), and this includes the salvation of the Old Testament saints (Heb. 10:4, 12). The heir then is man, or more precisely, that elect portion of the human race with which God has chosen to deal in each of the successive periods of history (John 6:37a). Human nature likewise exhibits little change throughout its historical course. Three aspects, however, remain: the effectuation, which is by grace; the conditions, which consist of commitment; and the inheritance, which is reconciliation.[32] Each of these possesses a fundamental changelessness, which is due to their ultimate nature as related to the changeless Christ; yet at the same time they exhibit marked differences of representation in the successive historical periods. The effectuation and the inheritance may be considered together as the objective features of the testament, meaning the historical arrangements that are accomplished by God for man's redemption. The conditions, however, are to be seen as subjective features, which means that while determined by God they yet consist of responses that are made by men (cf. John 6:37b).

The objective side of the testament may be summarized under five leading features. The most outstanding is *monergism,* or accomplishment by "one worker." It is God the Testator, and not man the heir, who makes the testament:[33] "By grace are ye saved, not of [your own] works" (Eph. 2:8, 9; cf. Rom. 5:6-11; 3:24; Titus 3:5). The New Testament bears witness to the way in which Christ stood alone in His redemptive work (Matt. 26:31, 40, 56; though cf. John 16:32), with which may be compared Isaiah 63:3, 5 in the Old Testament (even though it refers to the work of judgment):

[32]"Reconciliation" is used throughout this study in its New Testament significance of the relationship of God toward men. It concerns primarily the removal of His alienation from us, and only secondarily the removal of our feelings of enmity against Him. Cf. John Murray, *Redemption—Accomplished and Applied* (Grand Rapids: William B. Eerdmans Publishing Co., 1955), pp. 39-48.
[33]Cf. the preference in Greek for *diathēkē* over *sunthēkē*, p. 75.

> I have trodden the winepress alone; and of the peoples there
> was no man with me. . . . And I looked and there was none to
> help: and I wondered that there was none to uphold: therefore
> Mine own arm brought salvation unto Me.

Thus Christ, monergistically, by His active obedience in a perfect
life, earned salvation, making righteousness available (Gal. 4:4; Matt.
3:15). He furthermore touches men's hearts with His Spirit and
regenerates us (John 3:3), so that we may be found in Him, not
having our own righteousness, which is insufficient, but His (Phil.
3:9). For Christ was the "Son of man" of Dan. 7:13 (cf. Mark 14:
61, 62) with whom the saints are to be identified (vv. 22, 27).

A second feature, that is by its very nature essential to the effectuation of a testament, is *the death of the testator* (Heb. 9:16, 17).
So Christ offered Himself as the once-for-all sacrifice (7:27). This
was His passive obedience, His penal suffering and death for our sins
to satisfy the justice of God (Rom. 3:26). He identifies Himself with
us as sinners and takes our place as the "atoning cover" (Rom. 3:25).[34]
His was thus a two-fold action, that men might stand in His righteousness and He in their condemnation (II Cor. 5:21; I Pet. 2:24).
The feature of the Savior's death is marked by a progressive clarification during the unfolding of God's revelations concerning the testament. Its earlier expressions were simple but dramatically pictorial,
emphasizing that without the shedding of blood there can be no
remission of sins (Heb. 9:22). Its later expressions, however, as they
developed in reference to the Messiah (Dan. 9:26 AV) and the Son
of man (7:13; cf. v. 21) became more direct.

It is the inheritance aspect of the testament that suggests its third
objective feature: *the promise that is made*. For God promises us
salvation in terms of reconciliation to Himself. From the first book
of the Bible to the last, moreover, one statement in particular is
employed to characterize the reconciled status of the heirs of the
testament. John Murray explains it as follows:

> The promise which epitomizes the unity, and which summarizes
> the constitutive principle, of the church is, "I will be their God,
> and they shall be my people" [Gen. 17:7 to Rev. 21:3]. This is
> the promise of grace upon which rests the communion of the
> people of God in all ages.[35]

That God is indeed our God was demonstrated when "the Word
became flesh and dwelt among us" (John 1:14). Our reconciliation
to Him was guaranteed when, with the crucifixion, resurrection, and
ascension of Christ, Satan was cast from heaven no more to accuse
the brethren (John 12:31; Rev. 12:5-11). The relationship becomes
a reality for the individual when in the spirit of adoption he cries

---

[34]See below, topic 27-B.
[35]*Christian Baptism* (Philadelphia: The Presbyterian and Reformed Publishing
Co., 1952), p. 47; cf. *The Covenant of Grace*, pp. 4, 17, 28, 32.

to God, "Abba, Father" (Rom. 8:15-17) and relies upon the ascended
Christ to intercede in heaven for him (Heb. 7:25). It will be finally
accomplished in that glorious home which the Lord has gone to prepare for His Church and into which He will receive us to Himself
(John 14:2, 3; 17:24).

The fourth objective feature, which likewise relates to the aspect
of heirship, is the *eternity of the inheritance* (John 3:16; 10:27-29;
17:3). Leviticus 2:13 speaks pictorially of "the salt [eternal preser-
vation] of the testament of thy God"; and I Chronicles 16:15 and
Psalm 105:8-10 talk directly of God's "remembering His testament
forever." The prophecy of Daniel 7 climaxes in the univeṛsal and
everlasting dominion that is to be received by the saints (vv. 14, 27);
and the present session of Christ at the right hand of God has as its
more comprehensive goal thaᵗ eternal victory when His enemies shall
be made His footstool (Ps. 110:1).

Finally, along with these four, is the always-present feature of the
confirmatory sign, some visible demonstration of God's ability to perform what He has promised. The ultimate such sign is Christ's victory
over the grave, which serves as a pledge of His deity (Rom. 1:4), of
justification (Rom. 4:25), and of immortality and resurrection (I Cor.
15:20-22). Other signs, however, have been introduced with each
historical revelation of the testament.[36] Certain of these were somewhat modified at Christ's first coming, but God has never repealed
His earlier signs.

On the subjective side, God requires a human response, a meeting
of the conditions that He has laid down for inheritance under His
testament. This response may be summarized by the term "commitment." The one great requirement for status under the Hittite suzerainty testaments was that of loyalty to the king. So on the higher
plane, adoption into God's family comes about as a result of justification, which is itself accomplished only as men turn to God in repentance (Luke 13:1-3), and receive Christ by faith (John 1:12).
God keeps the testament with those who are faithful and remember
Him (Deut. 7:12; 8:18; Dan. 9:4), even though it is God who wills
human conversion in the first place (II Tim. 2:25). Three leading
subjective features of the testament appear 1) The most basic feature,
changeless in every manifestation of the testament, is *faith* (Genesis
15:6; John 6:28, 29); "Believe on the Lord Jesus Christ, and thou
shalt be saved" (Acts 16:31). Faith, with repentance, is God's own
gift (Rom. 12:3; Acts 11:18), and without it, it is impossible to
please Him (Heb. 11:6).

But faith, if it is genuine, must be demonstrated by works of
obedience (Matt. 5:48; 7:24; James 2:14-26). Ephesians 2:9, for ex-

---

[36]Note for example Shultz's reference to God's "mighty deeds" at the leading
of Israel from Egypt, *Old Testament Theology,* II:5, 6.

ample, which denies salvation by works, is followed by Ephesians
2:10, which assumes that salvation will necessarily result in works.
So Daniel 2:44 speaks of Christ's incarnation in the days of the
Roman Empire to set up a *kingdom*; and Ezekiel 20:37 describes "the
bond of the testament." Obedience, in turn, is seen in its two com-
ponent features: moral obedience, reflecting the character of the
sovereign God, and ceremonial obedience, reflecting the work of
Christ in which the sinner trusts as a substitution for his own life
of failure. 2) *Moral obedience,* as a feature of the testament, is the
response of men to God's revealed moral standards. These standards,
moreover, because of their origin in God's own moral perfection, are
inherently changeless, though progressively revealed because of man's
limited capacity to receive and obey. They culminate in the teachings
(John 1:18) and personal example of Christ (I Pet. 2:21; I John 2:6;
cf. Jer. 31:34), but the more restricted moral legislation of Moses is
still wholly binding upon God's people (Mark 10:19; Rom. 13:9). 3)
The third subjective feature, *ceremonial obedience*, shows a marked
augmentation from stage to stage in the revelations of the older
testament. But with the realization of the older testament's ceremonial
anticipations in the newer testament, many of its rites were fulfilled
and ceased to be observed (Heb. 9:8, 9; Col. 2:16, 17). The veil of
ceremony was rent away (Matt. 27:51). Yet some of its rituals were
maintained, though in a transmuted form (cf. Col. 2:11, 12), as sacramental seals of righteousness by faith (Rom. 4:11). Their performance, therefore, continues to be obligatory, as a commemoration of
Christ's past work, as a witness to His present salvation, and as an
anticipation of His future redemptive activity (I Cor. 11:23-26). But
whether by augmentation, transmutation, or abrogation, the ceremonies of Scripture do exhibit a number of changes from one stage
of God's dealings with men to the next. A sub-dispensation in His
redemptive revelation may thus be defined as "a period within which
faith in Christ is manifested by a distinctive form of ceremonial
obedience."

But the testamentary features as such remain the same in all
stages. Thus the later revelations of the testament are but clarifications
and extensions of the earlier. John Murray, to take a concrete example, has pointed out that:

> The church in the New Testament is founded upon the cove-
> nant [testament] made with Abraham. The specific covenant
> administration under which the New Testament church operates
> is the extension and unfolding of the Abrahamic covenant.[37]

This is the force of Galatians 3:9, that we are "blessed with faithful
Abraham" (and cf. v. 17). As Murray goes on to state, "It is the
blessing of Abraham, a blessing secured to him by the covenant

[37]*Christian Baptism*, p. 46.

administered to him, that comes upon the Gentiles through Christ (Gal. 3:14)."[38]

Furthermore, these features of the testament stand in marked contrast with those of the covenant of works, which preceded it and which is still operative for all who are not under the blood of the testament. Certain of these testamentary features appear also in the covenant; that is true. Both arrangements reflect the same fundamental situation of divine justice: that man's chief end is to glorify God (Rom. 11:36; I Cor. 10:31);[39] and that as it originally was in Eden, so at the final judgment, all men will be judged on the basis of works (Gen. 3:11; Rev. 20:12). Under the testament, however, it is Christ who provides the justifying works, not man himself. Even in the first revelation of the testament (Gen. 3:15), the aforementioned testamental features are truly present, though in a most rudimentary form.[40] Genesis 3:15 is, in fact, not even called a b'rîth; but it is necessarily assumed to be so, both because of the presence of all the important features and because of the development of all subsequent redemptive b'rîths from it. The following tabulation then presents both the similarities and the contrasts that exist between the features of the covenant and those of the testament:

Gen. 2:15-17	Gen. 3:15 ff
Designation:	
Called a b'rîth (Hos. 6:7), the covenant of works.	God's first redemptive disposition, the Edenic testament.
Fundamental Justice:	
Works: Adam was given a test of obedience (Gen. 2:17), "Thou shalt not eat."	Works: The seed of the woman, Christ, the last Adam, gains merit by crushing the serpent.
Objective Features **Monergism:**	
—(God had made man good, but Adam's works were also necessary for his probation to succeed; and this is "synergism," [41] not monergism).	God alone carries out the testament, "I will put enmity."
Death of the Testator:	
—(no substitutionary way to righteousness is yet provided)	The heel of the seed of Woman is to be injured by the conflict.

---

[38]*Loc. cit.*
[39]So Israel's position and blessings were not for her own sake (Deut. 7:6-9) but for God's glory (Isa. 43:7). Cf. Westminster Shorter Catechism Question 1.
[40]Schultz's observation is thus confirmed, that the origin of the testament must be placed earlier than Sinai, though hardly in Gen. 1, *op. cit.*, II:6
[41]Synergism is here used in the broad sense of mutual activity between God and man for the effectuation of the covenant, not in its more limited application (as found in sixteenth century church history) to the cooperation of human effort and divine grace in regeneration. The very concept of regeneration was inapplicable prior to the fall.

Promise:

That Adam would die for disobedience (2:17) indicates a corresponding confirmation in life for obedience.[42]

That enmity would be put between man and the serpent (Satan) indicates a corresponding reconciliation with God.

Eternity:

3:22, Adam could have lived forever.

5:24, Enoch was eternally translated to be with God.

Confirmatory Sign:

2:9, the tree of life

3:16, childbirth, the means through which the seed would come.

Subjective Features
Faith:

— (no such gracious way to God)

3:20, Adam trusted God's promise that Eve would bear seed;
4:1, Eve recognized God as her strength; her hope rested in her association with the victorious seed.

Demonstrated by Obedience,
Moral:

— (so there can be no such works-of-gratitude)

4:7, Cain should do well; 6:9, Noah walked with God in righteousness.

Ceremonial:

— (and no symbolical expression of deliverance)

4:4, sacrifice, anticipating the atonement of Christ for sins.

In theory, a successful relationship with God could be obtained through a man's conformity to God's fundamental standards of justice (Rom. 2:14, 15; Lev. 18:5; cf. Gal. 3:12; Rom. 10:5). But Adam failed and was condemned to death (Gen. 3:19), and all men since Adam have likewise sinned and come short of the glory of God (Rom. 3:23). Furthermore, Adam's rebellion left the whole human race depraved and guilty by nature (Eph. 2:3), destroying even the theoretical possibility of salvation. Man lay doomed to physical death and eternal damnation (Rom. 5:15, 18). By the works of the law no flesh could be justified (Rom. 3:20). Thus for a man to stand at the last before God's throne on the basis of his own works means his automatic rejection (Rev. 20:15). But under such conditions, God's unmerited love sent His Son with the gracious testament. Jesus Christ was the one man who did live a perfect life (Heb. 4:15), and then died as the Lamb of God to take away sin (John 1:29). Those who are "in Christ" by faith have the hope of glory (Col. 1:27). Those whose names are written in the Book of the Lamb, and only those, are in the Book of Life (Rev. 20:12; 13:8).

F. THE ESSENCE OF THE TESTAMENT. The record of God's dealings with Noah contains the first appearance in Scripture of the actual

[42]Cf. E. J. Young's appreciation of man's greater need for the negative warning than for the positive promise, *The Study of Old Testament Theology Today*, pp. 66-67.

term *b'rîth* (Gen. 6:18; 9:9). The Noachian *b'rîth* was, moreover, specifically testamentary.[43] It was preceded by bloody sacrifice (Gen. 8:20-22), which is a "type," an acted prophecy of Christ's death; and its redemptive significance is indicated by its purpose of preserving seed (9:9), which included that of the woman, through whom it was understood that deliverance would some day arise (3:15). The Noachian testament, moreover, demonstrates more clearly than any other of the Old Testament revelations what constitutes the essence of the testament, namely: the promise, the unconditional grace, and the eternal effect.[44] (a) The promise of no more destruction was indeed limited to the sort of catastrophe that is caused by universal flood waters (9:11), but the Noachian promise became proverbial for the general redemptive protection that God swears to His own (Isa. 54:9). (b) The monergistic character, the unconditioned grace of the testament, appears at all points. The Noachian *b'rîth* was conceived, devised, and disclosed by God (Gen. 6:8; 9:9, 11). It was sanctioned wholly by God, because its sign, the rainbow (9:12-14), is produced by conditions over which God alone has control, and the primary reference of which is Godward (to "remind" Him, not men; vv. 15, 16).[45] The *b'rîth* must finally be fulfilled by God (v. 15). It was, moreover, made with all the living and their posterity, even the animals (v. 10), which demonstrates that an understanding on the part of the beneficiaries is not required for the testament's validity. The basic explanation for the testament is that Noah found *hēn,* grace, in the eyes of Yahweh (6:8). From this it must not be assumed that the moral character of the one to whom grace is disclosed is irrelevant, once it has had the opportunity to display itself; for the following verse notes that the testament was given to Noah in his integrity. (c) Finally, the testament with Noah is specified to be everlasting (9:16). While the earth remaineth,[46] God's word is sure and God's word is applicable! These, and the other basic features as they appear in the eight successive Biblical revelations of the testament, are outlined on the page that follows.

For Further Reading:

Geerhardus Vos, "Hebrews, the Epistle of the *Diatheke*," *Princeton Theological Review* 13:4 and 14:1 (Oct. 1915 and Jan. 1916) 587-632 and 1-61. Much on the use of the Greek term in Hebrews.

Henry S. Gehman, "The Covenant — the Old Testament Foundation of the Church," *Theology Today,* 7:1 (April, 1950) pp. 27-41; and, "An Insight and a Realization," *Interpretation,* 9:3 (July, 1955), 279-293. Neo-orthodox studies on the nature of the testament and its historical development.

Robert H. Pfeiffer, "Facts and Faith in Biblical History," *Journal of Biblical*

---

[43]As opposed to Vos' analysis that it did not directly relate to the prosecution of redemption, *op. cit.,* p. 62. But cf. his recognition that blood sacrifice signifies redemption, p. 63, though he fails to associate this with the Noachian testament.
[44]Cf. Vos' analysis, *ibid.,* pp. 66-67, and Murray, *Covenant of Grace,* p. 15.
[45]Murray, *op. cit.,* pp. 12-14.
[46]See below, topic 32-D.

THE SUCCESSIVE REVELATIONS OF THE TESTAMENT

Reference, and 1st appearance	Objective Features					Faith	Subjective Response Faith manifested in obedience:	
	Testamental nature (death of Christ)	Reconciliation (the promise)	Graciousness (monergism)	Effective range (eternity)	Sign of confirmation		Moral	Dispensational
THE ANTICIPATORY OF THE OLD TESTAMENT								
Edenic, Gen. 3:15	Satan shall bruise Christ's heel	Enmity between Satan and mankind	I will put enmity	Enoch translated, did not see death (5:24)	Childbirth, sign of the seed (3:16)	Eve *will* bear seed (3:20, cf. 4:1)	If thou doest well (4:7)	Sacrifice (4:4)
Noachian, Gen. 9:9	Noah's offering accepted (8:21)	Seed protected (9:9)	I establish My testament (9:9)	All flesh no more to be cut off (9:11)	The rainbow (9:13)	Blessed be the God of Shem (9:26)	A just man with God (6:9)	Sacrifice (8:20)
Abrahamic, Gen. 15:18	Sacrifices laid before God (15:9)	I will be God unto Thee & thy seed (17:7)	I will make My testament (17:2)	An everlasting testament (17:7)	God's self-maledictory oath (17:7, cf. Jer. 34:20)	Abraham believed God (15:6)	Be thou perfect (17:1)	Circumcision (17:10)
Sinaitic, Ex. 19:5, 6	Blood of the testament sprinkled (24:8, cf. Heb. 9:18)	Israel a peculiar treasure of God (19:5)	I brought you unto Myself (19:4)	A statute for ever (27:21)	The exodus (19:4)	Believe forever (19:9, Deut. 6:5)	An holy nation (19:6)	Mosaism (25:8)
Levitical, Num. 25:12, 13	Peace came as Phinehas has made atonement	The priest turned wrath away (25:11)	I give unto him My testament	An everlasting priesthood	Aaronic priesthood	Zealous for his God	He thrust the sinner through	Mosaism (25:7)
Davidic, II Sam. 7:13 (cf. 23:5)	Christ's soul not left in death (Ps. 16:10, cf. Acts 2:31)	Salvation in David's kingdom (II Sam. 23:5)	I have sworn unto David (Ps. 89:3)	His kingdom established for ever (II Sam. 7:13)	David's continuing line (II Sam. 7:12)	Come unto Me & live, in David's mercies (Isa. 55:3)	Walk in My judgments (Ps. 89:30)	Mosaism (Jer. 17:25, **26**)
THE COMMEMORATIVE NEW TESTAMENT								
Future testament anticipated in Hos. 2:18-20								
New Testament, Jer. 31:31-34 (cf. Heb. 8:6-12)	My blood of the testament, shed for many (Matt. 26:28)	Least to greatest all shall know Me (Jer. 31:34)	I will make a new testament (31:31)	I will remember their sin no more (31:34)	Christ's resurrection (Rom. 4:25)	Whosoever believeth in Him (John 3:16)	My law in their hearts (Jer. 31:33)	Lord's supper (I Cor. 11:**25**)
Testament of Peace, Ezek. 16:60 (cf. 34:25)	The Lamb that was slain receives power (Rev. 5:12)	I will cause evil beasts to cease out of the land (34:25)	I, Yahweh, do sanctify Israel, (37:28)	They shall no more be a prey to the nations (34:28)	I with you, face to face (20:35)	Remember and **be** ashamed (16:61)	Walk in His ordinances (37:24)	My sanctuary in the midst (37:26)

Literature, 70:1 (March, 1951), 1-14. Radical historicism: facts and faith are not to be mixed; and the testamental concept, invented in 621 B.C., is an example of the latter, not of the former.

Colin Alves, *The Covenant*. Cambridge: University Press, 1957. A school manual surveying the O.T. Accepts liberal criticisms, but finds in the covenant the unifying principle for the Old Testament and the bond of its relation with the New.

7. The History of the Testament: the Older Established*

A. and B. THE EDENIC AND NOACHIAN TESTAMENTS. God's redemptive revelations during the primeval period were distinguished by universalism. They were presented to men on a universal basis. Be it noted, however, that these initial disclosures of the older testament were then rejected by those who heard them, because of man's almost equally universal antagonism toward God and toward His gracious offers.

Man, at his creation, had been placed on probation under the covenant of works. Adam, however, had both failed the test himself and had bequeathed to his posterity a depraved nature, equally prone to fail, and already adjudged guilty (Rom. 5:18). God then, in justice, might well have terminated human history at its very inception; but in His grace He provided the testament for man's restoration. Its first revelation, as has been described above, was the Edenic.[1] It included all men in its scope. But as men multiplied upon the earth, most of them in pride mocked its gracious provision and thoroughly corrupted themselves (Gen. 6:5). God, therefore, destroyed all but eight souls in the deluge and went on to elaborate His redemptive purposes with the revelation of the Noachian testament.[2] This, too, was universally directed to embrace the nations of the world. But, when the nations arose as outlined in Gen. 10, they turned to the construction of the tower of Babel, which became the climactic demonstration of the pride of the human heart and of its disdain for God's mercy.

The universal presentation of divine grace had failed, and God

---

*BIBLE READING: Nehemiah 9; Judges 2
Collateral Reading: J. B. Payne, *An Outline of Hebrew History*, pp. 1-3, 19-22, 36-39, 56-58, 67-73.
John H. Raven, *The History of the Religion of Israel*, pp. 156-158, 164-186

[1]See pp. 92, 93 for the comparative chart of the covenant of works and the Edenic testament
[2]See above, pp. 93, 94.

henceforth directed His proclamation of redemption under the older testament of an elect minority. He thus made the preparation of this select group a prerequisite to the ultimate appearance of Christ the testator. Only then could the universalism of the Edenic and Noachian testaments be re-enunciated by One who would say, "Come unto Me, *all* ye that labor" (Matt. 11:28).

C. THE ABRAHAMIC TESTAMENT. The revelation of the particularistic testament commences with God's choice of Abraham (Neh. 9:7, 8).[3] Called first in Ur of the Chaldees (Gen. 11:31; cf. 15:7; Neh. 9:7; Acts 7:2-4; Heb. 11:13-16), and then again in Haran (Gen. 12:1-3), this foremost of the patriarchs stepped out in faith at the age of 75 and came to Canaan in 2091 B.C. There he was granted the Abrahamic testament. Its description is found particularly in Genesis 15 and 17, though certain of its elements appear in other passages as well. It was later repeated to Isaac (26:3, 24) and to Jacob (28:15; cf. 35:12).

With the Abrahamic revelation, the objective features of God's testament come into clear focus. Abraham's salvation depended fundamentally upon the future work of Christ, whose "day" he rejoiced to see (John 8:56). His rejoicing, however, seems to have been in anticipation of Christ's general ministry, rather than in any detailed knowledge of His person. The necessity of a death for the ultimate effectuation of the testament is shown by the atoning blood that was shed in the accompanying sacrifices (15:9, 10). It is shown even more strikingly in the confirmatory sign of God's self-maledictory oath[4] (v. 17; cf. Jer. 34:18, 19), for the association in Abraham's vision of the dismembered bodies with the presence of deity is a bold picture of the violent execution of the Son of God. The monergism and eternity of the testament, as well as its promise appear together in Genesis 17:7. Here for the first time in history were spoken the words which constitute the classic expression of the testamental promise: "And I will establish My testament between Me and thee and thy seed after thee in their generations for an everlasting testament, to be a God unto thee, and to thy seed after thee" (cf. Ex. 6:7; Hos. 2:23; Jer. 31:33; Rev. 21:3).

This promise of spiritual reconciliation with God was accompanied by secondary, but confirmatory, material promises. Specifically, Abraham was promised a numerous seed (Gen. 12:2; 13:16) through whom would come the future testator (22:18) and he was promised the possession of the land of Canaan (12:7; 13:15; 15:5, 18). The Bible is thus concerned with realistic redemption: its doctrines not

---

[3]In a sense, the Noachian testament might be considered particularistic, because its first announcement involved selectivity (Gen. 6:18); but by the time of its establishment, the elected men had become mankind universal (9:19)!
[4]Vos, *Biblical Theology*, p. 100; cf. Murray, *Covenant of Grace*, pp. 16-17.

only spring from, but result in, historical situations. Its keynote is the reality of God's activity in history. The New Testament insists that if Christ is not risen from the dead, then is our faith vain (I Cor. 15:17); and the Old grounds its hope upon the historicity of the deliverance from Egypt and of the conquest of Canaan. Confidence in the reality of such miraculous happenings characterized the belief of those who were closest to the events described. Moreover, to deny the reality of divine intervention not only removes the proof for the doctrinal teachings involved; it ultimately denies the objective reality of the teachings themselves, and labels them as being contrary to fact. Even from a pragmatic viewpoint, to deny the historicity of the testament is to leave without adequate explanation many of the phenomena of the subsequent history of Israel. The presence, for example, of reforming leaders like Samuel or Isaiah; of a national cohesiveness, despite the chaos of the times of the judges; of the ethical law; of a social conscience; of Israel's continuous opposition to the Canaanitish fertility cults; and of their belief in a monotheistic God, who was transcendent to control and yet imminent to redeem — all these phenomena demand the historicity of God's testamental revelations for their valid explanation.[5]

But lest the promise of the land of Canaan be misapplied, as if its possession by Israel were inviolable, a further distinction from the preceding Noachian testament must be stressed. The Abrahamic testament was indeed particularistic, as opposed to universalistic, a characteristic which was confirmed by the way in which it granted a defined territory to a certain chosen people. But it was also specifically conditional, as opposed to the unconditioned grace that had marked the revelation of Noah's testament. A gift given by grace may yet possess stipulations; and even Noah went on to exhibit words of faith (Gen. 9:26), moral character (6:9), and ceremonial obedience (8:20). Abraham, however, provides the supreme Biblical example of faith, as the basic condition through which men are granted testamental righteousness and without which no man may be saved (15:6). He was also ordered to walk before God in moral obedience (17:1); his faith, that is, had to be demonstrated by his works (22:12; cf. James 2:21-24). The distinctive form of ceremonial obedience that was revealed to Abraham was that of circumcision,[6] and the one who refused the rite thereby broke the testament and was cut off from the people (Gen. 17:14). In reference, then, to the land of Canaan,

---

[5]So Walther Eichrodt, *Theologie des alten Testaments* (Leipzig: J. C. Hinrichs, 1933-1939), I:2:II. The approach of this and of the following topic are indebted to Eichrodt's tracing of the history of the testament concept in Israel, though his neo-orthodoxy causes him to deny much of the Biblical material and seriously to dislocate its historical order. Cf. Vriezen's similar understanding, *An Outline of Old Testament Theology*, p. 31.
[6]See below, topic 27-D, for its discussion.

God's promise as such was unconditional: its conquest by Joshua was accomplished in dependence upon testamental rights (Neh. 9:8); its partial repossession by Nehemiah was made possible because of God's keeping His testament (Neh. 9:32, 36); and the occupation of its capital, Jerusalem, by God's elect Church both during the millennium and throughout the eternity of the new heavens and the new earth is guaranteed by His prophetic word (Rev. 20:9; 21:2). But history demonstrates how Israel also lost the land — first in 586 B.C., for despising the word of God's prophets (II Chron. 36:16); and again in A.D. 70 for rejecting and crucifying God's Son (Matt. 21:41). Genesis 18:19 specifies that only as Abraham's children do justice and judgment will God bring upon them what He has spoken. In other words, the participation of individuals and groups in the promise *is* conditional.[7] Zionist Jews of today who persist in rejecting Christ have no more claim to Palestine than those who were expelled from it by the Roman general Titus nineteen hundred years ago (cf. Ezek. 21:27).

After Abraham, his son Isaac and then his grandson Jacob continued to live in Canaan, despite the occasional appearance of idolatrous terephim within their families (Gen. 31:19; cf. Judges 17:5). Jacob's twelve sons became, in turn, the ancestors of the nation Israel, into which Christ would some day be born (cf. Gen. 49:2-27). Joseph's providential rise in Egypt enabled the chosen group to be preserved in that land from a famine that was overwhelming Canaan (Gen. 45:7). God, moreover, provided that they remain in Egypt from 1876 to 1446 B.C., so that the family might increase in size to become a great nation (46:3). In Egypt, however, they drifted into idolatry (Josh. 24:14; Ezek. 20:7, 8; 23:8, 19) and, because of their rapid increase, were enslaved and oppressed (Ex. 2:9-11; cf. Gen. 15:13). They were faced eventually with national extinction (Ex. 2:16; Ezek. 16:5).

D. THE SINAITIC TESTAMENT. At this point, the God of history raised up a crucial leader in Moses. Moses was skilled in all the knowledge of Egypt (Ex. 2:10; Acts 7:22). His life had been twice preserved from the Egyptian government (Ex. 2:6-8, 15-21), and he had been humbled by forty years of menial service in the desert (Acts 7:30). Thus prepared, he was called of God to deliver Israel (Ex. 3:10). God's historical intervention was based upon His promise in the gracious testament as previously revealed (Ex. 2:24; 6:5). For contrary to most of the liberal and neo-orthodox interpretations,[8] Scripture makes it clear that God's testamental relationships with Israel did not begin at Sinai. He had been the God of their fathers

---

[7]Cf. G. H. Lang, "God's Covenants Are Conditional," *Evangelical Quarterly*, 32:2 (1958), pp. 86-97.

[8]Kohler, for example, says bluntly, "God willed to make Himself known to Israel at the time of Moses and through him—that is the first sentence of the history of God," *Old Testament Theology*, p. 60.

(3:13); and it was because He was their God, from the very first
(v. 18), that He acted through Moses to accomplish their deliverance
by the miraculous plagues and the crossing of the Red Sea (Ps. 77:20;
78:13; Isa. 63:11). Having arrived at Mt. Sinai in the summer of
1446 B.C., Israel was granted the fourth of God's testamental revelations in history, the Sinaitic.

Like the Abrahamic, the Sinaitic testament was particularistic.
But its distinguishing characteristic lay in this, that its particularism
embraced an entire nation, rather than an individual or a family:

> Now therefore, if ye will obey my voice indeed, and keep
> My testament, then ye shall be a s'ghullā ["peculiar (special)
> possession,"] unto Me above all people . . . and ye shall be
> unto Me a sovereignty of priests and an holy nation (Ex.
> 19:5, 6; Deut. 5:2, 3).

For the ratification of the Sinaitic testament, Moses erected twelve
pillars "according to the twelve tribes of Israel" (Ex. 24:4). He then
ordered the preparing of animal offerings to signify the testamental
death (Heb. 9:16-20). Half of the sacrificial blood was offered to
God, but the other half was sprinkled on the people: the whole nation was thus literally "under the blood" and identified with its saving
power (vv. 6, 8). Finally, the seventy elders, as representatives of
the nation, participated with God in a meal of fellowship (v. 11).
This sealed the testament and marked the fulfillment of the gracious
promise of reconciliation that had been first anticipated in Exodus 6:7.
Its result is expressed by the phrase, "Yahweh, God of Israel."

The large group involved, over two million people, explains the
necessity for the detailed Mosaic legislation that follows. For the law
had to spell out both the moral requirements of the testament (Neh.
9:13, 14) and also the forms of ceremonial obedience that made up
the ritual of the Tabernacle, which became the testamental sanctuary.
A family may indeed conduct itself on the basis of principles, but a
nation must have codified procedures and applications. The fundamental law of the Decalogue (Ex. 20:2-17), for example, was immediately elaborated in the judicial and the ritualistic specifications of
the book of the testament that comes after it (Ex. 20:22-23:33). For
in Israel, church and state, religious life and political life, were united
in one theocratic community. It should be noted, however, that membership in the testamental nation, essential as it was for reconciliation with God (Eph. 2:12), no more automatically guaranteed salvation than it had in Abraham's family (cf. Matt. 3:9). The conditional
nature of the Sinaitic testament appears from the very "if . . . then
. . ." phraseology of its initial revelation. Thus, though Israel as a
whole had accepted its conditions (Ex. 19:8; 24:3, 7), any man who
acted with presumption and refused to humble himself before God
and His law was thereby cut off from the people (Num. 15:30).

Moreover, the "chosen people" as a whole were subject to rejection in the case of apostasy. God was not mechanically bound by the testament — He could cast them off, and even at that very time almost did (Ex. 32:10). Balaam, it is true, saw Israel as set apart among the nations (Num. 23:9). God walked among them, He was their God, and they were His people (Lev. 26:12). But when they refused Him, their house was left unto them desolate (Matt. 23:37, 38).

This points up the fact that the essential features of the Sinaitic testament are identical with those of all other testamental revelations that appear in Scripture. Its *monergism* is declared by God Himself, "I bore you on eagles' wings and brought you to Myself" (Ex. 19:4). He speaks, and no advice is asked (20:1)! Deuteronomy 7:7, 8 and 9:4-6 in particular stress that the basis of the testament is God's love, His free grace. It is not Israel's merits, as if they were, as so often claimed by liberalism, a people with a "genius for religion." Their history, in fact, demonstrates the exact contrary to have been the case. This gracious nature of the testament was one of the unique features in the faith of Israel. It preserved humility on the part of the inheritors and checked all tendencies toward legalistic distortions or toward any necessary equating of God with the national interests.[9] Its *promise* concerned the nation, that they should be the people of God (Ex. 19:5). But immediately thereafter, Israel is defined as a "sovereignty of priests" (v. 6), which points to God's ultimate purpose of using this nation to mediate the promise of salvation abroad. The *eternity* of the truths revealed in the Sinaitic testament is indicated by Ex. 27:21 and 28:43 — "a statute for ever." Finally, it had as its *confirmatory sign* the exodus from Egypt (Ex. 20:2; Neh. 9:10, 11), an event which had, in fact, preceded the testament itself! The most fundamental of the subjective features of the testament is, as always, *faith* in the redeeming God (Deut. 6:5). The demonstration then of their faith by their obedience is summarized in Israel's description as a "holy [separated, Lev. 20:26] nation" (Ex. 19:6). Moses wrote much on *ceremonial* holiness. But, since the whole nation was separated to God, all of life became correspondingly sacred; and *moral* conduct, summarized in love for one's neighbor, constituted as much a part of holy living as did holy prayer and sacrifice (Lev. 19:18).

Israel left Sinai as God's people. The ark of the testament went before the line of march "to seek out a resting place for them" (Num. 10:33), and this concrete symbol of their redemption continued to lead them to the promised land (except in Num. 14:44, where they

---

[9]Cf. G. Ernest Wright, *The Old Testament Against its Environment*, ch. 11. Mendenhall thus stresses the close parallel between Sinai and the Hittite "suzerainty covenant," with its obligations to the one who is already one's benefactor, "Covenant Forms in Israelite Tradition," *The Biblical Archaeologist*, 17 (1954), pp. 63-64.

had failed). Moses anticipated that some day a human king would arise to act as God's regent in the theocracy. The king, however, was to reign in strict conformity to God's revelation (Deut. 17:16-18) and to consider himself no better than his brethren (v. 20). Israel had shown the need for such God-fearing human leadership in the past (Ex. 16:2); and, though many of Israel's future kings failed to live up to the standard set for their position, princes like David could and did do much to preserve public piety (cf. I Chron. 29:14).

But even under Moses in the wilderness, the children whom God had brought up rebelled against Him. As a result, they were again almost destroyed (Num. 14:12; cf. Isa. 1:2). That generation, moreover, was condemned to forty years of fatal wandering and were denied admission into the land of Canaan (Num. 14:34, 35). Still their failures continued. Instead of being Y'shūrūn, "upright little people," Israel waxed fat and kicked (Deut. 32:15); they carried images of the gods Molech and Kewan [Remphan] (Amos 5:26; Acts 7:43); and they kept not the testament (Ps. 78:10, 37; Neh. 9:17). Thus at the close of the forty years, early in 1406 B.C., God commanded Moses to make a renewal of the testament on the Plains of Moab, just prior to the entrance of the new generation into Canaan. Moses' words have the appearance of an addition to the Sinaitic testament (Deut. 29:1). Their real purpose, however, was to confirm the conquest of trans-Jordan, which had just been successfully completed (vv. 7-9), and to furnish the generations yet to come with one more reminder of their need for faithfulness to the testament (vv. 15, 18, 19). This renewal consisted actually of a reaffirmation of Israel's national testamental status (v. 13) and is not to be considered as a testament distinct from that of Sinai. Such repetitions and renewals, moreover, were characteristic of Hittite suzerainty-testaments. Indeed, the whole book of Deuteronomy, in its present form, corresponds to their six basic sections, the full classic pattern of which is documented only in the Syro-Anatolian treaties of the fourteenth-thirteenth centuries B.C.:[10] 1. Preamble (Deut. 1:1-5). 2. Historical prologue (1:6-4:49). 3. Stipulations (5-26). 4. Curses and blessings of ratification (27-30). 5. Enlisting of witnesses (31:19-22, 31:28-32:45). 6. Succession arrangements (32:46-34:12, plus parts of 31), including directions for the disposition and public reading of the text (31:9-13, 24-27; cf. chap. 27).

E. THE LEVITICAL TESTAMENT. At the same time, however, God did grant the fifth revelation in history of His redemptive testament (Num. 25:12, 13). This Levitical testament had been anticipated in Numbers 18:19 when Aaron and his family had been granted certain

---

[10]Meredith Kline, "Dynastic Covenant," *The Westminster Theological Journal,* 23 (1960), p. 15. He thus drives home the impossibility of the older critical attempts to dismember the book of Deuteronomy or to date the whole in a later period.

offerings as "a testament of salt." Indeed, their very right to the offerings was indicative of the reality and the objectivity of the reconciliation with God that came about through the services of the priesthood in making atonement for the people. The occasion for the historical revelation of the Levitical testament arose out of a heroic action by Phinehas, the grandson of Aaron and son of the contemporary high priest Eleazar. There on the Plains of Moab Phinehas personally destroyed Zimri, a leader in national apostasy and immorality (Num. 25:8). In recognition God then granted (note the monergism) to him and to his descendants what was styled the "testament of peace" (Lev. 25:12), or the "testament of life and peace" (Mal. 2:5). For the sake, however, of avoiding confusion with Ezekiel's subsequent testament of peace,[11] this revelation is designated as the Levitical testament.

The promise of the Levitical testament lay specifically in God's bestowal of the priestly office to this particular, limited group of Levites (Lev. 25:13) and, in the resultant reconciliation that they experienced with God, of the privilege to walk with Him in peace (Mal. 2:6). But the Levitical testament had a broader redemptive significance; for it was through the priesthood that God's wrath was turned away from Israel as a whole (Num. 25:11), and it was through the priest's teachings that the men of Israel were turned away from iniquity (Mal. 2:6). The atoning work of the Levitical priests (Num. 25:13) became ultimately effective because it anticipated Christ's testamental work of divine propitiation (Heb. 7:11, 19). The Levitical testament was explicitly stated to be an everlasting one, the very existence of the Aaronic priesthood being its confirmatory sign (Num. 25:13). In reference to the subjective testamental features, Phinehas was noted for his faith, "the fear with which he feared Me" (Mal. 2:5). Correspondingly, his descendants were warned that their continuation in this redemptive office was contingent upon their obedience (I Sam. 2:30). Still, the Levitical testament itself was irrevocable. Levites have a permanent significance; and in the kingdom that is yet future their ministry is coterminous with that of Christ, namely, eternal (Jer. 33:21; Isa. 66:21).

After the death of Moses in the spring of 1406 B.C. Israel under Joshua followed the ark of the testament into Canaan (Josh. 3:3, 11, 14; 6:6). That they should march in the train of this symbol of the testament was in itself highly appropriate, for both the increase of the people (Deut. 10:22) and the conquest of the land (Josh. 11:16; 21:43-45; cf. Neh. 9:22, 24, 25) came about in fulfillment of the material, corollary promises of the Abrahamic testament (Gen. 15:5, 18). At his first opportunity, Joshua accordingly reaffirmed the testament on Mt. Ebal (Josh. 8:33), precisely as the ancient suzerainty treaty

---

[11]See below, topic 8-H.

guaranteed dynastic succession by ceremonies in two stages, both before and after the death of the testator (in this case, God's representative, Moses).[12] His last recorded act, moreover, was to lead his people in another such national rededication at Shechem (24:25-27).[13] His concern was justifiable. Israel's future apostasy to the testament had been predicted by Moses (Deut. 31:16, 20); and Joshua shared similar forbodings (Josh. 23:16).

THE ALTERNATIVE TO THE TESTAMENT: BAALISM. The possession of Canaan was not an unmixed blessing,[14] for it brought Israel into direct contact with the pagan Canaanites. This Hamitic people possessed a settled culture which was superior to that of the nomadic, invading Hebrews. But their notoriously debased morality (Gen. 15: 16; Deut. 9:4) dated back to the very curse of Noah upon Canaan the son of Ham (Gen. 9:25); it constituted an antithesis to the Mosaic ideals of social equality, of personal and property rights, and of sexual purity. Canaanitish religion has received thorough illumination through the discovery in 1929 of the Ugaritic tablets at Ras Shamra in Syria.[15] These poems, myths, and rituals show it to have been a corrupt polytheism devoted to agricultural deities. _Ba'al_, meaning "master" or "owner," was the local god of each field, who was considered to give it its annual productivity. He was associated with storms and with the cycle of the agricultural year and was worshiped in the stone _massēvā_, or "pillar." Female deities included both _Ashērā_, a consort goddess who was believed to reside in a wooden pole[16] of the same name, beside each local Baal-pillar (Deut. 7:5), and _Ashtōreth_ (Astarte, Ishtar), a goddess of fertility, sex, and war. All these were worshiped in the _bāmā_, "high place" (Deut. 12:2), with obscene rites and even human sacrifice (Deut. 18:10; 12:31). The Israelites, however, made a very human but false association between what was good and what was evil in Canaanitish society. If the crops of the Canaanites were better than those of Israel (and they probably were, at first), then their crop gods must be superior to Israel's God (Hos. 2:8; Judges 2:3), at least in respect to insuring agricultural fertility and blessing.[17]

More serious, however, than the direct appeal for "conversion" to Baalism, were the theological concepts that lay behind the Canaan-

---

[12]Kline, _op. cit._, pp. 10-11.
[13]This, too, Mendenhall associates with the Hittite "Suzeranity covenants," in their need for renewal, _op. cit._, p. 67.
[14]Note Raven's analysis of the ways in which the conquest was damaging to Israel's religious life, _The History of the Religion of Israel_, pp. 157 ff.
[15]Cf. Herbert F. Hahn, _Old Testament in Modern Research_, pp. 109-115, 129-130, and accompanying bibliography.
[16]Not "grove," as translated in the Authorized Version.
[17]Kohler, on grounds of radical criticism, even denies that Yahweh was considered a God of "blessings" at all, prior to the conquest; _Old Testament Theology_, pp. 71-75.

itish practices. For even at the moment that Baal's idolatrous pillar was being broken into bits, his theology was being assimilated into the Yahweh-thought of many of the less discriminating of God's people. Yahweh could come to be treated more and more like Baal. Distortion was thus threatened within Israel's own concept of her testamental relationship with God, even though it was upon the preservation of this relationship that Israel's very existence depended.

Specifically, (a) the Canaanitish concept of deity opposed the monergism of the testament. Out of the Canaanites' belief in local gods with restricted spheres of influence arose a tendency to minimize the extent of God's claims and to bind Him by necessity to the people of a given area. God and His people came increasingly to be felt to exist for each other and to be mutually dependent. As certain of the false prophets expressed it, "Is not Yahweh among us? None evil can come upon us!" (Micah 3:11). Again, while Israel might reject the pagans' belief in the *massēvā*, or pillar, they could and did transfer the *massēvā*-concept to the ark. With God thus "contained," they fell prey to the delusion of being able to control God's power for their own ends. The capture of the ark as related in I Samuel 4:4-11 should have invalidated such ideas once and for all, but it did not. The Canaanites' belief, moreover, in ecstatic and even orgiastic communion with their deities minimized the idea of God's sovereignty and, of course, of His testamental moral requirements.

(b) The Canaanitish concept of religion as centering in ceremonialism ran counter to the testamental concept of man's spiritual obligations. It is true that most of the contemporary religious thought of the ancient Near East was devoted to matters of ceremony. But as the influence of the surrounding cultures led the Israelites to place more and more emphasis upon this one subjective feature of the testament, it resulted in the minimizing, if not the exclusion, of its other two features, namely faith and morals.[18] The Canaanites, furthermore, used bull-forms to depict their gods. Even if disassociated with idolatry, the use of similar "worship aids" among the Israelites detracted from their concept both of God's exalted power and of His moral claims. Elaborate rituals tended to externalize faith and to replace it with self-seeking formalism. The testamental promises were thus corrupted into a brand of religious commercialism: "I give, God must respond" (cf. Judges 17:13). Such an attitude makes confident surrender impossible. True faith and morals must be based upon devotion and not a "cash-register" concept of reward (Ex. 20:2, 3).

Finally, (c) the Canaanitish concept of the religious authority

---

[18]This is not to deny that some Canaanitish rituals did reflect true theology. For example, even human sacrifice indicated a sensing of the fact that the wages of sin is death (Rom. 6:23). But from the earliest patriarchal days, when Yahweh deliberately revealed His opposition to Abraham's offering up Isaac (Gen. 22:11), Scripture demonstrates the primacy of morality over ceremonial.

of political rulers tended to undermine Israel's commitment to the absolute moral standards of the testament. For in Canaan, the various independent kings, if not actually deified, were at least held to be divinely adopted and to be installed upon their thrones as representatives of the local Baal. The voice of the king became the voice of deity; and, as a result, no prophet in Canaan could criticize the ruler. He would become by this very act not simply a traitor, but a heretic! In Israel, on the contrary, obedience to God's testament was demanded of ruler and people alike (Deut. 17:19, 20). True prophets, however, found it increasingly difficult to enforce God's moral standards upon kings whose personal bent toward unchecked rule was being constantly reinforced by Canaanitish precedent (cf. II Kings 21:7). The temptation of identifying God with state interests remained persistently present.

At Joshua's death Israel reaffirmed her loyalty to God (Josh. 24: 16-18); and national fidelity continued briefly under the elders that outlived Joshua (24:31; cf. also the zeal of Phinehas, Judges 20:1, 28). God, moreover, had ordered the utter destruction of the Canaanites (Deut. 20:16-18), both to remove them from becoming sources of temptation to Israel and also to punish the sons of Ham for their own gross sins (Deut. 9:4). Israel, however, disobeyed and destroyed neither the Canaanites nor their idolatries (Judg. 2:2). Disastrous results followed. The period of the judges, in fact, almost witnessed the religious and national dissolution of Israel. Judges 17 alone records the violation of over half of the ten commandments in just one private family. Yet the faithless Levite involved, who deserted his benefactor to become the leader of a tribe's idolatry, was no less than a grandson or great-grandson of Moses himself (18:30). The generation that arose after the conquest lapsed into a general non-observance of the Mosaic law (2:10)[19] and wilfully transgressed the testament (2:20; Neh. 9:28). At Shechem there even appeared a temple in honor of *Ba'al* of *b'rîth* (8:33; 9:4), who is identified with *El* (God) of *b'rîth* (9:46). The meaning is uncertain. At its worst it would describe the complete syncretism of Baal and the testament, with the equally complete disintegration of the moral standards of the latter. For within the chambers of this temple were enacted crimes of rebellion, murder, arson, and perfidy. At its best, assuming *b'rîth* to mean only "treaty,"[20] it would describe a god bound by treaty to the town of Shechem. This, in turn, involves the Canaanitish deification of the state; for when "the master of the treaty" is a local Baal idol,

---

[19]But cf. Judg. 21:19; I Sam. 1:3; 2:13. There was some observance of the law, vs. the liberalism of Wellhausenism, which attempts to reason from its disregard to a theory of its non-existence, until forged in the name of Moses as much as a millennium later.

[20]Cf. the use of this same term, "masters of the treaty," for the Amorite allies of Abraham (Gen. 14:13).

his representative, the king, has in fact become the deity. Then he, or any other leader, rewrites the treaty as he pleases (9:5, 23, 26, 44, 49). But when Israel thus compromised her testamental religion, she threatened her own existence as a nation; for her survival, humanly speaking, depended on national unity (cf. 5:16, 17), and only a common loyalty to the testament could motivate an effective inter-tribal cooperation.

But all this served a purpose; for when Israel was weak, she became strong (II Cor. 12:9, 10). In her desperation she turned to God, and God raised up judges. These were not primarily judicial officers (though cf. Judges 4:5), but divinely empowered military and administrative leaders sent to save God's people (2:16). Repeatedly, during this period Israel experienced the cycle of sin, servitude, supplication, and salvation. The need for its repetition demonstrates human depravity (2:19), but at the same time the trials served a positive goal in the proving of Israel (2:22). The very attack upon the testament served to clarify its distinctive features and to hasten the appreciation of its nature.

Slowly but surely, consolidation did take place. The book of Ruth pictures a bright side to the period of the judges with graciousness, devotion, and piety (Ruth 2:8, 14, 20). Above all else, it teaches the potential inclusiveness of the testament as Ruth the Moabitess left her own people and land, choosing rather the people and the God of Naomi (1:16; 2:12). The fiasco of the ark's capture led directly to the twenty-year revival under Samuel, 1070-1050 B.C. (I Sam. 7:2). The founding of the kingdom under Saul in 1050 B.C., was, from a human viewpoint, motivated by Israel's sinful rejection of the theocracy of the judges (I Sam. 8:7; 12:12). But it was in fact the work of God's overruling providence (9:17). Negatively, Saul himself proved to be the punishment for Israel's sinful request (I Sam. 8:18; cf. 31:7). But positively his coronation set the pattern for a limited "constitutional" monarchy under God's testamental requirements (10: 25), which was unique in world history. His conquests (14:47) were a prelude to the final successful occupation of Canaan that was experienced under David, which marked the undisputed material establishment of the older testament. Moreover, his very position as anointed king meant the creation of that office through which the eyes of expectant men would be directed forward to a newer testament and to the ultimate Testator, who would give His life under the title, "The King of the Jews" (Mark 15:26).

For Further Reading:

Merrill F. Unger, "The Patriarchs and Contemporary History," *Bibliotheca Sacra*, 110:438 (April, 1953), 121-129, an evangelical discussion of patriarchal historicity.

H. H. Rowley, *Recent Discovery and the Patriarchal Age.* Manchester: 1945. A neo-orthodox study of the increasing modern respect for the validity of Genesis materials.

John Bright, *Early Israel in Recent History Writing.* Studies in Biblical Theology, No. 19. London: Student Christian Movement Press, 1956. A survey of recent scholarly thinking, mostly liberal, on Israel prior to the monarchy.

8. The History of the Testament: the Newer Anticipated *

F. THE DAVIDIC TESTAMENT. During the period of David, the testamental relationship came to be seen as that of a kingdom. Following a seven-year reign over his own tribe of Judah, David in 1003 B.C. became king over a united Israel. He marked this event by his capture from the Jebusites of the city of Jerusalem, which he proceeded to make his political capital (II Sam. 5:6-10). Shortly thereafter he brought within its walls the ark of the testament, thereby also making this city the religious center of his realm. Only his record of bloodshed prevented him from building the Temple in Jerusalem as well (I Chron. 22:8; 28:3). But though forbidden to erect this house of the testamental presence of God (17:1; 22:19; 28:2), he did organize Israel's service of worship and song around the ark in its tent on Zion (16:6, 37). Mount Zion thus became the city of God (Ps. 48:3) and the symbol of life in Him (vv. 12, 13; Ps. 87; 125:1, 2). To be "born in Jerusalem" (Ps. 87:5) expressed the truth that one was a redeemed son of God (cf. Gal. 3:26). David, moreover, conquered the surrounding territories and extended the borders of his kingdom to the Euphrates River (II Sam. 8:3; cf. I Kings 4:21), thereby fulfilling this last corollary aspect of the Abrahamic testament. The older testament was established.

It was at this point, about 995 B.C., that God decreed the sixth and last aspect of the older testament, the Davidic (II Sam. 7:12-16).[1] But though the Davidic testament had an immediate contemporary application, it contained other elements that were anticipatory of a new testament yet to come. Its essence lay in God's promise of salvation, mediated through the kingdom of David. The testament spoke, however, of the continuance of David's dynasty after him (7:16, 19) and of its particular culmination in that greater Son who would be also the Son of God (v. 14; Heb. 1:5). Other passages indicate that

---

* BIBLE READING: II Kings 17; Hosea 2:18-20; Isaiah 42
Collateral Reading: John Murray, *The Covenant of Grace,* 32 pp.
Payne, *An Outline of Hebrew History,* pp. 203-208.

[1]The designation "testament" appears in a number of parallel statements, such as II Sam. 23:5; Ps. 89:3, 132:12.

David's hope (Ps. 16:9, 11) lay specifically in Christ's death and resurrection (v. 10; cf. Acts 2:30, 31). The Davidic disposition is, therefore, literally a testament. This culminating rule of Christ would mean blessings like sunshine after rain (II Sam. 23:4). But for the saints in David's own day, too, God's choice of Zion meant salvation and joy (Ps. 132:13, 16). For the enemies of the Davidic dynasty, however, God's word threatened a fate of shame and of being burned like thorns (v. 18; II Sam. 23:7).

The monergism of the Davidic testament appears from Psalm 89:17, "In *Thy* favor our horn shall be exalted."[2] God, moreover, confirms His promise with an oath (v. 3). II Samuel 23:5 is, therefore, best translated:

> "For is my house not so with God? For He hath made with
> me an everlasting testament, ordered in all things and sure:
> for this is all my salvation, though all *His* desire, for will He
> not make it to put forth a shoot?'"

The everlasting nature of the Davidic testament is frequently repeated (Ps. 89:28). It is referred to as a "testament of salt" (II Chron. 13:5; cf. 7:18; 21:7). This feature, in turn, was closely associated with the testament's confirmatory sign, namely, the objective continuance of the Davidic dynasty (Ps. 89:4). As long as Christ lives, one possesses the "sure mercies of David" (Acts 13:34). It is stated in so many words that God will not break His testament (Ps. 89:34).

Equally unchanging in testamental thought, however, are the features of the heir's subjective response, which must be carried out if any given individual is to participate in the inheritance. One must incline his ear and hear, or have faith, if he is to participate in the sure mercies of David (Isa. 55:3). Furthermore, he must walk in God's ordinances, moral and ceremonial (Ps. 89:30); or God will so punish him as to appear to have abhorred His testament (v. 39; cf. Ps. 132:12). It is doubtful that God's followers in the time of David distinguished clearly between the Zion present and the Zion future, or between the earthly and the heavenly Jerusalem. But still, when a man qualified for the inheritance of reconciliation with God under the Davidic testament, he was blessed with divine guidance in this life, with reception to glory at death (Ps. 73:24), and with participation in the kingdom of Zion when the "horn of David" should bud (Ps. 132:17).

In the latter part of David's reign, his double sin of adultery with Bath-sheba and the murder of Uriah reflects the influence of Canaanitish standards of morality and royal absolutism. But David's subsequent condemnation by a prophetic watchman (II Sam. 12:7)

---

[2]Murray thus emphasizes the Davidic as the clearest Old Testament example of God's sovereign grace, *The Covenant of Grace*, p. 23.

and the king's sincere repentance that followed upon the prophet's rebuke (Ps. 51) would have been inconceivable elsewhere in the Near East. They stand as powerful witnesses to the reality and to the vitality of the testamental faith.

The period of the disruption of David's kingdom was a time of general triumph for Canaanitish thought over the religion of the testament. Solomon's reign, 970-930 B.C., was one of outward peace (I Kings 4:25), building (11:27), and commerce (9:26; 10:22). The king himself believed in the God of the testament (I Kings 3:6-9; Prov. 1:7; Eccl. 12:13). He furthermore executed David's plans for the Temple, the visible evidence of the testamental promise that God would be with Israel. But his very devotion to the Temple opened the way for a Canaanitish over-emphasis upon ritualism; and its expense, plus that of his own private luxuries, led to autocracy and oppression by the central government (I Kings 12:4). Solomon's personal life, moreover, degenerated into one of apostasy (11:1-8; cf. II Kings 23:13). The lēs, or religious scoffer, who had existed in David's time (Ps. 1:1), increased greatly in numbers (Prov. 21:24). Solomon's reign ended with Yahweh telling him, "Forasmuch as thou hast not kept my testament, which I have commanded thee, I will surely rend the kingdom from thee and will give it to thy servant" (I Kings 11:11).

But Jeroboam "who made Israel to sin" proved even worse as a ruler. In 930 B.C. this Ephraimite gained the throne in northern Israel, which consisted of ten tribes that had seceded from the Davidic kingdom. For political reasons, he raised up Dan and Bethel as sanctuaries to counteract the influence of Jerusalem (I Kings 12:29). Other rival sanctuaries, such as Gilgal, appeared, too (Hos. 4:15; Amos 5:5). Jeroboam then followed the example of the Canaanites and of Aaron in the wilderness (I Kings 12:28; cf. Ex. 32:4) and placed in his shrines golden bull-images. These he indeed connected with the historic God of Israel; but they were actually "other gods" (I Kings 14:9; II Chron. 13:8), and not just symbols for the true Yahweh. All the kings of Israel and most of those of Judah (the two southern tribes that maintained allegiance to the house of David) then perpetuated the sins of Solomon and Jeroboam (II Kings 17:8). The most notorious was Ahab in the north. Ahab's wife, moreover, was the Sidonian princess Jezebel (I Kings 16:30, 31), under whose influence he attempted to introduce Phoenician Baalism as the state religion of Israel (16:32). Jezebel, meanwhile, persecuted and killed the prophets of Yahweh (18:4). But though Ahab was checked by Elijah, and though both his dynasty and his foreign religion were overthrown by Elisha (II Kings 9:1, 2), local Baalism lived on, masquerading under the name of the worship of Yahweh (13:6).

Even in these troublous days, however, evidences of the historical reality of the testament continued to manifest themselves. The indirect influence of the testament, "common grace," is shown by the reputation that Israel's kings had for mercy (I Kings 20:31). Ahab, for all his apostasy, never questioned, for example, Naboth's property rights, which were guaranteed to him by the testament (21:4). Murder and robbery, however, came naturally to the mind of Jezebel, as they would have to any other pagan monarch at that time (vv. 5-10). Equally noteworthy is Ahab's repentance subsequent to these crimes when he was condemned by Elijah (v. 27). Indeed, the very fact of the appearance of reforming prophets (like Elijah), or priests (like Jehoiada), or kings (like Asa and Jehoshaphat), is inexplicable apart from the truth of the testament. Asa's national reaffirmation of "the testament of . . . Yahweh the God of their fathers" holds particular significance. It demonstrated Judah's faith, "seeking Him with their whole desire," and at the same time God's grace in being "found of them" and granting them "rest round about" (II Chron. 15:12-15).

The reigns of Jeroboam II (793-753 B.C.) in the North and of Uzziah (790-739) in the South were marked by outward prosperity but by inward decay, as is shown by the testimony of the eighth century prophets. The few lived in luxury by the oppression of the many (Isa. 1:21, 23; 2:7, 17). The prophets were generally corrupt (56:10-12). They worked for those who fed them (Micah 3:5) and prophesied peace. Religious forms were conscientiously observed, but they consisted of dead externalities (Amos 5:21-24). The people were blind (Isa. 42:18-20), and though true prophets were sent by God (II Kings 17:13), their messages were disregarded (v. 14). Near the end of this period, Ahaz of the South appealed to the Assyrians to intervene in Palestine on his behalf (II Kings 16:7). This had disastrous results. His entreaties brought about the fall of the North, as Assyria carried its inhabitants captive, first in 733 B.C., and then finally in 722. It proved almost as serious for the South, for in 701 B.C. Sennacherib carried the residents of the Judean towns into captivity as well. Only the miraculous intervention of God in history saved the capital city, Jerusalem, from a similar fate (II Kings 19:35, 36). Yet, even while the fire burned him, Israel laid it not to heart (Isa. 42:24, 25). The land lived in harlotry against its divine husband (Hos. 1:2); it was faithless to the testament (8:1). But history proved itself to be the acted revelation of God: the North's unstable faith had produced the unstable government that became its downfall (II Kings 15:10, 14, 25). More fundamentally, it was their rejection of the testament that constituted the cause for God's rejection of Samaria and the northern kingdom (II Kings 17:15; 18:12).

It may, therefore, appear strange that of the seven eighth century prophets (Hosea through Micah, plus Isaiah), only Isaiah makes consistent reference to the testament. Five do not even mention God's b'rith. The prophecies of Obadiah and Jonah have, of course, a foreign

orientation, but in Hosea, Joel, Amos, and Micah there appears to be
a deliberate neglect of this concept. It is evident that they knew of
it, for it is mentioned in Hosea 2:18; 6:7; and 8:1. The first of these
references, moreover, is highly significant, as noted below. Also, in
Amos 3:2, though the actual term "testament" is not employed, God's
choice of undeserving Israel is spoken of in such a way as to assume
its existence.[3] But still these prophets made little use of the testamental concept. The explanation seems to be this. They were faced
in their contemporaries with a dead externality of religion: the facts
were known, but the life was not lived. So the crying demand of the
prophets was for the restoration of a personal relationship with God,
based upon love and surrender. The judicial testament might conceivably have been perverted into a substitute for inner experience.
The eighth century prophets, accordingly, chose to stress God's gracious deliverance of His people from Egypt rather than His written
word upon Sinai. They defined His relationship with Israel as being
like that of a husband or a father (Hos. 2:15, 19; cf. Jer. 3:4) rather
than like that of a testator.[4]

Isaiah was nonetheless used of God to develop the truth of the
testament in three significant ways.

First, the monergism of the testament was by Isaiah related to
God's sovereign activity in contemporary history. The consistent theme
of this prophet was that Judah must trust in God and in Him alone
(Isa. 26:4). God would then keep those who trusted Him in perfect
peace (26:3). As applied to the immediate presence of Assyria, however, this thesis developed in four apparently contradictory stages. In
734 B.C. Isaiah opposed the appeal of the weakling Ahaz to Assyria
for help. He pointed out that Israel's hope lay in trusting God — and
in keeping Assyria out of the picture! (Isa. 7:9). But after Assyria
had once assumed the suzerainty over Judah, he condemned his people's resistance to Assyria and criticized the counter plots that were
made with the collaboration either of Egypt (30:1, 2) or of Babylon
(39:5, 6). He identified such plots as perfidious, as being in opposi-

---

[3]Note also the "contract" terminology, appealing to heaven and earth as judicial
witnesses, Isa. 1:2; Micah 6:1; cf. Deut. 32:1 and Jer. 2:12, Herbert F. Huffmon,
"The Covenant Lawsuit in the Prophets," *Journal of Biblical Literature,* 78
(1959), pp. 286-295.
[4]Cf. Vos' reference to "something deeper and more fundamental" lying back of
the *b'rith,* namely, the nature and will of God. *Biblical Theology,* p. 280. Mendenhall concludes that while the prophets favored the Sinaitic "suzerainty covenant,"
with its obligations based upon previous benevolence, they yet opposed the
Davidic testament, with its seeming approval upon a corrupt dynasty; so they
ignored the whole concept, "Covenant Forms in Israelite Tradition," *The Biblical
Archaeologist,* 17 (1954), pp. 72-73. Kline, however, demonstrates the unreality
of any such tension between Moses and David, since the Sinaitic testament contained provisions for "dynastic succession" (Joshua) and the Davidic testament,
like the Abrahamic before it, involved responsibility as well as promise, "The Two
Tables of the Covenant," *The Westminster Theological Journal,* 22 (1960), pp.
143-144, and "Dynastic Covenant," *ibid.,* 23 (1960), p. 11.

tion to God, and as constituting a rupture of the everlasting testament. He warned that they would only bring desolation upon the land (24:5), and this was exactly what happened with Sennacherib's attack in 701 B.C. But when Assyria had exacted her punishment and had gone on to defy the living God (36:15), Isaiah turned and demanded resistance and proclaimed the inviolability of Zion (37:21-25). God, so said Isaiah, would defend the city for the sake of His testamental promise to David (37:35). And He indeed did so, by direct intervention (37:36, 37). Finally, under Manasseh, Isaiah again opposed his people's appeal to temporal supports (55:2) and maintained his consistent demand for trust upon God's testamental mercies (v. 3). Isaiah even proclaimed that these mercies would prove sufficient for the foreigner, as well as for the Israelite, if only he would hold fast the testament (56:4, 6). Each of these four stages was but a specific application of his one basic plea for testamental commitment.

Second, major facets that contribute to our understanding of the person of the Testator were revealed through Isaiah. The personality of the Redeemer had come to the fore in the anticipatory aspects of the Davidic testament, where His death and resurrection had been first revealed (Ps. 16:10). The facts of His humiliation then received their fullest Old Testament description in Isaiah's remarkable predictions of the "Suffering Servant." See below, topic 19. In reference to the *b'rīth*, however, a high point was reached in Isaiah's personalization of the testament in the Servant. Yahweh says of Him, "And I will give Thee for a testament of the people, for a light of the Gentiles" (42:6; 49:8). That is, what had so far been considered as a legal disposition is here summed up in a Person. Christ is not only the everlasting Son of God who *establishes* the testament, but He is the priest who *officiates* at the death (52:15). He is also the Testator, the offering that *dies* (53:8), and He becomes Himself the living blessing of reconciliation; indeed, He *is* the inheritance that is bestowed (49:6): "Thou art my salvation!" Christ is the testament.[5] This accomplishment of the Servant, moreover, fulfills the universalistic, priestly purpose of Israel, for He becomes at the same time the light of the Gentiles (cf. Luke 2:29-32).

Third, Isaiah builds upon a revelation initially given through Hosea, by which God's people were led to anticipate a newer testament. This was a *b'rīth* which did not yet have contemporary application, but which was to be divinely executed in a future consummation. Seemingly in despair because of his immediate, Baal-worshiping surroundings (Hos. 2:17), Hosea looked forward to a better time ahead, as Yahweh said, "And I *will* make a testament for

---

[5]Cf. Murray's description of the embodiment of the testament in the Messiah, *op. cit.*, pp. 24-25. Vos' statement, that through the Servant the testament will be realized, *op. cit.*, p. 277, is true; but it is inadequate for doing full justice to the force of the words.

them" (2:18). This testament would have two aspects: an internal —
"And I will betroth thee unto Me in righteousness[6] . . . and thou
shalt know Yahweh" (2:19, 20); and an external — "And I will make
a testament for them with the beasts of the field . . . and I will break
the bow and the sword and the battle out of the land, and will make
them to lie down safely" (v. 18). These aspects reached complete
expression, respectively, in Jeremiah in the later prophetic period of
revelation and in Ezekiel in the exilic (see below). But Isaiah, in
the latter part of his life, carried forward to some extent the external
portion of Hosea's revelation. He first assigned it a name, the "testament of peace," which signified the mercy God would yet bestow
upon Israel (54:10). Isaiah then specified its everlasting character
(61:8; cf. 59:21). It remained, however, for Ezekiel to develop its
specific characteristics and significance.

In the seventh century the kingdom of northern Israel no longer
remained on the scene. The remnants of the more pious of its people
had become incorporated into the Southern Kingdom of Judah (II
Chron. 30:6; cf. 35:18), and much of its former territory was also
added in the days of Josiah (34:6). All twelve tribes again supported
the true worship in Jerusalem (34:9). But the Assyrians had repopu-
lated Samaria itself with foreigners whose religion consisted partly of
the debased Bethel type of Yahweh worship (II Kings 17:28) and
partly of their native paganism (v. 29). Though claiming to be the
legitimate successors of Jacob (cf. John 4:12), the Samaritans were
not true followers of Yahweh (II Kings 17:34; John 4:22).

In the Southern Kingdom, Manasseh (696-641 B.C.) proved to
be the worst of Judah's kings (II Chron. 33:9). He encouraged star
worship, perhaps because of the influence of his Assyrian masters (v.
5), and practiced human sacrifice in the valley of Hinnom south of
Jerusalem after the manner of the Canaanites (v. 6). Manasseh's
conversion late in life took away the pagan names from Jerusalem,
but the people still kept the pagan forms in the name of Yahweh
(v. 17). Josiah (639-608), however, was the last great king of Judah.
His significant reform of 621 B.C. was based upon his reaffirmation
of the testament, as written in the book of Moses (II Kings 23:3).
The people, however, continued their perverted trust in the external
sign of the temple (Jer. 7:4), rather than in the true reformation of
the heart (vv. 5-11). Josiah's four successors were evil, especially
Jehoiakim, who oppressed the poor that he might live in luxury (Jer.
22:13-17). Actually, Josiah's faithfulness had only postponed the end
(II Kings 22:20) that Manasseh's sins had made inevitable (24:3).
It was a fate, moreover, that had been predicted from the very days
of Moses (Deut. 28:36, 37). Judah had failed to meet the subjective
requirements of the testament; and, as a result, the God who is master

---

[6]God's righteous (saving) character, not man's, cf. topic 12.

of history brought in Nebuchadrezzar of Babylon, who in 586 B.C. destroyed Jerusalem, burned the Temple, and took most of the people captive (II Kings 25:15). The murder of Gedaliah, the governor of the remnant (vv. 25, 26), extinguished the last hope of those whose kings had reigned in the power of the Davidic testament. Such refugees as remained fled to the southwest; they compelled Jeremiah to accompany them, and they were last seen in Egypt engaged in willful idolatry (Jer. 44:11-12).

G. THE NEW TESTAMENT. It was through Jeremiah, however, that God revealed what is in fact the high point of all Old Testament theology. Jeremiah had preached on behalf of the Sinaitic testament in Josiah's reformation of 621 (Jer. 11:1-13; 22:9); and he appreciated the concepts of eternal priesthood and kingship that characterized, respectively, the Levitical and Davidic testaments (33:20-25). But he seems to have become disillusioned as he saw the practical deficiencies in the external, typical religion that marked the whole of the older testament. He looked forward instead to the day when the ark would be unnecessary and unmissed (3:16). Righteousness was the solution (7:23), but the heart of man is depraved and desperately wicked (17:9). As Hosea had suggested in the first revelation of a future testament, there would have to come a time when God would intervene in person and betroth men to Himself so that they may know Him directly (Hos. 2:19, 20). Through Jeremiah, then, God revealed the truth of the new testament (Jer. 31:31-34), the seventh in the series described in Scripture. Yet this new testament was fundamentally distinct from the preceding six, from the Edenic to the Davidic. It would belong, not to the older dispensation of anticipation, but to a newer, which should look back upon redemption as already historically accomplished. It is the gracious testament under which Christians are living today.

Jeremiah specified four elements in the new testament. It would be internal — "In their heart will I write it" (31:33). It would be reconciling — "I will be their God, and they shall be My people" (v. 33), the same promise that is found in all other revelations of the testament. It would be direct — "They shall all know Me" (v. 34), through personal faith made possible by means of the incarnation, rather than through the anticipatory rites of the older testament. Finally, it would be explicit in forgiveness — "For I will forgive their iniquity" (v. 34). The ultimate, ransoming death would have taken place; and the testament would have been effectuated for man's inheritance of righteousness. In the words of Jesus Christ for use at the Lord's Supper, "This cup is the new testament in My blood" (I Cor. 11:25).

Jeremiah had predicted an exilic period of seventy years duration (Jer. 25:11; 29:10; cf. II Chron. 36:21, 22, 605-538 B.C.), figuring from the first small deportation (Dan. 1:1) in 605 B.C. The future hope of the Jews lay in the second, or select, deportation of 597 B.C., Jeremiah's "good figs" (Jer. 23:3), rather than in the third, largest deportation of 586, which was generally "bad." Sadness and home-sickness for Zion characterized the early exiles in Babylon (Ps. 137), but the whole experience served to further God's providential plans for the good of His own (Jer. 23:5). For the exile acted as a great sifting process, once and for all breaking the grip in which Canaan-itish idolatry had bound Israel for eight centuries. All the Jews did not, of course, give up their pagan attachments. Quite to the con-trary! But only those who submitted faithfully to the testament found themselves with the motivation to return to Palestine at the close of the period (Ezek. 14:11).

In the exile, pious Jews gathered around God's leaders (Ezek. 3:15; 33:30, 31), and it was here that local synagogues seem to have had their inception (cf. the exilic Asaphite Psalm, 74:8). The external appeal of the one central temple was gone. Instead, Israel's non-localized observances, such as the sabbath (Ezek. 20:12-24), dietary laws (Dan. 1:8), and stated times of prayer (6:10), came increasingly to be stressed. Above all, the exile taught that only a life of commit-ment to the God of historic revelation could prevent death, both nationally and individually (Ezek. 18:31).

H. THE TESTAMENT OF PEACE. The exile marked a development in both of the aspects of Hosea's future testament. In reference to the first, the new testament, Daniel 9:26, 27 provided a date for the termination of the animal sacrifices of the older testament and for the confirming of the new. It revealed also that the latter would be inaugurated by the rejection, the "cutting off" of the Messiah. After His termination of the sacrificial system, however, the Messiah's activity in confirming the testament to Israel nationally (cf. v. 24) would be limited to a period of approximately 3½ additional years (cf. Acts 2:38).[7] The second aspect of Hosea's future testament, which had been named "the testament of peace" by Isaiah (54:10), was also mentioned briefly by Jeremiah in the later prophetic period (Jer. 32:40); but its full exposition was left to the exilic prophet Ezekiel. Ezekiel appre-ciated the value of the older testament for his contemporaries (Ezek. 16:8); for, even though the Israelites had broken its conditions (v. 59), he foresaw their post-exilic return to Palestine and their recon-struction of its sanctuary (43:10, 11).[8] But his real hope lay in the

[7]See below, topic 21-B, for the discussion of Daniel's 70 weeks of years.
[8]To see in this section, as some do, the prediction of a still future millennial temple not only opposes the above cited directions to Ezekiel's contemporaries for the rebuilding of the temple but raises serious theological difficulties by in-troducing literal blood atonement (Ezek. 43:20) and sin-offerings (vs. 21), that have now become impossible in the light of Heb. 9:20; 10:10. Cf. the discussion by Martin J. Wyngaarden, *The Future of the Kingdom in Prophecy and Fulfill-ment* (Grand Rapids: Baker Book House, 1955), pp. 76-78.

future, as he transmitted God's revelation of the testament of peace (34:25; 37:26), the eighth and final disposition of God's redemptive testament. Like the seventh, Jeremiah's new testament, it was not to be effectuated in his own anticipatory dispensation (Ezek. 20:37); but it was to constitute the latter stage of that newer dispensation which would be commemorative of Christ's accomplished act of redemption, "when I *have* forgiven thee all that thou hast done" (16:63). It is still future for us today.

Like all other revelations of the testament, the testament of peace possesses basic objective features as follows: the promise of reconciliation — "Ye My sheep, the sheep of My pasture, are men, and I am your God" (34:31; cf. 37:27); monergism — "I will establish My testament with thee . . . be confounded and never open thy mouth any more" (16:62, 63; cf. 37:28); and eternity — "It shall be an everlasting testament with them" (37:26; cf. 16:60). This testament requires also the same subjective response of faith — "I will purge out from among you the rebels" (20:38; cf. 16:61); and the faith demonstrates itself in obedience — "the bond of the testament" (20:37; cf. 37:24).

In particular, however, the testament of peace will bring to fulfillment the four features that have already distinguished Jeremiah's new testament, the testament which constitutes our earlier, present day stage of the new dispensation of realized salvation. Like the new testament, the testament of peace will be internal — "they shall walk in Mine ordinances and observe My statutes" (37:24); it will be reconciling, as always — "I will be their God, and they shall be My people" (v. 27); it will be marked by direct faith — "My sanctuary in the midst of them forever more" (v. 26); and it will grant explicit forgiveness — "the nations shall know that I am Yahweh that sanctifieth Israel" (v. 28). But the testament of peace goes further, beyond the present, Christian Church age, to God's final eschatological kingdom.[9] Whereas in the new testament we "know" God (Jer. 31:34), the confirmatory sign of the testament of peace will be communion with Him, "face to face" (Ezek. 20:35); whereas in the new testament the law is "in their heart" (Jer. 31:33), in the future testament God, externally, "will cause evil beasts to cease out of the land," as well (Ezek. 34:25); and whereas in the new testament God doth "forgive their iniquity" (Jer. 31:34), then it is stated in addition, "And they shall no more be a prey to the nations . . . but they shall dwell securely, and none shall make them afraid" (Ezek. 34:28).

Even at the fall of Jerusalem, Jeremiah had predicted a post-exilic restoration (Jer. 33:10-14); the faithful among the Jews would

---

[9]Part of the confusion in dispensational thought over the fulfillment of Jeremiah's new testament in the Church is due to its failure to distinguish the new testament from this still future testament of peace. Cf. Ryrie *The Basis of the Premillennial Faith*, pp. 122-124, and John F. Walvoord, "The New Covenant with Israel," *Bibliotheca Sacra*, 110:439 (July, 1953), 196-197.

return so as to join in the testament on Mount Zion (50:5). Ezekiel, moreover, had been granted the vision of the dry bones, indicating that Israel's national life would experience a God-given revival (Ezek. 37:11). In fact, this revival had become a necessity: both to vindicate Yahweh's honor as the testamental God of Israel (36:20, 21); and, as Moses had predicted long before, to prevent pride on the part of the conquering pagans (Deut. 32:27). The historical instrument for the accomplishing of this return had likewise been predicted far in advance. It was Cyrus of Persia (Isa. 44:28) acting through his decree of 538 B.C. Ezekiel had, moreover, predicted the return of all twelve tribes (Ezek. 37:21, 22). There seems to have been an intermingling of both Northern and Southern exiles in Babylon (16:53-58; cf. v. 51); Ezra speaks of the returning groups in both the sixth and the fifth centuries as offering "twelve sacrifices, according to the number of the tribes of Israel" (Ezra 6:17; cf. 8:35); and members of all twelve tribes were indeed presented in the restored Palestine (cf. Luke 2:36; Acts 26:7). The name "Jew," however, which had applied originally to the tribe of Judah, and then to those Hebrews who lived in the Southern Kingdom of Judah, came by this time to be applied to anyone who had embraced Judaism, irrespective of his origin. "Jew" thus became a religious rather than a national term.

Actually, the majority of Jews never returned to Palestine. The first return, in 537 B.C. under Zerubbabel and Jeshua, consisted of about 50,000 former exiles. The work of rebuilding progressed slowly. Zerubbabel's council refused to accept the religiously syncretistic Samaritans into the community of God's chosen people (Ezra 4:3), and the latter succeeded in delaying the reconstruction of the temple for some twenty years. The second return, under Ezra in 458, consisted of only about 1500; but these possessed more wealth, as well as more religious vision, than the former, larger group. But despite the wide political powers granted to Ezra in his commission from Artaxerxes (Ezra 7:18, 25), the Samaritans were able to thwart his efforts at rebuilding the walls of Jerusalem (4:23). The city's refortification was, however, accomplished by Nehemiah fourteen years later (Neh. 6:15).

First Ezra alone (Ezra 10:1-3), and then Ezra with the help of Nehemiah (Neh. 9:3), struggled to maintain the purity of God's people, but with only partial success. Except for sporadic cases (Zech. 13:2), idolatry was overcome; but an externalized and hypocritical formalism (Mal. 1:6-8), that was to develop into New Testament Pharisaism, became more and more apparent. The anticipation of a newer testament in the future, aroused by the prophecies of Jeremiah and Ezekiel, became dimmed in the minds of the nation's leaders. So, too, the revelations of Moses, that had established the older testament in the present, were increasingly disregarded as many of the temple officials defiled their own Levitical testament (Mal. 2:10; Neh. 13:29). Israel as a whole proved unfruitful in its status as God's vineyard (Isa. 5:1; Jer. 2:21; Ezek. 15:6). The vineyard would have to be given to others to carry on as the true Israel (Matt. 21:43) until the coming of a far distant national repentance and reingrafting into the faith (Rom. 11:23). But within the nation were to be found humble, godly folk, whom the centuries and the millennia under the older testament had prepared to be eager recipients of "the consolation of Israel" (Luke 2:25). Thus the last of the Old Testament prophets spoke both of the enduring present relationship of Moses (Mal. 4:6), and yet at the same time of the inadequacy of present institutions and of the need for that future relationship foreseen by Hosea and his successors. Malachi was looking forward to a future activity of the Messenger of the testament (Mal. 3:1). Both Moses and Hosea, both present and future relationships, were true. The synthesis becomes fully accomplished in Jesus Christ, for "he that hath the Son hath [present] life" (I John 5:12); and yet "the Lord shall [future] give them light, and they shall reign for ever and ever" (Rev. 22:5).

For Further Reading:

Geerhardus Vos, "Christian Faith and the Truthfulness of Biblical History," *Princeton Theological Review*, 4:3 (July, 1906), 289-305. An evangelical analysis of the historicity of revelation.

John F. Walvoord, "The Kingdom Promises to David," *Bibliotheca Sacra*, 110: 438 (April, 1953), 97-110. A dispensational treatment of the Davidic testament.

James Oscar Boyd, "The Davidic Dynasty," *Princeton Theological Review*, 25:2 (April, 1927), 215-239, and "The Davidic Covenant," *ibid.*, 25:3 & 4 (July & Oct., 1927), 417-443 & 587-607. Studies, respectively, on the history of David and on the oracle granted to him.

III. The Testator: God

"Know therefore that Yahweh thy God, He is God, the faithful God, who keepeth the testament and the *hésedh* [the loyalty to its obligations]" (cf. pp. 156-157; Deuteronomy 7:9).

9. The Personality of God*

The first of the five major aspects involved in the testament[1] is that of the reality of the testator: God, actively communicating His will in history. His existence is assumed in Scripture, never argued. In such statements as Ps. 14:1 — "The fool hath said in his heart, There is no God" (cf. Ps. 94:8-10) — the emphasis lies not upon a theoretical denial of His existence but upon a practical disregard of His lordship (Jer. 5:12 — "not is He [relevant]"). The "fool" (*nāvāl*, the hardened ungodly man[2]) does not know God (I Sam. 2:12), in that he simply shuts God out of his life. He acts as if God did not exist, but he is not an atheist; his very godlessness assumes its significance because of the man's prior awareness of God's existence (Ps. 14:4). God's nature is not formally discussed in Scripture either, for His existence as true Personality is likewise assumed throughout. An appreciation of the nature of God may, however, be gained from the descriptions of His activities. Because God is active in history, and particularly because He has come to man with the revelation of His saving testament (Parts I and II above), men may, as a result, come to understand something of the Testator Himself.

A. ANTHROPOMORPHISM. This term concerns the Biblical descriptions of God "in the form of man." In the primeval age, for example, God is described in a straightforward way as walking and talking with men (Gen. 2:6, 19; 3:8). The descriptions are anthropomorphic. God is also spoken of as having "human" feelings, such as being grieved and regretting (6:6), or feeling pleased (8:21). These latter are examples, technically, of anthropopathism. On the basis then of

---

*BIBLE READING: Deuteronomy 4:14-40; Leviticus 20:1-9, 20-27
Collateral Reading: Vos, *Biblical Theology,* pp. 253-257, 264-270.
    A. B. Davidson, *The Theology of the Old Testament,* 2, pp. 106-115.
    William F. Albright, *From the Stone Age to Christianity* (Baltimore: The John Hopkins Press, 1940), pp. 196-207.

[1]See p. 87.
[2]See p. 56.

the Biblical anthropomorphism and anthropopathism, the most fundamental truth about the Testator is that He is a real person!

In the time of the patriarchs God was first called *hai*, the "living One" (Gen. 16:14). Furthermore, though His suprahuman greatness as "Judge of all the earth" (18:25) then receives its initial expression (cf. Deut. 10:14), some of the revelations of God are still very simple. He comes down to see (Gen. 18:21), He eats (v. 8), and He goes His way (v. 33). He appears to Abraham as a smoking, portable furnace-oven (15:17);[3] though He is, at the same time, free from geographical limitations and able to appear anywhere (28:15; 46:4).

From the time of Moses and onward, God's qualitative distinction from man is clear (Ex. 19:12, 13), even in such anthropomorphic references as concern the movement of His glory (Ex. 33:20-23). Still, His being alive is the most certain of all conceivable facts; for this is what He, and others, swear by (Num. 14:21, 28). He is, in short, the ultimate personality: "I am He" (Deut. 32:39; cf. Isa. 43:10). But He yet "comes down in the sight of all" (Ex. 19:11), with "face" and "back" (33:23); compare the much later mention of His "hand" and "ear" (Isa. 59:1). The anthropopathisms continue as well: God becomes angry (Deut. 4:21) or jealous (Ex. 20:5), like a jealous husband (Num. 5:14; Prov. 6:34).[4] He is a consuming fire (Deut. 4:24). These descriptions, too, continue in the later periods, especially in the Old Testament poetry and prophecy. But with them appears an explicit denial of any human limitations or imperfections within God: He "sleeps" (Ps. 44:23), but does not slumber (Ps. 121:4) and is not weary (Isa. 40:28); He "repents" [regrets] (I Sam. 15:11, 35), but does not lie or repent (v. 29).

The following explanations relate to the anthropomorphisms of Scripture. 1) Some are due to the necessary limitations of language and human thought. They are "inevitable if men will think about God."[5] To "see" or to "hear" cannot but suggest human sense organs, even though none may actually be intended. 2) Some are poetic, as Exodus 15:8, "the blast of Thy nostrils." This same phenomenon, for example, is described in prose as a strong east wind (14:21). But 3) anthropomorphism as a whole serves the positive purpose of underlining the basic fact of God's personality. Even from the general revelation of creation the personalness of God is evident: "He that formed

---

[3]Or is this just a dream?

[4]The noun *qin'ā* comes from the root, "to become intensely red, or black." It is, therefore, the color produced in the face by deep emotion, especially the ardor of jealousy of a husband (Prov. 27:4). It develops to mean, however, anger or zeal in general. In the second commandment of the Decalogue, *qin'ā* is God's reaction to men's hating Him and to their not keeping His commandments; and the original connotations should not be pressed too far, as is perhaps done in Vos' *Biblical Theology*, p. 152.

[5]Davidson, *The Theology of the Old Testament*, p. 108. This section constitutes a generally valuable discussion.

the eye, shall He not see?" (Ps. 94:9). In the special revelation of
the testament, therefore, God acts like a person simply because He
is a Person! The Septuagint, it is true, attempted to remove certain
of these anthropomorphisms in its translation of the Old Testament
into Greek;[6] but the New Testament takes as its major premise that
the fullness of the Godhead is personal, dwelling in Jesus Christ (Col.
2:9). Salvation by the testament requires a Person.

B. SPIRITUALITY. God, the Testator, is essentially spirit (John
4:24), but this fact was not specified in the earliest revelations of
Scripture. Jacob, in the patriarchal period, indeed put away the material idols that his family had brought from Padan Aram (Gen. 35:2,
4); but whether he completely disassociated God from the stone of
Bēth-Ēl, "the house of God" (28:18), is not clear.[7] The various patriarchal theophanies were not spirit appearances but real, even though
they were only temporary and not descriptive of God's essential
nature. Moses, however, in the next period, emphasized that when
God spoke on Sinai there was no form seen (Deut. 4:12, 15). Command II of the Decalogue then expressly prohibited any representation of the Divine Being (Ex. 20:4-6). God was not to be associated
or confused with His creation. The massēvā, the memorial and sacrificial pillar of the patriarchs (Gen. 28:18; 35:14), Moses ordered
henceforth to be destroyed (Ex. 23:24). Originally, it had been a
helpful symbol; but now it might influence Israel toward a materializa-
tion of deity and lead to Canaanitish forms of idolatry. The pagan
ashērā poles and teraphim (hearth-gods) were of course to be destroyed (Ex. 34:13; cf. I Sam. 15:23). Aaron's golden calf, like Jeroboam's five hundred years later, was truly intended to represent God
(Ex. 32:4); but that was the very thing that made it so wrong
(vv. 7-10; cf. I Kings 12:30; Hos. 8:6)! Job (revealed in this same
disruption period) explicitly taught that God is not of flesh (Job 10:
4; cf. Isa. 31:3, "spirit and not flesh"). Hezekiah, in the eighth century,
was forced to destroy Nehushtan, which is what Moses' brazen serpent had come to be called (II Kings 18:4). The point is this: what
had once been a symbol of salvation (Num. 21:8) and a type, indeed,
of Christ lifted up on the cross (John 3:14) had through human
perversity, become an idol and a threat to the people in their doctrine
of the spirituality of God. At the same time, however, the informed
leaders of Israel knew that God could not be likened to His creatures

---

[6]In about 250 B.C. cf. C. T. Fritsch, *The Anti-anthropomorphisms of the Greek
Pentateuch* (Princeton: Princeton University Press, 1943).
[7]True, Yahweh had stood above the ladder (Gen. 28:13); but this was in the
dream in Jacob's head (v. 12), and Jacob's head was on the stone (v. 11)!
Neither, it must be carefully observed, does this passage teach the material nature
of God. It simply states that God had been there. Later revelation clarifies, never
contradicts, earlier revelation.

(Isa. 40:18), and they heaped ridicule upon the folly of idolatry (vv. 19, 20; 2:8, 20).

C. HOLINESS. In the Old Testament, holiness is more than just one of the many attributes of God. It is descriptive rather of His whole divine personality. The first specifically recorded revelation of God's holiness occurred during the Mosaic period. For at the time of Israel's deliverance from Egypt, the term "holy" was used to distinguish the true deity of Yahweh from the demonstrated impotence of the gods of the defeated Egyptians (Ex. 15:11; cf. 12:12): "Who is like unto Thee, oh Yahweh, among the gods? Who is like Thee, glorious in holiness?"

The noun qôdesh, "holiness," appears to have the basic meaning of "separateness" (Lev. 20:26). Its opposite is hōl, "profane," meaning not separate (Lev. 10:10; Ezek. 22:26).[8] Those who seek to explain Scripture on the basis of comparative religion have attributed much of the qôdhesh material that is found in the Old Testament to the primitive concept of taboo. It is asserted that "holy" objects were once thought to contain "other, separate" spirits in themselves and were therefore to be let alone. Such superstition, however, is unworthy of Scripture. It is true that certain holy objects were required to be kept separate and that contact with them could mean death, as when Uzzah touched the ark. But Uzzah died because God struck him, not because of an intrinsic taboo. The only relevance of the taboo concept to the Old Testament is this: qôdhesh items that were permanently separated to God, to the extent of losing all further connection or consequence in respect to mankind, were called hērem, gifts "devoted" to God (Lev. 27:28).[9] The objects, then, that the pagan Canaanites had considered qôdhesh or taboo, God commanded Israel to make hērem. But this was just another way of placing paganism under the ban, for to "devote" in the sense of hērem means simply to destroy! (cf. Josh. 6:17).

From the basic idea of "separation," there appeared in Israel in this same Mosaic period three other derived aspects of holiness.[10] 1) Since God the Testator is most "separate" from His creatures (Ex. 20:19), holiness becomes equivalent to deity (cf. Isa. 5:24; Hab. 3:3). The worship of other gods profanes His *holy* name (Lev. 20:3). "Holy" is thus synonymous with "divine": "There is none *holy* [uniquely divine] as Yahweh; for there is none beside Thee" (I Sam.

---

[8]*Tāhōr*, "clean," also means "separate," but *tāhōr* items are still found in natural association with the unclean. They have not yet been dedicated so as to become qôdhesh, see below, topic 26-D.

[9]Norman H. Snaith, *The Distinctive Ideas of the Old Testament* (Philadelphia: The Westminster Press, 1946), p. 39. Ch. II of this work surveys the concept of holiness, in a history of religion framework.

[10]Cf. Vos' four-fold treatment of holiness as separation, divine unapproachableness, the entourage of deity, and sinlessness, *op. cit.*, pp. 265-268.

2:2). Since God is the Holy One, He asks correspondingly, "To whom then will ye liken Me?" (Isa. 40:25); and for an incomparable oath, God swears by His holiness (His own deity, Ps. 89:35). It is because of His divine holiness (separateness), His dwelling in "the high and holy place" (Isa. 57:15), that there is no searching of His understanding (40:28; 55:8, 9; cf. Job 26:14; 37:23; Ps. 145:3). Holiness, then, is what characterizes God, and it includes all His other attributes. Noteworthy in this regard are the three parts of Psalm 99: on God's power, on His justice, and on His love. Each of the parts, however, concludes with the explanation, "For He is holy" (vv. 3, 5, 9). Holiness is, in fact, a fearsome thing. Death was expected to follow contact with God (Ex. 3:6; 33:20; cf. Isa. 6:5); and after Yahweh had struck down the men of Beth-shemesh for looking into the ark, they cried, "Who is able to stand before Yahweh, this holy God?" (I Sam. 6:20).

But there is another aspect to holiness which would be incredible were it not demonstrated by the fact of the testament: "Thus saith the high and lofty One, that inhabiteth eternity, whose name is Holy: I dwell in the high and holy place, *with him also that is of a contrite and humble spirit*" (Isa. 57:15). That is 2) God shares His holiness with those who inherit the testament;[11] they, too, are "separated" unto God (Ex. 19:10, 14; Lev. 20:24). Divine holiness is not exclusive, but it reaches out to draw others to God's separation. Hence God is called "the light of Israel" and "his [Israel's] Holy One" (Isa. 10:17; cf. Ps. 78:41). Such holiness may even extend to inanimate objects if they, too, become separated unto God. Thus the Mosaic tabernacle, where God met with Israel, was "sanctified" by His glory (Ex. 29:43-45; cf. Ps. 93:5); its inner chamber in particular, where the *sh'khīnā* rested, became the "holy of holies [most holy]." Similarly, the spot where God appeared to Moses in the burning bush was "holy" ground (Ex. 3:5). Zion became God's holy mountain. The priests had holy garments. The holy (divinely powerful) bones of Elisha actually raised a dead man (II Kings 13:21). Such holiness possessed, of course, no essential moral quality. In fact, it was God's "holiness," His sovereign election, that prevented the punishment of the immoral Israelites (Hos. 11:9). The nations at Christ's second coming even *qiddēsh*, "make holy," that is, separate themselves religiously for war *against Him*! (Joel 3:9). An extreme example of non-moral holiness was the Canaanitish temple prostitute, who was separated for this "religious service," and was called a *q'dhēshā* (Deut. 23:18). But when God destroyed the Jerusalem Temple in 586 B.C., there came a reaction against associating God's holiness with created objects. Commencing with the exilic period, pious Israelites came to

---

[11]Cf. Jacob's illuminating discussion, *Theology of the Old Testament*, pp. 89-90.

think of God as more removed, more transcendent. Thus Ezekiel in his vision had contact, not with God directly, but with "the appearance of the likeness of the glory of Yahweh" (Ezek. 1:28).

But since holiness means separation to God, and since, from the first, God's will has opposed sin and has sought righteousness in mankind (Gen. 6:5, 6), 3) holiness takes on a third meaning: that of conformity to God's moral standards (Lev. 20:7, 8). Furthermore, it is God's moral purity that leads Him to separate Himself from evil (Hab. 1:13). But man can experience no greater loss than this separation from the divine favor. The punishment, therefore, of a man's moral infractions must stem ultimately from the fact of God's holiness (Amos 4:2; Ezek. 38:23). So in the call of Isaiah, the prophet's natural reaction to God's holiness (Isa. 6:3) was to experience conviction about his own sin (v. 5). His submission, however, eventuated in his forgiveness, the imputation to him of moral holiness (v. 7). This developed aspect of holiness as morality is treated below in topic 25; and the specific requirement of consecrated separation from all compromise, whether with worldliness or with theological apostasy, is treated in topic 29-E.[12]

D. MONOTHEISM. From the greatness and the uniqueness of the testamental revelation, there should follow a knowledge of the unique deity of the Testator. Historically, however, this truth was only progressively revealed by God and grasped by fallen man. Before the fall Adam knew God, but most of his descendants became polytheists (Josh. 24:2). The patriarchs, in the next period, worshiped only the one God (Gen. 35:2), though this practice technically constitutes only monolatry and not monotheism. At one point Abraham did make the statement to Abimelech, "Gods caused me to wander" (20:13). This plural terminology, however, seems to indicate no more than an act of accommodation on the part of Abraham. He had been caught in an embarrassing situation of his own making; he became guilty of a sinful concession to the pagan thought forms of the Philistine Abimelech, under whose obligation he stood. The terminology, however, is not expressive of his own belief. Though he appreciated God as the "possessor of heaven and earth" (14:22), which indicates a practical monotheism, he did not deny the possible existence of other gods, in theory.

Theoretical monotheism, the conscious exclusion of even the possibility of other gods, was explicitly revealed in the Mosaic period: "Yahweh, He is God, there is none else" (Deut. 4:39; cf. v. 35).[13]

---

[12]Especially pp. 321, 322 and 432, 433 respectively.
[13]Liberalism, of course, denies the Mosaic authenticity of these verses. It recognizes an incipient monotheism, beginning with some of the eighth century prophets, and allows for a full-fledged monotheism only in the "deutero-Isaiah" at the end of the exile. In the collateral reading for this topic, therefore, the admission by Albright (who does not accept the authenticity of Deuteronomy)

Not only does sacrifice to other gods draw the death penalty (Ex. 22:20), but the pagan deities are relegated to the category of motionless idols, called *elīlīm* (Lev. 19:4; 26:1), "things of naught." They are made with hands, as contrasted with the true God (Ps. 96:5). Idols are more than helpless (Deut. 32:37, 38); they are "no God" (vv. 17, 21). By such statements, Moses of course becomes subject to the charge of misrepresenting pagan symbolism: he ignores the mythology of gods who fight and love and function astrally or in nature. This phenomenon, however, Yehezkel Kaufman grasps as indicative of a monotheistic vigor in Israel that rendered incomprehensible any sort of rival belief, beyond a shallow fetishism.[14] The first command of the Decalogue, "Thou shalt have no other gods before Me" (Ex. 20:3), is a command to monotheism: the "other gods" are limited to mere images.[15] This same explanation applies to Exodus 15:11; Deuteronomy 10:17; 32:12, 39; and Psalm 96:4, for the latter verses belong in contexts that explicitly assert theoretical monotheism. The fact of the Exodus served historically to demonstrate the unique reality of Yahweh, as contrasted with the lifeless gods of Egypt (Ex. 12:12; Num. 33:4). Scripture's classic statement of monotheism, which has become the practical motto of Judaism, is the "Shema" (from its opening Hebrew word, *sh'ma*, "hear"): "Hear, oh, Israel, Yahweh our God is one Yahweh"[16] (Deut. 6:4). The teaching of this passage does not primarily concern a divine unity of simplicity: that God constitutes a unity within Himself, in contrast, for example, with Baal, who was splintered up so as to exist separately in countless individual plots of ground (hence the plural, the Baalim). It concerns rather the divine unity of singularity; that God constitutes the sole deity, as opposed to others, which is the essence of monotheism. The validity of this interpretation is evidenced 1) by the logic of the context: because of the Shema, man is to love God with his whole heart (Deut. 6:5). But this is a command which is relevant because God is the only one, not because He might be an undivided one. The monotheistic meaning is then rendered certain 2) by the inspired New Testament commentary, "He is one, and there is none other but He" (Mark 12:32). Moses reiterated that to serve other gods is to transgress and to deny

of Mosaic monotheism, even of his rather poorly defined variety, is quite significant. Cf. the analyses by Leon J. Wood, "Present Trends in Old Testament Theology as Represented in the Albright Influence," Evangelical Theological Society, *1952 Papers*, pp. 30-34; and by Martin J. Wyngaarden, "Present Trends in the Biblical Studies of Old Testament Theology," *ibid.*, p. 24.

[14] *The Religion of Israel*, pp. 9-11, 18-20, 147, 221.

[15] Kaufman stresses that Yahweh's "competitors" are never living beings, "put to flight," but only idols, Num. 33:4; Jer. 51:44, 47, 52; *ibid.*, pp. 11-12.

[16] This translation is the one authenticated by our Lord's words as recorded in Mark 12:29. Others, grammatically possible, are: "Yahweh is our God, Yahweh is one," "Yahweh is our God, Yahweh alone," or "Yahweh our God, Yahweh is one."

the uniqueness of the testament altogether (Deut. 4:23; 17:2; II Kings 17:38).

The Old Testament's subsequent periods of revelation simply reaffirm the monotheism of Moses, though their history demonstrates Israel's frequent declensions from it. Religion was at a low ebb under the judges, in the period immediately following. That Jephthah should say to his enemies that as the idol Chemosh had given Moab to them, so Yahweh had given Canaan to Israel (Judges 11:24), at best indicates compromise and, at worst, explicit polytheism. It is clear that David, in the next period, was a monotheist[17] (II Sam. 22:32), as was Solomon after him (I Kings 8:60), at least before his sin through his thousand wives. With the national disruption came apostasy, though Elijah's victory on Carmel served as a marked demonstration of the fallacy of polytheism (I Kings 18:39). Isaiah, among the eighth century prophets, marks the high point of monotheistic revelation. He predicted that with Babylon's fall would come the corresponding breaking of the images of her gods (Isa. 21:9). This, in turn, meant Isaiah's denial of the existence of the gods themselves; for it was on the assumption of the gods' identification with their idols that he condemned the practice of idolatry in the first place (44:9-20; cf. Jer. 10:3-5). Positively, Isaiah's presentation of theoretical monotheism is both thorough and brilliant (41:24; 43:10; 45:5-18; and the whole of chapter 46). To it, moreover, corresponds the faith of his king, Hezekiah (II Kings 19:15). The exilic author of II Kings roundly censures the Samaritans for their religious syncretism, serving their own gods and yet attempting to fear Yahweh (17:30-34). Zephaniah, however, looks forward to the second coming of Christ and to the establishment of the testament of peace when Yahweh will "famish all the goods of the earth; and men shall worship Him, every one from his place" (Zeph. 2:11).

For Further Reading:

G. Ernest Wright, *God Who Acts*. Studies in Biblical Theology, No. 8. Chicago: H. Regnery, 1956. Chapters II-III stress God's nature as drawn from His activity; Neo-orthodox.

Wilhelm Vischer, "Words and the Word," *Interpretation*, 3:1 (Jan., 1949), 3-18. Neo-orthodox, on the anthropomorphism of the Biblical revelation.

Theophile J. Meek, *Hebrew Origins*. Revised edition; New York: Harper and Brothers, c. 1950. Chapter 3 is an unbelieving, evolutionary explanation for the origin of God in the Old Testament.

---

[17]Raven is guilty of an invalid admission of polytheism at this point, *The History of the Religion of Israel*, p. 206. Theoretical monotheism existed long before David; and the king's inspired words of praise, "There is none like unto thee among the gods" (Ps. 86:8) is no more polytheistic than is I Cor. 8:5, 6: "For though there be many that are called gods, yet for us there is one."

10. The Works of God*

A. PROVIDENCE. God truly exists, as the personal, spiritual, unique Testator; but this is not all. He proceeds to carry out specific acts on earth, first to establish and then to enforce His testament. In the very pre-redemptive period, God revealed His providential care for man (Gen. 1:28); and even immediately after the fall He provided Adam and Eve with the necessities of life, the clothing that they needed (3:21).[1] God's sovereignty in history in respect to the duration of man's life had been central in the promissory feature of the covenant of works (Gen. 2:17). Under the subsequent gracious testament, He not only continued to cause men's physical death (3:19); He set a 120 year period in the time of Noah, after which He destroyed all but eight souls in a universal deluge (6:3). He is "the God of the spirits of all flesh" (Num. 16:22; Job 12:10). His will includes even the lives of the animals (Ps. 104:21). But from the opening pages of Scripture, the works of God are seen as accomplished through an indirect providential activity as well as through His direct intervention. As Ramm has stated it: "The laws of nature, under the direction of the Holy Spirit, actualize over a period of time and through process, the plan of God."[2] Thus God's first words to man were for him to multiply, by regular means (Gen. 1:28). With this may then be compared His later Mosaic revelation of the function of the heavenly bodies, to mark off the regular progression of the seasons (1:14, 16, 17). The Noachian testament expressly guaranteed nature's orderly succession of seedtime and harvest (8:22; cf. Neh. 9:6). Even God's curse on fallen man is carried out, at least in part, through the natural appearance of thorns and thistles (3:18).

The patriarch Abraham expressly designates God as "the possessor of heaven and earth" (Gen. 14:22; cf. Deut. 10:14). The Lord occasionally intervened in His creation, particularly to save the weak, such as Ishmael (21:17), or to punish the wicked, such as the inhabi-

---

*BIBLE READING: Genesis 1; II Chronicles 32
Collateral Reading: Paul Heinisch, *Theology of the Old Testament,* pp. 146-163.
    Bernard Ramm, *The Christian View of Science and Scripture* (Grand Rapids: Wm. B. Eerdmans Publishing Co., 1954), pp. 96-117, 347-351.

---

[1]Though Gen. 3:21 is sometimes adduced to prove the requirement of death for man's reconciliation with God (in this case depicted by the animals whose skins were used for the clothing), the clear force of this passage concerns God's providential care. Blood sacrifice appears rather in chapter 4, see topic 27-C.
[2]Bernard Ramm, *The Christian View of Science and Scripture* (Grand Rapids: William B. Eerdmans Publishing Co., 1954), p. 116.

tants of Sodom (19:24). More characteristically, however, God accomplished His will through secondary means: He revealed to Abraham that when his later descendants should return to Canaan after their Egyptian sojourn (15:16), they would serve as the instruments to execute God's curse on Ham and Canaan (9:25). The historical fulfillment, as it worked out, was the conquest of Canaan by Joshua. God provided Rebekah as a wife for Isaac by the means of a providential timing (24:15, 16). Finally, both Jacob's receipt of Isaac's blessing (27:1-29) and Joseph's preservation of his family in Egypt (45:7, 8; 50:20) illustrate God's overruling providence, "the wrath of men" praising God (Ps. 76:10). In the case of Jacob particularly, Jacob's overcoming of Isaac's preference for his brother Esau (27:4; 25:28) became the means for effectuating the divine prediction that God had made even prior to the birth of the children. This, however, did not exonerate Jacob from his crimes of deception (27:20). In fact, he suffered a twenty-year exile from home as a result. But this exile, in turn, became God's means of bringing into existence the twelve tribes of Israel (28:13, 14; 32:10). The principle of providence is summed up in Abraham's expression *Yahwe yir'e*, "Yahweh will see (to it)": *Jehovah-jirah*, the LORD will provide (Gen. 22:14, 8).

The Sinaitic testament, in the Mosaic period, based its redemption of Israel upon the fact of God's possessing all the earth (Ex. 19:5). God had, in fact, already proved His care for Israel by the Exodus and by the specific provisions for His people furnished by the "spoiling" of the Egyptians (Ex. 3:21, 22; 11:2, 3; 12:35, 36). Note that *shā'al*, the verb that describes the action of the Israelites (11:2), means "ask," or even "demand," not "borrow." For it is not that the Israelites gave promises of repayment that they later violated; it is that God simply gave them favor in the sight of the Egyptians (v. 3). Moses made it clear that there are no accidents with God. What may appear as "accidental" comes about because of God's ordination (Ex. 21:13). Only pagans seriously entertain the idea of "chance," and even here God may correct them (I Sam. 6:9). In the Mosaic period God moreover revealed His responsibility for physical evils, especially for the purpose of chastening (see topic 29), and even for moral evil, to the extent of its inclusion within His decree (see topic 15). God directs the nations for the punishment of contemporary Israel (Num. 14:43) and determines their future contacts with His people, down through the Roman Empire itself (24:20-24). The basic standard required of men (Ex. 21:24), because it is true of God (Ps. 18:25, 26), is that of judicial retribution. He will "avenge the testament" (Lev. 26:25). Leviticus 26:23-31 and Deuteronomy 28:15-68 constitute two of the most detailed predictions of this providential work of God.

Israel's period of consolidation in Canaan demonstrates in history what Moses had predicted in word. On the one hand Judges

2:6-3:6 points out that God punishes the people who sin, a philosophy of history which is confirmed by the nation's decline after each judge. But on the other hand, Israel's very possession of the land of Canaan was a testimony to divine providence. God hardened the hearts of the Canaanites that they would resist Israel and be destroyed (Josh. 11:20); and later "the stars in their courses fought against Sisera" (Judges 5:20). These words may well constitute a poetic description of some divinely-sent storm, a phenomenon from heaven that immobilized the Canaanites' chariotry and made possible Barak's victory (v. 21; 4:15). Canaan, moreover, was not simply a good land (Ex. 3:8; Dan. 8:9; 11:16); it was the "holy land" (Zech. 2:12), divinely selected to carry out God's redemptive purpose. Even as the table of nations in Genesis 10 shows how God prepared His people out of all the rest, so the conquest brought Israel into a land that was also providentially made ready. Its dry summers and lack of major rivers forced men to look to God for their water (Deut. 8:7; I Kings 8:35), rather than to irrigation ditches as in Egypt (Deut. 11:10). Its eastern frontier, open to nomadic attack, not only furnished a way for its conquest by Israel, but also for its subsequent plundering by other nomads, which drove Israel to her knees before God (Judg. 6:6). Its location between the civilization centers of the Nile and the Tigris-Euphrates valleys provided it with cultural opportunities. But at the same time its geographical divisions made it a separated land (Num. 23:9; Deut. 33:28); and, as successive invading armies moved along its coast, they generally marched by Israel rather than through her. Finally, its position on major highways and trade routes (Ezek. 5:5) made it a radiating center from which the Gospel of the ultimate testament of Christ could be proclaimed in all directions (Acts 8:4).

David, in the next period, wrote of God's care for the earth (Ps. 65:9). He broke forth into thanksgiving, because "Thou crownest the year with Thy goodness" (v. 11). He wrote too of God's care for mankind. Man's whole life is foreordained "in God's book" before birth (139:16); and particularly, the heirs of the testament are to live in trust, "under His wings" (91:4; cf. topic 29-F.). It was God who raised up David himself and prospered him in his kingdom (II Sam. 12:7, 8). But at the same time, because of David's sin with Bathsheba, God brought upon him corresponding punishments (vv. 9, 10) that determined the events of most of the rest of his reign. Amnon, Absalom, and Sheba (II Sam. 13-20), each in his own way, were used as instruments for accomplishing God's purposes.

Solomon and the disruption period elucidate the revelation of God's providential work in the world in three important respects. 1) The work of directing the world is specifically associated with God's wisdom (cf. Prov. 8:16). The storm clouds are directed by His counsels (Job 37:12; cf. Isa. 40:26); the animals' cry to God is answered as He provides their food (Job 38:41; cf. Ps. 104:21, 27, 28; 147:9); and the days of a man's life are determined by His decision (Job 14:5). This direction is a total control: "The lot is cast into the lap; but the whole disposing thereof is of Yahweh" (Prov. 16:33; cf. v. 9). 2) God's wisdom, furthermore, is first clearly described as operating in various natural laws: for the ocean (Job 38:10, 11), the weather (28:26), the circulation of wind and water (Eccl. 1:6, 7), and the migrations of animals (Job 39:26; cf. Jer. 5:22; 33:20; Ps. 104:9; 148:6). But law-abiding nature may still carry out particular spiritual ends. For example, the famine that Elijah had predicted served as a testimony against Baal worship (I Kings 17:1). Think also of Joel's designating a plague of locusts as "God's army" (Joel 2:11). 3) During the disruption period, Israel's increasing involvement in the power politics of the ancient world brought to the fore God's providential control of history. This control concerned both the state of Israel and the neighboring states. There was, for example, the specific statement that Jehu's dynasty would endure for four generations (II Kings 10:30; 15:12). Elisha's deathbed instructions to Jehoash of Israel (798-782 B.C.) to shoot and to strike with the arrows demonstrated God's foreordination and control of battles (II Kings 13:15-19). The Lord pitied northern Israel, apostate as it was (14:26, 27), and directed its restoration through the home ministry of the prophet Jonah (v. 25).

The eighth century prophets were the first to draw detailed applications from God's direction of international politics. They showed that God was responsible for the civil conflicts within Egypt (Isa. 19:2). More particularly, He had raised up the Assyrians to be "the rod of His anger" (10:5) against His own people Israel. But when the Assyrians should overstep their function as an instrument of divine punishment, when the axe should begin to boast itself against the One who was handling it (v. 15; II Kings 19:25), then God would deliver them to their fate. In the same way, Isaiah predicted that God would stir up the Medes against Babylon (13:17) and that the Medo-Persian leader, Cyrus, would then become God's anointed leader for the restoring of the Jews to Palestine (45:1, 2). God's power is equally effective in the impersonal forces of nature, as shown by His first raising and then stilling the storm that frustrated the flight of Jonah (1:4, 15).

In the next century (the later prophetic period), Jeremiah emphasized that God's arrangements for men are as sure as those that He determines for the earth in its rotation (Jer. 31:35, 36). He ordains a man's course before He creates him (1:5). Similarly for the nations, He had determined a set period for Babylon's sovereignty (27:6, 7), during which time disobedience to Nebuchadrezzar would bring down His wrath upon any and all transgressors (v. 8). Then

to Habakkuk God revealed not simply the ministerial function of
Babylon to punish the sins of Judah (Hab. 1:6) but also Babylon's
eventual downfall for attributing its achievements to its own power
rather than to God (1:16; 2:5). Thus the whole earth should be
filled with the knowledge of the glory of Yahweh (v. 14; Num. 14:21).

When the exile came about, Judah was forced to recognize her
destruction as an act of God for the punishment of her own sins
(Lam. 3:37-39; II Kings 23:26; cf. Isa. 39:6, 7). Likewise, on the
beneficial side, the exilic author of II Kings 13:5 could speak of the
defeat of Israel's Syrian enemy by the Assyrian king Adad-nirari III
back in 803 B.C., as Yahweh's having raised up a "saviour" for Israel.
Ezekiel went on to describe how God would bring Nebuchadrezzar
against Tyre (Ezek. 26:7-11) and then, because of Nebuchadrezzar's
limited compensation at Tyre's conditional surrender in 573 B.C.[3] (29:
18), against Egypt. This latter prediction seems to have been fulfilled
by a brief invasion in 568 B.C. (vv. 19, 20). The prophecies of Daniel
center about God's sovereign providence in controlling the nations of
the world as a whole. Note, for example, his God-given description
of the course of world events for almost four centuries after his own
time (11:2-39).

Ezra notes how God accomplished the post-exilic restoration, first
prophesying it through Jeremiah and, second, stirring up the spirit
of Cyrus (whether Cyrus was conscious of it or not) to fulfill the
prophecy (Ezra 1:1). The whole book of Esther illustrates the
providential activity of God so clearly (cf. 4:14; Rom. 8:28) that His
name need not even be mentioned. Thus it is that from the display
of God's providence in the accomplishment of His testament, His
attributes, such as His knowledge, His power, and His love, come
to be revealed. The redemptive purpose, moreover, of God's providence is that, from His care, men may be led to trust Him and to
glorify His name (Ps. 145:15).

B. CREATION. When Moses questioned the possibility of God's
contemporaneous providential activity (through himself), God answered with a revelation that concerned His creative activity: "Who
hath made man's mouth? Have not I, Yahweh?" (Ex. 4:11). The fact
is that Scripture not infrequently introduces God's original creation
as a corollary to His present deeds; for creation is in essence but
an initial demonstration of His continuing creative providence (Ps.
104:30; cf. v. 2; Isa. 42:5).[4] The Bible cites the former as a confirma-

---

[3]Note that Ezek. 26:12-14 then seems to shift to Tyre's total destruction by
Alexander in 332 B.C.
[4]Thus Jacob (citing Karl Barth) rightly insists that the idea of creation must be
considered as secondary to that of the testament, *Old Testament Theology*, pp.
136-139, 148-149.

tory illustration of the latter.[5] Both are accomplished through the same instrumentalities, His word (Ps. 147:18; 33:9) and His Spirit (Ps. 104:30; Job 26:13). The former instrument, the word, seems simply to describe God's commanding speech, His fiat by which the various aspects of creation came into being (Gen. 1:3, 6, etc.). The creative activity of Christ the Word, while true, does not appear to be taught in these passages. The latter instrument, however, relates directly to the Holy Spirit as the effectuating agent in creation (Gen. 1:2); see below, topic 13-D. [producing]

Creation is the first event recorded in Scripture, but God's revelation of creation as a divine work was granted only in the Mosaic period, long after the revelations of His providence to primeval men and to the patriarchs. Moses taught that God is eternally existent. God is prior to creation (Ps. 90:2; cf. Job 38:4-6), and He is, therefore, distinct from creation. These facts rule out, respectively, all forms of theological dualism and pantheism. The Hebrew verb "create," bārā, in Gen. 1:1 does not necessarily imply creation ex nihilo, creation from nothing (cf. Ps. 51:10), though the term does signify divine activity. The opposite doctrine, however, that of the eternal existence of matter, is opposed by the New Testament (Heb. 11:3). Furthermore, the summary statement in Genesis 2:1, which indicates the completion of heaven and earth, demands that Genesis 1:1 be considered as a part of the narrative on the sequence of creation; for otherwise there would be no verse descriptive of the creation of heaven.[6] Genesis 1:1 may, therefore, not be treated as a mere title prefixed to the chapter. Neither may it be subordinated to verse 2. This latter and more dangerous rendering, that is advocated by liberalism, produces the translation, "When God began to create heaven and earth, then the earth was formless . . .,"[7] which suggests the prior, eternal existence of unformed matter. Equally necessary of rejection are the many liberal attempts to find in Genesis 1 reflections of the Babylonian creation myths, with their polytheistic dualism of good and evil deities. The word, for example, in Genesis 1:2 that describes the early chaotic condition of the earth is t'hōm. T'hōm, moreover, is related etymologically to Tiāmat, the name of the Babylonian dragon-goddess, from whose body the earth was supposed to have been formed. The Bible, however, incorporates t'hōm into its vocabulary

---

[5]Cf. Kohler's statement that creation is a deduction from, rather than a premise of, Old Testament revelation, Old Testament Theology, p. 85.

[6]Gen. 1:6-8, on the rāqi'a, refers to the appearance of the "expanse" of the atmosphere between the clouds and the newly formed waters on the earth. It does not refer either to the creation of heaven or to a "firmament," as if heaven were some firm or hard dome (!). Rāqi'a is also applied to the "expanse" of the upper heaven of solar space, as in vv. 14-17. A final use of "heaven" is to describe the home of God, which may account for Paul's reference to the "third" heaven (II Cor. 12:2).

[7]As in the Revised Standard Version, footnote to Gen. 1:1 (New York: Thomas Nelson & Sons, 1953), p. 1.

simply as the word for "the deep," an ocean of water, while the
word's pagan etymology was bypassed and forgotten.[8]

As to the process of creation, it must be first observed that Scripture commits itself to no precise explanatory theory. The Holy Spirit
in inspiration restricted the speculations of the Bible's human, secondary authors; and He thus prevented the inclusion within its pages of
the grotesque, ancient "scientific" ideas, in which these men may
personally have believed.[9] But it must be maintained, second, that
such Scripture as *was* written is equivalent to God's words; and God
is truth. Whenever Scripture does refer to scientific matters, therefore, what it says is accurate and constitutes the simple but fundamental basis for all modern scientific refinements.[10]

Recognizing then the limited scope of the Bible's evidence, but
also the historical validity of what is found in its opening chapters,
modern evangelicals have worked out four major theories of chronology to serve as tentative explanations for the process of creation.[11]
1) Some hold that Adam was created on the sixth consecutive day
of universal creation. Upon this basic approach, Archbishop Ussher
reached the well-known date of 4004 B.C. for the creation of heaven
and earth. This particular date, of course, depended upon his dating
of Adam; and Ussher's chronology is now generally recognized as
outmoded.[12] But the theory of creation in the same week as the appearance of man continues to be held by such evangelical scholars
as H. C. Leupold,[13] who considers it the most natural interpretation
of the Genesis data. The chief drawback to this theory is its failure
to square with the data of geology, which seems to indicate the exist-

---

[8]So the modern use of "Thursday" implies no belief in the god Thor. See Ramm,
op. cit., p. 101. Others feel that the name "Tiamat" may have been derived from
the natural phenomenon of "the deep," Charles F. Pfeiffer, "Figures of Speech
in Human Language," *Bulletin of the Evangelical Theological Society*, II:4
(Fall, 1959), p. 20.
[9]*Ibid.*, p. 349.
[10]Serious issue must be taken with Ramm's limitation of Biblical inerrancy and
relevance to matters of faith and morals, *Protestant Biblical Interpretation*, p. 182.
Jesus Christ and the Biblical writers committed themselves to all Scripture, scientific or otherwise (Ex. 20:11; Matt. 24:37-39). To admit such a theory of partial
inspiration is to mark an end to the Bible as a self-consistent authority.
[11]The numerous modern attempts to disqualify Gen. 1-11 from serious historical
consideration by treating it as if it were poetry or a parable, or some form of
theological mythology, cannot be considered as legitimate interpretative theories.
Such views automatically disqualify themselves as contrary, both to the literary
form of Genesis, which is straight-forward historical prose, and to the analogy of
the rest of Scripture, which assumes throughout the literal historicity of Genesis;
cf. our Lord's own statement (Matt. 19:4-5). Allan A. MacRae, "The Principles
of Interpreting Genesis 1 and 2," *Bulletin of the Evangelical Theological Society*,
II:4 (Fall, 1959), pp. 1-2; and G. Douglas Young, "The Effects of Poetic and
Literary Style on Interpretation of the Early Chapters of Genesis," *ibid.*, pp. 15-16.
[12]See below, pp. 219-220.
[13]*Exposition of Genesis* (Columbus, Ohio: The Wartburg Press, c. 1942).

ence of long ages prior to man. The attempt to account for stratified rock on the basis of the Noachian flood appears ill-advised.[14]

2)Other evangelicals suggest the passage of a great length of time during Genesis 1:2, which was then followed by six consecutive days of creation. This approach is recognized, for example, by L. Berkhof,[15] and it does allow the "In the beginning" of v. 1 to be as early as the scientists may wish to put it. But to assume that the earth continued formless for ages, followed by the remainder of creation in just one week, appears incongruous both with the symmetry of Genesis 1 and with the evidence of fossilized life. A variation on this view is the "restitution theory": that the earth was slowly created as postulated by modern science (Gen. 1:1); but that the earth "became" without form and desolate by a great cataclysm, perhaps to be associated with the fall of Satan (v. 2). The earth is then said to have been *re*created in six days, according to Genesis 1:3-31. This approach, widely advocated in dispensationalist circles,[16] gives free rein to any and all hypotheses of secular geology, but at the expense of divorcing Scripture from science. Genesis 1 becomes silenced, having been denied relevance to historical geology, while science can contribute no evidence that might bear upon the so-called restitution that is portrayed in Scripture. Exegetical data also militate against this theory in the following ways. (a) The verb of Genesis 1:2, *hā-y'thā*, "was," is in an unstressed position, which makes the translation "became" unlikely. That is, Genesis 1:2 seems naturally to describe the condition of primeval creation, rather than a process by which subsequently the earth was plunged into a ruinous state. (b) The nouns *tōhū* and *bōhū*, "formless" and "empty," indicate simply the absence of a detailed creation up to this point. Their meaning is not "desolation,"[17] as if some catastrophe had overtaken the earth between verses 1 and 2.[18] (c) The condition of creation as described in Genesis 1:31 was still "very good." The fall of Satan, therefore, whenever it may in fact have occurred,[19] could not yet have taken place.

3) Modern evangelicals have come increasingly to equate the "days" of Genesis 1 with geological eras. The Hebrew word for day does often indicate a period of more than twenty-four hours. In Psalm 95:8, 10, for example, the "day" equals forty years; or in the very next chapter of Genesis (2:4) it equals the total period of creation. On this approach, evangelicals such as Wilbur Smith have been able to develop detailed harmonizations between the Biblical creation

---

[14]Cf. Ramm's analysis of "flood geology," *Science and Scripture,* pp. 179-188.
[15]*Systematic Theology,* p. 152.
[16]Cf. C. I. Scofield, ed., *Reference Bible* (New York: Oxford University Press, c. 1917), p. 3.
[17]So in Isa. 45:18, God created it not to stay *tōhū, tōhū* being the first step toward the goal of habitation.
[18]Ramm, *Science,* pp. 194-210, gives a thorough discussion of the "gap" theory.
[19]As to the time of the fall of Satan, see below, p. 294.

record and modern scientific reconstruction.[20] It is this very possibility that lends attractiveness to the "day-age" view. The chief question that is raised against it, however, is whether the Biblical context
permits the word "day" in Genesis 1 to be understood as "age."

4) The alternative theory that has therefore been proposed is
that of the non-consecutive nature of the days of Genesis 1. Over fifty
years ago John Urquhart stressed that, except in the case of the sixth
day, the Hebrew noun for "day" has the indefinite form, "a second
day," "a third day," etc., not the definite form, "the second day,"
etc. It has therefore, been concluded that the days are not to be
taken consecutively but that they may be understood as separated
by long ages.[21] Each day would then indicate a normal, twenty-four
hour period, by the time of the arrival of which, the major phenomena
which God had been creating since the previously mentioned day,
had at length come into being. This view combines the advantages
of the literal day of theories 1 and 2 and the scientific harmonization
of theory 3. But confessedly, it would not have been as readily de-
duced from the Genesis text had it not been for the evidences advanced by secular science.

The most striking feature of the Biblical record of creation is its
progressiveness. Creation is described as a developing sequence.
Each stage of the sequence has, moreover, been confirmed by modern
historical geology.[22] It is marked by the six dividing days, though if
we accept Urquhart's observations as valid, these days need not be
taken consecutively: long periods of time may have intervened until
"there came a day" when the events previously described were completed.[23] To define these days other than normal twenty-four hour
days does, however, seem to wrest Scripture, with its description of
the "evening and morning" (Gen. 1:5; and cf. Ex. 20:11). A parallel,
moreover, exists between the geological separations recorded on the
first three days and the subsequent developments on the second three.
Each three-day sequence stresses sky, then water, then land. Specifically there first appeared the heavenly universe, and the earth with it
(1:1). After a time water was able to collect upon the earth, thus
separated from the water vapor that was still in the clouds (v. 7). Psalm
104:8 may refer to the accompanying geologic rise and fall of mountains. After considerable water action, however, soil was made and
God created plants.

---

[20]*Therefore Stand* (Boston: W. A. Wilde Co., 1945), pp. 311-325.
[21]*The Bible: Its Structure and Purpose* (New York: Gospel Publishing House,
c. 1904), II:69-70; cf. John D. Davis, *A Dictionary of the Bible*, p. 152.
[22]Cf. Edwin Walhout's article, "Sequence in the Days of Genesis One," *Journal
of the American Scientific Affiliation*, 11:2 (June, 1959), pp. 6-8.
[23]For other theories on the days, see Ramm, *Science and Scripture*, Chapter VI,
Part II, but in opposition to Ramm's own view of "pictorial-relevatory" days, see
Martin J. Wyngaarden, "Phenomenal Language According to Dr. Bernard Ramm,"
Bulletin of the Evangelical Theological Society, II:4 (Fall, 1959), pp. 11-12.

In the course of the second three days, the clouds eventually diminished to allow the heavenly luminaries to shine on the earth's surface (v. 14), though the light itself had been created long before (v. 3). God then created animal life, first in the water, but then the great *tannīn*, the monstrous reptiles (vv. 20, 21), some of which seem to have been land-going creatures (Ex. 7:9; Ps. 91:13), and the related birds. Lastly came the land mammals (v. 25). As a caution against a theistic evolution that would limit God's creative activity to basic categories only, appears the frequent phrase that He created each form of life according to specific subdivisions, "after its kind," Hebrew *mīn*. In the creation record the specification of *mīn* seems to reach only to families within the biological orders (for example, the cattle, rodents, and carnivors of Gen. 1:24, 25). But its usage elsewhere in Scripture shows that Moses meant by *mīn* about what we today call species (for example, the various "kinds" of falcons and locusts in Lev. 11:14, 16, 22).[24] But while Scripture suggests a mediate method of divine creativity, "Let the earth bring forth living creatures after their kind" (Gen. 1:24), rather than direct creation (as in the case of man), it remains silent both as to the means by which each creature at first appeared and as to the possibility of subsequent speciation. The climax of creation was the creation of man (see topic 17-A). All the earth is given to man (Ps. 115:16). The fact, however, that man is created in God's image (v. 26) shows that the ultimate purpose of all creatures is to manifest the Creator's glory. Likewise, the repeated statement that all was created was good (vv. 10, 21; Eccl. 3:11) suggests as its basic reason that Yahweh should rejoice in His works (Ps. 104:31). On the seventh day God enjoyed sabbath rest (Gen. 2:2).

Genesis 2:4 commences, not a second and conflicting creation account, as claimed by liberalism,[25] but rather the record of the man Adam, whom God had placed in the Garden of Eden. Adam was charged to keep the garden (2:15), which implies that the creation in itself must have been then much like it is now. Genesis 1:30, for example, does not restrict animals to a vegetarian diet, though this is often claimed. After Adam's fall, nature was indeed cursed; but the curse seems to have affected primarily nature's relationship to man (3:17; 5:29). There is no indication that thorns and thistles had not

[24]Cf. J. B. Payne, "The Concept of 'Kinds' in Scripture," *Journal of the American Scientific Affiliation*, 10:2 (June, 1958), pp. 17-20.
[25]In answer to the liberal criticism, it is to be noted that Gen. 2:9 refers to God's creation of the garden, not to the creation of all plants, as if plants appeared subsequently to man. 2:19 is perhaps best translated, "Yahweh had [previously] formed every beast." It is also to be observed that this section commences with Gen. 2:4, not 2:4b. Liberal writers are indeed embarrassed by the way in which 2:4a of the so-called P Document stands at the beginning of the so-called J Document that follows; but 2:4a is undeniably the title to the following section. Cf. MacRae, *op. cit.*, pp. 5-8.

previously existed, but previous to this time they had been no impediment to man. A final point that is stressed in the Mosaic period is that man is not to worship the creation, especially the heavenly bodies, but must serve the one Creator and Him alone (Deut. 4:19; 17:3; cf. Job 31:26, 27).

In the main, the periods of revelation subsequent to the Mosaic period simply reaffirm the Genesis outline of creation (Amos 4:13; Isa. 48:13; Ps. 104:5-7; 121:2). Two of the most important single sections are Job 38 and 39 and the creation Psalm, 104. David particularly rejoiced in the way in which God holds the "fountain of life," though he applies these words in reference to God's providence (Ps. 36:9). On the negative side, however, David's writings have often been distorted so as seemingly to bring into question the validity of the Biblical descriptions of creation. On the one hand, certain of his poetic expressions have been associated with the geographical misconceptions that were current in Babylon and among the surrounding Canaanites.[26] David, for example, wrote that God had "founded the earth upon the seas and established it upon the floods" (Ps. 24:2), in which some have seen the Babylonian idea of an egg-like world floating in an abyss. Actually, the phrase might better be translated "above" the seas; for the reference is to Genesis 1:9, the point at which God collected the waters in the depressions of the earth and shaped the land masses above sea level. Prior to the formation of these oceans, the water, of course, "stood above the mountains," in the form of steam (Ps. 104:6; cf. II Peter 3:5 on the earth's creation "out of and through water"). Concerning the land, when the Psalms speak of the "foundations of the earth" (as of 104:5), the reference is simply a poetic one to earth's established order. The Bible nowhere teaches that the world is held up by literal, solid, supporting posts. On the contrary, Scripture, in God-given knowledge, declares, "God hangeth the earth upon nothing" (Job 26:7). Indeed, for David's associate, Asaph, the "foundations of the earth" mean no more than the principles upon which human society rests (Ps. 75:3). Finally, concerning the sky when the Bible speaks of the "heavens of heavens," as in the anonymous 148th Psalm (v. 4), it is simply employing the Hebrew superlative (cf. S. of Sol. 1:1). The reference is to "highest heaven," hardly to the seven concentric stone vaults of the sky in which the Babylonians believed.

David and his friends have also been accused of incorporating pagan mythology into Scripture. Particularly, it is asserted that they describe the chaos monster Tiamat under the name of *Ráhav*[27] (Ps. 87:4; 89:10). But as Isaiah 51:9, 10 indicates, *ráhav* simply signifies

[26]So Heinisch, *Theology of the Old Testament*, pp. 146-147; and cf. Ramm, *Science*, pp. 97-98.
[27]*Ibid.*, pp. 155-157.

the crocodile, which serves in turn as a symbol for Egypt. Thus *Ráhav* was wounded by God when Israel escaped Egypt and Pharaoh's army was destroyed at the crossing of the Red Sea. David's Korahite singers speak in the same way of *Ráhav* as a parallel expression for Babylon (Ps. 87:4); and his wise man, Ethan, makes it clear that breaking *Ráhav* is but a poetic description of the scattering of the enemies of God's people (89:10). Similarly, in Job 26:12, where the smiting of *Ráhav* occurs at the dividing of the sea, the crocodile symbol is best retained, rather than to translate *ráhav* as a common noun, "the proud," as in the Authorized Version. In Job 9:13, however, there is no reference to the Exodus and the translation "proud helpers" is to be retained. To attempt to find "the army of Tiamat" in this verse is far-fetched indeed!

The Book of Job, written in the disruption period that followed David, has been twisted even more than the Psalms by those who attempt to discover mythological figures with which to discredit Scripture. In addition to the *ráhav* verses just noted, three other terms are persistently cited. (a) The subject of Job 41 is *liwyāthān.* "Leviathan," however, is again simply the powerful crocodile (vv. 1, 2, 12), though poetically described (vv. 18-21; cf. vv. 27, 31). So in the exilic Asaphite Psalm (74:14) leviathan is used, just as *ráhav* had been, as a symbol for Egypt at the Exodus (cf. Ps. 74:13). The "giving of him for meat to the people of the wilderness" may refer to the opportunity that the Israelites had for plundering the corpses of such of the Egyptian soldiers as were washed up on the shore of the Red Sea. It can hardly apply to the mythological Tiamat. In Isaiah 27:1, *liwyāthān* is used for a serpent (cf. Amos 9:3) that is punished, representing in symbol earth's sinful inhabitants (Isa. 26:21). This verse then serves to explain Job 3:8, which mentions men (magicians, like Balaam, Num. 22:5, 6) who are to curse the day of Job's birth and "who are ready to raise up *liwyāthān.*" But, far from suggesting the waking up of a mythical monster, the parallelism with the magicians suggests nothing more nor less than the oriental snake charmer (cf. Ps. 58:3). (b) Similar to the first use of *liwyāthān* in the verses where it means "crocodile" is the use of *tannīn. Tannīn* has already been noted as the word that describes reptiles in creation (Gen. 1:21); compare also its symbolic employment for Egypt in Psalm 74:13. *Tannīn* then appears in Job 7:12 as an animal that is "watched over." But, rather than picturing Tiamat kept in submission by Marduk or some other "good" god, this verse suggests nothing more than the vigilance of a zoo keeper in some Egyptian reptile garden! (c) Finally, Job 40:15-24 describes another powerful beast, the *b'hēmōth.* "Behemoth," moreover, looks in every respect, except for a poetically described tail (40:17), like a hippopotamus. To attempt to find in *b'hēmōth,* not this truly awe-inspiring mammal, but rather Kingu, the associate of Tiamat, does credit to the imagination of those who would mythologize Scripture.

Other passages in Job that have been similarly subjected to mythological distortion include 38:31, where Orion is simply a constellation of stars, not a "real" giant (9:9; cf. 26:13); 26:5, which refers to the unsaved dead, not to imprisoned water-ogres; and 7:12 and 38:8-10, which describe the bounds of the sea, not a divinely restrained chaos monster. Mythology is not only false, it is evil. For it robs nature by transferring its glories to fictitious beings. Scripture keeps nature distinct from persons, though it may occasionally personalize it in poetry (Ps. 98:8, 9). Thus it is Scripture alone that truly appreciates nature, both for its own God-reflecting beauty (Ps. 133:3; 147:9, 18) and for its purpose of leading men to God (Ps. 8:3, 4; 19:1; 84:3; 121).

The disruption period also contributes certain additional revelations on the process of creation. Job 38:7 specifies what had been implicit in Genesis 1:1, namely, that the stars of heaven were created before the earth. Verse 17 then goes on to suggest the creation of hell, "the gates of death," somewhere in the depths of the earth (cf. v. 16 and topic 30 below). The transcendent superiority of the Creator to His creation is poetically expressed by the statement, "the stars are not pure in His sight" (Job 25:5). Finally, "Wisdom" is noted as the One by whom God made the world (Prov. 8:30; cf. 3:19). It is on the basis of this passage that John 1:3 says of the Word as the Second Person of the Trinity, "All things were made by Him."

The last significant Old Testament contributions to the truth of creation were revealed through Isaiah in the period of the eighth century prophets. In accordance with the monergism that is so characteristic of testamental thought, Isaiah spoke of the God who "stretcheth forth the heavens alone, that spreadeth abroad the earth by Himself" (44:24). But Isaiah then proceeded to predict, by inspiration, God's final destruction of the present creation (34:4; 51:6; cf. the undated Psalm, 102:26). As early as Genesis 9:11, God's words had hinted at the possibility of the world's destruction, by some means other than that of a flood of water. Isaiah specifically defined the future dissolution (24:19, 20, 23; 54:10; cf. v. 9) as taking place in connection with God's final judgment (vv. 21, 22). There would be preserved, however, a certain continuum, those things which cannot be shaken that will remain (cf. Heb. 12:27). For Yahweh will continue to reign in Zion in the presence of the saved of all ages (Isa. 24:23), even though the environment will be that of the new heavens and the new earth (65:17; 66:22) that will mark the final accomplishment of the testament of peace, see below, topic 32-E.

C. MIRACLES. The miracle, like creation, constitutes a particular aspect of God's providential work in carrying out the testament. Four words are commonly used in Hebrew for miracles. Two of these, *péle* and *niflā'ā*, come from the root that means "to be wonderful" and therefore suggest certain extraordinary manifestations of power. They may occasionally refer to great happenings of a natural character, such as storms (Ps. 107:24) or birth (139:14). But for practical purposes, the term "miracle" may be restrictively defined as meaning unique acts of God, wonders that are performed without reference to natural means, or even in opposition to them.[28] Pure supernaturalism of this sort forms an inevitable stumbling block to the unregenerate mind. Liberalism, accordingly, persists in its denial of the historicity of the miraculous as this is found in the Old Testament, and also in the New Testament. For the sake of rational consistency, however, it must be observed that the non-natural becomes the truly natural for the one who is "holy," who is separate from creation (Ex. 15:11; Ps. 77:13, 14).[29] Furthermore, God's unique miracles appear appropriately as His workings on the behalf of those who are holy (separated) to Him (Ps. 77:15; 98:1-3). God's elect need not fear the arm of flesh, for our God is far greater than men and has acted with according wonderfulness (II Chron. 32:7, 8). A third term for miracle is *mōfēth*, which seems to possess a similar idea of "extraordinariness."

The fourth of the Hebrew words for miracle is *ōth.* This word differs in its meaning from the three terms previously noted, but it is equally significant. For *ōth* means a "sign" (Ex. 4:8; cf. Isa. 8:18). Miracles, that is, have a demonstrative aim: they occur for the purpose of testifying to God. For example, the retrogression of the shadow ten steps, or degrees, was shown to Hezekiah as a proof that God would heal him as He promised (II Kings 20:8-11); and the virgin birth of the Messiah was revealed to Ahaz as a proof of God's power to deliver, or to replace, both him and his household (Isa. 7:14). For this reason God usually announced or explained His miracles through a chosen, prophetic, human instrument. Furthermore, since these miraculous testimonies to God were usually performed in opposition to some specific challenge of heathenism, most of the Biblical miracles were concentrated in three periods. Under Moses and Joshua, 1450-1400 B.C., God's power demanded vindication against Egypt, against Israel's wilderness revolts, and against the opposition of the Canaanites. Under Elijah and Elisha, 860-800 B.C., God's representatives depended upon His supernatural aid as they fought back against the Baalism of Jezebel. Finally, under Christ and the apostles, A.D. 25-60, God's miraculous intervention was needed to overcome Satan's direct opposition to the founding of the Christian Church.

Though God had executed certain miraculous acts in the primeval

---

[28]*Ibid.*, p. 163.
[29]Rowley thus confesses, though guardedly, that belief in miracles is fundamental to belief in God Himself, *The Faith of Israel* (London: The Westminster Press, 1956), p. 58.

age (cf. Gen. 11:8, 9), the first recorded miracles to occur through a prophetic human instrumentality took place under Moses (Ex. 3:20; 4:2-9). The first nine plagues against Egypt, from mid-1447 to the spring of 1446 B.C. (Ex. 7:14—chap. 10), possessed a somewhat natural character and order, following upon the annual inundation of the Nile. For example, the possibility is sometimes stated that the changing of the water to blood may refer to coloring matter in the flood waters (Joel 2:31; cf. II Kings 3:22), for the red could be filtered out (Ex. 7:24). But the speed, the universality, the deadliness, and the distinctions that are found within the plagues (cf. 8:22; 9:26) are all miraculous. The tenth plague, the death of the firstborn, was purely supernaturalistic.

Subsequent miracles of particular note were Israel's crossings, first of the Red Sea in 1446, and then of the Jordan in 1406. In the former, God's east wind divided the sea (Ex. 14:21), leaving ground that was relatively dry, as described at the analogous crossing of the Jordan (cf. Josh. 3:17; but also 4:18). The waters of the Red Sea were then said to be "a wall unto them on their right hand and on their left" (Ex. 14:22). The indication, however, is one not so much of shape (perpendicular) as of use (protection against flank attack, cf. I Sam. 25:16; Ex. 15:8 is poetic). For when the Egyptians were forced to follow behind Israel, their chariots stuck in the bottom (14:25), and as the water returned they were all drowned. This was no shallow marsh water! The event was clearly a miracle, not simply because of the timing, but also because of the fact that when such winds occur (rarely) today, the water is blown in only one direction and not divided. At the Jordan, on the other hand, Scripture states that the waters were dammed a few miles upstream at Adam (Josh. 3:16), a narrow part of the valley where collapsing banks as recently as July, 1927, blocked the water in identical fashion for some 21½ hours.

But though the crossing of the Jordan may have been a miracle only of God's timing, subsequent events, such as the fall of Jericho (Josh. 6:20) or the prolongation of the daylight at the battle of Beth-horon (10:13), are furnished with no contributory explanations of a natural sort.[30] The purpose of such miracles was to establish Israel's faith in God's fulfilling of His testament (Ex. 6:7; 8:19; 14:31; cf. Ps. 78:43-51); and the effectuation of the testament, it must be remembered, was a matter of pure monergism, God's grace operative without natural assistance. (Cf. the similar purpose of supernaturally predictive prophecy for the establishing of faith, Isa. 43:10). The

---

[30]In the latter case, though the earth may well have continued its rotation unaffected, there must have been (at least locally, by some divinely-produced refraction?) a unique prolongation of daylight. Anything less, such as the explanations noted in Ramm, *op. cit.*, pp. 156-161, appears to be inadequate to satisfy the demands of the context.

miracles served to vindicate the true God against the claims of pagan polytheism (Ex. 12:12) and to create within Israel the anticipation of His further victories (15:14, 17). The possibility of "miracles" that might be performed through the ungodly is noted (Deut. 13:1-3). But Israel, at the same time, possessed a basis for discriminating against such lying signs. The analogy of the faith as previously revealed would readily expose the false message.

Miracles occurred in great number under Elijah and Elisha in the disruption period, when Israel was wavering between the two parties of Yahweh and of Jezebel's Baal (I Kings 18:21). The result of the miracles, then, was to produce a conviction on the part of the people that Yahweh, He was God (v. 39); and this was the basic subjective response that God required for the eternal inheritance of the testament. Perhaps the two most remarkable miracles of this period were those that were performed on the meal and oil that were not used up (17:16) and on the axehead that floated (II Kings 6:6). Both occurred in direct contradiction to natural law, as it is otherwise understood. In 701 B.C. (eighth century period) there took place the miracle of the destruction of Sennacherib's host, an example of national deliverance. For Israel, that had been equalled only by their crossing of the Red Sea 750 years before. In that night the Angel of Yahweh destroyed 185,000 in the Assyrian camp (II Kings 19:35; II Chron. 32:21). Egyptian legends[31] contain a record of mice that spread at night in Sennacherib's camp and destroyed the Assyrians' equipment. Rodent-carried plague seems probable (cf. I Sam. 6:4), but such a plague as was supernatural both in its speed and in its degree of mortality. The miracle's purpose was one of divine vindication. The Assyrians had classified Yahweh along with the pagan gods of other nations they had defeated (II Chron. 32:13-15, 17); but, as Scripture asserts and as the miracle demonstrated, *they* were but the work of men's hands, while Yahweh was lord of all history (v. 19). Of similar purpose were the God-given, post-exilic restoration of Israel (Ezek. 36:21-24) and the final accomplishment of the testament of peace (37:28), both of which take place to vindicate God's name. Much of God's work is beyond man's comprehension (Job 26:14). But it is this very supernaturalistic sort of redemption that man must have if he is to triumph over the relentless decay of life as it is presently constituted (I Cor. 15:17). It is the miracle that demonstrates historically the adequacy of the testament to meet human need.

For Further Reading:
> Wilbur Smith, *Therefore Stand*. Boston: W. A. Wilde, Co., 1945. Up-to-date evangelical apologetics, Chapter VII being devoted to the validation of the Biblical description of creation.

---

[31]Herodotus, ii:141, *History* (London: J. M. Dent, 1949).

Alexander Heidel, *The Gilgamesh Epic and Old Testament Parallels.* Chicago:
University of Chicago Press, 1949. An evangelical evaluation of Babylonian
mythology in relation to Scripture.
Ernest Gordon, *The Fact of Miracle.* Francestown, N. H.: Marshall Jones Co.,
1955. A neo-orthodox vindication of miracles; they may even happen today.

11. The Names of God *

In the Orient a name is more than an identification. A man's
name is not only descriptive of its bearer, it may stand as the equivalent to his very nature and individuality. Thus to change a man's name
indicates power over his person (II Kings 23:34; 24:17). In reference
to the divine testator, God's "name" may stand for His general revelation (Ps. 8:1, 9): "How excellent is Thy name in all the earth" (cf.
89:12). More often, however, it refers to God's special theophanic
revelation. His "name" comes to punish (Isa. 30:27), or it may equal
the glory cloud in the Tabernacle or the Temple (Deut. 12:11; I
Kings 8:29; Jer. 3:17; 7:12). Zion became "the place of the name of
Yahweh of armies" (Isa. 18:7), and the presence of God in Christ
involved a manifestation of His name (John 17:6). God's "name" may
even refer to specific attributes, as His might (Ps. 54:1; 76:1) or His
mercy — "The name of the God of Jacob set thee up on high, send
thee help . . . and strengthen thee" (20:1, 2). So, negatively, Commandment III of the Decalogue (Ex. 20:7) not simply forbids false
oaths (Lev. 19:12) or careless oaths (Lev. 5:4);[1] it condemns any
abuse of the person of God Himself. Correspondingly, idolatry becomes a profanation of God's "name" (Lev. 18:21); and oaths in any
other name are prohibited. Such utterances signify the swearer's recognition of other gods and constitute an affront to Yahweh's very Godhead. To "blaspheme the [divine] name" brought down the death
penalty upon the blasphemer (Lev. 24:11, 16). Positively, too, the
names of God as they are revealed in Scripture serve to depict His
Person and His attributes (Ps. 23:3). They show the way in which
He wishes Himself to be recognized. Above all, they are descriptive
of His activity in establishing the testament (Ps. 111:9).

* BIBLE READING: Exodus 3; 6:1-8
Collateral Reading: Edmond Jacob, *Theology of the Old Testament,* pp. 43-64.
    Robert Dick Wilson, "Critical Note on Exodus vi. 3," *Princeton Theological
    Review,* 22:1 (Jan., 1924), pp. 108-119.
    George A. F. Knight, *A Christian Theology of the Old Testament,* pp. 40-51.

[1]The oath, after all, invokes God's activity in punishment upon the man who
fails to live up to his obligation (Ex. 22:10, 11). See Vos' *Biblical Theology,*
p. 154, on the seriousness of such an invocation by oath, either of God's blessing
or of His damnation.

A. ELOHIM (and related forms). The two most significant names of God are El (or Elohim) and Yahweh. Both of these occur in the primeval period of revelation; in fact, they or their equivalents[2] were used by the first generation of mankind. But though the latter name, Yahweh, was revealed in the primeval period (Gen. 4:1, 26),[3] it was not "known" (fully appreciated; cf. Ex. 1:8) until the Exodus (Ex. 6:3); see below, Section C. The former name, El, seems to have arisen from the root ūl, the probable meaning of which is "to be strong" (cf. Gen. 31:29 "power").[4] The nominal form, Ēl, is found generally in combination-names, for example, the "Ēl who sees" (Gen. 16:13). A closely related noun is Elóah, which may be simply an augmented form of Ēl, or which may derive from a separate root, ālah. Both names, however, express the same general concept, that of "God." Similar divine names appear throughout the related Semitic languages (except Ethiopic), for example, in the Akkadian (Babylonian) ilu; and in the Arabic, Allah. The shorter noun is used in the earliest theophoric names, as Mehuja-El (Gen. 4:18). Though stressing God's power, Ēl may be used to show not simply God's interest in man but also His testamental requirements that bear upon man; e.g., Eliab, "God is Father," or Daniel, "a judge is God."

The plural of Elóah, Elōhím, represents Eve's earliest name for deity (Gen. 3:3) and is thus the first name of God known to have been uttered in history (compare Noah's compound usage, 9:26). The grammatical form of Elōhím is that of an abstract plural of greatness or majesty,[5] and not a true numeric plural. Unless referring to the gods of the pagans, Elōhím is construed with other words in the singular.[6] It signifies God as the one who bears the fullness of divine life. This same "plural of majesty" appears in reference to a single god in the Ras Shamra texts of Ugarit, north of Palestine, and in reference to the Egyptian Pharaoh in the Tell el-Amarna tablets from Palestine itself. Both instances belong to the time of the Hebrew conquest of Canaan. Therefore, though the original Canaanitish etymology of Elōhím may well have been one of henotheism, in which one deity represented the class (the totality of the gods), still, by the

---

[2]In whatever language was spoken by Adam and Eve.
[3]Cf. its appearance in pre-Mosaic names (Ex. 6:20; I Chron. 2:25; 7:8). Liberal criticism indeed attempts to assign Ex. 6:3 to the so-called P. Document and to maintain that P considered the name as one that was first revealed to Moses. But for a telling exposure of the inconsistencies of the liberal position, see R. D. Wilson's "Critical Note on Exodus vi. 3," *Princeton Theological Review*, 22:1 (Jan., 1924), p. 108. Cf. also Edmond Jacob, *Theology of the Old Testament*, pp. 49-50.
[4]For a summary of the proposed etymologies of "El," see Jacob, *op. cit.*, pp. 43-44.
[5]Cf. similar plural forms for "heaven" and "water" and plural terms for God as Maker or Creator in Eccl. 12:1; Job 35:10; and Isa. 54:5.
[6]In Josh. 24:19 the unusual modifying adjective in the plural is followed by a modifying pronoun in the singular.

time the name was naturalized into Hebrew, *Elōhīm* had come to connote only eminence.[7] It is not legitimate to use this plural to advance a theory of primitive Israelitish polytheism.[8] Similarly, Elohim ought not to be adduced as a proof for the Trinity, because Christians believe in only one God! Only in the quoted speeches of pagans is *Elōhīm* used as an actual plural while referring to the true God (I Sam. 4:8 and so probably Deut. 5:26 and II Sam. 7:23 and Ps. 58:11). In the Aramaic of Daniel, the singular alone is employed for God; and the plural form *elāhīn* is always a true plural. Elohim may, however, be used to describe certain persons with a divine relationship, for example, human judges when exercising God's function (Ex. 21:6; Ps. 82:1; John 10:34, 35), or the supernatural appearance of Samuel when brought back from the dead (I Sam. 28:12). *Elōhīm* is a more meaningful and specialized name than *Ēl*; witness the ascending order in Joshua 22:22 and Psalm 50:1 of El, then Elohim, and finally Yahweh.

Abraham, in the patriarchal period, knew and used the names Elohim (Gen. 17:7) and Yahweh. Through him, however, three additional names were revealed as valid for referring to the God of the testament, even though all of them had wide usage beyond Israel. The first two are compounds of *El. El Elyōn*, "God most high," appears in Genesis 14:18 ff. It was first employed by Melchizedek. The origin of "God most high" may lie in the dominating position that some god had come to assume in an early polytheism or henotheism. But Abraham accepted it for God, retaining only the significance of elevation: God the "possessor of heaven and earth" (14:22). This meaning of *El Elyōn* as the God of the universe thus signalizes an advance over the preceding period in its greater appreciation of divine transcendence. A form in the plural of majesty, *Elyōnīn*, occurs in the Biblical Aramaic (Dan. 7:18, 22, 25).

El Shaddai, "God almighty" (cf. the Septuagint translation, *Pantokratōr*), occurs in Genesis 17:1. *Shaddai* seems to come, not from the Hebrew, but from an Akkadian word, *shadu*, "mountain"; for in Akkad the gods were thought of as standing on mountains.[9] *El Shaddai* became the characteristic divine name for patriarchal religion (Ex. 6:3) with its sense of the "overpowering" God (as Ruth 1:20, 21). But though transcendent, *El Shaddai* is yet associated with the ethical requirement of the testament (Gen. 17:1). God's sovereign power is thus seen as providing man with the basic assurance that is needed for practical living.

B. HA-ADHON, this third divine name to be revealed through Abraham, means "the lord, the master." It is related to the pagan

---

[7]Cf. Heinisch, *Theology of the Old Testament*, p. 37; and Vos, *op. cit.*, pp. 77-78.
[8]As is done by Meek, *Hebrew Origins*, pp. 89, 196.
[9]Wilson, *op. cit.*, *p.* 113, though this is rightly noted as not altogether certain, p. 114.

name "Adonis." Most frequently, *hā-ādhōn* occurs in a special plural-of-majesty form with a pronoun suffix as *Adhōnāi*, "my Lord." It appears first in Genesis 15:2, 8. In the Pentateuch and in Joshua the "my" suffix has meaning, for *Adhōnāi* is used to address God by those who have been reconciled to Him through the testament, so that He had indeed become "their" Lord. Later the suffix ceased to have meaning and was preserved as an arbitrary sign to distinguish the divine Lord from human masters. The final long "a" vowel, *Adhōnāi*, as opposed to *adhōnai*, may even be a post-New Testament, rabbinic means of intensifying this same distinction. Thus in Genesis 18:3 the syntactical use of *Adhōnāi* with singular pronouns and verb shows that it means the "Lord." Abraham recognized God. But *adhōnai* in 19:2 construed with the plural, means simply "my masters." Whatever Lot may have thought of the two angels, the Masoretic pointing of the text does not ascribe to them deity. Jacob twice referred to God as *Páhadh*, "terror," (Gen. 31:42, 53), a term which suggests God's transcendence even more than does *Adhōnāi*.

C. YAHWEH. In the Mosaic period was revealed the most important single definition of God's name (=His nature; cf. Hos. 12:5). This was the tetragrammaton YHWH, God's personal name. YHWH was originally pronounced *Yahwe*, but in post-Old Testament days Yahweh ceased to be pronounced aloud in the synagogue reading and was replaced orally (but not in writing) by *Adhōnāi*. This exchange took place because of the superstitious reverence in which the scribes held the ineffable name of God. Next, when the medieval Jewish scholars, the Masoretes, began to write in vowels to accompany the consonatal Old Testament text, they added to the original consonants of Yahweh the Masoretic vowel points of *Adhōnāi*, and the actual written result became the impossible Y-H-W-H. In the American Standard Version,
$$a \quad o \quad a$$
it is rendered "Jehovah." In the Authorized Version, Yahweh is represented by "LORD" (or "GOD," when following the word "Lord"), written in full capitals to distinguish it from *Adhōnāi*, "Lord." The abbreviated forms — *yāhū*, or — *yāh* may stand at the ends of proper nouns, and *Y'hō* —, or *Yō* — at the beginnings. The form *Yāh* may occasionally stand alone, as in Ex. 15:2 or in the exclamation *Hall'lū-Yāh*, "Praise Yahweh!"

As to the meaning of Yahweh, etymological speculation is rather fruitless. It is the Biblical definition found in Exodus 3:14 and in the surrounding context that must be determinative. These verses indicate that the root of "Yahweh" is the verb "to be," used in its simple, rather than its causative,[10] stem: "God spoke in the first person and

---

[10] As in Albright, *From the Stone Age to Christianity*, p. 198 (and see the further reading suggestions below), or David N. Freedman, "The Name of the God of Moses," *Journal of Biblical Literature*, 79:2 (June, 1960), pp. 151-156, which has been criticized by Norman Walker as "Conjuring up a non-existent hiph'il form," *ibid.*, 79:3 (Sept., 1960), p. 277.

said unto Moses, 'I AM THAT I AM'" (Ex. 3:14; cf. Hos. 1:9). Then, when someone would speak about God in the third person, the form became, "He is," or, in Hebrew, in the archaic spelling, "Yahweh." Some have suggested that the name's meaning must be that of God's unchangeableness toward His people, (Ex. 3:15).[11] But, as Moses indicated in 3:13, the fact that He was the changeless God of the fathers was not enough to answer Israel's need at that time. A more fundamental objection to the "changelessness" concept is that the theology of the older testament is preeminently one of redemptive activity, and speculative thought on matters such as God's eternal self-existence is foreign to its nature.[12] Instead, the redemptive requirement of that moment in 1447 B.C. was for a God who would be present to visit and deliver the enslaved Israelites from Egypt (v. 16). Furthermore, God's immediately preceding promise to Moses had been, "Certainly I will be with thee" (v. 12). The best translation for Exodus 3:14 seems, therefore, to be this: "I am present is what I am."[13] This description is, in fact, the fundamental inheritance promise of the testament, "I will be their God, and they shall be My people." "Yahweh" ("faithful presence") is God's testamental nature, or name (Ex. 6:2, 4; Deut. 7:9; Isa. 26:4).

Scripture speaks of the tetragrammaton as "this glorious and fearful name" (Deut. 28:58) or simply "the name" (Lev. 24:11, 16). It carries the connotation of God's nearness, of His concern for man, and of His redemptive, testamentary revelation. So Moses selected Elohim as the appropriate term for Genesis 1-2:3, God transcendent in creation; but Yahweh for Genesis 2:4-25, God immanent in Eden's revelations. Similar shifts in names, corresponding to God's shift in activity from general sovereignty to personal redemption, appear in the Genesis passages that follow. For example, Elohim gave commands, but Yahweh shut the door for Noah. In Genesis 9:26, 27, Elohim enlarges Japheth, but Yahweh is the God of Shem. In Psalm 19 (vv. 1-6), the heavens declare the glory of Elohim; but (vv. 7-14) the law of Yahweh is perfect, and Yahweh is my Strength and my Redeemer.[14] The implications of the name Yahweh gain ultimate fulfillment only in the final testament of peace, when the God who has been present from the first will be fully present at the last (Isa. 41:4;

[11]Vos, op. cit., p. 134; and Oehler, Theology of the Old Testament, sections 36-42.
[12]Though note that Christ in the New Testament did use this verse to introduce the new thought of His eternal divine existence (John 8:59).
[13]Cf. Edmond Jacob's stress upon "Yahweh" as meaning life in its actuality, God livingly present "with" His own, op. cit., pp. 51-54, and Knight's phrase that Yahweh is to "become" to Moses, by being with him, A Christian Theology of the Old Testament, p. 42.
[14]This distinction of using Elohim for the world and Yahweh for Israel (and for all special theophanic and anthropomorphic revelations) is not always to be insisted upon. For example, compare the otherwise almost identical 14th and 53rd Psalms. Book I of the Psalter (Psalms 1-41) simply prefers Yahweh; and Book II (Psalms 42-72), Elohim.

48:12). "I will set My sanctuary in the midst of them forevermore" (Ezek. 37:26).

D. MELEKH. Another term, first employed as a name for God in the Mosaic period, is *Mélekh*, "king." Corresponding to the national character of the Sinaitic testament, Exodus 15:18 speaks of God as "reigning"; and *Mélekh* is first used to designate God in Numbers 23: 21 (cf. Deut. 33:5). *Mélekh* emphasizes God's position as "king of Israel." In the Davidic period with the full establishment of the Hebrew kingdom, its usage became frequent, both in reference to God as king over His people in Zion (Ps. 24:7-10) and as king over all nature (Ps. 29:10). Later, however, *Mélekh* came to be avoided as a name for God because of its use in the idolatrous paganism that surrounded Israel. It seems, for example, that the name of the idol "Molech" (I Kings 11:7; II Kings 23:10) must originally have been *Mélekh*, though the name of the "king" came to be pointed with the vowels of the Hebrew word *bósheth*, meaning "shame." Even to mention the name *Mélekh* was a shame! An exception appears in the phraseology of the eighth century prophet Isaiah who, with his stress upon divine sovereignty, often used it for God, both as king of Israel (Isa. 43:15) and as king of angels (6:5). In the post-exilic days when idolatry had been just about overcome, *Mélekh* regained something of its frequency in usage as a name for God (Mal. 1:14). It relates particularly to God's reign as king in the final testament of peace (Zech. 14:16).

E. DIVINE NAMES FROM THE CONSOLIDATION PERIOD. Although we cannot always distinguish descriptive phrases from actual divine names, there do appear to be four designations that come for the first time in this period to be used as regular names of God. *Ēl Hai*, "living God," may have been suggested by Hagar's description of God as *Hai-rō'ī*, "the living One who sees me" (Gen. 16:14) or by Moses' reference to living gods who could speak (Deut. 5:26; cf. I Sam. 17:26; Jer. 23:36). But in Josh. 3:10 *Ēl Hai* is used in the singular number, without definite article, as a proper noun. The name is synonymous in meaning with Yahweh, "the One livingly present in your midst."

Elōhīm Q'dhōshīm (Josh. 24:19) is an unusual plural of majesty that means "Holy God." It is possible, however, that these words may be a descriptive phrase of God's holiness and not a proper noun. Later, *Q'dhōshīm* (alone) is used in parallelism with God (Prov. 9:10; Hos. 11:12), though it is still not certain whether it serves as a name for God or has its more usual meaning of "holy ones" or "holy things." In any event, a phrase that uses this term in the singular, *Q'dhōsh Yisrā'ēl*, "the Holy One of Israel," was brought into currency by the associates of David, Asaph the chief musician (Ps. 78:41), and

Ethan the wise man (89:18). This name was extensively employed
by Isaiah (cf. II Kings 19:22) in the eighth century to emphasize
God's moral transcendence.

Yahwe (Elōhē) S'vā'ōth means Yahweh (God) of hosts, or armies.
As a name, "LORD God of Sabaoth," was first revealed in connection
with the worship at Shiloh under Eli, shortly before 1100 B.C. (I Sam.
1:3). As to its meaning, *s'vā'ōth*, "hosts, armies," is used in Scripture
in at least three different ways: for the armies of Israel, as God's hosts
(Ex. 7:4; I Sam. 17:45); for the stars, as God's heavenly host (Deut.
4:19; Ps. 33:6; Neh. 9:6); and for heavenly spirits, God's angelic hosts
(Gen. 32:1, 2; Ps. 103:20, 21). The earliest Biblical usage of "Yahweh
of Hosts" was the first of these three. Specifically, God fulfills His
testamental promise by adopting the armies of Israel as His own. He
marches with them and brings them victory (Ex. 12:41; II Sam. 5:24).
This fact explains the presence of the ark of the testament in battle
(I Sam. 4:3; II Sam. 15:24) and the militaristic praises that were
sung at its entrance into Jerusalem under David (Ps. 24:8). But the
disruption after David demonstrated the unworthiness of national
Israel to be considered as the hosts of Yahweh. Under the eighth
century prophets, therefore, a substitution in meaning was effectuated
to the third of the usages of *s'vā'ōth*. It was the holy angels that
formed the royal train in Isaiah's vision of "the King, Yahweh of
hosts" (Isa. 6:1-5). The name thus shifted to become significant of
the heavenly monergism of the testament. As Isaiah pointed out,
"The zeal of Yahweh of hosts will perform it" (Isa. 9:6).[15] "Yahweh
of hosts" was particularly used in this way in the post-exilic period
(Hag. 2:6-9; Zech. 4:6).

The basic meaning of *Bá'al* is "owner, or husband." The name
Bá'al thus constituted an appropriate description of the relationship
sustained by God to His testamental people, and it was so used in
certain personal names in the later consolidation period. Esh-baal
means, for example, "man of the Master" (I Chron. 8:33). But because of the name's inevitable association with Baalism, the prophets
opposed its employment altogether (Hos. 2:16, 17), and it fell into
disuse. From some texts, *Bá'al* was even removed and the Hebrew
word for shame, *bósheth*, was substituted, producing in the above-
mentioned example the name Ish-bosheth (I Sam. 2:8), "man of
shame" (cf. 9:6).

The revelation of new names for deity ceased with the consolidation period. During the exile, however, a final Old Testament development occurred when "God of heaven," a descriptive phrase dating

---

[15]Cf. Heinisch, *op. cit.*, p. 42; and Edward J. Young's excellent discussion of the
differences between Isaiah's vision and the apparently similar events recorded in
pagan Near Eastern religion, *The Study of Old Testament Theology Today*, pp.
50-52.

from early days (Gen. 24:3-7), was adopted by Daniel to emphasize God's universal sovereign power (Dan. 2:37). Shortened to "heaven," this term developed into a name of God in itself, as appears from the expression "the Heavens do rule" (4:26). In post-Old Testament days when the divine name came to be considered as too sacred even to pronounce, "Heaven" was increasingly substituted for it.[16] On this basis may be explained why Matthew, in writing to strict Jews, used "kingdom of heaven" instead of "kingdom of God," the phrase that is found in the identical passages in the other gospels.

For Further Reading:

Robert Dick Wilson, "The Names of God in the Psalms," *Princeton Theological Reveiw*, 25:1 (Jan., 1927), 1-39. A study in the use of the divine names that also demonstrates the authenticity of the Psalm titles.

William F. Albright, "Contributions to Biblical Archaeology and Philosophy, 2, The Name *Yahweh*," *Journal of Biblical Literature*, 43 (1924), 370-378; "Further Observations on the Name *Yahweh* and its Modifications in Proper Nouns," *ibid.*, 44 (1925), 158-162; and "The Names 'Israel' and 'Judah'," *ibid.*, 46 (1927), 175-178. A series of linguistic studies on the tetragrammaton; Neo-orthodox.

12. The Attributes of God *

As the redemptive activity of God unfolded itself in history, this very process entailed a certain revelation of the characteristics of the divine Redeemer. These revelations of God's attributes, however, were always corollary to those of His works. Scripture does not discuss the divine virtues in the abstract; it begins with the fact that God is the Testator, one bequeathing a gift (Heb. 9:15). The reality of His testamental bestowment, then, points Him out as free in His activity, as specifying qualifications for inheritance, and as blessing the heirs. Within each of these qualities, in turn, are revealed the specific attributes of God.

A. COSMIC SOVEREIGNTY. The freedom of the Testator is summed up in the words of the psalmist, "Our God is in heaven; He hath done whatsoever He pleased" (Ps. 115:3). God's control of the world is, in fact, implicit in His setting up the basic covenant of works in the primeval period. Even the tempter did not question that God *could* kill (Gen. 3:3), only whether He *would*. Cain, it is true, thought

---

* BIBLE READING: Psalm 139; Isaiah 45
Collateral Reading: Vos, *Biblical Theology*, pp. 257-258, 263-264, 270-276.
  Norman H. Snaith, *The Distinctive Ideas of the Old Testament* (Philadelphia: Westminster Press, c. 1946), pp. 90-98, 109-120, 135-139, 152-155, 162-169.

---

[16] I Macc. 3:18, 19, and other references in the Apocrypha.

that when he was cursed he would be left beyond God's geographical reach (4:14); but the Lord speedily corrected this misapprehension (v. 15). God's judgments, both in the flood (6:13) and at the tower of Babel (11:8), demonstrated His world sovereignty.

In His revelations to the patriarchs, God truly localized Himself, for example, in the making of the testament (Gen. 15:17). But such localizations were subject to three important qualifications: they were instituted by God's own free choice, they were temporary, and they did not preclude His simultaneous domination of the world (14:22; 18:14). Though He appeared at certain spots in Palestine, He was still able to answer prayers in Haran far to the north (24:12), and to maintain His infinite power as "the mighty One of Jacob" in Egypt beyond the southwestern desert (49:24). God's eternity was first revealed in Genesis 21:33, where Abraham called on the name of "Yahweh, Ēl Ōlām," the "everlasting God." The term ōlām, however, did not suggest to the Hebrews God's transcendence of time, but rather His endless duration in time (cf. 6:4) — "everlasting."

In the next period, Moses began his inspired record of creation, not with the thought suggested by the English versions, "In the beginning, God," but, as Genesis 1:1 reads literally, "In the beginning He created, namely God, heaven and earth." The teaching of the verse is limited to that of His creative activity and does not concern His pre-existence. The latter is a doctrine that rarely comes within the practical scope of Biblical theology. Moses' closest approach to it is to be found in his poetic comparison that a thousand years are but a day to God (Ps. 90:4) and in his exclamation that "before the mountains were brought forth, even from ōlām to ōlām Thou art God!" (v. 2). His words correspond to the expressions of Job (Job 10:5) and of his authoritative counselor Elihu (36:26) that God's duration is limitless, reaching far beyond the years of man. These verses describe eternity, but again in the sense of continuation, not timelessness. The concern of Scripture is with man's redemption, not with the communication of abstract truth, even of God; and man's redemption transpires in time (Isa. 40:28, 29).[1] It is, on the other hand, significant that Scripture never suggests a doctrine of theogony, of a temporal "birth" of God.

Moses emphasized the cosmic sovereignty of God. God's will produced the light (Gen. 1:3); His perfection, moreover, is proclaimed by the total goodness of creation (1:31). God's awesome transcendence was evidenced by the phenomena on Sinai (Ex. 19:16, 18). The mountain, as a result, was not to be touched (vv. 12, 13; cf. Heb. 12: 18-21), an injunction which demonstrates that reverence toward Him is still a most valid principle for those who would receive an eternal

[1]Cf. Oscar Cullmann's commendable study, *Christ and Time*. Trans. by Floyd V. Filson (London: S.C.M. Press, 1951).

kingdom (vv. 26-29). As God controls mountains, so too He controls men, inspiring even their inner desires (Ex. 35:34). Yet this sovereign God bound Himself to Israel by the testament! His presence came and dwelt over the ark (25:22), though He remained free to reject those who should prove faithless (19:5). For contrary to Canaanitish theology, the testament did not put God "in a box." Israel in the consolidation period may indeed have succumbed to a belief in the magical efficacy of the ark. (It is mentioned four times in the three verses, I Sam. 4:3-5). But to treat the ark as a "container" of God became in itself nothing short of a violation of the testament concept; and how God reacted to this sort of externalization, they learned to their sorrow (v. 11). "Man looketh on the outward appearance, but Yahweh looketh on the heart" (I Sam. 16:7).

Some of David's contemporaries felt that God was limited to Israelitish territory. They told him as he went into exile, "Go, serve other gods" (I Sam. 26:19). But David didn't (30:8)! For David, God's "temple" was heaven (Ps. 11:4), from which He would laugh at human opposition from any quarter (2:4). Compare Habakkuk 2:20, "Yahweh is in His holy temple; let all the earth keep silence before Him." Psalm 139 constitutes David's classic statement of God's infinity: He is omniscient (vv. 1-6), omnipresent (vv. 7-12), and omnipotent (vv. 13-19). God has knowledge even of contingent events that never take place (I Sam. 23:11; cf. Jer. 38:17, 20; Ps. 147:5). Yet the very fact that men must keep silence before God in His heavenly temple is an indication that God carries on a corresponding activity on earth. Specifically, God's temple is also (simultaneously) the tent that David pitched for the ark on Mount Zion (Ps. 20:2; cf. v. 6 and Isa. 63:15).

Solomon, too, in the following period, taught of God's transcendence. For at the very time that he was dedicating the Jerusalem Temple as a sacramental sign of God's immanence, the king exclaimed, "Highest heaven cannot contain Thee, how much less this house that I have built!" (I Kings 8:27). Elijah, however, met God, not at Solomon's temple, but back on Mt. Sinai (Horeb, 19:8); and the meeting occurred, not in a storm, as before, but in stillness (v. 12). God can reveal Himself by any means at any place. As the seer told Asa, "The eyes of Yahweh run to and from throughout the whole earth" (II Chron. 16:9). It was also in this period that the sovereign wisdom of God was fully revealed and was related to His freedom as the Testator.[2] He is "wise in heart and mighty in strength . . . which doeth wonders without number" (Job 9:4, 10; cf. 42:2; Prov. 15:3). By His wisdom He freely created heaven and earth (Prov. 3:19, 20). He possesses the wisdom for which men seek in vain (Job 28:23). Men cannot deceive God, though this was in fact what Job's friends at-

---

[2]His granting of wisdom to men had been revealed under Moses (Ex. 31:3).

tempted to do (13:7-9). God has the knowledge of the hearts of men, even as He has of hell (Prov. 15:11; cf. the Korahite Psalm, 44:21); and His insights are more accurate than the knowledge men have even of themselves (Prov. 16:2).

The eighth century prophet Jonah attempted to flee from God (Jonah 1:3); but he was forced to recognize Him, both on the sea and in Nineveh. The whole people of Israel, in fact, succumbed to a false trust in a God whom they felt to be limited to the temple and who must, therefore, be under a corresponding compulsion to protect both it and the surrounding city (Mic. 3:11). This Canaanitish theory was repeatedly exploded by the prophets (v. 12; cf. Jer. 7:4). Isaiah, more than any other prophet, revealed Yahweh as the One who can do all things. He stressed His dominion over the nations (Isa. 17:13), over space ("earth is His footstool," 66:1), over human thought (55:8, 9), and over time and change (31:2; 41:4; 46:6; 48:12). A classic expression of God's sovereignty over the last of these is the statement in the anonymous exilic Psalm, 102:27 that describes Christ: "But Thou art the same, and Thy years shall have no end."[3] The goal of creation and election is the glory of God (Isa. 43:7). Similarly, for the later prophet Jeremiah, God is the one who fills heaven and earth (Jer. 23:24). His ordination is both total and free — "I have purposed it, and I will not turn back from it!" (4:28).

During the exilic period, Daniel's prophecies marked a high point in the enunciation of the fact of divine sovereignty. "He doeth according to His will, and none can stay His hand" (Dan. 4:35; cf. v. 3). Ezekiel indeed faced the contemporary criticism that God's ways were not equal, that He was guilty of changing His punishments and blessings (Ezek. 18:25, 29). But, as Ezekiel proceeded to point out, it is men's actions that change, and then each human change leads to a changelessly corresponding divine response. Thus the post-exilic restoration came about only because Yahweh changed not in His testamental promises (Mal. 3:6) and because of His power to execute what He had once determined. He is "the great, the mighty, the terrible" (Neh. 9:32). He must "lower Himself" to see things in heaven (Ps. 113:6)! But at the same time, corresponding to the reconstruction of the Temple, there came a renewed post-exilic emphasis upon God's localized presence (Hag. 1:8; Zech. 1:16). To this Temple Christ Himself would some day come (Mal. 3:1), and a similar localization is revealed as true for that kingdom of the Church which is yet future (Zech. 14:16).

B. ETHICAL SOVEREIGNTY. A testator stipulates the conduct he requires of his heirs (cf. Gen. 12:1, 2). God's ethical testamentary

---

[3]The reference of the Psalm is to Yahweh, up through v. 22; but it shifts in v. 24 to *El*, which here signifies the Second Person of the Trinity, according to Heb. 1:8, 10-12. Cf. Payne, "So-called Dual Fulfillment in Messianic Psalms," *Evangelical Theological Society,* 1953 *Papers,* p. 66.

requirements become, moreover, a reflection of His own ethical attributes (Deut. 32:4); for God has but one consistent standard. He cannot behold evil (Hab. 1:13). Divine injunctions that embrace moral conduct began to be revealed from the earliest primeval period (e.g., Gen. 9:1-7); but it was with the particularization of the testament to Abraham in the patriarchal period that God's ethical standard became explicit. Two significant terms appear at this point: "Yahweh is the God of *tōrā* (Gen. 26:5) and of *mishpāt* (18:25). *Tōrā* means basically "instruction," and then, because God is the king as well as teacher, "law." *Tōrā* came in time to refer to God's written words, the Old Testament,[4] and particularly to the law of Moses, the Pentateuch. *Mishpāt* is the decision of the *shōfēt*, the "judge"; hence "custom," or codified *tōrā*. But *mishpāt* in the Old Testament cannot be separated from God, who is the basis for all ethical decisions.[5] It is often used as an equivalent for righteousness.

In the third, the Mosaic period, there occurred the initial revelation of two other fundamental ethical qualities of God: *yōsher* (cf. Ex. 15:26) and *s'dhāqā* (cf. Ex. 9:27).[6] *Yōsher*, "uprightness," is that which "stands up" in conformity to God's standards. Conceivably such *yōsher* might not necessarily be ethically right; but simply, what "pleased" God. Thus in Numbers 23:27, Balak assumed that his request to Balaam to curse Israel could "please," *yāshar*, the latter's deity. But such an eventuality did not take place. In God, *yōsher* is equated with justice and perfection (Deut. 32:4); and, therefore, as Abraham implied without using the term *yōsher*, the Judge of all the earth must do right (Gen. 18:25). God will not change or repent (Num. 23:19; I Sam. 15:29). Statements apparently to the contrary (e.g., I Sam. 15:11, 35 in this same aforementioned chapter; or Gen. 6:6) indicate genuine, divine sorrow, but not fickleness. They describe God's grief at sin or an ending of His wrath upon men's repentance (Ex. 32:10). But God changes only as men meet His own underlying conditions (Jonah 3:10; Jer. 26:19).

S'dhāqā is similar to *yōsher*, as is witnessed by the identical usage of the two nouns in Deut. 9:5 (cf. 32:4 which applies their adjectival forms to God). But the concept of *s'dhāqā* exhibits an extensive development in Old Testament revelation and may indeed be traced through nine stages as numbered below. The last three of these, moreover, stem from God's beneficent rather than from His ethical sovereignty. They, therefore, extend beyond this present section on God's

---

[4]So John 10:34 appeals to the "law," though the quotation that follows it actually from Psalms.

[5]Norman Snaith, *The Distinctive Ideas of the Old Testament* (Philadelphia: Westminster Press, 1946), p. 94, and cf. the detailed accompanying discussion of the meaning of these terms.

[6]This latter term does find mention in the patriarchal period (Gen. 15:6; 30:33), but in reference to men, not to the nature of God.

ethical attributes into the following section on His beneficence, see below, under "C."

1) The root meaning of s'dhāqā appears to be "straightness" in a physical sense; though there is some uncertainty at this point. Some sources suggest "excellence,"[7] while others refuse to commit themselves to a root meaning at all.[8] In any event, this physical meaning comes before the time of the Old Testament.

2) The Biblical usage of s'dhāqā commences already in the patriarchal age with the abstract meaning of objects or actions that are in conformity with some standard. The norm may be either God's standard, e.g., the testamental requirement which Abraham met through faith,[9] (Gen. 15:6), or man's standard, e.g., Jacob's "honest" living up to his sheep-contract with Laban (30:33). Even inanimate objects may be described as sédheq if they measure up to the standards that are appropriate to them. For example, "paths of righteousness" are walkable paths (Ps. 23:3), and "trees of righteousness" are beautiful trees (Isa. 61:3).

3) The root of s'dhāqā, as has already been noted, was first applied to God in the Mosaic age (Deut. 32:4). It indicates divine "straightness." That is, since there can be no standard more absolute than His own, God's s'dhāqā means simply His acting in accordance with His own will. The classic illustration of this divine, ethical sovereignty is that of the potter forming the clay according to his own desires (Isa. 45:9-12; Jer. 18:1-12). But this "righteousness" is not equivalent to arbitrary desire, for in the latter reference it is to be noted that the potter broke down the vessel because the clay was marred (v. 4). The potter acts in harmony with his own standard, which is at the same time the right standard. S'dhāqā in this sense is a manifestation of God's holiness, His separate, unique deity (Isa. 5:16). It is, moreover, an activity and not just a quality or attribute. God's s'dhāqā, His actions of consistency with His own will, includes His preservation, both of animals and of men (Ps. 36:6). It prevents activities which might otherwise be carried on in vain (Isa. 45:19). In both of these last two verses, the English versions translate s'dhāqā as "righteousness," but they might more appropriately render it as "regularity" or "reliability."[10]

---

[7]Brown, Driver, and Briggs, A Hebrew and English Lexicon of the Old Testament, p. 841.

[8]Ludwig Kohler, Lexicon in Veteris Testamenti Libros, p. 741. But cf. Snaith's preference for "straightness," op. cit., p. 91.

[9]Faith itself may be said to be "righteous" because it is the action which God requires of men. It is the standard to which He expects men to conform. But in Gen. 15:6 Abraham's faith is not what was imputed to him as "righteousness." His faith was simply the means through which he was granted the righteousness of Christ, see below, p. 160.

[10]Vos' "forensic" or "judicial" righteousness of Yahweh, Biblical Theology, pp. 270-271.

4) When s'dhāqā describes the moral standards which are inherent in God's nature and will, and by which He ever observes and evaluates human conduct, then its natural translation becomes indeed "righteousness."[11] For example, s'dhāqā may consist of a man's restoring to his debtors certain pledged items of which they now have need (Deut. 24:13); or it may consist of obeying God's laws in general (6:25). The eighth century prophets, with their passion for social justice, gave particular stress to this aspect of s'dhāqā (Amos 5:7; 6:12). But for a Biblical synthesis of the detailed standards that God requires of men and to which the moral attributes of God Himself correspond, see below, topic 25.

5) From the Mosiac period and onward, God's "righteousness" proceeds from abstract moral evaluation to include also the punishment of moral infraction. Thus, after experiencing God's plague of hail, Pharaoh states, "Yahweh is saddīq, and I and my people are wicked" (Ex. 9:27). From the very first, in fact, God had punished Adam for breaking the covenant of works (Gen. 3:17); and He had carried out vengeance for the murder of Abel (4:10). God hates evil doers (Ps. 5:5). The most extreme example of God's punitive righteousness was the universal destruction that He executed through the Flood (Gen. 6:5-7). Later, Israel's disobedience caused God in His righteousness to sentence His rebellious people to forty years of wilderness wandering (Num. 14:33, 34; Ps. 78:32, 33; 95:8-11; cf. I Cor. 10:5; Heb. 3:7-11). Idolatry particularly aroused His indignation (Ex. 34:14; Deut. 32:21); and the cycles of judges are thus a continuing demonstration of God's righteous punishments (Judges 2:6-3:6). Zeal in maintaining the right meant even more to God than did Israel's national existence (Ex. 32:10; Num. 14:12). This punitive aspect of God's righteousness is expressed in His wrath (Deut. 6:15), "a consuming fire" (4:24; 32:22). His wrath is emotional, and its description constitutes a form of anthropopathism, though this in no way detracts from its reality (see above, topic 9-A). But God's wrath is not vindictive. It is always under His control (Hos. 11:9), and it is aroused in particular by men's breaking His testament (Deut. 31: 16, 17). The deadened moral sensitivity of modern man may lead him to deny the doctrine of eternal punishment in hell — it is said to be incongruous with the loving nature of God. But such reasoning is utterly opposed to the historical revelation of God as found in Scripture.

In the Davidic period, "the man after God's own heart" extended this principle of God's righteous judgment to include all nations, because of their oppressive acts against Israel (Ps. 9:8). Then Amos in the eighth century, provided the first detailed explanation of divine

---

[11]Vos' "righteousness of cognizance," ibid., p. 271, beyond which point his list generally follows the points noted below.

judgment. In particular, he showed how the punishments that God inflicted upon the Gentile nations were based upon *any* immoral acts and were not limited to those that they committed against His chosen people (Amos 2:1). God's righteous judgment is universal in scope (Amos 2:1).

6) Commencing with the period of consolidation, "righteousness" is also applied to those acts of God by which He vindicates the deserving among Israel. Deborah sang that when men recounted the victory that God had just granted to Barak's deserving men, they would "rehearse the righteous acts, s'dhāqā [plural], of Yahweh" (Judges 5:11; cf. Ps. 35:28; Isa. 58:2). Actually, the truth of divine intervention on behalf of the upright had been revealed long before its explicit description as s'dhāqā (Gen. 18:25); and such vindication is indeed but the opposite side of righteousness in the previous (fifth) sense, namely, the righteousness of punishment. Scripture often combines both of these aspects in one statement; for example, that God is righteous toward the righteous and "perverse" toward the perverse (Ps. 18:26; Prov. 3:34). He will, in fact, some day judge the whole world, both good and bad, "with righteousness" (Ps. 98:9). God's zeal in executing both punishment and vindication is described as His qin'ā, His "jealousy" (Ex. 20:5). God will brook no infringement of His ethical sovereignty. Thus His qin'ā of punishment is illustrated by the above reference to Command II of the Decalogue: God will tolerate no rivalry, in this case, from idols. His qin'ā of vindication is first explicitly enunciated by Joel in the eighth century: "Then was Yahweh jealous for His land and had pity on His people" (Joel 2:18; cf. Zech. 1:14).

C. BENEFICENT SOVEREIGNTY. A testament is a matter of gift; it demonstrates the goodness of the testator. So God's testament, though witnessing to His freedom — "I will be gracious to whom I will be gracious" (Ex. 33:19) — likewise witnesses to His beneficence. He graciously cares for His own. As Nygren has explained,

> "God was the God of love because He was the God of the Covenant; the establishment of the Covenant [testament] and the giving of the Law had been the supreme expression of His love."12

Even before the testament of Genesis 3:15, God's love had been shown by His placing of man in Eden (2:8, 9). His very questioning of fallen Adam, rather than immediately destroying him (3:9), was in itself a gracious act. But God's graciousness is first openly declared in the proto-evangel of this fifteenth verse, see below, topic 20. Subsequent examples of His grace appear in Genesis 4:1, 25. Also

---

12Anders Nygren, *Agape and Eros.* Trans. by Philip S. Watson (Philadelphia: The Westminster Press, 1953), p. 48. Used by permission.

noteworthy is Genesis 5:29, Lamech's inspired prediction of Noah's "comforting" the human race, a comfort which was accomplished as God through Noah spared a remnant from the Flood's destruction. Specifically, then, God's beneficent sovereignty under the older testament is to be appreciated under four groups of Hebrew terms, each group of which describes this quality of graciousness within the divine attributes.

Beginning with the Davidic period, s'dhāqā, "righteousness," takes on three additional meanings that make up the first of these four groups;[13] for these later meanings relate to matters of unmerited goodness rather than to matters of precise ethical conformity.

7) In Psalm 51:14 s'dhāqā develops into a distinctly non-moral activity of God. David beseeches, "Deliver me from bloodguiltiness, Oh God, Thou God of my salvation; and my tongue shall sing aloud of Thy s'dhāqā." Though s'dhāqā is here translated "righteousness," what David was actually seeking was not vindication; for he had just acknowledged the guilt, not simply of his crime with Bath-sheba, but of his whole nature, which had been depraved from his very conception (v. 5). His real need was for unmerited forgiveness; and a better translation would consist of a simple repetition, "Oh God of my salvation, my tongue shall sing aloud of Thy salvation!" At this point, that is, s'dhāqā has become a redemptive, divine attribute. It is God's fulfilling His own gracious standard of salvation, irrespective of the merit of the human recipient. The basis for such unmerited favor lies in the truth that "Yahweh thy God, He is the faithful God, who keepeth the testament" (Deut. 7:9) and who may, in particular, be relied upon to keep its promise for the reconciliation of man to Himself. This is the meaning of "righteousness" as it appears also in Psalm 31:1; 103:17, and 143:1 (Davidic), in Psalm 85:9-11 and 89:16 (by, respectively, David's Korahite singers and his wise man, Ethan), in Psalm 71:2, 15, 16, 19 (anonymous, but known by its inclusion in Book II of the Psalter to be Solomonic or earlier), and in Psalm 116:5 (anonymous).

The eighth century prophets carried on this redemptive usage of s'dhāqā. Hosea, for example, made his prediction of the future testament, with Yahweh's promise to Israel: "I will betroth thee unto Me in [My] righteousness." (2:19; cf. Joel 2:23 and Mic. 7:9). Isaiah, in the latter part of his ministry, gave particular emphasis to the fact of God's redemptive righteousness. A probable historical reason for his emphasis is that God's saving intervention had been so clearly displayed in the destruction of Sennacherib's host in 701 B.C. Noteworthy examples include the following: the parallelism of s'dhāqā

---

[13]Kohler thus disregards the chronological development of revelation that the Old Testament itself presents when he asserts the original sense of s'dhāqā was not "juristic," as outlined above, but was the beneficent concept of God's offering fellowship with Himself, *Old Testament Theology*, pp. 34-35.

with salvation, in Isaiah 45:8; 46:13; the application of s'dhāqā to
the anticipated gracious deliverance of the Hebrew exiles, in 45:13;
and the force of s'dhāqā in such familiar verses as 41:10, "Fear thou
not for I am with thee, be not dismayed for I am thy God. I will
strengthen thee; yea, I will help thee; yea, I will uphold thee by the
right hand of my [not righteousness, but] salvation." So Isaiah 45:21
should be read, not "a saddîq, 'just' God, and yet at the same time a
Savior," but rather "a saddiq God, and therefore a Savior" (cf. Zech.
9:9).[14]

8) As a development out of this redemptive concept, Scripture
goes on to use s'dhāqā to describe the standing that is enjoyed by the
inheritors of the testament, which comes into being as a result of
God's saving s'dhāqā. The existence of such an imputed righteousness
had been suggested by the status granted to the patriarch Abraham
— "He believed in Yahweh, and He reckoned it to him for s'dhāqā"
(Gen. 15:6). At the same time, this revelation might have been confused with others in which s'dhāqā carried merely its second sense,
namely, that of human conformity to (God's), standards. As John Murray has paraphrased it,

"It might appear that it was the faith of Abraham which
was reckoned as the righteousness on the basis of which he
was justified, that faith itself was accepted by God as fulfilling the requirements for a full and perfect justification."[15]

But as Murray goes on to explain,

Scripture itself never uses such terms. It speaks always of our
being justified by faith, or through faith, or upon faith, but never
speaks of our being justified on account of faith or because of
faith. . . . We are justified by grace. It is not the reward of any-

[14]Similar meanings may be found in the New Testament (for example, in I John
1:9), cf. Vos, op. cit., p. 275. Further, Rom. 3:21 states that "A 'righteousness'
[salvation] of God hath been manifested." S'dhāqā has here entered its eighth
meaning, a condition granted by God, not merely an attribute of His. But care
must be exercised that only true applications of this sort be made. C. H. Dodd's
interpretation of Rom. 3:21, as if it taught a universalistic acquittal of guilty men
neglects the following verse, which specifies that the salvation (not just man's
realization of it) is only upon those who believe, cf. The Epistle of Paul to the
Romans (Moffatt Commentary; New York: [n.d.]), pp. 52-53. Equally false is the
application of s'dhāqā as a redemptive attribute to Rom. 3:26. Such would remove the antithesis, "that He might be just, and yet at the same time the justifier
of him that believeth in Jesus," and make the verse read, "that He might be
just, and therefore the justifier," as in William Sanday and Arthur C. Headlam,
A Critical and Exegetical Commentary on the Epistle to the Romans (New York:
Charles Scribner's Sons, 1911), pp. 90-91. But this produces a violation of context. Righteousness is doing what is right; the preceding chapters of Romans
have concerned God's righteous wrath against sin, and the preceding verse, 3:25,
concerns the propitiation of that wrath through the shed blood of Christ. Therefore, "what is right" in 3:26 is punishment, not forgiveness, and the translation
must be retained, "that He might be just, and yet the justifier of him that
believeth in Jesus."
[15]Redemption—Accomplished and Applied, p. 155. For the common view that the
faith was righteousness, cf. Snaith, op. cit., pp. 219-220.

thing in us or wrought by us but proceeds from God's free and unmerited favour (Rom. 3:24ff.). . . . . The righteousness of justification is the righteousness and obedience of Christ (Rom. 5:17, 18, 19).16

It remained, however, for Isaiah in the eighth century period to first use s'dhāqā for a humanly possessed righteousness, which is at the same time distinctly declared to have been God's own moral attribute (s'dhāqā in the fourth sense described above), but which was then granted by imputation to the inheritors of the testament as a result of God's beneficent sovereignty. Isaiah proclaimed: "This is the heritage of the servants of Yahweh and their s'dhāqā which is of Me, saith Yahweh" (54:17). As A. B. Davidson has defined it, "It is not an attribute; it is a divine effect, a condition of the world produced by God."17 There is, then, in Yahweh, a righteousness that, by His grace, becomes the possession of the saved (Isa. 45:24). Israel's own righteousness was inadequate (64:6; Dan. 9:18), but "in Yahweh" they sādhaq, "are righteous" (Isa. 45:25). In the later prophetic period Jeremiah with the pen of inspiration proceeded to combine the Messianic doctrine with this inheritance concept of s'dhāqā. For he described the Messianic Branch out of the house of David by saying, "This is His name, whereby He shall be called: Yahweh our righteousness" (Jer. 23:6; cf. 33:16). That is, the Messiah's function of effectuating Yahweh's plan of justification not only equates Him with deity but also identifies Him with the divine righteousness that is granted to God's people. As Calvin long ago commented:

"Righteousness is not in Christ as though it were his own, but we have it in common with him, for he has nothing separate from us. . . . Christ possesses a righteousness which He communicates to us."18

This is nothing less than the imputed righteousness of Christ, as I am "found in Him, not having a righteousness of my own, but that which is from God, by faith in Christ" (Phil. 3:9; cf. I Cor. 1:30).19

9) Finally, during the exilic period, s'dhāqā entered its latest stage in which it came to designate benevolence, and specifically "charity, or alms-giving." In Daniel 4:27, for example, "righteousness" is the equivalent of "showing mercy to the poor" (cf. Ps. 112:9). Thus in New Testament times our Lord cautioned, "Do not your 'righteousness' before men" (Matt. 6:1).

A second Hebrew word that describes God's beneficent sovereign-

16Op cit., pp. 155-157.
17The Theology of the Old Testament, p. 143.
18Commentary on the Book of the Prophet Jeremiah and the Lamentations. Trans. by John Owen (Grand Rapids: William B. Eerdmans Publishing Co., 1950), III:146.
19A meaning which as indicated in footnote 12 may also be found in Rom. 3:21, cf. Charles Hodge, Commentary on the Epistle to the Romans (Grand Rapids: William B. Eerdmans Publishing Co., 1950), p. 88.

ty is the term *hésedh*. *Hésedh* is often rendered "lovingkindness," but such a translation can be misleading. For example, Psalm 136:10 states that God "smote Egypt in their firstborn; for His *hésedh*, lovingkindness [!] endureth for ever." The fundamental idea of *hésedh* seems rather to be that of "strength" (Ps. 62:11, 12; 144:2; Isa. 40:6; and, used negatively, Prov. 25:10), from which develops the concept of a strongly binding social tie — "the mutual liability of those who are relatives, friends, master and servant, or belonging together in any other way; [it means] solidarity, joint liability."[20] So in secular thought, *hésedh* describes a man's faithfulness to his treaty obligations (Gen. 21:23; II Sam. 10:2). In reference to deity, from the time of the patriarchs onward (Gen. 24:12), it concerns God's faithfulness to the testament and its promises: "He is the faithful God, who keepeth the testament and the *hésedh* [His loyalty to the testamentary obligations]" (Deut. 7:9; cf. v. 12; I Kings 8:23; II Chron. 6:14; Neh. 1:5). In fact, God's *hésedh* is both prior to and serves as the basis for His testament. "*B'rîth* comes about by a ceremony, but *hésedh* results from the beginning of belonging together."[21] That is, the testament is the action of God that springs from His free relationship with certain men whom He has elected to reconciliation and "belongingness" with Himself.

Hésedh is frequently best translated as "loyalty." To "do *hésedh*" (Gen. 24:27) is to prove loyal; "abundant in *hésedh*" (Ex. 34:6) means to be thoroughly loyal; and *hésedhs* (in the plural, Isa. 55:3) are the single proofs of God's continual solidarity with His own, the deliverances that result because of His always proving loyal. *Hésedh* generally expresses God's love for the heirs of the testament (Gen. 24:12); but it also includes in its connotations God's consistent vengeance upon their enemies. Hence the action of God in smiting Egypt and Transjordan is described as *hésedh* (Ps. 136:15, 17-20). God's *hésedh*, because of His very nature, is eternal, a feature that Psalm 136 states twenty-six times in as many verses. Even after the fall of Jerusalem in 586 B.C. Jeremiah could say, "It is of Yahweh's *hésedhs* [plural] that we are not consumed, because His compassions fail not. They are new every morning; great is Thy faithfulness" (Lam. 3:22, 23).

But as is indicated by these verses from Lamentations, there exists a third aspect within God's beneficent sovereignty that lies behind *hésedh*. This is God's *emûnā*, or "faithfulness." The Hebrew root that is involved is *āman*, "Amen," which means to "be steady, or firm." From this root then are derived the two nouns *emûnā*, "faithfulness," and *emeth*, "truth." Sixteen times, beginning in the days of Abraham the patriarch (Gen. 24:27), the Old Testament employs the

20Kohler, *Lexicon*, p. 318.
21*Loc. cit.*

combination expression "*hésedh* and *emeth*." But it is the *emeth* that is the fundamental divine attribute of which the *hésedh* is the particular expression, in relation to the testament. Faithfulness is the idea of the very name Yahweh, the One who can be counted upon to be present. This concept is further expressed in God's title of *sūr*, "rock," a sure refuge (Deut. 32:4; II Sam. 22:32).[22] God is "truth," and, therefore, He will not lie (Num. 23:19). The greatest single demonstration, however, of divine *emeth* lay in the historical conquest of Canaan (Josh. 21:43-45). God was true to the word that He had sworn (Deut. 31:8). God's truth is thus not limited to logical abstractions. His "firmness" results practically in the salvation of His own. As David could so confidently respond, "Into Thy hand I commend my spirit: Thou hast redeemed me, Oh Yahweh, Thou God of truth" (Ps. 31:5).

Finally, the ultimate category of God's beneficent sovereignty is His *ahavā*, His "love." Indeed, it is God's love that explains why His faithfulness should be directed toward lost men in the first place. As Moses explained to Israel, "Because He loved thy fathers, therefore He chose their seed after them, and brought thee out with His presence, with His great power, out of Egypt" (Deut. 4:37; cf. 7:7, 8, 13). Love is the divine attribute that produced the testament, though it is here in the Mosaic period that this fact is for the first time explicitly revealed. David later spoke of God's loving concern for every living thing (Ps. 145:9, 16); the whole earth is full of His goodness (33:5). He provides for the beast and the raven (147:9; cf. Jonah 4:11), though His particular care is directed toward men (Ps. 139:17). Among the eighth century prophets, Hosea became the outstanding advocate of the love of God for Israel. God's love is like a husband's love for his bride (Hos. 3:1). God keeps patiently leading with "the cords of love" (11:4). His is a superhuman love that will not give up, even in the face of love's rejection (11:9). Then in the same period it was through Jonah that God's great love for the pagan nations was revealed (Jonah 4:2; cf. Isa. 54:7; Jer. 18:8; 49:11). Jeremiah, in the later prophetic period, again stressed God's love for Israel, revealing its eternal aspect — "Yea, I have loved thee with an everlasting love" (Jer. 31:3); while Malachi, in post-exilic days, traced God's love back to His initial concern for Esau's unworthy brother Jacob (Mal. 1:2).

Three phrases in the Hebrew of the Old Testament serve in particular to characterize the nature of God's love. 1) God is *érekh appáyim*, literally, "long of nostrils." That is, His snort of anger (anthropomorphism!) is delayed before it displays itself. The phrase *érekh appáyim* was first used by Moses (Ex. 34:6; Num. 14:18),

---

[22]Note the use of *sūr* in proper nouns, as Elizur, "God is a rock" (Num. 1:5; cf. vv. 6, 10).

though the truth it conveyed had been known long before, cf. God's delay in sending the flood (I Peter 3:20). David suffered three days of divine anger in the form of a pestilence because of his sinful census (II Sam. 24:13, 14); but at his subsequent dedication of the site for the Temple on the threshing floor of Araunah (where the plague was arrested), he emphasized how God's favor far outlasts His anger (Ps. 30:5). Nahum, however, in the later prophetic period, reminded the world that even God's longsuffering has limits (Nahum 1:3).

2) In the same Mosaic passage that first spoke of longsuffering (Ex. 34:6), there also appeared the initial Biblical description of God as *rahūm,* "merciful."[23] Mercy is goodness, but as expressed particularly toward those in trouble: God "executeth justice for the oppressed and giveth food to the hungry" (Ps. 146:7; cf. vv. 8, 9). As the next Psalm states, in an almost incredible combination, the same God who calleth the stars by name "healeth the broken in heart and bindeth up their wounds" (147:3, 4). Isaiah, in the eighth century, notes that the testament of peace will stand eternally because of the fact that God has mercy on His own (Isa. 54:10).

3) Perhaps the most significant term of all is God's *hēn,* His "grace." Grace consists of love, but for the undeserving. In the very primeval period, Noah found *hēn* in the eyes of Yahweh and so was preserved during the Flood (Gen. 6:8). Then in the following period on this same basis of *hēn* (grace), Lot with all his failures, was saved from Sodom's destruction (19:19). It was grace alone that rescued Israel in the Mosaic period after they had broken the testament (itself of grace) at Sinai (Ex. 34:6; cf. v. 7 on God's characteristic of forgiveness). David, out of his own bitter experience, could pray to God as "good, and ready to forgive" (Ps. 86:5; cf. 103:3); and Isaiah, in the eighth century period, exalted God as the one who will "abundantly pardon" (Isa. 55:7). Snaith compares God's grace with his *hésedh* or testamental faithfulness as follows:

> *Hen* is undeserved favor at the hands of a superior, where there is no bond or covenant between the parties, and no obligation on the superior to do anything at all. *Hésedh,* by contrast, presupposes a covenant, and has from first to last a strong suggestion of fixedness, steadfastness, determined loyalty.[24]

Thus God sovereignly formulates and executes His testament for lost men; but the divine attribute that motivates His redemptive activity is His boundless love, even for the least deserving. As God

---

[23]This had been approached in the patriarchal period when Jacob had prayed that God might grant his sons mercies in Egypt (Gen. 43:14).

[24]*The Distinctive Ideas of the Old Testament* (Philadelphia: Westminster Press, 1946), pp. 165-166. Used by permission. But note that in a few passages *hésedh* is used for God's love that exceeds the testamental obligation. *Hésedh* may, in fact, repair the testament which man has broken and to which God is thus no longer bound (Isa. 54:8; Jer. 3:12; Hos. 2:19).

cried out through Ezekiel in the exilic period, "I have no pleasure in the death of the wicked, but that the wicked turn from His way and live: turn ye, turn ye from your evil ways, for why will ye die, oh house of Israel!" (Ezek. 33:11; cf. 18:23).

D. THE TENSION. God's cosmic, ethical, and beneficent attributes synthesize historically in His sovereignly administered testament. But the very anticipatory nature of the older testament leaves within the pages of the Old Testament a series of unresolved features that constitute a genuine theological tension. Moses, for example, described God as transcendent, hidden behind curtains in the Most Holy Place, or commanding the Decalogue from the thunder clouds that gathered over Sinai. Yet he also described God as immanent, with His tabernacle dwelling in the center of the camp of Israel, and with the ark of His testament marching before their armies through the wilderness. This tension increased with Solomon's construction of the Temple. The temple could demonstrate God's transcendent power, witness Isaiah's proclamation of its inviolability against Sennacherib (Isa. 37:33-35); and yet the temple could at the same time undermine Israel's appreciation of divine transcendence, witness Jeremiah's denunciation of Judah's materialistic confidence that God was under "compulsion" to protect it (Jer. 7:4-15). Again, the temple services could lead to Israel's joyful fellowship with the immanent God (Ps. 132:7-9); and yet an overemphasis upon the rituals that were performed within its courts could take the heart out of truly yielded devotion (Amos 5:21-23). According to the prophets, God was both greater than Israel thought and yet nearer than Israel thought!

At the same time, God's beneficent sovereignty seemingly relaxed the penalty imposed by His ethical will. For example, divorce (Deut. 24:1) could take the place of death (22:22) as the punishment for immorality on the part of those within the marriage bond (cf. Matt. 19:8, because of "the hardness of your heart"). Or again, God's love could cause the postponement of God's punishments, as in the cases of His threats to overthrow faithless Judah in the days of Solomon and Josiah (I Kings 11:12 and then II Kings 22:20). Yet on the other hand, these relaxations were only delays; and eventually God's ethical will prevailed, both in the condemning of the guilty party in divorce (Matt. 19:9) and in the destroying of the kingdom of Judah (II Kings 23:26). Again, divine s'dhāqā seemed in its beneficent stage (7) to forgive the very crimes it punished in its ethical stage (5)!

The solution to this tension, however, lay in the future in the person and work of the Lord Jesus Christ. He was the divine Angel of the testament, whom Israel sought and desired, even without fully understanding what they did (Mal. 3:1). In Christ dwelleth all the fullness of the Godhead, and yet bodily (Col. 2:9). He is the ultimate tabernacling of God with men (John 1:14) toward whom the temple in both its misunderstood transcendence and misunderstood immanence pointed. Furthermore, His ethical will climaxed the Old Testament revelation of the moral attributes of God, far exceeding the perverted though seemingly lofty righteousness of the scribes and the Pharisees (Matt. 5:20). Yet He who commanded men to be perfect, even as their heavenly Father is perfect (Matt. 5:48), and who personally lived up to His own exalted ethical standard (Heb. 4:15), at the same time exhibited that love for which there is no equal, as He laid down His life for His undeserving friends (John 15:13). It was when He, His own self, bare our sins in His body upon the tree (I Peter 2:24) that the older testament was fulfilled, the veil of the Temple was rent in twain (Matt. 27:51), and the way into the holiest was made plain (Heb. 9:8). Here was s'dhāqā, "righteousness," in its ethical stage (5), in its redemptive stage (7), and in its imputed stage (8), all united in one. He came that God might be just, and yet the justifier of him that believeth in Jesus (Rom. 3:26) and that we might be found in Him, who is made unto us righteousness and sanctification and redemption (I Cor. 1:30).

For Further Reading:

Norman H. Snaith, *Mercy and Sacrifice.* London: Student Christian Movement Press, 1953. A neo-orthodox study on God's requirements and character in Hosea.

John A. Bollier, "The Righteousness of God," *Interpretation,* 8:4 (Oct., 1954), 404-413. A neo-orthodox article, emphasizing righteousness as a quality in God, without proper recognition of it as an effect in man.

Gottfried Quell and G. Schrenk, *Righteousness.* Translated by J. R. Coates. London: A. & C. Black, 1951. A translation of the thorough article on righteousness in both the Old and New Testaments from G. Kittel's *Theologisches Wörterbuch.*

13. The Persons of God *

The Old Testament places its emphasis upon the unity of God. A revelation of the Trinity at this early stage in human thought might have led to polytheism; and trinitarianism depended, in any event, upon the incarnation of Christ for its demonstration. There are, however, in the theology of the older testament genuine suggestions of the Persons that make up the Godhead. For example, it was revealed to Moses that God had said at the creation of man,

* BIBLE READING: Judges 6; Proverbs 8
Collateral Reading: Vos, *Biblical Theology,* pp. 85-89, 122-123.
  Heinisch, *Theology of the Old Testament,* pp. 102-115, 122-127.
  A. B. Davidson, *The Theology of the Old Testament,* pp. 115-129.

"Let *Us* make man in *Our* image" (Gen. 1:26); and all explanations
for this plural number, except the trinitarian explanation, must be
rejected as inadequate. The so-called "royal we" usage is foreign to
Old Testament thought. Moreover, though in some passages the
plural pronoun "us" may indicate God plus angels (as 3:22; 11:7 [cf.
18:2; 19:1] or Isaiah 6:8 [cf. vv. 2, 6]), here it is only in God's
image, not in angels' images, that man is made (Gen. 1:27). The
Trinity is implied.[1] Sometimes evangelical writers have, indeed, gone
too far, and some of the evidence that has been advanced to support
the doctrine of the Trinity is invalid. A well-known example is the
attempt to argue from the plural of the divine name *Elōhīm*.[2] But
there are yet four Old Testament figures that stand as significant
witnesses to the truth of the Trinity: the Angel of the Testament,
the Wisdom of God, the Spirit of God (which are considered below),
and the divine Messiah (in topic 21-B).

A. THE ANGEL OF THE TESTAMENT. The Hebrew noun *malākh*
means "messenger" or "angel,"[3] from which comes the phrase *malakh
Yahwe*, "the angel of Yahweh." *Malakh Yahwe* may refer to any of
God's angels (I Kings 19:7; cf. v. 5). But at certain points, though
the Angel of Yahweh may seem initially to be no more than any
other angel (as Judges 6:11), He soon transcends the angelic category
and is described in terms that are suitable only to a distinct Person
of the Godhead (Judges 6:12, 14). The divine Angel first, and most
frequently, appears in the patriarchal period, the period of theophanies.[4] His appearance to Hagar in Genesis 16:7 is the first such
instance. Here the Angel speaks about Yahweh as if He were a third
party (v. 11), and yet Hagar calls this angelic speaker by the names
of Yahweh and God (v. 13; cf. 21:17). In 22:11 the Angel again
speaks, but as being Himself *God* (v. 16; so too in 31:11, 13). It was
He who redeemed Jacob from all evil (48:16). The explanation that
some have offered is that the Angel simply acts for God and speaks
in God's name, just as did the prophets (cf. Isa. 1:2).[5] But while
such an interpretation might account for some of the above references,
it proves inadequate for others; for example, the very first reference.
For it states in context that Hagar followed Yahweh with her eye-
sight and that she gave a name to the God who was speaking with
her, things that are never said of any prophet.

[1]Heinisch's denial of the Trinity at this point, *Theology of the Old Testament*,
p. 102, hardly agrees with his recognition that God is "taking counsel as it were
with Himself," p. 103; and G. A. F. Knight too, despite repeated affirmations in
respect to the "complex" nature of God, *A Christian Theology of the Old Testament*, pp. 26-27, 67, really understands the "we" as a mere collective allusion
to God and His family of creatures.
[2]See below, p. 146.
[3]See below, topic 23-A.
[4]See above, p. 45.
[5]Cf. Edmond Jacob, *Theology of the Old Testament*, pp. 75-77, who admits that
the figure is "elusive and perplexing."

The evidence from the Mosaic period renders it impossible to view the Angel as a mere representative of deity. The Angel of Yahweh who appeared to Moses in the burning bush (Ex. 3:2) not only says He is God (v. 6), but, as the One who called from the bush, He is designated "God" by the inspired text (v. 4). It is specifically said of Him that Moses was afraid to look upon *God* (v. 6); and the place of His localization received divine reverence (v. 5). If, as an alternative explanation, it is suggested that the Angel might be simply Yahweh, the Father Himself, in some temporary manifestation,[6] v. 4 proceeds to declare: "And when Yahweh saw that he [Moses] turned aside to see, Elohim called unto him out of the bush." That is, the Elohim-Angel is, in the text, differentiated from Yahweh. Exodus 23: 20, 21, moreover, describes the Angel as sent by Yahweh (and so, distinct from Him);[7] but it then goes on to state that God's name (Person)[8] is in Him and that the Angel has the uniquely divine power to forgive sins (cf. Luke 7:49; Mark 2:7). Again, in Numbers 22:31, Yahweh opened the eyes of Balaam to see the Angel of Yahweh (distinct); but what the Angel says (v. 35) is what God says (v. 38). Compare also Exodus 14:19 and Numbers 20:16 in which the Angel is said to lead Israel, while in other passages it is God who so leads. It is indeed possible that when visible appearances of God occur elsewhere in Scripture (as Ex. 33:22; cf. Gen. 18:1) 'the actual subject may again be the *Malakh Yahwe*, even though the term itself may not be used. For no man can see God and live (Ex. 33:20), but Christ is the One who declares Him (John 1:18).

At the outset of the consolidation period, the "prince of the host of Yahweh" who appeared to Joshua (Josh 5:14) cannot be the commander of Israel's host (who was Joshua himself), nor of God's starry host. He must, therefore, be the commander of Yahweh's angelic host,[9] namely, the supreme Angel. Yet He accepts worship as no mere angel may (Rev. 19:10). The conclusion again appears inescapable that we have to do with a distinct Person of the Godhead. Judges 2:1 contains the significant revelation that it is the Angel of Yahweh who made and who enforces the testament (in this case, the Abrahamic).[10] In Judges 6:12, moreover, Gideon was told by the

---

[6]Cf. Knight, *op. cit.*, pp. 75-83, who considers the "angel" as but the pictorial and inconsistent form of an abstract idea (revelation).

[7]Davidson's position on the Angel, *The Theology of the Old Testament*, p. 298, is generally commendable; but his description of the distinction as "between Jehovah manifest for purposes of redemption and Jehovah in Himself" does scant justice to passages such as this.

[8]See above, p. 144.

[9]See above, p. 150, on the three-fold usage of "hosts of Yahweh."

[10]Cf. Davidson, *loc. cit.*, "In ordinary angelic appearances one may discover Jehovah present on some side of His being, in some attribute of His character; in the Angel of the Lord He is fully present, as the covenant God of His people, to redeem them."

Angel of Yahweh that Yahweh (as distinct from the Angel?) was with him. Gideon, at that moment, may not have appreciated how literally true these words were; but two verses later his angelic Companion is identified as Yahweh Himself! The Angel accepted sacrifice from him (v. 21); Gideon feared for his life because of his proximity to deity (v. 22); and it was Yahweh who finished the conversation (v. 23; cf. Judges 13:22, 23). The destroying angel of Yahweh at the time of David's census (II Sam. 24:15, 16; cf. Isa. 37:36) may not have been a unique angel; but the *malākh mēlīs*, "interpreting Angel," of Job 33:23 in the following period is no ordinary angelic being. He is not, as some have suggested,[11] "one of a thousand [such]," but "One [unique] out of a thousand"; for v. 24 goes on to describe how this Angel becomes a ransom that God may be gracious to sinners. The "interpreting Angel" not only shows God to man (John 1:18), He also mediates between God and men and brings man back to God. He is the one Mediator (I Tim. 2:5, 6).

Among the eighth century prophets, Hosea reveals that the Man who wrestled with Jacob was an Angel (Hos. 12:4), but Moses makes the identification complete because he wrote that Jacob saw *p'ni'ēl*, "the face of God" (Gen. 32:30). Isaiah calls the *Malakh Yahwe* the Angel of God's *pānim*, His "face," or theophanic presence (Isa. 63: 8, 9).[12] Daniel in exile had visions of the "Man" (Dan. 8:15; 10:5), who seems to give orders to the angel Gabriel (8:16) and is described in a way that is similar to Christ's description in Revelation 1:13-15 (Dan. 10:5, 6). It is possible that He is to be identified with the Messianic "Son of man" (Dan. 7:13). Finally in the post-exilic days, Zechariah describes the Angel of Yahweh as distinct from Yahweh (Zech. 1:12), and yet giving orders to ordinary angels (1:11; 3:4); and as pleading for the elect before God (1:12), and yet sitting in God's place (3:1, 2) and forgiving sins (v. 4). God and the Angel of Yahweh are equivalent expressions (12:8). Malachi makes the same identification (Mal. 3:1) and goes on to designate the divine Angel as the "Angel of the Testament," the One who will accomplish redemption by serving as the historical testator. His coming is further identified as preceded by that of God's messenger, Elijah (4:5), namely, John the Baptist (Matt. 11:14). Actually, it is this association of God with the testament that furnishes the key to the whole phenomenon of the *Malakh Yahwe*. The Old Testament, true to its nonspeculative nature, does not discuss the essence either of the Angel or of His relationship with Yahweh. But, true to the redemptive promise of the testament — "I will be their God, and they shall be My people" — it does describe the execution of the testament by a figure who is literally God with men. It makes it clear that —

[11]Gustav F. Oehler, *Theology of the Old Testament*, p. 442.
[12]See above, p. 30.

"... the Angel is truly divine, for otherwise He could not
have discharged the sacramental function of assuring man
that God was with him ... In the incarnation of our Lord
we have the supreme expression of this fundamental arrangement."[13]

That is, the Old Testament revelations of the unique Angel of the
Testament can be appreciated only when understood as pre-incarnate
appearances of Jesus Christ, the Second Person of the Trinity and
the one Savior of mankind.

B. THE WISDOM OF GOD. As has been already noted under the
subject of "revelation," the Old Testament Hebrew term for "wisdom,"
hokhmā, exhibits a considerable development in meaning: from ordinary skillfulness in applied knowledge, through morality, to the
fullness of reverence and faith (Job. 28:28).[14] Biblical wisdom, moreover, embraces more than human mental effort. Solomon, early in the
disruption period, cautioned men not to be "wise in their own eyes"
(Prov. 3:7). For human wisdom cannot equal God's wisdom (Job
15:8) or maintain itself against God (Prov. 21:30). In fact, true
wisdom is contrasted with what lies in one's own heart (28:26).
Rather, wisdom must spring ultimately from God. For though God
has prepared it for His own (2:6, 7), it is yet an essentially divine
attribute (Job 12:13; 28:23, 27). But neither does this recognition
exhaust the Biblical concept of *hokhmā*. Wisdom appears further to
be more than an attribute and to become actually objective to God.
On the one hand, throughout Proverbs 1-9 there recurs a persistent
personification of wisdom that is unique in Scripture.[15] Some of the
statements are simply poetic, as is demonstrated by contrasting sym-
bolisms in one and the same context: "Length of days is in her[16]
right hand" (personal, Prov. 3:16); but, "She is a tree of life to them
that lay hold upon her" (impersonal, v. 18). In certain of the passages, however, the description exceeds normal personification. Wisdom is set in personal contrast (7:4) to the sinful woman (vv. 5-27);
men are to cry after and seek for her (2:3, 4); and she is more
precious than any other desire (8:11). On the other hand, there are
described a number of activities as carried on by wisdom that ex-
ceed the function of a specific divine attribute or of an impersonal
mental effort on the part of either man or God. Wisdom not only
sets up kings (8:15, 16), but she exercises love (v. 17). She goes out

[13]Vos, *Biblical Theology*, p. 88.
[14]See above p. 55.
[15]Elsewhere personification does appear (cf. Ps. 85:10-13), but only rarely, and
then only in isolated statements.
[16]*Hokhmā* is a feminine gender noun, so "her" is simply a matter of grammatical
agreement and is not ultimately significant.

preaching (1:20), and reproves (v. 23) and advises (v. 30);[17] and she laughs at the calamity of those who refuse her (v. 26).

In Proverbs 1:20-33 and 8:22-36 *Hokhmā* passes the limits of even the most elaborate personification and is actually hypostatized by the inspired writer. That is, *Hokhmā* is revealed as an objectively existing person and, indeed, as a divine Person. "Wisdom," Solomon teaches, existed prior to the creation of the world (Prov. 8:23-25) and is thus not a created work at all (v. 22). He lives as One eternally possessed of God.[18] Wisdom was Yahweh's instrument in creation (3:19), His *āmōn*, His "artificer, architect, master-workman"[19] (8:30). A possible parallel that appears later in Proverbs, though perhaps poetic and not to be pressed, is found in 30:4: "Who hath established all the ends of the earth? What is His name, *and what is His Son's name*, if thou knowest?" Wisdom also answers prayer (1:28) and gives men life and the testamental favor of Yahweh (8:35).

Yet these divine characteristics of Wisdom involve the activities of a Person who is at the same time distinct from Yahweh, as the last verse makes clear. Proverbs 8 further notes that Wisdom was with Yahweh from the beginning: "When *He* established the heavens, *I* (distinct Person) was there" (v. 27). Wisdom rejoiced before Yahweh and was His delight (v. 30), but His own delight was with men (v. 31). His relationship with Yahweh was that of One eternally "brought forth" (v. 25). Since He is contrasted with the Spirit (1:23), He must Himself be the only begotten Son of the Father, Jesus Christ, the Second Person of the Trinity. Our Lord used the phrase, "the Wisdom of God," as interchangeable with a simple reference to Himself (Luke 11:49; Matt. 23:34). All wisdom is, in fact, in Him (Col. 2:3); and Scripture entitles Him "the Wisdom of God" (I Cor. 1:24, 30). The most direct New Testament connections of the Proverbs verses, however, are found in John 1:1-18. There Christ, as the *Logos* (Greek for "Word"), is described as the One who was in the beginning with God. He was God, and through Him all things were made. By Him, moreover, the men who receive Him may be reconciled to God as adopted sons. In the Apocryphal writings of the Intertestamental Period (Wisdom of Solomon 7:22-8:3; 7:12; 8:8, 13 and especially 9:1, 49; cf. Baruch 3:28, 29; I Enoch 42:1, 2) and in the

---

[17]Even casual reading indicates how much further this personalizing has gone than has, for example, the description of love in I Cor. 13, which is the closest Biblical parallel.

[18]The alternative translation to "possessed Me," namely, that Yahweh "created Me," (as in the Revised Standard Version), not only reflects the low Christological presuppositions of the Aryan heresy; it also runs counter to 1) the general meaning of the verb *qānā*, which is "get, possess," and not "create" (with the possible exception of one passage, Ps. 139:13), 2) the context, which separates Wisdom from the creation, and 3) the New Testament analogy of Christ as the only-begotten of the Father, who is begotten and not made.

[19]Brown, Driver, Briggs, *A Hebrew and English Lexicon of the Old Testament,* p. 54.

works of the Jewish philosopher Philo of the first Christian century, creative Wisdom is called the "Word," *Logos*. The correspondence of John 1 to Proverbs 8 thus receives pre-Christian validation. The place of God's creative word in the Old Testament (Deut. 8:3; Ps. 33:6; 104:7; 147:15-18; cf. Gen. 1:3) has already been mentioned;[20] but in these references the "word" does not appear to represent a distinct Person, though Christ did in fact act as is described.

C. THE SPIRIT OF GOD. After having noted a number of Old Testament verses on the Holy Spirit, A. B. Davidson came to a twofold and, to Bible believers, a self-contradictory conclusion:

> [1.] The language used . . . might be used, and no doubt is now used, to express the conception of the Spirit as a distinct person. [2.] But . . . it is doubtful if any passage of the Old Testament has this sense, if by the sense of the Old Testament we mean the sense intended by the writers of the Old Testament.[21]

Davidson's skepticism about the Holy Spirit, however, involves deeper questions that concern the nature of Scripture and, as a result, the definition that one gives to Biblical theology as a whole. The points at issue come into focus when the subject of Biblical theology is distinguished, in particular, from the two studies that are the most closely related to it in the investigation of religious phenomena.[22] The first of these, systematic theology, asks, "What is true of God?" and concludes that the Holy Spirit was indeed active in Old Testament events (Acts 1:16; 2:16). The other of these studies, namely, the history of the religion of Israel, asks rather, "What did men believe?" It concludes that, without the incarnate revelation of the Second Person of the Trinity, Old Testament Israelites could hardly have been aware of the essence of the Third Person; and so it denies to Him any consideration within its own subject matter. Davidson, however, by tacitly limiting the writers of Scripture to its secondary, or human, authors, has thus restricted himself to a history of religion. But Biblical theology is expected to ask this: "What did God reveal?" By "the sense of the Old Testament," therefore, Biblical theology means the sense that was intended by the primary, *divine* Author. So if the Holy Spirit now means by the language of the Bible to teach about the reality of His own distinct Person, He

---

[20]See above, p. 133, "lively personifications," Heinisch, *op. cit.*, p. 125.

[21]*Op cit.*, p. 127. Occasionally evangelical writers have fallen into a similar error. Cf. John H. Raven, *The History of the Religion of Israel*, p. 164: "Although these expressions resemble what is said about the Holy Spirit in the New Testament, there is here no distinction of persons in the Godhead. The Spirit of God in the Old Testament is God Himself exercising active influence and imparting divine life." Oehler, however, has well stated, "Though we must not read the New Testament doctrine of the Trinity into the Old Testament, it is yet undeniable that we find the way to the economic Trinity of the New Testament already prepared in the doctrine of the Malakh and of the Spirit," *op. cit.*, p. 142.

[22]See above, p. 21.

doubtless meant no less a view of Himself when He spoke in Old Testament days!

The Hebrew word that the Holy Spirit chose for Himself was *rûah*, which means "breath." Job 27:3, for example, reads, "My breath is in me and the *rûah* of God is in my nostrils." But here *rûah* seems to refer to the breath of life that God gives man and not to the Holy Spirit (cf. Hab. 2:19). Breath, moreover, implies life and then power (cf. Josh. 2:11). The writer of I Kings thus states that there was no more *rûah* in the queen of Sheba as she viewed the splendor of Solomon, meaning that she was "breathless"; she was overwhelmed (I Kings 10:5). From this concept comes the further derived thought of *rûah* as signifying the direction or the attitude of a person's mind (cf. Ex. 35:21; Num. 14:21). Scripture speaks of a "spirit of perverseness" (Isa. 19:14) or a "spirit of whoredoms" (Hos. 4:12). In a few Biblical passages, accordingly, God's *rûah* may refer simply to His active life or His intention. Isaiah 40:13 serves to exemplify this usage: "Who hath directed the spirit [attitude] of Yahweh, or being His counselor hath taught Him?" But at most points in the Old Testament, the immediate context approves, or favors, and the New Testament analogy strongly suggests, that the *Rûah* of God is to be understood as a distinct Person, the Holy Spirit.

The personality of the Spirit was first revealed to Moses. Specifically, God informed Moses relative to the seventy elders who were to assist him in government: "I will take of the Spirit who is upon you and I will place [Him] upon them, so they may bear the burden of the people with thee" (Num. 11:17). This statement indicates that the Spirit is distinct from Yahweh, that He is personal (giving judicial advice), and that He is divine (guiding Israel). So Hermann Schultz, when commenting on Moses' words in Genesis 1:2, observes, "The Spirit appears as very independent, just like a hypostasis or person."[23] David, two periods later, was the first to call Him the Holy Spirit (Ps. 51:11; cf. Isa. 63:10, 11); and it should be noted that "holy" is not used of the Spirit in His general activity, but only in His holy (separate) work with those who are the elect under the testament. Isaiah, in the eighth century, describes how Israel grieved the Holy Spirit (63:10), which is a strong indication of His personality (cf. Eph. 4:30). Isaiah 48:16, moreover, reads: "Yahweh hath sent me and His Spirit." The Spirit is thus seen to be distinct from Yahweh and to be personal, in whichever way the verse be understood, whether the Holy Spirit sends Isaiah or is sent with him as a fellow speaker. As A. F. Kirkpatrick has remarked, "Passages like these which imply that the spirit of Jehovah personally acts, prepare the way for the New Testament revelation concerning Him, and can be used in the

[23]*Old Testament Theology*, II:184.

fullest Christian sense."[24] Zechariah, in the post-exilic period, speaks poetically of the Spirit as the "seven eyes" of God (3:9; 4:10; cf. Rev. 4:5), but there is still only one Spirit (4:6).

The Old Testament reveals a four-fold work of the Spirit. 1) In the world in general, the Spirit serves as the effectuating agent in creation[25] (Gen. 1:2, of the Mosaic period; cf. Job 26:13). He continues, moreover, to function in a similar way in God's day-by-day sustaining providence (Ps. 104:30): "Thou sendest forth Thy Spirit, they are created: and Thou renewest the face of the earth."[26] David revealed the Spirit's omnipresence (Ps. 139:7), described in synonymous parallelism with God's own *pānīm* (face, Person). It is God's Spirit who gives life to men (Job 33:4; disruption period) and who makes the waters flow (Isa. 59:19, R.V.) and the flowers fade (40:7; eighth century prophetic period). As the post-exilic prophet Zechariah poetically phrased it, He "runs to and fro through the whole earth" (Zech. 4:10). 2) On His work in regenerating the elect (Ezek. 11:19), see below, topic 18.

3) David, in his intimate personal communion with God, was the first to reveal the activity of the Holy Spirit as indwelling and guiding the believer.[27] For the king prayed, "Teach me to do Thy will, for Thou art my God: Thy Spirit is good; lead me into the land of uprightness" (Ps. 143:10). Isaiah, in the eighth century period, described how Israel collectively had vexed God's Spirit during the wilderness wanderings (Isa. 63:10); but Isaiah looked forward to the day when this same indwelling Spirit would purge away the people's pollution, though as "the Spirit of judgment and the Spirit of burning" (4:4). The chastening of the Spirit is for Israel's own good (Micah 2:7). In a similar way Ezekiel, during the exile, spoke of how the Spirit would be active in reviving the community life in the post-exilic days that lay ahead (Ezek. 37:14). Then in that post-exilic period, Haggai noted that even as Yahweh's Spirit had indwelt Israel as a part of their inheritance under the Sinaitic testament (cf. Neh. 9:20), so in his own day the "Spirit remaineth among you: fear ye not" (Hag. 2:5). As Warfield summarizes it,

> "The Spirit of God, in the Old Testament, is not merely
> the immanent Spirit, the source of all the world's life and

---

[24]*The Book of Psalms* (The Cambridge Bible for Schools and Colleges; Cambridge: The University Press, 1914), II:293.
[25]See above, p. 133.
[26]*Rûah* might possibly here again mean life-breath (cf. v. 29 and Gen. 6:17). Such an impersonal meaning does seem clear in such verses as Ps. 33:6, "the *rûah* of His mouth," and Job. 34:14, 15.
[27]His indwelling of God's people had, of course, been true in the earlier periods (cf. Neh. 9:20); but it had not been contemporaneously revealed, as far as is known.

all the world's movement . . . He is as well the indwelling
Spirit of holiness in the hearts of God's children."[28]

4) The most mentioned of the four Old Testament activities
of the Spirit is that of His infilling the leaders of God's people for
their special protection or guidance. Even in the time of the patriarchs, Joseph's gift in interpreting Pharaoh's dream came about because the Spirit of God was in him (Gen. 41:38). In the next period
Moses and his associates judged Israel through His power (Num.
11:17). Bezaleel's skill in constructing the Tabernacle came because
of his being filled with the Spirit of God (Ex. 31:3; 35:31). The
seventy elders of Israel were able to prophesy because the Spirit
who had rested upon Moses had come to rest upon them as well
(Num. 11:25). The Spirit's instrumentality produced even the oracles
of disreputable Balaam (24:2), whom He rendered powerless to
follow his own greedy desire (22:38). Finally, when Joshua was
appointed Moses' successor as leader of Israel, Moses laid his hands
upon him and he was filled with the Spirit (Deut. 34:9).

Infilling by the Spirit was a phenomenon particularly in evidence
under the charismatically anointed judges of the consolidation period.
The Spirit literally "clothed Himself with Gideon" (Judges 6:34) and
"broke in upon Samson" (14:6, 19; cf. 3:10; 11:29; 13:25; 15:14; I
Sam. 11:6; I Chron. 12:18). A noteworthy restriction, however, is to
be seen in the periodic rather than permanent nature of this infilling
(I Sam. 16:14); and David, in the next period, feared that the fullness of the Holy Spirit might be taken from him (Ps. 51:11). At the
same time, however, it is significant that David's concern was in
reference to his being currently upheld in his position of leadership
and in reference to the *joy* of his salvation (v. 12). The salvation itself,
by the *indwelling* of God's Spirit, was not under question.

The ceremony of anointing by means of oil was the sacramental
sign and seal of the coming of God's Spirit. The oil upon the head
represented the Spirit's filling of the prophets, the priests, and the
kings for their leadership of God's people (I Sam. 10:6; 16:13).
Elisha, in the disruption period, sought and received a double portion of the Spirit who had rested upon Elijah (II Kings 2:9; cf. v. 16;
I Kings 18:12), and Isaiah, in the eighth century, prophesied that the
Messiah-Servant in particular (Isa. 11:2; 42:1; 61:1) would be in
possession of the Spirit (cf. John 3:34). For the highly significant
work of the Spirit in inspiring the sacred Scriptures of the Old Testament, see above, topic 4; in fact, the continuance of the Spirit with
the prophets became a very pledge of the testament (Isa. 59:21).
But in their general ministry as well, namely of preaching, these eighth
century prophets could say, "Truly I am full of power by the Spirit

---

[28]B. B. Warfield, *Biblical and Theological Studies* (Philadelphia: The Presbyterian
and Reformed Publishing Co., 1952).

of Yahweh, and of judgment, and of might, to declare unto Jacob his transgression, and to Israel his sin" (Micah 3:8). It was not by might nor by power (of man) but by God's Spirit that Zerubbabel was able to rebuild the Temple after the exile (Zech. 4:6). Particularly significant is the fact that the fullness of God's Spirit was bestowed consistently, not for the personal gratification of the individual receiver, but for the service of God's kingdom (cf. Num. 11:17); compare our Lord's own explanation: "Ye shall receive . . . Holy Ghost power, *and* ye shall be witnesses unto Me" (Acts 1:8). As Oehler has summarized it, "Those gifts of office in the Old Testament are similar to the gifts of grace in the New Testament.[29] But with all this spiritual blessing, a better hope yet lay ahead; for Old Testament Israel reaches its fulfillment in the New Testament Church. Joel (eighth century) accordingly prophesied, "It shall come to, pass afterward that I will pour out My Spirit upon *all* flesh" (Joel 2:28), not just upon the leaders (Num. 11:29), and not just temporarily (I Sam. 16:14), as in the older dispensation. But with the newer dispensation of Pentecost, *all* of God's people who would be willing to pay the price of full surrender to Him (Acts 5:32) and who would pray the Father in faith believing (Luke 11:13), would be enabled, yea, commanded (Eph. 5:18) to be filled with the Spirit!

Just as in the case of the Angel of the Testament, the Old Testament has little to say about the essence of the Spirit or about His relationship with Yahweh.[30] In general, God within is the Spirit, and God in external manifestation, the Angel. There are, however, two significant Old Testament passages that combine the Persons discussed above and suggest the Holy Trinity in its divine fullness. In Proverbs 1:23-29, *Wisdom* predicts, "I will pour out My *Spirit* unto you," but censures Israel because they "did not choose the fear of Yahweh." Likewise in Isaiah 63:9, 10, "The *Angel* of His presence saved them; in His love and in His pity He [*Yahweh*] redeemed them; but they rebelled and vexed His Holy *Spirit*." God is in three Persons, which were, and are, and evermore shall be!

For Further Reading:

Aubrey R. Johnson, *The One and the Many in the Israelite Conception of God.* Cardiff: University of Wales, 1942. Includes discussion of the Angel of Yahweh as God Himself.
Charles T. Fritsch, "The Gospel in the Book of Proverbs," *Theology Today,* 7:2 (July, 1950), pp. 169-183. A concluding section recognizes the Person of Christ in Prov. 8.
Edwin Lewis, "God with Man," *Interpretation,* 7:3 (July, 1953), 281-298. On the Holy Spirit; neo-orthodox.

[29]*Op. cit.,* p. 141.
[30]Cf. Köhler's repeated reference to the Old Testament's doctrine of the Spirit as "an unsolved problem," with "no adequate language." *Old Testament Theology,* pp. 111-112, 118-119.

Part IV. The Heir: Man

"The land is polluted under the inhabitants thereof; because they have transgressed the laws, violated the statutes, broken the everlasting testament" (Isaiah 24:5).

14. Election*

Once one is given the fact of a testator, a second major aspect[1] that arises in any will or testament is that of an heir. So God, by His very revelation of the testament, marks out an object that is to receive the inheritance. This object is man "for not unto angels did He subject the world to come, but one hath testified saying, 'What is man, that Thou art mindful of him'" (Heb. 2: 5, 6).

Further qualification, however, is required. The Word goes on to say, "For verily not to angels doth He give help, but He giveth help to *the seed of Abraham*" (v. 16). That is, there exists an election within the general body of mankind (I Pet. 1:1). The "inheritance incorruptible, and undefiled, and that fadeth not away (is) reserved in heaven for *you*," namely, those who are chosen and kept of God through the faith of Abraham (I Pet. 1:4, 5). This Biblical concept of election has, indeed, been criticized as a "contradiction of the Christian faith in the impartiality and reasonableness of God."[2] But the fact that God marks out the heirs of His testament cannot cast a moral reflection upon God: any favor He might show would be wholly of His mercy, for no man in himself deserves to be saved. It is only God's great love that reaches out and rescues His elect.[3] Even the truth of the love of God must not be distorted into implying the unscriptural doctrine of an indiscriminate and universal salvation. As Warfield has well explained,

> The love of God is in its exercise necessarily under the control of his righteousness; and to plead that his love has suffered an

---

*BIBLE READING: Isaiah 43; Jonah 4

Collateral Reading: Vos, *Biblical Theology*, pp. 68-72, 89-93, 108-111, 127-129, 139-141, 280-284.

H. H. Rowley, *The Biblical Doctrine of Election* (London: Lutterworth Press, 1953), pp. 69-89, 111-120.

[1]See above, p. 87, on the five major aspects entering into the testament.
[2]Cf. the discussion by Carl F. H. Henry, *The Protestant Dilemma*, p. 50, as previously noted above, p. 28; and that by Vos, *Biblical Theology*, p. 90.
[3]See above, pp. 163, 164.

eclipse because he does not do all that he has the bare power to
do, is in effect to deny to him a moral nature. . . . God in his
love saves as many of the guilty race of man as he can get the
consent of his whole nature to save. Being God and all that God
is, he will not permit even his ineffable love to betray him into
any action which is not right.[4]

Election thus constitutes a major corollary to the doctrine of the
sovereign freedom of the divine Testator. But election is also a primary element in the testamentary feature of heirship. It becomes,
furthermore, the historical basis for the Bible's discussion of man,
the heir of the testament, as this doctrinal area comes to expression
in the Old Testament.

A. INDIVIDUAL ELECTION. Although the Edenic and Noachian testaments (primeval period) were universalistic rather than particularistic,[5] the inheritance that took place under them still manifested
divine election. Even in Genesis 3:15, when God first promised to put
enmity between the seed of the serpent and the seed of the woman,
not all the natural seed of Eve actually entered into the promise,
as history itself demonstrates. On the contrary, our Lord Christ explicitly identifies the unregenerate as being "of your father the devil"
(John 8:44). They are seed of the serpent (Matt. 23:33).[6] This division of the race into the elect and the non-elect, once established,
continues henceforward. Speaking in reference to individuals, God
looked with favor on Abel, Enoch, Noah, and Shem; but not on Cain
or on Enoch's and Noah's contemporaries, or on Ham (Gen. 4:4, 5;
5:22 [cf. 4:24]; 6:7, 8; and 9:25, 26). The case of Shem is particularly
instructive, for while he, like the other chosen ones, had received a
blessing on the basis of his previous ethical superiority (9:23), he is
then specifically distinguished from his brother Japheth, whose meritorious action had been identical with his own. True, it is promised
that Elōhīm will enlarge Japheth (9:27), but it is Yahwe, the immanent God of redemption, who is named in respect to Shem. Yahweh
is further said to be "the God of Shem"[7] which is the characteristic
phrasing of the promise of reconciliation as it is found in the testament (9:26). Historical confirmation for the religiously privileged
position of Shem is provided by the fact that the world's three great

[4]*The Plan of Salvation* (Grand Rapids: William B. Eerdmans Publishing Co.,
1942), p. 74.
[5]See above, p. 96.
[6]Cf. Matt. 13:38, 39; II Cor. 11:14, 15; I John 3:8; Rev. 12:9, and Hengstenberg, *Christology of the Old Testament*. Trans. by Theodore Meyer and James
Martin (Grand Rapids: Kregel Publications, 1956), I:17-19.
[7]The rendering of the *Revised Standard Version*, "Blessed by the LORD my God
be Shem," p. 9, is unjustifiable. Though *Elōhē*, "God of," may be repointed
Elōhai, "my God," it is not so rendered in parallel passages in the RSV. (cf.
Gen. 24:27); and in order to say, "Blessed *by*," in Hebrew, one employs a preposition (cf. 14:19). There appears to be a theological bias against election in the
RSV's treatment of this verse.

monotheistic religions, Judaism, Christianity, and Islam, are all known
to have originated among the Semites.[8]

The particularistic testament, beginning with the patriarchal Abrahamic testament, brought into clear focus the truth of the divine
election of certain individuals to salvation. Abraham was the "friend
of God" (II Chron. 20:7; Isa. 41:8) and the particular object of God's
love (Deut. 4:37). When God chose him in Ur of the Chaldees (Neh.
9:7), this choice took place without reference to any prior distinction
on Abraham's part. It was an unconditional election. Abraham was,
in fact, unworthy (Gen. 12:13),[9] but God "knew" ($y\bar{a}dha$) him. To
"know" carries the idea of elective grace and is equivalent to saying
"choose" (cf. Ex. 1:8; 33:12; Hos. 13:5; Amos 3:2; and Rom. 8:29
where "foreknow" = "elect"). Only later did Abraham exhibit the
faith (Neh. 9:8) and works (James 2:23) which were so closely
related to his testamental standing. God's own description of Abraham as $\acute{e}vedh$, "servant," of Yahweh conveys both of these aspects of
election: the privilege (cf. Deut. 32:43; Ps. 89:50) and also the
responsibility. God's choice of Isaac over Ishmael, the "child of
promise" over the "child of the flesh" (Rom. 9:8), is similarly significant of God's unconditioned grace. But the most outstanding example
of unconditional election to be found in all of Scripture is that of
Jacob (Gen. 25:23). He was chosen before birth. He was one of
twins, so humanly equal. He was the younger of the two and, in his
personal character, he was an unethical trickster — from his very birth
in fact: "that the purpose of God according to election might stand,
not of works, but of Him that calleth" (Rom. 9:11).[10] God even
granted him the promise of the testament at the very moment he was
fleeing from home as a result of his crimes (Gen. 28:15).[11]

Malachi's post-exilic explanation, "I loved Jacob, but Esau I
hated" (Mal. 1:2, 3), then raises the question of the other side of
predestination, namely, that of a corresponding reprobation as applied
to the other twin. Jacob's election was indeed to salvation (he received the testament) and not merely to service or status in this
world;[12] but Malachi 1:3 relates. God's hatred of Esau simply to

---

[8]This, however, hardly warrants Vos' theories of a Semitic "inherited racial disposition," etc., *op. cit.*, pp. 72-76.
[9]Note also his unwarranted delay in Haran, Gen. 11:32.
[10]Rom. 9:16 goes on to exclude even the meritorious *attitude*, let alone any actual
works; for the very question of v. 19, "Why doth He yet find fault?" is meaningless if human worth or decision is allowed to enter into the picture.
[11]Cf. the renewal of the testament in conjunction with Jacob's own admission of
unworthiness (Gen. 32:10-12).
[12]Issue must here be taken with Rowley's claim: "They are not chosen for
what they are, or even primarily for what they shall be, but for the specific task
that is assigned them and for the service God requires of them," *The Biblical
Doctrine of Election* (London: Lutterworth Press, 1953), p. 95. On the contrary, the fundamental promise of the testament is that of personal reconciliation
with God.

the desolation of his earthly land of Edom. Esau himself may truly have participated in the testamental inheritance of redemption, for several generations later Edom still had pious men, such as Job of Uz and Eliphaz of Teman. But separation from Israel meant that eventually the Edomites became lost idolators; and the "reprobation" of Esau thus became an example of the true reprobation, that is, from salvation (Rom. 9:3; 10:1).

God's activity in personal reprobation received its first historical revelation in the Mosaic period, in respect to Pharaoh: ""For this cause have I raised thee up, to show thee My power, and that My name may be declared throughout all the earth" (Ex. 9:16). Compare in this regard Solomon's later conclusion, "Yahweh hath made everything for its¹³ own end, yea, even the wicked for the day of evil" (Prov. 16:4). Two points should be noted in this matter of reprobation, which Calvin himself called "the dreadful decree." The first is that God's eventual power in judgment is displayed because of the wickedness that men themselves do. That is, even though God raised up Pharaoh and makes the men who are wicked (the essential fact being that they are a part of His eternal decree), He is still not Himself the author of evil, as if it were He who made the men wicked. God must not be considered as a tyrant "pushing men down into hell"; for reprobation commences simply with preterition, God's decision to pass by some of lost mankind without applying to them the saving grace of His testament. The second point is that when the men He has thus raised up, sin, their sin, far from frustrating God, exists within His decree so as to declare His ultimate glory (Ps. 76:10). The permanent good that resulted from Pharaoh's temporary tyranny is a clear case in point.

The Old Testament brings out the truth of the eternal predestination of individuals to life or to death by means of the picture of God's "book of life." Its nature was first revealed through Moses (Ex. 32:32), who spoke of it as containing his own name: the book was significant of his standing as sinless before God. David used the "book of life" to indicate those who were accounted as righteous in God's sight (Ps. 69:28); and its anticipatory nature was shown by Isaiah's phrase which described the elect as literally "written for life in Jerusalem" (4:3). During the exile, Daniel predicted that deliverance at the end time would be for "every one that shall be found written in the book" (12:1).

B. NATIONAL ELECTION. With the Sinaitic testament (Mosaic period), God adopted Israel as His own, elect people (Ex. 6:7), and He is henceforth distinctively denominated, "Yahweh, God of Israel" (20:2). Moses, however, explained that even prior to this point God

---

¹³Or "for His own end." The "end" in either event is determined by God.

had been dealing with the nations on the basis of what their relations
would some day be with Israel (Deut. 32:8). From the first, the
primeval, period this fact had been shown on the one hand by God's
curse on Canaan (Gen. 9:25). The curse had come about, it is
true, because of the immoral conduct of Canaan's father Ham (v. 22;
cf. Hab. 2:15) and because of Ham's shameless publicizing of Noah's
disgrace, in which lewd characteristics the Canaanites came notoriously to participate.[14] But the curse was, at the same time, fulfilled by
the Israelitish national conquest of Canaan. On the other hand, the
table of nations (Gen. 10) had narrowed down and focused attention
first on Shem (cf. 9:26); then on Arpachshad in the Tigris-Euphrates
valley; then on Eber, whence comes the name "Hebrew" (10:21;
14:13), though other desert wanderers seem to have been descended
from him as well; and finally on Abraham. From the outset of the
patriarchal period, Abraham had been predicted to be the ancestor
of an elect nation (12:2), and Jacob had been named *Yisrā'ēl*, "he
who strives with God [and prevails]," not simply in a personal sense
(32:28) but also as the progenitor of the twelve elect tribes. Thus,
though God's choice of Israel was based upon His previous election
of the patriarchs (Deut. 7:9; 8:18; not on the people's own merit,
9:6), still the formation of the "holy" (separated) nation (Ex. 19:6;
Num. 23:9; Deut. 33:28) had been His goal from the very beginnings
of primeval history.[15]

Israel became the "people of inheritance" of the testament (Deut.
4:20). They were called of God to be His (Isa. 43:1). The Old Testament then employs a whole series of meaningful symbols to describe
the relationship of salvation that resulted. God is the "Rock of their
salvation" (Deut. 32:15), or their "Maker" (Isa. 45:11), just as the
potter who works the clay (64:8). God is their Caretaker, who provides for His vineyard (Isa. 5:4), or their Shepherd, who guides His
flock (Ps. 78:52; Isa. 40:11; Jer. 23:3). Israel, in turn, becomes God's
"peculiar treasure" (Ex. 19:5) or, as *s'ghullā* is more accurately expressed, His "special property" (cf. Ps. 135:4). Their relationship is
that of prized servants toward a loving master (Deut. 32:36) or of
a wife toward her husband. This last concept was first developed by
Hosea in the eighth century (3:1; cf. Isa. 50:1; 54:5; Jer. 2:2), though
it is implied in the Mosaic period when apostasy, and especially
idolatry, was defined as harlotry (Lev. 20:5; Num. 14:33). Apostasy
thus became punishable by death (Deut. 13:5; cf. Isa. 1:21; Ezek. 16).
Again, as the heir of the testament, Israel is called the adopted son
of the Father (Ex. 4:22; Deut. 32:6, 19, and frequently in the

---

[14]Gen. 15:16; Lev. 18:3; Deut. 9:4, 5; cf. Hengstenberg, *op. cit.*, I:35.
[15]The family, *am*, became also a *gōy*, or political state. Israel thus illustrates in
its own status a progressiveness of divine revelation, E. A. Speiser, " 'People' and
'Nation' of Israel," *Journal of Biblical Literature*, 79:2 (June, 1960), pp. 157-163.

prophets, Isa. 1:2; cf. Rom. 9:4).[16] It is noteworthy that the theory of a fatherhood of God for all mankind is nowhere taught in the Old Testament, not even of a universal fatherhood resulting from creation.[17] Only as many as receive Him under the testament have the right to become the adopted sons of God (Jer. 3:19; cf. John 1:12). Non-Israelitish nations, the gōyīm, are, accordingly, not simply foreigners, but "Gentiles [lost pagans]." Israel, on her part, was thus to make no alliance with her Canaanite neighbors because of the danger of apostasy (Ex. 34:16). To be separate, moreover, from the comonwealth of Israel meant to be "strangers from the testaments of promise, having no hope, and without God in the world" (Eph. 2:12). Scripture states bluntly that God loved Israel but hated the Edomites (Mal. 1:2, 3). The other nations of the world are reprobate, a "ransom" for the sake of the salvation of Israel (Isa. 43:3, 4).[18] Cyprian truly declared (minus, of course, the Romanist implications!) that there is no salvation outside of the Church.

Israel, furthermore, was a theocracy, a union of church and state. As demonstrated by the scope of the miracles in Egypt, God's election included the whole nation (Ex. 6:6, 7). He was the leader of the political group in its battles (Ex. 14:14; 15:1; 17:8; 23:22; Num. 10: 35), and one of Israel's collections of national poems was called "The Book of the Wars of Yahweh" (Num. 21:14). The nation was God's army (Ex. 7:4; 12:41), and God became in fact the King of Israel (Deut. 33:5). The early recognition of this divine rule appears in Balaam's oracle: "Yahweh his God is with him, and the shout of a King is among them" (Num. 23:21; cf. Ex. 15:18; Isa. 44:6). In the days when an additional human king should come, the choice of a monarch could fall only upon one of the election nation (not a foreigner), and then only upon that man whom God Himself should choose. His position would be that of a vice-regent under God (Deut. 17:15). Similarly, all legislative and judicial power lay in the hands of God; government did not originate, but was only mediated, through Moses (Ex. 18:16) and his assistants (v. 22). For this reason, Israel's judges[19] were called Elōhīm, divine representatives (Ex. 21:6; 22:8; cf. Ps. 82:6; John 10:34); and later David's sons as rulers were styled kōhēn, "priest," authorized ministers for God (II Sam. 8:18). This

[16]For elaboration on the Old Testament doctrine of adoption, and particularly in its individualistic application, see below, pp. 416, 417.

[17]Even Jer. 3:19, "I will put thee among the children and give thee a goodly heritage of the hosts of the nations," does not imply that the nations are the children, only that all Israel may join the elect children that are the Church; cf. Theo. Laetsch, Bible Commentary Jeremiah (St. Louis: Concordia Publishing House, 1952), p. 60. So Mal. 2:10, "Have we not all one father?"

[18]For this world-wide application of these verses, see J. A. Alexander, Isaiah (Grand Rapids: Zondervan, 1953), II:148-150.

[19]So the Authorized Version; the Revised Version reading, "God," appears to be influenced by the belief that early Israel held to a primitive concept of deity.

same administrative concept may apply to the Israelitish "priests," as they existed prior to Aaron (Ex. 19:22, 24), to Ira the Jairite (II Sam. 20:26), and to Zabud the son of Nathan (I Kings 4:5). As Isaiah summed it up, "Yahweh is our judge, Yahweh is our lawgiver, Yahweh is our king; He will save us!" (Isa. 33:22). Such theocratic election constituted, moreover, an effective basis for organized social control (cf. Ex. 21:20, as opposed to the former unlimited patriarchal power over life, Gen. 38:24); and in truth this union of civil and religious life *is* the ideal social relationship. As a form of government, it will some day be fully carried out in God's yet future theocratic kingdom (Zech. 14:20).[20]

Under the judges, in the period of consolidation, Gideon refused to accept the kingship that it might not reflect against Yahweh's theocratic rule (Judges 8:23). In Saul, Israel did at length gain a king. The rise of the kingdom was a development that was according to God's ultimate plan;[21] but the people's motivation in seeking the king made their actual request sinful. Specifically, they desired to "be like other nations" (II Sam. 8:5, 20); and this, in itself, constituted a repudiation both of the theocratic system and of its underlying principle of Israel's unique election under God. Yet even as the conquest and the victories of the judges had brought home to Israel the truth of their national election (Josh. 21:44; Judges 5:20, 31), so the leadership of Saul and David came to be recognized as a proof of God's primary rule over the people. The position of the kings was that of theocratic deputies, "fighting the battles of Yahweh" (I Sam. 18:17; 25:28). The king was God's minister to promote the faith. One of Saul's duties had been the destruction of God's enemies (15:3); David labored to prepare God's sanctuary (I Chron. 22:2); and the good among the kings carried out major reformations on the basis of God's law (though evil ones did about as they pleased).

God's having chosen a king was symbolized by his being anointed by a prophet (I Sam. 10:1; 16:3; I Kings 1:13), or high-priest (I Kings 1:39). The king was thus subject to God's directives: Saul, through Samuel (I Sam. 10:8); David, through Nathan (II Sam. 12:7); and Jeroboam, through Ahijah (I Kings 11:38). Refusal to sub-

---

[20]So in the original form of the Westminster Confession of Faith, on the obligation of the magistrate as a mediator of God's authority, chapter 23:3 reads, "It is his duty to take order . . . that the truth of God be kept pure and entire, that all blasphemies and heresies be suppressed . . . and all ordinances of God duly settled, administered and observed" (cf. Deut. 17:19). Vos' objection to the idea of the union of church and state, presently considered, as "an intolerable defect," *op. cit.*, p. 141, seems justifiable only when the condition is such that the true religion is *not* kept in a position of political dominance (cf. Acts 4:19, 20). When, however, evangelicals come to be in the minority and without political control, as is now generally the case, then a separation of church and state seems to be the only way to guarantee to the Christian the opportunity of rendering unto God that which is God's (Matt. 22:21).
[21]See above, p. 107.

mit to the will of God as declared by the prophet meant punishment
— for example, the rejection of Saul's dynasty (I Sam. 13:14). God
through His prophets and priests could depose one ruler and anoint
another — for example, Saul's personal rejection which followed upon
his dynastic rejection when the latter proved insufficient for his dis-
ciplining (I Sam. 15:26; 16:1; cf. I Kings 11:13; II Kings 9:6; 11:12).
But the king, as "Yahweh's anointed," was highly revered, and his
person was inviolable (I Sam. 12:3; 24:6; Ps. 20:6). Yet at the same
time Israel's monarchy was a "constitutional" one, in that the king's
authority was limited by God's law; cf. Samuel's written description
of the government that was laid up before Yahweh (I Sam. 10:25).
Furthermore, Israel occupied a unique position in the history of the
Near East in its demonstration of an essential democracy. For all
Israelites were potentially God's elect under the testament; and with
this God-given standing they could, by their own election, confirm
the anointing of an approved king (I Sam. 11:15; II Sam. 2:4; 5:3[22]),
or they could refuse to submit to a ruler who flouted God's standards
(I Kings 12:1, 4, 16). But Israel's was not a pattern of government that
is capable of wide application, for it is only when self-interest has
been subordinated to God's law that men can be trusted to govern
themselves. A later lawless democracy (as in II Kings 15:10, 14; Hos.
8:4) produced anarchy. Only a vital, Christian experience of submission to God as King can make men good enough for a democracy!

David's associates, the Korahites, poetically demonstrated the
truth of Israel's national election by equating a man's being "born in
Jerusalem" with his salvation (Ps. 87:5, 6). Isaiah, moreover, explicitly stated that the purpose of Israel's national existence was for
the glorifying of God (Isa. 43:7, 21). But the eighth century prophets
went on to condemn the way in which Israel mixed in with the life
of the surrounding pagans, which amounted to a denial of their election with its national distinctives (Hos. 7:8). This, in turn, led to
God's rejection of Israel as a unique group (Amos 9:7, 8). National
disaster then became but a matter of time, for they had violated the
statutes and broken the everlasting testament (Isa. 24:5).

C. THE REMNANT. Even with the appearance of the national
election of Israel, individual election continued; for in every period
each individual, as he was enabled by God, had personally to meet
the testamental conditions in order to receive the divine inheritance
(cf. Gen. 17:14). Primeval sin thus left only an eight-person remnant after the flood (Gen. 6-8). Then within the elect family of Abraham (patriarchal period), only Isaac of all his sons was chosen to
receive the promise (17:19-21). Next, as Rowley goes on to state,

---

[22]David's covenant with Israel in this verse indicates a definite and mutually
formulated compact, on the basis of which he was to reign and they were to be
ruled.

". . . of the children of Isaac one inherited the election and the other did not. Here, so early, was the seed of the doctrine of the Remnant. The heritage of the promises was not automatic, but something that needed to be accepted."[23]

Among Joseph's sons, God's choice of Ephraim over Manasseh (48: 14) concerned political prominence in the period of settlement (Judg. 12:1-4), not religion; but Judah's election in preference to his three older brothers did involve spiritual privileges. The initial selection of Judah was indeed due, negatively, to the sins that his elder brothers had committed — Reuben's of incest (Gen. 49:4) and Simeon's and Levi's of violence (v. 7); and subsequently Judah's distinction concerned only his position of national leadership (I Chron. 5:2). But eventually this selection came to involve the appearance of Christ in Judah's line and the preservation of this one tribe as the largest single element of the post-exilic remnant of Israel.

The true remnant doctrine, however, concerns the salvation of a small, faithful group out of a larger, original group to whom the revelation of election had been extended. The concept of the "remnant," therefore, first appears from Moses' threats, after the fulfillment of which would come deliverance for a faithful minority (Lev. 26:39, 44). The wilderness wanderings then went on to demonstrate that though many are called, only a remnant are really chosen (Ps. 95:10, 11; cf. Matt. 22:14). In fact, only two, Caleb and Joshua (Num. 14:30), were allowed to "enter into God's rest"; though Canaan's existence as a symbol of heaven (Heb. 4:11) need not mean that *all* who failed to enter the land, as Moses himself, were automatically deprived of heaven. Judgment for sin would not thus frustrate election (Lev. 26: 44); Israel would never be completely destroyed or the testament broken (Deut. 30:1-5). Moses also specified certain, select groups from among the whole nation as potential "remnant leaders." The Nazarites (Num. 6:1-8) took their name from the Hebrew word *nāzîr*, meaning "one in consecrated separation." They were a group set apart,[24] though the nation later corrupted them (Amos 2:12). The Levites distinguished themselves as men "who were on the Lord's side" (Ex. 32:25-28) and who remained faithful to the testament during the golden calf apostasy (Deut. 33:9). They, too, were particularly set apart (10:8). Finally the Aaronic priests (Ex. 28:41) were specially chosen under the Levitical testament (Num. 25:13) and received the priesthood as a gift of service by divine election (18:7).[25]

During the consolidation period and the rise of the united kingdom, there was little occasion to speak of a remnant. But, in the disruption that followed, and particularly in opposition to the wide-

---

[23]*Op. cit.*, p. 71.
[24]See below, topic 29-E.
[25]See below, topic 27-A, for further detail.

spread ninth century apostasy that was led by Jezebel, there appeared a remnant of 7000 who, as Elijah was told, had not bowed the knee to Baal (I Kings 19:18). A leading group within this remnant were the Rechabites, led by Jonadab, who later assisted in Jehu's reform against the house of Ahab in 841 B.C. (II Kings 10:15-23). The Rechabites, however, kept a mental association between their preservation of the true faith and their preservation of their own Kenite, nomadic background (I Chron. 2:55). They thus rejected the custom of living in permanent houses and the practice of agriculture, along with the worship of Baal (Jer. 35:7). Still, such social "props" for religion are not without value. If religion can be maintained only at the sacrifice of certain standards of living, then it is much better that those standards give way. The Christian must make no provision for the desires of the unregenerate nature (Rom. 13:14): the spiritual needs are far more important than the physical (Matt. 5:30). So the Rechabites eliminated all grape growing, as well as the specific act of drinking wine (Jer. 35:6). If the remnant were to preserve their testimony and win over the wavering, error had to be eliminated drastically. Subsequent examples include Elijah's slaying of the 450 prophets of Baal (I Kings 18:40) and Jehu's similar zeal against Baal's worshipers (II Kings 10:25).

Isaiah became God's preeminent voice for the revelation of the remnant doctrine. He commenced his ministry by noting that political disaster had already left Judah only a small "remnant" (Isa. 1:9); though the Hebrew term that is here employed, *sārīdh*, is used only this once in Isaiah and concerns simply a quantitative, rather than a spiritual remnant. The term Isaiah chose for describing the faithful remnant is *sh'ār*. *Sh'ār* appears, significantly, in the descriptive title that Isaiah gave to one of his sons, *Sh'ār yāshūv* (7:3). The name means, "A remnant shall return," the returning being not only from exile, but primarily to Yahweh (10:20-23). The main body of the people, that is, would be destroyed in punishment for sin (3:16); and their destruction would be thorough: one man left for every seven women (4:1); or, only a part of one-tenth (6:13); or, like the gleanings left on a harvested olive tree (17:6; cf. 30:17). Israel had been selected to be God's servant (49:3); but the servant was proving himself to be blind and deaf to his divine Master (42:18-20; 43:8), had become weary of God (v. 22), and was refusing Him the honor to which He was entitled (vv. 23, 24). To use another figure, Israel was God's bride, but because of her faithlessness she would have to suffer "divorce," being sold to conquering pagans (50:1; Hos. 2:2). But in the midst of apostasy there yet persisted a faithful remnant, including Isaiah himself, the disciples of the Messiah. They would be God's real servants and preserve Yahweh's "law," *tōrā* (teaching), even though others disregarded it (Isa. 8:16). Fundamentally, the saved status of this remnant group was due to their individual election as members of Christ's Church, for our Lord Himself spoke of them saying, "Behold, I and the children whom Yahweh hath given Me" (v. 18).[26] Their very existence was a miraculous sign, ōth, of God's continuing election (v. 18); and as the Messiah "waited" (v. 17), they became the hope for the eventual restoration of the whole nation.[27] Even the faithful few, however, were to prove insufficient for effectuating the testamental redemption; and the "Servant" is finally reduced to one Person (49:5). This One was the heir of all things (Heb. 1:2), who would truly "restore the preserved of Israel" (Isa. 49:6) by becoming Himself the personalized testament (v. 8).

In the later prophetic period the northern kingdom was replaced by the Samaritans, who showed themselves to be eclectic (II Kings 17:28) and ultimately pagan (vv. 29-32). Though they claimed Jacob as their own father (cf. John 4:12), they came to be excluded from the remnant of Israel (cf. Ezra 4:3). But the remaining Southern Kingdom had also to face the day of God's wrath in the form of the exilic desolation (Zeph. 1:14-18); from Judah too it would be but a "remnant" that would afterward return (2:7, 9; Jer. 31:1-7). In the same vein, the exilic prophets predicted the return of a remnant to rebuild Israel (Ezek. 17:22, 23), though such a restoration could transpire only after the nation's sinners had been purged away in captivity (20:40-43). But upon the historical return in 538 B.C., it developed that there were still sinners, thieves and false swearers among the "elect" nation. These then would have to be eliminated (Zech. 5:3); and at that same period, some seem to have removed themselves from the faithful remnant, being naturally attracted to Babylonian Shinar (vv. 8-11). They were providentially "drained off." In time, however, Israel would climax her sin by smiting the very "Good Shepherd" whom God would send to them (13:7). Thus, even as God had to give them up until the time that "she who travaileth" (the virgin Mary) had brought forth (Micah 5:3), so the Jews would have still to pass through what has proved to be two millennia of refining fire (Zech. 13:9). The main body, in fact, has not yet submitted to Yahweh and to His Christ, though some day they will recognize Him (v. 9). But in that day, when the Son of Man comes again (Dan. 7:13), He will no longer appear alone, as the epitome of the remnant; but He will stand as the representative figure for all the saints of the Most High (cf. vv. 22, 27; Zech. 13:1). Meanwhile, how-

---

[26]As demonstrated by Heb. 2:13, the speaker in Isa. 8:18 must be the "my" immediately preceding, the stone (v. 14) and divine redeemer, Christ, and not Isaiah himself, whom He addresses as "thou" (v. 16); cf. Alexander, *op. cit.*, I:126.
[27]Thus Scripture can speak of a "second" election, "choosing Israel again" (Isa. 14:1; cf. Zech. 1:17), the initial election of the group having been frustrated by their own apostasy and resultant rejection.

ever, the New Testament fulfillment shows that when the Messiah
came the first time He was accepted by only an elect remnant of the
nation of Israel (Rom. 11:5). Many of the descendants of Israel (the
patriarch Jacob) proved that they were not really of Israel (the true
Church, 9:6). Micah, however, had predicted long before that there
would then arise another remnant, not previously a part of Israel, to
take their place — "Then the residue of His brethren shall return unto
the children of Israel" (Mic. 5:3). This residue must be the elect
Christians from among the Gentiles, which serves to introduce the
next section:

D. THE UNIVERSAL MISSION. Man's election is to glorify God
(Rom. 11:36). Within this overall purpose, however, Biblical election
serves a two-fold aim: first, to bring wandering men back to God, to
gain salvation for those who are lost; but also, to employ the men
thus saved in the performance of service for God (Titus 2:14).[28] So
Israel was elect, first, as a means by which men should be saved prior
to the coming of Christ, but also as a means by which to prepare for
that saving advent of the Lord. With the privilege of particularism
there thus appears the responsibility of service, of a mission on the
part of the elect. This mission, moreover, proves to be nothing short
of God's original goal of universalistic evangelism. The initial two
testaments, the Edenic and Noachian, had been universal in their
scope. But then God's association with mankind had become more
restricted and He was distinguished as being particularly the God of
Shem. Simultaneously, however, there appeared the first indication of
the ultimately re-enlarged goal. This restored inclusiveness for revelation and redemption was expressed by the words "And let him
[Japheth][29] dwell in the tents of Shem" (Gen. 9:27). The phrase,
"dwell in the tents of," may carry the idea of conquest (Ps. 78:55);
and, since the time of the conquest of Babylon by the Persians in
538 B.C., the descendants of Japheth *have* generally exercised political
domination over the Semites. But the phrase may also refer to a
sharing in hospitality (Ps. 84:10; 120:5); and, since Genesis 9:26, 27 is
intended to be a blessing on Shem and Japheth, and not a curse, this
latter meaning appears to be the preferable one. Genesis 9:27 thus becomes a prediction of a participation by Gentiles in the gracious
blessings of the testimonial promise that was given to Shem (Rom.
11:11).

---

[28]See above, p. 179, and note 12.
[29]Against the alternate rendering, "But let Him [God] dwell in the tents of
Shem," it should be noted: 1) it is not Yahweh, the immanent Saviour (cf. v.
26), who would do the dwelling, but Elohim, for whom the thought would be
less congruous; 2) to "dwell in the tents of" is a recurrent idiom, but never with
God as the subject; 3) in v. 27, the first and third clauses concern Japheth, so
presumably this center clause should as well; 4) even as v. 25 concerned Canaan,
and v. 26 Shem, so poetic balance suggests Japheth for all of v. 27; and 5) a
statement marking Japheth as inferior to Shem would be out of order in a context of blessing such as this is.

The earlier universalism had failed in the Flood and then at the tower of Babel; but the particularistic preparation of a spiritual nucleus would make effective a restored inclusiveness when the fullness of time should come (Gal. 4:4).

Abraham, in the patriarchal period, represented the extreme of particularism — the restriction of the testament to one person. But even the Abrahamic context contains two indications of a more ultimate universalism. 1) Others could share in Abraham's blessing. The following are the most prominent examples: Abraham's servants, hundreds of them (Gen. 14:14) who were circumcised so as to participate in the testament (17:13, 27); Hagar, the Egyptian, who came to have a genuine faith in Yahweh (16:13); and Melchizedek, whose commitment to *El Elyōn* was recognized by Abraham as constituting a form of the true worship of Yahweh (14:14).[30] Then 2) it was predicted that because of Abraham's election, all the families of the earth should be blessed (12:3; 18:18). The verb *nivr'khū*, "be blessed," has a possible alternative rendering which appears in the Revised Standard Version, namely, "bless themselves" (and cf. 18:18). That is, according to the RSV, Abraham would be so prosperous that people would seek him as the means for invoking blessings on themselves.[31] This less spiritual meaning, however, must be rejected. In the first place, there exists another form which arises from this same verbal root and which does mean exclusively "bless themselves" (26: 4),[32] with which *nivr'khū* would thus seem to be contrasted. In the second place, the inspired New Testament quotes *nivr'khū* as having a passive meaning (Gal. 3:8), which shows that the one Holy Spirit intended to convey this same meaning, namely, "be blessed," in Genesis 12:3 and 18:18 also. [33] The promise of universal blessing was later repeated to Jacob (28:14), where God specified that it would be effectuated by the Messianic seed.[34]

At Sinai, with the establishment of the theocracy of the elect nation of Israel, universalism was necessarily pushed into the background. For the sake of her own faith, Israel was ordered to shun both Canaanitish religion and those who practiced it. A non-Israelite

[30]Though Melchizedek may still have been saved on the basis of the older (universalistic) Noachian revelation.
[31]On the basis of Jer. 4:2, the meaning is not "to use him as a comparison for invoking blessings on themselves," cf. Oehler, *Theology of the Old Testament*, p. 62.
[32]This *hithpa'el* form is also used in 22:18. The quotation of this latter verse as a passive in Acts 3:25 suggests that the Holy Spirit was at that point combining the ideas of two different verses: the Messianic character of Gen. 22:18, "the seed," and the universalistic blessing of 12:3. The latter fact, however, was not contained in the original Gen. 22:18 revelation. Cf. Vos, *op. cit.*, p. 91.
[33]On the anti-evangelical bias of the RSV, see Payne, "The RSV of the O.T. and Higher Criticism," *Evangelical Theological Society*, 1952 Papers, pp. 6-10, and his pamphlet, *A Criticism of the Revised Standard Version of the Bible*, 1952.
[34]See below, topic 20-A.

was called *nokhrī,* "a foreigner," if he was not permanently associated with Israel, or *gēr,* "a stranger," if he had taken up residence in the land. The *gēr* might be rich (Lev. 25:47); but he seems more often to have suffered under low economic status (Deut. 29:11), and hence to have become subject to oppression. The Mosaic legislation accordingly protected him, along with the widow and the orphan; and Israel was reminded that they too had been a *gēr* in the land of Egypt (Deut. 10:19).

But the Sinaitic testament, though particularistic, was not exclusivistic. A large "mixed multitude" had been allowed to come up with Israel out of Egypt (Ex. 12:38), even though these proselytes later caused considerable trouble (Lev. 24:10; Num. 11:4). Moses' Kenite brother-in-law, Hobab, was invited to share in Israel's blessing (Num. 10:29); and the faith of his descendants later became noteworthy (Judges 4:11; 5:24). Finally, the Kenizzite brothers, Caleb and Othniel (Num. 32:12); Judges 1:13), not only were adopted into the tribe of Judah; they proved themselves to be spiritually superior to most of the native Israelites. No *nokhrī* or hired servant could eat the passover (Ex. 12:43, 45). But, as in the case of Abraham's men years before, purchased servants were to be circumcised; and they could then share in the full blessings of the testament (v. 44). The *gēr* also was invited to receive circumcision and to enter into the testament (v. 48). Once, moreover, having thus become a proselyte, he was granted full equality in Israel and was subject to no further discrimination (v. 49; cf. Gal. 5:3). Only Ammonites and Moabites, and of course Canaanites, were excluded from Israel (Deut. 23:3); while the full participation of Edomites and Egyptians was put off to the third generation (vv. 7, 8). Some of the statements that Moses recorded in the Pentateuch have a universalistic application, for example: "All the earth shall be filled with the glory of Yahweh" (Num. 14:21). But, though this expression was later amplified by the prophets to include the concept of universal blessing (Isa. 11:9), its original meaning was one of universal punishment (cf. Ex. 9:16; Hab. 2:14)! Still, the very terms of the Sinaitic testament included the thought of a broader mission. For Israel's purpose was one of service — they were to become a "sovereignty (not a self-contained 'kingdom') of priests" (Ex. 19:6), so that through Israel salvation might be mediated to the world as a whole.[35]

During the conquest, the Gibeonites saved themselves from destruction and were enabled to live with Israel (Josh. 9:15). But Gibeon achieved this toleration only by deceit (v. 9), and its people were degraded to a menial status in Hebrew society (v. 23). More commendable were the exceptional cases of Rahab, a Canaanite and

---

[35] G. A. F. Knight particularly stresses the missionary call of Israel; cf. *A Christian Theology of the Old Testament,* p. 8.

a harlot, yet spared because of her faith and works (Josh. 2:11),[36] and of Ruth, the Moabitish widow, who accepted Yahweh as her God (Ruth 1:16) and "under whose wings she came to take refuge" (2:12). These two women are among those who are singled out for mention in the geneology of Christ Himself (Matt. 1:5). David, in the next period, recognized the obligation, both of himself personally and of Israel nationally, to witness to God among the *gōyim*, the pagan nations (Ps. 18:49; cf. 9:11; 57:9). Thus Ittai the Philistine was but one of the king's faithful foreigners who had come to know Yahweh (II Sam. 15:21); and David foresaw the day when princes should come unto God from the lands of Egypt and Ethiopia (Ps. 68:31). Indeed, all the nations that God had made (86:9; cf. 22:29) would some day come and worship before Him. Solomon, too, in his prayer at the dedication of the Temple, anticipated a universal worship of Yahweh in Jerusalem (I Kings 8:41-43); and he wrote of the divine Wisdom who cries out to all peoples (Prov. 8:4; cf. 1:20; 9:3). Elijah, though the bitter enemy of Sidonian Baalism, yet performed great miracles for the Sidonian widow (I Kings 17:8-24), who trusted Yahweh (v. 24); and Elisha, by his cure of Naaman's leprosy, gained a sincere proselyte out of the ranks of Israel's enemies. It is interesting that the Syrian's imperfect view of God's localization led him to take home with him a two mules' load of Palestinian soil so he could worship the Lord! (II Kings 5:17). Such cases were exceptional, but they kept alive the truth that there lay within Israel a salvation that was for all who would receive it.

The ultimately universal direction of the Gospel received its highest Old Testament expression in the writings of the eighth century prophets. Amos saw that both divine punishment (Amos 1:3-2:3) and divine guidance (9:7) embraced the Gentile nations just as it did Israel. Isaiah, the most universalistic of all the prophets, saw that the Jews who had been scattered into other lands in his own time, and those who yet would be (the "Diaspora," John 7:35; James 1:1), would serve as voices for the glorifying of God (Isa. 24:14-16). Egypt, in particular, would be granted a witness, even an altar (19:18, 19), which may perhaps have been fulfilled in the erection of a Temple at Leontopolis (of doubtful legality) by Onias IV in the second century B.C. But Isaiah's prophecies went on to include direct, divine appeals to all people:: "Look unto Me, and be ye saved, all the ends of the earth" (45:22). In Isaiah the *nokhri* who loves Yahweh and keeps His sabbaths is encouraged to lay fast hold on the testament (56:6);[37] and the Lord Himself promises, "My house shall be called

---

[36]For a similar exception to the curse on Canaan, cf. Matt. 15:22 and the acceptance of the Canaanitish (specifically, Phoenician) woman by Christ.
[37]In a similar vein, Isa. 56:3-5 grants permission to eunuchs who keep the sabbath and the testaments to participate in the congregation in a way that had not been previously allowed (Deut. 23:1).

a house of prayer for all nations" (v. 7). This universal invitation would be proclaimed in a preeminent way through the life of the Messianic Servant who would be a light to the Gentiles (42:6; 49:6). They would, as a result, become an engrafted part of Israel, "calling themselves by the name of Jacob" (44:5). Egypt, Assyria, and Israel together would be God's people (19:25). The climax would come when, with the establishment of the testament of peace, converted Gentiles would be appointed missionaries to the rest of the world (66:19) and every knee should bow to the God who had come to reign (25:7; 45:23).

So Hosea predicted that the Gentiles would become sons of God, even as Israel had been (Hos. 1:10; cf. Rom. 9:24-26); Obadiah (v. 21) widened the kingdom concept to extend beyond the geographical borders of Israel; and Micah painted the picture of many nations going up to Jerusalem to hear the word of Yahweh (Mic. 4:1-4; cf. Isa. 2:2-4; 11:10). The book of Jonah, in particular, served to heap ridicule upon nationalistic exclusivism (Jonah 1:17); and while other prophets simply predicted, Jonah actually went to Assyria and preached to the Gentiles. His life indeed constitutes the most significant missionary activity that is recorded prior to New Testament times (3:10; 4:11). He succeeded in accomplishing a valid, though brief, reformation in Nineveh, probably during the unsettled period of Assyrian history that climaxed in the confusion surrounding the eclipse of 763 B.C.[38] Meanwhile at home in Palestine, a certain missionary awareness is shown to have existed in Judah when the gēr from the formerly northern Israelitish territory were welcomed by Hezekiah to participate in his great passover of 725 B.C. (II Chron. 30:25).

The later prophets were less emphatic about Israel's universal mission, but they carried on the same message. Jeremiah noted that all nations possessed the same opportunity for repentance (Jer. 18:7) and could be built up as a part of God's people if they would but forsake their pagan vanities (16:19) and "learn the ways of Israel" (12:16; though cf. Isa. 16:2, which cautions that the prayers of idolatrous pagans will not be heard). Zephaniah looked forward to the day when other gods would be removed and all nations would worship Yahweh (Zeph. 2:11) with a "pure [non-idolatrous] lip" (3:9).

In the exile, Ezekiel noted a greater receptivity to the things of God on the part of Gentiles than on the part of Israel (Ezek. 3:6). Ezekiel assigned to the gēr (presumably converted) an equal share with the native Israelites in the post-exilic distribution of the land of Palestine (47:22). Then, in the final testament of peace, he recognized the participation of other nations as "daughters" of Israel. This participation, however, became possible only upon the basis of their association with Israel; for the nations were essentially extra-testa-

---

[38]Cf. Payne, *An Outline of Hebrew History,* pp. 132-133.

mental, while God had promised to Israel, "I will establish My testament with thee" (16:61, 62).[39] Hence Ezekiel demanded the exclusion of the *nokhri*, the foreigner, "uncircumcised in heart[40] and uncircumcised in flesh," from the post-exilic sanctuary (44:9).[41] It is interesting, though, to observe Ezekiel's description of Israel's former willingness to admit them, even to the extent of breaking the testament (44:7). Daniel, too, as he was inspired to predict the profanation of the Temple by Antiochus IV in 168-165 B.C., warned against the opposition of the foreign world to God's testament (Dan. 11:28, 30, 32).

Thus there existed in post-exilic days a tension. On the one hand, the very restoration of Judah had as one of its goals the providing of a witness to the nations of the truth of God (Ps. 102:15; 126:2). Isaiah had indeed predicted this very thing (48:20). Psalm 117:1, accordingly, calls on all nations to praise God; and Esther 9:27 speaks of numerous proselytes joined to Israel. Zechariah explicitly predicted the conversion of the remnant of the Philistines to God (Zech. 9:7), an event which took place, forcibly, under Jonathan the brother of Judas Maccabaeus in 148-46 B.C. (I Macc. 10:86-89; 11:60-62). Zechariah spoke also of the way in which many nations would join themselves to Israel at the time of God's incarnation, when He Himself would be with them (2:4, 5, 10, 11); and he described how, in the ultimate kingdom, God would be worshiped in Jerusalem by all of those that should be left of the nations (14:9, 16). Finally, Malachi foresaw the universal Church when "from the rising of the sun even unto the going down of the same My name shall be great among the Gentiles" (Mal. 1:11). Yet on the other hand, Esther 3:8 makes it clear that the dispersed Jews as a group did not integrate with society; they had "laws that were diverse from those of every people." Ezra and Nehemiah maintained a constant emphasis upon Israel's separation from the Samaritans, and from every other type of foreigner, as being necessary for the preservation of the faith (Ezra 10:3; Neh. 10:30; 13:25).

In time, two groups arose, both of which were extreme and actually perverted the testamental concept. There were the compromisers who included most of the priests, who mingled with the world (cf. Neh. 13:4) but had no witness to it. They eventually forfeited their own salvation. This group developed into the New Testament Sadducees. But the exclusivists, which included most of the scribes,

---

[39]Cf. Keil, *Biblical Commentary on the Prophecies of Ezekiel* (Grand Rapids: William B. Eerdmans Publishing Co., 1950), I:230-232.
[40]The exclusion of such godless foreigners, therefore, constitutes no contradiction of Solomon's invitation to pious foreigners (I Kings 8:41).
[41]This injunction was carefully observed in New Testament times (Acts 21:28, 29); and archaeology has produced one of the inscriptions that warned foreigners, on pain of death, against entering the prohibited areas of Herod's temple.

degenerated into a sect of the proudly self-righteous. Thus, though they compassed sea and land to make one proselyte, their zeal succeeded only in making the convert twofold more a son of hell than themselves (Matt. 23:15). From this group arose the hypocritical Pharisees. But in the Church, Israel's purpose of universalism lies fulfilled. The Church is in all the world, but it is not of the world (John 17:14-16). Christians are both the elect remnant out of the world (I Pet. 2:8, 9) and yet also the sovereignty of priests who are to mediate salvation to the world (Rev. 1:6) and who are some day to reign in glory over it (2:26; 5:10). We are elect, both to privilege and to responsibility.

For Further Reading:

Oswald T. Allis, "The Blessing of Abraham," *Princeton Theological Review,* 25:2 (April, 1927), 263-298. A thorough discussion of the passive vs. the reflexive meanings of the blessing.
John Bright, *The Kingdom of God.* Nashville, Tenn.: Abingdon-Cokesbury Press, 1953. Neo-orthodox, but includes an up-to-date discussion on theocracy in the Old Testament.
J. H. Y. Phythian-Adams, *The Call of Israel.* London: Oxford University Press, 1934). *The Fulness of Israel.* London: 1938. And other volumes. Neo-orthodox studies on the Church as the fulfillment of Israel.

15. The Sinful Race*

The doctrine of divine election would have raised questions relative to the fairness of God's dealings with mankind only if all men had possessed a neutral standing before God.[1] Mankind has, however, forfeited any right it may once have had to an impartial treatment by the Father, for men today are members of a sinful race and are guilty, specifically, of violating the gracious testament (Mal. 2:10). In fact, the very existence of the testament, which grants reconciliation with God, assumes man's need for such a reconciliation. The testamental concept, therefore, implies the prior reality of sin and of man's alienation from God.

A. THE NATURE OF SIN. The uniform presentation of Scripture is that sin is man's failure to conform to the will of the divine Testator. In its first appearance, sin consisted of disobedience to the *b'rith* conditions (Gen. 2:17; 3:11); and subsequently, "they, like Adam

---

*BIBLE READING: Psalm 51; II Chronicles 36:5-21

Collateral Reading: Vos, *Biblical Theology,* pp. 56-64, 284-285, 294-303.
Otto J. Baab, *The Theology of the Old Testament* (Nashville, Tenn.: Abingdon-Cokesbury Press, c. 1949), pp. 84-113.

---

[1]See above, p. 177, and note 2.

have transgressed the covenant: there have they dealt treacherously against Me" (Hos. 6:7; cf. Josh. 7:11, 15; Ps. 50:10 [Asaph's]; Jer. 11:10; Ezek. 16:59). "They have transgressed the laws, violated the statutes, broken the everlasting testament" (Isa. 24:5). Men may, it is true, commit disobedience to the testament in thought as well as in act (Ex. 20:3, 17), since evil comes from the heart (Gen. 6:5). But whether concealed or overt, disobedience is always dependent upon God's word, "the authority which validates all regulations," whether secular or religious.[2] Vos, for example, points out that the strength of Biblical humanitarianism lies not in a humanitarian but in a religious motivation.[3] Thus, even the greatest social commandment, "Thou shalt love thy neighbor as thyself," is grounded in religion and becomes compulsive because, specifically, "I am Yahweh" (Lev. 19:18); and Yahweh means "the One who is present" checking up! Hence David, after breaking Commands VI and VII of the Decalogue, could say, "Against Thee, Thee only have I sinned" (Ps. 51:4). Again, it was feelings of *religious* insecurity that seem to have prompted the first sacrifice (Gen. 4:3) and that certainly produced Cain's concern when his own particular offering was rejected (v. 5). On this same basis, moreover, any failure to do the right which has been commanded by God, becomes as serious as an actual commission of wrong (cf. I Sam. 3:13). Similarly, man's ritual sin, or error, consists of an identical failure to conform to God's, perhaps arbitrary (though often typical), prescriptions (Gen. 9:4; 17:14; I Sam. 14:33). Though conceivably involving neither "moral judgment or reflective reason,"[4] and even when committed in ignorance (Lev. 4:2), his sin produces a guilt that is nonetheless real.

The Old Testament terms for sin demonstrate the reality of this theocentric orientation. All seven of these terms were revealed early, and they show little development in meaning throughout the course of sacred history. Used in the Biblical record of the primeval period to represent whatever may have been the actual words employed before the linguistic disruption at Babel are the three Hebrew nouns, *hattāth, āwōn,* and *ra. Hattāth*[5] is translated "sin." It was first used in Genesis 4:7 and comes from the root which means *to miss the mark in shooting* (Judg. 20:16; cf. Job 5:24). Hence, the *hattāth* is what misses God's standard. *Āwōn* is rendered "iniquity" (Gen. 4:13; 15:

---

[2] This uniformity of dependence upon the authority of God's word explains the otherwise almost indiscriminating mingling of secular and religious ordinances within Israel's law codes, Baab, *The Theology of the Old Testament* (Nashville, Tenn.: Abingdon-Cokesbury Press, 1949), p. 92.
[3] Vos, *Biblical Theology,* p. 295.
[4] Baab, *op. cit.,* pp. 99-100, fails to grasp the full import of this fact that law consists of divine, testamental requirements. "Behavior patterns" and "the ideal of community integration," which he suggests, cannot substitute for the will of God.
[5] The same word is later used for "sin-offering," see below, topic 27-C.

16) and has as its basic idea that of crookedness (Lam. 3:9). The *āwōn* is thus what twists away from God's straightness; and it goes further than *hattāth* in that it indicates a wrong intention. Its extended meanings include the guilt that arises from iniquity (Gen. 44:16), or even the punishment that must result from it (as in the initial reference, 4:13). *Ra*, "evil," is the earliest term of all (2:9); but its root meaning is uncertain. It may perhaps signify a loud noise. *Ra* would thus suggest a physical calamity or a violent breaking (of God's orders).

Under the patriarchs, there appeared two additional terms. *Résha* is translated "wickedness." The adjectival form of *résha* occurs in Genesis 18:23 and comes from the idea of "loose," or "ill-regulated." The noun thus signifies a raging (Job 3:17) against God. *Pésha* means "transgression" (Gen. 50:17) and comes from the root "to rebel" (I Kings 12:19). It, therefore, describes man's rebellion against God. Since the *pésha* is a deliberate and premeditated transgression, it becomes more serious than the earlier terms for sin. Job 34:37 therefore speaks of adding *pésha* to *hattāth*.

Moses, in the next period, seems to have been the medium for introducing two final terms descriptive of man's sin. *Má'al* is translated "trespass" (Lev. 5:15). The verb form in Numbers 5:12 is used to identify marital faithlessness; so *má'al* means basically treachery or faithlessness to the God of the testament (I Chron. 9:1). *Awel*, or *awlā*, is rendered "perversity" (Lev. 19:15). Both nouns stem from a verbal root that means "to deviate." The verb itself is not used in Scripture, but it suggests that *awlā* is best understood as signifying man's deviation from the right course marked out by Yahweh.

Scripturally, the most condemned sinful practice is that of idolatry; for idolatry amounts to one's substituting another loyalty for that which he owes to God. Moses, accordingly, calls this breach of faith "harlotry" (Lev. 20:5). For though the idols are essentially *elīlīm* (Lev. 19:4; 26:1), "things of naught,"[6] they still drew Israel away from her true, divine Husband. Samuel, in the consolidation period, took up the idea of the futility of idolatry by applying to it the term *āwen* (I Sam. 15:23). The root meaning of *āwen* is "to be tired" (cf. Ezek. 24:12), and in earlier periods the word had meant simply "trouble" (Gen. 35:18; Num. 23:21). But since there are no other gods, and since idols are but "weary shadows," Samuel could, with appropriateness, use it for idolatry. Then with David and subsequently, *āwen* came to mean "wickedness" in general. Hosea, however, in the eighth century, took advantage of the presence of a small town near Bethel named Bethaven (*bēth āwen*, Josh. 7:2) to condemn Bethel's having become a seat for idolatry: he repeatedly called the city not *Bēth-Ēl*, "house of God," but *Bēth-āwen*, "house of naught

6See above, p. 126.

(idols)" (Hos. 4:15; 5:8; 10:8; cf. 12:11). The prophets, furthermore, looked behind Israel's idolatrous acts to the hearts of those who were involved. Just as in the writings of Moses, they labeled such sin as harlotry (Isa. 1:21). Again, they marked it down as the failure of the filial love that was due to their heavenly Father (1:2, 3), or they condemned it as symbolizing Israel's ingratitude toward their Redeemer from bondage (Micah 6:2-4).

But basic to idolatry, and indeed to all other transgressions, is the sin of pride, the desire of the rebellious race to become as God. In the primeval garden, this furnished the original temptation to mankind (Gen. 3:5). Pride was the cause for the tower of Babel (11:4); and Elihu's authoritative analysis of Job's problem explained suffering as an aspect of God's attempt to "withdraw man from his purpose: [namely,] pride" (Job 33:17). Isaiah saw Babylon's sin summed up in her "making herself like the Most High" (Isa. 14:13, 14; cf. Tyre, Ezek. 28:2); and Hosea grieved, "My people are destroyed for lack of knowledge," not for a lack of factual information, but for their lack of a submissive heart-acknowledgment of God (Hos. 4:1, 6).

B. THE RELATIONSHIP OF GOD TO HUMAN SIN. God, who lays down the standards of the testament, is Himself sovereignly free in His actions.[7] He may smite, or He may bind up (Hos. 6:1). He is King over all that transpires (Dan. 4:35); yet He always acts in accordance with His own inherently righteous standard (Gen. 18:25). It therefore becomes necessary to define the exact relationship that God sustains to the sinfulness of the human race, particularly when the Word makes statements about reprobation, such as "Yahweh hath made everything for its own end, yea, even the wicked for the day of evil" (Prov. 16:4).[8]

The theological difficulties that seem to be contained in certain verses are actually more apparent than real, being due to misleading English translations of the Old Testament. Amos 3:6, for example, asks, "Shall there be evil in a city, and Yahweh hath not done it?" But the word for evil comes from the Hebrew root *ra* and means "calamity," not "sin." Again, in Genesis 22:1, one should dismiss the reading of the Authorized Version, "God did tempt Abraham," and read rather with the Revised, "God did prove Abraham." The Lord was merely testing Abraham's love.

But God does ordain acts, in the commission of which men become guilty. The book of Job begins by describing Satan's persecution of Job (1:12) and the Sabeans' plundering of Job's property (v. 15); but the book concludes by speaking of all the "evil" (from the root *ra*) that *God* brought upon Job (42:11). The solution to this problem is to be sought in an analysis of God's purposes in such ordination. On

---

[7]See above, topic 12-A.
[8]See above, p. 180.

the one hand, God may ordain an evil act for the sake of the object of that activity. Moses, for example, justified God's sending of false prophets because they became a means of proving Israel, "whether ye love Yahweh your God with all your heart" (Deut. 13:3). Of a similar purpose were His leaving of the Canaanites in the Promised Land during the consolidation period in order to harden Israel (Judges 3:1, 2); His humbling of David by Shimei's cursing (II Sam. 16:11); and His trial of Hezekiah at the close of the eighth century by means of the Babylonian ambassadors (II Chron. 32:31). As Job could say (sometimes!), "But He knoweth the way that I take; when He hath tried me, I shall come forth as gold" (Job 23:10); cf. topic 28-F on the values of suffering.

On the other hand, God may ordain an evil act for the sake of the subject of the activity. Such ordination may have as its specific purpose to reveal to the subject his own heart and to bring him to repentance. David furnishes an outstanding example of this kind of situation. God had incited David to take a military census (II Sam. 24:1); but the king's action was based upon his own sinful trust in the numbers of his troops (v. 3, 4), rather than on God. But the final outcome of the incident was to produce in David a sincere repentance and submission to the will of God (v. 10; cf. Ps. 30:6).[9] Or again, David's crime with Bath-sheba led the king to a deep contrition (Ps. 51:4) and ultimately to his vindication of God, "that Thou mightest be justified when Thou speakest, and be clear when Thou judgest." At other times God's ordination of such acts may have as its purpose to lay bare the corrupt heart of the sinner and to bring him to punishment. In the Mosaic period, God thus hardened Pharaoh's heart. This hardening on the part of God is stated ten times in the context (first historically in Ex. 9:12); and, though it is previously stated that Pharaoh hardened his own heart (stated three times, first in Ex. 8:32), the very raising up of Pharaoh in the first place is said to have been divinely planned so as to display God's power upon him (9:16). Similarly, God hardened the spirit of Sihon, king of the trans-Jordanian Amorites (Deut. 2:30), so that Moses would destroy him and thus accomplish the fulfillment of Genesis 15:16. In the consolidation period, God dispatched evil spirits to bring destruction upon wicked Abimelech (Judg. 9:23) and upon Saul (I Sam. 16:14; 18:10; 19:9); and, in the disruption period He sent Satan himself to rouse up Ahab to the death he so richly deserved (I Kings 22:22). In the same way, when Rehoboam refused to listen to the just demands of his people, "it was a thing brought about of Yahweh, that He might establish His word [of punishment] by Ahijah the Shilonite" (I Kings 12:15). Isaiah with some of his fellow prophets spoke, among other reasons, so as to deaden the hearts of his unyielded countrymen (Isa. 6:10;

---

[9] Ps. 30 belongs historically at this point; cf. its title with I Chron. 22:1.

29:10; Jer. 1:19; 18:11, 12; Ezek. 2:3). Zedekiah's sin in the following period, that provoked the final destruction of the Southern Kingdom, is explained on this basis: "For through the anger of Yahweh did it come to pass" (II Kings 24:20). Even in the exile God "deceived" the false prophets that they might be destroyed from the midst of His people (Ezek. 14:9; cf. 20:25).

Two further facts contribute to the explanation of the divine ordination of evil. First, the inferior instruments who simultaneously commit the sinful acts are judged as guilty because of their sinful motivation. God, however, is not so judged, because His motivation is always s'dhāqā, righteousness (Lam. 3:37, 38; but cf. v. 39). For example, in the disruption period, God, through Ahijah, ordered the destruction of Jeroboam's house for its sins (I Kings 15:29, 30); but He punished Baasha for destroying it, when the latter did this with an attitude that was antagonistic to God (16:7). Similarly, He commanded the annihilation of Ahab's house (II Kings 9:7) but then punished Jehu for his unnecessary bloodshed in the execution of the divine orders (Hos. 1:4).[10] On the national scale, eighth century Assyria was ordained to be the ministerial rod of God's anger against Israel (Isa. 10:5, 6). The Assyrians, however, had other, self-centered ideas (vv. 7-11). "Wherefore," said Isaiah, "it shall come to pass, that, when the Lord hath performed His whole work upon Jerusalem, I will punish the fruit of the stout heart of the king of Assyria, and the glory of his high looks" (v. 12).

A second fact that is significant in explaining the divine ordination of evil is that such conflicts in motivations never thwart God, but actually perform His will. In the patriarchal period, Joseph's brothers hated him; but God had in mind the preservation of His own elect people and used their sinful selling of Joseph into slavery to accomplish His beneficial ends. As Joseph later concluded, "So now it was not you that sent me hither, but God!" (Gen. 45:8; 50:20). Nine centuries later Shimei cursed David through personal malice, but God had actually sent him to carry out a part of the divinely ordained punishment on David's sin (II Sam. 16:11). Most instructive of all is the multiple motivation when Satan is involved as well as sinful men. David, for example, ordered the census because of his false trust in armies (II Sam. 24:3, 4); Satan, at the same time, moved David to do this because of his own hatred for God's people, Israel (I Chron. 21:1); but Satan's maliciousness became in fact God's tool for His righteously angry punishment of the wayward people of Israel (II Sam. 24:1). Furthermore, although the reason for God's anger is not explicitly stated, it presumably arose because of Israel's sinful desertion of Yahweh's anointed at the time of Absalom's rebellion against David, which God had in turn ordered so as to punish

---

[10]This may, however, refer to his further bloodshed in II Kings 10:13, 14.

David for his sin with Bath-sheba (II Sam. 12:11), and which God
then overthrew because of Absalom's pride and wickedness (17:14)!
Again, in the case of the plundering of Job, the motivation of the
Sabeans against Job was one of greed for the plunder (Job 1:15), but
Satan used their greed to further his own ends of opposition to God
and to His elect (vv. 9-11). Simultaneously, however, God had ordained this same destructive act, though with His own righteous motive of proving Job. God thus made use of the sinful motivations of
both of the other parties to accomplish His over-all goal. "Surely the
wrath of men shall praise Thee, and the remainder of wrath shalt
Thou restrain!" (Ps. 76:10).

But this very verse in Psalm 76 raises the question, "Does God
indeed manifest His justice by restraining the rest of the evil of the
human race?" That is, can there be a God who is at the same time
both all-powerful and all-good in the midst of the obvious corruption
that fills today's world? This is the question of theodicy, the justice
of God; and the question is one that is discussed primarily in the wisdom literature of Israel's early disruption period. The Old Testament
is committed to the fundamental position of divine retribution:[11]
"For Yahweh knoweth the way of the righteous, but the way of the
ungodly shall perish" (Ps. 1:6; cf. Job 8:20). The moral structure of
the whole book of Proverbs is based upon this concept of divine
recompense, and David said flatly, "I have been young, and now am
old; yet have I not seen the righteous forsaken, nor his seed begging
bread" (Ps. 37:25). But certain of the Old Testament characters, taking a less long-range view of the subject, seemed to feel otherwise.
Job thus denied a distinctive treatment for the righteous (Job 9:22;
21:23-26), and Solomon insisted that the wise man went to the grave
exactly as does the fool (Eccl. 2:15, 16). In fact, said Job, the wicked
prosper and seem to be particularly blessed of God (12:6; cf. Eccl.
7:15 and especially Job 9:23): "They spend their days in prosperity,
and in a moment they go down to the grave [an easy death]. So they
say unto God, Depart from us; for we desire not the knowledge of
Thy ways" (21:13, 14).

Thus arose the question, why? (Ps. 10:1; 13:1). A preeminent
example is that furnished by Jeremiah, who suffered great persecutions and who then bitterly reproached God for apparently deserting
him (Jer. 12:1, 2; 15:15, 18; 20:7). Solomon generalized by saying
that everything under the sun (that is, on earth) was "vanity," *hével*,
which means futility (literally "a breath," Eccl. 1:2; 12:8). Compare
Malachi's question (Mal. 2:17), "Where is the God of justice?" On
occasion, the Old Testament saints even took exception to God's decree for their lives and wished for death (Job 3:3; Jer. 20:14), or
were tempted, at any rate, to give up His service (Mal. 3:14; Ps.

---

[11]As is also the New Testament (Gal. 6:7; Rev. 20:12).

73:13). To turn against God, however, was something that they did not do. Initially, perhaps, this may have been because of the responsibility they felt toward their society (Ps. 73:15); but eventually it was because they came to realize the error of such a temptation (v. 22). On the one hand, it was God's orders not to envy the wicked (Ps. 37:7; Prov. 3:31). Like the clay in the hands of the potter, a man is not to strive with his Maker (Isa. 45:9). Man's present duty is rather to submit and not to question (Job 37:21-24). But on the other hand, God revealed to His saints that the solution lay in His sure, even if not always immediate, retribution against sinners — "They sow the wind, and they shall reap the whirlwind" (Hos. 8:7).

From the very first, alienation from God makes the way of the transgressors hard (Prov. 13:15). But their actual punishment comes (sometimes) without too much delay: "Bloodthirsty and deceitful men shall not live out half their days" (Ps. 55:23). Even if it be postponed, "Though a sinner do evil a hundred times, and prolongs his days, yet surely I know that it shall not be well with the wicked, neither shall he prolong his days, which are as a shadow; because he feareth not God" (Eccl. 8:13). Eventual retribution is the force of the dialogue on theodicy that makes up the prophecy of Habakkuk, in the later prophetic period:

Habakkuk's statement		God's answer	
1:2	I cry of violence, why does God not hear?	1:6	I will punish sinful Judah by the Chaldeans [Nebuchadrezzar, 586 B.C.]
1:12 1:13	This I recognize; but they are more wicked than we: can God allow such?	2:3	Their day will come, after a short delay
		2:4	You are to live by faith
		2:6	They shall fall, for
3:2	Show us mercy in Thy wrath;	2:20	God is in His heaven
3:17, 18	I am confident in Thee, though all else fail.	—	(No answer needed!)

On this same basis of retribution, God granted ultimate vindication to Job (42:10). But He also condemned Israel to its exilic desolation that the nation might stand as a witness to God's retributive power (Ezek. 12:16; 17:24).

It is as illustrations of this truth of God's ultimate vindication of the righteous that the Biblical imprecations are to be understood. An imprecation may be defined as a prayer for the overthrow of the wicked. Such prayers most characteristically find their place in the Old Testament revelation at points in history when the inspired writers found themselves confronted by the opposition of the ungodly. As leaders of God's people, they felt themselves entitled to vindication; and they pled, reasonably enough, that God in His justice would eliminate their enemies. Best known are the imprecatory psalms of David and of others of the psalm writers, though Jeremiah, four centuries later (15:15; 17:18; 18:21-23; 20:12), and Nehemiah, in post-exilic days (6:14; 13:29), were impelled to equally strong statements. Similar prayers appear in the New Testament (II Tim. 4:14; Gal. 5:12; Rev. 6:10).

Writers with liberal theological tendencies have united in condemning the Biblical imprecations:

> "They must be viewed as belonging to the dispensation of the Old Testament . . . they belong to the spirit of Elijah, not of Christ; they use the language of the age which was taught to love its neighbor and hate its enemy" (Matt. v. 43)."[12]

In respect, however, to the passage cited, it should be clear that what Matthew 5 is condemning is the anti-Biblical tradition of the Pharisees, and not the Old Testament Scriptures. The latter do *not* teach hate for the enemies (cf. Ex. 23:4, 5; Lev. 19:17, 18). Three things must also be positively observed — that the Biblical imprecations are not hasty, emotional expressions, but careful literature; that they are prayers and songs to God, written in good conscience; and that they are not, in the last resort, human products but are rather inspired works of the Holy Spirit.[13]

---

[12]A. F. Kirkpatrick, *The Book of Psalms*, I:1xxxix.

[13]The following five explanations present themselves for the justification of these divinely approved words. 1) *Poetic statements.* Some imprecations exhibit but contemporary color, or hyperbole, as Ps. 68:21, 23: "that thou mayest crush them, dipping thy foot in blood" (cf. 58:10). Again, that God should destroy is sometimes but a poetic way of speaking of destruction by (brutal) men. Thus, as a commentary on the prayer to God in Ps. 137:9, compare Jeremiah's description of the fall of Jerusalem (Jer. 13:14), "I [God] will dash them one against another." Actually, in the historical fulfillment, it proved to be the Babylonians, and not God, who did the dashing down.

2) *Abhorrence of sin.* What Scripture essentially curses is the Satanic evil of sin (Nah. 3:19); and when the man is condemned (as Ps. 50:21), it is because the punishment of the sin inevitably involves the individual sinner (101:8; 139:21).

3) *The resignation of vengeance into God's hands* (Deut. 32:35; Rom. 12:19). An historical example of such imprecation is found in I Sam. 25. Vengeance had been planned by man (v. 22), but it was left with God (v. 29) and was divinely carried out (vv. 32, 33). Thus, even as Ps. 37:8, 9 teaches the committing of sinners into the hands of God for justice, so Ps. 104:34, 35 (cf. 58:11) carries this principle into application.

4) *Positive goals beyond private vindication.* David is noted for the way in which he often forgave Saul; and similarly, in Ps. 109:2, 4, 5, he disclaims any personal thirst for vengeance. But he then follows this statement with one of his most thorough-going prophetic imprecations! That is, a man's zeal for God and for the vindication of His righteousness may involve as a corollary the vindication of the individual himself: "Mine eye also hath seen my desire on mine enemies . . . to show that Yahweh is upright" (Ps. 92:11, 15; and cf. 54:7). So in II Chron. 24:22, the dying words of Zechariah, "Yahweh look upon it and require it," may seem to compare unfavorably with those of Stephen at his death, "Lord, lay not this sin to their charge" (Acts 7:60). But Zechariah was the high priest

One concludes that the imprecations found in Scriptures are truly normative examples of the proper human appreciation for the vindication of divine justice. As W. T. Davison has stated,

> It may indeed be well to consider whether the Old Testament saints, in the vigor and simplicity of their piety, did not cherish a righteous resentment against evil which the more facile and languid moral sense of later generations would have done well to preserve. "Oh ye that love Yahweh, hate evil," is an exhortation that belongs, not to one age, but to all time.[14]

God both vindicated Job and punished Eliphaz, and the Christian can well pray for both these aspects of justice.[15]

But it might be asked, what if Job had died in his sickness? Or what if a sinner dies before punishment? One could indeed reply, with Scripture, that the wicked man's descendants would suffer (Ps. 37:28) or his memory be dishonored (Job 18:17); but, as Job observed, these penalties are not too serious for the evil-doer himself (21:21)! Thus it was seen that the vindication of divine justice must reach its climax in God's dealings at death and in the life after death.[16] Even in a negative sense, death served to take the righteous away from earthly evils that were to come (Isa. 57:1, 2): "There the

---

who had just officially condemned the sinful king; and for his martyrdom, official vindication was required. This justification for imprecation particularly applies to David, God's anointed; for as he himself said, "The righteous shall see it, and fear" (Ps. 52:6). Again, God's vindication could involve the vindication of His nation. Just as in Ex. 32:12, Moses besought God not to destroy Israel because of what Egypt might say of him, so Ps. 83:3-5 states as the reason for prayer against Israel's enemies, "They take counsel against thy people . . . against thee do they make a covenant" (cf. 137:8).

5) *Prophecies of God's attitude toward sin.* The very curses contained in the Biblical imprecations may be duplicated elsewhere by divine prophecies. In a number of passages even the form of the Hebrew verb may be ambiguous, whether jussive, "Let him suffer," or imperfect, "He will suffer." On the one hand, some prophecies appear much like imprecations (55:2, 3; 125:4, 5; 145:20; cf. the New Testament references; Matt. 13:49, 50; John 5:29). On the other hand, some imprecations are simply prophecy. For example Ps. 109 has been condemned as one of the most violently imprecatory of the Psalms. But in the body of the composition (vv. 6-19), the object of the description shifts from the plural, which is found in the rest of the Psalm, to a singular, preeminent embodiment of evil. We have, therefore, nothing more nor less than a detailed, inspired description of Judas Iscariot, the betrayer of Christ (Acts 1:20).

[14] "Book of Psalms," James Hastings, editor, *A Dictionary of the Bible*, IV:158, though cf. John R. Sampey's caution, "We ought to use the imprecatory psalms in the light of our Lord's teaching. We cannot pronounce curses on our personal enemies. This heavenly artillery may be turned upon the saloon, the brothel and the gambling hell, though we must not forget to pray for the conversion of the persons who are engaged in these lines of business," "Book of Psalms," James Orr, editor, *The International Standard Bible Encyclopedia* (Grand Rapids: Wm. B. Eerdmans Publishing Co., 1939), IV:2494.

[15] See particularly Howard Osgood, "Dashing the Little Ones Against the Rock," *Princeton Theological Review*, 1:1 (Jan., 1903), 23-37; and Chalmers Martin, "The Imprecations in the Psalms," *ibid.*, 1:4 (Oct., 1903), 537-553.

[16] On the relatively limited Old Testament revelation on this matter, compare its general deficiency on the subject of life after death. Christ's resurrection had not yet taken place and opened up more clearly this area of truth. See topic 30, below.

wicked cease from troubling; and there the weary are at rest" (Job 3:17). But positively, death came to be understood as providing for such outworkings of God's justice as had not been completed during life: "I know that my *Gō'ēl,* 'Vindicator' liveth, and at the last He will stand upon the earth . . . whom I, even I, shall see, on my side" (Job 19:25, 27).

At this point a striking progression in revelation is demonstrated by four psalms of the Davidic period.[17] 1) Psalm 37, by David, states that evil doers will soon be cut down (vv. 2, 13), and the meek shall take over the land (vv. 11, 12). 2) Psalm 73, by Asaph, commences with the same thought that was found in Psalm 37, namely, that the wicked will soon perish (vv. 18, 19). But it goes on to state that the righteous are continually with God (v. 23); He is our portion forever (v. 26), guiding us now and afterward receiving us to glory (v. 24). The contribution of the 73rd Psalm consists, therefore, in its stress upon a personal reward after death, rather than upon the meek's taking over of the land in the future kingdom of God. 3) Psalm 49 is by David's Korahite singers. They observe that all die alike (v. 10), which is significant because this indicates that the emphasis is no longer placed upon an immediate punishment on the wicked. Subsequently, however, the wicked consume in hell, but the upright have vindication over them (v. 14), being saved from hell and received by God (v. 15). Finally, 4) Psalm 17, by David, concedes that the wicked may have domination in this life (v. 14), which is the opposite thought to that found in Psalm 37 and 73. But the righteous shall be satisfied, when they awake in glory, with beholding the likeness of God (v. 15).

> "For [whether in life or in death] the work of a man will
> He render unto him, and cause every man to find according
> to his ways. Yea, of a surety, God will not do wickedly,
> neither will the Almighty pervert justice (Job 34:11, 12)."

C. THE PRESENCE OF SIN IN THE HUMAN RACE. But though God's relationship to sin is right, man's is not. The reality of man's failure is shown, in fact, by his standing need for God's redemptive testament (Gen. 3:15). Furthermore, this evil presence of sin appears as practically coextensive with the historical existence of the race (see the following topic, on its origin). It reaches a climax in the very opening chapters of Genesis. Adam's firstborn son was guilty of envy, of murder, of lying, and of non-repentance (Gen. 4:4-14). Cain's early descendant, Lamech, then became the first polygamist, proud and boastful,[18] and exacted ten times the vengeance that God Him-

---

[17]Cf. A. B. Davidson's well-worked-out discussion, *The Theology of the Old Testament,* pp. 459-466.

[18]On the basis of the description in the preceding verse (Gen. 4:22) of Lamech's son as a metal worker, the poem has been interpreted as a "sword song," Lamech's reaction to swinging the newly forged weapon.

self had required (4:24; cf. v. 15). Sin, moreover, did not restrict itself to the line of Cain but came to dominate most of humanity. Among the Sethites, particularly at first, there was embraced the godly portion of the human race, the true "seed of the woman."[19] An outstanding example was Enoch, who walked with God in the fellowship of the testament and was then translated directly to heaven so that he should not see death (5:24; cf. Heb. 11:5). But subsequently the *b'nē hā Elōhīm*, the "sons of God" (Gen. 6:2, 4) involved themselves in unholy marriages, and sin soon became the dominant characteristic of the race.

The nature of these unholy marriage alliances is a much debated question. The phrase "sons of God" has in scripture two possible meanings[20] — either "angels" (Job 1:6; 38:7), or "godly men" (Hos. 1:10; Ps. 73:15; cf. Deut. 32:5, where the ungodly are *not* God's sons).[21] In support of the angelic identification, the context of Genesis 6 has been adduced as requiring a generic use of *ādhām*, "man" both in verse 1 and in verse 2. The *b'nē Elōhīm*, "the sons of God" would then seem to stand in generic contrast to humanity.

> "When men (*ādhām*) began to multiply, and daughters were born unto them (v. 1), the sons of God saw the daughters of men (*ādhām*); and they took them wives of all that they chose (v. 2)."

The sons of God would thus be non-human, or angelic. There exist, however, three alternative explanations which make it possible for the sons of God, as well as the daughters of men, to be considered human. 1) Moses may have shifted from a generic use of *ādhām* in verse 1 to a specific use (referring to only the *ungodly* men's daughters) in verse 2.[22] The sons (godly *ādhām*) then married the daughters (ungodly *ādhām*). 2) Or both uses may be generic (*all* men's daughters, in v. 2). The point would then be that the sons of God married *any* women, "All that they chose," indiscriminately, but not necessarily into a class of creatures different from themselves.[23] 3) Or both may be specific: both the men who multiplied (v. 1) and their daughters

---

[19]See above, p. 178.

[20]Rabbinical exegesis has indeed suggested a third alternative, namely, "nobility." But while *elōhīm* may have the meaning of "judges" (Ex. 21:6; Ps. 82:6), *b'nē Elōhīm* is not used for human nobility; and the interpretation seems untenable.

[21]It is true that in these verses the phrase "sons of God" has reference to God's people, subsequent to the granting of the Sinaitic testament. But Scripture presents a unified plan of salvation from Gen. 3:15 onward; and, since it sees the men of all ages as saved under one testament in Christ's blood, it follows that all should have the same status as sons of His Father (John 1:12).

[22]Keil lists a number of parallel passages for such a shift, *Biblical Commentary on the Old Testament: The Pentateuch*. Trans. by James Martin (Grand Rapids: Wm. B. Eerdmans Publishing Co., 1949), I:130.

[23]So H. C. Leupold, *Exposition of Genesis*, p. 250.

(v. 2) being limited to the ungodly.[24] The Genesis context, moreover, favors the identification of the b'nē hā-Elōhīm as godly men. For while there is no reference to angels in the immediate context, there is reference to the distinct godliness of the Sethites (5:22; cf. 4:26; 5:29).[25] Furthermore, it is men that are judged for the sin (v. 3), and not angels.

At the time of the translation of the Pentateuch into Greek (the Septuagint, 250 B.C.), and perhaps under the influence of the Greek myths with their tales of marital relations between gods and men, "sons of God" was first rendered as angels.[26] The analogy, however, of the New Testament leaves little room for the angelic hypothesis. 1) Angels are spirits (Heb. 1:14), who assume material bodies only on special occasions, and then only as commanded by God. 2) Angels in heaven do not marry (Matt. 22:30);[27] but the relationship of Genesis 6:2 was a permanent one, a "taking of wives," not a case of exceptional fornication. 3) The angels involved would have had to be fallen angels, though in a condition distinct from that of those in the original fall (II Pet. 2:4).[28] But even if such a "second fall" did take place, it could not concern Genesis 6:2, where the subjects are still called "the sons of God." Evangelicals who are committed to the

---

[24]So John Murray, *Principles of Conduct* (Grand Rapids: Wm. B. Eerdmans Publishing Co., 1957), pp. 244-45.

[25]This assumes the unity of Genesis, that it is not a patchwork of unrelated "source documents."

[26]The intertestamental literature elaborated this angelic concept. I Enoch 6 and 7 speaks of 200 angels, the tenth of whom was named Azazel, producing giants 3000 cubits high. (It should be noted, however, that the n'fīlīm, Gen. 6:4, are not to be equated with "giants," see below, p. 207; and they are not offspring of the sons of God in any event.) Cf. Jubilees 5:1, and others, as well as certain of the Church Fathers.

[27]To attempt to restrict this to "in heaven" is a feeble argument (cf. Luke 20: 35, 36).

[28]This verse speaks of sinning angels "cast down." But the reference appears to be to the original fall of angels. The "pits of darkness" in which they are now found may then equal the *abussos* (Luke 8:31), the abode of all demons. Another New Testament passage often cited is Jude 6, 7. Jude elsewhere quotes I Enoch, but this does not warrant an a priori expectation of Jude's following the I Enoch angelic identification. For Jude is inspired and true; Enoch is not inspired, and generally false. The presumption is against Enoch's interpretations. Specifically, then, the references in Jude are these. 1) "Angels left their habitation" (v. 6). But this was not to molest women on earth. They left, literally, their *arche*, or "authority," seeking God's, in pride (I Tim. 3:6). Again the reference is to the original fall of angels. 2) They are "kept in bonds" (v. 6). This description might seem to favor a second fall, the members of which are found in a different state from those of the original fall. But this reference resembles II Pet. 2:4 and could be poetic. 3) Certain cities were guilty of "fornicating like to *toutois*, 'these'" (v. 7). This, in turn, may mean that: (a) Other cities fornicate like to Sodom and Gomorrah. (b) All the cities fornicate like to the angels. But such a thought could not refer to Gen. 6:2, which concerns marriage, not fornication; and would imply that angels go after *sarx hetera*, "other flesh," as if they were flesh themselves. (c) All the cities, sinning in general like angels, fornicate. (d) All the cities fornicate like to the ungodly men (v. 4). This last explanation seems the most plausible in light of the subsequent demonstratives (vv. 8, 14) and of the fact that these men were immoral (v. 8).

unity and the credibility of Scripture, therefore, generally identify the sons of God with the godly portion of the descendants of Seth who involved themselves in indiscriminate mixed marriages.[29] The teaching of the passage is thus, "Be not unequally yoked with unbelivers" (II Cor. 6:14; cf. Ex. 34:16). But this historical example of Genesis 6:2 is then a negative one, for all men failed. The single exception was Noah (Gen. 6:8), with whom is to be included his immediate family.

God, therefore, made the pronouncement: "My Spirit shall not always rule, *yādhōn*, in man; in his going astray, *b'saggām*, he is flesh" (6:3). This verse could be stated in paraphrase, "My Spirit, who providentially sustains life,[30] will not keep on staying with man, because by sinning he had made necessary the exposure of the temporary nature of his bodily existence."[31] God proceeded to allow humanity 120 years grace before He should send the Flood to destroy all but His elect (6:3).[32] The presence of the *n'filīm*, both prior and subsequent to the marriages of the sons of God with the daughters of men (v. 4),[33] furnishes further evidence as to the dominating power of sin. The noun *n'filīm* can be taken in two different ways. It may be understood as describing men of violence, from its verbal root, *nāfal*, which means "to fall upon"; or it may refer to heroes who struggled against the rising tide of lawlessness.[34] In either event, their existence

---

[29]Modern interpreters fall into the following groups. 1) Those who believe that the "sons" are godly men and that the record is historical. This group includes most conservative writers (Keil, Leupold, Aalders) and some dispensationalists (Scofield *Reference Bible*). The motive is to maintain the consistency and the truthfulness of Scripture. 2) Those who conceive of the "sons" as angels, and the record as false. So most liberals (Driver, Skinner, *Westminster Study Bible*), with whom must be included Franz Delitzsch. The motive is to discredit Scripture and to strengthen a theory of religious evolution out of primitive superstition: "What it was found possible for men to believe . . . about the holy angels, is impossible for us now," J. B. Mayor, "The General Epistle of Jude," W. Robertson Nicoll, editor, *The Expositor's Greek Testament*, V:243. 3) Those who conceive both of the "sons" as angels and of the record as true. So a few conservatives (Alford, Pieters) and some dispensationalists (Larkin; Chafer is sympathetic, *Systematic Theology* [Dallas, Texas: Dallas Seminary Press, 1948], II:114-117.) The motive is to do full justice to the New Testament passages in II Peter and in Jude and to account for a second fall of angels. But see Note 28 above.
[30]See above, p. 174.
[31]This is a difficult verse. *Yādhōn* may mean "strive"; but such a usage would suggest "flesh" as something evil, against which God struggles (cf. Rom. 7:18). But such a conception is foreign to Old Testament thought, which treats of flesh as simply temporary, and sometimes desirable (see below, topic 17-B). Also *b'shaggām* may mean "in that also"; but to say, "My Spirit will not rule in man and keep him alive, in that also he is temporary," is pointless. For further discussion see Vos, *op. cit.*, pp. 61-62.
[32]"His days shall be 120 years" cannot refer to life span (cf. 11:11, 13).
[33]Note that the *n'filīm* were not the products of the mixed marriages. Neither does Num. 13:33 require that they be "giants" (the LXX rendering), for it is the related Anakim who are stated to have been of the large stature (cf. Deut. 2:11).
[34]Gen. 6:4, 5 would then be translated, "The *n'filīm* were in the earth . . . men of renown, but still God saw that. . . ."

illustrates why God found it necessary to send the Deluge with its destruction.

But even the Flood could not eliminate sin from the human race. The same sweeping description of sin that had been given earlier as the reason for the Flood (Gen. 6:5) is repeated after it as the reason for the uselessness — and hence the prohibition — of any further flood (8:21)! The explanation seems to lie in this. Genesis 8:21 contains the additional phrase that man's heart is evil "from his youth." That is, sin is inalterably present in the heart of man, a fact which the fiasco of the tower of Babel proceeded to demonstrate. Even the ancestors of Abraham were polytheists (Josh. 24:2, 14), though Yahweh could still be spoken of as "the God of Terah" (Gen. 31:53).

Subsequent history serves only to underline the continued *hattāth*, the "missing of the mark" by Adam's race. The call of Abraham the patriarch indeed marked a turning point in human history. The downward trend, which had climaxed at Babel, received a check, and Abraham's faith became the basis upon which God slowly built up that elect society into which His Son should one day come. But Abraham himself failed, by cowardice, by lying (a "half" truth, Gen. 20: 12!), and by opening the door to adultery (12:18, 19) — and that repeatedly (20:13). Jacob, prior to Peniel, consistently stole and deceived — his very name, *Ya'qōv*, means "he grasps at the heel" (25:26). Joseph then capitalized on a natural calamity to reduce the Egyptian people to serfdom (47:16, 20, 26). Outside of the elect family, crime abounded. Sodom in particular (18:20) is noted for its sexual perverts (19:5), though the city's basic sin, as always, was one of pride (Ezek. 16:49, 50). Moses, in the next period, began his career with murder and its concealment (Ex. 2:12); and at the last his sin of smiting the rock, as if he could perform miracles in his own power,[35] kept him from entering the Promised Land (Num. 20:2-13). Israel's "murmuring" in the wilderness has become proverbial (cf. 20:3).

In the succeeding periods, sin retarded the conquest of Canaan (Josh. 7:11) and almost destroyed Israel under the judges (Judges 10:13). Saul's rashness, his jealousy, and his pride marred his victories and occasioned his ultimate destruction (I Sam. 14:29, 30; I Chron. 10:13).[36] David committed adultery and murder (II Sam. 11), though his subsequently composed penitential psalm (51) constitutes the greatest confession to be found within Scripture.[37] Solomon then precipitated the disruption of Israel because, for all his wisdom and moral

[35]His sin lay in his pride and in his failure to glorify God (Num. 20:12). Scripture nowhere suggests that it lay in a violation of typology, as is sometimes claimed: for example, that Christ (the rock) was to be struck only once (not twice!); though it is true that the rock produced life-giving water, which is typical of the life that believers receive from Christ (I Cor. 10:4).
[36]Cf. Payne, *An Outline of Hebrew History*, p. 96.
[37]See below, topic 23.

instruction of others, he himself violated the testament and proved to be one of the greatest of fools (I Kings 11:11).[38] The eighth century prophets spoke of Israel's goodness "as a morning cloud, and as the dew that goeth early away" (Hos. 6:4). They described "Ephraim as a cake not turned" (7:8), burned to a crisp on the one side (punished for her foreign associations) but still unfit on the other! Judah, too, polluted the land with her willful transgression of the testament (Isa. 24:5): "Thou art obstinate, and thy neck is an iron sinew, and thy brow brass" (48:4).

As for the pagan gōyim, David had long before observed how they had forgotten God and must therefore sink into the destruction of the grave (Ps. 9:17). Instead of chastising Israel, according to God's directives, they cast off all restraint in their aggressions and raged against the Lord Almighty (Isa. 10:5, 12; 36:20; 37:27; 45:5-7; cf. Hab. 1:6, 11; Zech. 1:15). Amos went on to condemn their crimes, not simply against Israel (Amos 1:3, 11, 13), but also against each other (2:1). So Nahum, in the later prophetic period, predicted the gloating of all nations over the fall of Nineveh (Nahum 3:19); and Jeremiah went on to raise his voice in imprecation, "Pour out Thy wrath upon the gōyim that know Thee not, and upon the families that call not on Thy name; for they have devoured Jacob" (Jer. 10:25; cf. its quotation by the exilic Asaphites in Ps. 79:6, 7). According to Esther 3:8, it was the way in which elect Israel differed from the rest of the nations that particularly provoked their attack. Yet Ezekiel in exile condemned Israel's lawlessness (from the root résha; Ezek. 5:6) as worse than that of the pagans. Ezra analyzed the final destruction of his nation as due to its violation of the oath it had taken before God, by which it was to have stayed obedient to Nebuchadrezzar (II Chron. 36:13). But the officers who should have been Israel's spiritual leaders were the very ones who had led it in this fatal trespass against Yahweh (v. 14).

D. THE EXTENT OF SIN. The Bible's most penetrating description of the extent of man's sin is found in its opening pages (Gen. 6:5, in the primeval period). That is to say, human depravity is total and shows no "progress" in Biblical theology. Genesis 6:5, with the addition of two other statements that follow closely upon it, reveals that human sin was great in at least seven major respects: 1) in its extent, "in the (whole) earth"; 2) in its inwardness, "the thoughts of the heart"; 3) in its inherence, "the yéser," that is, "the very forming" of those thoughts; 4) in its exclusiveness, "only ra, evil"; 5) in its continuousness, "all the day"; 6) in its inclusiveness, "all flesh" (Gen. 6:12); and 7) in its earliness, "from his youth" (8:21). Subsequent revelations simply elaborate upon this sweeping description. In the patriarchal period, the performing of circumcision at a date only

---

[38]Payne, op. cit., pp. 114-115.

one week after birth (17:12) served as a constantly re-enacted sermon upon the need for the removal of uncleanness from even the littlest life.[39] Similarly, the Mosaic association of uncleanness with procreation and with birth (Ex. 19:15; Lev. 12) actively taught this same lesson. God specifically cautioned Moses about the hopelessness of the human heart (Deut. 5:29); and Moses, though there were none closer to God than himself (34:10), yet spoke repeatedly of his own faithlessness (1:37; 3:26; cf. 32:51; Ps. 106:32, 33). In the consolidation period, the depravity of man then appears as the very theme of the book of Judges (cf. 2:19). When man does that which is right in his own eyes, he necessarily does wrong (17:6; 21:25).

Solomon, in the disruption period, saw that behind the "vanity" (*hével* = futility) of life there lay the total sinfulness of mankind (Eccl. 7:20, 29). In his dedicatory prayer for the Temple, he spoke of the universality of sin (I Kings 8:46; cf. Prov. 20:9); and the book of Job, written in the same period, describes man as a worm before God (Job 25:6). During the eighth century the divided kingdoms of Israel, though spared by God's grace (II Kings 14:26), exhibited to the full the insensitiveness of human depravity. The upper classes in particular became proud and tyrannical (Amos 4:1). They lived "at ease in Zion" (6:1) and preserved their confidence despite the partial destructions they had already experienced (Isa. 9:9, 10; 28:3). So when even Isaiah responded to God's holiness with automatic guilt (Isa. 6:5; cf. I Kings 17:18), it is little wonder that the prophet confessed of his depraved people, "We are all as an unclean thing, and all our righteousnesses are as filthy rags; and we all do fade as a leaf; and our iniquities, like the wind, have taken us away" (64:6). But as for Israel's sins (v. 5), "in those is continuance," *ōlām* or "limitlessness."[40] Liberalism has indeed claimed that —

> "The idea of total depravity, in the sense of such complete corruption of human nature that no man can either will or do what is right without redemption by divine grace, is unsupported by the Bible."[41]

Perhaps the clearest refutation of this claim, however, is to be found in the revelation that God gave in the next period through Jeremiah, one of the most spiritual of the prophets. He saw that beneath the surface, the heart of man is "deceitful above all things, and desperately wicked: who can know it?" (17:9; cf. 5:23; 16:12; 18:12). Man's nature, in fact, drives him to sin like the compulsion of an animal in heat (2:24, 25; cf. 5:31). He can no more change himself and

---

[39]See below, topic 27-D.
[40]For other renderings of this confessedly difficult verse, see J. A. Alexander, *Isaiah* (Grand Rapids: Zondervan Publishing House, rep. 1953), II:431-432.
[41]Millar Burrows, *An Outline of Biblical Theology*, p. 170.

do good than an Ethiopian can change his skin or a leopard his spots (13:23). Hence arises the need for the new testament (31:31-34).

The depravity of the human race, however, does not, according to Scripture, relieve man of his responsibility. Man ought to choose the right, even though he does not. Cain, for example, prior to his murder of Abel, was cautioned by God that though sin, like a wild beast with designs upon him, was crouching at his door, still he should rule over it (Gen. 4:7). Moses, likewise, put the decision before his people, "See, I have set before thee this day life and good, and death and evil" (Deut. 30:15). He had, moreover, already assured them that "This commandment which I command thee this day, it is not too hard for thee" (v. 11). His approach was similar to the exhortation for choice between the "two ways" that is so common in Proverbs. Even when the conscience becomes dead after repeated hardenings of the heart (Ex. 8:32), the responsibility, the guilt, and the punishment continue in force (9:2, 3; cf. I Sam. 6:6). The people may not hearken to God, with the result that He lets them go after the stubbornness of their hearts to walk in their own counsels (Ps. 81:11, 12, by Asaph, of the Davidic period); but the theoretical possibility of choice still stands. Most remarkable is the combination of insensitiveness and yet of responsibility that is found in Ezekiel 3:27 (exilic): "He that heareth, let him hear; and he that forbeareth, let him forbear: for they are a rebellious house." Through Amos, however, in the eighth century, God revealed that a greater responsibility for depraved conduct lay with those (Israel) who were the most privileged with revelations and with election (Amos 3:2). Depravity, finally, does not mean that the unregenerate man never makes a right choice; but it insists that when he does make such a choice, it is still not with the right motive of glorifying God. An accurate description of total depravity might, therefore, be simply total inability. As David expressed it, "In Thy sight no man living is righteous" (Ps. 143:2). Cf. 130:3, "If Thou, Yahweh, shouldest mark iniquities, oh Lord, who could stand?"

E. THE RESULTS OF SIN. As just stated by the above verse, the hopeless standing of the human race comes about as the direct result of its sin. There appears, first, the guilt, $\bar{a}w\bar{o}n$ (Ps. 32:5),[42] or $\bar{a}sh\bar{a}m$ (Gen. 26:10; Ps. 69:5),[43] that follows automatically upon one's disobedience to the law of God. For when sin is committed, God knows about it, and men shall know about it (Josh. 22:22)! The crime of Joseph's brothers, in the patriarchal period, haunted them years later (Gen. 42:21); the Mosaic law repeatedly brought to the sinner's attention his guilt before God (Lev. 5:3, 4); and Moses' curse spoke of the doubts and fear that would follow upon a man's disobedience

---

[42]See above, p. 196.
[43]$\bar{A}sh\bar{a}m$ is also used for the guilt, the "trespass" offering. See below, p. 388.

(Deut. 28:66-67). The sinner's heart "smites him" (I Sam. 24:5; II Sam. 24:10). David's conscience thus gave him no rest until he confessed his great sins (Ps. 32:3; cf. Prov. 28:1). Though people's ears may grow heavy against understanding the truth (Isa. 6:10; cf. Zech. 11:5's description of "possessors who slay them, and hold themselves not guilty"), they still carry their iniquity like a heavy burden (Isa. 1:4; cf. Gen. 43:9). What became almost a refrain with Isaiah is his realization that "There is no peace, saith Yahweh, to the wicked" (48:22; 57:21).

Punishment follows upon guilt, as the further result of sin. It does so, moreover, inevitably: "If ye sin against Yahweh, be sure your sin will find you out"! (Num. 32:23; cf. Hos. 8:7). A man's sin may often bring its own judgment (Jer. 7:19; cf. Ezek. 22:31). Jacob's robbery of his brother, for example, forced him into a twenty year exile from home (Gen. 27:42, 43). Again, Israel's very refusal to enter Canaan under Moses was what condemned the rebels to wander for forty years in the wilderness (Num. 14:28, 29). Or again, at the close of the consolidation period, the people's sinful request for a king brought retribution upon their own heads in the form of Saul (I Sam. 8:18). They got just what they deserved!

But sin is rebellion against God, and therefore its punishment consists fundamentally in the separation of man from his Maker (Isa. 59:2). Saul in his sin found that at the time of his need he had no prayer access to God (I Sam. 14:37; 28:6). Moreover, at the last judgment, since the earth is the Lord's, sinners must be consumed out of this earth (Ps. 104:35). Nationally, both of the Hebrew kingdoms were destroyed because of their sin (Hos. 13:16; II Chron. 36:16); and individually, the soul that sinneth it shall die (Ezek. 18:4). Sometimes destruction would fall immediately and supernaturally (Num. 16:30-32; 21:5), or it might be delayed for a stated interval. God, for example, allowed one year to Hananiah the false prophet (Jer. 28:16, 17); and 120 years before the Flood (Gen. 6:3). Sickness may be due to sin (Lev. 26:16; Ps. 38:3); and the wicked, accordingly, are threatened with living out but half their days (Ps. 55:23; cf. Isa. 18:5). Similarly, the decreasing life span of man in the primeval period may have been due to the progressive effects of sin[44] (cf. Prov. 10:27). In the Mosaic period human life expectancy was fixed at its present limit of 70-80 years; but even our maximum span "is soon cut off, and we fly away," consumed by God's anger (Ps. 90:10). There remains, however, something more serious than death itself: the fact that the unrepentant sinner is able to find no place of inheri-

[44]Note that its greatest percentage of drop, almost in half, occurred in the days of Peleg (Gen. 11:17-19). But if this man's name *péleg*, "division" (10:25), refers to the contemporaneous confusion of tongues at Babel (and there appears to be no other contextually valid interpretation), then the drop in age is seen to coincide with this climax to human sinfulness.

tance under the testament. His name is "blotted out of the book of life, and not written with the righteous" (Ps. 69:28). Thus his "beauty shall be for hell to consume" (49:14), where separation from God is complete.

It is, therefore, little wonder that Solomon writes in Ecclesiastes that all life apart from God is futile, a failure (1:1, 2). Pleasures (2:2), wisdom (v. 3), buildings and property (vv. 4-7), wealth (v. 8) — death levels all (vv. 15, 16). With eternal potentialities, the natural man cannot attain unto eternal life (3:11); but he must face God's righteous judgment (12:14), depraved, guilty, and lost.

For Further Reading:

James I. McCord, "Know Thyself," *Interpretation,* 3:2 (April, 1949), pp. 142-153. A neo-orthodox study on human depravity in the Bible.

James Stuart Candlish, *The Biblical Doctrine of Sin.* Handbooks for Bible classes and private study; Edinburgh: T. and T. Clark, [n.d.]. A brief but noteworthy survey.

Georgia Harkness, *The Dark Night of the Soul.* Nashville, Tenn.: Abingdon-Cokesbury Press, 1945. A recent study, characteristic of the renewed neo-orthodox interest in the subject of sin.

16. The Origin of Sin*

A. ORIGINAL SIN. As Jeremiah stated, the heart of the members of the human race is deceitful above all things and desperately wicked (Jer. 17:9). But the question arises, "Why? And how?" Scripture, with its practical approach, is understandably more concerned with the problem of sin as already existing and with the good news of God's activity in history to overcome it through His testament, than it is with the problem of how it originated. Victory over sin in the present may, however, be aided by a knowledge of its origin in the past; and therefore Scripture's opening discussion of human history concerns the fall of the first human pair. Then, although the theory of the connection of each individual's sin with that of Adam does not constitute a topic of Old Testament discussion, the fact of the historical development of all human sin from this original failure does become a subject of repeated reference.

Most fundamentally, a man's sin lies in the decree of God (cf. Gen. 45:8); but still God is not the author of sin (James 1:13).[1] Temptation may indeed arise from without, from Satan and his le-

---

* BIBLE READING: Genesis 3; Ezekiel 28:11-19

Collateral Reading: Vos, *Biblical Theology,* pp. 43-55.
  Burrows, *Outline of Biblical Theology,* pp. 165-172.
  Ludwig Kohler, *Old Testament Theology,* pp. 166-181.

[1]See the preceding topic, sec. B.

gions; and we recognize that evil spirits function, in the long run, as agents of the decretive will of God (cf. I Kings 22:22). The responsibility for sin, however, on the basis of which man will be judged, rests in his own heart (Prov. 4:23). The question is then, what makes the human heart so wicked? The uniform answer of Scripture is that the heart is thus because the individual shares a part in the human race. He is an offspring of Adam and is therefore subject to condemnation, prior to any activity of his own (cf. Rom. 5:16). That is, he stands condemned as guilty on the basis of original sin.

The earliest periods of Old Testament revelation, in line with the generally rudimentary nature of the truths that they convey, are silent on this subject. Moses was the first to emphasize the fact that Adam begat sons in his own likeness (Gen. 5:3). The most striking aspect of this likeness, moreover, and one that becomes almost monotonous in its repetition in the paragraphs that follows, is that of man's mortality, of his necessity to face death (vv. 8, 11, 14, etc.); and death was the punishment received by Adam for sin (2:17; 3:19; 5:5).[2] Corresponding passages, such as Exodus 20:5 and 34:7 (cf. Gen. 15:16; Lev. 26:39; Jer. 32:18; Lam. 5:7) speak of divine punishment as continuing from generation to generation. But this punishment does not arrive simply because the parties concerned hold external membership in a certain group. Those who are punished are characterized by a collective depravity: the sons are guilty of hating God, even as did their fathers (Ex. 20:5). The iniquities of the fathers persevere among them. Thus the revelation of Genesis 8:21 (conveyed through Moses) taught that the very formation, *yéser*, of man's thoughts is evil from his youth, and apparently naturally so rather than learned, though this latter fact is not stated.

It remained for David, two periods later, to reveal the explicit truth that the cause of man's depravity lies in his original nature. It is not simply that the *wicked* are estranged from God from the womb (Ps. 58:3), but that he himself as one of God's elect (and errant) people "was shapen in iniquity," and in sin conceived by his mother (Ps. 51:5). Man, by virtue simply of being conceived as a man, is a sinner by nature and subject to the wrath of God. So Job's friends, in words that were seemingly revealed to Israel in the following (disruption) period, explained that the child of woman cannot be innocent (Job 15:14; 25:4). Isaiah later uttered a somewhat similar statement, "Thou wast called a transgressor from the womb" (48:8), though his words seem simply to personify the house of Israel (v. 1) and to refer to the nation's sin from its first wilderness days. They may yet serve, however, as an introduction to the thought of 43:27, "Thy first father hath sinned, and thine intercessors have trans-

[2]Liberalism struggles desperately (though in vain) to escape this fact of the dependence of man's death upon Adam's sin; see below, pp. 219, 220.

gressed against Me." Since the "intercessors" refers to Israelites like Moses, Samuel, and Elijah, it appears that the "first father" signifies, not Adam, but either Abraham or Jacob as the father of the Hebrews. The first point then is that, that even the best men in Israel's history were sinners.[3] But Yahweh continued His rebuke, in the next verse by saying, "Therefore I have put Israel to reproaches." It follows, accordingly, as a second conclusion, that within the human race there exists a connection between sin today and sin at the first.[4] The explanation for man's present dilemma lies in the original sin.

B. THE FALL OF MAN. The occasion of this original sin and of the fall of man into that state which causes us to be "by nature children of wrath" (Eph. 2:3) presented itself in primeval Eden. There God in His goodness concluded His *b'rîth* with Adam (cf. Hos. 6:7), the "covenant [of works]." The situation was preredemptive; that is, this *b'rîth* was a covenant of performance, not the later saving testament of grace. As a covenant, it was synergistic even though monopleuric;[5] and it was marked by mutual obligations that were laid upon the two parties concerned, namely, God and Adam. The whole arrangement, in turn, served as a means for the necessary probation of mankind; for it is only by the passing of a test that true character is to be demonstrated (cf. Rom. 8:24, 25). God's action, moreover, was designed to bring about men's voluntary glorification of Himself (Isa. 43:7); automatons would never do![6] The obligation of Adam was to obey God by not eating from the "tree of experiencing good and evil" (Gen. 2:17). This latter constituted a sacramental sign through which the doing of good or of evil would be accomplished, respectively, by the man's not eating, or eating. The tree, in other words, became the medium through which Adam would exercise discrimination and, by his free choice, come to know good, or evil, experientially.[7] The obligation of God, should Adam obey, was to grant him an everlasting, irrevocable life (Gen. 2:9); compare its final accomplishment in Revelation 22:2. Man even then held dominion over creation (Gen. 1:28), possession of the wonderful Garden of Eden, including its pleasant trees (2:9) and precious stones (Ezek. 28:13; cf. Gen. 2:11, 12), and a real fellowship with God; for only

---

[3]Contrast in the Apocrypha the denial to the patriarchs of the need for repentance (Prayer of Manasses 8).

[4]The Apocryphal book of Ecclesiasticus (25:24) first makes explicit this inference from the Old Testament, that the cause of sin is to be found in the Edenic transgression.

[5]See above, pp. 80, 87, 92.

[6]Cf. Vos, *Biblical Theology*, p. 43, "Some form of subjecting man to probation would have to be found."

[7]It is true that "knowing good and evil" may sometimes equal "knowing everything" (Deut. 1:39, Revised Version; II Sam. 14:17); cf. 13:22 and Cyrus Gordon, *Introduction to Old Testament Times* (Ventnor, N. J.: Ventnor Publishers, c. 1953), pp. 22-23; but the point here is discrimination (cf. Isa. 7:15), not factual knowledge.

sin introduced his need of hiding from deity (3:8). But he would have been confirmed in eternal life, approved by God, had he only obeyed. The "tree of life," finally, stood in Eden as the confirmatory sign of this covenant. It too was sacramental, actually mediating the promised life. For though man was not mortal prior to his probation, God had willed that, as a reward for passing the test, he should gain permanent immortality by eating of its fruit (3:22).

Into this setting came man's temptation to sin.[8] To experience temptation, however, is not in itself wrong. This particular experience could have been successfully passed and would then have become a matter of unsurpassed blessing (cf. Job 23:10). The source of man's fall lay in an external tempter, for sin did not then exist in man. Sin is thus by no means a necessary feature of human nature, nor can man's constitutional limitations be invoked as the essential element of sin. But behind the snake as tempter lay the evil personality of Satan. This latter fact is primarily a matter of New Testament, rather than contemporary, revelation (Rom. 16:20), though see below, topic 22-C. The object of the tempter's attack, moreover, was not Adam himself, but his wife Eve. It is not that woman is in any way the moral inferior to man. But 1) it was with Adam that God had talked; 2) it was Adam who stood as the representative head of the race (2:17) and who would thus be more on his guard; and 3) it was in Adam's position as a husband, through the person of the one whom he loved, that he could most effectively be overcome.

The primary aim of the tempter was to induce Eve to a sympathetic entertainment of the act of disobedience. This would, per se, constitute the true, spiritual fall; for it would signify the fundamental sin of pride in one's self, as opposed to God. The physical act would then be secondary, external; the eating of the fruit, in fact, seems not to have been inherently harmful or wrong.[9] The method of the tempter, though of seeming simplicity, was astute in the extreme. He began with an apparently harmless question of fact, "Yea, hath God said, Ye shall not eat of any tree of the garden?" (Gen. 3:1). But the psychological potentialities of this question were far-reaching. 1) To it, Eve was able to provide an answer that showed a knowledge superior to that of the tempter, and she was thereby furnished with an initial experience that was gratifying to the pride. 2) Eve was, moreover, from the outset placed in the position of an arbiter be-

---

[8] The interpretations of liberalism have indeed denied to Gen. 3 all significance in reference to the sinfulness, the fall, or the depravity of mankind, seeing in it rather anything from aetiological legends (e.g. why snakes go on their belly and men dislike them) to polytheistic myths (e.g. Adam, the earth god, and his companion Eve, the earth serpent), cf. Ludwig Kohler, *Old Testament Theology*, pp. 175, 177, 250. One could hardly discover, however, a more utter disregard of the analogy of Scripture (Rom. 5:12).

[9] Cf. Gen. 3:6, "good for food." Whether the fruit was the traditional apple is not stated and is in fact irrelevant.

tween God's word and some alternate possibility. Her unavoidably truthful answer, "Of the fruit of the trees of the garden we may eat" (v. 2), gave her the satisfying experience of "defending" God and thwarting the tempter; though it may also have begun to elicit within her an unconscious sympathy for the rebuffed questioner. 3) Next, by Satan's clever exaggeration of the divine prohibition, "not eat of *any* tree of the garden?" Eve was pushed into an explicit admission of her own restricted status.[10] "But of the fruit of the tree which is in the midst of the garden, God hath said, 'Ye shall not eat of it'" (v. 3). Thus came the implication that she too was being humiliated and thwarted. 4) By Satan's asking, moreover, "Hath God said?" the woman was forced to consider the exact form of God's words, and she was stimulated to express the charitable reason that God had given in justification of His prohibition, namely, "Ye shall not eat of it . . . *lest ye die.*" This quotation thus introduced the very subjects that Satan wished considered. Eve, furthermore, was thereby provided with a means for saving face in respect to God's limitation of her rights: it was for her own good. But who wants to "save face" if there exists some more positive alternative? 5) Satan accordingly replied, "Ye shall not surely die" (v. 4), but then immediately shifted the conversation to the question of God's "real" reasons for the original prohibition. Eve's curiosity was thus brought into play, and she was encouraged to defend the feeling of mistrust toward God on the basis of what *might be* the divine motivation for so restricting mankind.[11]

Satan's corresponding arguments possessed both a positive and a negative side. Positively, he resorted to a series of half truths (3:4, 5). Each of these was in a sense valid, but not in the way in which he suggested that they be understood. The half truths were as follows: 1) that the knowledge of good and evil, as acquired by disobedience, was desirable; 2) that God already possessed this knowledge and, selfishly, wished to keep men from it; and 3) that the knowledge thus acquired would give to man experience like God Himself possessed and would put them on a parity with God. Once this sort of distrust was insinuated, then the tempter's basic assertion, his denial of punishment, would seem relatively plausible.[12] Negatively, moreover, Satan concealed the real issues: he never directly asked for disobedience, he never questioned God's sovereign right to rule, and he never sought to investigate the reality either of God's threat of death (2:17) or of God's power to execute it.

---

[10]The popular interpretation, that when Satan asked, "Hath God said?" he thereby became the first "higher critic," thus misses the force of the sequence in the temptation. The tempter was here seeking, not man's *question* of God's command, but rather his admission of it!

[11]Cf. Kohler's well phrased analysis, *op. cit.*, p. 168.

[12]Cf. Vos' description of the temptation in these two states, *op. cit.*, p. 45.

Ezekiel 28:15 proceeds to state the sad truth that iniquity was found in man.[13] There remains, however, some uncertainty as to the precise point at which the fall occurred, namely, that point at which Eve's sympathetic entertainment of disobedience came into actual being. The following exist as possibilities within Genesis 3. Verse 1: the Fall might have occurred at the tempter's question, "Hath God said?" though Eve could have taken the tempter's query quite innocently.[14] Verse 3: the Fall might be suggested by the woman's adding that they were "not to touch" the tree, though God could have made just such an unrecorded prohibition. Verse 6a: it could have transpired when she recognized the fruit as "good for food," though the fruit may well have been thoroughly edible; or, verse 6b, when she appreciated the tree as "pleasant to the eyes," although the tree probably was just that. But in the next phrase, verse 6c, when Eve made the admission that eating of the fruit was "to be desired to make one wise," it becomes clear that the fall had occurred: the tempter *had* been believed and disobedience *had* definitely become a matter of her desire. But, as Professor John Murray has observed,[15] its appearance is most likely to have occurred following verse 5. When Satan blasphemously denied God's threat of death, and Eve yet raised no objection to his words, she could not longer have been God's true follower. So she ate of the fruit, Adam followed her lead, the covenant was transgressed, and man had fallen.

C. THE RESULTS OF THE FALL. When Adam and Eve partook of the forbidden fruit, their eyes were opened (Gen. 3:7). As the tempter had predicted, they now had come to know by experience good and evil and its guilt. They had matured, though hardly to the parity with God that they had coveted (v. 5). The first result of the fall appeared in their loss of innocence, a loss which was expressed in fear (3:10). Adam, it is true, sought to assign the cause of their fear to an awareness of bodily nakedness. God, however, assigned its cause to the voice of their conscience, answering to their having experienced evil (3:11). Actually, God was right and Adam was wrong. Sex is not evil (cf. 2:24); and nakedness becomes a matter of shame only because of sin-burdened minds. Their sense of nakedness seems rather to have arisen as an afterthought to the fear. Sewing the fig leaves was thus merely an escape mechanism, a futile attempt

[13]Ezek. 28:13-16 consists of a comparison of the king of Tyre with something (s), though interpreters differ as to what. The fall of Satan raises serious difficulties, see below, topic 22-C; and the most natural subjects for these verses appear to be, alternately, Adam (vv. 13 and 15) and the cherubim on the ark in the Temple on Mt. Zion (vv. 14 and 16).
[14]Note Vos' excellent analysis, especially of the implications of Satan's phrase, "of every tree of the garden," which proposes too sweeping a prohibition by God, *loc. cit.*
[15]In classes at Westminster Theological Seminary.

to find recourse for a moral evil in the form of a physical covering (cf. Job 31:33).[16] Further, their loss of innocence meant broken fellowship with God: they felt required to hide from the Divine Presence (v. 8).

But men, at the very time they fell, become the objects of God's gracious search (v. 9). They became also the objects of His interrogation (vv. 11, 13). God's questions, moreover, were presented in an opposite order to that of the previously committed sinful acts, so that the order of causation might be made very clear. Thus Adam was first called upon to answer, and he did with the truth (cf. I Tim. 2:14) but with an attempted evasion of responsibility. Then Eve answered, with the same unworthy sort of attitude. It appears significant, however, that God did not carry the interrogation further, so as to question the tempter. The relationship, that is, between God, Satan, and evil is at some points beyond the scope, both of God's historical revelation, and also of legitimate discussion within Biblical theology!

Immediately after His words of questioning, God uttered a series of curses, in the order in which the deeds had been committed: upon the serpent, then upon the woman, and lastly upon the man. Each was appropriate to the individual concerned; each, moreover, affected that party's most central function. For the curse upon the serpent, see below, topic 22-C. But even at this point the basic truth must be observed that the enmity injected between man and Satan implied a corresponding reconciliation of man with God. Herein lay the beginnings of the gracious testament.[17] In Eve's curse (3:16), the statement that "her desire should be to her husband" may be interpreted in either of two ways. It might be understood as relating to the clause that follows, namely, that she would desire to rule her husband, but that he would in fact rule her. Or, as seems more likely, it may be related to the preceding clause, namely, that she should suffer pain in pregnancy and in childbirth, yet that her sexual desire toward her husband would so drive her to render these curses inescapable.[18] Adam's curse likewise affected his most basic activity: he was condemned to sweat and sorrow in his labor as he provided for life, until he should work no more (vv. 17-19).

For, stemming from the original threat of the covenant of works came God's ultimate curse: "In the day that thou eatest thereof thou shalt surely die" (Gen. 2:17). Man, could have gone on living (cf. 3:22). It is true that Adam had not yet eaten of the tree of life; but even though he had not yet attained to this state of eternally con-

---

[16]"The reflex of the ethical," Vos, op. cit., p. 53; cf. Kohler, op. cit., p. 168.
[17]See above, p. 92.
[18]It is noteworthy in this regard that when sin ceases, childbearing ceases also (Mark 12:25) — men in the resurrection neither marry nor are given in marriage, but are become like the angels. Further, redemption even now works against the curse in alleviating both woman's pain in childbirth and man's in his work.

firmed, unlosable life, he was yet bestowed with an unhampered fellowship with God, which thereby entailed a life that continues. (Ps. 73:23; Mark 12:27). There was thus no natural reason why man had to die.[19] Death came rather as punishment for sin. The meaning, therefore, of the clause, "in the day that thou eatest," cannot be that of premature death, as though Adam would have died anyhow. Neither can it refer to his spiritual death, the separation of mankind from God that took place at the precise time of the Fall; for the emphasis of the context is upon man's body and its return to dust (3:19). Vos's explanation, moreover, of "the inevitable eventuation" of death[20] seems to correspond insufficiently to the words "in that *day*." Most likely appears Keil's suggestion, that on the day of man's eating, the germ of death entered him — though not death itself — so that he came under its power and became mortal[21] (Rom. 5:12a).

These overwhelming results of sin, however, are not limited in their application to that first couple thousands of years ago. When Adam acted, he acted as representative head of the race: the curse that fell on him has fallen on us all. Among the patriarchs, Abraham too was "but dust and ashes" (Gen. 18:27). Moses saw his contemporary generation passing, like grass that is cut down and withereth (Ps. 90:5, 6; cf. 103:15, 16; Isa. 40:6,7). He described death as "the visitation of all men" (Num. 16:29). So Solomon uttered his conclusion that "There is no man that hath power in the day of death: and there is no discharge in that war" (Eccl. 8:8).

But even more serious, as a result of the fall, is the terrifying picture that ensues of Adam's soul in its relationship with God. That first sin in the Garden of Eden (Gen. 3:6) led immediately to another (v. 8) and to another (v. 12). It accounted indeed for the man's total depravity. This curse, too, as it fell on him, has fallen on all of us. Job in desperation cried, "Who can bring a clean thing out of an unclean? Not one!" (14:4). The apostle Paul, moreover, truly gloried in the hope of the Gospel that, by the obedience of One, many should be made righteous (Rom. 5:19). But his hope took its meaning from that parallel, but catastropic, event in Eden: for just as by one man sin entered into the world, and death by sin, "so also death passed

---

[19]God's words, "Dust thou art, and unto dust shalt thou return" (3:19) can be appealed to as substantiating a "natural" inevitableness of death only by twisting the words from their context. For they constitute a judicial sentence, uttered *as the result* of man's fall; they would lose their very significance as a curse were they to be considered descriptive of man's previous, natural state. Kohler, *op. cit.*, p. 177, is thus guilty of what Vos styles "careless exegesis," *op. cit.*, p. 47; for the point of God's curse is to introduce as a new factor the penalty of human death, not to prevent any disturbance of the "natural" operation of death, should man take of the tree of life. The removal of man from the garden and from the tree of life appears only subsequently, almost as an afterthought.
[20]*Op. cit.*, p. 49.
[21]*Biblical Commentary on the Old Testament, the Pentateuch*, I:105-106.

upon all men, for all sinned [in Adam]" (2:12b); and "by the offense of one, judgment came upon all men to condemnation" (v. 18).

For Further Reading:

Leander S. Keyser, *Man's First Disobedience.* New York: The Macmillan Co., 1924. An evangelical defence of the Biblical record of the Fall.

John L. McKenzie, "Mythological Allusions in Ezekiel 28:12-18," *Journal of Biblical Literature,* 75:4, (Dec., 1956), 322-327. A thoroughly liberal article, but one that well associates this passage with Gen. 2 and 3.

H. Sheldon Smith, *Changing Conceptions of Original Sin.* New York: Charles Scribner's Sons, 1955. A historical study of this aspect of American theology since 1750, Chapter 9 noting the modern revival of interest therein.

17. The Nature of Man*

The Old Testament presents no systematic discussion of the abstract nature of man, any more than it does of the nature of God. Man's testamental heirship, however, does involve corollaries in respect to his nature that assume a considerable place within Biblical revelation. The fall of man, in particular, presupposes and reveals certain qualities in reference to human kind itself. This fact then causes the Old Testament's discussion of the nature of man to appear at a point that is completely contrary to the order suggested by the speculative approach of Greek thought: for the discussion of man's nature comes logically, not as the introduction, but as the conclusion to the Biblical doctrine of man.

A. THE ORIGIN OF MAN. Though Scripture presents the origin of man only as explanatory to his present heirship (Gen. 1:29, 30), it yet magnifies man's appearance in history as being the climax of God's general creative work. Man's creation is summarized by Moses in Genesis 1:27, with more detail being given in chapter 2. Some of these truths, however, must have been appreciated by Adam himself in the primeval period. The name Adam, *ādhām,* means "man, mankind"; and Scripture makes it clear that Adam and his wife Eve were indeed the original human pair. Mankind was created by special, divine fiat. Eve is expressly stated to have been formed from Adam by the direct act of God (2:21), and Adam's breath came into being by a similarly direct act (2:7). It is true that the statement relative to Adam's body, that "God formed man of the dust of the ground" (*ibid.*), has been adduced by some as supporting the theory of theistic

---

*BIBLE READING: Genesis 2; Ezekiel 18

Collateral Reading: A. B. Davidson, *The Theology of the Old Testament,* pp. 182-203.

Schultz, *Old Testament Theology,* II:242-269.

evolution, that God "created" man out of "living dust." Romanist theologians, for example, who on many doctrines tend to be conservative, regularly state about man's origin:

"Relative to the human body the exegete need not reject as contrary to Sacred Scripture the teaching that God equipped an organized body with a reasoning soul after the former had undergone a long period of development."[1]

This, however, is not the teaching of Genesis 2:7, which states that it was not until after God had breathed His spirit into man that man became a "living being." The analogy, moreover, of the obviously non-evolutionary return of the body *to* the dust (3:19), as well as the analogy of the creation both of Eve's body and Adam's soul, demonstrates the un-Biblical nature of such evolutionary theories.

The date of Adam's creation is not given. William Henry Green and John D. Davis interpreted the genealogical date of Genesis 5 and 11 so as to understand the generations that are listed in these chapters as successive rather than as overlapping; and their system, with modification, produces a date for Adam of about 15,000 B.C.[2] Other evangelicals, however, have posited gaps in the Genesis records which would allow for Adam's creation at 100,000 B.C., or 1,000,000 B.C. if necessary![3] But actually the latest assured results of dating human remains, by the radio-active carbon 14 process, give a date of no earlier than 10,000 B.C. for New World Indians (post-diluvian?) and 14,000 B.C. for the famous Lascaux cave paintings of France, though the earliest Eastern Hemisphere evidence may take us back to about 30,000 B.C.[4] The sexual distinction within mankind existed as part of God's original pattern (Gen. 1:27), and the marriage relationship was monogamous (cf. Matt. 19:6). Finally, as opposed to all of humanity since that time, with the exception of Christ (the sinless last Adam), Adam and Eve were by nature good (Gen. 1:31).

As to the origin of the human race subsequent to the first pair, Scripture confirms the observable fact that men's bodies are produced by natural generation. God's first orders to mankind included their obligation of filling the earth (1:27, 28; Hebrew, *mālē*, "fill," not "refill," as suggested by the Old English of the Authorized Version).

---

[1]Paul Heinisch, *Theology of the Old Testament*, p. 165. Yet cf. Allan MacRae's more Biblical conclusion, "Man becomes animate only after he is man." "The Principles of Interpreting Genesis 1 and 2," *Bulletin of the Evangelical Theological Society*, II:4 (Fall, 1959), p. 5.
[2]For an elaboration of this "successive counting" of generations (Gen. 15:13, 16), see John D. Davis, *A Dictionary of the Bible*, though the names must be of individuals rather than of family groups.
[3]Byron Nelson, *Before Abraham* (Minneapolis: Augsburg Publishing House, 1948), p. 16. Note especially Luke 3:36 compared with Gen. 11:12.
[4]Cf. Edwin A. Olson, "Radiocarbon Dating," *Journal of the American Scientific Affiliation*, 11:1 (March, 1959), p. 8.

Eve thus became the mother of all the living (3:20),[5] and all men who are alive today are descended from the three sons of Noah (9:19; 10:32). In respect to the mind, "the thing that thinks" and really makes the man, Eve, in the very primeval period, recognized that her children came as a gift from God (4:1; cf. Job 33:4; Ps. 104:29, 30). The most important passage, however, stems from the Davidic period, namely, his famous Psalm 139. David stated that even as the body comes from the parents, having been created by God (v. 13), so the ordained days of the spirit commence at that point as well (v. 16). Man is a unified whole, created together (cf. Ps. 119:73; Job 10:8). Job (revealed to Israel in the early disruption period) contains the following poetic statement: "Naked came I out of my mother's womb and naked shall I return thither" (1:21). But this passage is simply comparing the grave and the womb as two similarly dark, unknown places (cf. Ps. 139:15). It should not be taken as teaching a pre-existent life of the soul prior to conception,[6] parallel to its life after death. But Job goes on to note that, since all men are created by God in the same way, all men are therefore essentially equal (31:15).

Subsequent periods show little additional progress in this doctrine. Jeremiah 1:5, of the later prophetic period, describes the creation of a man's body and spirit together in the womb, though it also reveals the reality of God's elective purpose for the individual long before his creation. Ezekiel 28:13 (exilic) reaffirms the truth of the creation of the first man, in Eden.

B. MAN'S CONSTITUENT ELEMENTS. God's words at the fall of man (primeval period) served to reveal the nature of the material human body — dust (Gen. 3:19); and Moses' subsequent description concerning Adam's creation then made explicit the truth of an additional spiritual element in the human make-up (1:26). Man's essentially dualistic nature[7] thus appears early in Biblical revelation. On the one hand is the body, Hebrew bāsār, "flesh," which is composed of āfār, "dust," and n'shāmā, "breath" (2:7). N'shāmā, furthermore carries the idea of life-breath and so comes to mean "life" (I Kings 17:17; Job 27:3; Isa. 2:22). This term is generally restricted in its application to humans (cf. Deut. 20:16, 17; Josh. 10:40), though it may also be used for animals (Gen. 7:22); and of course animals have, or are, bāsār (6:17; 7:15; cf. 7:21). "Flesh" in the Old Testa-

---

[5]The concept of "pre-Adamites," if it is held to describe true men, is thus opposed to the teaching of Scripture.
[6]Such beliefs, due to Greek influence, do emerge in the non-canonical Apocrypha (Wisdom of Solomon 8:19).
[7]Note Davidson, *The Theology of the Old Testament*, p. 192, *spirit* and *soul* in antithesis to the *flesh*; p. 199, "The *soul* as well as the spirit is used to designate the whole immaterial part of man." Cf. L. Berkhof, *Systematic Theology*, pp. 191-195.

ment does not connote man's unregenerate nature, as it does in the Pauline writings, but only his temporariness: "All flesh is grass" (Isa. 40:6; Ps. 78:39).[8] This is true even in such a verse as Jer. 17:5, "Cursed is the man that trusteth in man, and maketh [impermanent] flesh his arm." "Flesh" may, on the contrary, carry a positive connotation, signifying that which is soft and yielded to God, and being contrasted with what is stony (Ezek. 36:26).

On the other hand, in man's dual composition, is the spirit, Hebrew, *rûah,* "wind, spirit," which is the active power that comes from God (Isa. 42:5). A man's spirit is said to be consumed when he is sick or faint (Job 17:1), but it comes back as a "second wind" and he "revives" (Judg. 15:19; I Sam. 30:12). Beasts too have *rûah* from God (Ps. 104:29, 30). Their spirit, however, comes into being simply as the earth brings them forth (Gen. 1:24), while Adam's was bestowed by the special creative act of God (2:7). The Trinity took counsel in the creating of man, but not of the beasts (1:26). Man is unique (2:20). Man's spirit is thus one of personal intelligence; it is capable of receiving and appreciating abstract thoughts from God. After one of Daniel's tremendous experiences of revelation, for example, it is said that his *rûah* was distressed within its bodily *nidhne,* the Aramaic word for "sheath" (Dan. 7:15).

In Scripture, however, man is generally treated, not dualistically, but as a whole. The *nefesh,* "soul," is the entire man and *nefesh* may therefore often be translated simply as "self," a "person" (Gen. 12:5; 17:14). In poetry, a synonym used for a man's soul is his *kāvōdh,* or "glory" (Gen. 49:6; Ps. 16:9). The basic meaning of *nefesh* appears to be "breath" or "throat" (Isa. 5:14; Hab. 2:5).[9] So in passages such as Job 11:20; 31:39 to lose one's life is literally to "breathe out *nefesh,* soul." Then, since the breathing being is alive, *nefesh* comes to mean life (cf. Jer. 38:16) or living creatures (Gen. 9:12). This significance is demonstrated in Deuteronomy 12:23 where blood, meaning "life blood," has a similar connotation: "The blood is the *nefesh* [life], and you shall not eat the *nefesh* with the blood." Or again, perhaps from the "throat" etymology, *nefesh* may mean "appetite, desire" (Eccl. 6:9; cf. v. 7). In any event, *nefesh* comes eventually to equal what thinks and feels, namely, the whole man (Gen. 34:3; Ps. 42:2), an individual "soul." Though usually treated as immortal, the soul may thus be said to "die" (Judg. 16:30; Num. 23:10). As Schultz puts it:

> "Souls" just means men, persons. Hence since a dead person is still "somebody," it is strictly correct to call him "a soul." Thus a man can say, "let my soul die," "my soul lives"; while, on the

[8]Hence its application in Gen. 6:3, as previously discussed, see above, p. 207.
[9]Heinisch stresses the primary meaning as "gullet," *op. cit.,* p. 167.

other hand, death is the departure of the soul, and a person lives by his soul.[10]

Néfesh hayyā, "living soul," equals "a live man" (Gen. 2:7), or sometimes animal (1:20).[11]

Soul, *néfesh,* is generally felt as being a more personal and individual term than *rúah,* spirit. Man has a *rúah,* but he is a *néfesh*: he thinks with his *rúah,* but the thinker is the *néfesh.* Roughly speaking then, man's constitutional elements may be plotted as follows:

$$\left. \begin{array}{l} \text{\textit{āfār},\ dust} \\ + \\ \text{\textit{n'shāmā},\ breath} \end{array} \right\} = \textit{bāsār},\ \text{flesh} \left. \begin{array}{l} \\ + \\ \textit{rúah},\ \text{spirit} \end{array} \right\} = \textit{néfesh},\ \text{"soul," self}$$

At death the flesh returns to dust (Gen. 3:19; Ps. 103:14; Job 34:14, 15), for man is but dust and ashes (Gen. 18:27). The same process of physical decomposition is equally true for animals (Ps. 104:29). Man's body, however, serves as the instrument for his divinely breathed spirit and is therefore not without honor. Among the Hebrews it was a serious disgrace for a corpse to be mutilated (II Sam. 21:10; cf. Jer. 7:33) or to remain unburied (Isa. 14:20; Jer. 16:4). The permanent significance of the body is shown by the Biblical doctrine of its ultimate resurrection (Dan. 12:2).[12] At death the spirit returns to the presence of God Himself (Eccl. 12:7). In this regard, *rúah* and *néfesh* are often used interchangeably (Isa. 26:9; and compare Ex. 6:9 with Num. 21:4).[13] Both leave the body at death, and they then exist in a state separate from that of the body (Gen. 35:18; cf. I Kings 17:22 on the rare case of a soul's return to its body).[14]

Another Hebrew term that may stand for the whole person is *lēv,* "heart" (Gen. 18:5). More precisely, "heart" serves as a symbol for the focus of life (Deut. 6:5): "Thou shalt love Yahweh thy God with all thy *lēv.*" The real man, the "heart," is thus not to be judged by externals (I Sam. 16:7; cf. Lam. 3:33, "For God doth not afflict from His *lēv,* heart"). The *lēv* may therefore be said to consist of the

---

[10]*Old Testament Theology,* II:249, and note his many proof texts.

[11]Knight, however, notes that *néfesh* is not used for particular animals, *A Christian Theology of the Old Testament,* p. 35; but it still has a wider meaning than the term "person."

[12]See topic 30, on life after death.

[13]Cf. Knight, *op. cit.,* p. 36. The chart noted a few lines above is thus only a generalization. The Hebrew words for the constituent parts of man, it must be cautioned, are not used in Scripture as precise theological definitions, and considerable freedom is to be found. Views, however, of trichotomy — man in three parts: body, soul, and spirit — fail to square with the Old Testament (or N.T.) evidence. Cf. Davidson's excellent summary, *op. cit.,* p. 203.

[14]This latter case invalidates the liberal claim that the soul cannot exist without the body, L. Kohler, *Old Testament Theology,* p. 145; but since *néphesh* ordinarily suggests the combination of spirit and flesh, it is true that the word seldom occurs in the Old Testament for a disembodied spirit (though cf. Ps. 16:10; 86:13, and Davidson, *op. cit.,* pp. 200-201).

more inward feelings, which in expression constitute the *néfesh*, the soul (Jer. 4:19). Such connotations seem to have been associated with the heart because of its function in pumping the blood, which is so essential to life (Gen. 9:4). This is borne out by the figurative description in Ecclesiastes of the aging body (12:3-6), in which the heart is equated with the pitcher that carries the water at the well (v. 6).

Three particular usages of *lēv* appear in the Old Testament. 1) The heart may signify a man's motivating spirit (Prov. 4:23); it is the source of the issues of life. 2) The heart may be treated as the seat of a man's moral qualities. Thus Psalm 51:12 speaks of a "pure heart," and Job 27:6 refers to Job's heart as synonymous with his conscience. Of a negative moral quality is the "deceitful heart" (Jer. 17:9). 3) Most prominently, *lēv*, "the heart" in Hebrew, equals what is popularly "the head" in English. That is to say, the heart concerns the intellectual function of knowing (Deut. 8:5). "Men of heart" are wise men (Job 34:10, 34), and even Yahweh is said to consider "in His heart" (Gen. 8:21). Only the particular Biblical context can determine the exact force of *lēv* in a given verse. The emotional concept, however, which is represented by the English term "heart" is most generally symbolized in Hebrew by *mē'îm*, the intestines (Song of Sol. 5:4), and also by *k'lāyōth*, the "reins," or kidneys (Ps. 73:21).

C. THE IMAGE OF GOD. A testament requires certain correspondence between the testator and the heir. Man therefore was created "in the image of God" (Gen. 1:26). This creation of man in God's image was what distinguished him from the animals, in which the divine image does not appear. It constituted, moreover, the basis for Adam's fellowship with God (2:19); and it gave mankind a rank only a little below that of the angels (Ps. 8:5; Heb. 2:7). The "image" affects the entire pattern of human life. It bestows upon man his value in the eyes of God, and it thus became the factor that insured his divinely ordained protection, against both beast and fellow human (Gen. 9:5, 6). Again, it was man's position as distinctive from that of the lower forms of life because of his association with God,[15] that made his sexual defilement with animals punishable by death (Lev. 18:23; 20:15).

Little is said in Scripture about the original state of man in God's image, because this information was not of primary relevance to the current testament. But from the brief clues that are given, plus certain deductions that may be made by arguing backward from man's present condition,[16] certain facts about the initial image of God do

---

[15]Note how among all the beasts there was found no help "meet" (corresponding, appropriate) to him (2:20).
[16]Cf. D. Garth Whitley, "The Primitive Condition of Man," *Princeton Theological Review*, 4, 3 (Oct., 1906), pp. 513-534.

appear. In the first place, the terms "image" and "likeness" (Gen. 1:25; 5:3) are used interchangeably (cf. 1:27 and 5:1). Man's character is a "reflection" of the qualities of God. The image thus connotes "freedom" and "blessedness," as it reflects within man the cosmic, ethical, and beneficent sovereignty of the Testator Himself.[17] Contextually then, the quality most emphasized in the original revelation of the image of God is that of man's cosmic dominion (Gen. 1:27, 28). Adam's dominion, for example, is witnessed by his naming of the animals (2:20). Furthermore, although God and His image are spiritual,[18] the presence of this sovereign image gives meaning to man's body as well; for it is the body that constitutes the fitly designed instrument through which man is to exercise his dominion. The body's eternal significance, in fact, appears from its utilization, when resurrected mankind shall assume their ultimate rule over creation. Thus God's theophanic appearances occur consistently in human form (Ezek. 1:26). Man in the divine image possessed also the freedom of ethical choice (2:16), a necessary quality[19] even though it opened the way for his possible fall. But at the same time the image meant that man had been created good (1:31) — "perfect in thy ways from the day that thou wast created" (Ezek. 28:15). The divine image thus implies all the various aspects of God's reflected glory and honor — "sealing up the sum, full of wisdom, and perfect in beauty" (v. 12; cf. Job 15:7). It may be defined, in summary, as the totality of man's higher powers that distinguish him from brute creation.

But Ezekiel 28:15 goes on to say, "Perfect in thy ways . . . *till* unrighteousness was found in thee." Of the same effect is Ecclesiastes 7:29, "God made man upright, *but* they have sought out many inventions." The fall, therefore, seriously impaired the divine image in man. 1) His cosmic dominion was exchanged for a losing struggle against nature (Gen. 3:19). As a result, Psalm 8:6, which describes man's original dominion, is at present found to be applicable only to Jesus Christ (Heb. 2:6-8). He is the last (not "second") Adam. That is to say, Christ is the only true Man; He alone fulfills what man was intended to be (I Cor. 15:45). 2) Ethically, the fall destroyed man's freedom to control his way to do the right (Jer. 10:23). It is not simply that man proposes and God disposes (Prov. 16:9), but that *what* man proposes God has to dispose *of* (Jer. 17:9)! Finally, 3) human goodness is now but surface goodness and it vanishes rapidly away (Hos. 6:4).

But the divine image has yet a continuing significance that extends beyond the fall (Gen. 9:6). For the image of God, along with human depravity, was transmitted by Adam to his descendants (5:1,

---

[17]See above, topic 12.
[18]See above, pp. 122, 123; and note how the image appears equally in male and female, despite their differences in bodily form (Gen. 1:27).
[19]See above, p. 215.

3). Man's higher powers, therefore, though marred, still persist as a pledge of what may some day be (Col. 3:10). God has placed a cosmic fear of mankind in the lower creation (Gen. 9:2); man is yet called upon to make the ethical decisions (Gen. 4:7; Deut. 11:26-29; Ezek. 3:27); and, although in himself he is incapable of responding to the right, God's Spirit can and does regenerate him (Ezek. 11:19) and grant him an imputed righteousness[20] which is not of his own making.

D. SOCIETY. The testament serves to define man's individual status, but it has social implications as well.[21] The Sinaitic testament, in particular, dealt with men in a group, speaking of Israel as a "corporate personality," and using the name "Jacob" for the whole nation or its remnant.[22] It thus makes significant contributions to our understanding of the nature of man as a collectivity. The testament, from its outset, demonstrates the essential equality of all men. Paul later spoke of man's racial unity in Adam and Noah (Acts 17:26);[23] and Job, in patriarchal days, maintained the rights of his servants on the basis of their common human creation: "Did not He that made me in the womb make him?" (Job 31:13-15). Just so, at the very beginning of history, the testament of reconciliation reveals the basically equal standing (and equal need) of men; for it was originally granted to all without distinction (Gen. 3:15). There appears, it is true, a testamental particularism that extends from Abraham to Calvary. Indeed, even before Abraham, the table of nations of Genesis 10 indicates how God introduced racial differences among men;[24] and the revelation of Genesis 11:9 reveals how He added linguistic and geographical distinctions because of the tower of Babel. All these social differences, moreover, were designed for the furtherance of the interests of those chosen people who should inherit His testament, namely, Israel (Deut. 32:8; cf. Eph. 2:12). The particularism, however, was only temporary, and it had as its purpose the ultimate proclamation of the Gospel to all without distinction.[25]

[20]See above, pp. 160, 161.
[21]The liberal and neo-orthodox claim that the Old Testament thinks of man *only* in the plural, and that man is always reckoned within a group, cf. Kohler, *op cit.*, p. 129, 162, patently fails to square with even the earliest O.T. revelations, which speak of Cain separated from his fellows (Gen. 4:15) and of Abraham called by the testament to take an individual stand against his own kindred (12:1).
[22]Similarly, in Josh. 24:6-7, Joshua could address the second generation Israelites as if they had actually been present during the lives of their fathers; they shared in one continuing community, Russell P. Shedd, *Man in Community* (London: The Epworth Press, 1958), p. 6.
[23]Cf. B. B. Warfield, "On the Antiquity and Unity of the Human Race," *Princeton Theological Review*, 9, 1 (Jan., 1911), pp. 1-25.
[24]Contrary to the liberal claim, this table is based upon racial descent, not upon language families (though these often correspond, Gen. 10:38), cf. Payne, *An Outline of Hebrew History*, pp. 21-22.
[25]See above, topic 14-D.

Another corollary of the older testament is that of the social rights of women. For in the God of the testament there is not only "neither Jew nor Greek, neither bond nor free," but also "neither male or female" (Gal. 3:28). In the theocracy of Israel women had, in fact, a position of equality before God which was unique in the cultural patterns of the ancient Near East. Women held every office in Hebrew society: prophetess (II Kings 22:14; Neh. 6:14), judge (Judg. 4:4), and even queen (though a wicked usurper, II Kings 11:3). Only the priesthood had no feminine representative, perhaps because of the physical exertions required in the services (cf. "heave" offerings, Ex. 29:27!). Sex is right (Gen. 1:28; 2:18; cf. Prov. 12:4; 19:14; Gen. 38:9, 10). Marriage is thus the oldest and most important social relationship (Gen. 2:24), and children are one of God's greatest gifts (4:1, 25; 25:21; cf. Ps. 127:3). Proverbs 31:10-31 cannot say enough in praise of the virtuous woman; indeed, it was through the seed of woman that the testamental deliverance of mankind was finally to come (Gen. 3:15). Women were equally responsible for obedience to the law (Deut. 31:12; Neh. 8:2). The one stressed exception is that a woman's husband might cancel the wife's vow (Num. 30:6-8). This, however, appears to have been enacted because the welfare of the family as a whole might be involved; cf. similar regulations relative to daughters prior to the time of their marriage. Only the males among the Hebrews were required to attend the three annual feasts (Ex. 23:17), but this specification seems to have been a humane concession due to childbirth and to the woman's responsibility for the children (cf. I Sam. 1:22). She possessed full rights of participation when she could attend. Her restriction to a separate, lower "court of the women" was an intertestamental and un-Biblical innovation that developed out of corrupted Judaism.

Another feature of the testamental teaching in respect to man and society is that of group responsibility. Adam's original sin has thus plunged the whole human race into collective depravity, guilt, and condemnation; though it must be admitted that this relationship of "federal headship" was unique in kind. Scripture is, however, filled with instances of punishment for sin which affected an entire social unit (Gen. 20:7). Especially noteworthy were Achan's theft, in the consolidation period, that caused Israel's national defeat (Josh. 7:1, 10) and David's later census, that caused a nation-wide pestilence (II Sam. 24:17). History demonstrates with what frequency "the iniquity of the fathers is visited upon the children unto the third and fourth generation" (Ex. 20:5).

Subsequent to Adam's initial transgression, however, collective punishment must be carefully distinguished from collective guilt. It is true that Canaanites, and such Israelites as were influenced by them, believed in collective guilt. The Gibeonites, for example, sought the slaying of Saul's sons, the idea being that Yahweh's anger, which had arisen because of the sins of Saul, would be turned away from Israel by the death of Saul's "guilty" family (II Sam. 21:6, 7). This belief, however, can hardly be classed as the normative teaching of Scripture. God did honor David's contemporary repentance, so that His anger ceased (v. 14). But David's ordering of the death of Saul's seven sons and grandsons was due to his rash promise made to the Canaanites of Gibeon in a moment of weakness (v. 4), and it must be grouped with his other great failures of this same period.[26] The true Old Testament position rejected such pagan concepts. The Bible demonstrates, contrariwise, a clear moral awareness of the individual character of innocence and guilt, an awareness that is witnessed as early as the recorded prayers of Abraham (Gen. 18:25) and Moses (Num. 16:22; cf. the distinction in Jer. 14:20 and Dan. 9:16 between "our wickedness and the iniquity of our fathers").

The concept of the responsibility of the individual within the group is what underlies the very existence of the requirements of personal obedience, both moral and ceremonial, that bulk so large in the Sinaitic testament.[27] Moses, in this period, laid stress upon the individualized nature of guilt. When the land, for example, should be defiled by blood, only the blood of the individual murderer could make atonement for such a pollution (Num. 35:33). Again a man was allowed to suffer execution only for his own sins, not for those of his relatives (Deut. 24:16; II Kings 14:6). Certain cases, such as the execution of Achan's whole family in the subsequent consolidation period (Josh. 7:24), might at first glance seem to teach to the contrary. It was in the crowded quarters, however, of an oriental tent that Achan buried his spoil; and all who lived with the guilty man must have participated in his crime to the extent of sharing in its guilt (vv. 22, 23). David in his psalms is noted for his individualistic relationship with God (cf. I Sam. 30:6); and in the eighth century, Isaiah's remnant doctrine[28] (7:3; 8:16) stands as a primary witness to the significance of the individual as opposed to the group.

In the later prophetic period, Jeremiah became preeminently the "man against the crowd" (Jer. 15:17) and Scripture's greatest exponent of individualistic faith (cf. Jer. 1:9). His contemporaries in Jerusalem, for example, criticized God's allowing of the second, select deportation (597 B.C.) and quoted the proverb, "The fathers have eaten sour grapes and the children's teeth are set on edge" (31:29; cf. Ps. 79:8). But though collectivism was a true explanation for their

---

[26]Payne, op. cit., p. 107. Shedd's willingness to justify these murders on the basis of the Biblical concept of "corporate personality," op. cit., p. 10, would seem to reduce Scripture to the level of ancient Semitic injustice.
[27]See above, pp. 100, 101, 184, 185; cf. G. Ernest Wright, The Rule of God (Garden City, N. Y.: Doubleday, 1960), p. 43.
[28]See above, topic 14-C.

punishment (cf. Lam. 5:7), it was not for their guilt. Jeremiah was therefore quick to disabuse them of this misconception and to assert that everyone should die for his own iniquity (Jer. 31:30). This same message was proclaimed in greater detail by Ezekiel shortly thereafter (18:2-21). Even if the most righteous men of the past and of Ezekiel's contemporary exilic scene — Noah, Daniel, and Job — were suddenly to be found in Palestine, their righteousness would serve to deliver only their own souls (14:14), and nobody else's, not even the souls of their children (v. 20). Vicarious atonement would be possible only by One who possessed the unique righteousness of the Servant of Yahweh (Isa. 53:5, 11; cf. its typifying in Aaron the high priest Ex. 28:38). Otherwise, the unchanging principle of Scripture is: "The soul that sinneth, it shall die" (18:4, 20). Thus only the faithful remnant would be saved after the exile (20:38; 34:20). Mankind's future hope, accordingly, lay in that individualistic new testament, when "They shall teach no more every man his neighbor saying, 'Know Yahweh; for they shall all know Me, from the least of them unto the greatest of them' " (Jer. 31:34). God's goal for the earth is indeed the "kingdom" of His Son, but this community finds its basis in the commitment of the individual to Him.[29]

For Further Reading:

J. Stafford Wright, *Man in the Process of Time.* Grand Rapids: Wm. B. Eerdmans Publishing Co., 1956. Evangelical, on the nature of man.

Walther Eichrodt, *Man in the Old Testament. Studies in Biblical Theology,* No. 4. Trans. by K. and R. Gregor Smith; Chicago: University of Chicago Press, 1951. A neo-orthodox and philosophical discussion of man as living under obligation to God.

Ludwig Kohler, *Hebrew Man.* Trans. by Peter R. Ackroyd; Nashville, Tenn.: The Abingdon Press, 1957. Another neo-orthodox work, covering broad aspects of physical and social, but also spiritual, life in the Old Testament.

---

[29]Wright, *op. cit.,* pp. 43-45.

Part V. The Effectuation: Grace

"All we like sheep have gone astray; we have turned every one to his own way; and Yahweh hath laid on Him the iniquity of us all" (Isaiah 53:6).

18. Regenerating Monergism*

A testament is characterized not simply by a testator and an heir, but also by an active interest of the former in the latter. The testator must take the necessary steps, if the heir is to receive the inheritance. God's activity to effectuate man's redemption constitutes, therefore, the third major aspect of the older testament.[1] Furthermore, since man is totally undeserving of God's favor, both because of original sin and because of his universally practiced sin,[2] this effectuating activity may be summarized under the term "grace." Grace marks God's monergistic, "one-sided" dealings with mankind in general; and it characterizes His regenerating work with sinners, who are hopeless by nature, in particular. Grace, moreover, marks His commissioning both of the Messiah, to redeem His Church, and of the angels, those celestial spirits that are sent forth to minister for them who are to be the heirs of salvation (Ps. 91:12; Heb. 1:14). Above all, grace distinguishes God's willingness to forfeit the life of His own dear Son; for a testament can ultimately be effectuated only by the death of the Testator (Heb. 9:17).

A. GENERAL MONERGISM. God's redemptive testament is, by definition, monergistic, a fact that is indicated by the Septuagint's very choice of *diathēkē* rather than *sunthēkē* for its translation of *b'rīth*.[3] It is true that prior to the fall man's life was regulated by a *sunthēkē*, a covenant of works, and that history's earliest situation was thus one of synergism, with mutual binding obligations between God and man. It was not a testament of grace, exhibiting undeserved favor for the guilty. But since the time of the Fall, redemption has been effectuated by God's sovereign disposition through a *diathēkē*, a last

---

*BIBLE READING: Judges 7; Daniel 4
Collateral Reading: Baab, *The Theology of the Old Testament,* pp. 114-138.
  H. H. Rowley, *The Faith of Israel,* pp. 62-73.

[1]See above, pp. 81-87.
[2]See above, topics 15, C-D; 16, A.
[3]See above, p. 83.

232

will or testament; and a testament is of necessity monergistic, having just "one worker." Thus the omnipotent God has "saved and called us with a holy calling, not according to our works, but according to His own purpose and grace" (II Tim. 1:9). As Baab has described it:

"It is not surprising that Israel's thinkers and saints hailed God as a covenant-keeping God. The keeper of the covenant is the giver of salvation."[4]

The primeval Edenic and Noachian testaments, in particular, were devised, revealed, established, and effectuated by God. At the very first revelation of the term *b'rîth*, the verb that was employed was *hēqîm*: God will "establish" (not "work out in a mutually agreeable fashion") the testament (Gen. 6:18; 9:9, 11). Even the matter of conditions to be fulfilled by men as qualifications for the testamental inheritance finds no immediate contextual mention.[5] The curses, moreover, that God pronounced after the Fall involved at the same time His sovereignly redeeming grace.[6] By His curse on the serpent, God monergistically introduced enmity between His chosen ones and Satan and, correspondingly, the reconciliation that brought them back into favor with Himself (Gen. 3:15). By His curse on Eve, namely, that of childbirth, He established the very means that would produce the saving "seed"; and childbirth also became the focus of woman's "home-station" in life, that medium through which she should demonstrate faith and enter into salvation (I Tim. 2:15). Even His curse on Adam, while it involved man's living by the sweat of his brow, yet became the means for preserving his life, as long as that life should last (Gen. 3:17-19). God's grace subsequently provided the skin clothing needed by the fallen pair (3:21). Eve recognized that her children were seed of God's appointment (4:25), born "with the help of Yahweh" (v. 1; cf. 5:29); and Noah is specifically stated to have found *hēn*, "grace," in the eyes of Yahweh (6:8). The tower of Babel, on the other hand, constituted a vivid demonstration of the ineffectuality of human efforts (11:1-9).

In the next period, the Abrahamic testament stressed imputed, not earned, salvation (Gen. 15:6). Its monergism is indicated, first of all, by the oath form in which the divine promise was stated (22:17; cf. Heb. 6:17),[7] by which God made it clear that *He* would perform what *He* had promised. It is indicated also by Scripture's re-

---

[4]*The Theology of the Old Testament*, p. 138. In the light, however, of this comment that "No other aspect of Israel's faith is so conspicuous as this, and no more fruitful inquiry can be made than to search the Scriptures for light on the covenant idea," p. 136, it is remarkable how little attention he actually devotes to the testament idea.
[5]Such did, however, exist (cf. Gen. 4:4, 5).
[6]Cf. Vos, *Biblical Theology*, p. 55.
[7]Again, though conditions of human fulfillment are revealed later (Gen. 17:14; 18:19), none are mentioned at the time of the revelation of the testament (15:18-21).

peated stress on the personal inability of the man Abraham. He was "a Syrian ready to perish" (Deut. 26:5), a man, by his own statement, "who [was] but dust and ashes" (18:27). When Abraham was called in Ur of the Chaldees, he was required to abandon both country and kindred (Acts 7:2-4); and he went out not knowing whither he went (Heb. 11:8). When he was called in Haran to go on to Canaan (Gen. 11:31), he left behind him his father's household as well (12:1). It was God who graciously promised him Canaan and promised him numberless descendants (13:14-17). It was God, moreover, who furnished him an unwarranted protection in Egypt and Gerar (12:18-13:2; 20:14-16) and granted him a major victory in war (14:14, 15), not to mention Melchizedek's blessing (14:19). But Abraham, on his part, never did gain possession of the Promised Land, and he had to purchase even the plot for his own final grave (23:4; cf. Acts 7:5). Furthermore, Abraham's man-made suggestions for his own advancement were deliberately over-ridden by God on more than one occasion (15:2; 17:18). The supreme demonstration of divine monergism in respect to Abraham came in the birth, late in his life, of Isaac, the child of promise (12:7; 15:3-4; 17:16, 21) when, humanly speaking, the fulfillment of this promise seemed impossible (Heb. 11:11, 12).[8] Among the subsequent patriarchs, Jacob's own craftiness left him a penniless exile, but God then moved in and made "Israel" into twelve tribes (Gen. 28:3; 32:10). Joseph's strength too lay in his confession, "It is not in me: God will give Pharaoh an answer" (41:16). But the attempted raid on Gath by his grandsons, in their own strength, brought down disaster upon the family (I Chron. 7:21).

Moses was the greatest leader, humanly speaking, that Israel ever had; but Moses was yet the meekest of men (Num. 12:3).[9] By way of contrast, his first efforts to deliver Israel, performed in his own strength, proved a miserable failure (Ex. 2:12-14); and he had, as a result, to undergo forty years of spirit-breaking discipline in the wilderness (Acts 7:23-30). Even after this, Moses himself achieved nothing when he went before Pharaoh (5:2). It was God who was in control and had hardened Pharaoh's heart, as He had, in fact, informed Moses previous to the whole encounter (4:21).[10] But, as it developed, it was God's miraculous plagues that finally gained for Israel release from Egypt (7:14-12:33); and it was His pillar of cloud and fire that led them on their way (13:21, 22).

---

[8]Vos well emphasizes the monergism of God's dealings with Abraham, *op. cit.*, pp. 94-95, though his exegesis of Gen. 14:21-23, on what was simply "tainted money," seems open to question, and his etymologies for *El Shaddai* must be rejected.
[9]Meekness, however, is not weakness. It consists essentially in recognizing one's proper place, even if this be one of violence (cf. Ex. 32:19, 20).
[10]See above, pp. 180, 198.

The Sinaitic testament, then, was essentially monergistic, and not synergistic. As Rowley explains, "It was not a commercial bargain or legal contract, but rather Israel's pledge of loyalty to Him who had first chosen and saved her."[11] God's disposition at Sinai had been preceded by grace at the Red Sea (Ex. 14:13; 15:2; cf. 19:4; 20:2); it was revealed by grace (19:4, 5; cf. Lev. 11:45);[12] and it was subsequently preserved by grace, as often as Israel failed (Ex. 32:11, 12; 33:13, 14). At the very time of their first failure (relative to the golden calf) and of their restoration to divine favor that followed, God made it clear that His forgiveness was not a matter of necessity, but only "perhaps" (32:30). For He specifically reserved to Himself the decision of mercy: "I will be gracious to whom I will be gracious" (33:19; cf. Joel 2:14; Jonah 3:9). Even then, Moses' intercession was based, significantly, not on the principle of excusing human frailty but of preserving God's own reputation, (32:12; cf. 7:5; Ezek. 20:9). Baab sums up Mosaic monergism as follows:

"God as father is revealed to be the creator and fashioner of the nation. He cares for, and watches over, Israel and requires love and loyalty of his children; he is also redeemer and determiner of their fate."[13]

The fundamental recourse of men under the "law" was to grace, as they appealed to God's undeserved mercy, especially as it had been shown to their patriarchal ancestors (Ex. 32:13; 33:13, 14). All success, moreover, was seen as the direct result of the work of the Lord (Deut. 20:3, 4). Moses went on to predict that when they should settle in the Promised Land, it would be God who would protect their territories from foreign aggression. Specifically, during the times of the three annual pilgrimage feasts, when all the males of Israel would be gathered at the central sanctuary, God Himself would keep watch over the unprotected substance of His people. Indeed, He would so work in the inner hearts of their enemies as to prevent the latter from even desiring Israel's land at such times (Ex. 34:24). Both the freedom of God's elective act and the deficiency of Israel's own strength are stressed in such passages as Deuteronomy 7:7; 8:17; 9:4. The Israelites were, in fact, a "stiff-necked" and wrath-provoking people (9:6). Accordingly, when they attempted to advance into Canaan in reliance upon their own effort (leaving the ark of God's testament in camp), their forces were cut to pieces at the border of the land (Num. 14:42-45). In the wilderness, the manna by which the nation was enabled to exist served as a constant reminder of the

---

[11]*The Faith of Israel* (Philadelphia: The Westminster Press, 1956). Used by permission.
[12]Here again the testamentary arrangement is divinely devised, revealed, and administered (Ex. 19:5-8; 20:1; 24:3-7; Deut. 4:13, 14). God "declared" it and "commanded" it for Israel to "keep" and "obey."
[13]*Op. cit.*, p. 124.

testamental promise that Yahweh was their God (Ex. 16:4, 12). Indeed, the whole forty year period of desert wandering was designed to humble Israel "lest thou say in thy heart, My power and the might of my hand hath gotten me this wealth" (Deut. 8:16, 17). The entire experience was to "make [them] know that man doth not live by bread alone, but by everything that proceedeth out of the mouth of Yahweh" (v. 3). So Hosea spoke of Israel's discipline in the Babylonian exile as an example of God's bringing her again "into the wilderness" (Hos. 2:14), and Moses predicted that the final restoration of the testamentary people would be when their own strength was similarly exhausted (Deut. 20:3, 4).

The history of the judges, during the years of the consolidation, demonstrates a repeated cycle of human self-will and sin, with a corresponding time of judgment, followed by God's gracious deliverance (Judg. 2:16-18). The result of each period of "grace" is generally expressed in terms of Israel's regaining its hold upon the material land of Palestine. But it must be recalled that the possession of the land was in itself a symbol of their testamental status of reconciliation with God (cf. Gen. 17:7, 8), so that this grace of deliverance *was* a real, saving grace. The victories of Joshua (21:44) and of the judges (I Sam. 7:10-12) are summed up in the phrase, "Ebenezer," (*Éven hā-Ézer*, the stone of help), "Hitherto hath Yahweh helped us." Likewise, the triumphs of Saul and his heroes became evidences of divine grace and of God's monergistic salvation. Particularly noteworthy were the campaigns of two of Israel's greatest champions. To Gideon God had said, "The people that are with thee are too many, lest Israel vaunt themselves against Me, saying, Mine own hand hath saved me" (Judg. 7:2; cf. Isa. 9:4; 10:26); but then, with a mere token human force, God overthrew the heathen hordes. Of similar import were David's words to the gigantic Goliath — "Thou comest to me with a sword, and with a spear, and with a javelin: but I come to thee in the name of Yahweh of hosts, the God of the armies of Israel, whom thou hast defied" (I Sam. 17:45); and the outcome remained but briefly in doubt. Thus, all the judges were weak, humanly speaking (cf. Judg. 3:31; 6:15), but powerful in God (cf. Ps. 83:9). Saul too arose from a lowly status and preserved, at least initially, a humility that God honored with blessing from on high (I Sam. 9:21; cf. I Kings 16:2; Dan. 4:17). Canaanitish Baalism, on the contrary, stressed "salvation by works"; and, as it rested its hopes on human religious manipulations, it proved correspondingly futile (Judg. 10:13, 15). Thus Hannah explained at Samuel's birth, "For by strength shall no man prevail" (I Sam. 2:9); and the writer of I Samuel proceeded to point out how Saul's failures came when he forgot, on the one hand, God's power and, on the other, his own inability (15:17-19).

David acknowledged that the testament that bears his name was unmerited on his part (II Sam. 7:18; cf. Ps. 78:70, 71; I Chron. 29:14), and that his answering success in battle must be attributed solely to God's favor. As he stated in his various psalms: "Some trust in chariots, but we will make mention of the name of Yahweh our God" (20:7); and, "There is no king saved by the multitude of his host, a horse is a vain thing for safety, [but] the eye of Yahweh is upon them that fear Him" (33:16-18; cf. 44:3, 6). At the time of his military census, David did succumb to a false trust in Israel's armed forces (II Sam. 24:2, 3), that is, until he was brought to his senses by God's punishing pestilence. Rowley, while recognizing the clear monergistic teaching of this chapter, has objected:

> "There are, indeed, passages in the Old Testament which suggest that God is arbitrary, such as that in which we are told that he made David to number the people and then punished him, and indeed his people with him, for doing so."[14]

But David, who was in a better position to judge, saw in it all God's purposeful hand, driving him to an awareness of his own sin and pride, and of his need for confession: for he went on to explain, "As for me, I said in my prosperity, I shall never be moved" (Ps. 30:6;[15] cf. Ps. 131:1). Divine monergism, however, not simply mortified the self-made man, but it also vivified the self-despairing man. As David's associate Asaph expressed it, "My flesh and my heart faileth; but God is the strength of my heart and my portion for ever" (73:26).

Solomon, too, began his reign in the next period with a recognition of his own inadequacy, and it was this very recognition which became the basis for his unsurpassed wisdom (I Kings 3:7). Solomon spoke of the king's heart as being in the hand of Yahweh, as a watercourse is directed by God (Prov. 21:1). He warned of the calamity of pride (11:2); and he commenced his wisdom psalm (Ps. 127) with the famous words, "Except Yahweh build the house, they labor in vain that build it." The wisdom literature of Job, which appeared in Israel at this same time, likewise stressed the non-meritorious character of even the best that man can accomplish by his own efforts (Job 22:2, 3; 35:6, 7). Solomon's chief difficulty lay in a disregard of his own proverb that "pride goeth before a fall" (Prov. 16:18); and subsequent kings either rose or fell in accordance with their reliance upon, or disdain toward, the grace of Yahweh. Under Asa, in about 900 B.C. (II Chron. 14:11), and under Jehoshaphat, in about 850 (20:12, 17), two of God's outstanding demonstrations of moner-

---

[14]*Op. cit.*, p. 67. Used by permission. His only solution is that Scripture cannot be on a "flat level"; that is, he resorts to partial inspiration. Rowley's criticism, however, appears superficial; see above, pp. 198, 199.
[15]On Ps. 30's assignment to this point, see above, pp. 164, 198.

gistic salvation were enacted against the heathen, "that they may know that Thou alone, whose name is Yahweh ['He is present'], art the Most High over all the earth" (Ps. 83:18).[16] To this same end, Elisha prayed that his servant might behold God's encircling chariots of fire and so come to appreciate that "they that are with us are more than they that are with them" (II Kings 6:16, 17). Finally, the prophetic writer of II Samuel, late in the tenth century B.C., drew satisfaction from the ease with which God was able to thwart the counsel of Ahithophel (II Sam. 17:18; cf. I Kings 12:15), even though it possessed such compelling logic, humanly speaking.

The chief reason for the involvement of the eighth century prophets in the politics of their time lay in their concern over the tendency of the Hebrew kingdoms to seek safety in international alliances, rather than in a heartfelt commitment to the God who alone could sustain them. Hosea warned, "Assyria will not save us" (14:3; cf. 5:13), and decried his people's trust in Egypt as equally futile (7:11). Isaiah, too, made it clear that Assyria lacked the self-sufficiency of which it boasted (Isa. 10:13, 14). Sennacherib's defiance of God simply sealed his own doom (37:29): he would fall by the sword, but not by a sword of men (31:8; cf. 37:38 and 63:3, which speaks of God's treading the wine press alone). Likewise Moab's pride would be brought to naught (16:6, 7). No nation, in fact, could hope to stand against Yahweh, "the One present" with Israel (8:9, 10). The nations were all but a "drop in the bucket" (40:15); and some day, at the time of God's great future intervention, "the haughtiness of man shall be brought low, and Yahweh alone shall be exalted" (2:17; cf. v. 11).

By the same token Isaiah rebuked his own Jewish sovereign, Hezekiah, for having boasted in his treasure (39:6) and having trusted in his fortifications and water tunnel, rather than in the Lord, the creator of the universe (22:9-11). "All flesh is grass" (40:6), God proclaimed through Isaiah, "and beside Me there is no savior" (43:11). If Israel would but "take heed, and be quiet, and fear not," she would experience in God's intervening grace the longed-for victory over her enemies, which were already but "tail-ends of smoking firebrands" (7:4). As Isaiah summed up the hope, and yet also the failure, of Israel, "In returning and rest shall ye be saved; in quietness and in confidence shall be your strength; and ye would not" (30:15). Monergism had, indeed, characterized God's dealings from the very first: "Thou wilt ordain peace for us; for Thou *hast* also wrought all our works for us" (26:12). It is true that God's interventions came about, not primarily for Israel's sake, but for His own;

---

[16]On the historical background to Ps. 83, and on the assignment of the Asaphite Jahaziel as author of this psalm, see Payne, *An Outline of Hebrew History*, pp. 124-125.

they occurred as the result of His concern and indignation over the profanation of His own holy name (48:9, 11). But such divine zeal holds redemptive aspects; for "it is his holy intolerance of that which is not merely antithetical to his own character, but also hostile to man's deepest interest."[17]

On a more personal basis, Amos praised God's grace in His raising up the prophets and the Nazirites to lead His people (Amos 2:11); and Jonah discovered to his sorrow that he could not avoid his own call or hide from God (Jonah 1:3). The eighth century prophets as a group rebuked the synergistic notion that God's favor could be purchased by a man's ritualistic conformity (Hos. 4:15; Amos 5:21-23; Isa. 1:11-15); the sovereign Lord must remain at the controls. In fact, one of God's aims in uttering predictive prophecies was to bring men to recognize the inferiority of their own, human insights (Isa. 48:7). At other times, God's intention in prophecy was to harden transgressors in their sins (6:10). All were but clay in the Potter's hands (45:9). But though Israel proved to be as faithless as Hosea's wife Gomer (Hos. 3:1, 2), God's love remained unconditioned and would yet finally prevail (11:8, 9). Of the post-exilic restoration, *He* would be the moving cause (2:15). In the subsequent testaments of the Church, *He* (note the monergism) would betroth the people unto Himself (2:19, 20). Among the Jewish remnant in Jerusalem at Christ's Second Advent, would be others (Gentiles) whom *He* should call (Joel 2:32).

Among the later prophets, Jeremiah too employed the figure of the potter as a description of divine monergism (Jer. 18:9). At another point he used the figure of a journey: "The way of man is not in himself; it is not in man that walketh to direct his steps" (23:10). The later prophets noted that in the past God had acted according to His own free will in Israel, whether for good or for ill (2:21; 7:14); and so now, as Nahum prophesied, even the Assyrians would be unable to resist His decree (Nah. 3:14, 15). The Assyrian conquerors had served as God's instrument to humble Manasseh, the most apostate of Judah's kings; and thus, in his affliction, Manasseh had come finally to recognize God as the only help for frustrated and failing men (II Chron. 33:12, 13). In Jeremiah's day, however, God raised up a different instrument: "I have made the earth, the men and the beasts, by My great power; and I give it unto whom it seemeth right unto Me. Now have I given all these lands into the hand of Nebuchadnezzar king of Babylon, My servant, and the beasts of the field also" (Jer. 27:5, 6). But Nebuchadnezzar too would hold sway only for the period that God had delimited (v. 7). Jeremiah pled with God not to break His testament with Israel, but the prophet did so only upon the basis of the disgrace that such an act might bring

---

[17]Rowley, *op. cit.*, p. 65. Used by permission.

against His own glorious name and throne (14:21). God, however, had willed otherwise: because the Israelites had broken its conditions, the older, anticipatory testament would have to be abrogated. But God, in His grace, would then grant, first the new testament (31:31, 32), and then the everlasting testament of peace (32:40). In these future dispositions, which together would make up His newer testament of realized salvation, He, by His grace alone, would put His fear directly into men's hearts that they should not depart from Him (32:40).

The historical fact of the exile and the sifting out of the remnant that it served to accomplish were divinely ordained to teach men that it is God who does all things (Ezek. 17:24; 12:16). Daniel's visions and miracles likewise drove home this one great truth of divine monergism. They demonstrated in history the victory that lies in store for the submissive, but the folly of human pride that seeks to oppose God's decree (Dan. 4:24; 30-32). Ezekiel then went on to prophesy the theocentric purpose in the historical return of the Jews from Babylon (20:41; 28:25); for the revival of Israel's "dry bones" would witness to the power of God's word (37:13). Their return would be a matter of pure grace, and for His name's sake (36:21, 36; 37:28). Zerubbabel raised up the post-exilic temple, "not by [his own] might nor by [his own] power, but by My Spirit" (Zech. 4:6); and the shout of invocation, as its top stone was laid in place, was "Hen, hen (grace, grace) to it" (v. 7). The second temple was glorious, not because men had bestowed worldly wealth upon it, but because God would grant peace in its courts, through the ministry of His own Son (Hag. 2:9). Finally, the future testament of peace would be established only when God, by His grace, should sanctify Israel (Ezek. 37:28). Yahweh would then be vindicated as King over all the earth (Zech. 14:9); and Gog and his hosts would fall, when God should be "jealous for His holy name" (Ezek. 39:25).

B. REGENERATION. As indicated by Jeremiah's description of the testament of peace (32:40, cited above), God's monergistic activity for the effectuation of the testament is not limited to His molding of all things in the external world into conformity to His will. There must be also the internal, effectual calling of His elected people and the corresponding implanting of fear (reverence) of Himself in the hearts of His own. This aspect of monergism, however, demands a replacement of man's depraved, former nature with "a new heart and a new spirit" (Ezek. 36:26). Man, overwhelmed by his original sin and guilt and by the condemnation that he has inherited from Adam,[18] and personally "accustomed to do evil," simply cannot "do

---

[18]See above, topics 15-D, 16-A.

good" (Jer. 12:23). As I Corinthians 2:14 says, "But the natural man receiveth not the things of the Spirit of God: for they are foolishness unto him: neither can he know them, because they are spiritually discerned." To the same effect is Romans 8:7, "Because the carnal mind is enmity against God: for it is not subject to the law of God, neither indeed can be." The New Testament then goes on to teach, not simply that men must be born again (John 3:3), but that, actually, if any man be in Christ, he *is* a new creature (II Cor. 5:17).

This definition of regeneration as being "in Christ" by no means, however, eliminates the doctrine of the new birth from the Old Testament. There is but one, unified testament, God's sole plan of salvation, through which Christ offers a redemption that is equally effective for the saints of both dispensations. Christ states that Abraham, in the patriarchal period, rejoiced to see His day, "And he saw it, and was glad" (John 8:56). Jesus was the Mediator of the older testament, as well as the newer (Heb. 9:15); and, since it is true that no man cometh unto the Father but by Him (John 14:6) and yet, since the saints of the older dispensation did indeed come to the father (Ps. 73:24),[19] they must have been made perfect *in Him* (Heb. 11:40). Furthermore, though the truth of the union of the believer with Christ stood in a necessarily veiled form prior to the historic Incarnation, our Lord Himself bore witness to the reality of the doctrine of regeneration within the older revelation; for He countered the perplexity over the new birth that characterized the well-intentioned but still Pharisaically blinded Nicodemus with the question, "Art thou the teacher of Israel and understandest not these things?" (John 3:10). The Old Testament teaching is, per force, limited; but God *had* made known the doctrine of regeneration in the pages of the Old Testament. The application of its truth constituted a significant element in Israel's religious experience in the past, and the content of these pre-Christian messages remains equally relevant for God's people today.

The Biblical description of regeneration, in an acted form, begins with the institution of circumcision under the patriarch Abraham. The importance of the rite of circumcision is indicated by its very identification with the testament: "This is My testament: every male among you shall be circumcised" (Gen. 17:10). It's performance was essential, if God was to be one's God (v. 7). The explanation of the rite, however, appears first in the Mosaic legislation. There circumcision was associated with the removal of uncleanness (Lev. 12:2, 3), the external act thus signifying the more fundamental reorientation of one's heart toward God. The thought concerned was that God's elect were to be no more "stiff-necked," but should the rather be characterized by a new nature (Deut. 10:16). It is true that in this last

---

[19]Note also the outstanding cases of Enoch, Moses, and Elijah; see below, topic 30.

reference the circumcision of man's heart is presented as a command to be executed by Israel; it reflects more the doctrine of human sanctification than it does the monergistic activity of God. But Deuteronomy 30:6 then goes on to define God-given regeneration in all its essential features: "And Yahweh thy God will circumcise thy heart, and the heart of thy seed, to love Yahweh thy God with all thy heart, and with all thy soul, that thou mayest live." The words, moreover, refer to contemporary Old Testament times, not to the future New Testament dispensation; for the following verse goes on to mention the presence of Israel's national enemies, with their ancient hatreds and persecutions.[20]

During the consolidation period, Scripture describes frequent "instances of men's infilling by God's Holy Spirit,[21] which in most cases imply His prior work in regeneration. This, however, cannot always be assumed, as it demonstrated by the example of notorious Balaam, upon whom the Spirit of God is likewise stated to have come (Num. 24:2). A more valid instance is that of Samuel's prediction of what Saul was to experience when he encountered the company of the prophets: "The Spirit of Yahweh will come mightily upon thee and thou shalt prophesy with them, and shalt be turned into another man" (I Sam. 10:6; cf. v. 9). Here, for the first time, God's Holy Spirit is named as the divine instrument in what seems to be a natural man's regeneration. Because of Saul's subsequent failures, one might indeed be tempted to question the genuineness at his rebirth from above. It is possible, however, for a man to lose the blessing of the fulness of God's Spirit without, at the same time, ceasing to be one of God's elect (cf. David's prayer, Ps. 51:11). Moreover, even at the end of his checkered career, Saul was still opposing pagan spiritism (I Sam. 28:9) and was earnestly seeking divine guidance (v. 6). Burrows has therefore appropriately concluded:

> The idea of a new heart appears in I Sam. 10:9, an especially striking instance because the passage is part of a very ancient narrative of the beginning of the monarchy. The account seems to indicate a real conversion—not merely the enthusiasm of the ecstatic prophets Saul meets, but also an inner spiritual experience which fits him to rule as Yahweh's anointed.[22]

In the next period, David, in his greatest penitential psalm, prays, "Create [bārā] in me a clean heart, oh God; and renew a right spirit within me" (Ps. 51:10). The verb bārā, as previously noted,[23] does not necessarily imply creation *ex nihilo*; and therefore full force must be granted to the verb "renew" in the second line. That is, God's Holy Spirit (v. 11) must, long before, have granted to David

---

[20]For other significances in the ceremony of circumcision, see below, topic 27-D.
[21]See above, pp. 175, 176.
[22]Millar Burrows, *An Outline of Biblical Theology*, pp. 183-84.
[23]See above, p. 133.

his original "right spirit" and thus caused (from his earliest life?) David's fundamental regeneration. The king, furthermore, laid stress upon the necessity for all men to experience the heart cleansing of spiritual birth. As he admonished his people in song, "Who shall ascend into the hill of Yahweh? And who shall stand in His holy place? He that hath clean hands and a pure heart" (Ps. 24: 3, 4). But this cleansing could not be the work of men; it is God who, by His unconditional election, both chooses the man and causes him to approach unto Himself (65:4). As Baab summarizes it, "Repentance is a fraud without this regeneration of heart and conscience."[24]

Through Solomon, God proceeded to indicate the relevance of hypostatized Wisdom to the process of regeneration; for it is the Second Person of the Trinity who promises, "Whoso findeth Me findeth life, and shall obtain favor of Yahweh" (Prov. 8:35). Elijah then spoke of God's grace on a community scale. As he expressed it in his great prayer on Carmel, "Hear me, that this people may know that Thou, Yahweh, art God, and that Thou hast turned their heart back again" (I Kings 18:37). God then, a short time later, in characteristic monergism, assured Elijah, "Yet will I leave Me seven thousand in Israel" (19:18).

Among the eighth century prophets, Isaiah anticipated a change that would take place in the hearts of his people, when "thine eyes shall see thy teachers, and thine ears shall hear a word behind thee, saying, This is the way, walk ye in it" (Isa. 30:20, 21). The time of this change Isaiah went on to define as still that of the Old Testament dispensation, for it would result in the destroying of their contemporary idols (v. 22). The thought of the passage seems related also to the more general prophecy of Isaiah 1:18, "Though your sins be as scarlet they shall be as white as snow; though they be red like crimson, they shall be as wool." Snaith, accordingly, comments on 40:30, 31:

> "When strong and vigorous youths faint and are weary, then God gives new and wondrous strength. The prophet does not mean that God revives the strength they have, but that He gives them new strength, strength of a different kind."[25]

Isaiah became, moreover, the first prophet explicitly to reveal the hope of a national regeneration of Israel at the coming of the testament of peace. Then at last "the Spirit will be poured upon us from on high" (32:15) and the Lord will "wash away the filth of the daughters of Zion" (4:4). Joel went on to speak of others also (Gentiles?) as being among the saved people of God who should be

---

[24]Baab, op. cit., p. 148.
[25]The Distinctive Ideas of the Old Testament (Philadelphia: The Westminster Press, 1946), p. 105. Used by permission.

found in Zion in that day, and he described them as "those whom Yahweh doth call" (Joel 2:32). This then is God's effectual call, as opposed to the general, external call of Isaiah 30:21. For Isaiah indeed proclaimed, "This is the way, walk ye in it"; and his call was sincerely directed to all, even though it be heeded only by the regenerate (ct. Matt. 22:14). In Joel's prophecy, however, the "call" becomes equivalent to a divinely efficacious summons and is to be accompanied, correspondingly, by the inwardly operative saving grace of regeneration.[26] Herein appears the Old Testament expression of the truth found also in Romans 8:30, that "Whom He did predestinate, them He also called: and whom He called, them He also justified . . ."

Jeremiah, in the later prophetic period, spoke both of contemporary and of future regeneration. On the one hand, he described the contemporaneous pious captives of 597 B.C. under the figure of "good figs," to whom God would grant "a heart to know me," when they should return to Palestine at the close of the exile (Jer. 24:7). On the other hand, he prophesied, of course, of the regeneration within the Church under the new testament; for God had promised, "I will put My law in their inward parts, and in their heart will I write it" (31:33). Such regeneration is thus a matter of "irresistible (efficacious) grace." God, that is, will surely regenerate His elect. For those who are "written for life in Jerusalem," namely, those who are predestinated to salvation as their names are written in God's book of the living (Ps. 69:28; Dan. 12:1), *shall* be called holy (Isa. 4:3) and shall be cleansed of their filth (v. 4). Similarly, when God sets His eyes upon the "good figs" (Jer. 24:6), He will, without question, give them the heart to know Himself (v. 7). This, however, suggests no "saving a man in spite of himself"; for they, at the same time, voluntarily turn to Him with their whole hearts (v. 7). As stated elsewhere, those whom He regenerates will surely demonstrate their new heart by conscious conversion, "becoming a fruitful field" (Isa. 32:15). Just so, Jeremiah's new testament emphasizes the fact that "they shall all know Me" (Jer. 31:34), which again describes the active response of loving human hearts.

During the exile, God encouraged His people with explicit promises of regeneration. Ezekiel speaks, on occasion, of the work of the Holy Spirit in "reviving" community life, upon the return of the Jews from exile in 538 B.C. (37:14); but he looks more deeply into the inner life of the returning captives and predicts (36:27, 28),

A new heart also will I give you, and a new spirit will I put within you; and I will take away the stony heart out of your flesh, and I will give you a heart of flesh. And I will put My Spirit

---

[26]Cf. John Murray, *Redemption—Accomplished and Applied*, pp. 112-115. Evangelicals differ on the question of the priority of God's effectual call and of regeneration. The two are often treated without great distinction.

within you, and cause you to walk in My statutes, and ye shall keep mine ordinances and do them (cf. 11:19, 20, a similar, though earlier, prophecy).

The significant point of this message is that its verses are not predictive of the church but are descriptive of Ezekiel's own sixth century B.C. religion. The immediately preceding context speaks of Jewish life in the Babylonian exile (11:16; 36:23), of the return of Israel from Babylon to Palestine (11:17; 36:24), and of the religious issue of idolatry, which ceased to be a real problem in later periods (11: 11; 36:18). It is the temptation, then, of the idolatries of the exile that is overcome by regenerative grace (36:25); compare the descriptions of idolatry, both immediately preceding and immediately following the references to the "new heart" in chapter 11 (vv. 18, 21). As Snaith has so aptly remarked:

> Jeremiah and Ezekiel say that God will give men new hearts and will put His Spirit in them, not "in a dim and distant future," but in the days of the return from exile and of the rebuilding of Jerusalem. This immediacy is quite clear from the contexts. If the suggestion of a far-distant future be made because it is thought that the references are apocalyptic, then we have a most extraordinary misapprehension . . . the crisis is near at hand. To suggest otherwise is a most amazing error.[27]

Ezekiel, did however, like Isaiah before him, speak also of a yet future outpouring of the Spirit and of a national conversion of Israel at Christ's Second Coming (39:29).

Correspondingly, on the post-exilic scene, the last of the prophets spoke of the contemporary work of the Holy Spirit in transforming the hearts of their people and in giving them strength and courage to maintain their immediate, restoration-era faith (Hag. 2:5). But they spoke also of His future coming, as the Spirit of grace and supplication, so that when they should look upon the One whom they had pierced, they would turn to Him in repentance and in eschatological, kingdom-era faith (Zech. 12:10). The God who would effectuate the testament by the death of His Son would likewise effectuate its application to the hearts of His own.

For Further Reading:

John Murray, *Redemption: Accomplished and Applied.* Grand Rapids: Wm. B. Eerdmans Publishing Co., 1955. A thorough, scholarly, evangelical presentation, in the Princeton-Westminister tradition.

Leonard Hodgson, *Biblical Theology and the Sovereignty of God.* New York: Macmillan Co., 1947. Neo-orthodox, but with the commendable modern reemphasis upon salvation as a divine disposition.

George Nye Boardman, *Regeneration.* New York: Fleming H. Revell Co., 1891. A survey of the Biblical doctrine of regeneration as the monergistic activity of God.

---

[27] *Op. cit.,* p. 83. Used by permission.

19. The Death of the Testator*

The most basic single feature for the effectuation of a testament is the death of the testator (Heb. 9:16, 17). So Moses, after the slaying of the symbolic offerings at Sinai, cried, "Behold the blood of the testament!" (Ex. 24:8). But what was symbolized at Mt. Sinai was accomplished at Mt. Calvary. Thus Christ, at the Last Supper, in anticipation of His crucifixion the following morning, explained, "This is My blood of the testament, which is shed for many for the remission of sins" (Matt. 26:28).

A. PRIMEVAL AND PATRIARCHAL REVELATIONS. The penalty for man's violation of the original covenant of works was death (Gen. 2:17). Man, moreover, in the person of his representative head, Adam, did violate this covenant; and, since the covenant continues perpetually in force[1] (Rev. 20:12), it meant that the requirement of death in some way had to be met before man could be reinstated with his Maker (Ezek. 18:4; Rom. 6:23). As Hebrews 9:22 states it, "Apart from the shedding of [life] blood there is no remission." Thus, when in the proto-evangel of Genesis 3:15 God revealed that there would arise another representative head for mankind, Jesus Christ the last Adam, who would destroy the evil work of the tempter and bring men back to God, it followed inevitably that He would have to die. In other words, this redemption of Genesis 3:15 could come about only in the form of a bequest, through an Edenic last will or testament. Accordingly, this first redemptive note in all the Word contained simultaneously the figurative but yet ominous prediction that the heel of the seed of the woman must needs be bruised in the course of His effectuating man's reconciliation. From this point on, therefore, the entering of primeval men into God's favor was marked by the death of animals, symbolically anticipatory of God's ultimate sacrifice (4:4; 8:20).[2]

Among the patriarchs, such sacrifices continued. Their purpose, however, was clarified by the revelation that God granted to Abra-

---

* BIBLE READING: Job 33; Isaiah 53

Collateral Reading: A. B. Davidson, *The Theology of the Old Testament,* pp. 315-338.

    Erich Sauer, *The Dawn of World Redemption* (Trans. by G. H. Lang; Grand Rapids: Wm. B. Eerdmans Publishing Co., 1952), pp. 131-140.

---

[1]See above, p. 92.

[2]*The Dawn of World Redemption.* Trans. by G. H. Lang (Grand Rapids: Wm. B. Eerdmans Publishing Co., 1952), p. 135.

ham in connection with the proposed sacrifice of his son Isaac on Mt. Moriah. This event demonstrated two things: 1) that God has the unquestioned right to claim the life of fallen men, but 2) that He will not allow human sacrifice, however appropriate this might seem (22:12). Rather, the death of an animal is decreed to take the place of that of the man (v. 13). So early was the substitutionary nature of the testamental death revealed. But though men were thus relieved of the penalty that was their due, God in the ultimate expression of His love and grace (cf. Rom. 5:7, 8), involved *Himself* in the threat of testamental dismemberment (Gen. 15:9, 10; so Jer. 34:18-20; cf. I Sam. 11:7).[3]

B. MOSAIC REVELATIONS. With the national election of Israel, there appeared a specification in ritualistic procedure, which had become necessary for the conduct of worship in this larger group. Opportunity was thereby provided for detailed, enacted representations of the death of the Testator. As Sauer stated, after noting the basic unity of salvation in Christ throughout all ages,

> From this historical oneness connecting the millenniums it follows that even in the Old Testament time God was able to give a certain advance presentation of the coming salvation, certain prophecies in act and fact, in offices and institutions, in historical leadings and individual happenings, which had Christ and His redeeming work as their end.[4]

Even before the nation had left Egypt, God illustrated the way of divine salvation in the events of the Passover, by which He delivered His people from the last of the ten plagues. God had earlier proclaimed the death of all the firstborn of Egypt, without exception (Ex. 11:5). But He then made provision for a limited atonement. In the place of the firstborn of His own people, a lamb was to be substituted; its life constituted a "redemption" for the men who would otherwise have been themselves involved (13:13). The verb used is *pādhā*, "to buy (off), to ransom: the firstborn from being killed"[5] (cf. Num. 18:15-17). Specifically, the ransom price consisted of the life of the lamb as this was represented by the lamb's blood (compare Gen. 9:4, "flesh with the *néfesh* [life] thereof, which is the blood thereof"; cf. Lev. 17:14). The blood around the door of a house served, therefore, to exempt that house's occupants from the fatal visitation of the destroying angel (12:23). The death penalty had already been paid, by proxy. It is significant that this same verb, *pādhā*, is used by Moses as descriptive of God's redeeming the whole people out of Egypt (Deut. 7:8; 9:26; 13:5), though the ultimate

---

[3]Cf. John Murray, *The Covenant of Grace* (London: Tyndale Press, 1953), pp. 16-17.

[4]*Op. cit.*, p. 135.

[5]Ludwig Kohler, *Lexicon in Verteris Testamenti Libros*, (Leiden: E. J. Brill, 1951), p. 752.

nature of God's "ransom" is here left undisclosed. A somewhat similar verb is *gā'al*, to "lay claim to a person, claim back from another's
authority, redeem";[6] but the emphasis of *gā'al* falls more upon the
resumption of a right of a claim that has lapsed, than upon the
actual gaining of title through a payment (*pādhā*).[7] Thus *gā'al* is
likewise used for all Israel in Ex. 15:13: "Thou in Thy *hesedh* [in
Thy faithfulness to Thine already existing testamental relationship][8]
hast led the people that Thou hast redeemed" (cf. 6:6).

In respect to the Mosaic doctrine of redemption, Vos rightly remarks, "There is not yet any reflection on that element, so easily
associated with the conception, viz., that a redemption price is paid."[9]
Two contemporary indications do, however, exist that point to the
nature of the One who should, in the fulness of time, give His life as
a ransom for many (Mark 10:45). On the one hand, only God Himself was capable of making the sufficient, atoning redemption (cf.
Ps. 65:3; for when men are said to "make atonement," Ex. 29:36;
30:10, it is only as God's representatives or mediators).[10] Incredible
as this truth might have seemed to the Old Testament saints, one of
the Persons of God would have to give His own life to redeem men.
On the other hand, the symbolism of the Passover lamb serves as
a divinely intended analogy to what would some day constitute the
true redemption for the nation. Specifically, the ransom price represented by the lamb was One, a bone of whom would not be broken
(Ex. 12:46; cf. John 19:36), and who would be a male, without
blemish (Ex. 12:5). As I Peter 1:18, 19 later explained, "Ye were
redeemed, not with corruptible things, with silver or gold, but with
precious blood, as of a lamb without blemish and without spot, even
the blood of Christ." Thus Sauer remarks:

"*Without blemish* points to the holiness of the Lord Jesus.
His freedom from inherited sin through His miraculous birth
and His freedom from all actual sin through His holy walk."[11]

God's Son became the ultimate ransom that had been typified by the
lamb (Heb. 10:4, 10). The Holy Spirit accordingly spoke through
Paul, "Christ, our passover, is sacrificed for us" (I Cor. 5:7).

After the Sinaitic testament had been enacted, forgiveness was
shown to be obtainable upon men's repentance; but the penalty for
guilt had still to be exacted (Ex. 34:6, 7; cf. Num. 14:20-23). Moses
even expressed the willingness to bear, himself, the punishment for his
people's sin (Ex. 32:32). But God provided for another and more

---

[6]Kohler, *op. cit.,* p. 162.
[7]Cf. S. R. Driver, *A Critical and Exegetical Commentary on Deuteronomy* (New
York: Charles Scribner's Sons, 1895), p. 101.
[8]See above, pp. 162, 163.
[9]*Biblical Theology,* p. 129.
[10]Davidson, *The Theology of the Old Testament,* p. 321.
[11]Sauer, *op. cit.,* p. 136.

effective substitutionary death, which death was symbolized by the blood of the animals that were sacrificed on the altar of the tabernacle. For explanations in respect to the details of the Mosaic sacrifices, see below under ceremonial actions, topic 27-C. The basic underlying theory of sacrifice, however, is that of the death of the testator. As Moses expressed it in Leviticus 17:11, "For the life of the flesh is in the blood; and I have given it to you upon the altar to *kippēr* [make atonement] for your souls; for it is the blood that maketh atonement by reason of the life." The Old Testament, it is true, gives no systematic presentation of the way in which death, as typified by shed blood, serves to effectuate the testament. But its explanation does appear (characteristically) in practical contexts, the method of its accomplishment becoming particularly apparent from the meaning of this verb *kippēr*, "atone."

The Hebrew verb, *kippēr*, has sometimes been derived from the Akkadian and Aramaic root that means to "wipe." The thought would then be that of wiping out an object of wrath, or of wiping away its guilt (cf. Isa. 47:11). But the etymology that is now generally accepted arises from the meaning of the root as it is found in Arabic, meaning to "cover." For the cognate noun, *kōfer* (translated "ransom," Ex. 30:12; cf. its use with *pādhā* in 21:30) is the thing that "covers" or shields a man from harm. *Kōfer* may even mean a "bribe," the thing that *covers* the eyes of the judge so that he does not punish. Cross reference I Samuel 12:3, "Have I taken a *kōfer* to blind mine eyes therewith?" This thought of "covering" is then confirmed by the parallel expression in Genesis 20:16, "I have given thy brother a thousand pieces of silver: behold, it is for thee a *covering* of the eyes to all that are with thee; and in respect of all thou art righted" (cf. Neh. 4:5). The most recent lexicons therefore conclude:

> "The Hebrew, considered for itself, leads to 'cover' as the original meaning . . . The aim of *kippēr* is always to avert evil, especially punishment."[12]

The significant point, relative to *kippēr*, is that it defines atonement as a covering-over of one's sins (Lev. 16:30); atonement diverts the plague that would otherwise fall upon man, should God "see through" to the sinner (Num. 8:19; Ex. 32:30). Centuries earlier than Moses, this fundamental function of atonement to deliver one from punishment, even from simple, secular punishment, had become clear. Jacob said of Esau, "I will appease [Hebrew, *kippēr*] him with the present that goeth before me, and afterward I will see his face; peradventure he will accept me" (Gen. 32:20). Compare also Solomon's admonition, "The wrath of a king is as messengers of death; but a wise man will pacify [*kippēr*] it" (Prov. 16:14). The meaning

---

[12]Kohler, *op. cit.*, p. 452.

of "atone" in the Old Testament is therefore to "propitiate (placate),"
and not simply to "expiate (make reparation)";[13] for expiation specifies neither the why nor the how of atonement. Propitiation, by contrast, necessarily connotes the idea of an offended person (Person),
against whose wrath the propitiatory covering is sought for protection.
Professor John Murray has thus well stressed the point that —

> . . . it is before the Lord that both the covering and its effect
> take place (cf. especially Lev. 4:35; 10:17; 16:30) . . . the sin,
> or perhaps the person who has sinned, is covered before the sight
> of the Lord. . . . Sin evokes the holy displeasure or wrath of God.
> Vengeance is the reaction of the holiness of God to sin, and the
> covering is that which provides for the removal of divine dis-
> pleasure which the sin evokes.[14]

Liberal theology demonstrates a consistent antagonism against
the doctrine of divine propitiation. Moses, however, made it clear that
God does have righteous wrath against sin (Num. 25:3-13) and that
atonement then transfers to another, "covering" object the punishment that men would otherwise be due (Num. 16:47, 48; Ex. 30:12).
Reference to God's wrath against sin and of the necessity for punishment to satisfy His divine justice is found over 580 times in the
Old Testament alone.[15] The means that Scripture uses to depict this
process of penal, substitutionary atonement is the ritual of sacrifice;
and one of its most significant particular aspects is its requirement
that the guilty man lay his hand upon the head of the animal that
is to be offered (Lev. 1:4). Such action symbolized the transference
of guilt from the person of the offerer to that of his sacrificial substitute (cf. Lev. 16:21).[16] Liberalism, as might be expected, has exhausted itself in its efforts to explain away the obvious meaning of
this rite. Even Oehler has attempted to reduce its significance to a
matter of mere expiation, asserting that it represents the "self-surrender" or "self-sacrifice" that is necessary before a sinner can gain an
approach to God.[17] But though Oehler's recognition of the element
of self-surrender within the sacrificial concept is in itself a proper

---

[13]Some writers have claimed that in a restricted number of particular contexts
kippēr must be limited in meaning to the idea of expiation, for example in II
Sam. 21:3, David's simply "compensating" the injured honor of the Gibeonites,
or in the priestly writings (e.g., Lev. 19:22), the priests' making "reparation"
for its own sake, and not for God's sake, cf. Kohler, *Old Testament Theology*,
pp. 213-14. But Scripture makes it clear that what is really at stake, even in
these references, is man's personal relationship with his offended Deity, the
wrath of whom must be placated (cf. II Sam. 21:1).
[14]*Redemption — Accomplished and Applied*, p. 36.
[15]Leon Morris, *The Apostolic Preaching of the Cross* (Grand Rapids: Wm. B.
Eerdmans Publishing Co., 1955), p. 131. The same truth is fundamental to New
Testament revelation.
[16]Cf. the candid recognition of this fact by E. Jacob, despite his subsequent
attempt to subordinate the sacrifice's death as a punishment for sin, to its supposed use as a means for God's communicating His life to the sinner; *Theology
of the Old Testament*, pp. 295-296.
[17]*Theology of the Old Testament*, pp. 279-280.

one,[18] his expiatory view yet remains inadequate to serve as a total
explanation for the rite. For it fails to explain why sin makes such
a self-sacrifice necessary in the first place, namely, because God in
His wrath demands death as the punishment for transgression (Ezek.
18:4). It likewise fails to explain how the mere fact of a guilty man's
yielding himself in surrender can make that man fit for approach to
God without his moral disqualification being in some way removed.
Finally, it fails to take into consideration the fact that God punishes
by death whether a man tries to approach Him or not (Ezek. 18:20;
Deut. 21:6-9). The only comprehensive explanation for the atonement ritual is the following. There must be divine propitiation, not
simply to open a way by which men may approach God in fellowship, but first of all to satisfy heavenly justice through a payment that
will free man from the penalty that his failures are due (cf. Num.
35:31). He must present the kōfer (the ransom) to pādhā (to redeem)
his life (Ex. 21:30). Then it is that he will find forgiveness (Lev.
4:20) and that the way to divine fellowship will be open. As a final
requirement, however, the kōfer must be constituted an adequate one
(cf. II Sam. 24:24). The penitent might, and did, lay his hands on the
head of a sheep; but the dumb beast, not having the image of God,[19]
could not even appreciate guilt, let alone receive it by transference.
As in the case of the Passover, its death could serve only as a type
of the death of that Testator who was yet to come. Thus Sauer
concludes:

> The offering becoming one with the offerer through the *laying
> on of* hands, points to the acceptance of guilt by the Lord Jesus.
> In the reality, when Christ, the sinless, submitted Himself to "the
> baptism of repentance unto forgiveness of sins" (Mark 1:4), He
> fulfilled the typical declaration of readiness to accept the place
> of the sinner, to become one with him, and to bear the sins of
> mankind (Matt. 3:14, 15), a typical declaration of readiness which
> He then carried out historically on the cross (I. Pet. 2:24).[20]

Because of this same need for the propitiation of God through
a sacrificial death, the effectuation of the Sinaitic testament was
illustrated by the sprinkling of "the blood of the testament" on the
assembled Israelites. In this way the people were able to identify
themselves with the death of the ultimate Testator (Ex. 24:6, 8; cf.
Heb. 9:19-21). They were all, literally, "under the blood," and therefore justified heirs, able to receive the inheritance that was to be bequeathed them by their dying substitute. This action was, of course,
a limited atonement, designed only for God's elect church, Israel; cf.
similar New Testament statements in reference to the Church (John

---

[18]See below, topic 23.
[19]See above, topic 17-C.
[20]Sauer, *op. cit.,* p. 136.

10:11; Rom. 8:32, 33; II Cor. 5:14 RV; Eph. 5:25).[21] After this first initiatory ceremony, there were then held, year after year, the Day of Atonement services,[22] which became the regular memorial to Israel's shielding from the punishment of sin by the intervention of sacrificial blood (Lev. 16:16, 30). But it was not Israel who made the atonement. This could be accomplished only by the priest who stood as the representative, not now of the people, but of God, "hallowing the altar from the uncleannesses of the children of Israel" (v. 19).[23] In the last analysis, it must be God who propitiates Himself (Ps. 65:3; 79:9); for God "to atone" thus comes to mean "to pardon" (II Chron. 30:18; Ps. 78:38; cf. Jer. 18:23). So the divine Christ, "a high priest of the good things to come . . . through His own blood, entered in once for all into the holy place, having obtained eternal redemption" (Heb. 9:11, 12).

In the fall of 1407 B.C., after nearly forty years in the wilderness, Israel suffered under a divinely sent plague of deadly serpents because of their rebelliousness against Moses. God, however, commanded Moses to lift up for their deliverance a brazen serpent on a pole (Num. 21:8). Thus Moses once again carried out an action that was designed to be typical of the death of God's Son on the cross. Israel, then, by looking in faith at this standard, inherited life, both temporal and eternal (John 3:14). It is not to be supposed that Israel, at the time of Moses, understood all the details of God's way of atonement. But this event did serve its contemporaries as a simple means for their identification by faith with the redemptive plan of God and with His own preordained method for the effectuating of His testament. As a final saving event in this period, in 1406 B.C. on the Plains of Moab, God's revelation of the Levitical testament (Num. 25:12, 13) once more demonstrated that the testament depends upon the making of atonement. Whether by Phinehas, or by that greater Priest whom he typified, God's wrath against sinners is averted through testamental blood (v. 11; cf. Ex. 24:11).

C. REVELATION CENTERING IN DAVID. During the period of consolidation in Canaan, there continued the atoning sacrifices that had been prescribed by Moses (cf. I Sam. 7:9), but there was little additional revelation. In the next period, however, the psalms of David and his friends contain some of the most pointed anticipations of the death of Christ that are to be found in the entire Old Testament.

---

[21]The qualification "limited" must not be understood as in any way minimizing the *potential* efficacy of the atonement. But it does signify that the *actual* propitiation of God's wrath only occurs in reference to the elect. "Limited" atonement is simply "definite" atonement. There is no real atonement, unless it is efficacious; and therefore, since salvation is not universal, it is clear that God did not ordain the atonement of the sins of the non-elect. Cf. Murray, *op. cit.*, p. 74.
[22]See below, topic 28-C.
[23]Davidson, *op. cit.*, 321.

Asaph stated in so many words that the testament is effectuated by sacrifice (Ps. 50:5). Through David himself, then, came Psalms 16, 22, and 69. In Psalm 16:9, 11, David described the gladness, hope, and eternal life that were his; for (v. 10), "Thou wilt not leave My soul in death;[24] neither wilt Thou suffer Thy holy One to see *shâhath* [corruption]." This word *shâhath* may come either from the root *shâhath*, "to corrupt," or from the root *shû'ah*, "to sink down." The latter etymology would produce a noun meaning "pit, or grave" (as in the Revised Standard Version) and would limit the meaning of Psalm 16:10 to a simple preservation by God of David's life. The analogy of the New Testament, however, (Acts 2:27), shows that the noun that the Holy Spirit intended to be conveyed through David was indeed that which signified "corruption"; and Psalm 16:10 thus concerns the resurrection of the body, the preventing of its decay. The verse, therefore, cannot refer to David at all, since he was not resurrected and since his body did disintegrate. Acts 2:31 reveals, however, that David was thinking and speaking of the death and resurrection of Christ, the events which then constituted the source of his own hope.

Psalm 22 is unique because it is the only psalm in which David was so completely overshadowed by the Holy Spirit that all of its words became in fact the words of Christ. In this greatest of all passion psalms, the Savior pours out His grief at His desertion by God the Father (v. 1; Matt. 27:46); for when Christ gave His life and became sin for us (II Cor. 5:21) He was, per force, separated from Yahweh in His holiness (Hab. 1:13) and left to suffer the torments of hell alone (cf. Luke 22:44; but also 23:46). Nor was this all: He was reproached of men and mocked (Ps. 22:6, 7; Matt. 27: 39); He suffered thirst (v. 15; John 19:28); His hands and feet were pierced (v. 16; Matt. 27:35); and they cast lots upon His garments (v. 18; John 19:24). But such indescribable suffering was not in vain: His atonement would bring satisfaction for the meek (v. 26) and eventually cause all nations to turn to Yahweh (v. 27) in His eternal kingdom (v. 28).

In Psalm 69, on the other hand, only three of its statements are known to concern the passion of Christ. Verse 4 speaks of the way in which our Lord was hated without cause (John 15:25); verse 21 predicts the gall that was given Him to drink at the Crucifixion (John 19:28, 30); and verse 25 has reference to His betrayal by Judas and to the fate that shortly thereafter overtook the betrayer (Acts 1:16, 20). But though these particular verses are interspersed with other words that are simply David's own (cf. Ps. 69:5), these three do not appear to be readily applicable to the career of the man David (cf. v. 21); and the New Testament goes on to demonstrate the Messianic

---

[24]The meaning of *sh'ôl* in this context, see below, topic 30.

25

4 THE THEOLOGY OF THE OLDER TESTAMENT

meaning that God originally intended. For a more complete listing of statements in the Psalms that concern the death of Christ, such as His betrayal by Judas Iscariot in 41:9 (John 13:8) or His rejection by the nation Israel in 118:22 (Matt. 21:42) and for the evidences that suggest their exclusive application to Himself,[25] see below, Appendix B.

In the wisdom literature of Job (revealed to Israel in the disruption period), Elihu not only diagnosed the sufferings of his friend; he also spoke by inspiration of the ransom (*kōfer*) that God would provide as a redemptive substitute for Job, who must otherwise go down lost into the grave (Job 33:24). In the context, furthermore, the ransom appears to be none other than the interpreting Angel of Yahweh.[26] The Angel, moreover, both becomes the ransom price and at the same time shows man His own righteousness (v. 23); He then freely reckons this righteous standing to those whom He has redeemed (v. 26). In the same vein, Elijah laid stress upon the sacrificial altar, as the primary external indication of Israel's testamental relationship with God (I Kings 19:10, 14).

D. PROPHETIC REVELATIONS. Turning to the eighth century prophets, one finds in the history of Jonah how this disobedient minister was first swallowed by a great fish and then, in three days, cast out again on dry land alive (1:17, 2:10). Jonah's experience was subsequently used by Christ as an illustration of His own death and His resurrection on the third day (Matt. 12:40). It is doubtful, however, whether the event of Jonah holds any divinely intended typical meaning. For a genuine type must possess a basically uniform symbolism, both for its contemporaries and for the future; and, at the time, the prophet's strange captivity seems to have had no recognized symbolical significance,[27] unless it concerned the ridiculous situation into which Jonah's bigoted nationalism could plunge even a prophet of God!

Isaiah, on the other hand, ranks with David as marking a high point in the Old Testament revelation concerning the death of God's Testator. In the closing years of Isaiah's ministry, in his work of comforting ravished Israel after the repulse of Sennacherib in 701 B.C., this greatest of the prophets was used of God to reveal five "servant songs" (Isa. 42:1-7; 49:1-9; 50:4-9; 52:13-ch. 53; and 61:1-3).[28] The

---

[25]See also Payne, "So-called Dual Fulfillment in Messianic Psalms," *Evangelical Theological Society, 1953 Papers*, pp. 62-71.

[26]See above, p. 169.

[27]See above, p. 192. On the necessity of a corresponding contemporary symbolism for a type to be constituted as genuine, see below pp. 355-360.

[28]The first two songs are often limited to 42:1-4 and 49:1-6, and the fifth is generally rejected entirely by liberal writers, as being the work of a separate author, the so-called "trito-Isaiah." Cf. Oswald T. Allis, *The Unity of Isaiah* (Philadelphia: Presbyterian and Reformed Publishing Co., 1950), p. 82, and H. H. Rowley, *The Servant of the Lord and Other Essays* (London: Lutterworth Press, 1952), p. 6.

term, "servant of Yahweh," refers basically to one who fulfills God's
purposes (cf. Nebuchadnezzar, Jer. 25:9). In these songs, however,
there may be traced an eight-stage development of thought relative
to God's servant. 1) The identification of the servant moves from
Israel as a whole (49:3), through the remnant concept, to that One
individual in whom the remnant is summed up (v. 5).[29] 2) This individual is then identified as a humanly born prophet (50:4; 49:2; cf.
49:1 and Jer. 1:5), empowered by God's Spirit (Isa. 42:1; 61:1), but
with a humble, non-self-assertive ministry (42:2, 3; Matt. 12:18-21).
Still, He who serves is greater than any other prophet, for Isaiah's
description of the Servant predicts not simply a personal sufferer,
but One whose suffering is vicarious, as He carries the cares and
sicknesses of His fellow men (50:4; 53:4). This is a function that
was fulfilled by Jesus Christ in His incarnate ministry of healing
(Matt. 8:17).[30] 3) The sufferer, moreover, meets disbeliefs (53:1)
and becomes subject to reproach: "I gave My back to the smiters,
and My cheeks to them that plucked off the hair: I hid not My face
from shame and spitting" (50:6; Matt. 26:67; 27:26; cf. Isa. 49:7;
53:3, 4, 7, 8). Yet in all His affliction, "He is brought as a lamb to
the slaughter; and as a sheep before her shearers is dumb, so He
openeth not His mouth" (53:8). 4) Condemned as a criminal and
treated as a wicked man in His death, the Servant gives up His life
as a voluntarily accepted punishment for the sins of others (53:8, 9):
"All we like sheep have gone astray; we have turned every one to his
own way; and Yahweh hath laid on Him the iniquity of us all" (v.
6; cf. vv. 5, 12). God will thus "make His soul an offering for sin

---

[29]See above, p. 187. The servant is thus "Israel" (41:8; 44:1, 2, etc.) in its
various aspects: glorifying God (49:3), or sinful (42:19, 43:22, 25, though the
term "servant" is not so used in the five songs), and then restored in the person
of its sinless representative Head, Jesus Christ (49:5; 53:9). The attempts of
both Jews and liberals to limit the Servant to Israel collectively, or to the
prophets, or to some other collective remnant within Israel (cf. 44:26), cannot
do justice to passages such as these last. Even the particularly pious, such as
Isaiah's own disciples (8:16), seem to have experienced no unique sufferings but
are rather included with the others who are blessed by the Servant's vicarious
sacrifice (53:6).

[30]Once the Servant is recognized as an individual, His Messianic identification
necessarily follows; for though the alternative proposals are legion, none appears
to satisfy with adequacy Isaiah's own contextual requirements. The objective
phraseology (cf. 42:1) demonstrates that the Servant cannot be Isaiah (or the
so-called "deutero-Isaiah") himself (cf. Acts 8:34); the future reference (as Isa.
52:13, 15; 53:11) demonstrates that He cannot be Moses, a king performing
ritualistic services, or some other past leader; and His sinless character (53:9)
and return to life (v. 10) and the magnitude of His work (setting "justice in the
earth," 42:4, accomplishing the eschatological regathering, 49:5, and "justifying
many" 53:11) demonstrates Him to be more than a merely human leader of
the future, such as Jehoiachin or Zerubbabel. The New Testament (John 12:38,
41; Acts 8:32-35), for those who accept its authority, settles the identity of the
Servant as being Messianic; and Christ Himself, before His death, said of Isa.
53:12, "This which is written must be fulfilled in Me" (Luke 22:37; cf. Isa.
61:1, 2; Luke 4:21).

[Hebrew, *āshām*, a guilt, or trespass offering[31]]" (v. 10), and by His atonement "shall He sprinkle many nations"[32] (52:15; cf. Heb. 10:22; 12:24; I Peter 1:2). 5) The Servant thereby accomplished God's pleasure (53:10) and is honorably buried with the rich (v. 9; cf. Matt. 27:57-60). But after His death, the Servant revives. He prolongs His days (v. 10) and receives a portion with the great (v. 12). 6) His sacrifice, moreover, avails to justify many (v. 11). He sees a numerous spiritual seed (v. 10)[33] and makes intercession for the transgressors (v. 12). He becomes a light even unto the Gentiles (42:6; 49:6; Luke 2:32; cf. Acts 13:47). 7) So at length Yahweh's righteous Servant accomplishes the universalistic goal of Israel: "He shall not fail nor be discouraged, till He have set judgment in the earth: and the isles shall wait for His law" (Isa. 42:4; cf. 52:15 and Rom. 15:21). 8) He thus constitutes in Himself the testament, effectuating it, but more: He both becomes the Testator who dies, and then the one who provides in His own revived life God's inheritance for the saints (42:6; 49:8).[34]

In the exile, Daniel for the first time specifically names the One who is to put to death as the Messiah (Dan. 9:26); but He goes on to explain that by this very act, the Messiah shall confirm the testament with many (v. 27). Finally, Zechariah (post-exilic period) revealed how the "Good Shepherd," God's associate, would be smitten, prior to the extending of God's hand on behalf of His little flock (13:7). Zechariah further described how Israel would look upon God in His glorious Second Advent, but would see in Him the One whom they had previously pierced (12:10) and valued at thirty pieces of silver (11:12; see the next two topics for elaboration on the details of these Messianic prophecies). Thus, though the revelations were scattered, the Old Testament consistently maintained the necessity of the death of the Son of God for the effectuation of the testa-

---

[31]See below, topic 27-C.

[32]Maintaining, on the basis of the New Testament analogy, the standard meaning for *nāzā* of "sprinkle," rather than the rare translation "startle," Revised Standard Version, cf. Edward J. Young, *Studies In Isaiah* (Grand Rapids: Wm. B. Eerdmans Publishing Co., 1954), Ch. 8, pp. 199-206. Note also the consistent position of limited atonement, a sprinkling designed not for "all" but "many." This in no way questions the theoretical sufficiency of Christ's death for all; but it follows naturally from the Biblical stress upon election that God's intention in sending His beloved Son was limited to the "laying on Him of the iniquity of *us* all" (Isa. 53:6). By His stripes *we* are healed (v. 5); and it is clear that His death made justification for many (v. 10), not all. Limited atonement is, accordingly, often clarified and stated positively as "efficacious atonement."

[33]The reading of the Masoretic text of Isa. 53:11, "He shall see of the travail of his soul," thus refers to this same fruit of His ministry and thereby appears to provide adequate meaning without resorting to the reading of the Qumran Isaiah, "Of the travail of his soul he shall see light." Cf. Martin J. Wyngaarden, "The Servant of Jehovah in Isaiah and the Dead Sea Scrolls," *Bulletin of the Evangelical Theological Society*, I:3 (Summer, 1958), p. 22.

[34]See above, p. 113.

ment. In the light, moreover, of the New Testament's fulfillment and explanation of the Old, there should no longer exist among Christian interpreters any such lack of exegetical discernment as occasioned the censure, given by our Lord to the two on the way to Emmaus, "Oh fools, and slow of heart to believe all that the prophets have spoken: ought not Christ to have suffered these things, and [only then] to enter into His glory?" (Luke 24:24, 25).

For Further Reading:

Edward J. Young, *Isaiah Fifty-three.* Grand Rapids: Wm. B. Eerdmans Publishing Co., 1952. An up-to-the-minute, scholarly, evangelical study on this crucial chapter. *Studies in Isaiah.* Grand Rapids: 1954. Chapters 4-5 are reprints of excellent articles on the Suffering Servant that appeared in the *Westminster Theological Journal,* 11:2 (May, 1949), pp. 135-155, and 31:1 (Nov., 1950), 19-33.

J. H. Y. Pythian-Adams, *The Way of At-one-ment.* Toronto: The Macmillan Co., 1944. Neo-orthodox and Anglican in reference to the Church, but finding the true fulfillment of Israel's redemption in Christ.

Christopher R. North, *The Suffering Servant in Deutero-Isaiah.* London: Oxford University Press, 1948. Obviously liberal in its Biblical criticism, but maintaining the Servant to be Messianic.

20. The Messiah: His Person *

The testament is effectuated by means of a mediator (Heb. 9:15). Specifically, it is by the One whom Scripture calls the Messiah[1] that the testament is literally, according to Dan. 9:26, 27, "caused to prevail, made efficacious."[2] The noun *māshíah* means "anointed one"; for a "messiah" was technically any man who had been consecrated to God's service by the application of holy anointing oil, which in

---

* BIBLE READING: Isaiah 7:1-16; 9:1-7; II Samuel 7

Collateral Reading: E. W. Hengstenberg, *Christology of the Old Testament* (Grand Rapids: Kregel Publications, 1956), I:149-159; II:26-31, 43-50.

Helmer Ringgren, *The Messiah in the Old Testament (Studies in Biblical Theology No. 18;* London: Student Christian Movement Press, 1956), pp. 25-38.

---

[1]Cf. Edward J. Young, *The Prophecy of Daniel, a Commentary* (Grand Rapids: Wm. B. Eerdmans Publishing Co., 1949), pp. 208-209: "This is the view which seems to be most tenable. To construe 'prince' as subject, does not appear to be the most natural reading, for the word occupies only a subordinate position even in vs. 26, where it is not even the subject of a sentence . . . Furthermore, the entire passage is Messianic in nature, and the Messiah is the leading character." Indeed it appears questionable whether Dan. 9:26 contains any reference whatsoever to an anti-christian prince, and whether the passage should not rather be translated with the variant Hebrew and versional reading, "Messiah shall be cut off, and shall have nothing: and the city and the sanctuary shall be destroyed, along with the Prince that is to come ['Messiah, the Prince,' v. 25]; and the end thereof shall be with a flood."

[2]See next topic, p. 277; and cf. *ibid.,* p. 213.

turn symbolized the enabling presence of the Holy Spirit in his heart. The Greek equivalent of *māshíah* is *christos*, an anointed one, from which comes the title "*the* Christ," and eventually simply "Christ." In the Old Testament, the term *māshíah* may be employed in reference to all of those who possess spiritual gifts, for example (Ps. 105:15), the founding patriarchs of the Hebrew people. But this title comes at an early point to be applied in particular to the person of Israel's future Deliverer, to the One who would confirm the testament. For as Warfield has stated,

> "The Messianic hope was aboriginal in Israel, and formed, indeed, in all ages the heart of Israelitish religion . . . It is an essential element in the eschatological system of the Old Testament and is inseparably imbedded in the hope of the coming of God to His kingdom."[3]

Liberal and neo-orthodox writers persistently attempt to limit the Messianic hope to a late development of reaction, caused by popular disillusionment subsequent to the decline and fall of the Davidic dynasty. But Scripture assigns the commencement of Messianic revelation to the Garden of Eden itself and focuses the testamental expectation, throughout its historic course, upon the Person of the Messiah, its ultimate, divine Testator.[4]

A. THE MESSIAH'S HUMANITY. The proto-evangel of Genesis 3:15 revealed to fallen mankind that their hope for deliverance would arise out of their own human race, out of the very "seed of the woman." The Hebrew text makes it clear that it is the seed who wins the victory not the woman (or particularly, the virgin Mary, as is maintained by Romanists).[5] Even the fact that it is the seed of the woman (Eve), as opposed to that of the man (Adam), seems to possess little theological significance. The thought is expressed in this way simply because it is the woman who bears the children. The phrase, "seed of woman," can thus hardly be said to imply the virgin birth (cf. 24:60). Indeed, Scripture is ambiguous as to whether it is even a single person that is intended. The Hebrew word for seed is *zéra*, which may be taken either as a collective (as 22:17) or as a singular: "It [He *or* they] shall crush thy [Satan's] head, and thou shalt bruise its [His *or* their] heel" (Gen. 3:15). Context does imply that since the serpent is to have a representative leader, "thy head," so also should the seed of the woman; but whether or not Adam real-

[3]*Biblical and Theological Studies* (Philadelphia: The Presbyterian and Reformed Publishing House, 1952), pp. 115, 124.
[4]Cf. Edward J. Young, *The Study of Old Testament Theology Today*, pp. 77-78; or even the guarded and mythologically oriented statements of Edmond Jacob, *Theology of the Old Testament*, p. 328, who insists that Messianism arose, not out of disillusionment, but out of divine victories already won and of the hope for fuller redemption to come, p. 317.
[5]Paul Heinisch, *Theology of the Old Testament*, pp. 338-339.

ized this fact cannot be determined. Vos' caution, however, that "we are not warranted in seeking an exclusively personal reference to the Messiah here,"[6] must not be misinterpreted. For though the individuality of the Messiah is not yet clearly revealed, neither is it ruled out. Progressive revelation does not invalidate or correct the earlier revelations, as though they were any less inspired; its purpose is rather to clarify them. The wording of Genesis 3:15 was thus providentially designed by the Holy Spirit: the verse is simple, but it is at the same time true, and congruous with its future fulfillment in the one person of Christ. It is this potentiality of individualistic reference that constitutes the point of Galatians 3:16, with its explanation that the promise was directed, not toward "seeds," as many, but toward "seed," one, which is Christ.

Genesis 9:26 then goes on to stress God's particularly Semitic association and limits the application of His testamental name, Yahweh, to the descendants of Shem.[7] Thus, within the human race as a whole, it would be particularly from the branch of the Semites that the Messianic deliverance would come.

To the patriarch Abraham it was revealed, not simply that all nations would be blessed in him personally (Gen. 12:3), but that they would find "in thy seed" their special object of hope (22:18; cf. the combination of these two elements in Gen. 28:14 and Acts 3:25).[8] Even yet, however, Scripture does not reveal the knowledge that the Messiah would be one individual; and Christ was careful to say that Abraham saw His *day* (but not necessarily His person, John 8:56). Neither does the individualistic hope appear in the repetition of the promise of the seed as it was given to Isaac (Gen. 26:4) or Jacob. Indeed, it was only to Jacob on his way to Haran (28:14) that God for the first time revealed, explicitly, that all the families of the earth would *be blessed* in this seed that was to come.

At Jacob's death, however, in 1859 B.C., this father of the sons of Israel included in his final predictive blessing (Gen. 49:2-27) three significant Messianic truths. He revealed that the anticipated deliverance would come about through one individual, that this One would hold office as a king (see next topic, 21-A), and that He would arise from among the tribe of Judah in particular. The initial kingly statement (Gen. 49:8), that the eleven other brothers would bow down to Judah, was adequately fulfilled when David acceded to the throne of all Israel at Hebron in 1003 B.C. (II Sam. 5:1-3). But Genesis 49:10 goes on to state, "The sceptre shall not depart from Judah, nor the ruler's staff from between his feet, until *shilō* come; and unto Him shall the obedience of the people be." *Shilō* cannot refer to the city

[6]*Biblical Theology*, p. 55.
[7]See above, p. 178.
[8]See above, p. 189 and note 32.

of Shiloh, as with the Authorized Version; for that town was destroyed before Judah ever rose to power (Jer. 7:14). The following clause, moreover, "unto Him shall be obedience," indicates an individual man. *Shīlō* is therefore best rendered in the way done by the Septuagint. For this earliest of our translations divided the term into its three elements: *she*, "whom"; *l'*, "to"; and *ō*, "Him." The thought expressed by "*shīlō*" is thus: "whom, to Him (it is)"; or, "to whom it is." The whole clause then reads, "The sceptre shall not depart from Judah until the One comes whose it is."[9] The same Hebrew syntax is repeated in the confirmatory Messianic prophecy of Ezekiel 21:27. Judah, accordingly, henceforward holds the significant place in Messianic prophecy (cf. Matt. 2:5, 6); and the Revelation describes Christ's victory by saying, "The Lion that is of the tribe of Judah hath prevailed" (5:5).

With the accomplishment of Israel's election at Mt. Sinai, the attention of God's people came to be concentrated upon the present, rather than directed toward the future Messianic hope. But Balaam still spoke of a star, a scepter, arising out of Jacob: "I shall see Him, but not now" (Num. 24:17). Baalam foretold the Star's smiting Moab, which could have been fulfilled (as was Gen. 49:8) in David's victorious leadership. But the added word that He should break down *all* the sons of *shēth*, "tumult," can have reference only to the final Messiah.

Finally, to David in about 995 B.C. was revealed the awesome truth that, within the tribe of Judah, it would be through him personally that the Messiah would come. II Samuel 7:13 speaks of David's son Solomon building the Temple, but the prophecy then moves on into the future and describes the throne of the Davidic dynasty as being eternal (cf. v. 25; 22:51). But before reverting to the more contemporary problems of the dynasty as a whole, inspiration proceeded to individualize the Davidic dynastic hope: there would be one particular descendant of David, and "that one shall be My Son" (II Sam. 7:14). Immediately subsequent to David, however, apostasy would arise within the royal line, a declension which first became marked in the latter years of Solomon (disruption period) and which brought adversity to the house of David. But this eclipse could be only temporary (I Kings 11:39). The eighth century prophets praised the future Messiah as sitting on the throne of David for ever (Isa. 9:7); and, without further elaboration, they designated Him simply "David" (Hos. 3:5), the "One head" of God's people (1:11; cf. Ezek. 34:23, 24; 37:24).

In his last words, David related his Messianic expectation to the

---

[9]Cf. Heinisch, *op. cit.*, p. 339. Note that the "until" does not necessarily imply that the scepter in Judah will then cease upon Messiah's appearance, cf. H. C. Leupold, *Exposition of Genesis*, p. 1181.

hope of salvation that he possessed through the testament. He praised the God who "hath made with me an everlasting testament . . . for it is all my salvation," but then asked rhetorically, "For will He not make my house to *sāmah*, to put forth a shoot?" (II Sam. 23:5; cf. Ps. 132:17). The prophets, therefore, starting with Isaiah, used the terms "shoot" or "branch," *sémah*, *hôter*, and *néser*, as descriptive designations for the coming Messiah (Isa. 11:1;[10] Jer. 23:5; 33:15).

With the onset of the exile, the house of David was removed from its position of absolute kingship until the Messiah should come (cf. Micah 5:3). But Ezekiel 17:20-22 yet speaks of a "tender young twig" from the stock of Jehoiachin (the Davidic ruler who was taken captive to Babylon in 597 B.C.) coming back to Palestine, a prophecy which perhaps refers to his grandson, Zerubbabel, who acted as governor of the land under the Persians. In this specific branch, then, is concentrated the future Messianic hope (v. 23). It was also in this period that *Māshiah*, without the article, came first to be used as a proper noun, as the personal name, "Messiah" (Dan. 9:25). Thus the New Testament exhibits a similar development, as "the Christ" (the anointed heir of David, Matt. 16:16) came later in our Lord's ministry to be shortened simply to "Christ" (26:68). So in the next (post-exilic) period, God delivered through Zechariah certain revelations that concerned "My servant, *Sémah*," "Branch" (3:8; cf. 6:12), where again an attributive expression of Jesus' Davidic descent has become a personal name without the article. Almost the last of our Lord's words in Scripture are, "I am the root and the offspring of David" (Rev. 22:16).

B. THE MESSIAH'S DEITY. At the time of David, when the human origin of the Messiah was being narrowed down to the family of this "man after God's own heart" (I Sam. 13:14), the Holy Spirit first revealed the parallel fact of the divine nature of the Messianic deliverer (see below, the concluding outline, page 283). The manna in the wilderness (Mosaic period) had indeed served as a type of Christ coming down from heaven (John 6:33-35), but it was to David that God made His first direct disclosure of the deity of the Messiah, saying, "I will be His Father, and He shall be My Son" (II Sam. 7:14; Heb. 1:5). Of similar import are the words of the Messiah himself in Psalm 2:7 — "I will tell of the decree: Yahweh said unto Me, Thou art My Son; this day have I begotten Thee" (cf. v. 2, which identifies the speaker with Yahweh's *Māshiah*). Liberals,[11] and occasionally conservatives,[12] have attempted to apply these references to the "Son

---

[10]The first reference. In Isa. 4:2 the *sémah* of Yahweh appears to refer to literal agricultural growth and prosperity.
[11]Ringgren, *The Messiah in the Old Testament* (*Studies in Biblical Theology* No. 18; (London: Student Christian Movement Press, 1956), pp. 11-13; and see above, pp. 22-24.
[12]Gustav F. Oehler, *Theology of the Old Testament*, p. 374.

of God" to some anointed human king of Israel, Hasmonean or earlier. But the Old Testament never uses the verb "beget" to describe God's relationship with individual men,[13] whether kingly or otherwise. In the light, moreover, of the teaching of the New Testament, which relates these passages to the doctrine of Messiah's deity (Heb. 1:5; 5:5), any theory of their merely human application becomes inadmissible for Bible-believing Christians.

Actually, the Old Testament itself so openly describes the Messiah in terms of deity, as sometimes to obliterate the line of demarcation between the Son of David and Yahweh God of Israel, and to produce what Warfield has called "the coalescence of the advent of the Messiah and the advent of Jehovah."[14] Because of the divine character of the Son, David could therefore call his Messianic descendant, who otherwise would have been his inferior, "Lord" or "Master" (Ps. 110:1; cf. Matt. 22:44); and he could define His office as eternal in its extent (Ps. 110:4). Of parallel significance is the anonymous (but Davidic?) Psalm 102. For after first describing Yahweh (through v. 22), it turns to the figure of Ēl (God, v. 24), and says, "Thou art the same, and Thy years shall have no end" (v. 27), words which are known to have reference to the eternal deity of Jesus Christ (Heb. 1:10-12). Finally, the Korahite singers of the early disruption period, in the midst of a love song (Ps. 45) presumably composed for a wedding of Solomon, were transported by the spirit of the occasion and by the inspiration of the Holy Spirit to lift their eyes from Solomon, their contemporary anointed king, and to address that future anointed One, the greater Māshīah (v. 7). They therefore exclaim, "Thy throne, oh God, is for ever and ever" (v. 6). Yet the God whom they address has been Himself anointed by God (v. 7). The Messiah must therefore be a distinct (Second) Person of the Trinity (Heb. 1:8, 9).[15] The Revised Standard rendering of Psalm 45:6, 7 admittedly eliminates this vocative reference to God: but it does so only by the artifice of substituting the reading, "Your divine throne endures, etc.," which constitutes an unabashed violation of basic Hebrew grammar.[16] But this much does appear to be true, that after the seventh verse, because of the reference to the ivory palaces and to the queens in vv. 8 ff., the subject of Psalm 45 becomes once again the merely human monarch, Solomon.

---

[13]Deut. 32:18 is a poetic reference to the nation of Israel.
[14]Op. cit., p. 100; and see below, p. 482.
[15]Cf. Oswald T. Allis, "Thy Throne, O God, Is for Ever and Ever," Princeton Theological Review, 21, 2 (April, 1923), pp. 236-266.
[16]Cf. the remark by C. A. Briggs, himself unfrocked from the Christian ministry because of Biblical heresies, "Such usage is improbable; there is no sufficient evidence for it," A Critical and Exegetical Commentary on the Book of Psalms (The International Critical Commentary; Edinburgh: T. and T. Clark, 1907), I:391.

Isaiah, in the eighth century, identified the virgin's Son as *Im-mānū-Ēl*, "with us, God" (7:14; Matt. 1:23). This name is not simply descriptive of Isaiah's confidence that "God will be with us (in the form of a providential victory against the Syrians)," but, as Hengstenberg has paraphrased Isaiah's revelation to Ahaz,

> "Your weak, prostrate faith may erect itself on the certain
> fact that, in the Son of the Virgin, the Lord will some day
> be with us in the truest manner."[17]

God's personal presence, that is, would be with Israel in the form of the Son, Immanuel, as is evidenced by the context of the four chapters of Isaiah that follow. For not only is "Immanuel" described as the owner of the land (8:8), this Messianic child is expressly equated with the Lord God almighty (9:6). The first phrase of this series, "Wonderful counselor," is in itself descriptive of deity (28:29); but the next two phrases, *Ēl gibbōr* and *Avī-adh*, "The mighty God" and "Everlasting Father" (cf. 57:15 and Gen. 21:33), are flat equations of the Messiah with God.[18] Attempts, moreover, to reduce the meaning of the former to simply "a God-like hero" are forbidden by the analogy of Isaiah 10:21 (cf. Deut. 10:17). The truth of the deity of the Messiah is then confirmed by the description of His universal divine power in 11:4. Ringgren's application of Isaiah 9:6 to some young prince, a contemporary of Isaiah, stands self-condemned, though even he makes the grudging admission, "It is not quite impossible that the prophet had in mind something more than the actual child"(!)[19] Micah's revelation, shortly thereafter describes the Bethlehem-born Messiah as One "Whose goings forth are from old, from everlasting" (5:2), a quality which constitutes further witness to His eternal deity.[20]

Through Jeremiah, in the later prophetic period, came three additional revelations of the Messiah that may suggest His deity. Jeremiah 30:21 speaks of the Messianic Prince as arising from the midst of Israel but then states an apparent contradiction, "He shall approach unto Me: for who is he that hath had boldness to approach unto Me? saith Yahweh." For this freedom in approaching God was, as Keil notes, a prerogative that was reserved to the priests; "even a David could not approach into the immediate presence of the Lord

---

[17]*Christology of the Old Testament*, II:43.
[18]Cf. Young, *The Study of Old Testament Theology Today*, pp. 97, 108-110.
[19]*Op. cit.*, p. 30. Cf. John D. Davis' excellent discussion, "The Child Whose Name Is Wonderful," in Princeton Theological Seminary, *Biblical and Theological Studies* (New York: Charles Scribner's Sons, 1912), pp. 91-108; and Warfield, *op. cit.*, pp. 104-112.
[20]The bias of the Revised Standard Version's rendering, "whose *origin* [as a created being, not God] is from old, from ancient days," is indicated by its translation of the very preceding line of this verse. For there, a word that is derived from the same root as the term it renders "origin" is translated correctly (but inconsistently) as "coming forth," not "originating."

to ask His will."[21] But with the Messiah, a greater than David would
some day be here!

Again, Jeremiah 23:6 speaks of the righteous Branch that would
be raised unto David and declares, "And this is his name whereby
He shall be called: Yahweh our righteousness." Keil comments,

> The older Christian commentators understand that the Messiah
> is here called Jehovah, and must therefore be true God, and that
> He is called our righteousness, inasmuch as He justifies us by His
> merit. But . . . we are bound to take the name by the parallel
> passage, xxxiii. 16, where the same name is given to Jerusalem,
> to convey the thought that by the Messiah the Lord will make
> Jerusalem the city of righteousness, will give His righteousness
> to it.[22]

That is, the name may be rendered, "Yahweh *is* our righteousness";
this very function however, of conveying God's imputed righteousness
to mankind suggests the supernatural character of the Messiah.

Finally, Jeremiah 22:30 pronounces a curse on Jeconiah (Jehoiachin), the young king who was about to suffer permanent exile in
Babylon, by saying, "Write this man childless, a *géver* [strong man]
that shall not prosper in his days; for no more shall an *īsh* [human
man] of his seed prosper, sitting upon the throne of David." Jehoiachin did, in fact, have children (I Chron. 3:17); so the curse must
have reference to his childlessness in respect to *reigning* seed. Yet
at the same time Jesus Christ, who does occupy the throne of David
(Luke 1:32), was a lineal descendant of Jehoiachin, through both
His legal (Joseph) and actual (Mary?) genealogies.[23] The implication is that Jesus, having escaped the curse of Jeconiah, must have
been more than human in His nature.

Among the exilic authors of prophecy, Daniel described the future Messianic dominion under the figure of the "Son of man" (7:13).
The contextual stress rests upon the function of this "Son of man" as
the representative of the whole group of saints of the Most High (cf.
vv. 22, 27); and liberalism therefore generally denies the presence

---

[21]*Biblical Commentary on the Old Testament, the Prophecies of Jeremiah.* Trans.
by James Kennedy (Edinburgh: T. and T. Clark, 1874), II:12. Keil's subsequent attempt to refer this passage to the "prince of Israel" in general, rather
than to the Messiah, cf. Theo. Laetsch, *Bible Commentary, Jeremiah* (St. Louis,
Mo., c. 1952), pp. 242-243, is difficult to understand.

[22]*Ibid.,* I:352-353.

[23]This seems to be the most plausible explanation for harmonizing the genealogies
of Matt. 1 and Luke 3. Matt. 1:12 traces Christ's descent through Jehoiachin,
Shealtiel, and Zerubbabel, the last of whom was actually the son of Shealtiel's
brother Pedaiah (I Chron. 3:19). Zerubbabel presumably carried on the name
of his childless (?) uncle, according to the levirate law; see below, p. 331. Thus,
though Luke 3:27 traces Shealtiel's ancestry through a certain Neri (his real
father?) rather than Jehoiachin (who may have adopted Shealtiel prior to the
birth of his own sons), Zerubbabel was in any event a direct grandson of
Jehoiachin through Pedaiah.

within Daniel 7 of any reference to an individual Messianic Person.[24]
Rowley conceded,

> "It is probable, however, that before the days of our Lord
> the term 'Son of Man' had been individualized to stand for
> a divinely sent leader and establisher of the kingdom."[25]

It is, furthermore, a historical fact that Jesus Christ claimed to be
the "Son of Man" (Mark 14:62) and, as the ultimate point of the
remnant doctrine,[26] did indeed constitute the only true (Son of) man.
For He not only represented the saints; He is, in fact, the only actual
"saint," in whom all others must be found if they are to be classified
as "sanctified" in God's sight (I Cor. 1:30). Recognizing then the
truth of the divinely intended individuality of the Messianic "Son of
man," one observes the following characteristics of the Son's deity:
His exalted personality as the One who comes from heaven and opposes the beastly human powers, which come from the earth (Dan.
7:3); His advent in conjunction with the reappearance of the theophanic
glory cloud (v. 13); His free access to the "One who is an ancient
of days" (God the Father, v. 13); and His universal and everlasting
reign (v. 14). As has been already noted,[27] the Son of man in Daniel
7 may be identified with the divine Angel of Yahweh who appears
in chapter 10 (vv. 5, 6). Because of the suffering that elsewhere in
Daniel is associated with the name Messiah (9:26), the Son of man
is not specifically called Māshîah (but cf. 7:25). The equation of the
two figures does, however, appear in the intertestamental literature
(cf. I Enoch 48:2, 10).[28] Rowley confessedly argues, "That our Lord
identified the Messiah and the Son of Man may be concluded from
Matthew xxvi. 63 f., but that the identification had not been made by
any before Him is equally clear."[29] His argument, however, opposes
his own admission that has already been cited above.

Finally, in the post-exilic period, Zechariah describes the Messianic (though smitten) Good Shepherd as God's āmîth, which means,

---

[24]H. H. Rowley, *The Re-discovery of the Old Testament* (Philadelphia: The
Westminster Press, c. 1946), pp. 268-69. Used by permission.
[25]*Ibid.*, p. 269.
[26]See above, p. 187.
[27]See above, p. 169. In this regard, note particularly Warfield's discussion, *op.
cit.*, pp. 116-123. "In the 'one like unto a son of man' of Dan. vii 13, we have a
superhuman figure, a figure to whose superhuman character justice is not done
until it is recognized as expressly divine . . . On every occasion on which our
Lord called Himself the Son of Man thus, He bears witness to the transcendental
character of the figure presented to Daniel. There is no reason apparent today
why His judgment of the seer's meaning should be revised," pp. 122-123.
[28]Cf. R. H. Charles, *Religious Development Between the Old and the New Testaments* (New York: Holt, Rinehart and Winston, [n.d.]), pp. 84-90.
[29]*Op. cit.*, p. 268, though the logical arguments that he adduces in support of
his contention are worthy of note.

His "associate, fellow, or relation"[30] (Zech. 13:7). Further, he makes even a flat equation between the crucified Messiah and the God who is speaking to him: "They weighed for *My* hire thirty pieces of silver" (11:12, cf. 13 and Matt. 26:15; 27:9, 10) and again, "They shall look on *Me* whom they have pierced" (12:10).[31] In the immediately preceding context, Zechariah had predicted that "the house of David shall be as God, as the Angel of Yahweh before them" (12:8). The reference is, of course, only comparative; but as Oehler says, "If the house of David is . . . compared even to the angel of the Lord, what will the second David himself be?"[32] Malachi, the last of the Old Testament prophets, then concluded by stating that the coming One,[33] who accomplishes the Messianic work of establishing the testament, is none other than the Angel of the Testament (Mal. 3:1), distinct from God the Father and yet possessed of full deity.

C. THE MESSIAH'S INCARNATION. The union of the true deity of the Messiah with His full humanity is brought about through the historic event of His incarnation. The fact of the Messiah's birth had indeed been implicit in His original description as "the seed of the woman" (Gen. 3:15). The existence of His human mother is, moreover, alluded to by the Messiah Himself, in Psalm 22:10. But it was only in the eighth century, after God had granted considerable opportunity for men's reflection upon the doctrine of the deity of the Messiah, as this had been revealed under David and Solomon in the two proceeding periods, that the time had become fully ripe for God's revelation of this explanatory doctrine. But at length Isaiah was empowered to speak directly of the Messiah's incarnation and of His being born as a little child (9:6). Micah was able even to add the place of His birth, at Bethlehem (5:2). Both of these prophets, moreover, associated the Messiah's deity with His birth. For Isaiah, the Incarnation became the means by which God would fulfill the testamental promise of His presence with men. As he stated it in his famous words to Ahaz (Isa. 7:14), "Behold, a virgin shall conceive, and bear a son, and shall call His name Immanuel," meaning *God with us.* Isaiah's prediction was then fulfilled by the birth, seven centuries later, of the divine Christ, made incarnate through the person of the

---

[30]Brown, Driver, Briggs, *A Hebrew and English Lexicon of the Old Testament,* p. 763.

[31]The Revised Standard Version renders this phrase: "look on him [not Me] whom they have pierced." Such a rendering effectively denies the deity of the One who is pierced, but it does so only at the sacrifice of valid textual criticism. For the "him" reading is based, not on the original Hebrew, or even on the old Greek translation, but on the work of Theodotion, an early antagonist of Christianity who consciously revised the Old Testament in Greek so as to remove its distinctively Christian passages.

[32]*Op. cit.,* p. 528.

[33]In the immediate context He is not, it is true, expressly designated as "Messiah," though the work He is described as accomplishing lends probability to this identification.

virgin Mary (Matt. 1:23). His mother was human, but Jesus had no human father. Isaiah's younger contemporary, Micah, also associated Christ's deity with His birth, for he predicted how the people of the One "whose goings forth were from everlasting" would be given up (to the Romans and others) "until the time that she who travaileth hath brought forth" (Mic. 5:3). This prophecy thereby constitutes the earliest human commentary on Isaiah 7:14. Even Ringgren concedes, "This verse is difficult; but we notice that the motif of the pregnant woman who is to bear, is in full agreement with the Immanuel passage in Isaiah."[34] The very emphasis that the Gospel writers placed upon Mary's virginity was designed to show that Christ was fully God, conceived by the Holy Spirit (Luke 1:35).

Liberalism of course, bound as it is by its antisupernaturalistic prejudice, rests under an antecedent obligation to deny the virgin birth. It must, in fact, deny both the miraculous occurrence and (the matter that particularly concerns Old Testament theology) the miraculous prediction of that occurrence. Commenting on Isaiah 7:14, Ringgren therefore declares flatly, "The words are not messianic in the proper sense of the word."[35] Two approaches are then generally adopted by liberal scholars to accomplish this necessary denial. On the one hand, the Hebrew word that Isaiah employed to describe the virgin, namely almā, is broadened in its meaning to include any "young woman." In the Isaiah 7:14 context, the young woman is presumably married; and she is certainly not a virgin, cf. reading of the Revised Standard Version. There does, indeed, exist in Hebrew a more technical term for virgin, namely b'thūlā. But after his exhaustive study of the noun almā, Robert Dick Wilson stated:

> Two conclusions from the evidence seem clear; first, that alma, so far as is known, never meant "young married woman"; and secondly since the presumption in common law was and is, that every alma is virgin and virtuous, until she is proven not to be, we have a right to assume that Rebekah and the alma of Isa. vii 14, and all other almas were virgin, until and unless it shall be proven that they were not.[36]

Thus even the RSV elsewhere translates almā as "maiden" (Prov. 30:19), and it includes the translation "virgin" as a footnote to Isaiah 7:14. Moreover, Matthew 1:23 in its New Testament context leaves no doubt as to the meaning that God's Holy Spirit intended in Isaiah.

> If the events recorded in Matthew . . . and Luke . . . are true and the Holy Spirit of God really overshadowed the virgin Mary, all difficulties are cleared away. The language itself is not the difficulty. The great and only difficulty lies in disbelief in predictive

[34]*The Messiah in the Old Testament*, p. 34.
[35]*Ibid.*, p. 27.
[36]"The Meaning of Alma (A.V. 'Virgin') in Isaiah VII. 14," *Princeton Theological Review*, 24:2 (April, 1926), p. 316.

prophecy and in the almighty power of God; or in the desire to throw discredit on the divine Sonship of Jesus.[37]

On the other hand, the surrounding context in Isaiah is claimed by liberalism to require a specifically contemporary fulfillment. This approach has an equally damaging effect upon the virgin birth concept; for, as one of its advocates has confessed, "To admit the possibility of an immediate application and still to insist on 'virgin' would put one in the awkward position of holding to a virgin birth in the time of Ahaz."[38] This latter insistence no one, of course, maintains.[39] The chief contextual evidence appears in Isaiah 7:15, 16, "Butter and honey shall He eat [that is, Immanuel would grow up during years of privation and affliction; but] . . . before the child shall know to refuse the evil, and choose the good, the land whose two kings thou abhorrest shall be forsaken." This "forsaking" of which Isaiah spoke was actually fulfilled within the next two or three years as the armies of Assyria executed a series of desolating attacks (734-732 B.C.) against Ahaz's northern enemies. Some evangelical writers have advanced the explanation that the period of the infancy of the Messiah is simply "made the measure of the time of the desolation," and that the prediction of Christ's future babyhood becomes "a symbol of the situation existing in His [Isaiah's] own day."[40] But if it be granted that the time of Immanuel's eating "butter and honey" refers to the years just before 732 B.C., then to deny the corresponding presence of the divine child, does seem to lay one open to the charge that is made by the liberal critics, of "mental gymnastics involved in ignoring the clear sense of immediacy in the mind of Isaiah."[41]

---

[37]*Loc. cit.*

[38]Dewey M. Beegle, "Virgin or Young Woman?" *Asbury Seminarian,* 8:1 (Fall-Winter, 1954), p. 34.

[39]This verse thus constitutes one of the primary evidences on the futility of resorting to hermeneutical theories of "dual application," "double meaning," or "multiple fulfillment." Utterly apart from the single meaning taught by the New Testament as it describes the historical fulfillment of this and other prophecies (cf. Acts 2:29-31), and the havoc wrought by "double meanings" on hermeneutics as an objective discipline, the fact remains that the *almã* of Isa. 7:14 either was a virgin or was not. Evangelicals cannot afford to force Scripture into a neo-orthodox irrationalism so as to "have their cake and eat it too"; see above, p. 37.

[40]Edward J. Young, *Studies in Isaiah,* pp. 195, 197.

[41]Beegle, *op. cit.,* p. 31. This, however, hardly supports his further criticism of evangelicals that "they are inclined to deny any human element in the Scriptures," unless by "human element" he means (and he does!) man-made errors, whether Isaiah's or Matthew's, in Scripture. The "immediacy" even of the destruction of the people of Samaria was by no means clear to Isaiah's hearers (cf. 7:8, "within 65 years"); and, while the first deportations of Damascus and Samaria did in fact follow rapidly upon the contemporaneous birth of Isaiah's son (8:1-4), attempted equations of "the prophetess" with the Virgin, or of Maher-shalal-hash-baz with Immanuel, the "mighty God," present serious contextual difficulties.

The explanation seems rather to be as follows. The birth of Immanuel was expressly defined as an *ōth*, a miraculous sign[42] (7:14); and with this miracle no contemporary event is known adequately to coincide. Furthermore, King Ahaz had been guilty of pious hypocrisy and had wearied God; so the demonstrative *ōth*, or sign, was intended, not as a promise but as a threat. This threat, moreover, was directed not simply against Ahaz, but against the whole human house of David (v. 13). That is, when the Messiah should be born, He would eat "butter and honey," which was the sign of an afflicted land (the affliction, as it worked out, was caused by the Romans), and which therefore meant that the house of David would have been reduced to impotency. The Messiah would then Himself replace once and for all the merely human Jewish kings of Ahaz' house and character. Isaiah's prophecy, furthermore, showed no inaccuracy when it predicted that Ahaz' enemies would be destroyed "before the child knew how to refuse the evil and choose the good"; Immanuel did not, in fact, appear for over seven centuries! But this extended lapse of time does not diminish the contemporary relevance of Isaiah's threat. On the principle of "prophetic telescoping," the prophets not infrequently described, as if in immediate succession, events that later proved to be separated by even millennia (cf. Isa. 11:1-6; 61:1, 2). Actually, moreover, a threat may serve as a valid force in motivating conduct, no matter how distant its historical fulfillment may really be, provided the contemporary audience does not know when this fulfillment is to take place. A present day instance of such motivation appears, for example, in I Thessalonians 5:2-6: "The day of the Lord so cometh as a thief in the night. When they are saying, Peace and safety, then sudden destruction cometh . . . so then let us not sleep as do the rest, but let us watch and be sober." Even as the Lord's Second Coming should motivate our faithful conduct, no matter how distant it may in fact be, so Isaiah 7:14, on His miraculous first coming, was equally valid for motivating Ahaz, 730 years before Christ's advent actually took place.

Other prophetic revelations that relate to the incarnation of the Messiah include the following: Hosea (still in the eighth century period) looked back on the early days of his nation and spoke for God, saying, "When Israel was a child I loved him." But Hosea then went on to predict, "*and* it is out of Egypt that I will have called My Son" (Hos. 11:1). This latter clause predicts Jesus' babyhood refuge from Herod in Egypt and His subsequent return to Palestine (Matt. 2:15). Some have seen in Hosea 11:1 an example simply of synonymous Hebrew parallelism, so that both of its clauses would seem to refer to the same event, namely, to God's care for Israel in Egypt prior to the national Exodus (cf. Ex. 4:22, 23). Christ's

---

[42]See above, p. 141.

experience would then be, at best, only a similar one. But the parallelism of Hosea 11:1 does not have to be synonymous; it might be progressive: God did love Israel in the past in Egypt, *and* He will yet bring for their salvation His Son from Egypt. For Matthew 2:15 makes it clear that the holy family's sojourn in Egypt was "that it might be fulfilled [Greek, *hina plērōthē*] which was spoken by the Lord through the prophet." The grammatical construction is that of a purpose clause: Christ stayed in Egypt, not parallel to, but *because of,* what Hosea had said. Hosea 11:1, in other words, required His going to Egypt; and no interpretation short of this will be found adequate to the New Testament context.[43] Isaiah then spoke of the humiliation that would characterize Christ's incarnate childhood, using an agricultural figure to describe the harshness of His environment: "He shall grow up as a root of a dry ground" (53:2). Again, in his designating Christ as "the Branch" Isaiah used, not the word *sēmah* (as in 4:2), but *nēser* (11:1). This latter term became peculiarly significant, for it seems to have served as the basis for the naming, in post-Old Testament times, of the newly founded and lightly esteemed village of Nazareth, Galilee's "sprout-town." Matthew, accordingly, could say that the holy family "came and dwelt in a city called Nazareth; that it might be fulfilled which was spoken through the prophets, that He should be called a Nazarene" (Matt. 2:23).

Jeremiah, in the later prophetic period, went on to describe the persecution that accompanied our Lord's incarnation. Specifically, he foresaw "Rachel weeping for her children" (Jer. 31:15), a prediction that was accomplished, in all its horror, when Herod slaughtered the innocent children of Bethlehem (Matt. 2:18).[44] As discussed

---

[43]Some have proposed the explanation that Hosea's statement about God's calling His Son out of Egypt referred fundamentally to the Exodus, but that this event then stood in a necessary typical relationship to Christ's childhood, which thus fulfilled the purpose of the Exodus; C. F. Keil and Franz Delitzsch, *Biblical Commentary on the Old Testament, the Twelve Minor Prophets,* I:137. Such an assertion possesses some validity. For God did call Israel in order to prepare for Christ; and God did, therefore, have to maintain and deliver Israel, in this case from Egypt. But the fact that Israel's maintenance was prerequisite to the Messiah's advent does not prove that Christ had to be called from *Egypt,* which is the point that Matthew makes. Israel's preservation could adequately have been justified by His being kept alive anywhere. Keil, indeed, posits a *detailed* typical relationship: "Just as Israel grew into a nation in Egypt, where it was out of the reach of Canaanitish ways, so was the child Jesus hidden in Egypt from the hostility of Herod." But this kind of argument represents a degeneration into man-made and fallacious allegorization. Scripture teaches no such necessary point-by-point correspondence between Israel and Christ. Furthermore, its consistent application would lead to absurdities such as 40 years of wilderness wandering for the holy family to make the return journey. Hos. 11:1, moreover, would then have to refer, not to Christ's safety in Egypt from Canaanite ways, but to His salvation from Egyptian persecution (Ex. 4:22, 23). By this same token Christ would have had to escape from Egypt to fulfill Hos. 11:1! To invoke typology for the interpretation of this verse is neither warranted nor possible.

[44]Rachel, in her life time, had been particularly concerned over children (Gen. 30:1). She had then been buried on the way to Bethlehem (Gen. 35:19) by the

above (pp. 264, 265), Daniel's exilic identification of the divine Son of man with the human saints of the Most High (Dan. 7:13, 14, 18, 22, 27) implies the true union of both deity and humanity within the person of Christ. Finally, Zechariah 6:12 (post-exilic) says of the Messianic Branch, "He shall grow up out of His [lowly] place" (cf. Ex. 10:23). This verse, that is, describes the humble growth of Him who is one Person but who is yet possessed of two natures, the one that was in the beginning with God and was God (John 1:1), and the other that increased in wisdom and stature and in favor with God and man (Luke 2:52).[45]

For Further Reading:

  B. B. Warfield, "The Divine Messiah in the Old Testament," *Princeton Theological Review*, 14, 3 (July, 1916), pp. 369-416. A fundamental study by this master theologian. Reprinted in his *Biblical and Theological Studies*, Philadelphia: 1952), pp. 79-126.

  Edward J. Young, *Studies in Isaiah*. Grand Rapids: Wm. B. Eerdmans Publishing Co., 1954, Chapters 6 and 7 are reprints of a two-part article, "The Immanuel Prophecy," that appeared in the *Westminster Theological Journal* and that carry on the tradition of Robert Dick Wilson in thorough, orthodox scholarship.

  Wilhelm Vischer, *The Witness of the Old Testament to Christ*. Trans. by A. B. Crabtree; London: Lutterworth Press, 1949. Vol. I. Neo-orthodox, but generally worthwhile and evangelical in its conclusions.

  Sigmund Mowinckel, *He That Cometh*. Trans. by G. W. Anderson; Nashville, Tenn.: The Abingdon Press, 1956. A radical work that interprets the New Testament writers as reading back their own Messianic ideas into the pre-exilic materials of the Old Testament, which were really intended to describe Israel's concepts of her kings.

21. The Messiah: His Work*

In the Old Testament, the term *Māshíah*, "anointed," is applicable to kings (I Sam. 2:35; 10:1; 24:6; cf. Judg. 9:8, 15), even heathen kings, like Cyrus of Persia (Isa. 45:1); to priests (Ex. 29:7; 30:30; Lev. 4:3); and to prophets (I Kings 19:16; cf. Ps. 105:15, referring to the patriarchs). The work then of Christ in confirming, and in

---

* BIBLE READING: Daniel 9; Psalm 110

Collateral Reading: J. B. Payne, "So-called Dual Fulfillment in Messianic Psalms," Evangelical Theological Society, *1953 Papers*, pp. 62-70.

Hengstenberg, *Christology of the Old Testament*, III:129-148, 313-327.

---

tribal border of Benjamin (I Sam. 10:2). Jer. 31:15 has indeed often been interpreted figuratively, as describing the tribal mother, Rachel, grieving over the Babylonian exile of her "children." But the preceding verses describe the post-exilic restoration; and it is most natural to refer v. 15 to the literal children killed by Herod, which constituted the cloud of grief that marred the otherwise dominant comfort and joy (vv. 13, 14) at the Messiah's birth. Cf. Theodore Laetsch, *Bible Commentary, Jeremiah*, pp. 248-251.

[45]Keil and Delitzsch, *op. cit.*, II:299.

being, the testament, involved and ultimately combined all three of these "Messianic" offices.

A. KINGLY WORK, *Christ's executing of the testament*. Along with the primeval declaration of the person of the Messiah (Gen. 3:15) came the first description of His work: He would *shūf*, "trample upon, crush" the serpent's head.[1] This same verb reappears in the next clause, "And you [serpent, Satan] will *shūf* His heel." The meaning, "trample," is here, however, clearly inappropriate; the repetition of the verb seems rather to be for the sake of poetic balance and effect. The latter clause may thus more legitimately be rendered, "The serpent will bruise, or injure, His heel." The point then is this: Christ's redemptive work would require genuine labor, sacrifice, and grief on His part, but not permanently so. His sovereign overthrow of Satan, on the other hand, and His re-establishment of mankind with God, would be complete and would be eternal.

Jacob, in the patriarchal period, and Balaam, in the Mosaic, both spoke of the Messiah as wielding the sceptre — breaking down human opposition (Num. 24:17)[2] and gaining the obedience of peoples (Gen. 49:10). The concluding verse in Hannah's consolation period song of thanksgiving (I Sam. 2:10) then becomes the first passage in Scripture in which the coming Deliverer is specifically designated *Māshīah*, "the anointed One"; and it becomes also the first in which He is explicitly called *mélekh*, "king": God "will give strength unto His king, and exalt the horn of His anointed." The Person to whom I Samuel 2:10 refers cannot be King Saul (who was not yet born), for the reign of the king to whom the reference is made takes place in that yet future age when Yahweh shall judge the ends of the earth. The subject of *Māshīah* must indeed be the Christ.

David likewise refers to the anointed eschatological king as *Māshīah* (Ps. 2:2). He predicted the Messiah's ascension to heaven (68:18) and His session upon the right hand of Yahweh (110:1). David anticipated also the time when He should return to the earth to assume its total rule (v. 2). Three points of particular interest are associated with the passage from Psalm 68 which has just been cited. The verse (68:18) reads, "Thou hast ascended on high, Thou hast led away captives; Thou hast received gifts among men, yes, among the rebellious also, that *Yāh Elōhīm* might dwell with them." It appears that 1) the subject to whom these words are addressed must be the divine Messiah. In the preceding verses of the Psalm, Yahweh,

---

[1]There has existed some uncertainty about the actual meaning of this rare verb, *shūf*. The LXX translated it with *tēreō*, meaning "watch," or "lie in wait." But the Holy Spirit's intention through Moses is shown by His New Testament rendering, *suntribō*, which means to "break in pieces" (Rom. 16:20). Cf. Geerhardus Vos, *Biblical Theology*, p. 54.

[2]Edmond Jacob, *Theology of the Old Testament*, pp. 329-330, presents a commendable defence of the antiquity of Baalam's Messianic concept.

God the Father, has been described in the third person. But with verse 18 comes a sudden shift to the second person, and the One who is addressed is a Person distinct from *Yāh Elōhīm*. He must be Jesus Christ the Son (Eph. 4:9). 2) Christ is already a king. He victoriously overcame all opposition by His life, by His death, and by His resurrection. The result is that now God and sinners may meet together and dwell together. The effecuation of God's testament means reconciliation for mankind. 3) Following His earthly victory, Christ ascended to *mārōm*, the height of heaven. The Revised Standard Version renders *mārōm* as "the high mount." But while this earth-bound meaning remains lexigraphically possible, it still represents a deliberate rejection both of *mārōm's* standard lexical definition and also of the clear intention of the divine Author, as this has been revealed in the analogous New Testament passage of Ephesians 4:10.

David then, in other writings, looked on to that more complete realization of the kingdom of God when the conquering Messiah should return to Zion and break the nations with a rod of iron (Ps. 2:6, 8, 9). From this, His holy city, He should rule, empowered by the testament (132:12, 17); and He would establish righteousness among men (II Sam. 23:3). In a similar vein, Solomon, in the next period, after praying for wisdom to lead his people (Ps. 72:1-4), looked far beyond his own time and predicted, "They shall fear Thee while the sun endureth" (v. 5).[3] He then foretold the coming of the perfect King, who would deliver the needy (v. 12) and whose kingdom would take up where his own had terminated: "He shall have dominion from sea to sea, and from the River [Euphrates] unto the ends of the earth" (v. 8). In a similar fashion, Psalm 45:6 addresses itself to the divine Messianic King, saying, "A sceptre of righteousness is the sceptre of Thy kingdom."

Isaiah predicted that the Messianic child would bear the governmental authority upon the throne of David (Isa. 9:7). Micah, however, spoke of Christ's birth in the humble village of David's family in Bethlehem, rather than in the royal city of Jerusalem (Micah 5:2). Amos too, anticipating the destruction that would come upon Israel prior to the Messiah's appearance (Amos 9:9, 10), described God's establishing the kingdom in terms of His "raising up the tabernacle of David that is fallen, and closing up the breaches thereof" (v. 11). This last verse referred to Christ's spiritual rule in the hearts of men and to His kingship in the Church rather than over the nations of the world (Acts 15:16, and see below topic 31-C). Of corresponding significance is Isaiah's general statement on the security that is

---

[3]The Revised Standard phraseology seeks, however, to convert the rest of this Psalm into a mere continuation of Solomon's prayer for himself; and it thus misses the main point of the revelation.

afforded to believers by their membership in the kingdom, that is, the Church: "Behold, I lay in Zion for a foundation a stone, a tried stone, a precious corner-stone of sure foundation: he that believeth shall not be in haste" (Isa. 28:16; cf. Rom. 9:33; 10:11; I Peter 2:6). But Isaiah went on to describe Messiah's final universal reign. He spoke of it as "the day of vengeance of our God" (61:2; cf. Micah 5:6), and yet at the same time, as a day which was designed "to comfort all that mourn" (Isa. 61:2), and in which He would "judge with equity for the meek of the earth" (11:4; cf. Jer. 8, Jer. 23:5, 33:15). So too in the exile, Daniel spoke of the Son of man's receiving world-sovereignty (Dan. 7:14); and Ezekiel depicted His universal kingdom as a great tree, in the shade of which would dwell "all birds of every wing" (Ezek. 17:23). Under the testament of peace, "David" would be personally present to shepherd His people (34:23-25) and to keep them from sin (37:23, 24); see below, topic 32-C and E. Zechariah's post-exilic description of the King, however, reverts to His first coming, humbly, riding upon an ass (9:9; Matt. 21:5).[4]

B. PRIESTLY WORK, *Christ's being the testament* (see above, topic 19, on the death of the Testator). The Messiah's priestly function is seen both in His work as the sacrificer, who officiates at the altar, and also in His constituting in His own person the sacrifice, the One who is slain to atone for sin. In the earlier, more elementary periods of Old Testament revelation these truths were taught by acted prophecies (types) rather than by spoken ones. Indeed, Adam's initial headship of the human race, which brought about the condemnation of his descendants (Gen. 2:17; 3:19), served as an enacted symbol of that last Adam, who should come to work redemption for His own (Rom. 5:18). So also Melchizedek, in the patriarchal period, lived his life as a type of Christ's priesthood. His specific pre-figuring of Christ lay in the fact of his becoming a priest who legitimately officiated at the altar, not by right of Levitical (!) descent, but by the matter of simple, divine decree (Gen. 14:18; Heb. 7:6). Both Psalm 110:4 and Hebrews 7:3, 8 stress the fact of Melchizedek's continuous life of service, "having neither beginning of days nor end of life." His service thus became typical of the priestly Messiah's eternal existence. This similarity, however, must not be interpreted to mean that Melchizedek was either eternally pre-existent or deathless, but merely that his life was undefined. It had no expressly stated boundaries, either before or after; and his birth neither gave him his priesthood nor took it away. The one distinctive point is

---

[4]Ringgren, failing to distinguish the two comings of the King, makes the strange attempt to find in Zech. 9:9 the very opposite to its natural meaning of humiliation: "It is difficult to get away from the suspicion that the word 'lowly' or 'meek' in some way belongs to the royal sphere, though at present we cannot establish its exact meaning." *The Messiah in the Old Testament*, p. 37.

this, that the Melchizedek of the record does nothing but live.[5] The typical significance of the Passover, in the period of Moses, has already been noted;[6] and the typology of such other Mosaic matters as the tabernacle veil, through which men passed to God (typical of Christ's flesh, Heb. 10:20), or of the sin-offerings, that were burned without the camp (typical of His crucifixion outside the walls of Jerusalem, 13:12), is discussed below; cf. topics 26-28.

Through David, the Holy Spirit first revealed the truth of the eternal agreement that was established between Yahweh, the Father, and the Messiah, His Son, which is often called the "covenant of redemption." This covenant constitutes, in fact, the basis for the subsequent testament made between God and the elect of mankind. For in this original agreement between Yahweh and the Messiah, the latter, as "the last Adam," undertook both to earn salvation for mankind under the covenant of works and also to give Himself as the ransom for the sins of which the elect should become guilty. Psalm 2:7, 8 thus quotes the Messiah (v. 2) speaking of this agreement, as it was made within the Trinity, "I will tell of the hōq, statute or decree: Yahweh said unto Me, 'Thou art My Son . . . Ask of Me, and I will give thee the nations for Thine inheritance.'"

The Messiah, moreover, did so ask! For Psalm 40:6-8 proceeds to indicate how Christ assumed His position as representative head of the elect heirs of the testament, and it describes how He would work out their salvation by His active obedience: "Sacrifice and offering Thou hast no delight in, Mine ears hast Thou kārā [literally, 'dug out,' 'opened up,' in obedience] . . . Then said I, Lo, I am come . . . I delight to do Thy will." It is in truth the Messiah who is here speaking. The narrative style of these verses marks a distinct break from the style of the Davidic praises that both precede (vv. 1-5) and follow them (v. 9 f.). The claim, moreover, of this speaker's submission to, and delight in, God's will contrasts both with the known facts of David's life and with the statements that David makes in his own part of the Psalm (v. 12). Finally, the New Testament makes it clear that the Holy Spirit intended these words to be understood as spoken by Christ (Heb. 10:5-7).[7] The Messiah thus agreed to come to earth, to live in obedience to God's law, and thereby to establish the testament (Heb. 2:9).

The covenant of redemption involves also Christ's passive obedi-

---

[5]Cf. Franz Delitzsch, *Commentary on the Epistle to the Hebrews* (Edinburgh: T. and T. Clark, 1871), I:333-336.

[6]See above, pp. 247, 248.

[7]Note the additional concept of the *Incarnation* revealed in Heb. 10:5, "A body hast thou prepared for me." But since this phraseology is of LXX origin, the writer is careful not to base his contextual arguments on the "body" reading; cf. Roger R. Nicole, "The Old Testament Quotations in the New Testament with Reference to the Doctrine of Plenary Inspiration," Evangelical Theological Society, *1954 Papers*, p. 47, and footnote 5, p. 54.

276 THE THEOLOGY OF THE OLDER TESTAMENT

ence, His offering of Himself as the surety for the guilt of His own
(v. 10). Psalm 22:1 thus quotes our Lord's cry, which was later repeated on the cross, "My God, My God, why hast Thou forsaken
Me?" These grief-stricken words indicate the Messiah's actual separation from the Father as He bore the penalty for sin (Matt. 27:46).
As the Holy Spirit said through Paul, He "became sin for us" (II Cor.
5:21). But His very use of the phrase, "My God," demonstrates that
His sufferings were to come about as the result of His agreement with
the Father, in the eternal counsel of redemption. So it was that He
was able to act as our priest and to save His elect children, the
Church (Ps. 22:22; Isa. 8:18; Heb. 2:11, 12).[8]

Among the eighth century prophets, Isaiah's description of the
priestly activity of the Servant of Yahweh has already been noted.[9]
The Servant makes intercession for the transgressors (Isa. 53:12; cf.
Heb. 7:25; I John 2:1) and thus, by His justifying work, comes to
see a numerous seed who gain an inheritance under the testament
(Isa. 53:10).[10] So too Hosea prophesied that the very God who had
smitten Israel in His justice would subsequently bind them up in His
gracious redemption (Hos. 6:1). Hosea then went on to describe the
divine priestly means by which Israel's salvation would be effectuated.
"After two days will He revive us; on the third day He will raise us
up, and we shall live before Him" (v. 2). The "revival" that is here
anticipated is that of Hosea and his saved friends; but the fact remains that it is only because Christ lives that we have hope of living
also (John 14:19). Pusey therefore states, "The Resurrection of
Christ, and our resurrection in Him and in His Resurrection, could
not be more plainly foretold";[11] and he proceeds to elaborate on
Hosea's prediction of the exact two days that were involved. Hosea
6:2 may thus be the point of reference of Paul's statement in I Corinthians 15:4, Christ "hath been raised on the third day *according to
the Scriptures.*"

One of the most significant passages in the Old Testament on
the priestly work of the Messiah is the exilic prophecy of Daniel
9:24-27. The subject of these verses is stated to be (the) Messiah
(v. 25 and 26). His mission is then described in six categories: "to
restrain transgression, and to make an end of sins, and to make reconciliation for iniquity, and to bring in everlasting righteousness, and
to seal up vision and prophecy, and to anoint the Most Holy" (v. 24).
The applicability of the first four to Christ's incarnate ministry is clear
(Heb. 9:26). The "sealing of vision" most probably refers to Christ's

[8]See above, p. 187.
[9]See above, pp. 255, 256.
[10]Thus Kohler is willing to allow, though only at this point, an exception to his
general conclusion that the Messiah, by His own action, does *not* contribute to
the coming of salvation(!), *Old Testament Theology*, pp. 237-238.
[11]E. B. Pusey, *The Minor Prophets* (New York: Funk and Wagnalls, 1885), I:63.

THE MESSIAH: HIS WORK

termination of that anticipatory, prophetic mode of revelation which reached its climax in John the Baptist (Matt. 11:13);[12] the phrase need not require His fulfilling of all known prophecies. Finally, Daniel's reference to "the anointing of the Most Holy" can, in the light of the Messianic prophecy that follows, signify nothing other than Christ's personal anointing by the Holy Spirit (John 3:34).[13]

The Messiah accomplished this six-fold mission by "causing a testament [the new testament] to prevail with many" (Dan. 9:27): That is, He makes the testament efficacious[14] with His elect people (cf. Isa. 53:11). His testamentary action then brings to an end the anticipatory sacrificial system of the older testament (Dan. 9:27), a termination that was accomplished when the veil of the Temple was symbolically rent in twain at Christ's crucifixion (Matt. 27:51; cf. Heb. 9:8). But before the testament could be effectuated, the death of the Testator had to take place: Messiah Himself would be cut off (Dan. 9:26). "For a testament is of force where there hath been death: for it doth never avail while he that made it liveth" (Heb. 9:17). The additional qualification that is stated in the Authorized Version, namely, that Messiah should be cut off, "but not for Himself," states indeed a true fact relative to our Lord's vicarious atonement. The AV translation, however, does not appear to be as satisfactory a rendering of the Hebrew as the reading of the Revised Version, "and shall have nothing."[15]

A final noteworthy feature of Daniel's prophecy is the inspired prophetic calendar in which it is embedded. Daniel predicted a span of "seventy weeks of years," or 490 years, for the accomplishing of the Messiah's priestly work (Dan. 9:24). The beginning point was fixed at the going forth of the commandment to restore Jerusalem (v. 25). In 538 B.C., the very year of Daniel's prophecy, Cyrus of Persia did in fact, issue a decree that encouraged the return of the Jewish exiles to Palestine and that authorized the rebuilding of the Temple (Ezra 1:1-4; cf. Isa. 44:28). But Cyrus' decree did not mention the rebuilding of the city or its walls. This latter restoration came to pass a century later, in the reign of Artaxerxes I (465-424 B.C.), under Nehemiah in 444 B.C. There had been, however, an earlier beginning of restoring the walls under the same monarch, which had been thwarted by the Samaritans (Ezra 4:11, 12, 23). This original attempt must have occurred under Ezra (458 B.C.), whose decree from Artaxerxes granted him just such extended powers (7:18, 25; 9:9).

Daniel then went on to predict that from this commandment to the time of the Messiah there would elapse "seven weeks, and three

[12]Hengstenberg, *Christology of the Old Testament*, III:102-105.
[13]Edward J. Young, *The Prophecy of Daniel, a Commentary*, p. 201; cf. Hengstenberg, *op. cit.*, III:105-114.
[14]See above, p. 257.
[15]Cf. Hengstenberg, *op. cit.*, III:131-137.

score and two weeks" (9:25). This equals sixty-nine weeks of years, or a total of 483 years. From 458 B.C. this figure brings one to the year A.D. 26, the time of the descent of the Holy Spirit upon Jesus Christ and of the beginning of His incarnate ministry. Verses 26 and 27 then describe how, in the midst of the final seven year period, or in the spring of A.D. 30, Christ would bring the Old Testament economy to an end by His death. One could hardly discover a more miraculously accurate prediction! The full 490 year period then concluded with a final 3½ years, during which the testament was confirmed to Israel (cf. Acts 2:38). It terminates in A.D. 33, which is the probable date for the conversion of Paul. At this point, the Jews, by their stoning of Stephen, deliberately cut themselves off from the priestly mediation of Christ and from the eternal blessings of inheritance under the newer testament (cf. Rev. 12:6, 14). Then within that generation, the Roman legions destroyed apostate Jerusalem, A.D. 70 (Dan. 9:26).

The above generally traditional interpretation of Daniel 9:24-27 is opposed by a number of modern interpreters, who may in turn be grouped into three classifications. Liberal writers consistently attempt to assign the "fulfillment" of Daniel's seventy weeks to the unfulfilled hopes of the book's supposedly Maccabean author. Dispensationalists have invented a special 360 day year, which brings the sixty-nine weeks down from 444 B.C. to Palm Sunday, and after which they introduce the Church age as a parenthesis before the purportedly still future seventieth week. Certain symbolical interpreters, finally, reject definite chronology altogether. The very meaningfulness of the prophecy, however, seems to demand that the years be actual, that they be of normal length, and that they follow each other consecutively,[16] from the first right through the 490th.[17]

In the post-exilic period, Haggai spoke of the second Temple, which was then under construction, as the place in which Yahweh

---

[16]Cf. *ibid.*, III:143: "The period of seventy hebdomads, or 490 years, is here predicted as one that will continue uninterruptedly from its *commencement* to its *close*, or completion, both with regard to the entire period of seventy hebdomads, and also as to the several parts (7, 62 and 1) into which the seventy are divided. What can be more evident than this? *Exactly* seventy weeks in all are to elapse; and how can anyone imagine that there is an interval between the sixty-nine and the one, when these together. make up the seventy?"

[17]See Appendix C. pp. 520-522 for point-by-point outline of these four schools of interpretation.

The outline on pp. 520-522 in the Appendix surveys the point-by-point conclusions of the four schools of interpretation of Daniel 9, as they are elaborated in the following representative studies: liberal, James A. Montgomery (*A Critical and Exegetical Commentary on the Book of Daniel*, New York: 1927); traditional, E. B. Pusey (*Daniel the Prophet*, New York: 1891); dispensational, Joseph A. Seiss (*Voices from Babylon: or, the Records of Daniel the Prophet*, Philadelphia: c. 1879), with supplementation from A. C. Gaebelein (*The Prophet Daniel*, New York: c. 1911); and symbolical, H. C. Leupold (*Exposition of Daniel*, Columbus, Ohio: c. 1949). The page numbers in each column then refer to these respective books.

would give peace (Hag. 2:9); and it is a fact that within the courts of this building the Lord Jesus, who brought reconciliation with God, did indeed walk and teach. Zechariah, similarly, spoke of the day of Christ's incarnation, when the very glory of God would dwell in the midst of Jerusalem (Zech. 2:5, 10, 11). Zechariah then went on to predict that the post-exilic priests would, despite their failings, yet have a place of access to God (3:7). For, in the exercise of their function at the altar, they even then constituted a *mōfēth*, or miraculous sign (v. 8), of that ultimate priest, the Messianic Branch, who would remove men's sin in one day (v. 9; Heb. 9:12; 10:10).

But even as the Old Testament records the development of God's revelation of the priestly Messiah, it is careful, at the same time, to point out the essential unity that exists between this Priest and the person of the Messianic King. For just as the Christ, the Son of God, was simultaneously the human son of David (II Sam. 7:12, 14; cf. Ps. 89:27, 29; 110:1), so His special priestly work was yet concentrated, along with His kingly function, in the One supernatural Person. Variety in activity did not signify a plurality of Messiahs (see below, the concluding outline, p. 283). Thus, even in the patriarchal times, Melchizedek, the type of Christ, existed as both king and preist: *malki-sédheq*, "king of righteousness," and *mélekh shālēm*, "king of (Jeru)salem," or, as *shālēm* also signifies, of the priestly blessing "of peace" (Gen. 14:18; Heb. 7:2). David, in his writings, went further and presented a two-fold combination: 1) the One who was of the order of Melchizedek would possess eternal deity (Ps. 110:4) and yet would come forth from earthly Zion (v. 2); and 2) He would be both priest (v. 4) and yet, at the same time, kingly ruler (v. 2). Correspondingly, Psalm 22:27 speaks of the One who would suffer in His function of priestly sacrifice, as being simultaneously the royal effectuator of the Messianic age.

Just before the fall of the Jewish kingdom, in the later prophetic period, Jeremiah predicted that Jacob's "Glorious One shall be one out of their midst, and his Ruler shall come near to Me" (30:21). But having made this translation, Laetsch then adds the following paraphrase: "The Noble One will arise out of their midst, the Ruler prophesied in Micah 5:2, the Messiah, who will as the representative of His people and their Priest be permitted to approach the Lord."[18] Daniel, in exilic days, similarly united the offices of king and priest; for it is "Messiah *nāghīdh*, the prince" (9:25), who is cut off (v. 26) and makes reconciliation for iniquity (v. 24).

One of the most crucial questions that concerns the combined offices of the one Messianic Person is whether the Suffering of Isaiah's five Servant Songs[19] is to be identified with the Davidic Messiah. At

---

[18]Theodore Laetsch, *Bible Commentary, Jeremiah*, p. 242.
[19]See above, pp. 254-256.

the outset, both figures are characterized as divinely chosen and uniquely righteous (Isa. 42:1, 6; cf. Ps. 89:3, 4; Isa. 9:7; Jer. 23:5). The Davidic Messiah is, moreover, described as a "witness to the peoples" (Isa. 55:4), a function which is identical with that of the Servant, who is to be "a light to the Gentiles" (49:6). The Servant is also called a *nāghīdh,* a prince, which is the very term later used by Daniel to describe the *priestly* Messiah. Again, the same Holy Spirit who is to rest upon the Davidic "Branch," so that He may decide with equity for the meek of the earth (11:1-4), rests upon the Servant, that He may bring forth justice to the Gentiles (42:1). The humiliation of the Messiah at His first coming (7:15, cf. Zech. 9:9, 13:7; Dan. 9:25, 26) is closely paralleled by the unpretentiousness of the Servant (53:1, 42:3).[20] Most significant, however, is the final exaltation that is to be experienced by the Servant. "Him whom man despiseth . . . a servant of rulers, Kings shall see and arise; princes, and they shall worship" (49:7 and cf. v. 5). "Kings shall shut their mouths because of Him" (52:15); and, "Therefore will I divide Him a portion with the great" (53:12). Isaiah even says, in so many words, that the Servant is "anointed" (61:1);[21] He and the Messiah can only be one and the same. Zechariah, in post-exilic days, therefore associates the Messianic Branch with the priestly function of removing men's iniquity (Zech. 3:8, 9); and he specifically equates the two offices in his phrase, "My servant the Branch" (v. 8). He further identifies the deity who is pierced (12:10) with the deity who will yet descend upon the Mount of Olives to reign (14:4). Christ Himself provides the final answer to this question by revealing His identity both as Messiah (John 4:25, 26; cf. 1:41) and as the Suffering Servant of Isaiah 53:12 (Luke 22:37; cf. Acts 8:35).

A final passage of significance in respect to the combined priestly and kingly work of the Messiah is Zechariah 6:12, 13: "Behold, the man whose name is the Branch . . . He shall sit and rule upon His throne; and He shall be a priest upon His throne; and the counsel of peace shall be between them both." The Branch is thus both King and Priest. It is true that the Revised Standard Version changes the latter clauses so that they read, "And there shall be a priest by his throne, and peaceful understanding shall be between them both," a rendering which eliminates the personal union of king and priest. This rendering, however, while grammatically possible, is yet opposed

---

[20]Ringgren identifies the Messiah and the Servant on this basis, *op. cit.,* pp. 65-67; while Mowinckel concludes that "The Servant displaces the king and himself becomes king," *He That Cometh.* Trans. by. G. W. Anderson (Nashville: Abingdon Press, 1956), p. 256.
[21]Cf. The Qumran Isaiah A reading of Isa. 52:14, "I have anointed His visage more than any man." F. F. Bruce adds that Daniel's triumphant Son of man (see above, p. 265) seems to have been intentionally patterned on the Messianic Servant of Isaiah, *Biblical Exegesis in the Qumran Texts* (Grand Rapids: Wm. B. Eerdmans Publishing Co., 1959), pp. 58, 81.

to the total context of the passage. First, it is the priest (v. 11) who wears the crown, not someone else who is setting by him (unless the standard, but unwarranted, practice of liberalism is followed of introducing emendations into the text). Second, the phrase that occurs twice in v. 13, "upon his throne," is inconsistently rendered by the RSV. In the first instance, the RSV translates it "upon his throne" (the king) but in the next instance, "by his throne" (the priest); so that two persons come to be distinguished. As distasteful, however, to the unregenerate mind as this accurate prediction of the two-fold work of Christ must be, Scripture states that there *will be* a harmonious rule of both the king and the priest, united in the one person of the Messianic Branch.

C. PROPHETIC WORK, *Christ's proclaiming the testament.* Our Lord came to this earth, not simply to rule and to redeem, but also to teach to men the truths of God's testamental revelation. His very incarnation was a revelation of the Father (John 1:18), God visibly present in history. It was Moses who first predicted, "Yahweh thy God will raise up unto thee a prophet from the midst of thee, of thy brethren, like unto me; unto Him ye shall hearken" (Deut. 18:15; cf. 18). The description of the Prophet's origin as "of thy brethren" is a characteristic one; for, though the Messianic king and the Messianic priest were foretold, sometimes as human and sometimes as divine (or both), no reference ever appears about the deity of this great anticipated prophet of the future. In fact, it has been questioned whether the "prophet" of Deuteronomy 18 is Messianic at all. Verse 14 had forbidden Israel to consult the contemporary pagan diviners; and verse 15 appears to present the "prophet" as an equally contemporary substitute for the former group. Similarly, in verses 20 and 21, the problem in Israel's mind seems to be one of how they are to distinguish the contemporary false prophets from "the prophet." The conclusion reached by Schultz, among others, is therefore:

> I cannot see in this passage a prophecy of a Messianic prophet of the last days, nor even a promise of the "ideal prophet, of whom Moses knew that he would culminate in an actual person, Christ." The context and the contrast with heathen soothsaying absolutely require us to understand it of the prophets as a class.[22]

It must be recalled, however, not simply that the Old Testament prophets spoke of "these [New Testament] days" (Acts 3:24), but also that the Spirit of Christ who was in them was the One who testified to them and enabled them to speak for God in the first place (I Peter 1:11). Essentially then, the one real prophet is Christ; only He declares the Father (John 1:18). Thus Acts 3:22 and 7:37 were inspiredly correct when they treated Deuteronomy 18:15, 18 as a prediction of Christ, the one ultimate prophet, though for Moses' con-

---

[22]*Old Testament Theology,* II:425.

temporaries He spoke through His servants, the prophetic class of Israel, as well as in His own Person.[23]

David's colleague Asaph thus spoke on behalf of Christ, when he foretold the Lord's teaching ministry by saying, "I will open my mouth in a parable; I will utter dark sayings of old" (Ps. 78:2). This verse cannot refer to Asaph's own Psalm that follows, which is neither problematic or obscure (though it could have been said, for example, of Ps. 49:4 or Ezekiel 17:2). Rather, as the New Testament shows (Matt. 13:35), its reference is to the methods that were to be used by Christ in His incarnate, prophetic ministry. But this knowledge, let it be said, could probably not have been gained from the Old Testament context alone, a situation which is true of five others out of the seventeen Messianic Psalms; see below, appendix B, pp. 519-520.[24]

In the eighth century, Isaiah revealed the following aspects of the Servant-Messiah's work as a prophet. The source of His teachings would lie in Yahweh Himself (Isa. 50:4). The instrument by which He should be empowered to preach would be the anointing of the Holy Spirit (11:2; 42:1; 61:1). The scene of His teaching was predicted as the underprivileged land of Galilee (9:1, 2; cf. Matt. 4:15); and the methods of His activity, as most unpretentious (42:2-4; cf. Matt. 12:18-20). The effect, however, of His ministry would extend even to the enlightening of the Gentiles (42:1, 6). In fact, the subject of Isaiah's five Servant Songs is a consistently prophetic, as well as priestly and kingly figure. Isaiah also disclosed that his ministry would be preceded by the preparatory work of another prophet, "the voice of one crying in the wilderness" (40:3). This reference to John the Baptist (Mark 1:3)[25] was given its final development by the post-exilic prophet Malachi (3:1), who identified Christ's forerunner as a second Elijah (4:5, 6; Mark 1:2). But though Luke 1:17 revealed that John the Baptist was to embody Elijah's spirit and ministry, John himself seems not to have been aware of this fact (John 1:21). Christ, however, specifically identified the two figures (Matt. 11:14).

Psalm 22 concerns basically the priestly work of the Messiah; but it goes on, not simply to identify the priest with the honored king (vv. 27, 28), but also to equate this Messianic figure with that of the anticipated prophet, who declares God's name in the midst of the Church (v. 22; Heb. 2:12; cf. the equation of the preacher, the priestly Servant, and the anointed vindicator in Isa. 61:1-3).[26] Conceivably, of course, an Israelite in David's day might have believed in "five Messiahs": the human prophet, the divine and the human king, and

---

[23]The Angel of Yahweh; see above, p. 168.
[24]Also see Payne, "So-called Dual Fulfillment in Messianic Psalms," p. 67.
[25]Cf. John Davis, "An Interpretation of Isa. xl, 3," *Princeton Theological Review*, 18, 4 (Oct., 1920), pp. 645.
[26]Cf. Edmond Jacob's appreciation of this combination of offices, *Theology of the Old Testament*, pp. 340-341.

the divine and the human priest. The whole development, indeed, of the Messianic expectation, from man's fall[27] to the time of David (about 1000 B.C.) may be plotted as follows:

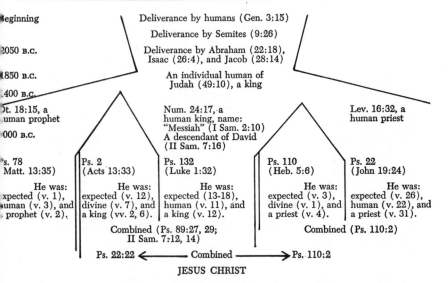

There had been, first, a gradual narrowing down and clarification of the revelation that identified the human person of Christ: from "the seed of the woman" (humanity in general) to the particular royal family of which David became the head. But there had been subsequently a broadening out and amplification of aspects in respect to the work of Christ as prophet, priest, and king, plus the revelation in David's day of His divine person as priest and king. Actually, however, these various aspects were synthesized, almost as soon as they were revealed, into the one glorious picture of Jesus Christ. This is not to say that all, or even many, in the days of ancient Israel grasped this truth. In our Lord's own time many, including apparently John the Baptist, considered "the Christ" and "the prophet" (Deut. 18:15) as distinct figures (John 1:20, 21, 25). Even Christ's own disciples, prior to His resurrection, could not comprehend both the humiliation and the glory of the Messiah (12:34). But the total synthesis had been

---

[27]Before man's fall there were certain unspoken but acted prophecies (types) of Christ. Adam's dominion, for example (Gen. 1:26-28), which he lost, anticipated the dominion that Christ gained after His death, resurrection, and ascension (Heb. 2:8, 9; Ps. 8:3-8); cf. Edmond Jacob, op. cit., pp. 327, 342; and see above, p. 274.

revealed, and it should have been understood from the Word (cf. Matt. 22:45, 46; Luke 24:25-27; Acts 18:28). Then finally, on Easter morning, the radiance of the empty tomb brought light to the disciples:

> "In Jesus they saw all the lines of Messianic prediction converge; and they declare Him no less the Jehovah who was expected to come to save His people, than the Son of David or the Suffering Servant of God."[28]

Jesus Christ's own life and work became the historical and demonstration of the one Savior, who is prophet, priest, and king.

For Further Reading:

Edward J. Young, *The Messianic Prophecies of Daniel.* Grand Rapids: Wm. B. Eerdmans Publishing Co., 1954. A recent thorough work of believing scholarship in this needy field.

John D. Davis, "The Reclothing and Coronation of Joshua," *Princeton Theological Review,* 18:2 (April, 1920), pp. 256-258. A scholarly, orthodox study on these passages in Zechariah.

H. H. Rowley, *The Servant of the Lord and Other Essays on the Old Testament.* London: Lutterworth Press, 1952. Chapters 1 and 2 concern the recent criticism of the Servant concept and of its relationship to that of the Davidic Messiah.

22. Other Supernatural Agents*

A. ANGELS. Although the chief mediator of the testament is the Messiah, Scripture yet describes other supernatural beings, the angels, who were concerned in God's testamental revelation at Sinai (Deut. 33:2; Acts 7:53) and who minister generally in the effectuation of the testament (Heb. 1:14). Theological liberals are inclined to dismiss the entire subject of angels as though it belonged to an outmoded pattern of thought. "Belief in angels," they insist, "is a part of the prescientific, mythological world-view of the Bible."[1] It is admitted, however, that "Jesus apparently accepted the current beliefs on this subject";[2] and, for those who take the mind of Christ seriously (Phil. 2:5), angelology comes to assume a corresponding significance.

From the patriarchal period and onward, the Old Testament designation for an angel is *malākh,* which denotes a "messenger";[3]

° BIBLE READING: Daniel 10; Job 1

Collateral Reading: Burrows, *An Outline of Biblical Theology,* pp. 113-129.
Merrill F. Unger, *Biblical Demonolgy,* pp. 14-20, 59-61, 107-115, 119-124.

[28]Warfield, *Biblical and Theological Studies,* p. 103.
[1]Burrows, *An Outline of Biblical Theology,* p. 119, cf. p. 123.
[2]*Ibid.,* p. 122.
[3]One must therefore exercise care against introducing the concept of angels where only a human *malākh* is concerned, cf. Isa. 44:26; Mal. 2:7.

cf. the Greek noun *aggelos,* which carries the same meaning. Angels, therefore, are couriers for God's use, agents who serve Him just as do wind and fire and other elements of nature (Ps. 104:4; cf. Heb. 1:7). Jacob referred to them as God's "Mahanaim," His "[two] camps" or military companies (Gen. 32:1, 2); and a similar term that appears in reference to these heavenly creatures is that of God's *sāvā,* His "host" or army (Ps. 103:21). Moses in the next period described Jacob's experience at Bethel by saying that "*Elohim* were revealed [plural verb] unto him" (35:7). He thus indicated that God and His angels, when envisioned together, may be called *Elōhīm,* supernatural beings. Compare the use of *elōhīm* in Psalm 8:5 (Heb. 2:7) for the angels alone. In Deuteronomy 33:2 Moses called them God's "holy ones," which means separated (from earth; cf. Job 5:1); and similarly, when Psalm 89:5, 7 speaks of the "assembly of the saints [holy ones]" the passage is best understood as referring to angels. In the book of Job (revealed to Israel in the disruption period) angels are characterized as "sons of God" (1:6; 2:1), sharing, that is, in certain divine attributes. Both of these latter terms, however, are also used for the elect of mankind (Deut. 14:1; Hos. 1:10; Gen. 6:2), so that care must be taken in the assignment of meaning in any given passage.[4] Daniel 4:13, and perhaps Isaiah 62:2, speak of them as "watchers," a descriptive title that is based on function.

As to the origin and nature of angels, Moses spoke of Yahweh's making heaven and earth "and all that in them is" (Ex. 20:11). His words suggest that the angelic creation is to be conceived of as occurring at the time of God's forming the heavenly systems, though it is true that angels are not specifically noted in Genesis 1:1. In any event, their creation must have taken place before that of the world, for Job 38:7 states that the "sons of God" rejoiced over this latter event. The number of angels is that of a great host (I Kings 22:19; Dan. 7:10). Their existence, moreover, in the celestial heights where they as personal beings associate with God Himself, indicate their essentially spiritual nature (Ps. 87:5, 7; 148:1, 2). Thus the description of the wilderness manna as "angels' bread" (Ps. 78:25) demonstrates, not their materiality (they do not eat it!) but rather their heavenliness (the manna had a heavenly source). Such material appearances as they may have assumed were but temporary and for the purposes of divine revelation. Finally, despite their great power, wisdom, and grace (Ps. 103:20), Scripture makes it clear that God is in no way dependent upon these His subservient creatures (Job 4:18; 15:15).

Knowledge of the distinctions and classes that exist within the angelic category as a whole generally appears late in the Old Testament revelation. The very first Biblical reference to angels, however (Gen. 3:24), speaks of one particular angelic type. This is the class

---

[4]Cf. the *b'nē ēlīm,* "sons of the mighty" (Ps. 29:1; 89:6).

of the cherub (plural, cherubim), the living personalities who guarded Eden. Ezekiel 9:3; 10:1 mentions them again and equates them with the "living creatures" that are described in Ezekiel 1 (cf. Rev. 4:6-8). The appearance that they assumed for conveying God's revelations was human (Ezek. 1:5), not that of the mythological winged sphinx or Assyrian-type lion, as is claimed by liberal historicism.[5] Ezekiel 10:20, 21 mentions wings and four faces, signifying the wisdom and power of the cherubim — they are able to see everything that goes on, in all four directions at once! In Exodus 25:18-20, however, they are represented with but single faces, directing men's attention to the cloud of God's presence that rested over the midst of the ark. Basically, the cherubim are spirits, presumably angels; and God made their visible appearances to differ, as each occasion might best be served. In II Samuel 22:11 the function of the cherubim is stated to be that of carrying God's throne (cf. Rev. 4:6, in which they are stationed by the heavenly throne), and in the Mosaic tabernacle God is therefore pictured as enthroned between the two cherub figures on the ark (Ps. 80:1). The cherubim do not appear as messengers (angels) to men; their purpose seems rather to be that of emphasizing the hallowed presence of God, sovereignly transcendent. Thus they were depicted in the ornamentation of the Tabernacle and Temple, and they served to keep fallen Adam and Eve away from the holy person of God and from the tree of life within the Garden of Eden.

The class of the s'rāfîm is mentioned only in Isaiah 6:2-7 (eighth century period). The same Hebrew term, which means "burning ones," is employed in Numbers 21:6-8 (cf. Isa. 14:29; 30:6) to describe darting serpents with a fiery bite. The function of the seraphim, however, is not to burn men but to burn away the sin that keep men from God (Isa. 6:6, 7). Their purpose therefore is to show forth Yahweh's holiness and ethical transcendence. For even the seraphim must cover their faces in holy reverence before God (v. 2).

The exilic revelations of Daniel 10:21; 12:1, serve to introduce the person of the one archangel of Scripture, Michael, *the* great prince (though Dan. 10:13 speaks of him as "one *of* the great princes"; cf. Rev. 8:2's reference to the seven angels that stand before God). Another specifically named angel is Gabriel (Dan. 8:16; 9:21). Liberal writers have tended to look upon this detailed angelology, along with certain other theological aspects of Daniel, as indicative of a Persian influence that was imported into the older Hebrew religion;[6] but

---

[5]W. F. Albright, "What were the Cherubim?" *The Biblical Archaeologist*, ɪ, 1 (Feb., 1938), p. 2. The only possible Biblical evidence of animal form is the uncertain statement of Ezek. 1:7 that they had a hard sole on their feet, like a calf.

[6]But cf. James A. Montgomery, *A Critical and Exegetical Commentary on the Book of Daniel* (New York: Charles Scribner's Sons, 1927), pp. 85-86.

both in their names and in their offices these angels are genuinely Hebraic in character.

The representation of angels that has had the widest popular influence occurs in Zechariah 5:9 (post-exilic). There we find the picture of a woman with the long white wings of a stork (cf. Gabriel's description as "flying swiftly," Dan. 9:21). The sex distinction, however, does not appear to have valid application to angels, with their essentially spiritual character.[7]

The purpose of angels is to act as God's agents for effectuating the testament and for carrying out its provisions for the elect. Commencing with the period of the patriarchs, their activities become a matter of occasional Biblical reference.[8] Two angels in human form (Gen. 18:2; 19:1), for example, accompanied Yahweh (18:17) on His visit to Abraham to announce the joyful message of Sarah's impending conception. Then, though the angelic pair preceded to rescue Lot (19:15, 16), their ability as agents of destruction is shown by the way in which they struck down the men of Sodom with instantaneous blindness (19:11). Their warning to Lot, moreover, indicates the power that God had committed to them, as they stated simply, "We will destroy this place" (v. 13). Later, God sent His angel before Abraham's servant to prosper this man in gaining a wife for Isaac (24:7, 40); and the providential success which the servant experienced illustrates the general, ministerial function of angels on behalf of God's own (if this passage, that is, does not refer to *the* "Angel of Yahweh"). In the case of Jacob at Bethel, as he dreamed of the ladder set up between earth and heaven, it was the angels who mediated the communion with God to this heir of the testament (28:12).[9] Jacob then, on his return to Palestine spoke of them as God's protecting army (32:1; cf. II Kings 6:17). They attended the giving of the law on Sinai (Deut. 33:2), constituting the multiplied thousands of "God's chariots" in a way that corresponded to their presence in later days with Yahweh on Zion (Ps. 68:17). It was an angel who restrained Balaam against Israel (Num. 22:22) and who executed the cursing of those who would not come to the assistance of Deborah and Barak in their great battle of the consolidation period (Judg. 5: 23). It was also an angel, however, who condemned Israel for their national apostasy (2:1-4).[10]

David was the first Biblical character to provide us with extensive information about angels. God's postponement of such revelations until this time may well have been due to their lesser degree of rele-

---

[7]See above, p. 206.
[8]The "Angel of Yahweh," or "the Angel of the Testament" passages are not here discussed, for they seem to refer to Christ. See above, topic 13-A.
[9]Cf. Geerhardus Vos, *Biblical Theology*, pp. 110-11.
[10]If again the angels who are described in these instances are not Christ, the Angel of Yahweh, cf. Num. 22:31-35.

vance in respect to the testament; for redemption, after all, constitutes the organizing principle of divine revelation. To David, angels
were defined as being superior to man in wisdom (II Sam. 14:20;
19:27) and in strength (Ps. 103:20). Their basic function is stated
to be that of praising God (Ps. 89:7; 150:1) and of doing His pleasure
(103:21). Through David's contemporary Asaph, it was revealed that
"angels of evil" took part in the plagues against Egypt so that Israel
might be released from that land of bondage, and that the whole
sequence of events might redound to God's glory (78:49). Psalm
91:11, 12 states as a general principle, "He shall give His angels charge
over thee, to keep thee in all thy ways. They shall bear thee up in
their hands, lest thou dash thy foot against a stone." The book of
Job, which seems to have been revealed to Israel in the next reign,
spoke of the angels as God's servants (Job 4:18); and it described
how they stand before God to report on their assignments (1:6; 2:1;
I Kings 22:19; cf. Zech. 1:11). They number in the thousands (Job
33:23). An example of their ministry is the provision made by one
angel for Elijah's journey to Sinai (I Kings 19:5). The function of
angels as mediators in prophetic revelation is first suggested in this
same period (I Kings 13:18), though the particular disclosure claimed
in this verse was not in fact a valid one. The words of Yahweh at the
call of Isaiah, when He asked, "Whom shall I send, and who will go
for *us*?" (Isa. 6:8), suggest God's deliberation with His angelic "council" (v. 2; cf. Gen. 11:7). Isaiah, however, makes it clear that this
"consultation" occurred only because of God's gracious desire to share
His thoughts with the others that were concerned. God Himself needs,
and indeed takes, no advice (40:13, 14).

Daniel, during the exile, reveals much about angels. He quietly
corrected King Nebuchadnezzar's view of providence; for while the
monarch had come to believe that certain happenings were determined "by the decree of the (angelic) watchers" (Dan. 4:17), Daniel
removed any possibility of theological dualism by stating that future
events lay actually in "the decree of the Most High" (v. 24). But at
the same time he pointed out, both by his experiences and by his
teachings, the important role that angels do play in human history.
It was an angel who protected Daniel in the den of lions (6:22) and
his three friends in the fiery furnace (3:28). This latter angelic presence serves to explain Nebuchadnezzar's cry, "Lo, I see *four* men
loose, walking in the midst of the fire, and they have no hurt; and
the aspect of the fourth is like a son of the gods" (v. 25). The statement of the Authorized Version, that the fourth was "like the Son
of God," is precious in its thought, but it cannot be retained as a
legitimate rendering of the truly plural force of the Aramic *elāhīn*,[11]

---

[11]See above, p. 146.

"gods." This passage does show, however, both the human form and yet the supernatural qualities that are evidenced by a mighty angel.

In respect to guardian angels, the book of Daniel does not teach the particular assignment of angelic guardians to individuals; but it does so teach in respect to groups. An example is that of Michael, Israel's prince (10:21), who stands up for the chosen people (12:1; cf. Matt. 18:10), though Michael also assists the divine Angel of Yahweh in His more general activities in human history (10:13, 21). Finally, Daniel was the first Biblical writer to indicate his reception of divine revelations through a special interpreting angel (7:16; 9:21, 22). Daniel's exilic contemporary, Ezekiel, beheld in a vision the destruction of Jerusalem, as if committed into the hands of an angelic group (Ezek. 9:5, 7) which God had particularly assigned to the city (v. 1). Zechariah, in post-exilic days, made repeated reference to the interpreting angel who instructed him (Zech. 1:9, 19; 2:3, etc.). At the close, then, of his prophecies he made the prediction, "Yahweh my God shall come, and all the holy ones with Thee" (14:5). His words about the accompanying host seem to have primary reference to the presence of the holy angels at the Second Advent (so II Thess. 1:7). The thought of the verse is therefore similar to that of I Thessalonians 3:13: "May He establish your [human] hearts, at the coming of our Lord Jesus with all His [angelic] saints." These verses may, however, also include the presence of resurrected and raptured human saints with Christ at His return (so I Thess. 4:16).

B. DEMONS. Because of the dangers of polytheism and spiritism,[12] the Old Testament reveals little about demons, those angels that have fallen from goodness and that are now the instruments of evil. There has been a tendency, however, particularly on the part of liberals looking for evidence of religious evolution, to attribute to the Old Testament considerably more of a belief in evil spirits than the Scriptural evidence actually warrants. Through Moses came the first of God's revelations about demons. "They [Israel] sacrificed unto *shēdh* (plural), which were no God, to gods that they knew not, to new gods that came up of late" (Deut. 32:17). *Shēdh* is an Assyrian loan-word meaning "demon." This verse, therefore, shows that behind the practices of idolatry and polytheism there does lie a spiritual reality (cf. I Cor. 10:20), but one that is evil and to be shunned.[13] A similar demonic concept is sometimes attributed to Leviticus 17:7. This latter verse recounts how Israel sacrificed also to the *sā'ir*, which is the regular term in Hebrew for "he-goat." When wild, this animal was noted for inhabiting ruins (Isa. 13:21; 34:14). But goats are far

---

[12]See Unger, *Biblical Demonology* (Wheaton, Ill.: Van Kampen Press, 1952), chapters VII-IX.

[13]*Ibid.*, pp. 59-60; cf. Vos, *op. cit.*, p. 126, "A religious, demonic background is thrown back of the human figures that move across the canvas."

from being demons or ghosts; and the claim that Israel believed in "Pan," the satyr demon, can hardly be supported.[14] Elsewhere the *sā'ir* are connected with worship only in II Chronicles 11:15, in conjunction with Jeroboam's golden calves. In this verse therefore, as well as in Leviticus 17:7, they appear to be nothing more than goat idols. Israel was strictly charged to have no dealings with witchcraft or with similar matters that had demonic associations (Ex. 22:18; Deut. 18:10-12; cf. Isa. 2:6).

In the next period, however, when Israel entered into Canaan, the surrounding paganism did lead God's people astray into extensive demon worship, even to the point of human sacrifice (Ps. 106:37). Near the close of the period, the tragic case of Saul furnishes the chief Old Testament instance of demon possession. It is true that an "evil spirit" may mean no more than an unfriendly attitude (Judg. 9:23), but with Saul the personality of an evil, spiritual being was objectively present (I Sam. 16:14). David's harp playing seems to have soothed Saul and to have helped him to overcome this foreign power (v. 23); but twice, because of the evil spirit that troubled him, the king sought to kill David (18:11; 19:10). The significant point, however, is that the demon was, ultimately, but an instrument in God's hand for the unveiling of Saul's sinfulness and for the accomplishment of the latter's eventual replacement by David. The evil spirit was *from Yahweh* (16:14, 18:10) and is even described as "the spirit of God" (16:23).[15]

The book of Job, which was published in the disruption period, not only describes the work of Satan (see next section) but also gives certain indications about his demonic followers. Job 21:22 states that God judges angels; apparently, therefore, some angels are condemned. With this fact must be associated the thought of Job 25:2 which states, "He maketh peace in His high places." This verse suggests more than the calm that comes after physical storms; it serves as an allusion to an event that is rarely mentioned in Scripture, namely, the fall of the angels.[16] For though no basis exists for the assuming of "a cataclysmic judgment upon a pre-Adamite earth"[17] between Genesis 1:1 and 1:2, it is nonetheless clear that by the time, at least, of man's temptation in Genesis 3, some of God's angels had fallen and become demons. God thus judged "those that are high" (Job 21: 22). The angels that sinned were not spared but cast down to hell (II Peter 2:4; cf. Jude 6). Indeed, in Job's day there was not yet "peace in

[14]Unger, *op. cit.*, p. 60.
[15]See above, topic 15-B, on the relation of God to human sin.
[16]A. B. Davidson, *The Book of Job* (The Cambridge Bible for Schools and Colleges; Cambridge: The University Press, 1908), p. 180. Job 4:18 and 15:15, however, do not appear to be relevant to the question of the fall of angels; they are simply poetic descriptions of angelic inferiority to God (cf. 25:5, where moral purity cannot be involved).
[17]Unger, *op. cit.*, p. 17; cf. p. 15.

His high places" (25:2); for Satan was still able to appear in heaven
and to accuse the brethren (see next section). Job 25:2 was, however,
a prediction of the victory that Christ, at His ascension, would gain
over the dragon and his angels (Rev. 12:7). At that time, Satan would
be cast down to the earth, and his angels with him (v. 9); no more
would he be able to accuse, under the newer dispensation of the
Church (v. 10). But, even as Satan now concentrates upon persecut-
ing the Church on earth (v. 17), so even in Job's time, when demons
yet had access to heaven, their aim against men on earth was harm
and death. It is to such enemies that Job 33:22 seems to have had
reference: "His soul draweth near unto the pit, and his life to the
destroyers."[18] Isaiah, in the eighth century, speaks likewise of a judgment on fallen angels; but in Isaiah it is not simply to bring peace
in heaven, but also upon earth: "In that day Yahweh will punish the
host of the high ones . . . and they shall be gathered together, as
prisoners are gathered in the pit, and shall be shut up in the prison"
(24:21). With this passage should be compared Revelation 20:3,
which describes Satan's being bound, to deceive the nations no more,
until the thousand years should be finished.

A final reference to demons comes from Daniel 10:13, 20 (exile),
which speaks of certain princes of kingdoms, namely, the kingdoms
of Persia and Greece. Since, however, these "princes" correspond to
Michael, the archangel, who serves as the guardian angel for Israel,
and since they oppose both him and the Angel Christ, these verses
suggest the existence of a demonic hierarchy and of "guardian" (possessing) demons of pagan society.

C. SATAN. Just as the angels, Yahweh's ministering spirits, serve
Christ, the Angel of the testament, who is their particular leader
(Dan. 10:13, 21; Zech. 1:11), so the fallen angels, the demons, have
a representative head and chief in the person of Satan. The book
of Genesis contains no direct revelation of Satan; but it does describe
the serpent in Eden who acted as the instrument of man's temptation.
That a real serpent was present in the garden is shown in the Genesis
context by its comparison with the other animals (3:1), as well as by
the direct reference to the snake in God's subsequent curse (v. 14).
The snake's presence, moreover, is confirmed by the witness of the
New Testament (II Cor. 11:3). But behind the visible serpent there
lay an equally real, spiritual personality. This fact is shown in the
Genesis context, not simply by the snake's ability to speak,[19] but by
its very relationship with mankind. For man, as a part of His divine
image, held dominion over all the lower forms of life (1:28); but here
was a beast that assumed a position of full equality. The New Testament then makes the specific identification of the snake with the

18Davidson, op. cit., p. 230.
19Vos, op. cit., p. 44.

person of Satan (Rom. 16:20), "the great dragon, the old serpent" (Rev. 12:9). The underlying presence of Satan is further borne out by the nature of the curse. The serpent was indeed more seriously condemned than all the other animals (Gen. 3:14; for they too were about to suffer under the curse upon nature, v. 17; cf. Rom. 8:22). This beast's motion upon its belly would henceforward signify the failure of its attempt to exalt itself against man, as well as its fate of being trampled and crushed (Gen. 3:15). But its curse was to be a perpetual curse: "all the days of its life" (v. 14). The rest of God's natural creatures will some day be freed from the curse (Rom. 8:21), but even in the redeemed kingdom of the testament of peace, the serpent will still be "eating dust" (Isa. 65:25). The reason for this unique degradation of the serpent seems to lie in the correspondingly eternal punishment that remains in store for its master, Satan (Rev. 20:3, 10). His was the active, though unseen, force in Eden.

Moses, in his description of the day of atonement services, spoke of *Azāzēl* (Lev. 16:8). This Hebrew word is probably not, as the Authorized Version and in the Revised Version margin, a common noun with the meaning of "removal," or "the scapegoat." It is rather, as in the text of the Revised Version, a proper noun, the name Azazel. Here, then, is a personality that corresponds to, and yet opposes, Yahweh. This Azazel, moreover, is the ruler of the wilderness area outside the camp of Israel (v. 10), the prince, that is, of the world that lies outside the scope of God's testament. It is significant at this point to note how Scripture refers to the desert as the abode of evil spirits (Matt. 12:43; Rev. 18:2; cf. 17:3). Though the name "Satan" does not yet appear, the personality of the evil one is here first revealed. Confirmatory of this conclusion is the use of "Azazel" as the name of one of the leading demons discussed in the intertestamental literature.[20]

Azazel's function was to receive the second of the two goats that were used in the atonement service (Lev. 16:7, 8). The first, as determined by lot, was offered to Yahweh as a sin offering (v. 9; cf. v. 5). The second, or scape (escape), goat, however, is not called a sin offering nor was it killed: God's people are not to sacrifice to demons (Deut. 32:17). Its significance lies rather in the fact that the sins of the people were confessed over it (v. 21) and that it was sent away, allowed to escape alive, into the wilderness for Azazel. In this way, the scapegoat made atonement for the people (v. 10). The two-fold truth that is symbolized is this: the release of Israel from the grip of sin as caused by Satan, and the subsequent taking back of these sins to their demonic author. The fulfillment of this Mosaic type occurred when Christ took upon Himself the sins of the redeemed, thereby suffering separation from God the Father

---

[20] In the Pseudepigrapha, I Enoch 8:1; 10:4, etc.

(Matt. 27:46), but "through death bringing to nought him that had the power of death, that is, the devil; and delivering all them who through fear of death were all their lifetime subject to bondage" (Heb. 2:15, 16). Our Lord's penal sufferings were clearly a ransom to God, and not to Satan; but still, "to this end was the Son of God manifested, that He might destroy the works of the devil" (I John 3:8).

The term *sātān* was first applied to the preeminent evil one in Job 1-2 (disruption period). But *sātān* had not yet become a proper noun. It carries the definite article and reads, literally, the-*sātān*; for the noun is subject to translation and means simply, "the adversary." A similar phenomenon appears in Biblical Greek, where the descriptive adjective *diabolos*, "slanderous," exhibits development into the noun, "the slanderer," and thus into the name, "devil." The word *sātān* had been used earlier in Scripture, and without reference to Satan, for either an opposing angel (Num. 22:22) or an opposing man (Ps. 109:6; cf. v. 29). These opening chapters in Job, then, show "the Satan" to be powerful and self-determining by nature. He roams the earth at will, though he is not omnipresent (1:7). As opposed to the evolutionary reconstructions of liberalism, which picture Satan in the earlier revelations as differing little from any other angel,[21] he appears from the first as adopting an insolent attitude toward God (1:7). He is thoroughly corrupt.[22] "The adversary" insinuates untruth against Job (1:11; 2:4), for he hates men and, as in Eden, desires nothing less than their total fall. More basically, his opposition is directed against God, from whose glory he would detract by whatever means (1:9; 2:5).

In his work, however, the adversary is limited by God; for, though he appears to be called the fatal "king of terrors" (Job 18:14; cf. 33:22),[23] he cannot kill (2:6) nor do *anything* to God's elect, for that matter (1:12), without God's express permission. But he is still responsible for his own evil motivation and is subject to God's reprimand (2:3). Furthermore, though in this last verse he might seem to influence or to move God, the conclusion to the book of Job demonstrates that it was God who had been in sovereign control from the start. It was He who was actually responsible, though with a differing (righteous) motivation, for all the evil that befell Job

---

[21]Note Burrows' claim that Zechariah constitutes the first witness to Satan as a title for a supernatural being, and that even then "Satan" is not to be regarded as being hostile to God, *op. cit.*, p. 125.

[22]Cf. Jacob's more Biblical approach to Satan, as more than suspicious, and positively malicious, in his prosecutionist work. *Theology of the Old Testament*, pp. 71-72.

[23]See in this regard Franz Delitzsch, *Biblical Commentary on the Book of Job*. Trans. by Francis Bolton (Edinburgh: T. and T. Clark, 1876), I:326. He notes the possibility that 18:14 might refer to Satan, but he questions this meaning as probably beyond the knowledge of Job and his friends at the time.

(42:11). Satan is but a frustrated tool, executing the will of God for the heirs of the testament!

A situation similar to that of Job 1-2 is described in I Kings 22: 19-22. In this latter passage the evil one is identified as "the [well known] spirit" (v. 21), which indicated Micaiah's knowledge of, and dependence upon the Job context. In the same period there is mentioned the Philistine name Baal-zebub (II Kings 1:2, 3) which in the New Testament is applied to Satan (Matt. 10:25). In the Old Testament, however, "Beelzebub" is no more than the local god of Ekron. Of a somewhat similar significance are the references to the "sons of *b'lĭyá'al*" (Authorized Version, "Belial"; from Deut. 13:13 on). Belial indeed, in II Corinthians 6:15, identifies the person of Satan; but in the Old Testament the term merely connotes "worthlessness."

Isaiah described the king of Babylon, and said:

> "How art thou fallen from heaven, oh *hēlēl* ['morning star, Venus.'] . . . that didst lay low the nations! And thou saidst in thy heart, I will ascend into heaven, I will exalt my throne above the stars of God . . . I will make myself like the Most High. Yet thou shalt be brought down to hell" (Isa. 14: 12-15).

The proud Babylonian monarch is clearly compared to something; but the planet Venus, which does not try to raise its throne and become like God, hardly seems an adequate point of reference. In the light of Revelation 9:1, it appears likely that the fall of Satan is the real subject of this inspired comparison. For it was Satan who, in pride (I Tim. 3:6), attempted to rival God and was condemned.[24] On the strength of this understanding, the Latin name for the morning star, *lucifer*, "light bearer," (cf. Isa. 14:12, Authorized Version) has become a regular designation for Satan. The question then arises as to when this fall of Satan, into the demonic character that presently distinguishes him, actually took place. The only objectively relevant Biblical context is that of Genesis 3:1. In other words, lacking information to the contrary, we may well infer that Satan's attempt to win over the allegiance of mankind from God to himself constitutes the most natural incident with which to equate his "exalting his throne so as to be like the Most High." The hypothesis that the fall of Satan and the fall of man took place almost simultaneously is then substantiated by the fact that both were penally cursed at the same time (Gen. 3:14-17). Some interpreters have sought to adduce Ezekiel 28:13-15 as another comparative description of the fall of Satan, similar to that of Isaiah 14:12-15. In Ezekiel 28:13, however, the presence of the precious stones and gold and the fact that the subject was created in connection with the Garden of Eden suggest Adam (Gen. 2:

---

[24]Cf. Vos, *op. cit.*, p. 302.

7, 12), and not Satan; while in Ezekiel 28:14 the references to the mountain of God and to the cherub covering (the ark) suggest the Temple on Mt. Zion, but not the pride of the devil.[25] There thus appears to be no Biblical basis for assuming from Ezekiel 28:14 that Satan was once a member of the class of the cherubim.

In the post-exilic passage of Zechariah 3:1, 2, the definite article is still written with the noun *sātān*; it is still "the adversary." But with Ezra's composition of Chronicles in the following century, *Sātān* for the first time appears alone as a personal name (I Chron. 21:1). In the latter reference, Satan's function as an instrument of God may be clarified if one will compare the verse with its parallel representation in II Samuel (24:1). There, Satan's work is identified as the work of Yahweh Himself. What Satan does, in other words, is what God decrees! The Zechariah verses, on the other hand, picture Satan in the act of accusing the high priest Jeshua (who stands representing the heirs of the testament) before the judicial presence of Christ, the Angel of Yahweh. At that time, Yahweh did not more than rebuke our demonic accuser (Zech. 3:2). But the next stage of revelation, after the silent intertestamental period, would find Christ promising in connection with His crucifixion, "Now is the judgment of this world, now shall the prince of this world be cast out" (John 12:31; cf. Rev. 12:10). Under the newer testament, the members of the Church therefore no longer suffer heavenly accusation, as did Job and Jeshua. Instead, it is Christ who is in heaven, who ever liveth to make intercession for us (Heb. 7:25). Satan is still the prince of the power of this terrestrial air (Eph. 2:2); but the testament has been effectuated, the saints need only to respond in faith to receive the full inheritance, and if we resist the devil, he will flee from us (James 4:7).

For Further Reading:

William George Heidt, *Angelology of the Old Testament.* Washington, D. C.: The Catholic University of America Press, 1949. An S.T.D. thesis at the Catholic University of America.

Aubrey R. Johnson, *The One and the Many in the Israelite Conception of God.* Cardiff, Wales: University of Wales, 1942. Includes a discussion of angels and the Angel of Yahweh.

Edward Langton, *Essentials of Demonology.* London: Epworth Press, 1949. On the origin and development of this doctrine, both Jewish and Christian.

---

[25]See above, p. 218.

Part VI. The Conditions: Commitment

"Now therefore, if ye will obey My voice indeed, and keep My testament, then ye shall be Mine own possession, from among all peoples" (Exodus 19:5).

23. Repentance*

Though a testament is effectuated by grace (Part V, preceding), it may yet involve stipulations, requirements that are imposed upon the heirs and that must be met, if the latter are to qualify for the inheritance (Part VI, this section). God accordingly laid on Abraham, whom He had chosen by unconditional election,[1] this general obligation: "As for thee, thou shalt keep My testament, thou and thy seed after thee" (Gen. 17:9). Without any sense of incompatibility, the Old Testament asserts both the divine ordination of the testament (Ex. 6:7) and yet, at the same time, the human responsibility to accept its obligations and to fulfill them, (19:7, 8; 24:7, 8). Our finite minds may be unable completely to grasp this truth of the identity between the results of human freedom, on the earthly level, and the results of divine sovereignty, on the heavenly level. But as long as we remain unaware of the course that God has already plotted for each of us, the fact of predestination should in no way impair our own enthusiastic response to God's requirements. In fact, knowing that God ordains the ends through (not in spite of) the means,[2] we should confidently make our "calling and election sure" (II Pet. 1:10) by carrying out those God-given means to the best of our ability. Historically, men's belief in predestination has proven to be an incentive for them to put forth their greatest efforts; for it provides us with the assurance that our very response is the proof of our election and that the God "who has begun a good work in us will perfect it unto the day of Jesus Christ" (Phil. 1:6).

---

*BIBLE READING: Hosea 6; Ezekiel 33

Collateral Reading: Oehler, *Theology of the Old Testament,* pp. 455-463.
    Heinisch, *Theology of the Old Testament,* 180-185, pp. 264-268.
    Rowley, *The Faith of Israel,* pp. 74-88.

---

[1]See above, p. 179.
[2]Biblical predestination is thus opposed to the fatalism that is so characteristic of Mohammedanism, which affirms its belief in the divine ordination of the ends, irrespective of the means.

The fundamental requirement for inheritance under the testament is commitment to God: "Commit thy way unto Yahweh, trust also in Him, and He will bring it to pass" (Ps. 37:5). Commitment, moreover, begins with the experience of conversion and then follows through into a life of progressive sanctification in obedience to God's law, both moral and ceremonial. Conversion, for its part, embraces two basic matters: repentance (this topic) and faith (the next). True repentance involves a man's admission of his sins, his feelings of sorrow, and his decision to turn from a life of sin to a life that is dedicated to God. As Ezekiel proclaimed it: "Repent [shūv, 'return'] and turn yourselves from all your transgressions . . . and make you a new heart" (Ezek. 18:30, 31). True faith, then, consists positively in a man's sincere trust in the Lord. As Joshua resolutely affirmed, "As for me and my house, we will serve Yahweh!" (Josh. 24:15).

A. PRIMEVAL AND PATRIARCHAL REVELATIONS. After Cain, in the primeval period, committed his crime against Abel, he experienced sorrow (Gen. 4:13, 14), but only because of the penalty that fell upon him and not because of any real repentance for the wrong he had done. The patriarch Abraham, on the contrary, in response to God's enunciation of His moral testamentary requirements (17:1), fell on his face in earnest submission to the Lord (v. 3). A similarly contrasting pair of examples are presented by the histories of Jacob and Esau. Esau wept in sorrow at the loss of his blessing (27:38) but was rejected just the same (v. 39;[3] Heb. 12:17), because his conduct had demonstrated him as profane in his attitude (Heb. 12:16). Jacob, however, at a later date, when in fear over the approach of Esau, exhibited true submission to God and prayed fervently for divine deliverance, confessing, "Oh Yahweh, I am not worthy of the least of all the hésedhs [acts of loyalty to the testamental promise] which Thou hast showed unto Thy servant" (32:10). Shortly thereafter, Jacob had his experience of wrestling with God's Angel, which both demonstrated the validity of his prior conversion and which also marked, in itself, a turning point in his life.[4]

During the next patriarchal generation, the first step in repentance (a man's admission of his sins) is remarkably evidenced by the confessed guilty consciences of Joseph's brothers, which tormented them for having sold him (42:21; cf. 50:17). The next step (a man's feelings of sorrow for his sin) is demonstrated by Job, who gave an ex-

---

[3]Isaac's words to Esau were similar to those to Jacob: "Behold, from [Hebrew, min] the fatness of the earth shall be thy dwelling, and from the dew of heaven" (Gen. 27:39). Cf. his former statement to Jacob, "God give thee, min [from] the dew of heaven and from the fatness of the earth" (v. 28). But though these are often called Isaac's blessings, v. 39 was actually a curse: the min is separative, "away from the fatness," while in v. 28 it is partitive, "give you a part from the fatness," a seemingly intentional play on words.
[4]See below, pp. 419, 420.

ternal manifestation to this aspect of his repentance by marking his
body with dust and ashes before God (Job 42:6). Jacob's rent clothes,
however, at this period serve merely as indications of grief (Gen.
37:29, 34) and are as yet without relevance in regard to the matter
of repentance from sin.

B. MOSAIC REVELATIONS. When God enunciated the Sinaitic testament, He clearly stated the necessity for a human response to divine
grace: "If ye will obey My voice indeed, and keep My testament,
then [and only then] shall ye be Mine own possession, from among
all peoples" (Exodus 19:5). As Heinisch has expressed it, (his latter
quotation being from Deut. 6:5, of this same Mosaic period):

> "Divine love which 'drew them with cords of kindness, with
> bands of love, and was to them as one who presses an infant
> to his cheeks,' demands human love in return. 'You must love
> Yahweh, your God, with your whole heart, with your whole
> soul, and with your whole strength.'"[5]

So Moses, after he had predicted the future apostasy of his people,
explained to them the basis for restoration to God's favor: "And thou
shalt *shūv* [repent] and obey the voice of Yahweh" (Deut. 30:8; cf.
v. 2). The verb *shūv* is one of the most common in the Hebrew language and means "to turn" or "to return." In reference to the conversion experience, it expresses the thought of a man's return to the original hope that God granted to mankind: to the redemptive testament,
with its condition of a repentant submission to God and with a renunciation of all that fails to correspond to His will.[6]

Repentance was the feature of the law that made necessary, along
with the external forms of sacrifice, a more underlying and heart-felt
confession of sin (Lev. 5:5). The acts, that is, had to be accompanied
by a penitence of spirit that arose out of genuine conversion.[7]
Pharaoh indeed performed an outward confession of sin (Ex. 9:27;
10:16); but if repentance be defined as "being sorry enough not to
do it again," he had experienced no true repentance! When Moses,
however, confessed the deep sins of his people (32:31; 34:9), they,
in contrition, put away even their personal ornaments and mourned
from the heart (33:4, 6). The law, furthermore, required not simply
sacrifice but also practical restitution in whatever damages the sin
may have involved (Lev. 6:5). Humanly speaking, the effectiveness,
then, of the annual day-of-atonement service lay in the way in which
Israel "afflicted their souls" (Lev. 16:29-31; cf. 23:27; Num. 29:7). This
"afflicting of soul" is not to be simply identified with the external rite
of fasting, for it is noteworthy that the same phrase occurs in respect
to a variety of vows (Num. 30:13). But it did imply some type of

---

[5]Heinisch, *Theology of the Old Testament*, p. 183.
[6]Cf. Edmond Jacob, *Theology of the Old Testament*, p. 289.
[7]Rowley, *The Faith of Israel*, p. 87.

humble submission to God and soul-searching before Him. Only on such a basis then was the high priest authorized to confess the iniquities of the children of Israel over the scape goat, so that the typical animal could "bear upon him all their iniquities into a solitary land" (Lev. 16:21, 22).

C. REVELATIONS CENTERING IN DAVID. When defeated at Ai, at the commencement of the consolidation period (1406 B.C.), Joshua and the elders of Israel rent their clothes, fell on their faces, and heaped up dust on their heads in grief (Josh. 7:6). God, however, ordered them up; and He demanded, instead, a confessing and a forsaking of sin (v. 11). So under the judges, it was the cry to God and the turning from sin that saved Israel (Judg. 10:10, 16; I Sam. 7:3, 4). It was only this latter feature (repentance) that could give force to their external acts of offerings, libations, and — here mentioned for the first time in Scripture — fasting (Judg. 20:26; cf. I Sam. 7:6). Saul's words were commendable and exemplary, at least at the time when they were spoken — "I have sinned, for I have transgressed the commandment of Yahweh" (I Sam. 15:24); or again, "I have sinned: return, my son David; for I will no more do thee harm: behold, I have played the fool, and have erred exceedingly" (26:21). But Saul seems to have failed in the consistent application of his own words (cf. 27:4). Heinisch's analysis may not do full justice to Saul personally, but his basic point is sound:

> Conversion implies a break from one's former mode of life. It must be genuine "with all one's heart and with all one's soul"— an external acknowledgment of having sinned is wholly insufficient. Saul regretted not having observed Yahweh's command and Samuel's directions, but his sorrow proceeded merely from the evil consequences of his actions. There is no conversion without abandoning sin because sin breaks intimacy with God.[8]

In the next period, David's experience with Bath-sheba, while heinous, led to the greatest Biblical expression of what is involved in repentance, both in the king's personal confession (Ps. 51) and in what seems to have been his public admission (Ps. 32). For David not simply confessed his own sins (cf. Ps. 38:19), he recognized his sin as constituting a direct affront to God (51:4; 32:5; cf. II Sam. 12:13). He confessed the total depravity of his human nature, as well as of his overt acts (Ps. 51:5); and he submitted himself completely to God: "The sacrifices of God are a broken spirit: a broken and a contrite heart, oh God, Thou wilt not despise" (v. 17). But David then found, experientially, that the man who will throw himself wholly upon God's mercy will find sure forgiveness and will in no wise be cast out (86:5; cf. John 6:37a). Whosoever will may come! David recognized, of course, the corresponding truth that his repentance was, in itself, but the evidence of God's prior work of predestination and

---

[8]*Op. cit.*, p. 265.

regeneration — only God can create the clean heart (Ps. 51:10). As David's Korahite colleagues expressed this truth in their prayers, "Turn (shūv, 'repent') us, O God of our salvation . . . Wilt Thou not quicken us again? . . . Show us Thy lovingkindness (hésedh), O Yahweh, and grant us Thy salvation" (Ps. 85:4, 6, 7); compare Asaph's repeated refrain, "Turn us again, O God" (Ps. 80:3, 7, 19). In the same vein, Christ Himself explained in the first half of John 6:37, "All that the Father giveth Me shall come to Me." David then went on to identify the specific instrument of conversion: it is the word of God (Ps. 19:7), the external call of the truth of Yahweh's special, written revelation.

Other psalms by David express Israel's national repentance for their sins both past and present (cf. Ps. 106).[9] On the occasion of David's sinful census (c. 975 B.C.), the contrite king and the elders of Israel are described as clothing themselves in sackcloth (I Chron. 21:16). This becomes, therefore, the first Biblical mention of the use of sackcloth for the practice of religious humiliation. With it may then be compared David's recourse to fasting and sackcloth in another exceptional case (Ps. 69:10, 11). Fasting, however, as it is described in I Samuel 31:13 and II Samuel 1:12; 12:27, appears not as a religious function, indicative of repentance, but as an expression simply of sincere grief (cf. Ps. 35:13; 109:24).

Solomon, in the early disruption period, stressed the need of each man for the confession of his sin and for repentance, that he should shūv, (return) to God with all his heart (I Kings 8:46-48). "He that covereth his transgressions shall not prosper; but whoso confesseth and forsaketh them shall obtain mercy" (Prov. 28:13). Job "the patient," concluded his spoken words by confessing before God the rashness of his previous speeches (Job 40:3; 42:6). Rehoboam and his princes, moreover, found that God's blessing came only as they humbled themselves in His presence (II Chron. 12:6, 7, 12). A great national conversion of Judah is described under Asa (14:2-4; 15:12-15); and when his son Jehoshaphat was faced by an overwhelming invasion, c. 850 B.C., he experienced divine deliverance as he too sought Yahweh and even proclaimed a fast (20:3). Some fasts doubtless consisted of mere formalities, or may have involved thoroughgoing hypocrisy (cf. I Kings 21:9, 12). When Ahab was condemned by Elijah, however (v. 27), his rent clothes, the sackcloth, and the fasting evinced a true humbling of himself (so contrary to Canaanitish royal practice) and brought about a postponement of the divine punishment that had been threatened against him. This latter reference is the first Biblical example of the rending of garments as a sign of repentance. In addition, Elijah worked for a total national conversion (I Kings 18:21); he prayed for it too, because he also recognized that

---

[9]Davidic, as indicated by its quotation in I Chron. 16.

conversion could come about only as God "turned their heart back again" (v. 37).

D. Prophetic Revelations. In the troubled years of the latter half of the eighth century, national emergencies caused the Hebrew kingdoms to proclaim special fast days (Joel 1:14; 2:15; cf. Jer. 36:9); but the prophets insisted that the primary need was for the people to rend their hearts and not their garments (Joel 2:13). In fact, in their zeal for true repentance, they sometimes spoke as if they were rejecting the system of external symbols and types *in toto* (Amos 5:22). The actual prophetic feeling, however, is to be found in verses such as Hosea 6:6, "For I desire goodness, and not sacrifice; and the knowledge [acknowledging] of God *more than* burnt offerings."

> "Prophecy puts the question thus: How had the nation
> conformed to its Divine destination? How far has a commu-
> nity consecrated to God been really formed under the ordi-
> nances of the law?"[10]

Contemporary observations furnished a gloomy answer. The age of the prophets was characterized by a blind reliance upon external-ism, which was divorced from any real commitment to God.[11] The fasting and the "affliction of the souls" was on the surface, it was perpetuated for purely selfish ends, and God did not see it (Isa. 58: 3, 4; cf. Jer. 14:12). As opposed to such popular vanities, "in the teaching of the prophets the only foundation for man's well-being lies in obedience to the will of God."[12] These watchmen of Israel kept insisting that their people turn unto Him from whom they had so deeply revolted (Isa. 31:6), that the wicked man forsake his way and return unto God (55:7), and that the people establish justice and seek Yahweh (Amos 5:4, 6, 15). In the preaching of the prophets, the most emphasized object of repentance, in the sense of "turning from," was the worship of false deities. Practices that constituted a rivalry to Yahweh, such as the idolatrous service of the Baalim, must be abandoned (Hos. 2:17; 13:1). But for that matter, Israel must be willing to yield up anything that was incompatible with devotion to Yahweh. Thus Isaiah preached to his people, "In *shūvā* ["returning," from entangling foreign alliances][13] and rest shall ye be saved; in quietness and in confidence [in Yahweh] shall be your strength" (Isa. 30:15).

Just as had been true, however, for those before them, so the eighth century prophets recognized that such conversions could only come about as the Lord enabled. They spoke for deity and said,

---

[10]Oehler, *Theology of the Old Testament,* p. 456.
[11]See above, pp. 111, 112.
[12]Rowley, *op. cit.,* p. 63.
[13]The only instance in the Old Testament in which a Hebrew noun, and not a verb, is used to express the active truth of conversion; cf. Jacob, *op. cit.,* pp. 289-290.

"Return unto Me, *for* I have redeemed thee" (Isa. 44:22). They made their appeal to God's mercy (55:7) and to His grace (Joel 2:13; Amos 5:15). Also, like David, they recognized that the instrumentality of God's external call consisted of His revealed word, which would not return unto Him void (Isa. 55:11). If Israel would but hear, they might turn again (*shūv*, repent) and be healed (6:10). A remarkable demonstration of the effectiveness of the spoken word appears in the ministry of Jonah to Nineveh (Jonah 3:10), though the resultant Assyrian penitence was short-lived and seems to have been stamped out twenty years later by the ruthless aggressiveness of Tiglath-pileser III (745-727 B.C.).[14]

At the beginning of the last quarter of the eighth century, Hezekiah, guided by Isaiah, led in a major national revival in Judah (II Chron. 29-31). The long relapse that God's people experienced under Manasseh the son of Hezekiah (696-641) ended with the latter's conversion late in his reign. It took an Assyrian captivity, perhaps in connection with Ashurbanipal's reasserted power in 648 B.C.,[15] to bring Manasseh to his senses; but he did, belatedly, humble himself before God (II Chron. 33:12, 13). Josiah's famous reforms advanced in three stages, 631, 627 (II Chron. 34:3), and 621 B.C. (v.8); and they climaxed in the greatest revival of Israel's history (34:29-35:19). King and people pledged themselves "to walk after Yahweh and to keep His commandments, with all the heart, and with all the soul, to perform the words of the testament" (34:31). Jeremiah joined in the royal appeal for Israel to turn back from their evil doings and to make their way good (Jer. 18:11; cf. 11:6). Then indeed they might dwell in the land that Yahweh had given them (25:5; cf. 26:3; 36:3). This "turning back" makes up the essence of repentance; and it constitutes, as Oehler describes it, the negative side of faith:

> "It is a ceasing from all natural confidence in one's own strength and power, a renunciation of all trust in human support and assistance. Jeremiah xvii. 5; 'Cursed be the man that trusteth in man, and maketh flesh his arm.' "[16]

But Josiah's reformation failed in the long run to reach the people's hearts.[17] Judah returned to Yahweh only "feignedly" (Jer. 3:10). Jeremiah found that "no man [really] repenteth him of his wickedness" (8:6); Jerusalem was "slidden back by a perpetual backsliding" (v. 5). But since Israel had refused the word of Yahweh (v. 9) they would have to suffer the loss of their land (v. 10). Subsequently, however, God could yet turn them back so that they would

---

[14]On the political background to Jonah's ministry, see Payne, *An Outline of Hebrew History*, pp. 132-133.
[15]*Ibid.*, pp. 145-146.
[16]*Op. cit.*, p. 459.
[17]See above, p. 114.

repent (31:18, 19). After Jerusalem's fall, therefore, Jeremiah prayed, "Turn Thou us unto Thee, oh Yahweh, and we shall be turned" (Lam. 5:21). The prophet then went on to anticipate the post-exilic days, when Israel would return to the land (Jer. 31:21) and when, as he pictured it, "A woman shall encompass a man" (v. 22). That is, the virgin Israel would embrace and cling to Yahweh. Some day, moreover would come Christ and the newer testament:

> God will, according to the prospect held out, Dt. xxx. 6, of a circumcision of the heart, work in them a susceptibility for the Divine, a willingness to perform His will. The people no longer encounter the law in its rigid objectivity; but God will, in the times of the new covenant, write it in their hearts.[18]

The exilic prophet Ezekiel expressly identified himself as a watchman over Israel (Ezek. 33:7-9), warning the ungodly to repent and to turn from their evil ways (v. 11). In submission lay Israel's hope for divine forgiveness (v. 16); but without it, there could be no anticipation of repossessing the promised land (v. 25). Perhaps even more distressing to Ezekiel than the openly ungodly were the "church going" exilic hypocrites who were accustomed to sit before him: "For with their mouth they show much love, but their heart goeth after their gain; for they hear Thy words, but they do them not!" (v. 31, 32). The need for both of these groups was to submit to God and to make them a new heart (18:31), though it would, at the same time, be God who would give the new heart to them (36:26-29). Daniel was inspired, after a period of fasting (Dan. 9:3), to produce one of the great Biblical examples of national confession (vv. 4-19). Fasting came, in fact, to be increasingly stressed in the post-exilic days (Ezra 8:21; Neh. 1:4; 9:1; Esther 4:16; 9:31). It passed, indeed, beyond all meaningfulness in later Judaism (cf. Luke 18:12); but in the Old Testament period it still signified an honest attempt to deal with sin (Neh. 9:2) and led to heart-felt confessions before God (Ezra 9:6-15; Neh. 1:6-8; 9:16-37). The oft-repeated principle, therefore, which constitutes the fundamental condition for inheritance under the testament was, and still is, that of commitment: "Return unto Me, saith Yahweh of hosts, and I will return unto you" (Zech. 1:3; Mal. 3:7). So today, if America, or any other nominally Christian nation, is long to endure, its hope can only rest upon the basis of a God-given revival which turns hearts in repentance to Him and to His law. As it was expressed through the wisest man of all history:

> "If My people, who are called by My name, shall humble themselves, and pray, and seek My face, and turn from their wicked ways; then will I hear from heaven, and will forgive their sin, and will heal their land" (II Chron. 7:14).

[18]Oehler, *op. cit.*, p. 458.

For Further Reading:

Hiram D. Oxley, "Repentance of Believers in the Old Testament." An unpublished master's dissertation, Wheaton College, Ill., 1951. An analysis of the factors involved in this Old Testament doctrine and a treatment of some of the more significant individual examples.

Harry A. Ironside, *Except Ye Repent.* New York: American Tract Society, c. 1937. A Biblical and practical study that brings home the absolute need of every Christian to experience personal repentance.

William Douglas Chamberlain, "For Deliverance and Freedom, the Biblical Doctrine of Repentance," *Interpretation,* 4:3 (July, 1950), 271-283. A neo-orthodox survey that questions repentance as an Old Testament doctrine but gives an outline of recent thought on repentance in the Bible as a whole.

24. Faith*

A. PRIMEVAL AND PATRIARCHAL REVELATIONS. Although God laid down no explicit human response as a condition for a man's inheritance under the Edenic testament (Gen. 3:15), the proper heart attitude was still necessary if any given individual was to be reckoned with the seed of the woman rather than with the seed of the serpent. Adam demonstrated his faith in the divine promise (that the woman would produce redemptive offspring) by the very name that he gave to Eve (3:20); Eve confessed her dependence upon God as she then bore her seed (4:1); and Genesis 4:4 notes that God had respect unto Abel, but not unto Cain. The type of offering presented by each of these latter was significant;[1] but the stress of the Genesis context falls upon Cain's improper attitude of spirit (vv. 5,9). Thus Hebrews 11:4 summarizes the situation, saying, "By faith Abel offered unto God a more excellent sacrifice than Cain ... and through it he being dead yet speaketh." The general proposition then, that Abel yet speaks, is this, "Without faith it is impossible to be well-pleasing unto Him" (Heb. 11:6).

The patriarch Abraham believed in Yahweh, and He reckoned it to him for righteousness (Gen. 15:6; cf. Rom. 4:18). The Hebrew root of this verb "believe" is *āman,* "to be steady, firm, or trustworthy, trust in."[2] The basic idea is therefore that of "confirming," of causing

---

*BIBLE READING: Genesis 15; Habakkuk 2

Collateral Reading: Vos, *Biblical Theology,* pp. 96-102.

John H. Raven, *The History of the Religion of Israel,* pp. 459-474.

Norman H. Snaith, *Mercy and Sacrifice: a Study of the Book of Hosea* (London: Student Christian Movement Press, 1953), pp. 39-40, 50-69.

[1]See below, topic 27-C.

[2]Ludwig Kohler, *Lexicon in Veteris Testamenti Libros,* p. 61. Thus Raven, *The History of the Religion of Israel,* p. 468, well notes, "Isaiah was the great prophet of faith. Nevertheless it did not begin with him. The beginning of the doctrine of faith is in the story of Abraham," though cf. Abel.

oneself to find support. Vos terms it a "causative-productive";[3] and Warfield, in a similar vein, has stated:

> "It is a subjective causative, and expresses the acquisition or exhibition of the firmness, security, reliability, faithfulness, which lies in the root meaning of the verb, in or with respect to its object."[4]

This object, in Scripture's discussion of Abraham's faith, was none other than God Himself. The most generally satisfactory translation, therefore, of *āman* (believe) in Genesis 15:6, and the translation that best brings out this idea of "relying upon," or of "fastening one's confidence upon," is simply this: "Abraham trusted in God."

To such a definition of faith appear the following six corollaries. 1) Faith is a matter of personal commitment to God. As Vos well points out, the development of a man's faith in God does not consist of "assent to the veracity of a statement" followed by an ultimate trust in a Person; because the Person of God transcends human verification. "Back of the belief, the assent, therefore there lies an antecedent trust distinguishable from the subsequent trust."[5] Faith may therefore exhibit a quantitative development, but not a qualitative one. It does not evolve from doubt to trust. A man either has committed himself to the historical God of salvation or he has not.

2) Such faith composes the one preeminent condition for a man's inheriting the blessings of the testament. Faith constitutes the basic commitment from which all other aspects of commitment will follow, even the repentance which, in practical outworkings, precedes it. Abraham's receiving of the testament was thus conditioned by his "faithful heart" (Neh. 9:8). So also today, as 1900 years ago (or over 3900 years ago, in the case of Abraham), the question, "What must I do to be saved?" is answered by the same simple but profound truth, "Believe on the Lord Jesus, and thou shalt be saved, and thy house" (Act 16:31).

3) Faith in the Person, if sincere, will be followed by a faith in (that is, an assent to) His propositional declarations. Abraham therefore committed himself to the truth of the promise that he could receive a seed as numerous as the stars (Gen. 15:5), impossible as this promise seemed at the time (Heb. 11:12). Sarah, one must admit, laughed at first in disbelief at the prospect of a couple, as old as they were, having a child (Gen. 18:13); cf. Abraham's own, similar attitude (17:17). From this hesitancy, then, arose the ironical name given by God to the promised son, *Yishāq* (Isaac), "he laughs" (17:19). But, subsequently, Sarah went so far as to become guilty of falsehood, as she attempted to repudiate her own skepticism

[3]*Biblical Theology*, p. 98.
[4]*Biblical Doctrines* (New York: Oxford University Press, 1929), p. 468.
[5]*Op. cit.*, p. 98.

(18:15). Fundamentally, her acknowledgement of God was genuine; she became strong and consistent in faith, "since she counted Him faithful who had promised" (Heb. 11:11); and she ended by giving a happy turn to this name *Yishāq*: "God hath made me to laugh; every one that heareth will laugh with me" (Gen. 21:6). So today, Christ demands of His own their conformity to His truth, particularly to the propositions of the Bible, to which He Himself was so thoroughly committed. Christ indeed considered faith in the Bible and faith in Himself inseparable: "For if ye believed Moses, ye would believe Me; for he wrote of Me. But if ye believe not his writings, how shall ye believe my words?" (John 5:46, 47). The Pharisees of Jesus' day did not really believe in the Mosaic supernaturalism that they professed, and, so they did not accept Christ; but similarly, any man who now questions Scripture, even this same Mosaic authorship of the Pentateuch, cannot possess a true conformity to the mind of Christ, in which this aspect of supernaturalism bulked so large.

4) Abraham's faith included both the negative renunciation of his own ability and his positive reliance upon God. Abraham was willing to go so far as to sacrifice his son Isaac when God ordered him to do so. He had faith in Yahweh's ability even to raise Isaac from the dead (Heb. 11:19),[6] as is witnessed by his statement of confidence, at the point where he and his son left the servants, saying: "*We* will come again to you" (Gen. 22:5).

5) Though qualitatively speaking, Abraham's faith remained constant, as a basic commitment to God, this did not mean that quantitatively speaking he stood without need of more faith. As a man once exclaimed to Christ Himself, "I believe, help Thou mine unbelief!" (Mark 9:24). The matter of Abraham's laughter over the birth of Isaac has already been noted, and just two verses after the supreme description of Abraham's faith comes a questioning on Abraham's part, a seeking of proof from God, that showed his need even then for additional faith (Gen: 15:8).

6) Abraham's faith involved both a subjective and an objective side. As Vos puts it, his faith was an "affirmation of divine omnipotence." It consisted, subjectively of an affirmation, that is, of a state of mind, "the attitude of faith"; but it consisted also of an affirmation that was directed toward the divine object. For anyone can possess faith, in the subjective sense of being sincere; but he may be a sincere communist! Abraham's faith, however, was directed; it involved an entering into God's objective promises, "to incorporate the supernatural."[7]

---

[6]The next statement, "whence also he received him in a figure," lends further emphasis to the reality of Abraham's faith in such a resurrection. It is not that Isaac exists as a type of Christ's sacrificial death in obedience to the Father, or as a type of His resurrection, which Scripture nowhere suggests. Rather, Isaac himself was the one who died "figuratively" in the ram and was thus figuratively restored.

[7]Vos, *op. cit.*, pp. 99-100.

In both of these respects, then, Abraham became the "father of the faithful." Subjectively, he establishes the pattern for our attitude of faith (Gal. 3:7; Rom. 4:16)); and objectively, he serves as an exemplary recipient both of the God-given righteousness that comes through faith and of a divinely granted heirship to the world (Gal. 3:29; Rom. 4:11, 13). When he was called of God in Ur of the Chaldees,[8] he stepped out in faith, "not knowing whither he went" (Heb. 11:8). His whole life, moreover, demonstrates a commitment, not to material values, for he and his family were "strangers and pilgrims on the earth" (v. 13), but to the spiritual side of life: "But now they desire a better country, that is, an heavenly: wherefore God is not ashamed to be called their God (the promise, in summary, of the testament): for He hath prepared for them a city" (v. 16). In the final analysis, the Abrahamic promise was directed only to Christ (Gal. 3:16), He who constituted in Himself alone the ultimate remnant of the seed of Israel.[9] But Christ "took on Him the seed of Abraham . . . that He might make reconciliation for the sins of the people" (Heb. 2:16, 17); "And if ye are Christ's then are ye Abraham's seed, heirs according to promise" (Gal. 3:29).

Two specialized Hebrew terms appear in Genesis as further descriptions of the faith of the patriarchs. Abraham spoke of the *yir'ā*, the "fear" of God (Gen. 20:11). The connotation of this noun *yir'ā* is not one of terror towards God, for this would not be true of those who trust in Him (I John 4:18), but rather of respect and reverence toward the Heavenly Father. "Fear" is faith, as it submits to His will. The heart of man's response to the testament is therefore to "fear" God (II Kings 17:35, 36, 38, 39). Scripture reiterates, "Fear [from the verbal root *yārē*], show faith in, God, and [as necessarily follows in *yir'ā*] keep His commandments; for this is the whole duty of man" (Eccl. 12:13). Jacob then employed a second, related term when he invoked God as the *páhadh*, the "Fear," of his father Isaac. That is, he conceived of God in terms of the One whom his father revered (Gen. 31:42, 53). Jacob's very citation of Isaac witnesses to the reality and depth of the latter's religion,[10] to the impression that a father's godly fear has upon his son, and to the lasting effect of one's paternal faith.[11] This faith then continued to characterize both Jacob and his son Joseph, down to their very deaths in Egypt. For

---

[8]See above, p. 234. Vos indeed maintains that Abraham continued to remain ignorant of his destination, after his call in Haran as well, claiming that God's designation of Canaan in Gen. 12:7 "came as a surprise to him," *ibid.*, p. 97. Before reaching Haran, however, Abraham and the rest of the party under Terah knew that their destination was to be Canaan (Gen. 11:31).

[9]See above, pp. 187, 264, 265.

[10]A point needed to qualify Vos' criticism of Isaac's, as a passive period in redemption, *op. cit.*, p. 106.

[11]Observations by Professor John Murray in classes at Westminster Theological Seminary, Philadelphia.

their trust in God's word, as it had first been revealed to Abraham, was evidenced by their commands to be buried in the Promised Land of Canaan, even though it had yet to be possessed (47:29; 50:2, 25; cf. Heb. 11:22).

B. MOSAIC REVELATIONS. Sinai, despite its external regulations, was basically a matter of heart-felt faith. The testamental condition was indeed stated in the following legalistic phraseology: "If ye will obey My voice indeed, and keep my testament, then . . . " (Ex. 19:5).

> But why must Israel obey the Ten Commandments? . . . The reason is given in the verse which precedes the Commandments: "I am the Lord thy God which brought thee out of the land of Egypt, out of the house of bondage" (Exodus 20:2). The essence of the faith, therefore, is . . . that Jehovah was and is their Savior, and He has saved them, saves them now in order that they may do His Will . . . being truly thankful to a Husband-God who has never been anything else than faithful from the beginning.[12]

So Moses' ministry was one that throughout its course placed the emphasis upon faith (cf. Heb. 11:24-29). The people believed Moses at the first (Ex. 4:31); and, following their deliverance at the Red Sea, "the people feared Yahweh: and they believed in Yahweh, and his servant Moses" (14:31). God's statement of this free, prior redemption from Egypt served as His introduction to the actual words of the testament (19:4); and the people, in correspondingly appropriate faith, accepted the testament before ever they knew its detailed, external conditions (v. 8). The legalities do indeed follow, but only as an application and as a demonstration of the fundamental requirement of grateful faith.[13] It cannot be emphasized too strongly that Exodus 19 (faith and salvation) precedes Exodus 20 (the fruitage of moral works)!

A fundamental failure of Scofield dispensationalism is its short-sighted inability to appreciate the Sinaitic law as a part of the one gracious testament, which had been revealed immediately after man's fall. This same grace continues and develops progressively throughout the rest of human history and the rest of the Bible. The New Testament makes it clear that the testament (to Abraham), "confirmed beforehand by God, the law, which came [at least the well-known][14] four hundred and thirty years after, doth not disannul, so as to make the promise of none effect" (Gal. 3:17). Yet the notes of the Scofield Reference Bible assert,

---

[12]Snaith, *Mercy and Sacrifice: a Study in the Book of Hosea* (London: S.C.M. Press, 1953), pp. 54-55, 57.

[13]See above, p. 91, and cf. Raven, *op. cit.*, pp. 469-470, and John Murray, *The Covenant of Grace*.

[14]Cf. Payne, *An Outline of Hebrew History*, p. 35, and John Murray, *op. cit.*, p. 22.

"The Dispensation of Promise ended when Israel rashly accepted the law (Ex. 19:8). Grace had prepared a deliverer (Moses), provided a sacrifice for the guilty, and by divine power brought them out of bondage (Ex. 19:4); but at Sinai they exchanged grace for law."[15]

As an initial criticism, however, one must object that since the testament is monergistically devised and imposed by God, such an assertion would suggest that God had in some way tricked Israel into accepting what was not really in their best interests. The context, on the contrary, makes it clear that there was nothing whatsoever "rash" about Israel's claiming heirship under the Sinaitic testament. Theirs was the automatic response of grateful hearts, trusting God and rejoicing in His gracious adoption. Sweepingly to dismiss the whole of the Sinaitic commandments as "a ministry of condemnation and of death,"[16] is grossly to misapprehend the Old Testament. The law was by no means an impossible burden (Deut. 30:11-14). Israel loved the law (Ps. 1:2; 119:167), which it lauds as "sweeter than honey" (19-10). After all, its statutes were their highway, albeit anticipatory, to heaven itself!

The fundamental requirement of the law was faith, belief in God (Deut. 1:32; 9:23). Moses explained: "And now, Israel, what doth Yahweh thy God require of thee, but to fear [have faith in] Yahweh thy God, to walk in all His ways and to love Him, and to serve Yahweh thy God with all thy heart and with all thy soul" (Deut. 10:12) Scofield, however, insists,

"As a dispensation, grace begins with the death and resurrection of Christ. The point of testing is no longer legal obedience as the condition of salvation, but acceptance or rejection of Christ, with good works as a fruit of salvation."[17]

The very existence, however, of Moses in heaven (cf. Matt. 17:3), is proof enough that good works were not "the condition of [his] salvation." Rather, as the verse previously quoted demonstrates, the essential matter both for him and for us is the fear and love of God. Then, that Israel should "walk in all His ways" became the natural expression of their love. Obedience constituted just as much a fruit of salvation for them as it does now for us. Compare the wording of Deuteronomy 6:2: "Fear Yahweh [the basic point], to keep all His statutes [the result]."

Christ declared that the essence of the law is this: "Thou shalt

---

[15]P. 20; contrast Murray's definition of obedience as simply reciprocated faithfulness, *op. cit.*, pp. 18-20.
[16]*Ibid.*, p. 95. For the true significance of II Cor. 3:7-9, see below, topic 25-period 3. Note also in this regard John Murray's excellent distinction of the three New Testament usages of the phrase "under law." *Principles of Conduct*; *pp.* 182-200, 263-65, and especially p. 190.
[17]*Ibid.*, p. 1115.

love Yahweh thy God with all thy heart, and with all thy soul, and with all thy might" (Deut. 6:5, cf. Mark 12:28-30). Thus the opening commandments of the "ten words" lay down the attitudes of mind toward God that the Lord expects of His own; for example, Command III, that men should show reverence for the name of Yahweh (— the very person of God);[18] and only subsequently appear the moral requirements of the Decalogue. In the same vein, Moses repeatedly stressed that the law's primary requirement was that of a circumcision of the heart (Deut. 10:16), of a seeking of God with one's whole being (4:29). It was this wholehearted commitment to God in faith that distinguished the heroes of the wilderness period (Num. 14:24; 32:12). The entire nation of Israel, in fact, found deliverance when those who were perishing looked in faith on the brazen serpent—no works involved! (Num. 21:9; cf. John 3:14).

Appeals, moreover, on the basis of the gracious Abrahamic testament, with its requirements of faith and of a humble and yielded heart, continued to be made by those who were living chronologically under the Sinaitic testament (Ex. 32:12,13; Lev. 26:40-42; Deut. 4:29-31). For the Sinaitic is identical with all other Biblical testaments in its basic features of faith and obedience.[19] Thus the New Testament affirms that the legalism of the Pharisees was actually a perversion of the faith that the law really taught (Matt. 23:23). God's design all along, as these students of the law should have known, was righteousness by faith, not by works (Rom. 9:32).

C. REVELATIONS CENTERING IN DAVID. The time of Israel's consolidation in Canaan was marked by a general departure from faith in God (Judg. 21:25), but the Lord continued to raise up great leaders of faith (cf. Heb. 11:30-32). At the very beginning of the period, for example, Joshua had recognized that Israel might readily be led astray into a reliance upon the gods of Canaan; but he made crystal clear the stand that he personally had taken (and which he expected the nation to take) — "As for me and my house, we will serve Yahweh" (Josh. 24:15).

David's early hardships taught him the basic necessity of faith. When in flight from Saul and having barely escaped with his life from the hands of the Philistines (I Sam. 21:13), he was led to compose such lines as these:

"This poor man cried, and Yahweh heard him,
And saved him out of all his troubles.
Oh taste and see that Yahweh is good:
Blessed is the man that taketh refuge in Him!" (Ps. 34:6, 8).

[18]See above, p. 144.
[19]See above, topic 6-E.

When even his few followers threatened to turn against him, we read
that David "strengthened himself in Yahweh his God" (I Sam. 30:6).
Later on, when betrayed by his own sinful nature, he revealed that
his confidence lay in a broken and a contrite heart, one which was
fully trusting in the mercy of God (51:17). His psalms abound with
sentiments such as "I love Thee" (18:1); "Hope thou in God" (42:5);
"Wait thou upon God" (62:5); "He only is my rock" (62:6); and
compare Asaph's meditation, "Whom have I but Thee?" (73:25).
David stands out as the greatest Biblical representative of personal
faith in God. His famous words in Psalm 37 summarize indeed
man's whole attitude of response under the testament:

"Commit thy way unto Yahweh,
    Trust also in Him, and He will bring it to pass.
Rest in Yahweh, and wait patiently for Him" (vv. 5, 7;
cf. 112:7; 131:2).

In the next period, Solomon's best known proverb (3:5, 6)
teaches this same principle of faith in God rather than of reliance
upon one's own understanding (cf. Prov. 16:3). Solomon emphasized
that the great need of Israel, and of all nations, is humbly to seek
God's face (II Chron. 7:14); and, the positive conclusion of his book
of Ecclesiastes states, as previously noted, that man's chief duty is
the fear of God (12:13). Eliphaz, whose words seem to have been
first revealed to Israel at about this time, indeed misjudged Job personally; but his general approach was a sound one: "Is not thy fear
of God thy confidence?" (4:6); and again, "If thou return to the
Almighty thou shalt be built up" (22:23). That "faith is the victory,"
even against overwhelming odds, was then borne out in experience
by the deeds of the pious among Judah's ninth century kings.
Specifically, Asa advanced against his Cushite foes with the resolute
prayer, "In Thy name we go" (II Chron. 14:11); and Jehoshaphat
experienced his greatest success, following upon his ringing charge,
"Believe in Yahweh your God, so shall ye be established" (20:20).
Equally victorious, though not outwardly so, was Zechariah the
priest, receiving a martyr's crown at the hands of Joash, as he remained faithful unto death (24:20).

D. PROPHETIC REVELATIONS. The prophets reacted against an
undue externalism in their people's religion and stressed the need
for their return to simple but heartfelt faith in Yahweh. Snaith puts
it this way, in respect to the earliest eighth century prophet to Israel:
"Hosea's contribution is that the relation between God and His people
Israel is personal."[20] God loves man; and, in respect to the correspondingly personal response,

---

[20]*Mercy*, p. 39. But when he qualifies this relationship of personal faith by claiming that Hosea is "beyond question the first prophet of a new tradition," he
demonstrates an almost total disbelief in the historicity of Abraham, David, and
others of those mentioned above, as they are described in Scripture.

". . . on man's side it consists of dutiful love and humble
trust . . . To love God with all that a man is and has, is more
than all burnt offerings and sacrifices, more indeed than anything else."[21]

Micah then composed what has been called the greatest verse in the
Bible, second only to John 3:16, as he described the response of
man's faith in terms of fear and humility: "He hath showed thee,
oh man, what is good; and what doth Yahweh require of thee, but
to do justly, and to love *hésedh* [loyalty to the conditions of the tes-
tament], and to walk humbly with thy God?" (6:8). Joel spoke of
"turning to Yahweh" (2:13); and Amos, of "seeking" Him (5:4; cf.
Zeph. 2:3). Hosea is further distinguished by a peculiarly meaningful use of the verb *yādha,* to "know," and its derivatives. He exclaims,
for example, "My people are destroyed for lack of knowledge: because thou hast rejected knowledge, I will also reject thee" (Hos.
4:6). Or again, "Let us know, let us follow on to know Yahweh"
(6:3). In reference to these passages, Snaith comments,

> "We are accustomed to follow the Greek tradition and to
> interpret knowledge as being mainly intellectual. The He-
> brews did not do this . . . Hosea here envisages a growing
> personal knowledge of God."[22]

It is true that Snaith's antithesis between faith and intellect is an unhappy one; and his thought is doubtless conditioned by his neo-orthodox limitation of revelation to an existential, non-propositional
knowledge of God.[23] Hosea himself makes it clear that faith is impossible apart from one's rational assent to propositions (cf. the stress
upon words in Hos. 14:2).[24] This axiomatic truth, the Hebrew Scriptures demonstrate throughout;[25] for faith is by definition a mental
activity. But Hosea, in these verses about "knowledge," is demanding
a consistent rationalism, knowledge that arises from God's special
revelation, that is validated by man's personal encounter with the
God who is trusted, that is truly believed with the mind, and that
produces the appropriate response in a man's life.[26] There is nothing
more vain than knowledge that is falsely professed but not really
believed. So Hosea insists, "It is time to seek Yahweh" (10:12); for
to experience the historical revelation of God, and to trust both Him
and it, is the heart of religion.

---

[21]*Ibid.,* pp. 40, 69.
[22]*Ibid.,* p. 62.
[23]See above, pp. 16, 33, 34.
[24]See Gordon H. Clark's incisive analysis, "Faith and Reason," *Christianity Today,* 1:10, 11 (Feb. 18 & March 4, 1957).
[25]See above, pp. 71, 72.
[26]E. Jacob thus speaks of the three-fold aspect of faith in the Old Testament:
faith as knowledge, as trust, and as active obedience, *Theology of the Old Testament,* p. 174.

With this emphasis upon faith, Isaiah's prophecies particularly abound.[27] His word to the vacillating Ahaz was, "If you will not believe [*āman* in the causative: consider God as steady or trustworthy], surely ye shall not be established [*āman* in the passive, be steadied, be able to last out]" (Isa. 7:9). Compare also the following verses: Isaiah 8:17, "I will wait for Yahweh, that hideth His face from the house of Jacob, and I will look for Him"; 26:3, 4, "Thou wilt keep him in perfect peace, whose mind is stayed [*sāmakh*, supported] on Thee; because he trusteth in thee: trust ye in Yahweh for ever"; 28:16, "Behold I lay in Zion a precious corner-stone [Messiah]: he that believeth shall not be in haste [or, be anxious]"; 30:15, "In returning and rest shall ye be saved; in quietness and in confidence shall be your strength";[28] 50:10, "Who is among you that feareth Yahweh, that obeyeth the voice of His servant? Let him trust in the name of Yahweh, and rely upon his God." The very troubles and uncertainties on the eighth century international scene tended to force Isaiah's contemporaries to a deeper faith in God (26:16). Isaiah's sovereign, Hezekiah, thus became Israel's preeminent king of faith (II Kings 18:5), even as Josiah, in the next century, became her preeminent king of the Book (23:25).

In the later prophetic period, Jeremiah, from his "lone-wolf" existence as a man against the crowd,[29] came clearly to perceive the necessity for individualistic faith in God. He observed, negatively, that man cannot trust in himself (Jer. 10:23) or in other men (17:5). Positively then, man must give glory to Yahweh (13:16), trusting in Him (17:7) and glorying in the fact "that he hath understanding and knoweth Me" (9:23, 24). His own bitter experiences during the reigns of Jehoiakim and Jehoiachin (608-597 B.C.) cast Jeremiah even more unreservedly upon the faithfulness of his God. He could thus be used the more effectively as the mouthpiece of the Lord, joyfully to proclaim, "Ye shall seek Me, and find Me, when ye shall search for Me with all your heart" (29:13). The reason for the rejection of the Samaritans was that during these years they tried to "fear" Yahweh and yet at the same time serve their own idols (II Kings 17:33, 41); and men simply cannot do both!

Perhaps the most famous single Biblical expression of faith came through Jeremiah's contemporary, Habakkuk. This man of God spoke of the pride of Babylon, the empire which was then rising to dominance, but also of that power by which the Babylonians, or any other force, could be overcome: "Behold, his soul is puffed up, it is not upright in him; but the just shall live by his faith" (Hab. 2:4). The meaning of Habakkuk's "faith" is not that of the "stiff upper lip," of

---

[27]Cf. Raven, *op. cit.*, pp. 470-474: "No other Old Testament book contains such a large element of the gospel as Isaiah," p. 459.
[28]And see above, p. 302.
[29]See above, p. 230.

a man holding out, in his own "powerful" faithfulness, until the crisis be past.[30] Rather, as the contrast with Babylonian pride demonstrates, and as the subsequent context illustrates, this faith consists of a commitment to God, of one's faithful trusting in Him to accomplish what is, humanly-speaking, impossible (3:18, 19; cf. Rom. 1:17).

It is necessary, however, to ask in each case of faith that is found in the Old Testament, faith for what?[31] Paul, in the epistle to the Romans, means faith for the Christian's justification from sin, while Habakkuk speaks simply of faith for his people's deliverance from the power of Babylon. Other examples of faith's more limited goals are Joel 2:13, 14, Judah's faith for recovery from a locust plague, and Jonah 3:9, 10, the Assyrians' faith for God's sparing of their city Nineveh (cf. Isa. 7:4). But Isaiah 1:18 preaches faith for the forgiveness of sins, just as does Romans 1:17; and Ezekiel in the exile stresses faith for a man's deliverance from the death that his transgressions would otherwise entail (Ezek. 18:30-32). The latter's contemporary, Daniel, went still further, teaching fidelity to God, even should one's life be forfeited. His three friends thus demonstrated their supreme faith to Nebuchadnezzar, by stating, "If our God whom we serve be able to deliver us from the burning fiery furnace, He will deliver us out of thy hand, oh king. But if not, be it known unto thee, oh king, that we will not serve thy gods, nor worship the golden image which thou hast set up" (Dan. 3:17, 18).[32] Here is a faith that looks beyond life to heaven itself. The point of all these passages, though, is this: Whatever the faith that was described in any given context might have been for, it was a faith in Yahweh; and it is this commitment to Him that constitutes the condition of the testament. Such commitment was indeed expressed and demonstrated in moral and ceremonial obedience (see the following topics); but "behind all demands of morality, and behind all sacrificial custom, there is a personal relationship with God,"[33] namely, that of saving faith. The undated 130th Psalm may serve then as a final exhibition of this indispensable relationship.

---

[30]Though this has become liberalism's standard interpretation of the passage, cf. Lanchester's handbook, *The Books of Nahum, Habakkuk and Zephaniah* (Cambridge: The University Press, 1920), p. 77, which speaks of Paul's "reading into it his own theory of faith."

[31]Cf. Raven, *op. cit.*, p. 465: "It is often difficult to determine whether there is any thought of salvation from sin as it occurs in certain connections, for example, Isa. 12:2, 3 . . . There are, however, a few passages in which the spiritual conception of salvation is certainly present. Such is Isa. 64:5, 6."

[32]This marginal translation in the Revised Version is not only a more natural rendering of the Aramaic than that found in its text — "If it be so, our God is able, and He will" — it also brings out the faith of the three, even if they were not delivered. To adopt the former reading need cast no reflection on the power of Yahweh; for should God refuse to deliver, it would be for good reasons known only to Himself.

[33]Snaith, *op. cit.*, p. 52.

Out of the depths have I cried unto Thee, oh Yahweh.
I wait for Yahweh, my soul doth wait,
    And in His word do I hope.
For with Yahweh there is *hésedh* [faithfulness to the testament],
    And with Him is plenteous redemption.
And He will redeem Israel
    From all his iniquities (vv. 1, 5, 7, 8).

For Further Reading:

Benjamin B. Warfield, *Biblical Doctrines.* New York: Oxford University Press, 1929. Chapter 13 consists of a significant study of the Biblical doctrine of faith.

William D. Kerswill, *The Old Testament Doctrine of Salvation.* Philadelphia: Presbyterian Board of Publication and Sabbath-school Work, 1904. The study tends to give insufficient attention to the fulfillment of salvation in Christ, but it contains much on the Old Testament teaching concerning redemption.

J. Gresham Machen, *What Is Faith?* New York: The Macmillan Co., 1935. A defence against Modernism of the Biblical concept of faith, in its various aspects.

25. Morals*

Genuine conversion eventuates in sanctification. The reality of Israel's personal relationship with God, the sincerity, that is, of their faith, was demonstrated by the actualization of their personal obedience to Him (Ex. 15:25; Deut. 8:2).[1] Faith without works is dead (James 2:17; cf. Deut. 13:3, 4), as truly in the Old Testament as in the New. The Sinaitic testament makes it clear that if, and only if, the Israelites obeyed God's voice would He be their God (Ex. 19:5). Indeed, "in every important affair of life the Israelite has to accomplish something which God demands."[2] On the one hand, God revealed certain demands, the execution of which served as acted symbols of the redemption that He was yet to accomplish. Herein arises "ceremonial obedience" (topics 26-28 that follow). But on the other hand, and without "claiming a difference of dignity,"[3] one seems justified in stating that God's ethical demands, His demands for "moral obedience" (this topic), constituted the more fundamental means for a man's demonstration of the validity of his faith (cf. Acts 10:35). The ceremonies in many cases were, in fact, added to

---

*BIBLE READING: Amos 5; Exodus 20
Collateral Reading: Vos, *Biblical Theology,* pp. 64-66, 102-103, 141-150.
    Oehler, *Theology of the Old Testament,* pp. 182-191, 451-455.

[1]See above, pp. 90, 91, 297.
[2]Oehler, *Theology of the Old Testament,* p. 182.
[3]*Loc. cit.*

provide a means for the man's restoration to God's favor, because of his having previously suffered a *moral* lapse (Lev. 6:1-7).

Two general qualifications must be stated at the outset if the Biblical position on sanctified morality is properly to be appreciated. In the first place, successful ethics cannot exist independently of faith in the redeemer-God. Cornelius' works of righteousness, for example (Acts 10:35), were acceptable to the Lord only because, prior to all his works, he feared God and was committed to the faith of Israel (cf. v. 2). Furthermore, as Gordon Clark so forcibly points out, a positive and effective ethic simply cannot be grounded on a naturalistic world-view.[4] The "Achilles heel" that is precipitating America's present moral dilemma is the impossibility of maintaining a self-disciplined, democratic government "under God" when the individual citizens are no longer characterized by a personal commitment to Him and therefore feel themselves under no compelling obligation to subjugate their selfish interests to the larger good. In the second place, however, genuine faith cannot long exist independent of ethical commitment. We fear God by keeping from sin (Ex. 20:20; cf. Job 1:1; 28:28); and only the man with a pure heart is able to abide with God (Ps. 15:1, 2). Scripture therefore admonishes us, "Trust in Yahweh, *and* do good" (37:3); or again, "Whoso confesseth *and* forsaketh his transgressions shall obtain mercy" (Prov. 28:13; cf. Ezek. 18:30, 31).

PERIOD A, PRIMEVAL. The significance of morals appears from the outset of human history. The pre-redemptive covenant depended on synergistic works (Gen. 2:17); and even the inheritance of the protoredemptive testament, while bequeathed by grace, could yet be attained only with the demonstration of good works. As God explained to Cain, "If thou doest well, shalt thou not be accepted? And if thou doest not well, . . ." (4:7). Indeed, just as in the covenant of works man had been under obligation to be fruitful and subdue the earth (1:28) and to keep the garden (2:15), so in the gracious testament man lived, not simply under the identical obligation of propagation (9:1), but under what was actually an intensified requirement, as he was ordered, literally, to "swarm" on the earth (9:7). The increased strictness of this demand may possibly have been caused by the destruction that was wrought by the Flood; but as Köhler points out, the very fact that God directs mankind about the activities he is to perform constitutes in itself the first, and at the same time a truly great, act of divine grace.[5]

Though God refrained from revealing a detailed ethical system until Period C, Mosaic, still, mankind's awareness of positive moral

[4]"Can Moral Education Be Grounded on Naturalism?" *Bulletin of the Evangelical Theological Society*, 1:4 (Fall, 1958), pp. 21-23.
[5]*Old Testament Theology*, p. 201.

requirements appears from the very beginning,[6] and with particular reference to the essentials of human life. The production of life is described in the phrase, "(the man) yādha, [knew] his wife" (4:1, 17, 25). This "knowing" was not just a matter of cognition, which would mean that man's sexual abilities were directed rather than seasonal, as with the animals. It appears to have involved human volition as well; that is, there seems to have been present an element of moral decision, an understanding of the divine purpose of multiplying and of working in harmony with God's standards. The purity of marriage, that it should not be mixed or polygamous, is then indicated positively by God's blessing on the two, that they should become one flesh (2:24; cf. Matt. 19:5), and, negatively, by the sinful contexts in which Scripture records the indiscriminate and plural marriages that all too soon occurred (6:2; 4:19).[7]

For the sustenance of life, God revealed the standard of work, that man must labor, in farming and in husbandry (3:17-19; 4:2). The moral sanctity of life is stressed too (4:9, 10), even of the life of the offending murderer, Cain (v. 15). It is significant, however, that subsequent to the Flood God found it further necessary to provide this legislation: "Whoso sheddeth man's blood, by man shall his blood be shed" (9:6). The Hebrew verb, yishshāfēkh, "be shed," might be taken either as an indicative description, "It will be shed by man" (cf. Matt. 26:52), or as a jussive requirement, "Let it be shed by man," which indicates capital punishment. The latter is the more probable interpretation. For the thought that is expressed in the preceding verse, namely, "I will require it," indicates that God has decreed a necessary enforcement (cf. Ezek. 33:6; Deut. 18:9). The addition then of the phrase, "at the hand of every man's brother" implies further the judicial responsibility of the brother's fellow man (compare the punishment of beasts which precedes): that he is to function as an "avenger of blood" for his family (cf. Num. 35:19). Also, as Vos points out,[8] the explanation that follows, "For in the image of God made He man," provides the divine reason for the authorization of capital punishment: the seriousness of the sentence is proportionate to the seriousness of the crime.

The means by which human kind was delivered from the Flood provides a practical illustration of the necessity for man's obedience to God: God saved Noah, but Noah still had to build the ark (6:14)! Then shortly thereafter, Scripture points out the seriousness of drunkenness (9:21). The example of Ham goes on to furnish a negative

---

[6]A needed qualification in the light of Vos' characterization of this period as basically negative, *Biblical Theology*, p. 58.

[7]Cf. Vriezen, *An Outline of Old Testament Theology*, p. 207.

[8]*Op cit.*, p. 65. As he further elucidates, the purpose of the "for" clause is not to explain how man's creation in the divine image authorizes him to take life, but how it justifies the extreme form of the penalty.

lesson in morality. Though it may not be apparent at first glance, guilt was involved in Ham's conduct, for a curse did follow (9:25). It is true that the spoken curse fell on Canaan, who seems particularly to have shared in his father's lack of modesty (cf. v. 22); but Ham too was cursed, to the extent of receiving no blessing along with those of his brothers. Ham's "looking upon the nakedness of his father" thus seems to imply more than a mere accidental glance. This phrase may have been an idiom for a certain gloating in immorality (cf. Hab. 2:15). Furthermore, Ham did then proceed to advertise Noah's shame by spreading the word to his brothers (Gen. 9:22), with which must be contrasted the modest and chaste conduct of the latter (v. 23).

PERIOD B, PATRIARCHAL. The moral obedience that God requires under the testament is expressed in this period by Yahweh's general directive to Abraham, "Walk before Me and be thou 'perfect,' tāmīn" (Gen. 17:1). The adjective tāmīn connotes, not sinless perfection, but rather a complete, "whole-hearted" dedication to the following of a sanctified life in the presence of God. Such a life, however, expressly constitutes one of the basic conditions of the testament: "Do righteousness and justice, to the end that Yahweh may bring upon Abraham that which He hath spoken of him" (18:19). In fact, the very purpose of Abraham's election was that his children should maintain this righteousness (ibid., cf. Titus 2:14). But Abraham recognized, at the same time, that morality must arise as a development that springs from faith and that ethical behavior could not be expected where there was no "fear of God" (20:11).[9]

Scripture describes Abraham as the évedh, "servant" (slave), of Yahweh (24:26). As such, Abraham serves as an example of Biblical morals in a number of major respects. He exhibits, for example, magnanimity (13:8, 9), as he allowed his inferior, Lot, to take the first choice at their division of the land of Canaan. He possessed loyalty, as is shown by his subsequent rescue of Lot (14:12-14) and by his intercession for Lot in Sodom (18:22-32), even though both of these acts involved personal risk for himself (v. 25). His loyalty appears further in his activity on behalf of Ishmael (17:18; 21:10, 11). Yet Abraham maintained a sense of justice, which balanced his magnanimity: he would not, as in the case of the reward for his Amorite confederates (14:24), "give the shirt off the back" of someone else! Abraham practiced slavery (17:23), though hardly in a reprehensible way. Slavery seems to have been an economic necessity, so as to maintain the solidarity of the social unit under the semi-nomadic living conditions of the patriarchs. The évedh was not a slave in the modern sense. He was treated with kindness (cf. Lev. 25:43), and all

[9]Cf. Vos' excellent discussion, ibid., pp. 102-10.

the Abrahamic household were enabled to share alike in the redemptive testament of God (Gen. 17:12, 13).

Scripture makes no attempt to gloss over Abraham's serious failures of cowardice, lying, and the possible occasioning of immorality (12:11-13; 20:11-13); but still this patriarch constitutes a preeminent example of testamentary obedience (17:27; 22:3). James 2:21 thus concludes, "Was not Abraham our father justified by works?" though his works were of course understood as the outworkings of his faith (vv. 22, 23). Faith therefore justifies the man, but the works justify the faith! As Christ Himself insisted (Matt. 7:20), "By their fruits ye shall know them."

Jacob's entire, earlier career was one of "grasping at the heel." It is negative as far as patriarchal morals are concerned. His wrestling, however, with the Angel of the testament at Peniel seems to mark the final surrender of Jacob's unyielded life.[10] The patriarchs contracted a number of consanguineous marriages, within the degrees that are later prohibited; but these unions were exceptional for the maintenance of religious purity (28:1, 2; cf. 24:3). Polygamy, on the other hand, was freely practiced; but it is nowhere condoned. Indeed, Genesis singles out this custom as a major cause of trouble wherever it appeared (30:1; cf. 16:5); and so it is throughout the Old Testament. Joseph stands as an example of moral steadfastness. He specifically condemned adultery as a sin against God Himself (39:9; cf. 20:17); and his love for his undeserving brothers, though disciplinary (44:12, 13!), is still outstanding (50:21).

PERIOD C, MOSAIC. The Sinaitic testament was likewise revealed as one of conditional fulfillment. The requirement of moral obedience was explicit in its very enunciation (Ex. 19:5, 6); and, after hearing the legal codes that were associated with it, the Israelites consciously agreed, "All the words which Yahweh hath spoken will we do" (24:3). This feature of conditionalness constitutes, indeed, the chief problem that concerns God's Sinaitic revelation, particularly as it is taken up in the New Testament discussion.

On the one hand, the old covenant of works has never been repealed; and it must be recognized that the Mosaic law does contain statements of the theoretical possibility of a man's justification by his works. For example, God said, "Ye shall therefore keep My statutes which, if a man do, he shall live in them" (Lev. 18:5). Compare His explanation in Galatians 3:10: "The law is not of faith; but, He that doeth them shall live in them" (cf. Rom. 10:5). That one's observance of the moral law constituted the ground for God's blessing was the position of the New Testament Pharisees. They taught, for instance, that alms-giving could substitute for sacrifice (cf. Ecclus. 3:30), and particularly so after the destruction of the Temple in A.D

[10]See below, topic 29-C.

70. Such was the legalism of the Judaisers, whose condemnation is
the subject of Galatians (cf. 3:3; 4:21), as well as of other portions
of Paul's epistles. Finally, today, it is this same position that is
peculiarly characteristic of dispensationalism's interpretation of the
Old Testament; so the Scofield notes bluntly define the status of the
Old Testament saints by saying, "At Sinai they exchanged grace for
law."[11] But the New Testament, as well as the Old, contains statements of the selfsame theoretical possibility of a man's justification
by works (Rom. 2:9-11). In practice, however, no man, and this
includes Moses himself, was ever saved under such a possibility of
works-righteousness, as noted either in the Old Testament or in the
New (Rom. 2:21-3:20). Jesus Christ is the only One "saved" under
the covenant of works (Gal. 4:4). In fact, one of the purposes of the
Mosaic law (though not its only one) was to show men their sin and
thus lead them to Christ (Deut. 32:28, 29; Rom. 7:13; Gal. 3:19,
24, 25). Especially under the prophets (Period G, on), the Old
Testament saints' conviction of moral failure drove them to confession and to a humble reliance upon the grace of the testament (Dan.
9:4, 5; cf. Micah 6:10-13; Jer. 3:4, 5). Thus the law's was, at points,
a ministry of condemnation (II Cor. 3:9). What Paul, therefore, in
certain passages, criticizes as "the law" is really that relatively small
proportion of the law which is concerned with the covenant of
works,[12] but which the Pharisees and the Judaisers had perverted
into representing the whole, thereby producing the "yoke upon the
neck which neither we nor our fathers were able to bear" (Acts
15:10). In a similar fashion, modern dispensationalism tends to force
the law as a whole into this same restricted and negative category.
It generalizes that "The law is not proposed as a means of life . . .
it was but a preparatory discipline . . . it was 'added' to convict
of sin."[13]

But on the other hand, (and more significantly) the law constitutes a major development within God's testament of grace.[14] The
Hebrew word for "law" is tōrā, which means simply "instruction"
(cf. Hos. 8:12); "the law of God" is therefore nothing other than
"the word of God" (Ps. 147:19).[15] It served as the means by which
Israel was enabled to manifest the faith that they had expressed in
Exodus 19:8. Thus Romans 10:5, which condemns the righteousness
which is of the "law" (the Pharisees' interpretation of Moses) is
followed by Romans 10:6: "But the righteousness which is of faith
speaketh on this wise," the verses which it then goes on to quote

[11]Reference Bible, p. 20; cf. p. 1115.
[12]Cf. Vos, op. cit., p. 142, "certain of the statements of the Pentateuch."
[13]Scofield, op. cit., p. 95; cf. the treatment of II Cor. 3:7-9, loc. cit.
[14]Cf. Vos, op. cit., pp. 128-129, 142 on Israel's (necessarily) unmeritorious adoption into sonship and previously accomplished redemption.
[15]Cf. Kohler. Op. cit., p. 207.

being Deuteronomy 30:11-14, taken from this same Mosaic law! The point, indeed of the Deuteronomy passage is that God's word, the law, "is not hidden from thee, neither is it far off"; it was not an unworkable system, but was one that was graciously effective (Deut. 4:6). The law was what gave Israel its distinction and its redemption (Deut. 4:8; Ps. 147:19, 20; Rom. 9:4). It caused rejoicing and illumination, not grief (Ps. 1:2; 19:8); and, as it lodged in the heart, it produced confidence and power (37:21; 119:92, 165). The motive which lay behind the keeping of its regulations was one of gratitude to God for salvation and for prosperity (Deut. 8:6-10).[16] "Oh, to grace how great a debtor, daily I'm constrained to be!" The law, in summary, is God's word, which was proposed as the way in which men are to be saved, both then and now.

Faith must eventuate in moral conduct. Among the ceremonies at Mt. Sinai, when Yahweh revealed His testament, were preparatory washings (Ex. 19:10, 14), which served as a sign of the sanctification of God's people. Similarly, those who were unclean were to be cut off from Israel's fellowship (Deut. 23:1-3). At Sinai, Israel then became God's s'ghullā (Ex. 19:5), His peculiarly elect possession from among all the peoples. But, even as the Levites had to be holy, as they devoted themselves to God's service (Num. 3:6, 7; 8:6-8),[17] so all Israel, as His "peculiar treasure," had to be a holy nation (Ex. 19:6). The term "holy," qōdhesh,[18] means "separated," from the profane (Lev. 20:26), and conformed to God's standards. Holiness was thus a necessary, consequent expression for those who were included in the testamental fellowship (Deut. 6:4-15). As Oehler summarizes it,

> The fundamental principle of the law, tora, "instruction," is expressed in the words, "Be ye holy, for I am holy," Lev. xi. 44 f., xix. 2; or more completely, xx. 7, "Sanctify yourselves and be holy, for I am Jehovah your God."—The impress of consecration to the holy God is to be stamped on the life of the Israelites in ordinances extending to all important relations and conditions.[19]

In Israel, therefore, every activity became sacred. For when a man's aim is that of conformity to the will of God, who executes moral righteousness for all, life cannot be divided between the secular and the sacred. Accordingly, our Lord Himself treated the commandments as one, "Thou shalt love the Lord thy God with all thy heart, and thy neighbor as thyself" (Luke 10:27, 28). The Mosaic legislation thus exhibits a frequent co-mingling of ceremonial and moral laws. Even the Hebrew terms for the different laws of Moses show

---

[16]Though, correspondingly, to keep it meant also that a man would not be punished (Ex. 23:22-27; Lev. 26; Deut. 28).

[17]In substitution for the firstborn of Israel, who had been redeemed to God at the time of the first passover (Num. 3:12, 13).

[18]On developing significance of qōdhesh, see above, topic 9-C.

[19]Op cit., p. 182.

no hard and fast application according to subject matter. The Scofield
Bible indeed suggests three divisions:

> The Commandments [*miswā* (?)], expressing the righteous
> will of God (Ex. 20:1-26); the "judgments" [*mishpāt* (?)],
> governing the social life of Israel (Ex. 21:1-24:11); and the
> "ordinances" [*hōq* (?)], governing the religious life of Israel
> (Ex. 24:12-31:18).[20]

Actually, however, the Hebrew words to which reference is apparently intended show great freedom in usage. They exhibit wide ranges
of meaning and are employed interchangeably. *Miswā* comes from
the verbal root "to command" and includes anything that God prescribes or prohibits. *Mishpāt* has, it is true, a primary reference to
rulings or decisions of the judge, the *shōfēt*;[21] but it came to connote
any claim that is legally justifiable (Deut. 10:18; Isa. 32:7), and
hence all of God's claims or demands (cf. Num. 35:24). *Hōq* is literally that which is "cut in," or "engraved," that is, a prescription,
whether moral (for example, Num. 30:16, concerning the binding
character of promises), or social (Gen. 47:26, concerning tax percent-
ages) or ceremonial (Ex. 12:24, concerning the sprinkling of the
blood at Passover.) All are "testimony," a standard term in the suzerainty-treaties of the ancient world for the stipulations of the testament.[22] The English terminology is even less exact, particularly in
respect to the word "ordinance," which translates all three of these
Hebrew terms, plus others. Finally, an examination, even of the passages listed in the above quotation, confirms Oehler's contention that
"Here there is no primary distinction between the inner and the outer
life; the holy calling of the people must be realized in both."[23] Such
holiness, arises not from "natural" purity of life but can proceed only
from a man's consciousness of divine election and regeneration. Leviticus 19:18 expresses this religious basis for holy living as follows,
"Thou shalt love thy neighbor as thyself: *I am Yahweh* [He who is
present, directing us]." The all-compelling motivation which determines both our "religious" and our ethical conduct must be one of
response to the grace of God, a motivation, not of reward, but of
gratitude. The prophets, at a later point in Israel's history, found it
necessary to draw the valid distinction which does exist between
morals and ceremonial; but for Moses, holy living had no distinguishable compartments.

Furthermore, since the Lord's moral nature does not change, the

---

[20]Scofield, *op. cit.*, p. 95: cf. p. 1244.
[21]See above, p. 155.
[22]Meredith B. Kline, "The Two Tables of the Covenant," *The Westminster Theological Journal*, 22 (1960), pp. 136-137. Cf. Köhler, *op. cit.*, pp. 203-209, who
notes also the term (*ēdhūth*, "testimony," originally a "witness, or reminder," and
hence any law that reminds of, or testifies to, the claims of God (Neh. 9:34).
[23]Oehler, *op. cit.*, p. 182.

ethical standards that God revealed through Moses to Israel remain as equally binding upon His Church today. What was right then is no less right now. Jesus indeed revealed the ultimate standard in holy living, not simply by His teachings but above all by His blessed exemplary incarnate life (I John 2:6; cf. III John 11, Revised Version). At the same time, however, Christ came not to destroy the law. Far from repealing the regulations of the Old Testament, our Lord actually "tightened them up" (Matt. 5:17) by driving home their inner significance (cf. vv. 21-26 on killing and 27-30 on adultery). Most regrettable is the tendency of dispensationalism to treat the moral law of Moses as a temporary measure that has become inapplicable to the Christian Church. The Scofield Bible, for example, insists:

> "The law was but a preparatory discipline . . . the Christian is not under the conditional Mosaic Covenant of works, *the law*, but under the unconditional New Covenant of grace."[24]

In respect to salvation it is patently true that the Christian is free from having to "earn" his redemption by the works of the law (Rom. 7:4-6); but then so was Moses, for that matter! Christ did this once, for all (Gal. 4:4). On the other hand, those who are not "in Christ" nor through faith written in the Lamb's Book of Life (Ex. 32:32; Rev. 20:12) both have been, but also will be, subject to judgment according to the original (Edenic) covenant of works (Rev. 20:15). In respect to ethical standards, however, believers (of both dispensations) and unbelievers together are expected to govern themselves by the same moral will of God. Nor may verses such as Colossians 2:14 be invoked as proof of dispensational antinomianism. For though this latter passage truly describes how "the bond written in ordinances" has been taken out of the way by Christ and nailed to the cross, still the preceding verse makes it clear that it is our guilt that is "taken away" (forgiven); the idea is by no means that God has repealed His standards of morality. The whole point of Romans 6 is that the Christian must not "continue in sin, that grace may abound." Israel's love for God was reflected in their obeying the commandments (Ex. 19:8); "and this is love," writes the apostle John, "that *we* should walk after His commandments" (II John 6). The Ten Commandments are quoted individually in the New Testament as still normative and binding upon us as Christians (Rom. 13:9; cf. 3:31), even Commandment IV, in its transmuted form (I Cor. 16:1, 2).[25] Now if ever, in this age of deadened moral sensitivity, the

---

[24]*Op. cit.*, pp. 93, 95; cf. his denial of the law as a means for the sanctification of the believer, p. 1245. He then concludes, "The believer is both dead to the law and redeemed from it, so that he is not under the law."
[25]See below, sec. 28-A.

evangelical Christian must honor the Biblical laws, especially the "ten words," and "teach them diligently unto his children" (Deut. 6:7).

Some of the particularistic applications of the Mosaic codes are confessedly limited to the communal and nomadic life of the 15th century B.C. For example, the law of the Levirate marriage (Deut. 25:5-10)[26] seems to have been required in those days to preserve patriarchal households as distinct, economic units; and the inheritance law, which gave a double portion to the first born (21:17), to assist the one to whom Hebrew society had committed the care of a household's dependents. These laws, however, are but instances of the general subject (which is taken up in Biblical hermeneutics) of the normativeness of particularistic injunctions. The relevance of the principles that underlie each such case is clear. Thus when our Lord was asked to sum up man's supreme obligation (Matt. 22:35-40), He selected as His ultimate formulation of human responsibility two quotations taken directly from the law of Moses: Deuteronomy 6:5 (on faith), "Thou shalt love the Lord thy God with all thy heart," and Leviticus 19:18 (on morals), "Thou shalt love thy neighbor as thyself."

The Sinaitic testament served to accomplish divine election on a national scope. The very size, however, of the inheriting group demanded that there be a detailed revelation of the moral requirements that were involved in the testament.[27] Here then for the first time God granted a specific corpus of ethical legislation. These more or less systematic lists of moral laws, together with certain intermingled ceremonial requirements, occupy about half of the Pentateuch; and they constitute for all dispensations the major revelation of God's moral will. Scripture organizes these laws into what may be called four major codes: the Decalogue (Ex. 20:2-17), the book of the testament (Ex. 20:22-chapter 23), the priestly codes (consisting primarily of Leviticus — except for the narrative sections in chapters 8-10 and 24:10-23[28] — Num. 5-6; 9:1-14; 10:1-10; 15; and 18-19), and the Deuteronomic codes (primarily Deut. 1-30, to which may be added Num. 28-30).

Of these codes, the Decalogue, the "ten words" (Ex. 34:28; Deut. 4:13; 10:4), is the most significant. Its subject matter was spoken aloud by God on Mt. Sinai at the time of the giving of the testament, 1446 B.C. The purpose of His audible voice was that all the people might hear (Ex. 20:18, 22; Deut. 5:22). The ten words were then repeated by Moses forty years later on the Plains of Moab (Deut.

---

[26]See below, p. 331.
[27]See above, p. 100.
[28]And even these two narratives are introduced primarily as background to legal material.

5:7-21). This latter statement consisted of a free quotation, with certain special applications that were suited to the situation (cf. v. 15). The Decalogue was also written by the finger of God on both sides of two tablets of stone (Ex. 31:18; 32:15, 16; 34:28).[29] This code was designed to be the fundamental moral law of God's people. Obedience to its standards served to demonstrate (not replace) their faith in God's testament. It is therefore called, in itself, "the words of the testament" (Ex. 34:28; cf. this same type of designation for various suzerainty testaments of the ancient world);[30] "His testament, even the ten commandments" (Deut. 4:13); and "the tables of the testament which Yahweh made with you" (9:9; cf. vv. 11, 15). Correspondingly, the sacred chest that contained the two tablets is described as "the ark, wherein is the testament of Yahweh" (II Chron. 6:11).

The book of the testament (so named in Ex. 24:7) was spoken by Yahweh to Moses on Mt. Sinai (Ex. 20:22); but it was written down, not by God, but by Moses, immediately after its revelation (24:7). Parts were subsequently repeated at the time of Moses' last trip up Sinai (34:17-26), and these too were written down by the hand of Moses (v. 27). The purpose of the book of the testament was to provide Israel with concrete applications of the principles of the Decalogue, in sufficient detail that God's moral requirements could be thoroughly appreciated and then accepted by the people. The book is therefore characterized by the following five main features. 1) It is explanatory, a feature that is seen, for example, by the way in which Exodus 21:12-17 illustrates the principles of Commandments V, VI, and VII of the Decalogue. 2) It is preliminary. Thus Exodus 20:24, 25 prescribes unhewn stones for the altar, in a way that is adapted to the nomadic state of Israel at this time, 1446 B.C.[31] 3) It is representative, rather than complete. For example, two particular types of stealing are singled out in Exodus 22:5 and 14; the problem of loss of life, when caused by animals, in 21:29; and the penalty for slave-kidnaping, in 21:16. 4) It is revelatory of God's basic ceremonial requirements, such as the prohibition of leavened bread, in connection with blood sacrifice, 23:18.[32] Finally, 5) it is indicative of God's standards of basic social (not personal) justice, the most quoted verse of the entire book of the testament being its law of

[29]Shortly thereafter, the original tables were broken (Ex. 32:19), and two more were made by Moses. But the writing on these latter was still done by God (34:1), to whom the "He" in v. 28b must refer.
[30]Kline, op. cit., p. 134.
[31]Ex. 23:10, however, on vineyards and oliveyards, appears to have been granted in anticipation of Israel's settlement in Canaan.
[32]The attempts, however, of liberalism to discover the "original" (ritualistic) Decalogue, particularly in chap. 23, constitute sorry examples of subjectivism in Biblical criticism.

equivalent punishment: "An eye for an eye, and a tooth for a tooth" (21:23-25).[33]

The appearance of this same *lex talionis* in the codes of Hammurabi, king of Babylon (1728-1686 B.C.)[34] as well as the existence of certain other similarities, have led some interpreters to question the divine origin of Moses' laws. It is true, moreover, that the book of the testament was revealed over two centuries after the time of Hammurabi. But on the one hand, God in His grace could, and did, grant to His people legal patterns with which they were already familiar. The only restriction would have to be, of course, that such laws as were concerned be just and good; and these were. On the other hand then, there are important points at which Moses' book of the testament and his other legal codes disagree with Hammurabi and with the other extant codes of the ancient Near East. These points of difference, moreover, constitute a strong witness to the unique inspiration of Scripture. Thus the Pentateuchal codes are divinely related; that is, they were spoken by God throughout, while Hammurabi's code exists in no such form.[35] Moses' laws, moreover, possess one standard of justice for all; while Hammurabi's present a series of class distinctions. Moses' insist strongly on sexual purity, with divorce, for example, permitted only for lewdness (Deut. 24:1); but in Hammurabi's, temple prostitutes constituted a recognized social class and divorce had become a matter of routine. Finally, Moses' laws exhibit a unique regard for natural resources (even in war, Deut. 20:19), a unique social sympathy (as for the poor, Ex. 23:11), and a unique quality of love, that reaches even to the enemy (vv. 4, 5) and expresses to him gratitude where it is due, even for events long past (Deut. 23:7). For this last point, a significant illustration is provided by Moses' own spirit of selfless concern for the very men who opposed him (Num. 14:2, 17).

God revealed the priestly codes to Moses in 1445 B.C. at Sinai,[36] immediately after the construction of the Tabernacle. The purpose of these was to provide professional guidance for the priests and a detailed liturgy for the new house of God. The Deuteronomic codes,[37]

---

[33]Actually, very few of the Mosaic Laws (as Deut. 25:12) involve real bodily penalties, particularly as these are compared with other ancient codes. Man, even his body, has value before God. Castration, for example, was opposed (Deut. 23:2), and Moses required the offender to be cut off from the people, though faith in the testament, and especially its sabbath, were later revealed as able to overcome this (Isa. 56:4, 5).

[34]Law 200. For an analysis of this, and of other parallels with the Mosaic laws, see George A. Barton, *Archaeology and the Bible* (7th ed.; Philadelphia: American Sunday School Union, c. 1937), pp. 378-406.

[35]Except for an initial reference to its supposed receipt from Shamash, the sun god.

[36]With the exception of Num. 15, 18, 19, which were revealed at miscellaneous points during the wilderness wanderings.

[37]Including Num. 28-30, on the calendar of worship, and on vows.

on the other hand, were revealed on the Plains of Moab almost forty years later, just before Israel entered Canaan, early in 1406 B.C. These "second laws" consisted primarily of two speeches by Moses (Deut. 1-4 and 5-26), with concluding blessings and curses, as God's injunctions should be kept or not (27-30). The purpose of the Deuteronomic codes was to guide the nation as a whole in its settlement in Canaan. They were popular instead of professional, as were the priestly codes. It is therefore the historical situation that explains the simple and hortatory approach of Deuteronomy, rather than an evolutionary theory which insists that "P" the (priestly codes) could only have arisen in exilic and post-exilic times, and at least a century after "D" (the deuteronomist). Deuteronomy's messages were designed to touch men's hearts and to stimulate them to a love and obedience of God, rather than to trace out the detailed prescriptions that applied to Israel's worship in the Tabernacle. Indeed, all of the Mosaic moral codes serve only to reflect, to apply, and to develop the fundamental principles that are contained in the second table of the Decalogue. It is on the basis, then, of these latter "words" that Moses' specific moral teachings may be surveyed.

Calvin's masterful "Exposition of the Moral Law" lays down two initial standards for one's approach to the Decalogue. He points out that —

> [1.] The law inculcates conformity of life, not only to external probity, but also to internal and spiritual righteousness. [That is, though only Commandments I and X teach directly about the heart-attitudes that are necessary toward, respectively, God and man, still there are eternal principles that lie behind the outward regulations contained in each of the others] . . . [2.] The commands and prohibitions always imply more than the words express.[38]

That is, even though the Decalogue (with the exception of Commandments IV and V) is phrased in negatives, there still exist throughout its prohibitions corresponding positive truths. Furthermore, the "words" serve as examples. In most instances only the most serious infraction is listed, but from each of these a whole class of related wrongs may then be apprehended.

While Scripture makes it clear that the commandments are ten in number (Ex. 34:28), no little question has arisen historically as to the exact organization of the Decalogue and as to the precise inclusiveness of the second (moral) table. At the outset, it must be noted that the text of the tables does include the introductory statement (Ex. 20:2; cf. Deut. 5:6, 22, in precisely the "I-thou" form of contemporary Hittite suzerainty-treaties).[39] This verse, however, is not contextually parallel with God's list of commands; and it is hardly

---

[38]*Institutes of the Christian Religion,* I:333, 335.
[39]Kline, *op. cit.,* p. 134.

to be included within the numbered ten words. Its exclusion then opposes the tradition of modern Judaism, which counts this introductory verse as commandment I, and then combines I (Ex. 20:3) and II, (vv. 4-6) as II. But the former of these combined verses (v. 3) combats polytheism while the latter (vv. 4-6) combats idolatry. The two are distinct matters, either of which may be practiced without reference to the other. This fact therefore renders equally improbable the approach of Romanism and Lutheranism, which connects Commands I and II, as I, and then splits X (v. 17) into two separately numbered commands on coveting, which it identifies as IX and X.[40] Such a division does then produce three commandments (the Trinity!) on duties to God and seven (perfection!) on duties to man. In context, however, the forced nature of this scheme is obvious. Others would make an equal division among the commandments, five and five. But this procedure requires Commandment V (v. 12, on honoring parents) to be classed with the duties of piety that precede rather than with those of social obligation that follow. Calvin's division of the Decalogue of four (duties to God) and six (duties to man) deserves the preference, both from the nature of the material and because of the New Testament analogy (Mark 10:19); for in this last verse Christ Himself apparently combined the latter six into one grouping.[41] Even so, there exists considerably more writing on the first table than on the second.[42] The duties to God are discussed elsewhere in this study: Commandments I and II in topic 9; III in topic 11; and IV in topic 28.[43] The moral duties to our fellow men, commandments V to X, are discussed on the following pages.

Commandment V reads, "Honor thy father and thy mother: that thy days may be long upon the land which Yahweh thy God giveth thee" (Ex. 20:12). These divinely revealed words establish the family as the primary social unit of mankind (Lev. 19:3; Prov. 23:22; Eph. 6:2, 3). It is an observable fact that where men "rise up before the hoary head, and honor the face of the old man," all society is given preservation and dignity. But more basically, the blessings come about because such obedience reflects the fear of our God (Lev. 19:32). The supreme importance of the family further is shown by the death penalty that Scripture invokes for striking or cursing one's parents (Ex. 21:15, 17) or for filial rebelliousness (Deut. 21:20, 21). This penalty gains in significance when it is realized that in the inspired codes of Israel, capital punishment was much more sparingly

[40]See Oehler, *op. cit.*, pp. 185-188, on the numbering of the commandments.
[41]Matt. 19:19 and Luke 18:20, however, list only V-IX, and Rom. 13:9, VI-X.
[42]See Oehler, *op. cit.*, pp. 188-191, for further information on the division of the tables. On the basis of the Hittite suzerainty testaments, which often specify duplicate copies, Kline has even made the proposal that both tablets contained complete texts of the Decalogue, one for Israel and the other (in theory) for God, the suzerain-testator, *op. cit.*, p. 139.
[43]And see "Index of Subjects," under "Decalogue."

employed than in the legal systems of the surrounding cultures. Even
in this case, however, the commitment of such judgments into the
hands of the government authority (Deut. 21:20, 21) represented a
restriction upon the formerly unchecked power of the individual patriarch (cf. Gen. 38:24). Children are one of God's greatest blessings
(cf. Ps. 127:3). Israel's sons were specifically preserved during the
death plague in Egypt by a divinely-revealed method of redemption
(Ex. 13:12; Num. 18:16). In this way, moreover, the fact that children are owed to God was made quite clear. But by the same commandment (Ex. 13:15), the sons of Israel were prohibited from
being sacrificed to the nation's deity, this rite which constituted one
of the most revolting practices of the pagan Canaanites. On the contrary, the greatest obligation of parents is to bring up their children
in the nurture and the admonition of the Lord (Ex. 12:26-28; 13:8;
Deut. 6:7; cf. Gen. 18:19).

Commandment VI, "Thou shalt not kill" (Ex. 20:13), concerns
the sanctity of life. It thus epitomizes the moral law, the general purpose of which is to preserve human society. The Hebrew verb that
is employed in this prohibition is *rāsah*, which concerns the concept
of "murder"; the authorized taking of human life is not the point at
issue. Furthermore, God Himself is not bound by the commandment:
He takes life as He sees fit. Indeed, it is as God delegates this responsibility to men that capital punishment, for example, for murder
(Ex. 21:12; Num. 35:31; cf. Gen. 9:9), receives its authorization. A
particularly illustrative figure is that of the "avenger of blood" (Num.
35:19), the responsible clansman of a man who has been killed and
whose divinely revealed duty is to slay the murderer on sight. Not
even a refuge sought by the horns of the altar could protect the
guilty in such cases (Ex. 21:14; cf. I Kings 2:28, 34). At the same
time, however, God indicated the distinction that exists between premeditated murder and unintentional manslaughter (Ex. 21:13). The
essence of crime lies, therefore, not in the external act, but in the
motivation; and the criminal must be judged accordingly. For the case
of manslaughter, God provided the "cities of refuge" (Num. 35:11,
12). These served as a needed check against the avenger of blood
(v. 24); but recourse could be had to a city of refuge only in true
cases of killing "unawares" (v. 15), "without intent to harm" (v. 23).

Life is precious. Even a burglar's life is protected in the course
of his apprehension (Ex. 22:3); and the interesting regulation of Deuteronomy 22:8, "When thou buildest a new house, thou shalt make a
battlement for thy roof, that thou bring not blood upon thine house,
if any man fall from thence," constitutes a standing requirement for
the provision of all necessary safety devices. On suicide, see below,
p. 452. Yet even as God's moral will and the good of society demanded the execution of the individual murderer (Num. 35:33), so

these same goals may require police action on a nation-wide scale, that is, the declaration of war against an ungodly, national enemy.

On a similar basis, God required any city that was found guilty of apostasy to be totally destroyed, including even its cattle (Deut. 13:15, 16). Such groups had to be cut out of the body politic, even as one would a cancer. The Hebrew word for this annihilation was *hĕrem*, "devotion" (the ban); and it particularly concerned the Canaanites. They were not simply to be driven out (Ex. 23:31, 33) and their idolatries destroyed (34:13); they were to be completely consumed (Deut. 7:2; 20:16, 17). They had been cursed (Gen. 9:25) and were dangerous idolaters (15:16; Lev. 18:27; Deut. 12:31). Just as in the case of Calvin's permission for the execution of the unitarian Cervetus, so Scripture describes it as better for some to burn on earth immediately, than to be allowed to live, with the result that many of their fellows will burn in hell eternally. Thus Jericho suffered the *hĕrem* (Josh. 6:17, 21), as did the household of Achan for violating its *hĕrem* (7:25); and the same fate was threatened against Israel, should they turn aside from God (Deut. 8:19, 20; Josh. 23:15).

Commandment VII, which reads, "Thou shalt not commit adultery" (Ex. 20:14), maintains the principle of sexual purity. Israel, in contrast with the morally lax peoples who surrounded her, possessed the highest standards in respect to sex. Adultery was punishable by death (Lev. 20:10; Deut. 22:21). Fornication (illicit sexual relations, but not in violation of the marriage vow) was equally wrong, though it did not entail the death penalty (Lev. 19:20). Brides were expected to be virgins (Deut. 22:14), and a man who forced a virgin by rape was required to marry her (v. 29; Ex. 22:16). The very desire for another man's wife was wrong; see Commandment X. Later, because of the hardness of the people's hearts (cf. Matt. 19:8), God legislated through Moses to relax the death penalty and to permit legalized divorce (Deut. 24:1). Divorce, however, became possible only on the grounds of *erwā*, serious reproach, or lewdness (cf. Matt. 5:32);[44] and at various points divorce is expressly prohibited (Deut. 22:19, 29). Even in such cases of unfaithfulness, divorce was not required. It could, moreover, only be accomplished with the proper written, legal procedure (Deut. 24:1), which served both as a safeguard against precipitous action and as a document of proof for all concerned. Numbers 5:11-31 provided for an ordeal by means of a curse for cases of suspected adultery; and the action seems to have been designed to protect a wife against an unduly suspicious husband. Since immodesty serves as a stepping-stone to sin (cf. II Sam. 11:2), the Old Testament emphasizes the necessity of proper bodily covering (Ex. 20:26); and this standard was con-

---

[44]With the exception of women taken as captives in war; these were instead granted their freedom (Deut. 21:14).

scientiously upheld (cf. II Sam. 10:4, 5). Prostitution was prohibited (Lev. 19:29). A priest was forbidden to marry a harlot (21:7); and if his daughter became one, she was to be burned (v. 9). Particularly banned were the Canaanitish sacred prostitutes, called the q'dhēshā, and homosexuals, the qādhēsh, a "dog" (Deut. 23:18). This sin of homosexuality had been especially prevalent among the Canaanites of Sodom (Gen. 19:5), hence the term "sodomy." Moreover, it soon infected the invading Israelites; cf. the crime of Gibeah (Judg. 19:22). Its practice was condemned (Lev. 18:22); and apprehension for it carried the death penalty (20:13), as did also beastiality (Ex. 22:19). To avoid even the suspicion of sodomy, men and women were forbidden to wear each others' clothes (Deut. 22:5). None of the above serves as pleasant reading, but that it is relevant to "Christian" America is all too plain.

The positive side of the seventh commandment concerns marriage. Marriage in the Old Testament often occurred because of a betrothal that was arranged by the groom's father (Ex. 21:9; cf. Gen. 24:2), though this was not always the case (cf. Gen. 26:34). In any event, the responsible Israelitish party was forbidden to contract marriage with a Canaanite (Ex. 34:16): mixed marriages were, and are, an open invitation to apostasy (cf. II Chron. 6:14). Only Rahab's faith (cf. Heb. 11:31; Matt. 1:5) succeeded in making her an exception. Approval was also granted in the case of captive women, after they had been granted a gracious time of delay for readjustment (Deut. 21:13). Polygamy is never sanctioned. On the contrary, its overall prohibition appears in John Murray's accurate rendering of Leviticus 18:18, "Thou shalt not take a wife to another, to vex her, to uncover her nakedness, besides her in her lifetime."[45] Polygamy is specifically prohibited to kings (Deut. 17:17), and its evils are uniformly opposed (Ex. 21:10, 11; Deut. 21:15-17). Leviticus 18:6-17 establishes the prohibited degrees of consanguineous marriages. The only exception allowed is that of the levirate marriage (Deut. 25:5-10). The term "levirate" comes from the Latin word levir, which means "brother-in-law." In this type of union, a man's widow was married by his surviving brother (cf. Gen. 38:8; Ruth 4:5, 6, 10; Matt. 22:24). The firstborn son would then carry on the name of the deceased party (Deut. 25:6). At the most, the levirate marriage was never compulsory; and its explanation appears from the fact that the brothers had to have been dwelling together (v. 5). In other words, there was not simply the humanitarian purpose of caring for the widow, there existed also the economic necessity of maintaining the unity and the normal functioning of a mutually dependent household group.

---

[45]*Principles of Conduct*, pp. 252; cf. his cogent arguments in support of this translation, pp. 253-256.

Commandment VIII, "Thou shalt not steal" (Ex. 20:15), provides the Scriptural basis for the doctrine of property rights. It establishes the principle of private ownership, for it condemns as criminal the attempt to take from a man that which is his own. Ultimately, of course, all property belongs to God. As the Lord stated, "The land is Mine; for ye are strangers and sojourners with Me" (Lev. 25:23). That is, men never hold the final title to worldly property; they are temporary stewards, as God in each case designates. Yet once God has delegated such possession, men are not to alter what He has granted. Such human usurpation would reflect against the very sovereign freedom of God the Testator. Yahweh, accordingly, assigned the various portions of Canaan to the families of Israel on a basis of permanent tenure: "The land shall not be sold for ever" (Lev. 25:23). If a man in the pinch of circumstances felt required to give up some of his property, his relatives were divinely empowered to redeem it back at any time (v. 25); and, in any event, it reverted to him automatically every fiftieth year, at the period of jubilee (v. 10).[46] It is this God-given right to the possession of property which explains Naboth's refusal to surrender his ancestral inheritance, even at the demand of the king (I Kings 21:3); and his divinely established title to the property was recognized in Israel, by even an Ahab (v. 4). But such an appreciation of values came about only as a result of Israel's previous recognition of God's right to ordain the moral standards of His redeemed people, and thus to maintain the principle of private ownership along with the other moral conditions of His testament. Such moral awareness existed, moreover, as a unique matter in the ancient world; contrast the "normal" (depraved) attitude of the Phoenician queen Jezebel toward Naboth's property rights (v. 7). The reason for the inalienability of Israel's land appears to have been typical; its possession by the individual and family owners served an acted prophecy of the blessings of the Messianic age (Isa. 61:1-3). It can hardly be made expressive of the socialistic economic theory that men are entitled to the ownership of goods on the basis of their need (in this case, ownership of the land which produced their living), irrespective of prior, individualistic property rights.

For Yahweh gives further voice to His testamentary sovereignty by consistently limiting the Scriptural acquisition of property to one of two means. 1) Property may be acquired on a basis of reward. As Moses expressed this concretely, "Thou shalt not muzzle the ox when he treadeth out the corn" (Deut. 25:4). Here is taught reward, even for animals; though the more basic teaching lies in the application of this principle to mankind (I Cor. 9:9-11). 2) Property may be acquired on a basis of assignment by those already possessing it, for

[46]See below, p. 401.

example, through an inheritance (Deut. 21:16).[47] Israel's judges were
thus specifically warned not to let economic need influence their decisions (19:15; cf. Ex. 30:15). It is not that God is unconcerned about
the poor, see below, Commandment X; but "Thou shalt not steal"
includes stealing, even by society as a whole! All forms of fraud are
condemned, together with the withholding of wages that are due
(Lev. 19:13), or with the exaction of usury (25:36). Honor is demanded in the administration of trust funds (6:2). God's economic
standards then are summarized in these words: "Ye shall do no unrighteousness in weight or in measure. Just balances, just weights,
shall ye have." The reason that God demands such economic justice
is not primarily because of expediency, or even for the general social
good. Honesty is the rather required because of the moral character
of God, which regenerated mankind accepts as the standard for its
own conduct. This acceptance, in turn, arises out of a man's gratitude
for his testamental redemption; for, as the verse just quoted concludes,
"I am Yahweh your God, which brought you out of the land of
Egypt" (19:35, 36).

An aspect of particular interest within the general subject of
property holding is that of slavery. God had redeemed His people
from bondage in Egypt (Lev. 25:42); and none of His own were
again to be reduced to the status of an *évedh,* or slave (v. 39; cf. Phi-
lemon 16). Poverty could, even at its worst, reduce an Israelite into a
status no less than that of a hired servant, a wage earner, and then
only until the year of jubilee (v. 40). God's chosen child was not to
be oppressed (vv. 43, 46). A unique arrangement appears in the case
of the Hebrew who bound himself to service on a stipulated basis.
His service, however, was limited to a term of six years. On the
seventh, he went free (Ex. 21:2; unless he voluntarily chose otherwise, v. 5). The entire situation exhibits a remarkable similarity to
that of the "indentured servant" in early American history. Heathen
Gentiles could, on the contrary, become slaves (Lev. 25:44). It must
be observed, however, that in practice, such instances seem to have
been relatively few; and, as previously noted, the status of bound
servants was not that of slavery as it would be considered today.[48]
Their masters did not have the right of life or death over them (Ex.
21:20), and they were given their freedom if abused (vv. 26, 27).
The prohibition against returning runaway slaves (Deut. 23:15, 16)
demonstrates the extent to which freedom served as the true Old Testament ideal. The existence of slavery as a system seems to have
come about to insure the economic preservation of the patriarchal
household unit. The slaves' participation in the true religion, and the
enlightened recognition by their masters of human equality before

---

[47]Though this verse also checks unfair discrimination in such assignments.
[48]Cf. Murray's careful analysis of Biblical slavery, *op. cit.,* pp. 94-103.

God (cf. Job 31:13-15), contributed to their fair treatment. Some gained high position and privilege (cf. Gen. 24:2) and could join their master's family by marriage (I Chron. 2:35). Finally, it should be observed that for culprits who could not pay their stipulated fines, slavery took the place of imprisonment (Ex. 22:3).

Commandment IX reads, "Thou shalt not bear false witness against thy neighbor" (Ex. 20:16). The serious responsibility that rested upon a witness to present the truth is shown by the way in which the Mosaic law singles out the witnesses who have been involved in a capital case as the first to act in the execution of the death penalty (Deut. 17:7). Human weakness and depravity in the matter of witnessing were to some extent checked by God's requirement for a plurality of witnesses before a conviction could be brought in (v. 6). The same end was also served by the principle of laying upon the witnesses the punishment for the crime to which they had witnessed, should they prove to have testified falsely (19:19). Judges also were admonished against being swayed by the crowd (Ex. 23:2) by a regard for a defendant's poverty (v. 3), or by bribes (v. 8). Commandment IX then naturally moves out beyond the sphere of witnessing in court to that of truth in general. Any falsehood in speech came, in fact, to be treated as on a par with falsehood in action (Lev. 19:11). Malicious gossip, for example, was strictly to be avoided (v. 16; Ps. 19:14).

Commandment X, "Thou shalt not covet" (Ex. 20:17), turns finally from matters of external conduct to the basic, inner feelings of the human heart. The believer must tolerate no desire that works to the detriment of his neighbor and his neighbor's household; whether of his wife, his children, his servants, or his property. "Thou shalt not avenge, nor bear any grudge against the children of thy people; but," Moses goes on positively to add, "thou shalt love thy neighbor as thyself" (Lev. 19:18). Thus appears the climax to the revealed moral will of God. Israel's divine Legislator enjoined a humanitarianism that went beyond the letter of the law and taught, for example, the return of pledged articles when such might be needed by poor, distraught debtors (Ex. 22:26; Deut. 24:12, 13). Indeed, the law forbade inconsiderate pledging altogether (vv. 6, 10, 11) and extended special consideration to the physically handicapped (Lev. 19:14). The law even expressed concern that "thou shalt not plow with an ox and an ass together" (Deut. 22:10), an action which would have placed an undue burden upon the smaller of the two beasts (cf. a similar regard of animals in vv. 6, 7 and Lev. 22:28).[49] In particular, the law extended its protective care to the weakest members of society, to the widow, the orphan, and the gēr, the foreign

---

[49] A symbolical illustration of holiness (separation) is probably also involved; see below, topic 26-D(5), pp. 370, 376.

resident (Ex. 22:21, 22, and so throughout Deut.). One of the purposes of the sabbatical year was that these underprivileged classes
might receive the produce of that particular season (Ex. 23:11). The
Israelite was to love the gēr as himself (Lev. 19:34), and all were
treated alike before the law (24:22).

The ideal of Israel was that of no poverty whatsoever (Deut.
15:4). The leaving of the corners of a reaped field and of the gleanings of harvest, while perhaps originating as an old Canaanitish superstition that involved pagan spirits, was yet applied in Israel to the
relief of the poor (Lev. 19:9, 10; Deut. 24:19-21). Debts were can-
celled at the end of every seven years (Deut. 15:1); and loans, furthermore, were not to be withheld in anticipation of the immediately
impending seventh season (v. 9)! The basis, moreover, of this Biblical
humanitarianism lay in Israel's gratitude for their own divine deliverance from Egypt (v. 15). Every Israelite, accordingly, was bound
for life to be an évedh, a devoted slave, of Yahweh (Lev. 25:55),
even as was Moses (Num. 12:7; Josh. 1:2). Love for the neighbor
thus reflected one's love for God. The people indeed wore fringes,
tassels of blue ribbon, so as to be sure not to forget Yahweh's laws
(Num. 15:38-40; Deut. 22:12); but all of them, like Caleb, should
rightfully have possessed that inner spirit to "follow Him fully"
(Num. 14:24), in sincere love toward God and hence toward each
other.

PERIOD D, CONSOLIDATION. The Mosaic standard of practical devotion to the will of Yahweh was illustrated historically in the personal careers of the judges. Especially was this true in this case of
the Nazarite Samuel, who literally owed his life in service to Yahweh
(I Sam. 1:28). The people as a whole, however, were marked by a
general assimilation of Canaanitish thought-forms, which had a thoroughly adverse effect upon public morals. Saul's later career constitutes a negative commentary on the truth that "to obey is better
than sacrifice" (I Sam. 15:22). But the two incidents which compose
the appendix to the book of Judges (chapters 17-21), and which
occurred at the very beginning of the period,[50] serve as perhaps the
clearest demonstrations of just how rapidly human morality can become corrupted. The first of these incidents, that of Micah and the
Danites, is marked by the violation of practically every commandment
on the two tables of Moses. Even if we restrict our observations to
the transgressions of the second table, the following violations at once
appear: Micah dishonored his mother (Judg. 17:2); the Danites
threatened murder (18:25); Micah both stole and was stolen from
(17:2; 18:24); Moses' great-grandson Jonathan was false to his contract and to his benefactor (17:10, 11; 18:20); and the Danites seem
to have been so covetous of Micah's idols as to have needed no more

---

[50]Cf. Payne, *An Outline of Hebrew History*, p. 81.

specific incitement for their expropriation of them than the simple suggestion (18:14), "Now therefore consider what ye have to do" (cf. v. 23). Nothing, indeed, appears about Commandment VII, adultery. But the second incident, on the Benjaminite outrage, commences with infidelity, prostitution, and the grossest sexual perversion (19: 2, 22, 24, 25); and it terminates with the abduction of two different groups of virgins (21:12, 23). Even men who were personally righteous, such as Eli, fell into condemnation for failing to restrain the immoralities of their children (I Sam. 3:13).

PERIOD E, DAVIDIC. David likewise was notoriously incapable of controlling his own family, as witnessed, for example, by his deserved censure at the hands of Joab for his weakness regarding Absalom (II Sam. 19:5, 6). Yet the unchecked conduct that was manifested by David's children seems to have been but a reflection of the monarch's own immorality. Significant in this regard is Amnon's decision to rape his sister Tamar, on the basis of his cousin's subtle suggestion, "Why, *oh son of the king*, art thou thus from day to day?" (13:3; cf. 12:10, 11). David's double crime of adultery and murder (11:4, 15) is difficult to comprehend. The king's failure seems to have been conditioned by his perversion of royal power to selfish ends, by his indifference over a prolonged absence from his troops (11:1) at a time of serious fighting (10:12), and by his unrestrained practice of polygamy. Plurality of royal marriages had been sharply prohibited by the law and seems particularly to have dulled his moral sensitivity (Deut. 17:17). David's unnecessary bloodshed (cf. II Sam. 8:2), furthermore, had already prevented his building of the Temple (I Chron. 22:8). Yet positively this same David taught that God showed His *hésedh*, His faithfulness to the testament, to those who kept its conditions (Ps. 25:10, 14; 103:18). He stressed the absolute necessity for indivdual uprightness, without which no man can dwell with God (5:4, 6). As the king summarized it:

> Depart from evil, and do good;
>   Seek peace, and pursue it.
> The eyes of Yahweh are toward the righteous,
>   And His ears are open unto their cry.
> The face of Yahweh is against them that do evil,
>   To cut off the remembrance of them from the earth
>
>   (34:14-16; cf. Ps. 1).

David, in fact, made a not infrequent profession of his own righteousness (7:8; 18:20, etc.). Kirkpatrick has explained:

> Readers of the Psalms are sometimes startled by assertions of integrity which appear to indicate a spirit of self-righteousness and self-satisfaction approximating to that of the Pharisee (Luke xviii. 9). . . . Some of these utterances are no more than asseverations that the speaker is innocent of particular crimes laid to his charge by his enemies (vii. 3ff.); others are general professions of purity of purpose and single-hearted devotion to God (xviii.

1ff.). . . . They breathe the spirit of simple faith and childlike trust, which throws itself unreservedly on God. Those who make them do not profess to be absolutely sinless, but they do claim to belong to the class of the righteous who may expect God's favor, and they do disclaim all fellowship with the wicked, from whom they expect to be distinguished in the course of His Providence.[51]

The contemporary Korahites asserted their loyalty to the testamental conditions in words of a similar nature (44:17). On the morality of the imprecatory Psalms, see above, pages 201-203.

PERIOD F, DISRUPTION. The man Job, whose record seems first to have been revealed to Israel in this period, is described in its opening verse as *tām*, a Hebrew adjective which means "complete, sound, wholesome, having integrity"[52] (1:1). Job himself consistently claimed to be characterized by such righteousness (6:29; 10:7; 12:4; 16:17; 23:11, 12; 31:5, 6), in his past life as well as in the present (29:12-17). He moreover concluded his defence by insisting, "My righteousness I hold fast, and will not let it go!" (27:6). He appealed to his own conscience (27:6; cf. I John 3:21); he was willing to appear before God and take whatever consequences might result (13:3, 13) — a thing which his three friends could not do (v. 9) — and his affirmation of righteousness was confirmed by the normative declaration of Elihu (33:8, 9;[53] cf. Eliphaz's earlier admission, 4:6).

---

[51]*The Book of Psalms*, I:lxxxvii.

[52]Brown, Driver, and Briggs, *A Hebrew and English Lexicon of the Old Testament*, p. 10, 71.

[53]The normativeness, that is, the inspired truthfulness and reliability of the words found in Job, varies according to the speakers. Satan and Job's wife may be generally discounted. God said of Job that he spoke "without knowledge" (38:2), and yet also "the thing that is right for me" (42:7). Job was correct in his describing of world conditions (evil, etc.) and in his analysis of his friends. He claimed also a true knowledge of God (27:11), which he seems to have possessed (cf. 42:7), except that he miscalculated and failed in his diagnosis of God's relation to his calamities (9:22-24). He put two and two together wrongly, forgetting the possibility of other factors (he was unaware of Satan's part). For God does not do wickedness (34:10). Elihu therefore put his finger on the truth, and yet the untruth, of Job's words: "Job hath said, 'I am righteous [which was correct], and God hath taken away my right' [which was not]" (34:5). That is, Job's words appear totally normative, except as they impugn God.

The three friends had not spoken what was right "of God" (42:7, 8) because, by their imputation of various crimes to Job (22:6-9; 32:3), they had limited God (13:7). In their very attempt to show partiality toward Him and to vindicate their interpretation of theodicy (v. 8) they limited the Lord to a position of immediate retribution (though cf. 20:5; 22:18). Still, some of the finest passages of the book of Job lie imbedded in the speeches of these men, especially of Eliphaz 5:8, 17-27; 22:12-15, 21-30), but even of Zophar (11:7). Their concept of God's justice and of His reaction to sin did not represent the whole picture. But retribution *is* fundamentally correct; see above, p. 200. From the very extended presence of their speeches in Scripture, it seems fair to conclude that their words are totally normative, except as they impugn Job and seek to explain his woes.

Elihu alone is not condemned, but he analyzes and condemns all the other speakers (35:4). He directly claimed inspiration (32:8, 18; 36:4); and his claim is validated by his correct appraisal of Job's situation as one of corrective suffer-

Yet Job's state was far from being one of sinless perfection. Job admitted his sins (7:20, 21; 9:2, 15; 10:6; 14:16, 17), even from his youth (13:26); and he confessed that he could not be held innocent (9:28). But such sins as Job had committed were limited sins: "And be it indeed that I have erred, mine error remaineth with myself" (19:4). Above all, they did not consist of the gross immoralities of which his "friends" had accused him (cf. 22:6-9). Job was undeniably in the wrong, temporarily, in his attitude toward his calamities (9:23; 27:2; 32:2); for he strove against the Lord and even condemned God's having given his life in the first place (3:20). Nevertheless. Job began right (1:21), he stayed (at points) right (23:10), and he ended right (28:23-28; 42:6). Job serves thus, in general, as the supreme Biblical example of the moral qualities of patience and endurance (James 5:11).

The greatest block of Biblical material on moral living, second only to the Pentateuchal codes, is that which is revealed in the Proverbs of Solomon. Though the proverbs are not presented in Scripture in an organized fashion, they may yet be synthesized so as to bring out their main contributions to personal, economic, and social ethics.

In respect first to personal ethics, the true basis for all effective morality is shown to lie in a man's devotion to God (Prov. 1:7). That is to say, a binding commitment to ethical conduct can be expected to follow directly upon a man's decision to place his faith in the Lord, but not otherwise. Fundamentally, then, faith demands of the believer that he recognize his proper place, that of submissiveness to God. "The fear of Yahweh is the instruction of wisdom; and before honor goeth humility" (15:33). Next, this recognizing of one's place produces two primary reactions. 1) Often it means effort (6:6-11), rigorous as some of these admonitions may sound: "Go to the ant, thou sluggard; consider her ways and be wise!" (v. 6; cf. 10:4, 5; 24:30-34; 26:13-15; II Thess. 3:10). Effort involves "getting dirty"; but, as Solomon subtly pointed out, "Where no oxen are, the crib is clean; but much increase is by the strength of the ox!" (14:4). 2) Such a recognition of place also means reliance, a resting upon God rather than upon self-sufficient pride (16:5). This "reliance" may then be manifested by humility (11:2; 16:18), by contentment (14:30), by deliberation (29:20, 22), or by one's resignation of vengeance to Yahweh (20:22; cf. 24:29). Solomon's explicit norms of personal effort or of reliance, as these are presented in Proverbs, may then, like those

ing (33:16, 19), by his appeal to Christ (33:23, 24), and by his introduction to, and explanation of, the coming of God in the storm (37:14, 15, 21, 22). Elihu corresponds to the best thought in Job the man (28:23-28), and is to be received as totally normative. The same is of course to be concluded for the speeches of God and for the words of the inspired writer of the book of Job.

of the Pentateuch, be organized around the subjects of the second table of the Decalogue.

In elaboration upon Commandment VI, on the sanctity of life, Proverbs stresses the need for a basic respect for a man's life and for the judgment to which he is entitled: "To punish the righteous is not good, nor to smite the noble for their uprightness" (17:26; cf. 18:5; 21:15; 28:21; 29:7). The use of force, however, is revealed to be justifiable for maintaining the right against those who would usurp it (20:30). Justice too must be done to one's own life: we must guard against self-overevaluation (16:2, 25)!

As with James 3:17, which states that "The wisdom that is from above is first pure," and with Commandment VII, so Proverbs insists on moral purity. In a position exactly opposite to that of personified wisdom stands the impure woman (7:4, 5). Prostitution (5:8 f.) and sexual promiscuity (6:25, 26) are condemned both in themselves, and because they lead to other sins (23:28; 29:3). Another aspect of purity is that of temperance. The proverbs in general censure over-indulgence (e.g., gluttony, 23:20; 28:7); but in particular, "Wine is a mocker, strong drink is raging: and whosoever is deceived thereby is not wise" (20:1). Total prohibition, because of particular attendant circumstances (23:27, 28; cf. v. 33), is taught in Proverbs 23:29-35. It must be noted, however, that in the simple, unmechanized society of the Old Testament, such situations were not ordinarily the case (cf. Judg. 9:13;; Ps. 104:15).[54] The valid use of alcohol as a narcotic is upheld by Proverbs 31:6, 7, though the immediately preceding context (vv. 4, 5) prohibits its use by those in authority or in other situations that demand the full use of one's facilities (cf. Lev. 10:9). In reference to the purity of amusements, Proverbs advocates the glad heart (Prov. 15:13, 15, 30), as well as the seeking of physical comforts (27:9), though not to excess (25:16, 27).

With Commandment VIII, Proverbs opposes theft (29:24). The seeming approval of thievery in 6:30 is only as a lesser evil in comparison with adultery (v. 29; and cf. v. 31). Dishonesty and fraud have no place in the Christian's life (11:1; 21:6), and bribery is outlawed (15:27; 17:23).[55]

Proverbs underlines the need for truth, which is the subject of Commandment IX. "Lying lips are an abomination to Yahweh; but they that deal truly are His delight" (12:22). Along with outright lying, hypocrisy is seen as equally abominable (26:23, 24). The unbridled tongue can bring disaster, both to others (11:9) and to oneself (12:13). The impartation, however, of needed truth becomes as important as life-giving food (10:21, 31, 32); and for a man to reprove the

---

[54]Cf. the balanced approach of Roland H. Bainton, "Total Abstinence and Biblical Principles," *Christianity Today*, 2:20 (July 7, 1958), pp. 3-6.
[55]Prov. 17:8; 21:14, appear simply as descriptive, not approving.

wicked merits the greatest of blessings (24:24, 25). But at other points, the virtue of the open eye is directly associated with that of the shut mouth (10:19; 11:12; 14:33; 18:2). Such restraint applies particularly to the guarding of secrets (11:13). Thought must be given to one's answers (15:28); but, above all else, they must be controlled by the principle kindness (15:26). Before a man speaks, he should always ask himself, "Is it true?" "Is it edifying?" and then, "Is it kind?" Correspondingly, a man must be willing to receive the truth (10:8, 17; 12:1, 15), while at the same time exercising critical judgment toward what he hears (14:15).

The inner desire of the born-again individual for the welfare of his neighbor, Commandment X, is given numerous practical applications in Proverbs. For example, in the ordinary matter of keeping up with one's correspondence, Solomon observed that "As cold waters to a thirsty soul, so is good news from a far country" (25:25). Compare his similar stress upon generosity (11:24; 19:6) and on peace-making (12:20). The highest of all the virtues is that of love; hence, "Better is a dinner of herbs, where love is, than a stalled ox and hatred therewith" (15:17). Love will overcome all opposition (10:12). Love is due in particular to the widow and the orphan (23:10), whom God Himself loves (15:25). God's people are concerned with the poor (14:21, 31; 17:5; 19:17; 22:9, 16, 22); for social rank merits no distinction in the eyes of the Lord (22:2; cf. Mal. 2:10). Love reaches out finally to the enemy (25:21), and not simply in external matters but in one's heart attitude toward him (24:17). The saints are kind, even to dumb animals (12:10).

In respect to the area of economics, Proverbs develops the implications of Exodus 20:15, "Thou shalt not steal"; and it thus comes to furnish one of the major Biblical justifications for the capitalistic system of free enterprise.[56] The private ownership of property (wealth) is encouraged throughout the book of Proverbs. As Solomon explains it, "The precious substance of men is to the diligent" (Prov. 12:27; cf. 13:8; 14:20; 21:20). As early therefore, as in Exodus 22: 7, 8 the right of a man's possession of property had been guaranteed, even though someone else might have been actually using the goods that were involved. Property is valuable. It gains friends (19:4) and power (22:7). It pacifies (21:14), it provides protection (10:15), and it outweighs social position (12:9). In this present-day, unregenerate society of this world evangelicalism (being as it is a minority movement) can only expect to suffer loss from systems of economic collectivism. If it were not, in fact, for the private possession of wealth and for the right of the God-fearing individual to dispose of it as he pleases, most Bible-believing institutions and organizations

---

[56]See particularly in this regard Carl McIntire, *The Rise of the Tyrant* (Collingswood, N. J.: Christian Beacon Press), chapter 4.

would long since have ceased to function. Ephesians 4:28 thus states
that one of the purposes of a man's possessions is "that he may have
whereof to give to him that hath need." At the same time, Proverbs
does not deify the dollar. Wealth at the price of righteousness is
worthless (15:16; 16:8), and the possession of a moderate amount
of property is viewed as the ideal (30:8, 9).

The acquisition of property by the private individual receives the
positive approval of Proverbs (3:9; 31:31). So also does the "profit
motive" (13:4; 14:23); for, "In all labor there is profit." As to the
means of acquisition, wealth is appreciated as coming basically from
God (10:22; 22:4, and especially 3:9-10; cf. Job 1:21). Humanly speaking, wealth is to be gained by wisdom (24:3; cf. 3:16), by one's application to corrections received (13:18), and by developing insight
(14:15), but preeminently by industrious labor: "The soul of the
sluggard desireth, and hath nothing; but the soul of the diligent shall
be made fat" (13:4; cf. 10:4; 14:23). So Psalm 104:23 takes it as
accepted that, "Man goeth forth unto his work and to his labor until
the evening" (cf. Eccl. 2:24, "man in his labor"). Our nation today
needs a revival of its pride in honest labor and of the innate satisfaction that arises from a job well done. Industriousness brings wealth
(10:4) and power (12:24). The need for honest labor becomes particularly clear in the pursuit of agriculture (12:11 (=28:19), 10:5)
and in the tending of flocks (27:23-27). The acquisition of property
by inheritance is specifically noted (19:14). But there must be no
illegal acquisition, such as by deceit (21:6; 20:17), by false weights
(20:10), by shifted landmarkers (22:28), or by oppression (23:10-
11) and usury (28:8). Such unjustly gained wealth will not last
(13:11; 28:22), and those who seek it will suffer punishment (v. 20).
Borrowing is dangerous and is discouraged (22:7).

The highest possible use of property is indicated in Proverbs 3:9,
"Honor Yahweh with thy substance, and with the first-fruits of all
thine increase." Concrete ways of using property for God then include one's support of public worship through the recognized offerings, e.g., the "first-fruits" (cf. 7:14) and one's dedication to the
general propagation of the faith (11:30). An even greater stress in
Proverbs, however, falls on such God-honoring matters as benevolence,
especially toward the poor (3:27, 28 [cf. James 2:16]; 14:21, 31; cf.
21:3). But at the same time, man is subject to the God-imposed
responsibility of making provision for his own posterity (19:14), as
well as for himself (30:24, 25; cf. I Tim. 5:8). Wealth, however, must
not be over-valued. Peace and piety are both of them preferable to
material treasures (17:1; 15:16); and, though property is better than
social position (12:9), still, "a good name is rather to be chosen than
great riches" (22:1). Possessions are not to become the final object
of a man's trust (11:28); for they will all, sooner or latter, pass away

(v. 4). But on the other hand, wealth must not be squandered (29:
3); and suretyship is to be avoided (22:26, and especially 6:1-5).
No believer, finally, is to engage in enterprises of a questionable
nature (22:16).

God desires not only high personal ethics and a responsible
economy, but also righteousness in human society (Ps. 133:1, 2). On
the social scene, Proverbs develops the implications of Commandment
V, not simply in respect to the family, but also in the broader areas
of community and state relations.

In reference to the family group, Proverbs emphasizes a happy
marriage as one of God's greatest blessings (18:22; 19:14). A man
should, in the first place (before getting married!) be able to provide
for his family (24:27). Above all, he should love his wife (5:15-19;
cf. Eph. 5:25). This latter passage is then immediately followed in
Proverbs by warnings against adultery (Prov. 5:20). The wife too
should remember that marriage is a covenant before God (2:17) and
maintain faithfulness. Her career rests in her home, where she should
become a crown to her husband (12:4; cf. I Tim. 2:15); and one of
the most beautiful passages in all Scripture is the praise of the virtuous woman of the house (31:10-31). Her potential failure, however,
lies in the same area (14:1; 30:21, 23). Nagging and strife are subjects of particular warning: "The contentions of a wife are a continual
dropping" (19:13); and, "It is better to dwell in the corner of the
housetop, than with a contentious woman in a wide house" (21:9;
cf. 9:13; 21:19; 27:15).

Children are the glory of a family (17:6) and are basic in a
home's happiness (10:1; 15:20). The primary responsibility of God-
fearing parents is to communicate their faith to their children (14:26).
The stress of Proverbs upon discipline is well known (22:15; 23:13).
Children must be kept from running wild (29:15). But at the same
time, the familiar verse, "Train up a child in the way he should go.
. . ." (22:6) reads more accurately, "Train up a child according to
his way, and even when he is old he will not depart from it." That
is, our teaching should be adapted to the capacity of the child. Scripture indeed departs from "modern education" in that it refuses to
recognize self-expression as the ultimate goal for a child; for growth
without conversion will serve simply to express innate depravity.
Rather, every thought must be brought into captivity to Christ (II
Cor. 10:5). But this goal of conformity can most effectively be accomplished by using progressive methods, graded to each child's
needs "according to his way," and seeking through his own motivation to bring about yieldedness to Christ. Children too possess responsibility before God (20:11). They must show respect for their parents
(19:26; 20:20); and the lament of Proverbs 30:11 sounds almost predictive of the twentieth century: "There is a generation that bless

MORALS

not their mother"! Children must ever be obedient (6:20), even in later life (23:22). Particularly is the child responsible to give heed to his parents' instruction (1:8; 4:1).

Reaching beyond the actual blood-relations, Proverbs speaks of the household servants who tend to become a part of the family. Their natural duty was thus one of faithful service to the group (17:2); but many, apparently, failed to attain this purpose (29:19). The corresponding duty of the master lay in treating his servants well, but he is cautioned not to over-indulge them (29:21).

Friendship is of great value (17:17), for as Proverbs reiterates, "There is a friend that sticketh closer than a brother" (18:24; cf. 27:10). The reproof of a friend is to be prized (27:6). But a man should not seek too many friends (18:24), for such may prove insincere (19:4). In social life one must exercise restraint, "Let thy foot be seldom in thy neighbor's house, lest he be weary of thee, and hate thee" (25:17). The believer must exercise care in his choice of companionship, avoiding fools (13:20), angry men (26:21), and talebearers (26:20).

On the national level, an abundant, prosperous, and holy people is revealed as the goal of the God-directed state (14:28): "Righteousness exalteth a nation, but sin is a reproach to any people" (v. 34; cf. 28:2). Heavy responsibility, accordingly, rests upon the person of the ruler, for disaster results if he be incapable or unworthy (19:10; cf. 30:22). The ruler must keep himself from such evils as lying (17:7) and oppression (28:16). He must be efficient in his administration (25:2), maintaining justice (16:10, 12; 29:14) and exacting such penalties as are due (20:26; though cf. 17:26). He must also, however, exercise kindness in his dealings (20:28). The citizen, on his part, must show reverence to the state (24:21); compare the words of Romans 13:1, "the powers that be are ordained of God." Diplomacy is thus not to be foregone (16:14; 20:2; 25:15). Reverence, however, does not equal blind submission. The Christian has the obligation to support reform insofar as he may be able: "Take away the wicked from before the king, and his throne shall be established in righteousness" (25:5).

The critics of Scripture have tended to minimize Proverbs as being mere "worldly wisdom"; and Proverbs *is* practical (thank God!), but the book is also divine. It declares its purpose as this: "That thy trust may be in Yahweh" (22:19), and that mankind should realize a wisdom that expresses itself in morals (1:3). The source of such wisdom is God (2:6); and, though some of the "wisdom" of Proverbs might seem restricted in its scope or even trivial, its basic content is forthrightly religious (2:5). Furthermore, "The fear of Yahweh is to hate evil: pride, arrogancy, and the evil way" (8:13); and God has been good enough in this portion of Scripture to grant specifications, concrete rules of conduct that are binding upon His people today. The doctrine of the two "ways" (which may perhaps have arisen from Moses' words in Deut. 30:15) dominates much of the thought of Proverbs. For example: "The way of the sluggard is as a hedge of thorns; but the path of the upright is made a highway" (15:19; cf. 2:13; 4:18; etc.). The comparison, then, of these two ways brings out the truth that the righteous man is rewarded (13:13). But this fact does not thereby reduce the ethics of Proverbs to that of mere self-interest, e.g., avoiding adultery because of what the jealous husband may do as a result (6:34, 35). Submission to God comes first; and then, without any sense of incongruity, Proverbs can go on to speak of "the reward of humility" (22:4). For ethical conduct must be judged, fundamentally, before God (cf. this same matter of adultery, 5:21, 22), who owes no man anything, but who subsequently, as the *gracious* testator, distributes to each man his "reward."

Solomon's violation of the law that forbade royal polygamy (Deut. 17:17) led him, in time, into serious failure in respect to God's whole testamental revelation (I Kings 11:11). Despite, however, his personal deviation, Solomon seems to have been able to recognize and to honor God's standards in respect to love and marriage, as these were observed by others. The result would appear to be his composition of the Song of Solomon. The historical setting of the Song concerns the king's wooing of a Shulamite maiden (S. of Sol. 6:13), who is probably to be identified with Abishag the Shunammite (I Kings 1:3). This beautiful country girl from northern Israel was brought to the royal court, originally, to cheer David in his old age. In this capacity, she is described as maintaining her chastity, under conditions that were hardly the most favorable (I Kings 1:3, 4). How she left the court of Jerusalem is not recorded in I Kings (though cf. 2:17). The Song, however, if understood as a three-act, semi-dramatic pastoral, with a heroine who refuses the royal harem so as to return to her shepherd lover in Shunem, not simply explains the literal event but also carries a high moral message which accords with its divine revelation.[57] Foremost is the Lord's own approval on human love: "For love is strong as death . . . a very flame of *Yah*. Many waters cannot quench love, neither can floods drown it" (S. of Sol. 8:6, 7). Also to be noted are Abishag's standards of purity and chastity (4:12; 8:9) and the tacit condemnation of Solomon's notorious polygamy (cf. 8:12). The repeated refrain of the book is, "I charge you, oh daughters of Jerusalem, that ye stir not up, nor awake love, until it please" (2:7; 3:5; etc.).[58]

---

[57]The allegorical interpretation which applies the Song to Christ and the Church, while widely held, seems to have no Biblical support.
[58]See Appendix D, p. 523, for plot of the book outlined as a three-act drama.

Shortly before 930 B.C., at the close of his life and the disruption of his kingdom, Solomon composed Ecclesiastes (12:1; cf. 7:10; 4:1). The primary purpose of this writing was to demonstrate the futility of a life that is lived apart from God (1:2). Positively, however, Ecclesiastes contains a number of significant moral revelations parallel to those that appear in the other books of Biblical wisdom literature. In general, men are urged to rejoice and do good so long as they live (3:12). The attainment of true wisdom is commended (2:13; 7:11), as superior to power (7:19; 9:14-18) or riches (4:13). Wisdom will deliver from death (7:12, 14), and it brings good to those who seek it (10:10). A man should be willing to take advice (4:13; 7:5), and a good reputation is to be desired (7:1). Among the many negative points that Ecclesiastes teaches us to avoid are: hypocritical goodness (7:16), or a prying attitude, for it cautions its readers, "Take not heed unto all words that are spoken, lest thou hear thy servant curse thee" (v. 21). Especially serious are acts of sexual immorality (v. 26), of oppression, and of dishonesty (v. 7). Among the points of character, the value of which receive confirmation from its pages, are the following: obedience, to the king (8:2-4); graciousness, in speech (10:12); charity (11:2); sociability (4:9-12); industriousness (10:18; 9:10; cf. John 9:4); efficiency, for, "If the serpent bite before it is charmed, then is there no advantage in the charmer" (10:11; cf. 11:1, 4, 6; 2:10); and love, toward one's wife (9:9). A particular emphasis of Ecclesiastes is that of the believer's need for rejoicing in this confessedly evil world: "He should eat and drink, and make his soul enjoy good in his labor. This also I saw, that it is from the hand of God" (2:24; cf. 5:18; 7:14; 8:15; 9:7; 11:9). Related subjects that are discussed in Ecclesiastes include the use of wine (9:7; 10:19) but also the need for sobriety (11:8; 7:2-4), and the qualities of patience (7:8, 9) and contentment (4:5, 6; 5:12; 7:10); cf. 6:9, "Better is the sight of the eyes than the wandering of the desire." God's people must guard themselves against any surrender to sin (7:17; 12:1), for someday Yahweh will judge the conduct of men (11:9; 12:13, 14).

Out of the histories of the ninth century kings comes the parable of the escaped prisoner: "And as thy servant was busy here and there, he was gone!" (I Kings 20:40), a dramatic incident which brings home the moral requirement of putting first things first. Jehoshaphat's appointment of judges emphasized Judah's need for judicial integrity (II Chron. 19:7), "For ye judge not for man, but for Yahweh" (v. 6). But this incident also marked the appearance of the first official distinction between the application of the moral and the ceremonial law. Deuteronomy 17:9, 12 had indeed suggested that for the deciding of legal cases, Israel should employ both Levitical priests *and* judges; but here for the first time God's word specified

346

THE THEOLOGY OF THE OLDER TESTAMENT

a prince to advise "in all the king's matters," and a priest "in all matters of Yahweh" (v. 11).

PERIOD G, EIGHTH CENTURY PROPHETIC. The prophets from Hosea to Micah (including Isaiah) were forced to contend with a general public disregard for social morality. The people were quite happy to observe, in fact overly so, the Mosaic ceremonial requirements (Amos 4:4, 5); but when it came to the basic matters of justice, mercy, and the humble walk with God (Micah 6:8), that proved to be another matter.

> Hence it is but a result of that tuition of the law which advances from the outer to the inner that prophecy should carry out the distinction between the ceremonial and the moral law, and emphatically declare that the performance of the external ordinances of the law, and especially the offering of sacrifice, were as merely outward acts, worthless; that the will of God aimed at the sanctification of the heart and the surrender of the will to God; and that the observance of the ceremonial law had no value except as the expression of a godly disposition.[59]

(Hosea 6:6; Amos 5:21-24). The prophets thus developed the essential distinction between the intrinsic significance of the moral law of Moses and the representative, symbolical value of his ceremonial prescriptions. The former laws thus remain perpetually binding upon the Church, while the latter have suffered transmutation, or actual abrogation, with the historical effectuation of salvation in Christ.

The prophets in general, including these eighth century prophets, made little original contribution to the content of Biblical ethics, for the primary goal of their moral preaching was to re-emphasize the various norms of conduct that had already been revealed through Moses and Solomon (cf. Isa. 8:20).[60] They demanded, for example, mercy for the oppressed (Isa. 1:17; in accordance with Deut. 14:29) and consideration, even for enemy prisoners (II Chron. 28:9-11, in accordance with Prov. 25:21). Among the more striking of their specific applications of God's ethical standards are the following examples. Jonah emphasized the value of human life by recording how, on his voyage of flight, even the pagan sailors hesitated to cast the guilty prophet (himself!) overboard, but rather prayed, "Oh Yahweh, we beseech Thee, let us not perish for this man's life" (1:14). Isaiah demonstrated his concern for the welfare of his fellows by demanding both a positive performance of acts of charity, "dealing one's bread to the hungry" (Isa. 58:7) and also a negative withdrawal from activities of oppression: the righteous man is "he that shaketh his hands from taking a bribe, that stoppeth his ears from hearing of blood" (33:15). Micah recognized, however, the basic lack of moral sensitivity that characterized the Israel of his day; and he therefore

[59]Oehler, op. cit., pp. 451-452.
[60]See above, pp. 49, 50.

cautioned his audience against patterns of conduct that placed undue confidence upon the rectitude of their fellows: "Trust ye not in a neighbor; put ye not confidence in a friend" (Mic. 7:5). But Jonah found that even the Assyrians could be influenced to turn from evil and from violence (Jonah 3:8).

The prophets thus accomplished much of their ethical teaching by illustrating, in their condemnations, the positive standards that should have been upheld but were actually being violated.[61] They condemned, for example, their people's refusal to return pledged garments (Amos 2:8), which Moses had enjoined (Ex. 22:26), and the drunkenness of their leaders (Isa. 5:11), against which Solomon had voiced his warning (Prov. 23:31). Thus in the personal realm, they spoke out against such sins as gluttony (Amos 6:4, 6) or sexual immorality (Hosea 4:14). In the area of economics, they censured such contemporary forms of corruption as commercial dishonesty (Hosea 12:7; Micah 6:10, 11) and greed for landed property until they "joined house to house" (Isa. 5:8; Micah 2:2). On the national scene, they denounced Israel's rebelliousness against its ruling dynasties (Hosea 8:4), the widespread practice of cruelty in warfare (Amos 1:3), the slave trade that so often followed in the wake of battle (Amos 1:6, 9; Joel 3:6), or simply the callousness of those nations that "stood on the other side, in the day that strangers carried away his [Israel's] substance" (Obad. 11). True morality would, however, be accomplished, in the Messianic kingdom (Isa. 11:3-5).

PERIOD H, LATER PROPHETIC. Morality reached a new low under Manasseh, when houses of "sacred" prostitution appeared within the very temple area (II Kings 23:7). International pledges came to be openly disregarded by the last of Judah's kings (24:1), even though this form of perfidiousness had been a major matter of condemnation by the prophets of the preceding century (Hos. 10:4; Isa. 30:15). But finally sin brought its own reward as the Babylonians moved against Jerusalem to destroy it (II Kings 24:2). At one point during the siege, the wealthy, in fear, released their Hebrew servants according to the Mosaic law (Jer. 34:9, 10), only to re-enslave them when the siege was temporarily lifted (v. 11)! Destruction had become inevitable (v. 17).

The prophets of this period — Nahum, Zephaniah, Jeremiah, and Habakkuk — despite popular disregard and opposition, continued to proclaim God's moral requirements by their reinterpretation and application of the great ethical principles laid down in the legal and poetic books of the Old Testament. Occasionally, their ministry assumed the form of direct moral instruction, though this was more true of Jeremiah than the others. For example, Jeremiah would teach,

---

[61]Cf. Raven's summaries of "The Morality of the Time" in his chapters on Amos, Hosea, Isaiah, and Micah, *The History of the Religion of Israel.*

"Execute justice between a man and his neighbor" (7:5), or, "Deliver him that is robbed out of the hand of the oppressor" (21:12; 22:3). But, as even this last statement indicates, their more characteristic approach was that of the negative condemnation of current evils. Thus Nahum spoke against drunkenness (Nah. 1:10; 3:11) and Zephaniah against the shamelessness of his unjust contemporaries (Zeph. 2:1, 5). Jeremiah inveighed against such evils as the tyranny of Judah's rulers (Jer. 23:1) and the falsehood of her citizens (5:1-3); and Habakkuk, against the slackness of law enforcement and perversion on justice (Hab. 1:4). A primary vehicle of ethical instruction, particularly for Nahum and Habakkuk (cf. Obadiah in the preceding century), was found in the lawless conduct of Judah's oppressors. Thus the former condemned Nineveh's lust for prey and blood (Nah. 2:12; 3:1); and the latter, Babylon's passion for conquest and for violence (Hab. 2:5, 17). So too Jeremiah illustrated moral principles for his own people by exposing the falsity of the standards upon which their pagan neighbors had come to base their confidence; for example, in Jeremiah 49, Ammon, upon material treasure (v. 4), Edom, upon human counsel (v. 7), Damascus, upon universal praise (v. 23), Kedar, upon temporal security (v. 31), and Elam, upon physical might (v. 35).

Jeremiah's personal experiences served as a preeminent demonstration of a man's commitment of his life and conduct to God. Jeremiah thus wept in sympathy for the Judah he was required to condemn (9:1; 13:17). He became willing personally to forego the satisfaction of marriage for the sake of proclaiming his message (Jer. 16:1-5). He risked his life when he took a stand against his murderous family in Anathoth (11:21). He sacrificed his substance by purchasing a field from which he could expect no return, so as to re-enforce his prediction of Israel's post-exilic restoration (32:9, 15); and he refused to compromise his position as a prophet, despite royal petitions, personal threats, constant persecutions, and well-nigh fatal imprisonments (cf. 37:3, 15, 17). But still Jeremiah, in the highest spirit of Moses and Solomon, prayed for his persecutors (Jer. 18:20) and requested a similar attitude on the part of other sufferers (29:7). He anticipated no immediate reform among his contemporaries (13:23);[62] but he did look forward to the days of the new testament when God would write His laws in men's hearts (31:33). Zephaniah correspondingly revealed God's timeless moral standards by describing that final time when "the remnant of Israel shall not do iniquity, nor speak lies . . . and none shall make them afraid" (Zeph. 3:13).

PERIOD I, EXILIC. Ezekiel in exile united with Jeremiah in Palestine in condemning the immorality, both personal and international, of his people. He explicitly assigned the fall of Judah to the nation's

[62]See above, pp. 210, 211.

faithlessness in respect to its treaty obligations (Ezek. 17:15-19), and he elaborated on various other moral failures of which it had become guilty. Chapter 22 of Ezekiel furnishes an outstanding example of ethical preaching, as it catalogs Judah's failures in such areas as the children's disregard of their parents (v. 7), crimes of adultery and incest (v. 11), the exaction of bribes and usury (v. 12), and a love for dishonest gain (v. 13).

The exilic book of Daniel, as well as the latter part of Ezekiel, exhibits that lesser stress upon contemporary morals, which constitutes one of the features of apocalyptic-type prophecy.[63] Yet even in these portions of the Word, Daniel spoke of showing mercy to the poor (Dan. 4:27), he exhibited faithfulness in his presidential post under Darius the Mede (6:4), and he confessed the wickedness of his exilic community (9:5); cf. Ezekiel's later moral admonitions (Ezek. 34:2, 3; 45:9, 10).

PERIOD J, POST-EXILIC. The prophets Haggai and Zechariah spoke not only of the rebuilding of the post-exilic Temple, but they emphasized God's timeless moral requirements as well, such as the keeping of the love of luxury — "ceiled houses" — in its proper place (Haggai 1:4) and the executing of true judgment, "to show kindness and compassion every man to his brother" (Zech. 7:9; cf. vv. 16, 17). Several decades later, in the Diaspora, the book of Esther served to present a vivid picture of the corruption of the Persian court of Xerxes (cf. 1:10-12; 2:14, 21; 3:11). But Esther's own standards of devotion and self-sacrifice are, thereby, revealed all the more clearly (cf. 4:16; 7:3). It is true that near the close of Esther, the Jews themselves are described as exercising violence (9:5); but its ethical justification rests upon a basis similar to that which had, a millennium earlier, required the destruction of the Canaanites. Such bloodshed became a necessary step for the preservation of God's people against those who hated them.

Nehemiah's broad reforms included certain matters of social ethics, such as his measures of assistance for the economically destitute among his people (Neh. 5:7-13). The governor, moreover, was willing to, and did, forego the governmental allowance to which he was personally entitled (vv. 14-16), which stands as a striking example of self-sacrifice for the common good. Mixed marriages constituted a problem that was faced by both Ezra and Nehemiah (Ezra 9:1 f.; Neh. 13:23-28; Mal. 2:11). Through Moses, the only mixed marriages that God had specifically prohibited were those of alliance with the Canaanites (Ex. 34:16). Nehemiah, however, citing the evil example of Solomon (Neh. 13:26), proceeded to lay down the eternally valid standard of no marriage with those who are not of the faith (v. 27; II Cor. 6:14). The contemporary prophet, Malachi, then went

[63]See above, p. 61.

on to describe true marriage as a covenant before God (Mal. 2:14). Its purpose is to raise up "godly seed" (v. 15); and no man is to deal treacherously against the wife of his youth. God hates divorce (v. 16).

The total Biblical picture, therefore, throughout the ten periods of the Old Testament is this: Morals form an inevitable concomitant of faith: "The fear of the Lord, that is wisdom; *and* to depart from evil is understanding" (Job 28:28). Furthermore ethical sanctification becomes the prerequisite to that further growth in faith that God desires and expects: "My son, if thou wilt lay up my commandments with thee . . . then shalt thou understand the fear of Yahweh, and find the knowledge of God" (Prov. 2:1, 5).

For Further Reading:

John Calvin, *Institutes of the Christian Religion*. Trans. by John Allen; Philadelphia: Presbyterian Board of Christian Education, 1936. Book II, Chapter VIII, "An Exposition of the Moral Law."

John Murray, *Principles of Conduct*. Grand Rapids: Wm. B. Eerdmans Publishing Co., 1957. An up-to-date survey in the scholarly, orthodox Westminster tradition.

William Brenton Greene, Jr., "The Ethics of the Old Testament," *The Princeton Theological Review*, 27:2, 3 (April and July, 1929), 153-192, 313-366. A survey of the fundamentals of the Old Testament ethics, followed by their detailed defence against liberal objections.

G. Ernest Wright, "The Old Testament Attitude toward Civilization," *Theology Today*, 5, 3 (Oct., 1948), 327-339. A neo-orthodox study, primarily on the prophets and social justice.

26. Ceremonial: Places*

A. THE SIGNIFICANCE OF CEREMONIAL. The testamental fellowship that Israel enjoyed with God was expressed in symbolical worship (e.g., Ex. 20:24). The Old Testament furnishes, indeed, no systematic explanation for the theory of its ceremonial; it simply describes the fact of its existence as a part of the revealed conditions for participating in the testament (cf. Ex. 20:22-26). Explanations, however, are not lacking, and the most basic interpretation is this: that if a man fails to keep the moral law — and all do fail, as was recognized by Moses himself (Deut. 5:29) — then he gains forgiveness through a ceremonial observance.[1] Leviticus, for example states,

---

*BIBLE READING: Exodus 19; 29:38-46; I Chronicles 21:18-25.

Collateral Reading: Vos, *Biblical Theology*, pp. 159-172, 190-200.

Patrick Fairbairn, *The Typology of Scripture* (Grand Rapids: Zondervan Publishing House, 1952), I:42-61.

---

[1]The ceremonial law frequently concerned unintentional sins of ignorance (Lev. 4:2, but it was not limited to such (cf. 6:2); cf. Leon Morris, "Asham," *The Evangelical Quarterly* 30:4 (1958), pp. 200-201.

> If any one sin, and commit a trespass against Yahweh, and
> deal falsely with his neighbor . . . he shall restore that which he
> took . . . and he shall bring his trespass-offering unto Yahweh
> . . . and the priest shall make atonement for him before Yahweh;
> and he shall be forgiven concerning whatsoever he doeth so as to
> be guilty thereby (Lev. 6:2-7).

The testament remains, still, a matter of grace; for, as the prophets emphasized, it was God's mercy alone that granted the forgiveness (Isa. 43:25; Micah 7:18, 19). But even a testament may have conditions, and it was through the medium of the ceremonies[2] that God felt pleased graciously to mediate His imputed righteousness (Deut. 6:25).

In its essential function, the ceremonial law foreshadowed the person and work of Jesus Christ (Col. 2:17). It served as a means by which faith in the coming Savior could be exhibited, prior to His actual incarnation. The question immediately arises, then, as to the extent to which this anticipatory character was actually appreciated by the Old Testament saints. To this inquiry, moreover, three types of answers may be made. 1) As symbolical of Israel's sanctification to God, the Mosaic ceremonial was well understood by its contemporaries, for like the moral law, the ceremonial served as a visible demonstration of the people's faith in Yahweh. Thus Moses said, "I command thee this day to love Yahweh thy God [the demonstration of this love being:] to walk in His ways, and to keep His commandments and His statutes and His ordinances" (Deut. 30:16). Similarly, Israel's failure in both their moral and ceremonial obedience was understood as indicative of heart declension and apostasy from Him (31:29). The fact of the matter is, as long as the ceremonial was accepted as a sign of sincere commitment to God and of the nation's reliance upon His monergistic redemption, then whether or not they understood the antitype of which its rites were typical, or even the fact that its rites *were* typical, becomes a matter of relatively minor importance. God would take care of them; and that was all they needed!

2) As symbolical, moreover, of the general substitutionary way of salvation, the Mosaic ceremonials had a meaning that could hardly have escaped even the most dull. Berkhof rightfully criticizes those interpreters of the Old Testament who

> . . . lose sight of the symbolical character of many of its insti-
> tutions and ceremonies. They see in the ceremonial institutions,
> rites, and transactions of the Old Testament, only external forms
> that had no spiritual significance, and bodily exercises that
> profited but little; while in fact these ceremonies were symbols
> of spiritual truths.[3]

---

[2]The Hebrews in the Mosaic period did not, in fact, consciously distinguish between the ceremonial and the moral law; see above, p. 322. In practice, all were equally valid and were equally to be observed (Deut. 27:26; cf. James 2:10).
[3]*Principles of Biblical Interpretation*, p. 135.

More specifically, the ceremonies symbolized not just human obedience and devotion, but also positive elements of divine reconciliation.
As Vos has said in reference to sacrifice,

> "Before the blood could act for the benefit of the people
> it had to do its work with reference to Jehovah, and this
> could scarcely consist in aught else than to make the pre-
> requisite expiation."4

Thus Berkhof goes on to affirm:

> The sacrifices that were brought spoke of the forgiveness of sin
> on the basis of the atoning blood of Christ, and the oft-repeated
> washings symbolized the purifying influence of the Holy Spirit.
> The tabernacle as a whole was a revelation of the way that led
> to God, and Canaan itself constituted a symbol of the rest that
> remains for the people of God. The following passages prove that
> the Israelites had some conceptions of the spiritual significance
> of their rites and ceremonies.5

and Berkhof then lists, among other passages, Psalm 51:7, "Purify me
with hyssop, and I shall be clean: wash me, and I shall be whiter than
snow." Their understanding of this verse must have been not simply
that blood sprinkled from hyssop related somehow to the forgiveness
of sins, but that this ritual performance symbolized an action of
justification that God Himself would yet carry out for His own.

3) As symbolical, therefore (even in its details), of the redemptive program of God which He had devised in His heavenly eternity,
the Mosaic ceremonial came to be appreciated by at least some
of its contemporaries. The point to be stressed is not only that what
really saved the Old Testament saints was the blood of Christ which
was yet to be shed (systematic theology = what is true); it is also
this: that God made known to the Israelites in their own Old Testament times (Biblical theology = what is revealed) that these ceremonials depicted His eternally ordained blueprint of redemption.
Moses and his associates are stated to have understood that their
construction of the Tabernacle would have to follow, precisely, the
revealed heavenly pattern (Ex. 25:40; Heb. 8:5). It is this fact, moreover, which accounts for the seriousness of seemingly minor devia-
tions from God's revealed ritualistic procedure, for example, when
the Lord slew Uzzah (II Sam. 6:7). Ceremonial detail, after all,
meant the way of salvation!6 God was providing acted predictions
of Calvary when He revealed the ceremonial law.

4*Biblical Theology*, p. 139.
5*Loc. cit.*, though most of the verses he lists have no anticipatory significance.
6Note that Uzzah's personal salvation is not necessarily involved: his intentions
were good (II Sam. 6:6), and he may well be in heaven today. But the very
shockingness of his death drives home the lesson that Old Testament ceremonial
is symbolical of divine redemptive activity, far more significant than the humanly
observable, ritualistic actions. That many of the less spiritual in Israel failed to
attain to a true understanding of the ceremonies cannot be gain-said; for even the
leaders must have been unaware of some of the meanings that the events of Calvary have now made plain to all.

It must, however, be cautioned that the value of the ceremonial was not intrinsic. The prophets had to contend sharply with what was a false reliance upon performance for its own sake (Amos 5:21). Ritualism arose as a heresy of Canaanitish origin; and it is illustrated, soon after the conquest, by Micah's claim (Judg. 17:13), "Now know I that Yahweh will do me good, seeing I have a Levite to my priest." Actually, even if Micah's Levite had been a priest (which he wasn't), and even if priestly mediation had been legally acceptable apart from the central sanctuary (which it wasn't), such a claim would still have reflected a pagan-like reliance upon externalities and would have been worse than useless for securing true, divine favor. The Old Testament contains more on morals, even in the Pentateuch, than it does on ceremonials. To obey is better than to sacrifice (I Sam. 15:22); and the man who would sojourn in Yahweh's tabernacle and dwell in His holy hill is the one who "walketh uprightly, and worketh righteousness, and speaketh truth in his heart" (Ps. 15:2).

The ceremonial possessed effectiveness only as it manifested a man's faith. Confession of sin had therefore to precede sacrifice (Lev. 5:5), and there was no offering sufficient for the "high-handed" sin (Num. 15:30). The sacrifice of the wicked was, on the contrary, an abomination to God (Prov. 15:8; 21:27). Numbers 15:30, however, does not mean that the Pentateuch contained no provision for the case of the sinner who was guilty of deliberate rebellion against the Lord, even though this criticism is one that is commonly advanced by liberal interpreters.[7] Rather the unpardonable transgression that is described in this verse consisted of the extreme case, of one who "blasphemeth Yahweh"; compare verse 31, "He hath despised the word of Yahweh." Rowley insists that the high-handed sin must be "something more than consciously sinning: [it is] sinning as the expression of the settled purpose of the heart."[8] Indeed, it was only exceptional sins that could not find atonement through the Mosaic ceremonial (e.g., I Sam. 3:14). The "high-handed" sin is thus equivalent to the unrepented sin, and the sin that remains inaccessibly so. It corresponds moreover, to the New Testament revelation of "the blasphemy of the Holy Spirit" (Matt. 12:31, 32) which was unforgivable by its very nature, because it denied a hearing to the God who might have convicted men of their sins, by identifying Him with Beelzebub (v. 27). The result was that the man who acted in this way thereby deliberately cut himself off from the only source of hope, namely, his eventual conviction by the gracious Holy Spirit. Correspondingly, any man who is honestly concerned about the unforgivable sin, Old Testament or New Testament, cannot have committed it! But without

---

[7]Cf. H. Wheeler Robinson, *The Religious Ideas of the Old Testament* (London: 1944), p. 145; but see above, p. 350, note 1.

[8]H. H. Rowley, *The Unity of the Bible* (Philadelphia: Westminster Press, 1953), p. 45.

such a concern, and without true faith, the sinner will find that the ceremonial forms of both Testaments become useless and are, in fact, prohibited to him.

Like the moral law, the ceremonial law developed from the simple to the complex. With the revelation of the Sinaitic testament, this larger, national heirship inevitably required a more detailed ritual and its more strict regulation. Some of the Sinaitic ceremonials, moreover, correspond to similar materials that are found in the earlier and surrounding pagan religions.[9] But, just as in the case of the similarity of Moses' moral codes to Hammurabi's,[10] so this correspondence in ritual is to be explained by the fact that God in His grace may simply have granted to His people certain legitimate, pictorial forms with which they had already become familiar. The differences between the inspired and the pagan ceremonies are far more significant than the points of agreement. Moreover, even where they do agree in form, they may well disagree in function. The important thing is not the prior existence of a given Biblical rite, but rather the transformation of the religious concept with which it may have been associated in paganism into that new meaning which God had assigned to it in reference to His own redemptive program. With but few exceptions, Scripture then exhibits very little progress in its rituals beyond the definitive revelations that God granted in the Mosaic period. The Lord did not change His way of salvation! The psalmists and the prophets may indeed add certain details; and they did move toward a more direct, inward expression of the truths that the ceremonial symbolized (cf. Ps. 51:17). But at the same time, they continued to accept the Mosaic ritualistic patterns (v. 19).

Once again like the moral law, the ceremonial law serves to express the *qŏdhesh*, the holiness, that is required of those who are in fellowship with God. This feature helps to explain the above-mentioned and seemingly indiscriminate mixing in the Pentateuch of moral and ceremonial legislation![11] The distinction between the two came about historically only when the people, after having satisfied the ceremonial, began to disregard the moral aspects of holiness. So Samuel, in the consolidation period, first spoke of obedience as separate from sacrifice (I Sam. 15:22). Jehoshaphat, two periods later, proceeded to make the first official distinction in enforcement between these two types of law (II Chron. 19:11); and the precedent that he established was then elaborated and applied by the strong preaching of the eighth century prophets (Amos 5:23, 24; Isa. 1:11-17; Mic. 6:6-8). Liberal interpreters have tended to assert that the prophets

---

[9]These similarities are particularly striking between the Ugaritic materials and the so-called "late" Priestly Code of Moses; cf. H. F. Hahn, *The Old Testament and Modern Research*, p. 112.

[10]See above, p. 326.

[11]See above, p. 351, note 2.

denied the divine origin of the ceremonials altogether (cf. Jer. 7:21-23). But the pronouncements that the prophets made indicate not a rejection of the ceremonial, but rather an almost undivided stress on that part of the law that most needed the stressing at the time, namely, God's ethical requirements. Amos' opposition, for example, was not to pilgrimages as such (Amos 4:4, 5; 5:5, 14), but to their taking the place of the more basic matters of faith and morals. Compare Hosea 6:6, which states that Yahweh desires the knowledge of God *more than* burnt offerings.

Holiness climaxes in Christ. Our Lord truly procured for mankind that separation from sin and that reconciliation to God, which had all along been the theme of the testament. Much therefore of the Old Testament ceremonial has been fulfilled in Him. For those who would seek to trust in it as intrinsically efficacious after once having looked into the face of Jesus Christ, its practice must be forbidden. The Jewish ceremonies are "weak and beggarly" anticipations (Gal. 4:9). At the same time, however, the principles (e.g., atonement) that the ceremonies symbolized are timeless; and the ceremonies, accordingly, where relevant, continue to be matters of obligatory observance in the Church, though in a necessarily transmuted form. An example is that of the Passover, which has become the Lord's Supper (Matt. 26:26, 27). Furthermore, holiness for the individual Christian is incomplete in this life. Some ceremonies, therefore, such as the Sabbath (though again with a shift in details of performance, namely, of the particular day of the week that is set apart) continue to possess binding significance; for they still anticipate that heavenly rest, when the believer's actual state will correspond to his present holy standing in Christ (Heb. 4:9).

B. TYPOLOGY. As a theological study, typology has been much abused. If one, therefore, is to discover the divinely intended meanings of the Old Testament ceremonials and the actual ways in which they foreshadowed Christ, he must do so on the basis of a consistent and valid methodology. One must have an objective standard for determining the existence of predictive elements in the ceremonies and, when such elements appear, in determining the precise redemptive truths to which they point. Prophecies consist basically of two kinds, either spoken or acted. Acted prophecies then include both object-lessons and types. The former are defined as self-evident (or immediately explained) predictions of events whose fulfillments were relatively close at hand, while the latter consist of predictions that related to God's still distant accomplishment of salvation. Types indeed symbolized for their contemporaries the same general truths that they came ultimately to express; but their detailed meanings became evident or explained only with the incarnate life of Christ. The well known Scofield definition, "A type is a divinely purposed illustration of some truth,"[12] therefore needs, at the outset, some qualification that relates typology to "future truth." Symbolism is the discipline that deals with representations of contemporary truth.

The justification for typology as an authentic medium for the revelation of futuristically fulfilled truth lies in the fact of the fundamental unity that exists within God's plan of salvation in general, and within the testament in particular. The Old Testament ceremonial "is a figure for the time present, according to which are offered sacrifices that cannot make the worshipper perfect, being only ordinances, imposed until a time of reformation," when Christ should come (Heb. 9:9, 10). As Fairbairn has well stated it,

"The realities of the Gospel . . . are the ultimate objects which were contemplated by the mind of God, when planning the economy of His successive dispensations."[13]

This emphasis upon the Gospel, far from minimizing the significance of the older forms, is actually what gives meaning to the Old Testament ceremonial. Otherwise its rituals at best would be arbitrary, and, at worst, would smack of outright magic. The ceremonial observances were designed from their very inception to be shadows (Heb. 10:1), ineffectual in themselves (vv. 4, 11), but inherently descriptive of the work subsequently to be accomplished by Christ (v. 12; cf. 9:28).

The unity of salvation then requires the existence of unified theological meaning in the revelations of that salvation. That is, since men throughout the ages have been saved in the same way, a given rite must have symbolized to the Old Testament saints the same general teaching that it now typifies to the New Testament saints. The preparatory stage would, of course, have to be "of more obvious meaning, and of more easy comprehension than the ultimate and final."[14] When God's wrath, for example, brought death upon Israel by fiery serpents, the salvation that the Israelites gained by looking in faith at the brazen serpent on the pole (Num. 21:9) served as a type of the final salvation from God's wrath that is gained (though less obviously) by looking in faith at Christ lifted up on the cross (John 3:14). Simultaneously, however, this pictorialness of typology makes the acted prophecy, in the last analysis, more obscure and difficult to interpret than the spoken prophecy:

"Prophecy . . . naturally possesses something of the directness . . . of historical description. But types having a significance or moral import of their own, apart from anything

---

[12]*Reference Bible*, p. 4.
[13]Patrick Fairbairn, *The Typology of Scripture* (Grand Rapids: Zondervan Publishing House, 1952), I:47.
[14]*Ibid.*, I:51, though Fairbairn carries this too far and sometimes ends up with the Old Testament saints finding meanings that are not the same as the general truth taught in the New Testament.

prospective, must, in their prophetical aspect, be somewhat less transparent, and possess more of a complicated character."[15]

Since typology, therefore, is not transparent, its presence and its limits must be determined with the utmost care. The specific definition, then, that is employed in this study on Old Testament ceremonial-places (topic 26) and in the following sections on ceremonial actions and times (topics 27 and 28) is as follows: a type is to be understood as *a divine enactment of future redemption.* From this definition, four corollaries appear.

1) A type must have a divine origin. Even as God was the One who planned out the ultimate redemption of mankind in Christ, and He alone; so only God could enunciate a type that would be predictive of that redemption, and He alone. All "discoveries" by human interpreters are nothing more than allegories, if they cannot be shown to have been a part of God's original intention. It was on this basis that Bishop Marsh enunciated his famous dictum:

"There is no other rule by which we can distinguish a real from a pretended type, than that of Scripture itself . . . expressly declared by Christ or by His apostles to have been designed as prefigurations of persons or things relating to the New Testament."[16]

This Marshian position is reflected by the Scofield warning:

"Nothing may be dogmatically asserted to be a type without explicit New Testament authority; and all types not so authenticated must be recognized as having the authority of analogy, or spiritual congruity, merely."[17]

From the first then, this much at least can be said: the most basic category within typology consists of those figures that are explained elsewhere in Scripture. About such, one may say, "I know they are types, and I know what they mean." They constitute, accordingly, sound doctrinal sources, insofar as they may be explained.

2) A type must be redemptive. To take an example of a Biblical passage that does *not* meet this qualification, God said of Eliakim, the son of Hilkiah, "I will fasten him as a nail in a sure place" (Isa. 22:23). This prediction was true, but it is not directly redemptive; it merely concerned Eliakim's government position under Hezekiah. It is not a type of Christ, as is sometimes claimed; and "the nail" eventually was pulled down (v. 25)! Moreover, since redemption requires a response and elicits worship, this redemptive quality, that is so characteristic of the known Biblical types, furnishes typology

---

[15]*Ibid.,* I:106.
[16]From his Lectures, as quoted in Fairbairn, *op. cit.,* I:19.
[17]*Op. cit.,* p. 100.

with an important general limitation, namely, "All that was really typical . . . stood related to a religious worship."[18] This fact, that the Biblical typology concerns the ceremonial and ritualistic worship of Israel, is well expressed in L. Alexander's detailed definition (one of the best):

> "Types are *symbolical institutes* expressly appointed by God to prefigure to those among whom they were set up certain great transactions in connection with that plan of redemption which, in the fulness of time, was to be unfolded to mankind."[19]

Because of this quality of redemptive ceremonialism, typology may *not*, therefore, be legitimately applied to individual Old Testament characters. The only exceptions would be the person of Adam, who was created as the federal head of the race and was hence intended as a type of Christ's own representative position in redemption, and the person of Melchizedek, the priest-king, who was, from the first, designed as a type of Christ's priestly superiority to Abraham and Levi. Other individuals that are sometimes proposed as types do not appear to be inherently redemptive of mankind and should not, in consequence, be considered typical.[20] There exist, however, a number of matters in Scripture that are clearly parts of redemptive contexts and that occupy, in parallel with other *known* types, a significant place in the ceremonial worship of Israel. Such items may then, by analogy, be recognized as genuine types, even though they may never be given explicit elucidation elsewhere in Scripture. One of these, for example, is the "candlestick" (lamp stand) in the Tabernacle. God intended this object as a main article in His testamentally significant sanctuary; and Hebrews 8:5; 9:5 demonstrate that the major parts of the tabernacle did have divinely intended meaning. Most evangelical scholars therefore feel that Marsh, by limiting types to those matters that are expressly declared to be so by the New Testament, went too far in his generally laudable attempt to prevent uncontrolled typology. About such ceremonial matters one may say, "I know they are types, but I am not sure what they mean." They cannot, therefore, serve as a source of doctrinal authority.

    3) A type must be a pictorial enactment. It must have existed,

---

[18]Fairbairn, *op. cit.*, I:189.

[19]From his *Connection and Harmony of the Old and New Testament*, 1841; as quoted in Fairbairn, *op. cit.*, I:25.

[20]David, for example, despite his Messianic psalms and his position as ancestor of Christ (so that Christ is sometimes called simply "David," cf. Hos. 3:5), never appeared to his contemporaries as a divinely intended prefiguration of Christ. Moses also is simply "like Christ" (Deut. 18:15), and God does not appear to have created Moses with this similarity to our Lord as the motivating factor in His designing of Moses' life.

from the time of its enunciation, as a symbolically acted-out prophecy of redemption. This feature of representativeness then produces what is perhaps the most important single principle in the delimiting of typology, namely, that a given item must be symbolical to its contemporaries before it can be considered typical for the future. As Vos so ably compares symbol and type:

> They are in reality the same things, only different in this respect that they come first on a lower stage of development in redemption, and then again, in a later period, on a higher stage. Thus what is symbolical with regard to the already existing edition of the fact or truth becomes typical, prophetic, of the later, final edition of that same fact or truth. From this it will be perceived that a type can never be a type independently of its being first a symbol.[21]

Far too many evangelicals have exhausted themselves in the invention of fine-spun theories about the typical significance in respect to Christ of, say, the details of the life of Joseph. To his contemporaries, if Joseph were considered symbolical at all, it would have been in respect to just one thing: the power of God's wonderful providence. We must not allow this basic, Biblical truth to be obscured by futile speculations over the "meaning," for example, of his Gentile wife in respect to the Church! Even concerning certain ceremonial matters, such as the colors that were used in the hangings of the Tabernacle, it is best simply to say, "I do not know whether they are types or not"; and until we do know, we had best leave them out of the doctrinal picture altogether.[22]

4) A type must have a future reference. If the full meaning, therefore, of a given matter appears to be limited to its immediate context, then that matter should not be treated as if it were typical. The Scofield Bible, for example, after stating its previously quoted, Marsh-like definition of typology, goes on to discover typical meanings in even the utilitarian hooks and boards of the Tabernacle . . . sometimes several, mutually exclusive meanings for the same items![23] Such fanciful typologizing constitutes another of the serious failures that are characteristic of modern dispensational interpretation; for, refusing as it does to recognize the presence of the Church in the literal prophecies of the Old Testament, dispensationalism seems to find compensation for this deficiency by having recourse to excessive typology. But this sort of a procedure tends to bring into disrepute the whole field of typology and the really valid explanations of true, inspired types, which are so necessary for the understanding of the

---

[21]*Op. cit.*, p. 162.
[22]Even Vos appears to have suffered from a guilty conscience over his "searching the field of prophecy" for types; for he adds, "Of course, it is inevitable that into this kind of interpretation of O.T. figures an element of uncertainty must enter. But after all this is an element that enters into all exegesis" (!), *ibid.*, p. 163.
[23]For example, in reference to the boards of the tabernacle; cf. *op. cit.*, pp. 103, 105.

place of the ceremonial in Biblical theology. As a procedure, it confuses genuine, acted prophecies with matters about which one should say flatly, "I know that they are not types."

C. SANCTUARIES. The ritualistic typology of the Old Testament is concerned first of all, with sacred places. The early patriarchs exhibited a reverence for particular spots that had been made sacred by theophanies (cf. Gen. 28:17). It is significant, moreover, for the theology of the older testament as it thereafter developed, 1) that the patriarchal sacrifices were consistently limited to these places, which had been chosen by God for the revelation of Himself, and 2) that the sacrifices then occurred only in one such place at a time.[24] The basic principle is expressed in Genesis 12:7, "And there builded he an altar unto Yahweh, who appeared unto him" (cf. 28:18). No sanctuaries, however, were as yet constructed.

God appeared to Israel on Mount Sinai (Ex. 19:3, 12, 16, 18, 20), on "Horeb, the mount of God" (I Kings 19:8). Moses accordingly "builded an altar under the mount" (Ex. 24:4). In fact, the opening ceremonial provision of the book of the testament was this: "An altar of earth thou shalt make unto Me . . . In every place where I record My name I will come unto thee and I will bless thee" (20:24). Wellhausenism has selected Exodus 20:24 as one of the key verses for its evolutionary reconstruction of the history of the religion of Israel. It draws from it the theory that, prior to the "discovery" of Deuteronomy (or its oldest parts) under Josiah in 621 B.C., Israel believed in a plurality of sanctuaries. This it "proves" from the legends of the patriarchs, which it conveniently dates to about 850-750 B.C. Archaeology has now done much to overthrow this classic Wellhausen reconstruction;[25] but the Biblical evidence alone, if it is allowed to speak for itself, shows that patriarchal worship does not describe the practices of the nation of Israel in 850-750! Furthermore, though Exodus 20:24 does allow for worship in more than one place, as Israel's tent-sanctuary moved about during the years of the wilderness wanderings

---

[24]The only example of a patriarchal theophany without the corresponding erection of an altar is that of Gen. 26:2, perhaps because of its occurrence in Gerar, a foreign place. Concerning the theophany at Hebron (17:1), an altar had already been erected there (13:18). As to altars without theophanies, such rare cases (there are 3) are to be explained in recognition, either of a theophany immediately preceding, or of some related type of divine intervention or activity. The altar of Gen. 13:18 was erected in recognition of God's blessing on Abraham, after his generosity in the matter of Lot's choice (vv. 14-17). Gen. 33:20 then constituted Jacob's first stopping place subsequent to the Peniel theophany (32:30) and his deliverance from Esau (33:16). This leaves Gen. 12:8, the one reference which remains without explanation, but for which it may be assumed that some divine activity must have prompted Abraham there to call on the name of Yahweh; cf. Moses' erection of the altar following the God-granted victory over Midian at Rephidim (Ex. 17:15).

[25]See above, the studies by Unger and Rowley; and compare the timely article by Cyrus Gordon on the fancifulness of the JEDP theory in toto, "Higher Critics and Forbidden Fruit," Christianity Today, 4:4 (Nov. 23, 1959), pp. 131-134.

(Num. 10:11; cf. II Sam. 7:6), the teaching of this verse, in parallel with that of the patriarchal materials, still does *not* authorize worship in more than one place at one time (Lev. 17:5). Moses' eventual stress on the one, fixed, centrally-located sanctuary then appears in Deut. 12:5, 11-14 (which is to be dated in 1406 B.C.), in natural anticipation of Israel's final settling down in Canaan, which was shortly to take place.

Immediately after the ratification of the testament in Exodus 24, God granted to Israel His pattern for the Tabernacle. This Tabernacle consisted of a movable sanctuary that was designed to replace the provisional tent of Exodus 33:7-10, where God had previously met with His people. The significance of the Tabernacle was defined by God Himself in Exodus 29:45 as follows: "I will dwell among the children of Israel and will be their God." The Tabernacle thus served as a sacrament, as the visible sign and seal of the reality of Yahweh's testamentary promise to be present as Israel's God and of the fact that He and sinners were now truly reconciled. Its function has been perpetuated by the sacrament of the Lord's supper, the sign and seal of the remission of sins (Matt. 26:28) and of spiritual communion with Christ (I Cor. 10:16).

The Hebrew names for the Tabernacle witness to this testamentally expressive purpose. The first of these is "*Mishkān*" which means "dwelling" (Ex. 25:9, Revised Version, margin). *Mishkān* signifies "dwelling" in its active sense of "living with" rather than in its passive sense of "a dwelling," as if God needed a "dwelling house." God was thus realistically described as dwelling[26] there in the Tabernacle, as King amongst His people. From this meaningful word arises the term "Shekinah," *sh'khīnā*, which derives itself from the same verbal root, "to dwell." *Sh'khīnā* as a word is not actually found in the Old Testament, but the term is descriptive of the reality of the theophanic glory-cloud which rested over the ark (Lev. 16:2).[27] A second name for the Tabernacle is *ôhel mō'ēdh*, "tent of meeting" (Ex. 29:42, 43, Revised Version); for it was here that God met with Moses. The primary reference of *ôhel mō'ēdh* is therefore to the place where God meets men, not (as in some churches today?) where men meet each other! The Tabernacle is called, thirdly, the "house of Yahweh" (34:26), that is, the place of His localized appearance. A final name for this sanctuary is "the tabernacle of the testimony" (38:21, Revised Version); because it constituted the place of revelation and because

---

[26]Cf. Vos, *op. cit.*, pp. 123, 168-170.
[27]Cf. Ex. 40:34-35; I Kings 8:10-11; II Chron. 7:1-3. Note also Rom. 9:4, the Jews, "whose is the glory." Lev. 16:13 mentions the cloud of incense brought in by Aaron; but this latter was to protect him from the Shekinah cloud, in which God appeared and which would otherwise have prevented his entering.

it contained the ark, in which were the tables of the law, the testimony, or reminder[28] of God's testamental conditions (25:21).

Yet the Tabernacle, even while it stood as a symbol of God's immanence, served at the same time as a symbol of God's transcendence; for it was the means by which He shut Himself off from the common people. This appears from the very structure and plan of the Tabernacle. The building itself was constructed of such materials as were available at hand, plus the treasures that had been removed from Egypt. It consisted basically of a two-roomed, windowless, wooden oblong, composed of portable, vertical frames, with four layers of coverings in the following order: linen, for beauty inside; a padding of goats' hair; dyed rams' skins, for protection; and a final coating of treated leather to withstand the climatic extremes of the wilderness. Thus isolated within the inner chamber, the "holy of holies [the place most separated]," God dwelt "in thick darkness" (I Kings 8:12). But the Tabernacle was, at the same time, prophetic of a better dispensation; for it served in its total function as a type of Christ. He it was who would be Immanuel, God tabernacling with us (John 1:14); and through His flesh (Heb. 10:20) men would yet have direct access to God under the newer testament (Jer. 31:34).

At the time of God's revelation of the Tabernacle, Moses was repeatedly cautioned that its construction must conform in every respect to the meaningful pattern which was made known to him on the mount (Sinai, Ex. 25:9, 40; Heb. 8:5). All of its distinctive elements may therefore be appreciated as possessing symbolical and typical significance. As the first object within the gate of the Tabernacle, the altar stands as mute evidence to the fact that God may be approached only by the way of sacrifice, which means, in the last analyses, the substitutionary and testamentary death of Christ (Heb. 8:2, 3; 9:12). But sacrifice produces power, which is then symbolized by the horns that are fixed to the corners of the altar (Amos 3:14). These horns thus came to have significance as a place of asylum in ancient Israel (cf. I Kings 2:28). Next is stationed the laver, which demonstrates the necessity for purity if one is to approach God (Ex. 30:21) and which points to the washing of regeneration and sanctification in Christ (Titus 3:5; Heb. 9:10).

Inside the "holy place, " the "show [presence]" bread is displayed on its golden table as a symbol of reestablished harmony and of Israel's sustaining testamental communion with Yahweh (Lev. 24:8; cf. Ex. 24:11). The bread serves also as a type and a pledge of that closer fellowship with Him, which is to be realized in the heavenly and eschatological kingdom of God (Luke 14:15). The "candlestick [lampstand]" appears to symbolize the perfection (seven lamps) with which God's Old Testament church must shine forth before Him

---

[28]See above, p. 322, note 22.

(Lev. 24:3), as enabled by the oil of the Holy Spirit (cf. Zech. 4:2-6). Its illumination is then typical of the present day light and truth that radiates from the heart of the consecrated Christian (Matt. 5:14), through the priestly ministration of the Lord Jesus (Lev. 24:4; John 8:12). The altar of incense seems to stand for the believer's communion with God in prayer (Ps. 141:2; Luke 1:10; Rev. 8:4).

The veil that divided the two chambers of the pre-Christian sanctuary had the function of sealing off the way into the "most holy place." It was thus emblematic of the truth that the way of access to God was not yet clear (Heb. 9:8), and would not be until the Messianic High Priest should come and take out of the way the anticipatory forms of the older testament (Matt. 27:51). The central object of the whole Tabernacle was the ark, which served first of all as a chest for containing the two inscribed stones of the Decalogue (Ex. 25:21), as well as a pot of the wilderness manna (16:33) and Aaron's rod that budded (Num. 17:7). By its side was placed Moses' book of the law (Deut. 31:26). Since these written documents were what constituted the objective basis for Israel's testament, the ark itself came to receive the title, "ark of the testament" (Num. 10:33). The cover of solid gold that rested upon the ark was given the special title of the *kappōreth*, the "mercy seat," or atoning cover; see the next topic for the details of its redemptive significance.[29] The basic thought of the *kappōreth*, however, was that of grace (the blood of the testament) intervening between the holiness of God and the inalterable verdict of divine justice upon the conduct of man (the Decalogue underneath). But the ark constituted more than a symbol; it was an authentic sacrament conveying the real presence of God to Israel. For the cloud of God's glory (Ex. 13:21) came to reside over its golden cover (40:34). Now, in this New Testament age, the visible, outward presence of the Shekinah has been transmuted into the believer's invisible and inward fellowship with the person of Christ in the sacrament of the Lord's Supper; but its observance still conveys the real though spiritual presence of our living Lord, "the communion of His blood" (I Cor. 10:16). Finally, the ark constitutes a type of the presence of God in heaven itself (Ps. 11:4);[30] for heaven is the pattern from which the whole earthly sanctuary was copied, and to which the saints will yet go marching home (Heb. 9:24). With this connotation of heavenly glory may be compared the ark's ceremonial continuation in the form of the Lord's Supper, which serves also as a type of that eschatological kingdom, when the saved shall feast in the presence of their Redeemer (Mark 14:25; I Cor. 11:26).

But beyond these confessedly many and wonderful depicted

---

[29]See below, p. 380.
[30]Cf. Vos, *op. cit.*, p. 171.

truths, Scripture suggests nothing about the allegedly inexhaustible, esoteric "meanings" of the Tabernacle. Its structure and ornamentation were for efficiency and beauty, but not, as far as we can tell, for symbolism and typology.

With the commencement of the consolidation period in 1406 B.C., the Tabernacle moved with Israel into the Promised Land of Canaan. The Mosaic sanctuary was first set up on the western bank of the Jordan at Gilgal (Josh. 9:6; 10:43) but was finally settled at Shiloh (18:1), where it remained for some 300 years. The ark, however, was moved about to some extent; and wherever it went, sacrifice could, of course, legitimately be performed (Judg. 20:27; 21:4; I Sam. 6:15). For a number of years Moses' commandment for the establishment of only one central sanctuary was strictly enforced. This is witnessed both by the concern of Israel over the possibility of a separate sanctuary in Transjordan, and by the emphatic denial on the part of the eastern tribes that they should ever become guilty of entertaining such ideas (Josh. 22:19, 26). It is true that under the judges, occasional theophanies led to the offering of special sacrifices (according to the principle of Gen. 12:7; Ex. 20:24) away from the Tabernacle at Shiloh. But these occurred only at the specific times of the divine appearances; no other sanctuaries were (illegally) set up (Judg. 6:18; 13:16). The same justification, however, cannot be adduced in reference to the partially paganized forms of worship that were practiced by the apostate among the people (Judg. 17:5), or even by the leaders (8:27).

By the time of Eli (1130-1090 B.C.) a permanent "house of Yahweh" had been built at Shiloh (I Sam. 1:7; v. 9). Here was situated the only altar that was legally recognized in Israel (2:28; cf. 1:3). But with destruction of this temple at the hands of the Philistines, as a result of the first battle of Ebenezer, c. 1090 B.C. (I Sam. 4:10, 11; Ps. 78:60; Jer. 7:12), sacrifice at Shiloh ceased. The ark was first taken as spoil to Philistia and was then, upon its return, kept at Kirjath-jearim (I Sam. 7:1). Nob in Benjamin seems to have come into being as the contemporary priestly center (21:1; 22:19); and the Tabernacle found its way, eventually, to Gibeon (I Chron. 16:39). Faced by such a breakdown of the official worship, Samuel, as God's charismatically anointed representative,[31] was forced to take over the religious leadership of Israel personally. He therefore conducted official sacrifices in various places as he moved about (I Sam. 7:9; 9:13). Saul, during the forty years of his reign (1050-1010 B.C.), neglected the ark (I Chron. 13:3; though cf. I Sam. 14:18) and ended by slaughtering the priests at Nob (22:19). The absence of a central sanctuary until the time of Solomon is thus specifically noted in Scripture as the justification for the localized worship of Yahweh which

---

[31]See above, p. 49.

arose in various "high places" throughout the century and a quarter preceding the completion of the Temple in the fall of 959 B.C. (I Kings 3:2).

Early in this reign over unified Israel, David brought up the ark of God's testament from Kirjath-jearim and established it in a tent that he had pitched for it in the city of David, which is Mount Zion (II Sam. 5:7; 6:17; Ps. 24). The king thereby produced two main centers of worship — Jerusalem, the city of God (Ps. 46:5; 48:3), with reference especially to Mount Zion, which was Yahweh's "holy hill" (9:11; 3:5), and Gibeon, the significance of which was concentrated in its high place, where the old Tabernacle was by this time located (I Chron. 16:39). It was in David's day, however, that God finally revealed that spot for the location of the central sanctuary which Moses had originally prescribed: "The place which Yahweh shall choose out of all your tribes, to put His name [His Personal presence] there" (Deut. 12:5). For, following upon David's sinful census, the Lord spoke through the prophet Gad and commanded the king to erect an altar on the threshing floor of Arauna, where God had revealed Himself, and there to offer up sacrifices (I Chron. 21:18, 28). This threshing floor was situated on Mount Moriah, just north of the limits of the city of Jerusalem as they then existed (II Chron. 3:1). Moriah was indeed the same hill on which Abraham had once been willing to sacrifice his son Isaac (Gen. 22:2). It thus became, even when occupied only by the king's altar, the "house of Yahweh" (I Chron. 22:1). Its designation as God's "house" seems to explain certain words which appear in the Psalms, which otherwise would have been quite inappropriate in the mouth of David and his friends, such as the following: "a song at the dedication of the house" (Ps. 30, title) and their expressions of love for God's house, which is His temple, hēkhāl (27:4; 65:4). But it was not for David, who had become guilty of much bloodshed, to erect the actual building on this sacred site; that would remain to be accomplished by his son Solomon (I Chron. 22:7-10).[32] Before his death, however, David did gather extensive materials for the sanctuary's construction (v. 5); and he strictly charged both Solomon (vv. 6, 11-16)) and also the princes of the people (vv. 17-19) with its completion. The plans for the erection

---

[32]God's words in I Chron. 22:10 that "He shall be my Son, and I will be his Father," hark back to the Lord's original revelation in II Sam. 7:13, 14, when David had first hoped to build the temple himself (v. 2). Instead, however, David had been promised that God would build up the king's "house," a building that would climax in the incarnation of the divine Messiah, see above, p. 261. The words of Sonship therefore apply to Christ alone; but their quotation in I Chron. 22:10 appears to be an example of "sandwich" structure, that is, the inclusion of certain words in the center of a quotation, when actually it is only the preceding and the following sections of that quotation that apply to the subject at hand (cf. Acts 2:17-21).

of the sacred structure were revealed to David in writing by the
Holy Spirit (28:12, 19).

At the opening of his reign, Solomon sought the face of God
at the high place of Gibeon, where the Tabernacle was set up (II
Chron. 1:3). Between the spring of 966, however, and the fall of
959, over a period of some seven and one-half years (I Kings 6:1, 38),
Solomon succeeded in accomplishing the construction of the *hēkhāl*,
the "temple" (6:3). Frequently this sanctuary is called simply "the
house (of God)." The basic plan of Solomon's Temple was similar to
that of the Tabernacle, but with double dimensions and triple height.
The stone walls of the building were lined with carved cedar, which
was in turn overlaid with gold (I Kings 6:22). Two huge cherubim,
that were designed to indicate God's settled presence and permanent
residence in the Temple, stood in the "oracle," its most holy place.
The altar of incense was now also associated with this inner sanctum
(v. 22; cf. Heb. 9:3, 4). The outer, holy place was equipped with
ten "candlesticks" (lamp stands) and ten tables of showbread. The
temple's porch supported two pillars, *Yākhīn*, "Hè establishes," and
Bō'az, "in Him is strength." They were thus indicative of God's power
in the Temple (I Kings 7:21; cf. Ps. 87:1). Outside lay the great
altar and the laver, or "sea," which was supported on twelve carved
oxen. This sea was then provided with ten smaller lavers that were
mounted on bases with wheels, so that water could be transported
to the points where it should be needed (I Kings 7:23-39). The surrounding court was now divided into two parts (II Kings 23:12), the
upper one being for the use of the priests (II Chron. 4:9; Jer. 36:10).
The basic truths, however, of the Temple remained identical with
those of the Tabernacle: at its completion the old "tent of meeting"
was brought up from Gibeon and actually placed inside the new
sanctuary (I Kings 8:4); and at the heart of the building rested the
same holy ark of the testament (I Kings 6:19; 8:1, 6, 21; II Chron. 5:
2, 7). At the Temple's dedication, the Shekinah cloud came and filled
the house (II Chron. 5:13); and God's fire fell from heaven upon its
altar (7:1), even as it had at the consecration of the Tabernacle (Lev.
9:24). Solomon's Temple became God's testamental dwelling (I Kings
8:12, 13).

At the division of the kingdom in 930 B.C., Jeroboam I hypo-
critically informed his people in north Israel, "It is too much for you
to go up to Jerusalem." Then, in clear opposition to the divine law
of the central sanctuary that was located on God's one holy hill,
Jeroboam proceeded to set up rival temples at Bethel and Dan
(12:28, 29). His real motivation was to circumvent a possible return
of Israel's loyalty to the house of David (vv. 26, 27). It is strange
how a man who had been ordained by God and who had been
promised permanency in his God-given position if he would but con-

tinue obedient (11:38) came to feel that he must provide for himself a human undergirding for that position, and at the expense of disobedience! As a result, even Yahweh's true leaders in the north were compelled to make recourse to altars other than the one that God had designated in Jerusalem (18:30), while the general populace proceeded to patronize countless, illegal high places that sprang up, either as outright revivals of the old native paganisms, or as supposedly Yahweh-centered places of worship that, for all practical purposes, differed in little more than name from the Canaanitish sanctuaries (cf. Hos. 8:12, 13).

Amos, in the eighth century, predicted the destruction of Israel's high places and the captivity of the land (Amos 7:9); and, even in southern Judah, weak King Ahaz "sacrificed and burnt incense in the high places, and on the hills, and under every green tree" (II Kings 16:4). At one point, Ahaz indeed went so far as to replace the brazen altar of the Temple with one of pagan design from Damascus (v. 14). Isaiah predicted the appearance of a temple to Yahweh in Egypt (Isa. 19:19). His prophecy may perhaps refer to the temple of the Elephantine colony of the Jews, which was destroyed in 410 B.C.[33] or, as seems more likely, to that of Onias IV in the Egyptian city of Leontopolis. Onias was a priest who, centuries later, was to be driven from Palestine in a period of similar apostasy, following the murder of his father, the pious high priest, Onias III, in 172 B.C.[34] Neither of these Egyptian "temples," however, may be considered as legitimate sanctuaries in the Biblical sense. Isaiah's true, spiritual experiences and future hopes centered in Zion, the temple of Yahweh's actual presence (6:1; 14:32). Hezekiah's reform of 725 B.C. once again laid stress upon the single, central sanctuary in Jerusalem (II Kings 18:4).

In the next period, Hezekiah's son and successor, Manasseh, openly converted the Temple of Yahweh to an Assyrian-like adoration of the heavenly bodies (21:5, 7; cf. 23:11). Furthermore, even though Josiah's great reform of 621 had as one of its primary objectives the purification of Judah's worship at the one central sanctuary (23:8), religious corruption immediately revived during the reigns of his worthless successors. The prophet Jeremiah felt a personal reverence for the Temple, "the throne of God's glory" (14:21; cf. 17:12); and he sincerely regretted its profanation by the leaders of his day (23: 11). Still, he roundly condemned his people's false reliance upon it (7:4); and he revealed that the externalities of sacred places, even of the ark itself, would yet be superseded by a more spiritual presence of God in the heart, under the newer testament (3:16). In 586 B.C. the armies of Nebuchadrezzar destroyed the Temple, together

---

[33]Cf. Payne, *An Outline of Hebrew History*, p. 123.
[34]*Ibid.*, pp. 179, 182.

with all its major furnishings, and carried off its plunder to Babylon (II Kings 25:9; 13-17).

Ezekiel in the exile exerted his utmost influence for the rebuilding of the Temple (Ezek. 43:10, 11; cf. Isaiah's prediction of over a century before, Isa. 44:28); and, with this goal in mind, he provided the Jews, in chapters 40-46 of his book, with inspired, detailed plans for its post-exilic reconstruction. What they eventually did failed, it is true, to measure up to Ezekiel's dreams; but the pre-New Testament sin-offerings that are described in these seven chapters (cf. 43:20-27) make it impossible to relate this material, as is sometimes done, to God's kingdom that is still in the future. For our own days, it is primarily only his concluding chapters (47-48) that appear to be still predictive. The Babylonian captivity, moreover, exercised a generally negative influence upon the whole concept of temple worship. For even as the previous participation of any given individual in the worship at the central Jerusalem sanctuary must have been necessarily infrequent, so now the exile demonstrated to the Jews that they could get along without the Temple and its ritual altogether. Synagogues rather began to take their place in the real religious leadership of Israel (cf. Ps. 74:8).

Upon the post-exilic return of the Jews to Palestine, the Temple's rebuilding proceeded slowly, both because of Samaritan opposition (Ezra 4:24) and because of popular indifference (Hag. 1:4). The altar was rededicated in 536 B.C. (Ezra 3:3, 6); but only because of the energetic preaching of Haggai and Zechariah did Judah finally manage to complete the Temple itself, early in 515 (6:15). In the next century, Nehemiah exiled from the Jewish community one of the apostate grandsons of the high priest, a certain Manassah, who had even married a daughter of Sanballat, Nehemiah's Samaritan opponent (Neh. 13:28). As a result, the Samaritans proceeded to erect an illegitimate, rival sanctuary on Mt. Gerizim in their own territory (cf. John 4:20).

In the sixth century, however, Haggai, while predicting the ultimate worship in the new Jerusalem (Hag. 2:7), had also foretold that in the courts of the post-exilic Temple of ancient Jerusalem, Yahweh would some day speak forth peace (v. 9). Haggai's words were then fulfilled in the person and ministry of Jesus Christ. The Son of God constituted in His incarnate presence the true "sacred place" (Matt. 12:6; cf. John 2:20). By His death, He rent away the temple veil and all the system of restricted access to God that had bulked so large in the Old Testament ceremonial (Matt. 27:51). His message to the woman of Samaria revealed that henceforth men were to seek God, neither in Gerizim nor in Jerusalem (John 4:21), but in the direct spiritual worship of the Father through Himself (vv. 24, 26). Jesus thus fulfilled the universalistic prediction of the last of the Old Testament prophets, when he foresaw and spoke for God that "from the rising of the sun even to the going down of the same My name shall be great among the Gentiles; and in every place incense [prayer?] shall be offered unto My name" (Mal. 1:11).

The Old Testament concept of the sanctuary as the sacred place of God's presence has thus now attained its universalistic accomplishment in the Christian Church, which is the body of Christ (Eph. 5:30). For where two or three are gathered together in His name, there is Christ in the midst of them (Matt. 18:20). Yet the particularistic truth of the sacred place of the testamental sanctuary continues to be expressed in the sacrament of the Lord's Supper. On the one hand, true believers, who come to the Lord's table with a faith that anticipates the real though spiritual presence of Christ, find that the bread "is His body, which is broken for us"; and they meet with God in a unique way (I Cor. 11:24). But on the other hand, unbelievers, who eat and drink unworthily, become subject to serious condemnation, not discerning the Lord's body (v. 28). The localization of the presence of God continues to be true, whether for good or for evil; compare I Corinthians 11:29 with Numbers 4:15 (on the furniture of the tabernacle): "They shall not touch any holy thing, lest they die." Scripture, moreover, foresees that yet future day of Christ's Second Advent when, in the testament of peace, our Lord will again be visibly present in His "house" on Mount Zion (Mic. 4:2; Jer. 17:26; Ezek. 37:27).

D. CLEANNESS. The Old Testament not only reveals the historical fact of sacred places, in the form of the sacramental sanctuaries where Israel was to seek her God, but it also identifies certain places, objects, and situations that were to be avoided by God's people. These latter are described as *tāmē*, "unclean"; while others, that are accessible or usable, are called *tāhōr*, "clean." Some critics have suggested that a very sacred object served also to make a man "unclean." But the Old Testament contains no such "taboo" concept.[35] It is the impure, the idolatrous thing, that is forbidden;[36] the *tāhōr*, the "clean," is what is fit for use. The *tāhōr* may, however, become, though it is not necessarily yet, *qōdhesh*, that is, a thing of holiness.

Unclean animals are mentioned as early as the primeval period in connection with the ark of Noah (Gen. 7:2), while a matter of holiness appears immediately thereafter in God's statement which prohibited mankind from eating blood (9:4). With the Mosaic codes, however, God revealed a series of detailed regulations on the things that men are to consider either clean or unclean. These may then be divided into six classes, in accordance with the reasons that seem to be involved in their selection.

---

[35]See above, p. 123.
[36]Cf. Vos's condemnation of such views of sacred totemism, *ibid*, pp. 192-193.

1) Some items are catalogued as unclean because of hygienic reasons. An outstanding example is the uncleanness of leprosy and of everything that is associated with it (Lev. 13-14). Factors other than that of a simple quarantine may also have been involved; for example, on rare occasions leprosy is associated with spiritual failure (cf. Num. 12:10). But to assert that "sanitary significance the distinction does not have"[37] is to fly in the face, both of the medical facts of the situation,[38] and of the known hygienic sensitivity of the Hebrew people (cf. Deut. 23:13).

2) A closely related explanation of the Old Testament thought on uncleanness concerns the avoidance of bodily injury (Lev. 19:28). That no iron, for example, was permitted to be used in the preparations for the construction of Israel's sanctuaries (Ex. 20:25; I Kings 6:7) may have been caused by the association of iron with the destructive instruments of war, and the avoidance of leaven may have arisen because of the association of this substance with physical corruption.

3) Another reason proposed for the Pentateuchal cleanness laws is that "certain animals, like snakes and birds of prey, awaken a natural aversion in the human mind."[39] Indeed, some of the foods that were prohibited as unclean appear equally loathsome today (Lev. 11:20, 41).

4) Of a similar, but more serious nature, is the fact that ethical questions may enter into consideration in reference to certain categories of Old Testament uncleanness (cf. Isa. 1:15). The prohibited degrees of marriage (Lev. 18:6), for example, forbid the impurity of incest; and the injunction against wearing forbidden clothes of the opposite sex seems to be a safeguard against homosexuality (Deut. 22:5; Lev. 20:13). Again, the reason for a woman's uncleanness and separation when ill or in the period that followed upon child birth is, at least in part, humanitarian, for the purpose of relieving her of what would have been her normal responsibilities (Lev. 12:1, 2). The direct application of these first four categories of cleanness should be clear in respect to modern Christian practice.

5) Somewhat less obvious in their explanation are the regulations that were designed to enforce holiness. The basic concept of holiness is that of "separation"; see above, topic 9-C. The prohibition, therefore, of the wearing of garments of mixed materials and the prohibition of sowing of mixed seed, while without justification by

---

[37]Vos, op. cit., p. 190.
[38]Some have indeed questioned the possibility of true leprosy (Hansen's disease) being known to Moses; cf. the pamphlet by Robert G. Cochrane of American Leprosy Missions, "Biblical Leprosy—A Suggested Interpretation," p. 3. The presence, however, of this disease in the days of the Old Testament and the accuracy of the Biblical statements relative to it have been confirmed medically by Harold M. Spinks, "Leprosy in Ancient Hebrew Times," Journal of the American Scientific Affliction, 11:1 (March, 1959), pp. 17-20 (with bibliography).
[39]Ibid., p. 199.

nature, are yet explained as striking pictures of this religious stress upon holiness in Israel (Lev. 19:19). Ultimately, holy separation involves the content of the entire unregenerate world. The natural life is both insufficient before God and is, indeed, hostile to Him. As an indication of this fact, sexual relations, while by no means wrong in themselves,[40] still kept a man from what was holy (I Sam. 21:4). Everything, moreover, which was connected with birth was treated as symbolical of original depravity, and was hence considered to be unclean (Lev. 12:1-8; 15:2, 3; cf. II Sam. 11:4). In a similar way, death, which comes as a result of sin, was designated as a matter from which God's people were to maintain complete separation, or "holiness" (Num. 19:11; Ex. 22:31).[41] Again, the lands of foreigners, pagan peoples who lived outside God's redemptive testament, were automatically identified as unclean in the eyes of God's people (Amos 7:17). Israel's holiness, furthermore, demanded their separation from all things that possessed idolatrous connotations (Ex. 23:13). For example, the pagan ritual, harmless in itself, of boiling a kid in its mother's milk was strictly prohibited (v. 19). The principles, however, that lie behind the specific cases of this fifth category of cleanness are still binding upon Christians today, who must "Abstain from all appearance of evil" (I Thess. 5:22).

6) Scripture mentions, finally, certain matters that are seemingly without inherent significance in respect to cleanness but which were chosen, almost arbitrarily, as media through which Israel's faith could be demonstrated and by the means of which their sanctity could, as a result, be promoted. Certain meat, for example, was prohibited to the people because it was reserved for holy sacrifices (Lev. 7:25). Compare also the repeated daily "sanctification" (the washing) of the clothes at Sinai, prior to the revelation of the testament (Ex. 19:10). Such ceremonial matters were typical foreshadowings of the work of Christ and are no longer binding upon Christians today (Col. 2:16, 17).

Often, indeed, one object may have involved several of the above reasons for its prohibition as unclean. Thus, cutting oneself (Lev. 19:28; Deut. 14:1) was both harmful to the body (#2) and it also carried pagan connotations (#5; I Kings 18:28); observe the way in which the later Jews continued to practice it in pagan-like mourning, despite God's prohibition (Jer. 16:6; 41:15). But the rule against cutting the corners of the beard was a purely anti-pagan injunction (#5; Lev. 19:27) and is thus no longer binding upon Christians, except in principle, even though it is elsewhere joined directly with the previous prohibition (21:5), which *is* still binding! For all such

---

[40]See above, p. 218.
[41]This is a more worthy explanation than that of the pagan concept of harmful ghosts hovering near dead bodies, cf. Vos, *op. cit.*, p. 195.

cases of uncleanness, the law then provided various purification rites, with washings, sacrifice, and other procedures.

Subsequent Old Testament materials contribute little to the development of the cleanness laws, beyond these detailed Pentateuchal revelations. Isaiah in the eighth century was the first to lend special emphasis to the Mosaic prohibition against eating swine's flesh (Isa. 65:4; 66:17), which later became one of the most distinctive of Israel's purity laws. The prophets of the exile gave particular stress to the matters of cleanness (Ezek. 4:16; 20:12, 21, etc.); they had, after all, been forcibly deprived of most of their other means of religious expression. Daniel's refusal to be defiled with the king's dainties[42] constitutes a well known example of exilic loyalty to these Mosaic standards (Dan. 1:8).

For Further Reading:

Bernard Ramm, *Protestant Biblical Interpretation.* Revised edition; Boston: W. A. Wilde Co., 1956. Chapter 9 is an up-to-date, evangelical survey of the subject of typology.

Walther Eichrodt, "The Right Interpretation of the Old Testament . . . a Study of Jeremiah 7:1-15," *Theology Today,* 5:3 (Oct., 1948), 327-339. On the nature of the Temple, with parallels in the New Testament and today.

W. O. E. Oesterley and T. H. Robinson, *Hebrew Religion: Its Origin and Development.* 2nd edition; New York: The Macmillan Co., 1937. Contains a radical discussion of Old Testament cleanness as an indication of Israel's evolutionary development out of primitive superstitions.

27. Ceremonial: Actions*

A. PRIESTHOOD. Although the first ceremonial action to be revealed in Biblical history was that of sacrifice, one must yet give prior consideration to the concepts of priesthood and of ceremonial atonement, both of which underlie and hence serve to explain the conduct of the sacrificial service. The Old Testament word for priest, *kōhēn,* appears to possess the fundamental meaning of "an authorized minister"; and the term may therefore be used to identify a non-religious government official (II Sam. 8:18). Ordinarily, however, the significance of *kōhēn* is restricted to God's authorized minister (cf. Heb. 5:4), the man who serves at the altar. The prophet speaks for God to the people; but it is the priest who speaks for the people to God.

---

* BIBLE READING: Leviticus 17; Genesis 17

Collateral Reading: Vos, *Biblical Theology,* pp. 103-108, 172-190.
Theophile J. Meek, *Hebrew Origins,* pp. 119-147.

[42] As ceremonially unclean, but not necessarily harmful to the body.

The primary functions of the priest were thus to officiate at the sanctuary (Deut. 18:5) and to pray on behalf of the people (Joel 2:17). Three other functions, however, also appear. 1) The priest was expected, in personal living, to set an example of faithfulness to the testament (Deut. 33:9). The priestly consecration therefore included an anointing upon the candidate's ear, thumb, and toe (Ex. 29:20): rightly to hear the word, to carry it out, and to walk therein throughout life. His need for "wholeness" in devotion was further symbolized by the exclusion from the altar of those who suffered from physical impairments (Lev. 21:17). 2) The priest, and particularly the high priest, was also to "enquire" of God for divine oracles. This function is specifically associated with his wearing of the urim and the thummin, the precious stones of the priestly breastplate;[1] for the man who wore these insignia officiated before the ark of the testament and thus came into the closest possible contact with Israel's testamental God (cf. Judg. 20:27). Because of the high priest's oracular status, this setting of stones came in turn to be described as "the breastplate of judgment" (Ex. 28:30). 3) The priest, finally, was responsible to teach the law (Lev. 10:11; Mic. 3:11; Mal. 2:7). He might even be required to travel about in his performance of this ministry (II Chron. 17:9). These latter two functions, of revelation and interpretation, made it natural for the priests to serve also as judges (Deut. 17:9).

In the tracing of the history of Biblical priesthood, it appears that during the earliest primeval times any man could serve as his own priest (Gen. 4:3). But already in the days of Noah the priestly ministration appears to have become the responsibility of the patriarchal head in any given family (8:20; compare Gen. 12:8 and Job 1:5, of the next period). In times of distress or emergency, however, the laity could still serve as priests. This fact is illustrated, for example, by the conduct of certain laymen of the consolidation period when they were encountered by special theophanies (Judg. 6:18; 13:16) or by the activities of the northern prophets of the disruption period, after the division of Israel, when the north was isolated from the services of the true Levitical priests (I Kings 18:30). Melchizedek, the priest-king of Jerusalem, possessed neither recorded genealogy, nor dates of service, nor limitation of life; and he thus exists as a type of Christ's non-Levitical priesthood (Ps. 110:4; Heb. 7).[2] In the days prior to Israel's arrival at Sinai, certain national leaders seem also to have occupied the office of priest (Ex. 19:22).

At Sinai, God restricted the legitimate priesthood to the family

[1] T. J. Meek, *Hebrew Origins*, p. 148, therefore concludes, "the Hebrew priests, like those of other peoples, were in the first instance shamans and owed their priestly office to their supposed possession of mantic power." For a more Biblical appreciation of this function, however, see above, p. 48.
[2] See above, p. 48.

and to the descendants of Aaron the brother of Moses, of the tribe of Levi (Ex. 28:1; 40:12-15; Num. 16:17; 17:8). For efficacious priesthood can alone exist when it is granted as a gift from the Lord (Num. 18:7); only God, that is, stands in the position to select the man who is to have access to Himself (Heb. 5:4). As Yahweh's chosen high priest, Aaron thus became the leader in the offering up of national sacrifice and the chief representative before God of the people of Israel. He wore the very names of the twelve tribes inscribed on his vestments (Ex. 28:12, 21, 29), so as literally to "bring them before God" as he appeared to accomplish divine propitiation and reconciliation (v. 38). Aaron continued to occupy the post of high priest, despite his failure at Sinai in reference to the golden calf (32:4, 21).

God's first revelation in respect to subordinate priests resulted in the naming of the four sons of Aaron for service in the Tabernacle. But Nadab and Abihu, soon after their appointment, were slain by Yahweh for violating their office (Lev. 10:2). Scripture thus furnishes a compelling initial revelation of the need for holiness on the part of priests (Lev. 21). It is possible that Nadab and Abihu may have been under the influence of liquor at the time, for its prohibition in reference to officiating priests appears in the immediately following context (10:9). Thus, out of Aaron's sons, Eleazar and Ithamar were left; and, unlike the charismatically appointed prophets, descent from these two men continued to be the basis upon which Israel henceforth distinguished her divinely authorized priests (Ezra 2:62). The preservation of Aaron's family in its position of perpetual priesthood was then guaranteed by the Levitical testament (Num. 25:13).[3]

Next in rank to the Aaronic priests, stood their fellow tribesmen, the Levites, who served as assistants before the sons of Aaron (Num. 8:13). Actually the Levites and their cattle were selected by Yahweh to take the place of the firstborn of Israel, who owed their lives quite literally to the grace of God (cf. Ex. 13:12, on the Passover; and Num. 3:45; 8:16). The sinfulness, however, of the rank and file of the nation incapacitated Israel as a whole from divine service (18:22). Levi too, for that matter, had been cursed at one point for his fiery zeal (Gen. 34:30) and had been doomed to be scattered among his brethren (49:7). But the zeal that Levi's descendants displayed for Yahweh at the time of the golden calf apostasy had provided the basis for their restoration. For when Moses had stated the issue, "Who is on the LORD's [Yahweh's] side?" (Ex. 32:26), Levi had rallied in faithfulness to the testament (Deut. 33:9); and they were therefore honored with the corresponding privilege of religious ministry (vv. 8, 10). The Levites were later dedicated to God by the laying on of hands, almost like a sacrifice (Num. 8:10). The patriarchal curse still held, for they received no tribal district of land in

---

[3]See above, pp. 102, 103.

Canaan (Num. 18:23). But, unlike the other cursed tribe of Simeon, which was scattered to vanish, Levi was allocated most of the leading towns in Palestine, including the six cities of refuge and forty-two others (Num. 35:6). These totaled a full forty-eight urban areas, though certain non-Levites were granted places in the towns as well (Josh. 21:11, 12; Lev. 25:33). Thirteen of these centers went specifically to the priests (Josh. 21:4). God had thus become the "inheritance" of Levi (Deut. 10:9). They were endowed with Israel's tithes and offerings, so as to be free to serve Him (Num. 18:21, 24-26). They were indeed scattered, but in such a way as to influence and to direct the lives of their fellow Israelites.

Specifically, "Yahweh set apart Levi to bear the ark of the testament" (Deut. 10:8; 31:9). It is true that the ministry of the altar and of the area within the veil was restricted to the Aaronic priests (Num. 18:7); the Levite Korah, as a result, died when he attempted to usurp these priestly functions (16:18). But the three Levitical clans of Kohath, Gershon, and Merari were appointed to specific tasks in the transportation of the Tabernacle and of its furniture (1:50). The Kohathites, who made up the clan of Moses and Aaron, held the honored assignment with respect to the major holy objects; but precise obedience was required, on pain of death (4:15; cf. the death of Uzzah, II Sam. 6:7). The Kohathites were not even to look at the holy things until the priests had insured that they were properly covered for the march (Num. 4:20).

Like most of the aspects of Israel's religion, the institution of the priesthood suffered injury as a result of the conquest of Canaan. The Levites did not retain possession of most of their allocated cities and were forced to wander about the country (Judg. 17:7; 19:1; I Sam. 1:1). More serious was the theological impact of Canaanitish religious practice. Even faithful Gideon came to feel no qualms about assuming to himself certain of the priestly functions; for he made an ephod, the priest's surplice that was decked with gold (Ex. 28:6-15), and employed it for a worship that was contrary to the law (Judg. 8:24-27). Eli's sons became so corrupt (I Sam. 2:12) that the line of Eli, which seems to have been that of Aaron's fourth son Ithamar, was cursed of God (vv. 30-36). Saul then slaughtered both the priests (I Sam. 22:18) and the temple slaves (II Sam. 21:1). These latter consisted of the Canaanites of Gibeon. For though the Gibeonites had saved their lives by trickery in the days of Joshua, they had been reduced to the status n'thīnīm, "given ones," for the sanctuary (Judg. 9:23; cf. Ezra 2:58).

David found himself with two high priests: Abiathar, who was presumably of the line of Eli and Ithamar, and who ministered before the ark in Jerusalem, and Zadok, of the line of Eleazar, who served at the Tabernacle in Gibeon (II Sam. 20:25). Scripture contains certain references to the king's "sacrificing" (II Sam. 6:17, and perhaps I Sam. 13:9); but these verses seem to indicate merely his designating a priest to perform the propitiatory act, and not to his personal execution of the sacrificial ceremony. David, more than anyone else, was responsible for the priestly organization that officiated at Israel's sanctuary. He systematized the priests into twenty-four rotating courses (I Chron. 24:3-19), and he assigned new functions to the 38,000 Levites, in ways appropriate to their now settled organization (chapters 23-26). Radical reconstructions, that seek to discover an opposition between David's Levites and the "image worshiping" Aaronic priests, have been advocated by writers such as Theophile Meek:

> Thus were the Levites ensconced in a position of supreme priestly authority in the religion and there came a temporary eclipse of the bull cult and its Aaronite priesthood. This did not mean the suppression of the bull cult nor of any other; it simply meant that Yahwism was now the state religion and Yahweh the national god. In their local sanctuaries the people could and did worship what gods they would.[4]

But though no evangelical would take Meek's theories seriously, it is true that the Levites were given the leadership in the new musical service which was created by David and which constituted a matter of his particular concern (I Chron. 15:16; II Chron. 29:25). David also made official the status of the n'thīnim (Ezra 8:20), and to this group Solomon proceeded to make further additions (2:58). The Davidic organization of the priestly courses was reinstituted after the exile (Neh. 12:1-7) and was perpetuated on into New Testament days (Luke 1:5).

Solomon, at the beginning of the disruption period, fulfilled God's curse upon the line of Eli by driving the latter's great-grandson Abiathar out of the high-priesthood (I Kings 2:27), and leaving Zadok, the prophesied "faithful priest" (I Sam. 2:35), in sole authority over the Temple. From the name "Zadok" comes the New Testament title for the priestly party, the "Sadducees." Jeroboam's illegal sanctuaries at Dan and Bethel brought about a corresponding appointment of illegitimate, non-Levitical priests (I Kings 12:31). The true but castoff priests and Levites then fled south and so came to strengthen the religious life of Jerusalem (II Chron. 11:13, 14; 13:9). The wholesome influence also in political life that could be exercised by faithful priests is witnessed by the revolt that was engineered by Jehoiada, which forced the wicked queen Athaliah off the throne of Judah in 835 B.C. (II Kings 11). However, Jehoiada's son Zechariah suffered a martyr's death while opposing the idolatry of her successor some years thereafter (II Chron. 24:21, 22).

During the exile, Daniel by inspiration predicted the career of the famous pre-Maccabean high priest, Onias III, and foretold his

---

[4]*Op. cit.*, p. 147.

position as the "prince of the testament" (Dan. 11:22). But Daniel also predicted that Onias would be overwhelmed and broken. This last prophecy was fulfilled by the latter's murder in 172 B.C. by Menelaus, one of his thoroughly corrupt successors in the priesthood.[5] For with organized, inherited religion there exists the ever-present danger of a lack of spirituality, or worldliness, and even of outright apostasy. Hezekiah, in the eighth century, found that "the Levites were more upright in heart to sanctify themselves than the priests" (II Chron. 29:34), and his contemporary Isaiah had to criticize sharply the drunkenness of Judah's priestly leaders (Isa. 28:7). The most consistent opponents of Jeremiah in the later prophetic period, as this man of God attempted to revive Israel's tottering faith, were the official priests (Jer. 1:18; 20:1; 23:33). Especially had Jeremiah to face the hostility of his own family, the deposed line of Abiathar, whose means of living (as extra-legal, local priests) seems to have been threatened by Jeremiah's activity in support of Josiah's reformation. For one of the goals of Josiah was the re-establishing of the one exclusive central sanctuary for all Judah (11:6, 21).

Ezekiel too described the thorough-going declension of the official priesthood (Ezek. 8:6; 22:26); but during the course of the exile he noted that the Levites had degraded themselves more than the Zadokite priests, even becoming guilty of the crime of idolatry (44:10; 48:11). In 538 B.C., after the exile, relatively few of the Levites returned to Palestine (Ezra 2:40-42), as contrasted with the comparatively numerous representatives of at least four of the courses of the priests (vv. 36-39). Ezra had difficulty getting any Levites at all to join in the second return, in 458 (8:15). With the reconstruction of the post-exilic Temple, the priestly class were promised a valid, redemptive access to God (Zech. 3:7). But the urim and thummin were no more (Ezra 2:63); and, in the fifth century B.C., priestly failures brought about an extensive corruption of the Levitical testament (Mal. 1:10; 2:8; Neh. 13:29).

The Old Testament priesthood constituted a type of Christ (Heb. 8:1), who is our "merciful and faithful high priest in things pertaining to God." He it was who performed the ultimate and real "propitiation for the sins of the people" (2:17), and there seems to have been a strong priestly element in the Early Church (Acts 6:7). Yet even at their best, the Old Testament high priests had to bring forward offerings for their own sins, as well as for those of the people (Lev. 16:6; Heb. 5:3). At worst, however, Aaron forged idols and conspired against Moses (Ex. 32:4; Num. 12:1); Eliashib strengthened the enemies of Israel and undercut the reforms of Nehemiah (Neh. 13: 4, 28); Caiaphas and the Jewish Sanhedrin persecuted the apostles and crucified the Lord Jesus Himself (Acts 4:27, 29); Leo X and

[5]Payne, *An Outline of Hebrew History,* p. 182.

the Roman Curia condemned Martin Luther as a heretic; and the leaders of the modern councils of churches seek to ban evangelical preachers from chaplaincies, pulpits, and from radio time, daily crucifying our Lord afresh. Prophecy does indeed suggest the reappearance of Levitical priests in the future testament of peace (Jer. 33:18); but it seems just as well that the present new testament of the Church is characterized, not by a hierarchy, but by the universal priesthood of believers (I Peter 2:5, 9; Rev. 5:10), even as Jeremiah had predicted (Jer. 31:34).

B. CEREMONIAL ATONEMENT. The principle of atonement has been already defined in topic 19 under the subject, "The Death of the Testator." In the above treatment, it was concluded that the verb *kippēr*, to "atone," comes from the root that means to "cover" and that it carries the primary thought of propitiation. Atonement thus serves to placate the wrath of God by transferring the punishment that is due the sinner to another "covering" object.[6] This basic truth is then depicted throughout the Bible by a series of ceremonial terms, objects, and activities. Together with the doctrine of priesthood, which concerns the human agency through which the atonement is accomplished, the idea of ceremonial propitiation (this Section) lies as fundamental to one's appreciation of the details of sacrifice, as these are historically revealed in Scripture (Section C, that follows).

From the earliest description of primeval sacrifice (Gen. 8:21), the Old Testament's enacted symbolism of atonement is explained as a *rē' ah han-nīhôah,* a "smell that placates." In Genesis 8, Noah's offerings concern man's protection from God's wrath as displayed in the Flood. So too in Job 1:5 and 42:8 (actions that were carried out in the patriarchal period), the ceremonies of sanctification, sacrifice, and prayer are performed to the end that God may not deal with sinful men "according to their folly." In the time of Moses, the mass-dedication of the Levites was designed to accomplish a substitutionary atonement for the Hebrew nation "that there be no plague among the children of Israel, when they come nigh unto the sanctuary" (Num. 8:19). In order to give repeated emphasis to this need for divine propitiation, Moses insisted that whenever an animal was to be slaughtered, it be presented through these Levites as an offering on the altar of the Tabernacle (Lev. 17:4); and even then, the animals had to be clean beasts (Lev. 27:11), that is, without "guilt" of their own, so as to teach in symbol what God requires in the way of a sin-bearing substitute.

In every case of ceremonial atonement[7] God's judgment of death as the punishment for sin was depicted by the shedding of (life-)

---

[6]See above, pp. 249, 250, and cf. Vos, *Biblical Theology,* pp. 183-185. Through atonement, the sinner is not just protected; rather, the guilt of his sin is actually obliterated by means of this transference.
[7]Cf. the discussion in topic 19 of the Passover and the Sinaitic testament.

blood. Even the preparation of the ashes of the red heifer, which were used to produce purifying water (Num. 19:10), involved a preceding manipulation of the animal's blood (vv. 3, 4); and the whole procedure thus became a type of the redemption finally accomplished by the shed blood of Christ (Heb. 9:13, 14). The other purifying libations and washings (cf. I Sam. 7:6) likewise pointed to the true cleansing that is effectuated in our Lord (Heb. 9:10). A particularly clear illustration of the substitutionary and symbolic character of the atonement ceremonial of the Old Testament is the enactment that was revealed by Moses in Deuteronomy 21:4-8. These verses describe the means for delivering from the burden of guilt a town near which a man has been murdered:

> And the elders of that city shall bring down a heifer into a valley with running water, and shall break the heifer's neck. . . . And all the elders shall wash their hands over the heifer whose neck was broken in the valley; and they shall answer and say . . . Forgive, oh Yahweh, thy people Israel. . . . And the blood shall be forgiven them.

The guilt for the crime was thus symbolically transferred to the animal and then carried away by the flowing stream.

In reference to the type of victim whose blood was to be shed, Moses stated that pigeons would be considered sufficient for those who lacked the means of purchasing a whole lamb (Lev. 5:7; 12:8); and this considerate provision was later illustrated by the offering presented by Joseph and Mary at the birth of Christ Himself (Luke 2:24). Such bloodless offerings as the law prescribed were limited to special matters, "meal-offerings" (cf. Num. 5:15), which were designed only to accompany other blood sacrifices. The one exception is found in Leviticus 5:11, where fine flour is designated as a substitute for blood, for those who were too poor to afford even pigeons. Hebrews 9:22 apparently has this verse in mind when it reads, "According to the law, *I may almost say,* all things are cleansed with blood." But, since even in this case it is the atoning death of Christ that is symbolized, to the best of the offerer's ability, the passage adds, "and apart from shedding of blood there is no remission." As a further illustration of the truth of Christ's propitiation, the census money, which was given as a ransom for the souls of the people, was instituted so that there should be no *plague* upon Israel (Ex. 30:12). It was then called "atonement money" (v. 16); and it was used to provide for the services of the tent of meeting, where the animals were killed in the regular sacrifices. The very historical basis for the Levitical testament lay in the making of atonement by Phinehas (Num. 25:13), so that God's wrath was stayed (vv. 8, 10). The propitiating blood shed in this case, however, was that of the guilty couple themselves (vv. 7, 8).

The most significant single object in Moses' rites of ceremonial atonement was the *kappóreth*, the "atoning cover," or "mercy seat," on the ark. This "atoning cover" consisted of a large plate of pure gold on which two cherubim were mounted, and above which the very cloud of God's presence rested (Ex. 25:17-20). But though the plate served as a literal "cover" for the ark (v. 21), the intensive verbal stem from which the name *kappóreth* is derived indicates that the meaning of this term must be that of propitiatory atonement, and not simply of physical covering. As the climax, accordingly, to the annual day of Atonement service (see next topic, 28-C-5), the high priest would sprinkle blood (substitutionary life) on the atoning cover (Lev. 16:14). In this way an intervening shield was introduced between the Shekinah, the presence of God, and the tables of the Decalogue below, which stood for the moral conditions of the testament, and which are ever being broken by sinful man. It was because of this merciful provision of God, by which He allowed the ceremonial fulfillment to make up for Israel's moral deficiency, that it became possible for God to commune with men over the ark (Ex. 25:22). The explanation for this particular ritual, and indeed the ultimate fact which made the whole ceremonial a truly effective and valid sacrament, is that the *kappóreth* stood as a type of Christ. Its translation into Greek, *hilastérion* ("propitiatory"), is employed in Romans 3:25 as follows: "God hath set forth Jesus Christ as a *hilastérion*, [an 'atoning cover'] through faith in His blood." For the lives of the animals that Israel offered up in sacrifice could never really atone for moral failure. Beasts could not assume into themselves, and so obliterate, God's wrath against guilty men (Heb. 9:9). But Christ's offering of Himself did, once and for all, make the effective atonement for guilt (v. 14), as He bore the penalty for our sins (Isa. 53:5, 6; I Peter 2:24).

C. SACRIFICE. The testament is made by sacrifice (Ps. 50:5). Its effectuation was to be accomplished, fundamentally, by the sacrificial death of the Testator (cf. Gen. 3:15 on). But prior to that event, the testament became valid, as far as any given individual's participation in it was concerned, when that individual responded to God's gracious bequest, through the ceremonial performance of typical sacrifice. One of the first recorded events subsequent to the primeval fall is the offering of sacrifices by Cain and Abel (Gen. 4:3, 4; cf. Noah's similar action after the Flood, 8:20). The term in Genesis 4 is *minhā* (v. 3), which here has the general sense of "sacrifice," but not the specific sense of "meal offering," which it was later to acquire in the Mosaic period (see below). An equally general term that came into early use is *zévah*, "sacrifice" (31:54).

The question that immediately arises in respect to this first known sacrifice, and one that is crucial for one's understanding of the system of sacrifice as a whole, is why Abel's offering was accepta-

ble to God and Cain's was not. As has been previously n
attitude of the offerers constituted an important factor in
Abel was characterized both by faith (Heb. 11:4) and by ιαιu..
demonstration in good works, while his brother was not (I John 3:12).
These points are made clear from the Genesis context itself (4:6, 7).
But the form of the sacrifice seems also to have been involved, along
with the attitudes of mind that the men possessed; for "Yahweh had
respect unto Abel *and* to his offering" (4:4). This conclusion about
form is then confirmed by the words of Hebrews 11:4, which state
that "By faith Abel offered a *more excellent sacrifice.*" The comparative degree of the adjective here employed shows that the "excellence"
must refer to the sacrifice, and not to the attitude; for that which lacks
faith can hardly be styled "less" excellent; it is not excellent at all
(v. 6)! Cain's *sacrifice,* however, was excellent — fruit grown from
God's own ground — though less excellent than the firstlings out of
Abel's flock. The analogy of Scripture, furthermore, demonstrates that
the crucial element in the superior excellence of Abel's sacrifice consisted primarily, not in the fact that his lambs were the first of his
increase, but in the fact that their sacrifice involved the giving up of
substitutionary life: for "without the shedding of blood there is no
remission" (Heb. 9:22). The implications that then arise from this
incident are two-fold: 1) that there must have occurred some revelation from God, perhaps in connection with His prediction of the
bruising of the heel of the seed of the woman,[9] which specified the
necessity of shed blood in any atoning sacrifice that was to be considered as valid by God; and 2) that bare faith is not the only factor
that counts in religion. Man must possess that saving faith which is
demonstrated by a mode of worship which is in compliance with the
will of God. Sincerity alone is not enough; there must be sincere faith
in the right thing, specifically in the blood (of Christ). As John 14:6
explains, no man cometh unto the Father but by Him.

The patriarchs offered up frequent sacrifices;[10] but the actual
record of these acts contributes little, by way of additional explanation, to our understanding of the subject. Genesis 15:9, 10 depicts
the sacrificial loss of life that is central in the making of the testament,
and it proceeds daringly to identify this sacrifice with that of the
very life of deity (v. 17).[11] The need for such a death is then brought
out in striking fashion by the events that are associated with Abraham's sacrifice of Isaac. Genesis 22:2 demonstrates the fact that God
is due everything that we have, including our own lives. Verse 3
records how Abraham submitted to God, immediately, and was willing to offer up to Him even his son, Isaac. But instead, the life of

[8]See above, p. 304.
[9]Gen. 3:15, though actually no such revelation has been preserved in Scripture.
[10]See above, p. 360 and footnote 24.
[11]See above, pp. 82, 97.

another (represented by the ram, v. 13) is given in Isaac's place; and the necessity, or even the possibility, of human sacrifice is put away (cf. Ex. 13:13). The Mosaic law specifically forbade the practice of child sacrifice, which was so common among the Canaanites (Lev. 18:21). The apparent demand to the contrary for the offering up of the firstborn (as this is stated in Ex. 22:29) had, moreover, already been defined as to its intent in respect to children by the laws which provided for their redemption (13:13; cf. 34:20). An indirect witness, furthermore, to its prohibition, arises from within the patriarchal period itself, in the form of the pride and joy with which the arrival of a firstborn child was greeted (Gen. 48:18; 49:3), not with sorrow, as if its death before an idol were impending.

Moses became the chief human instrument through whom God granted His revelations on the Biblical concept of sacrifices. The Mosaic law provides both for their theoretical explanation and also for their practical procedures. Sacrifices are called in general *qorbān*, "offerings," for *qorbān* means the things that are "brought near" and dedicated to God (Lev. 1:2; cf. Mark 7:11). But why are they brought? The evidence presented through Moses has led to four main theories for the explanation of Old Testament sacrifice.[12] 1) Leviticus 3:11 speaks of sacrifice as "the food of the offering made by fire unto Yahweh." The most crude liberal explanation is, accordingly, that sacrifice was intended to be a meal, nourishing the deity; compare Genesis 8:20, "Yahweh smelled the sweet savor," and then, in "gratitude," acted more favorably toward man (!). Such an explanation was undoubtedly the concept that was widely held in the ancient world even by such advanced pagans as the Babylonians;[13] but it is impossible as a serious interpretation for the true teaching of Scripture. Such a theory would be opposed to the consistent view of the Bible concerning the eminence of Yahweh. That God needed the sacrifices is outrightly denied (Ps. 50:9-13; Isa. 40:16); and milk products, which are the most important kind of food for herdsmen like the Hebrews, are significantly absent from Moses' sacrificial elements. The fact that "food" descriptions occur in even the latest of the Old Testament writings (cf. Ezek. 44:7; Mal. 1:7) is proof that, while Israel might have adopted the *terminology* of Canaan, this language could only have been understood poetically, and never realistically. The latter idea would have opposed the whole Biblical concept of God.

2) In circles somewhat less liberal, Old Testament sacrifice is generally explained as a gift. This second theory contains an element

[12]See, for example, Vos's discussion, *op. cit.*, pp. 174-178.
[13]Note the "hungry gods" in the Babylonian corruption of the flood record: "The gods smelled the savor, the gods smelled the sweet savor. The gods above the sacrificer collected like flies"; George A. Barton, *Archaeology and the Bible*, p. 330.

of truth, for the gifts of the "thank-offerings" occupied a recognized place in Israel's sacrificial system (Lev. 7:12-15). Vos accordingly states, "The two main ends served by sacrifice are expiation and consecration."[14] Moreover, though Vos' definition may not be a complete or a balanced one, Scripture does describe a number of offerings of consecration (such as Hannah's after the birth of Samuel) which served indeed as sincere gifts of gratitude to God (I Sam. 1: 24-27). A similar motive lay behind David's refusal to dedicate to God that which cost him nothing (II Sam. 24:24). But the "consecrated-gift" explanation fails to account for the Mosaic stress upon the necessity of blood. For, basically, it is the estrangement that exists between God and guilty, "bloody" man that establishes the need for the whole sacrificial procedure, and that then explains the details of the ceremonies as they were actually carried out. Furthermore, neither human sacrifice nor cultic prostitution are to be found in Israel, though both were prominent in the pagan gift-sacrifice theory. "Gifts" cannot, therefore, be considered as the fundamental explanation for the Biblical offerings.

3) The Canaanites considered sacrifice as a means of communion with deity, and that in a very physical sense: they ate the deity's blood, or they entered into covenants of blood-brotherhood with it. But though Scripture surely believes in communion with God (Ex. 24:11), this blessed communion transpires in a moral and spiritual sphere only. It arises, moreover, as a result of the sacrifice, not as the explanation by which to account for the sacrifice. The exalted nature of God, the free Testator, could never be made subject to such materialistic compulsion.

4) The true Biblical explanation is that sacrifice is propitiatory, or atoning.[15] It was, for example, the offerings that sealed the Sinaitic testament for the reconciliation of God and man (Ex. 24:4-8). Furthermore, each detailed stage of the sacrificial ceremony, as it was carried out in Israel, stands as typical of some aspect of the propitiatory work of Jesus Christ (Heb. 10:11, 12). First, in the choice of the sacrificial animal and of the other materials that were involved, there existed a general prohibition against defects (Lev. 22:21); for only One who was perfectly pure could bear the sins of others (I Pet. 1:19). Leaven or yeast, for example, was in most cases excluded, for the fermentation (leavened rising) of the baked things was suggestive of corruption (2:11). Salt, however, was required to be pres-

---

[14]Op. cit., p. 173.
[15]Vos correctly notes that consecration had existed as a necessary obligation, laid upon men prior to their sin in Eden. But with the fall, the requirement of atonement had become the more basic necessity for mankind; so that subsequently the externalized form even of consecration took on the bloody character that had arisen as a result of sin, loc. cit. To claim, however, that previously "no symbol intervenes between the worshipping creature and the Creator" perhaps fails to assign proper weight to the sacramental tree of life, and to other related matters.

ent, as a symbol of the permanently preserved salvation that was mediated by the testament (Lev. 2:13). Second, in the ritual the offerer presented his sacrifice and laid his hands on its head (1:4), thus appointing it as a proxy for himself (cf. Num. 27:18-21), to take the sinner's place (cf. 8:18, 19). The true substitute that this rite pictured was Christ, the Lamb of God whom the Father made to be sin for us (II Cor. 5:21).

As the third step in the Mosaic ceremony, the animal was immediately killed (Lev. 1:5). Its death took the place of the sinner's death; it was punished in his stead (Num. 6:11; cf. Lev. 19:20, 21). The particular symbol of the surrendered life was its blood (Gen. 9:4), "given to you upon the altar to make atonement for your souls: for it is the blood that maketh atonement by reason of the life" (Lev. 17:11). It is true that these daily, bloody ministrations by the priests were incapable, in themselves, of ever taking away men's sins (Heb. 10:11); but they stood as types of Christ's once-and-for-all sacrificial death (v. 12). Fourth, the sacrificed life was then committed to God by sprinkling and burning on the altar (Lev. 1:6-9).[16] For example, at the ceremonial ratification of the testament at Sinai, half of the blood of the offerings was scattered upon the altar (Ex. 24:6): it served as the ransom price paid to Yahweh, and it anticipated the work of Christ, "who offered Himself without spot to God," for the purging of His people (Heb. 9:14).

In the fifth and last place came a ceremonial indication of the fact that God's fellowship with men had actually been restored. Thus in Exodus 24:6, 8, the remaining half of the sacrificial blood was gathered into basins and literally sprinkled out over the people. As Moses explained, "Behold the blood of the testament, which Yahweh hath made with you." They knew themselves, by experience, to be under the blood! At the dedication of the brazen altar, the sign of Yahweh's acceptance of the atonement took the form of celestial fire which descended from God and fell upon the altar, thus sealing this sacred instrument as divinely efficacious (Lev. 9:24; cf. Judg. 6:19-21). The penalty of death had been paid, and the sacrifice had therefore become acceptable to the Lord. This God-given fire was then kept perpetually alive and burning (Lev. 6:12) as if preserving in its symbol the truth of Israel's favorable reception by Yahweh. The most common indication of men's acceptance, however, lay in a communion meal that followed upon the sacrificial rite (Ex. 24:11). The eating of the sacrifice served as a tangible proof of reconciliation, as God and the restored sinner sat down together at the same table. This ritual truth continues to be expressed today in the sacrament of the

---

[16]The objection that the guilt-laden blood might not come upon the clean altar of God is obviated by the fact that death of the animal had, symbolically, made full satisfaction for the guilt. Cf. Oehler, *Theology of the Old Testament*, p. 279.

Lord's Supper (I Cor. 10:16). In some of the sacrifices, spec...
of the "guilt offerings," the removal of men's sins was symbolized by
the taking away of the sacrificial victim's body and by its burning
outside the camp.

The ultimate demonstration, however, of God's acceptance of
atonement was provided by the empty tomb on that first Easter Sunday morning, when Christ was "raised for our justification" (Rom.
4:25). The living Savior becomes the final proof of the reality of
God's reconciliation with men. In Biblical theory, then, it is Christ's
propitiation that lies at the heart of sacrifice. God, the loving Father,
rejoices in forgiveness (Ps. 103:13; Hos. 11:8, 9); but, because of the
continued sin of mankind, the people were never allowed to approach
His holy presence without atonement first having been made. God's
warning was explicit: "None shall appear before Me empty" (Ex.
23:15).

Moses revealed not only the theory and the steps of sacrifice, but
also the ultimate number and variety of divinely sanctioned offerings.
All legitimate sacrifices had to be presented at the central sanctuary
(Deut. 12:6, 7), where God revealed Himself (Ex. 20:24). All varieties, moreover, involved some form of burning on the altar and could
therefore be called *ishshe*, a "fire offering" (Lev. 1:9). But there
existed within the general Mosaic concept of sacrifice five distinct
categories of offerings, a summarization of which is presented in
Appendix F, p. 526.[17]

The first three of the five Mosaic sacrifices may be grouped together under the title of "sweet savor" offerings (Lev. 1:9; 2:2; 3:5).
The Hebrew phrase for sweet savor, *rē' ah nîhôah*, is an anthropomorphic expression that means "a smell that placates" (cf. Ezek. 5:13;
20:41).[18] The phrase thereby signifies God's satisfaction in respect to
the offerings and the propitiation of His divine wrath, as He graciously
accepts these sacrificial tokens of the ultimate, redemptive work of
Christ.[19] The first specific category of sweet savor sacrifice is that

[17]For further details, the following commentaries will be found particularly
helpful: Samuel H. Kellogg, *The Book of Leviticus* (The Expositor's Bible; 3rd
edition London: Hodder & Stoughton, 1899), and Charles R. Erdman, *Book of
Leviticus: an Exposition* (Westwood, N. J.: Fleming H. Revell Co., 1951). See
also the suggestions for further reading at the end of this topic.
[18]See above, p. 378; and note Kohler's forthright recognition of this truth, *Old
Testament Theology*, pp. 186-87.
[19]This classification may be supported by the greater incidence of the descriptive
term "sweet savor," in reference to the first three types of sacrifice. It does not
mean, however, that the other two types were not placating (cf. Lev. 4:31), but
simply, as W. G. Moorehead points out, that the latter were concerned more
expressly with the "guilt" of particular sins; *Studies in the Mosaic Institutions*
(New York: Fleming H. Revell Co., c. 1895), p. 132. By the same token, the
"sweet savor" offerings may not be denied a primary relevance in respect to men's
guilt (vs. *ibid.*, p. 133), a fact which their very identification as "placating" makes
clear. For a summarization of other methods of classifying the Mosaic sacrifices,
see J. J. Reeve, "Sacrifice in the Old Testament," James Orr, ed., *The International
Standard Bible Encyclopedia*, IV:2641.

of the ōlā, or "burnt offering," literally, that which "goes up," in smoke. For, as the ōlā is described in Leviticus 1, its chief distinguishing feature consists of the requirement that it be completely consumed upon the altar. It is thus styled the kālīl, the "whole burnt offering" (6:22). Furthermore, the ōlā was the sacrifice that was offered every morning and evening on the main altar of the Tabernacle, as the tāmīdh, the "continual burnt offering" (Ex. 29:38-42); and it thus symbolizes the idea of complete and continuous atonement and consecration. Noah's offering after the Flood is defined as an ōlā (Gen. 8:20). In that early period, however, the word seems there to have been used in a more general way, and Noah's sacrifice may have served as a thank-offering as well.

Minḥā is the first term that was used for sacrifice in Scripture,[20] but the connotation of the word was specialized by Moses into that of the "meal-offering"[21] (Lev. 2). This sacrifice symbolized in particular the devotion of one's person and one's property to the Lord, as a recognition of the atonement that God sovereignly accomplishes for His own. Purely human tribute could thus be called minḥā (II Sam. 8:2, 6). The meal offering did not, in itself, involve the presentation of bloody flesh; but it always appeared in company with other offerings that did. As Leviticus 23:18 puts it, Israel was to present burnt offerings "with their meal offerings." The minḥā was not adequate when offered alone, as is shown by the rejection of Cain's bloodless sacrifice. A specialized form of minḥā was the nésekh, or "drink offering" (Num. 28:7). The ultimate points of reference of these first two sweet savor sacrifices may be distinguished as follows. The ōlā typified Christ's complete obedience; it signified His penal suffering and substitutionary death. But the accompanying minḥā was then typical of His living obedience, His corresponding life of dedicated righteousness in satisfaction of the demands of the moral law.[22]

The sh'lāmīm, "peace offerings" (Lev. 3), went on to symbolize the reconciliation with God that follows upon atonement. Their distinctiveness lay in this that, except for certain fat parts that were burned, most of the portions of the peace offerings were consecrated for use in a communion meal before Yahweh.[23] They were eaten by the sacrificers themselves, rather than being completely burned or turned over to the officials of the sanctuary (7:15). Only the "wave-breast" and the "heave-thigh," which were motioned toward God at the time of offering, were reserved for the priests (7:30-34). The underprivileged

---

[20]See above, p. 380.
[21]In the old English of the Authorized Version, "meat [food, not flesh] offering." This is now quite misleading, since the minḥā was the one offering not composed of meat.
[22]Moorehead, op. cit., pp. 153-154.
[23]It was this same feature of communion (with idols!) that made it necessary for Moses to forbid Israel from eating of the Canaanitish sacrifices (Ex. 34:15).

of the land, and the Levites too, were to share in the *sh'lāmīm* (Deut. 12:18; 16:11). The "peace" that this sacrifice represented was man's peace with God, either gained or hoped for (Judg. 20:26; 21:4). It stood, moreover, not just for the negative peace of forgiveness, but also for that positive peace of all-round soundness, of prosperity and of blessing from God.[24] In the peace offering there is typified the communion of the saints "in Christ" (Col. 1:27). This sacrifice thus stands as a close parallel to the present day Lord's Supper (John 6: 51), and it points forward still to that blessed final communion when we shall sit down together in the kingdom of heaven (Ps. 22:26; Luke 14:15; Rev. 19:6-10). Included under the *sh'lāmīm* were a variety of thank-offerings (Lev. 7:12-15) and votive offerings (which involved some specific request, v. 16), as well as free-will offerings, out of a love for God in general (Deut. 16:10).

After the three "sweet savor" offerings come the latter two of the Mosaic sacrifices, which may be grouped together as specific "guilt" offerings. Both were occasioned by some particular sin, on the basis of which divine condemnation had overtaken the offerer. The Hebrew word, *hattāth*, carries the original meaning of "sin"[25] and, by development, of a "purification from sin" (Num. 8:7; 19:9); but it comes to be applied in particular to the fourth Mosaic sacrifice, the "sin offering" (Lev. 4-5:13). This *hattāth* sacrifice was designed to propitiate the Most High because of the concrete sin that the man concerned had committed. The situations that could occasion both this offering and the trespass offerings (that appear next) include the commission of certain unintentional violations (4:2; 5:15). The guilt offerings, however, were not limited to such sins of ignorance, or even to those sins that were simply unpremeditated (5:1, 4; cf. 6:2, 3; 19:20). In the case of intentional sins, however, forgiveness *was* impossible, should the guilty party continue unrepentant (Num. 15:30; I Sam. 3:14). But for the truly penitent, the blood of the guilt offering did become acceptable upon the Lord's altar, because the death penalty for sin had thus, in token, been vicariously paid. Still, to emphasize the transference of the man's sin to the animal and the removal of the guilt of that sin, some of the guilt offerings had a requirement that the corpses concerned be taken outside the camp and burned (Lev. 4:12, 21). So Christ "suffered without the camp," as one reproached, bearing our sins (Heb. 13:11-13). Other animals, however, whose sacrifice did not involve the sins of the priests themselves, could be eaten by the Aaronites (Lev. 6:26); and, correspondingly, the blood could be considered holy (v. 27). But again, the sin that had been transferred to these offerings caused the pots in which they had been boiled to be smashed, or the metal ones scoured (v. 28).

---

[24]Cf. Vos, *op. cit.*, p. 187.
[25]See above, p. 195.

The term *āshām*, which may mean simply "guilt,"[26] was selected by Moses to designate the fifth, or "trespass offering" (Lev. 5:14-6: 7). This was a sacrifice which overlapped the *hattāth* in many respects (7:7). But while the stress of the latter rests upon the propitiation of God, the *āshām* includes a perhaps secondary but still very real emphasis upon the satisfaction of the injured human party. It teaches us, both of the need for our appeasement of the disobeyed God, but also for our social compensation of the wronged man (5:16; 6:5; I Sam. 6:3). Liberalism generally considers the sacrificial element in the *āshām* as a relatively late development, with the compensation constituting what was the original feature of the transaction (cf. II Kings 12:16).[27] But the witness of Leviticus to the reality of the sacrifice is clear, provided, of course, that one accepts the Mosaic authenticity of the Pentateuch. In fact, the *āshām* could take place without any restitution at all (Lev. 5:17, 18). It should be further pointed out that the atonement occurs in the sacrifice, rather than in the payment. However, the spirit of repentance that is demonstrated by the restitution takes precedence over the ceremony (II Sam. 15:22; Prov. 21:3; Eccl. 5:1). It is in this context then that our Lord uttered His command (Matt. 5:23, 24), "Leave thy gift before the altar, and go thy way; first be reconciled to thy brother, and then come and offer thy gift." As the Suffering Servant, Christ Himself became a propitiating sin offering; but Isaiah 53:10 also designates Him as an *āshām*, or trespass offering. "Both are fulfilled in the Lord Jesus Christ, who bore the penalty due to sin [our *hattāth*] and redressed every claim of God upon the sinner [our *āshām*]."[28] He thereby made atonement not only by His passive obedience in bearing our sin, but also by His active obedience in making compensation for us to God.

One Old Testament situation could, in fact, involve several different sacrifices. Noteworthy is Leviticus 14:10-20, on the cleansing of a leper, where four, or perhaps all five, of the varieties of Mosaic offerings appear.

After the death of Moses, Joshua inaugurated the period of Israel's consolidation by invading Canaan and by making of Jericho a *hérem*, a sacrifice to God.[29] Years later, Jephthah rashly swore a vow to sacrifice to God whatever came out first to meet him from the doors of his house (Judg. 11:31). Furthermore, despite the many more or less ingenious attempts made by uncomfortable expositors to explain the passage away, Scripture states that this judge then fulfilled his vow upon his only daughter (v. 39). Jephthah, however, had shown himself guilty of accommodation to Canaanitish patterns

---

[26]See above, p. 211.
[27]Cf. George Buchanan Gray, *Sacrifice in the Old Testament* (Oxford: Clarendon, 1924), p. 37.
[28]Moorehead, *op. cit.*, p. 171.
[29]See above, p. 330.

of thought in other respects as well (v. 24). Another man who became chargeable of the pagan practice of sacrificing his own children was Hiel, in the days of Ahab (disruption period; I Kings 16:34), as he fulfilled, though perhaps unintentionally, the curse that Joshua had pronounced on anyone who attempted to rebuild Jericho (Josh. 6:26). David did much to encourage the ritual life of Israel, by bringing the ark to Jerusalem, by establishing the courses of the priests and the singers, and by making preparations for the Temple (cf. Ps. 51:19). Yet he appreciated, at the same time, the priority of a man's repentance in his inner spirit over his performances of external sacrifice (Ps. 51:17). So too Solomon, in the next period, stressed that the sacrifices of the wicked were of no avail, and constituted indeed an abomination unto the Lord (Prov. 15:8; 21:3, 27).

During the eighth century, Israel lapsed into the shameful Canaanitish custom of human sacrifice, both in northern Israel (II Kings 17:17) and, with corrupt Ahaz, in the south also (16:3). Universally prevalent, moreover, had become a false, popular reliance upon ceremonialism (Isa. 1:11-15). The prophets therefore felt themselves compelled to condemn all types of Mosaic "sweet-savor" sacrifices (Amos 5:22), though, actually, only in the relative sense of being secondary to Moses' more basic requirement of a true heart knowledge of God (Hos. 6:6). Hosea was thus led· to predict that the day would come in which Israel would have its sacrifices taken away from it altogether (Hos. 3:4). This specific prediction seems to have been fulfilled in the Roman destruction of the Temple (A.D. 70),[30] though Isaiah still looked forward to a re-establishment of a visible, sacrificial service in the eschatological kingdom of the future (Isa. 60:7).

In the next, seventh century period, the wicked ruler Manasseh revived the practice of human sacrifice (II Kings 21:6) in the valley of the son of Hinnom outside Jerusalem (II Chron. 33:6). But then, even after such outright paganisms had been abolished, Jeremiah, like the earlier prophets, has still to condemn Judah's false reliance upon the externalities of continual offerings (7:22, 23). At the same time Jeremiah appreciated the value of divinely controlled ceremonialism, for he predicted that burnt offerings would again be presented by the Levitical priests in that day when the Davidic Messiah should come in glory to rule the world (33:18). The Babylonian captivity caused a distressing interruption of the sacrifices at Jerusalem, from 586 to 536 B.C. (cf. Lam. 2:7; 4:1); but, with the post-exilic return, the altar and ritual were restored. Daniel predicted a somewhat similar abeyance of sacrifice because of the persecutions of Antiochus Epiphanes, an event which was remarkably fulfilled in the three year

---

[30]The corresponding absence of idolatry, "ephod and teraphim," shows that the verse cannot refer to the idolatrous exilic period.

period, 168-165 B.C. (Dan. 8:11). During the Persian restoration, however, the heart again seems to have gone out of Israel's sacrifice: inferior animals were offered on the altar (Mal. 1:7, 8, 12-14) and men "robbed God" in His offerings (3:8).

In the fulness of time, Jesus Christ came and shed His precious blood as the perfect sacrifice. He thereby confirmed the newer testament and, once and for all, replaced its older, anticipatory predecessor. He caused the sacrifice to cease (Dan. 9:27). But though our Lord brought an end to the altar as a means of atonement (Heb. 9:12), His action does not thereby exclude the possibility of its future reestablishment in some other (memorial ?) capacity. Today, however, the Christian Church contains no altar, but rather a communion table. This latter object possesses in itself a three-fold significance. Each of these areas, moreover, is related to one of the Old Testament teachings on sacred ceremony. In the first place, the table represents the fulfillment of sacrifice; for the Lord's Supper was ordained as a memorial of that same redemptive death toward which the sacrifices of the older testament had pointed in anticipation (I Cor. 11:24).

In the second place, the communion service exhibits the continuation of the truth of the holy sanctuary. It serves as the sacramental means of grace through which the presence of the living God is experienced in a special way by His redeemed people (I Cor. 10:16). Herein exists a significant point of relationship, and yet an even more significant point of distinction, between the communion ritual of the New Testament Church and that of the contemporary and also prior ceremonialism of the Essenes of the Qumran community, by the Dead Sea. Fritsch has said of this sectarian group:

> The fact that the members were to eat and bless communally shows that the meal was sacramental in character. This is emphasized by the priestly blessing of the bread and wine. . . . Furthermore, this communal meal was Messianic in character, because the "Messiah of Israel" was considered to be present. . . . K. G. Kuhn believes that the background of the Lord's Supper must be sought in the communal meal of an Essenian group like the Qumran sect, rather than in the Passover meal.[31]

Actually, however, Christ at the Last Supper combined both the paschal sacrifice (Luke 22:15) and the sacramental communion into the one rite of the Lord's table. This ordinance is the sign and seal, both of His testamental death (a truth far beyond the limited grasp of Qumran) and of His living presence.

Then, in the third place, the Lord's Supper constitutes the continuation of the prophetic significance of the ark and of the most holy place, insofar as these symbols served also as types of the glory of

---

[31]Charles T. Fritsch, *The Qumran Community: Its History and Scrolls* (New York: The Macmillan Co., 1956), p. 123-124. Burrows, however, questions whether the Qumran meals had any particularly sacred character at all; *More Light on the Dead Sea Scrolls* (New York: Viking Press, 1958), p. 369.

Christ's future kingdom. For that day has yet to be revealed in which the testament shall be fulfilled and "God Himself shall be with them, and be their God: and wipe away all tears from their eyes" (Rev. 21:3, 4). But by the bread and the cup we do show the Lord's death *till He come* (I Cor. 11:26).

D. CIRCUMCISION. Though sacrifice had been practiced from primeval times, circumcision was revealed, and appropriately so, only with the particularization of the testament to the patriarch Abraham (Gen. 17:10). That is to say, it was when special revelation no longer proclaimed salvation in a universal fashion that the need arose for a sign that would distinguish God's own people. The historical origin of circumcision, as it was practiced in the religions of the ancient Near East, is unknown. The rite may first have been introduced as a substitute for child sacrifice, or it may have arisen as a means to promote human fertility (cf. Ezek. 16:7). Circumcision appeared early in Egypt, but its observance was not characteristic of the Canaanites (Gen. 34:22). But whatever this ceremony may have symbolized to others, to Israel it became the sign and seal of the testament (Gen. 17:11, 13). Indeed, in respect to circumcision, God said flatly, "This is My testament" (v. 10).[32] To neglect circumcision was a most serious offence (Ex. 4:24-26); it amounted, in fact, to breaking the testament (Ezek. 44:7). Any man who refused the rite was to be cut off from the people and to forfeit his testamental inheritance (Gen. 17:14).

As to the precise significance of this ceremonial action, it may be said negatively that uncircumcision expressed unfitness, and particularly that of the natural life (Ex. 6:12). When Moses referred to his "uncircumcised lips," he meant that he had poor native speaking ability. To specify therefore an "uncircumcised heart" (Jer. 4:4) was to picture a soul that was covered with its natural wickedness. In contrast, then, to circumcise meant to remove one's sin (Deut. 10:16) and "to love Yahweh thy God with all thy heart and with all thy soul that thou mayest live" (30:6). Circumcision thus became the earliest Biblical symbol of regeneration (Lev. 26:41). Some commentators, including even Oehler, have denied to circumcision its individualistic application and have looked upon it as a sign of mere external incorporation into the nation of Israel.[33] Now it is indeed true that membership in the elect community was involved in the idea of circumcision. But its chief contextual point of relationship concerns God's redemptive testament and the fundamental, associated

---

[32]The "blood" which is referred to in Ezek. 16:6, 8, if it were that of circumcision, would provide an interesting commentary on the sacramental significance of the rite; "When I saw thee in thy blood, I said unto thee, live . . . and I entered into a testament with thee, and thou becamest Mine." But this equation appears highly suspect (cf. v. 7).
[33]*Theology of the Old Testament*, pp. 193-194.

divine promise that Yahweh would be their God (Gen. 17:7). This testamental connotation, in turn, renders necessary its personal application as a sign of individual salvation from sin and of reconciliation to God. Circumcision, it must be observed, existed within the personal religious life of Abraham's family for centuries before the nation of Israel had even come into existence; and New Testament analogy specifically defines the sign of circumcision as "a seal of the righteousness of faith" (Rom. 4:11). For those whose hearts were in rebellion against God, the external ceremony was, of course, no more to be considered mechanically effective than was their vain offering up of sacrifices. The rite was designed as "an outward and visible sign of an inward and invisible grace"; and if a man remained uncircumcised in heart he lay still, in God's eyes, in his uncircumcision (Jer. 9:25, 26).

Circumcision was performed at eight days (Gen. 17:12), that is, as soon after birth as was practical. This early date possesses a two-fold significance. It demonstrates, on the one hand, man's need for redemption and regeneration, from the time of birth itself. David went even further and exclaimed, "Behold, I was brought forth in iniquity and in sin did my mother *conceive* me" (Ps. 51:5). As Ephesians 2:3 states it, we are by nature children of wrath and are totally depraved. Because of this natural sinfulness of life, the Mosaic law considered a mother to be ceremonially unclean until the circumcision of her son had been performed (Lev. 12:2, 3). But infant circumcision demonstrates, on the other hand, that the children of God's elect people may confidently be understood as included within the saving grace of His testament (Gen. 17:7, 10). Yahweh is their God; compare the assurance granted to believers by the words of I Corinthians 7:14, "else were your children unclean, but now are they holy." The naming of a child seems to have taken place at his circumcision (Gen. 17:5; 21:3, 4; cf. Luke 1:59; 2:21); and it is significant that the Biblical Hebrew names, especially for boys, generally carried a religious meaning. Often the name served as a forthright witness of the child's participation in salvation. The name of Isaiah, for example, *Y'sha-Yāhū*, means "Salvation, Yahweh [is]."

The form and function of circumcision continued unchanged throughout the course of the history of Israel. Abraham's household servants had entered with him, through the rite of circumcision, into full testamental participation (Gen. 17:12, 13, 27); and, just so, those who came to be attached to the nation of Israel in the times of Moses were similarly received into the household of faith (Ex. 12:44). Proselytes were accepted to the passover table on the basis of their first having undergone circumcision (v. 48); and the Mosaic priestly codes emphasized the continuing validity of the patriarchal injunctions, which had been given to Abraham over 600 years before (Lev. 12:3).

Circumcision was not observed in Israel during the four decades of the wilderness wanderings (Josh. 5:5). The reason is not stated in so many words, but Numbers 14:33 had revealed that the children were "to bear the whoredoms" of their fathers over the entire forty-year period. Israel's refraining from circumcision may then have been done intentionally, so as to provide the people with a concrete symbol of God's disfavor, or perhaps of their own physical sufferings. At Gilgal, however, at the commencement of the consolidation period in 1406 B.C., the rite was renewed; and Yahweh simultaneously announced, with significance, that He had "rolled away the reproach of Egypt from you" (Josh. 5:9). This "reproach" would thus seem to consist, not simply of the taunts of the Egyptians at Israel's having to wander in the deserts of Sinai, but more fundamentally of the opprobrium of sin. But with the entrance into Canaan, the punishment for the disobedience of the earlier generation had been completed; and it was the removal of just such guilt that constituted the uniform significance of circumcision.[34]

As a sacrament of salvation, circumcision is now prohibited to the Christian Church (Gal. 5:2). This once precious rite had been so distorted and had become so much a part of the un-Biblical legalism of the Pharisees (v. 3) that God felt constrained to replace it altogether. But the basic testamental feature of a ceremonial sign and seal for one's initiation into God's elect people is a matter of permanent validity. The New Testament specifically describes the transmutation of circumcision into the sacrament of baptism: "In Christ ye were circumcised with a circumcision not made with hands, in the putting off of the body of flesh, in the circumcision of Christ, having been buried with Him in baptism" (Col. 2:11, 12). The two sacraments possess an identical function; for both serve as symbols of regeneration by identification with Christ. God therefore, through Paul, described the way of salvation by saying that it is "not by works of righteousness which we have done; but according to His mercy He saved us, by the *washing* of regeneration" (Titus 3:5). Some evangelicals today seek to limit baptism to the function of symbolizing conscious conversion, rather than to that of symbolizing the more basic matters of regeneration and salvation. They must, accordingly, reject the sacrament of infant baptism. This rejection, however, not simply appears to be contrary to the primary meaning of baptism; but it serves also to create two rather awkward theological problems. 1) In the light of the above evidence on infant circumcision, the antipedobaptist is faced with the necessity of accounting, in some way, for the presence of a more extensive grace in the preparatory Old Testament than in the ultimate New Testament.[35] 2) He is then called

---

[34]Cf. John H. Raven, *The History of the Religion of Israel*, pp. 175-176.
[35]Cf. John Calvin, *Institutes of the Christian Religion*, IV, XVI, VI (Translated by John Allen; 7th American edition; Philadelphia: [n.d]), II:607.

upon to discover some means for justifying a belief in the salvation of the unconverted infants that are born within a Christian home, while at the same time refusing them baptism, which is the sign of the washing away of their sins (Acts 22:16). Father Abraham seems to have possessed a more adequate procedure, as he acted in faith upon the words of Yahweh, "Every man child among you shall be circumcised, and it shall be a token of the testament betwixt Me and you" (Gen. 17:10, 11).

For Further Reading:

Patrick Fairbairn, *The Typology of Scripture.* Grand Rapids: Zondervan Publishing House, 1952. Vol. II concerns the ceremonials under the dispensation of the law, Chapter III, Sec. 5, being concerned particularly with sacrifice.

Royden Keith Yerkes, *Sacrifice in Greek and Roman Religions and Early Judaism.* New York: Charles Scribner's Sons, 1952. Liberal, seeing sacrifice simply as surrender to God, not as death for sins.

Oscar Cullmann, *Baptism in the New Testament.* Trans. by J. K. S. Reid; Studies in Biblical Theology No. 1; London: Student Christian Movement Press, 1950. Chapter IV concerns the relationship of baptism and circumcision.

28. Ceremonial: Times*

A. THE SABBATH. The doctrine of Israel's "sacred times" develops directly from the basic truth of the testament. The special days of the Mosaic calendar, that is, were specifically designed to picture various aspects of the testamentary redemption that God had promised His people. The "times" therefore exist as matters of divine revelation; and they are not to be accounted for on the basis of purely natural phenomena, for example, on men's calculation of the duration of the phases of the moon. The agricultural cycle is no doubt related to the annual feasts, but only in a secondary way. As Oehler has well said,

> What made these feasts, feasts, and the Sabbaths holy days, was not human choice, guided by the order of nature, but the enactments of the covenant God, who on the one hand preserved by these festivals a lively remembrance of the great facts of His deliverance and guidance of His people (comp. Ex. xiii. 9, Lev. xxiii. 42sq., etc.), and on the other admonished the people to follow their earthly vocation to an agricultural life, in constant dependence on the Giver of all the blessings of nature, and to regard these blessings as inalienably connected with the ordinances of the covenant.[1]

° BIBLE READING: Leviticus 23; Isaiah 58

Collateral Reading: Oehler, *Theology of the Old Testament,* pp. 323-352.
W. G. Moorehead, *Studies in the Mosaic Institutions,* pp. 183-206.

---

[1]Oehler, *Theology of the Old Testament,* pp. 325-326.

The basis, therefore, for men's observance of the Sabbath (*shab-bāth*, "rest") lies not in any desire or plan on the part of man, but rather in God's revelation of how He rested on the seventh day of creation (Gen. 2:1-3). The truth of the sabbath was, indeed, first recorded only by Moses; but Babylonian parallels[2] suggest that the obligation of reverence for the seventh day had been granted as a matter of revelation from the beginning. Its original purpose, as Vos has pointed out, was for man's sanctification to the Lord.

> "God 'hallowed' the sabbath, not because it inherently pos-
> sessed a peculiar character, to which magic and superstition
> could attach themselves, but because it was His will that the
> day should bear a peculiar significance reminding of and
> binding it to the service of God."[3]

But though man failed and was expelled from Eden, his very sin, the Fall, and the curse served to accentuate both his need for rest in the present and his longing for a true rest in the future (Gen. 5:29). The people of Israel correspondingly observed the Sabbath before they ever reached Mt. Sinai, that is, before "the law" was ordained (Ex. 16:23-26).[4] Even at this early point, moreover, the nature of the sabbath is identified as a means of tangible grace; for the Lord prom-ised to Israel that what they sacrificed by abstaining from labor on the seventh day would be restored by a corresponding blessing from God (Ex. 16:29).

At Sinai, the observance of the Sabbath was singled out as one of man's fundamental duties to God, by being listed as Commandment IV of the Decalogue: "Remember the sabbath day, to keep it holy" (Ex. 20:8). The Sabbath served two major functions. 1) As a mat-ter of moral law, it guaranteed to men a needed day of rest from their labor: "Six days shalt thou labor and do all thy work; but the seventh day is a sabbath unto Yahweh thy God: in it thou shalt not do any work" (vv. 9, 10). One of its purposes, as the Book of the Testament shortly thereafter explained, was "that thine ox and thine ass may have rest, and that the son of thy handmaid, and the so-journer, may be refreshed" (23:12). Furthermore, when Moses re-stated the Decalogue forty years later, he reinforced this moral func-tion of Commandment IV by establishing it as a memorial of Israel's own deliverance from Egyptian bondage:

> "Observe the sabbath . . . that thy man servant and thy
> maid servant may rest as well as thou. And thou shalt re-
> member that thou wast a servant in the land of Egypt, and

---

[2]These, however, exhibit the usual corruption experienced by divine truth when left in pagan hands; for the seventh, and certain other days, came to be treated by them as unlucky, cf. Oehler, *op. cit.*, p. 329.
[3]Geerhardus Vos, *Biblical Theology*, p. 270.
[4]Moses, though, does appear to be the one who was responsible for its reinstitu-tion among the people (Neh. 9:14).

Yahweh thy God brought thee out thence: therefore Yahweh
thy God commanded thee to keep the sabbath day" (Deut.
5:12, 14-16).

But the seventh day was still a sabbath "unto Yahweh thy God"; and
Vos has rightly concluded that, "From what has been said about the
typical, sacramental meaning of the Sabbath it follows that it would
be a mistake to base its observance primarily on the ground of
utility."[5]

The more prominent function of the Sabbath, therefore, was
this: 2) As a matter of ceremonial law, the seventh day was to be
observed as a perpetual b'rīth (Ex. 31:16). This specific terminology
appears to indicate something beyond the mere fact of changeless
obligation. The expression seems rather to be a bold statement of
identification between the Sabbath and God's redemptive b'rīth, or
testament. The Sabbath constitutes, that is, a feature of the testament
that is so essential that it, like circumcision (Gen. 17:10), is actually
made equivalent to the b'rīth. Isaiah 56:4, 6 thus identifies a man's
keeping of the Sabbath as the very first characteristic of his keeping the
entire testament. Observance of the Sabbath serves, moreover, as a major element in the fundamental, testamentary concept of holiness; and
Scripture promises that it will result in a divinely given experience
of separation and of sanctification as God's own people: "Ye shall
keep My sabbaths: for it is a sign between Me and you throughout
your generations; that ye may know that I am Yahweh who sanctifieth you" (Ex. 31:13). Thus, in its moral aspect, the Sabbath serves
as a condition for testamental standing; for it constitutes a means of
demonstrating faith, through holy (ethical) obedience. But more
prominently, in its ceremonial aspects, it demonstrates an individual's
faith in the holy (divine) truths of the testament that the Sabbath
was designed to typify. For the Sabbath was not only a sacrament, a
means of grace by which believers were assured that "Yahweh was
sanctifying them"; it constituted, at the same time, the acted revelation of a number of great doctrinal truths. Most significantly, it serves,
on the one hand, as a symbolical reminder of God's creation rest
(Ex. 20:11; 31:17); and, on the other hand, it typifies that corresponding future rest which becomes the divinely-revealed anticipation
of the heirs of the testament. Compare the words of promise which
are expressed in Psalm 95:11, "That they should enter into My rest."
Vos concludes,

> "Before all other important things, therefore, the Sabbath
> is an expression of the eschatological principle on which the
> life of humanity has been constructed. There is to be to the

---

[5]Op. cit., p. 157.

world-process a finale, as there was an overture, and these two belong inseparably together."6

The Sabbath was, accordingly, observed in Israel as a day of special religious assembly (Lev. 23:3). It was marked by the setting in order of fresh "show [presence] bread" (24:5-8) and by the offering up of particular sacrifices (Num. 28:9, 10). Its regulations were scrupulously to be observed (cf. Ex. 35:3), even in the busy times of plowing and harvest (34:21). Indeed, the close association of the Sabbath with the testament, and its fundamental status as a medium for demonstrating one's obedient faith in the testament, caused its violation to be treated as a crime subject to death itself (31:14; Num. 15:32-36).

Subsequent to Moses, the actual observance of the Sabbath followed the usual pattern of "ups and downs" in the religious life of Israel. II Kings 4:23 (in the disruption period) first mentions the existence of local Sabbath meetings, conducted under the leadership of God's prophets. The eighth century prophets went on to record varied reactions on the part of Israel toward the Sabbath. Its observance could be a time of joyful assembly (Hos. 2:11), or it might be one of impatience to get back to the "important" business of the next day (Amos 8:5). Isaiah appreciated the Sabbath as a primary feature within Israel's testament (Isa. 55:4) and also, because Sabbath-keeping is geographically unconditioned, as a practical basis for appeal to foreign proselytes (v. 6). God's day thus became a means for the accomplishment of the universalistic goal of the testament, that "My house shall be called a house of prayer for all peoples" (v. 7). Scripture reveals that sabbaths will be universally observed in the future testament of peace (66:23). Isaiah 58:13 then constitutes the greatest single verse in all of Scripture on the nature of Sabbath observance. Such questions as, "Should I go driving on Sunday?" or, "Must I attend all the sabbath services in my church?" or, "Can I patronize sports on the Lord's day?" are answered in principle by these inspired words of the prophet:

> If thou turn away thy foot from the sabbath, from doing thy pleasure on My holy day; and call the sabbath a delight, and the holy of Yahweh honorable; and shalt honor it [or, *Him*], not doing thine own ways, nor finding thine own pleasure, nor speaking thine own words: then shalt thou delight thyself in Yahweh; and I will make thee to ride upon the high places of the earth; and I will feed thee with the heritage of Jacob thy father: for the mouth of Yahweh hath spoken it.

Every Christian must then, of course, make his own applications of this passage, honestly seeking before God to exemplify the standards that are laid down in His Word.

In the next period, immediately before the captivity of Judah, Jeremiah revived Moses' stress upon the observance of the Sabbath

6*Ibid.*, p. 156.

(Jer. 17:19-27). He cried out, "Take heed to yourselves, and bear no burden on the sabbath day" (v. 21). For with the exile, the faithful found that they were able to compensate for the ceremonial loss that had been entailed in the destruction of the Temple by their renewed emphasis upon the Lord's sacred day. Ezekiel emphasized that the Sabbath was indicative of the continuing testamental promise that Yahweh was their God (Ezek. 20:20), "a sign between Me and them, that they may know that I am Yahweh that sanctifieth them" (v. 12; cf. Ex. 31:13). He enjoined the hallowing of the sabbath (v. 20), as an essential part of the believer's overall way of life (v. 21). The Sabbath day is not mentioned by name in Esther, but, together with the other sacred times, dietary laws, etc., it may well have contributed to the popular reaction against the Jews, with "their laws, diverse from those of every people" (Esther 3:8).

Upon Israel's return to Palestine, strict observance of the Sabbath became a prominent feature in the life of the restoration community: no labor, as on week-days (Neh. 13:15); and no buying or selling (v. 16). Nehemiah exhorted his people, "Did not your fathers thus, and did not our God bring all this evil upon us, and upon this city? yet ye bring more wrath upon Israel by profaning the sabbath!" (v. 18). Thus today, the Christian Church should exhibit similar vigilance in the support of Sunday-closing legislation. It is true that the present evangelical minority in America cannot do as Nehemiah did, and lock the gates or threaten arrest against sabbath violators (cf. Neh. 13:19-22). But we could still at least resolve, as did Nehemiah and his followers, "if the peoples of the land bring wares or any grain on the sabbath day to sell, that we would not buy of them on the sabbath" (10:31).

The present-day significance of sabbath observance may be appreciated under four categories. 1) As carried on by the New Testament Pharisees and by their counterparts in modern Judaism, its practice is condemned. Their Sabbath had become a perversion of the joyful day of worship, praise, rest, and service that had been intended by the Old Testament and as is witnessed, for example, by the undated 92nd Psalm, "A song for the sabbath day." Instead, the first century Jews imposed on the sabbath a series of most burdensome regulations. During its hours, for example, they limited a man's travel to the "sabbath day's journey" (less than one mile, Acts 1:12), which is opposed, by the way, to the explicit descriptions of sabbath activities that are found in the Old Testament (II Kings 4:23; cf. Hos. 2:11)! Thus the Jews distorted God's Sabbath rest into a man-made weariness. Jesus Christ sharply condemned these legalistic perversions and stressed, not simply that He Himself was Lord of the Sabbath (Mark 2:28), but that "the sabbath was made for man, and not man for the sabbath" (v. 27). The spirit of worship far outweighs the form. Such pronouncements of His resulted in some of the bitterest Pharisaic opposition that our Lord experienced — hypocrisy cannot afford to be exposed! — though the enlightened Israelites who made up the true Church reacted, with Christ, against such religious near-sightedness (John 9:16). More serious, however, than the sophistry of any of the specific Pharisaic regulations, was the apostasy of the general Judaistic declension into works-righteousness: their reliance upon a legalistic way of salvation, which came to be associated in particular with their rigid observance of the Sabbath on the seventh day. It is this perversion, and not the revealed truth of a ceremonial Sabbath,[7] which is condemned in passages such as Galatians 4:9, 10, and which made it necessary for God's New Testament Church to abandon the seventh day observance altogether.

2) As a ceremonial type of the testamental rest accomplished by Christ at His first coming, Israel's sabbath has been fulfilled. For when our Lord cried, "Come unto Me and I will give you rest" (Matt. 11:28), the consolation of Israel was achieved, and its rites of antici-pation were necessarily terminated (Col. 2:16, 17), such as the presentation of the special burnt offerings that had been so charac-teristic of the ancient Sabbath services. But at the same time, our observance of the Church's sabbath, with its weekly assemblies of worship in commemoration of the finished work of Christ, is cor-roborated by apostolic precedent (Acts 20:7).

3) As a ceremonial type of the final testamental rest for be-livers, in heaven or at the Lord's Second Coming (Heb. 4:9-11), the Church's sabbath is as yet unfulfilled and is still binding. Here too, however, the apostolic shift in the chosen day of the week is a most fitting one; for Christ's resurrection on Easter Sunday serves as a type of the future hope of each individual Christian, when in the testament of peace our bodies of humiliation shall be conformed to the body of His glory (Phil. 3:21). The precise day of the week that is kept has indeed been shifted by New Testament revelation to Sun-day (Acts 20:7; I Cor. 16:1, 2), and this first day of the seven has now become "the Lord's day" (Rev. 1:10). But the appropriateness of Sunday as our new day of worship is patent; for our Lord's resur-rection on the first day of the week constitutes the seal of the newer testament and of our justification before God (Rom. 4:25). His words to the Jews about Saturday are thus even more appropriate to us in regard to Sunday: "Hallow My sabbaths; and they shall be a sign between Me and you, that ye may know that I am Yahweh your God" (Ezek. 20:20).

---

[7]Cf. Charles Hodge, *Commentary on the Epistle to the Romans,* p. 420. "It is obvious from the context . . . that Paul has reference to the Jewish festivals, and therefore his language cannot properly be applied to the Christian Sabbath."

4) As the fourth word of the changeless moral law, Sabbath observance remains permanently binding.

B. EXTENSIONS OF THE SABBATH. At Sinai God also ordained a series of seven special "convocation sabbaths" in the calendar of Israel. These sabbaths were days of rest from labor and of special sacrifices. They were to be observed in connection with the five Mosaic annual feasts: passover, pentecost, trumpets, the day of atonement, and tabernacles. The first and the last of these feasts, moreover, were assigned two such convocation sabbaths (Lev. 23:7, 8, 35, 36).

A day of rest that was observed monthly was that of the new moon. Moses' only specifications had been that on these days there were to be offered up special sacrifices (Num. 28:11-15) and that "in the beginnings of your months ye shall blow the trumpets over your burnt-offerings and the sacrifices of your peace offerings; and they shall be to you for a memorial before your God" (10:10; cf. Ps. 81:3). The point of the trumpet-blowing then is this: to remind God, anthropomorphically, of the needs of His people Israel. During the break-down of the services of the central sanctuary that climaxed in the days of Saul, the new moons appear to have become occasions for private family sacrifices (I Sam. 20:5, 6); and later (disruption period) they provided an opportunity for popular assemblies to hear sermons by the prophets (II Kings 4:23; cf. Ezek. 46:3). In the eighth century, the new moons seem to have been observed as days of rest, and hence as extensions of the concept of the weekly Sabbath (Amos 8:5; Isa. 1:13). Isaiah 66:23 notes that they will be again observed under the future testament of peace.

The sabbatic year, which is also called the "year of release" (Deut. 15:9), was revealed through Moses and was designed by God that the land might lie fallow every seventh year. The practice possessed agricultural value as "a sabbath of rest" (Lev. 25:4) for the land; but the more important feature, and the one that is more stressed by Scripture, is that of its function in aiding the poor (and even the wild animals!) by bestowing upon them whatever happened to grow during the seventh season (Ex. 23:10, 11; Lev. 25:1-7). This humanitarian factor receives further emphasis in the suspension, or cancellation, of loans on the sabbatic year (Deut. 15:1-15). Finally, at the feast of tabernacles in the seventh year, the law of Moses was publicly to be read (31:10-13). The central truth that is demonstrated by the ordinance of the sabbatic year is that the land, and indeed all creation, is subject basically to God's law, and not to men's desires. For almost five hundred years previous to the exile of Judah, this regulation was widely disregarded. As Oehler has explained:

> The omission of these ordinances was already contemplated in Lev. xxvi. 35, while how far they were really carried into practice in post-Mosaic times does not appear. It is evident from II Chron.

xxxvi. 21, where it is said that the land lay desolate during the captivity seventy years to make up for its sabbath years, that the celebration of the sabbatical year had been omitted during the last centuries before the captivity.[8]

A comparable Israelitish failure was their corresponding disregard of Exodus 21:2, which required the release of Hebrew indentured-servants on the seventh year after purchase (Jer. 34:8-10).[9] The sabbatic year was, however, observed again in the later post-exilic restoration (Neh. 10:31) and down into New Testament times.

After the passage of seven sabbatic years came the year of jubilee, the fiftieth year (Lev. 25:8-34). Moses stated that its purpose was to "proclaim liberty throughout the land unto all the inhabitants thereof" v. 10), for it possessed the features of an ordinary sabbatic year, plus the requirement of freeing all Israelitish servants and of returning all landed properties (cf. Ezek. 46:17). The legislation of the year of jubilee, with the permanent property rights that it guaranteed, helps to explain the conduct of Naboth and of Ahab in the later disruption period (I Kings 21:3, 4); for both of the parties concerned recognized its principle of permanent land tenure. Oehler, correspondingly, remarks:

> "Prophetic rebukes, like Isa. v. 8 sq. and Mic. ii.2, can only be fully understood from this point of view; while these very passages lead to the conclusion that a carrying out of the law of the jubilee was out of the question."[10]

But though disregarded throughout most of Israel's history, the year of jubilee yet served as a type of the deliverance that Israel anticipated in the Messianic times (Isa. 61:1-3; Luke 4:21; Heb. 4:9). See Appendix E, pages 524, 525, for a summary of "The Significance of the Sacred Times of the Old Testament."

C. THE ANNUAL FEASTS. Israel's five annual feasts were established of God in the Mosaic era. These feasts, moreover, though confessedly somewhat disregarded in periods of apostasy, yet constituted one of the most consistently significant forms of ceremonial response, by which the faithful among Israel sought to demonstrate their commitment to the God of the testament. Three of the five — passover, pentecost, and tabernacles — were pilgrimage feasts. They were points at which every adult male of the saved community was expected to appear before Yahweh at the central sanctuary (Ex. 23: 14-17; cf. Solomon's three annual sacrifices, I Kings 9:25).

The first of these, the passover, is called in Hebrew the *pésah*,

---

[8]*Op. cit.*, p. 343.
[9]See above, pp. 333, 334. This ordinance is not, however, to be confused with that of the sabbatical year, which concerned the release of debts. But the occasion for Jer. 34:8-10 might indeed have been the appearance of a sabbatical year, cf. Oehler, *loc. cit.*
[10]*Ibid.*, p. 344.

from which is taken our own term "paschal," which signifies a matter that pertains to this celebration (Ex. 12:11). *Pésah* is derived from the Hebrew verb that means to "pass over" (v. 13; cf. Isa. 31:5). For this "passover" feast originated with 1) the historical event of the by-passing of the homes of Israel, at the time when God smote the firstborn of Egypt, in the spring of 1446 B.C. But with the historical event came 2) the paschal ceremony. The passover, that is, consisted from its outset of a feast, of a heavy meal, to prepare Israel for the exodus journey that was to commence the following morning (Ex. 12:31-33). The meal then was designed of God to exhibit an extensive symbolism. Its employment of unleavened bread, for example, (v. 8) served as a symbol of Israel's holy separation from natural corruption[11] (cf. I Cor. 5:8), but also of the hastiness of their departure from Egypt (Ex. 12:34; cf. Deut. 16:3). The bitter herbs that accompanied the bread (Ex. 12:8) most likely reflected the bitterness of their previous bondage to the Egyptians (1:14); and the presence of laced shoes on their feet and of a staff, ready in their hand (12:11), again signified the haste of the exodus. The fact that they ate the meal by family groups (vv. 3, 10) and that no one was allowed to leave his home that night (v. 22) was in itself indicative of the communal nature of Israel's salvation and of the national testament that God was about to make with His people (6:7). Finally, the seven days' use of unleavened bread that followed (12:15; Lev. 23:6-8) gave added emphasis to the symbolical lessons that have been already observed (Ex. 12:34).

The most significant parts of the passover ceremony, however, consisted of the slaying of the paschal lamb, the marking of the two side-posts and the lintels on their doorways with its blood, the preparation of the body of the slain animal, and the final eating of its flesh (vv. 6-10). The blood in particular served as a token (v. 13); and Vos has suggested the following theories for its historical background, prior to the events of 1446 (cf. the feast that is assumed in Ex. 5:1):

> That the Hebrews had been previously accustomed to observe a religious festival in the Spring, we know from their request to Pharaoh (Ex. 8:1, 27). This may have been a feast of the sacrifice of the first-born. As to the theory of an ancient blood-rite this likewise God may have incorporated into the historically-instituted feast.[12]

But, although a hypothesis such as that of human sacrifice is not inherently impossible, since the Hebrews are known to have lapsed into pagan observances in Egypt (Josh. 24:14), still Genesis 22:12 had forbidden this practice; and verses like Genesis 29:32 show joy not sorrow, over the coming of Israel's firstborn. It appears unlikely,

---

[11]See above, pp. 370, 371.
[12]*Op. cit.*, pp. 136-137.

therefore, that God would thus tacitly have rested His approval upon such an unholy activity. A more satisfactory approach consists rather of relating any previous Israelitish beliefs about the token of the blood to the established truths of atoning blood sacrifices.[13] In any event, the significance that Scripture proceeds to assign to the Mosaic passover lamb is that of a redemptive substitute (Ex. 13:13). God's threat had been that *all* the firstborn in the land of Egypt should die; and this included, of course, the firstborn of Moses' own people (11: 5; 13:15). The death of the lamb, however, served to "redeem" the firstborn of the Hebrew children (13:15); but for the full significance of this fact, and for its influence upon our understanding of the Biblical teaching on atonement, compare topic 19, on the death of the Testator.[14] As a result then of this redemption, God promised, "When I see the blood, I will pass over you, and there shall no plague be upon you to destroy you, when I smite the land of Egypt" (12:13). The requirement of death had, in God's eyes, been met — vicariously. Not only could Israel live through that momentous night, but they could also live to inherit eternal salvation under the testament.

God, however, did not limit paschal observance to that original passover of 1446 B.C.; He proceeded to establish 3) a perpetual, annual passover feast (12:14). The passover was to commence on the fourteenth day of every first month (March or April), which meant, specifically, the time of the full moon that followed the first new moon after the vernal equinox; and it was to continue through the seven subsequent days of unleavened bread. This annually repeated service was designed, first of all, to serve as a memorial of Israel's deliverance from Egypt (vv. 14, 17, 24-27), "a night to be much observed unto Yahweh for bringing them out from the land" (v. 42). But its purpose exceeded that of a mere memorial. The reason that the passover feast and sacrifice had to be perpetual was due to the fact that Israel's firstborn children continued perpetually to be God's and stood, therefore, in constant need of divine redemption (Ex. 13: 2; Num. 3:13). The explanation, in turn, for this continuing obligation in respect to the children's lives is found in the fact of sin, specifically, of Pharaoh's rebellion against God (Ex. 13:15). The truth then is this: Even after Pharaoh disappears from the historical scene, men in general still do not obey God and so continue to stand in need of a sacrificial ransom. It is significant, therefore, that foreign proselytes were not allowed to take part in the passover (Israel's repeated sacrament of continued redemption) until they had first, as saved believers, undergone the rite of circumcision (Israel's initiatory sacrament of original redemption), which symbolized their regeneration by God's Holy Spirit (12:48).

---

[13]See above, pp. 381, 382.
[14]See above, pp. 247, 248.

With the passing of the years, 4) certain changes were made in the form of the paschal feast. Moses himself anticipated his people's settlement in Canaan and provided for the offering of the first sheaf of the grain harvest at passover time (Lev. 23:11). Then in 1406 B.C., at the close of the wilderness wanderings, he ordered the observance of the blood on the door-posts and of the family meal at home to be replaced by a ritual of sacrifice and of organized feasting at the central sanctuary, to the founding of which he looked forward (Deut. 16:5-7). Among the later Jews, moreover, the blood came to be represented in the form of four cups of wine. During the course of this ceremony, the "Hallel" (Ps. 113-118) was then sung; compare the statement of Mark 14:26, "And when they had sung a hymn they went out." In times of Israelitish apostasy, the ceremony of the passover was badly neglected; but, with the various Judean reformations, there occurred noteworthy revivals of the observance of its rites. Hezekiah in 725 B.C. was responsible for holding the greatest single passover since the time of Solomon (II Chron. 30:26). It is true that in that year, because of a lack of proper preparations, the people found themselves unable to celebrate the feast in the prescribed first month (v. 3); but the date was able to be satisfactorily shifted to the second month (v. 2). Such arrangements had been authorized by Moses (Num. 9:10, 11), and the spirit meant more than the exact calendar! Josiah in 621 B.C. then celebrated the greatest passover since the days of the judges (II Chron. 35:18; II Kings 23:22). Its observance constituted a primary demonstration of Israel's renewed faith in God's testament (v. 21).

In the fulness of time came 5) the fulfillment of the passover in the person of the Messiah; "For even Christ our passover is sacrificed for us" (I Cor. 5:7). On the very afternoon that the paschal lambs were being prepared (cf. John 13:1; 18:28), Jesus Christ gave His life on the cross in order that redemption might be accomplished once and for all. In His own person, He constitutes the final Lamb of God who was for sinners slain. The Savior, moreover, offered Himself without spot or blemish (I Pet. 1:18, 19; cf. Ex. 12:5), and not a bone of His body was ever broken (John 19:36).[15] In such a way was the Mosaic system of anticipatory sacrifice terminated that day on Calvary.

Yet on the evening previous to the regular celebration of the paschal ceremony,[16] Jesus Christ observed the ancient passover feast with His disciples in the upper room (Matt. 26:17). This meal thereby became, at the same time, history's last, valid Mosaic passover and also the first Lord's Supper; for the one was transformed into the other. The redemption that had been anticipated in the passover is now commemorated in the supper. Moreover, even as the passover

[15]God's reason for the original regulation of Ex. 12:46.
[16]Cf. C. H. Turner, "Chronology of the New Testament," James Hastings, ed., A *Dictionary of the Bible*, I:411.

constituted a sacramental seal, both of Israel's gracious adoption by God, so that He should be their Father (Ex. 4:22), and of their resultant, communal brotherhood under the national testament; so the supper has become the sacramental seal of our union with Christ (I Cor. 10:16) and of our union with one another in the new testament of His blood (v. 17, 11:25). The truth of Exodus 12:13 is *eternally* valid:

> "The blood shall be to you for a token upon the houses where ye are: and when I see the blood, I will pass over you, and there shall be no plague upon you to destroy you, when I smite the land (of Egypt)."

The second of the three annual pilgrimage festivals was the feast of weeks. It was later called pentecost, which means the "fiftieth [day]"; for it took place seven weeks and one day after the passover (Lev. 23:15, 16). It thus followed the wheat harvest and became the occasion for the presentation of two wheaten loaves as a new meal-offering (v. 17). In this symbolic way, the Hebrews were enabled to recognize Yahweh as the source of their daily food. A moral lesson was also contained in pentecost, because foreigners, servants, and the needy were invited to share in Israel's festivities (Deut. 16:11).

The third pilgrimage feast was that of tabernacles. It was so named because for seven days in the fall, commencing with the fifteenth day of the seventh month (September or October), Israel was commanded to dwell in temporarily constructed tabernacles, or outdoor booths. These in turn served as a memorial of the Exodus and of the nation's camping in the wilderness (Lev. 23:40-43). Tabernacles were also called the feast of ingathering, for it marked the termination of the Palestinian agricultural year (Ex. 23:16). This feast was instituted, therefore, as a time of special rejoicing (Lev. 23:40) and of sharing with the poor (Deut. 16:14); it was the Hebrew thanksgiving. The fifteenth day of the seventh month became an even further memorial of thanks when, with the post-exilic restoration, this date was chosen for the re-establishment of the sacrificial ceremonial in Jerusalem (Ezra 3:1, 4). Tabernacles is the one Old Testament feast that is specifically singled out for observance in the eschatalogical context of the testament of peace. Oehler explains it as follows:

> The admission of this festival into Zechariah's prophecy of Messianic times, Zech. xiv. 16, is undoubtedly founded on the kindred thought, that the keeping of the Feast of Tabernacles is an expression on the part of the nations, of their thankfulness for the termination of their wanderings, by their reception into the peaceful kingdom of the Messiah.[17]

The two other annual feasts, or set convocations, that were revealed through Moses took place shortly before the feast of taber-

---

[17] *Op. cit.*, p. 351.

nacles in this same seventh month. On the first day of the month, two weeks, that is, before the beginning of tabernacles, came the feast of trumpets (Lev. 23:24). This opening date may have marked the older, secular, new year's day of the Hebrews (cf. Ex. 23:16), as it could have been observed prior to the Exodus, when Moses moved it to the springtime and to the month of the passover (12:2). Under the divided kingdoms, the calendar year of northern Israel began in the month of March-April; but that of the south seems to have commenced in September-October, and hence at the feast of trumpets.[18] This observance of an autumnal new year's was then continued in Judah after the exile; and it accounts for the appearance of the present *Rōsh hashshānā,* "Jewish New Year's," in the fall. Just as in the case of the new moon sabbaths, the "memorial of blowing of trumpets" (Lev. 23:24) appears to have had an anthropomorphic import, to "remind" the Lord of the needs of His people. Correspondingly, Numbers 10:9 reads, "Ye shall sound an alarm with the trumpets; and ye shall be remembered before Yahweh your God, and ye shall be saved from your enemies" (cf. v. 10; and II Chron. 13:14).[19]

Then on the tenth day of this same fall month, five days before tabernacles, came the fifth of the annual convocations of the Mosaic calendars, namely, *Yom Kippūr(îm),* the day of atonement (Lev. 16). "Yom Kippur" was the day that was preeminently designated for national repentance on the part of Israel and for their sincere humiliation before God (v. 29). The precise divine command reads, "Ye shall afflict your souls." By the time of the New Testament, these words, had become popularly understood to indicate a practice of fasting (cf. Acts 27:9, "the fast"). But "affliction of the soul" does not necessarily carry this connotation; and fasting, as an observance, is nowhere prescribed in the Old Testament. Humble confession of sin, however, constitutes one of the changeless requirements of God (Prov. 28:13).

Yom Kippur served also as a day of ceremonial atonement for the tabernacle (which had been defiled by the sinful nation), for the priests, and for all the repentant people of Israel (Lev. 16:21, 33). Moorehead thus concludes:

> It was the supreme day of the whole Mosaic economy, and it signalized as no other rite in the entire complicated system did the vital New Testament truth that "Christ was once offered to bear the sins of many," and that he has "entered into heaven itself, now to appear in the presence of God for us."[20]

[18]Payne, *An Outline of Hebrew History,* p. 124; and cf. Edwin R. Thiele, *The Mysterious Numbers of the Hebrew Kings* (Chicago: University of Chicago Press, 1951).
[19]Rather than the position of Moorehead, *Studies in the Mosaic Institutions,* p. 226, who states, "We understand the expression, 'a memorial of the blowing of trumpets,' as relating to what was to come in the sacred calendar of Israel. It ushered in the Day of Atonement, which was observed nine days after."
[20]*Ibid.,* pp. 183-184.

The actual atonement ritual was performed by the Aaronic high priest over the ark of the testament in the most holy place of the Tabernacle. Moorehead calculates from the evidence of Leviticus 16, that "Three times on the Day of Atonement the high priest passed the veil and stood before the awful Presence at the ark."[21] He came first with incense, as an acted prayer for mercy "that he die not" (v. 13); then with the blood of a bull, as a sin-offering for himself and for his priestly household, to be sprinkled on the "mercy seat," the atoning cover of the ark (vv. 6, 11, 14); and finally with the blood of a goat (one out of two that had been originally set apart), as a sin offering for the people (vv. 9, 15). The blood of both of the slain animals was then used to make atonement for the altar of the tabernacle (v. 19).

After the ceremony at the sanctuary, the bodies of the bull and the goat were burned outside the camp (v. 27). They thus became typical of Christ's death outside the walls of Jerusalem (Heb. 13:12). The second goat however, was employed as a "scape [escape] goat" and Scripture designates it as intended "for Azazel" (Satan). It thus symbolizes both the sending of sin back to its demonic author and the breaking of the latter's claims over Israel.[22] It must, however, be noted that the goat is distinguished from Azazel himself. This second goat symbolized neither the getting rid of Satan or the laying of man's sins upon Satan. Nor does the scape goat constitute a sin offering, as did the first (v. 9); for men are not to sacrifice to devils. Rather, the second goat was presented alive before God for the purpose of depicting another aspect that is involved in men's atonement (v. 10). Specifically, it had the sins of the people confessed over its head (v. 21); and it was then allowed to "escape" into the wilderness, sent off to Satan in symbolical, substitutionary condemnation (v. 22).

Oehler, together with most liberal commentators, has denied to the scape goat any such idea of its vicarious suffering of the penalties that were due to men or of its functioning as a satisfaction. He seeks rather to establish that the sins that Aaron laid on its head had already been forgiven.[23] Context, however, demands that the confession that the high priest made over the goat be understood in relation to a real transference of guilt and of punishment. A parallel example is that of the bird that was released at the cleansing of a leper, which was allowed to fly away and thus, symbolically, to carry off the evil leprosy (Lev. 14:7).[24] As a result of this sin-bearing, even the man

[21]*Ibid.*, p. 191.
[22]See above, pp. 292, 293.
[23]*Op. cit.*, p. 313.
[24]Cf. Vriezen's admission of the truth of this interpretation, though he proceeds, with typical neo-orthodox subjectivism, to dismiss it as a primitive, "dynamistic" element in Old Testament religion; *An Outline of Old Testament Theology*, p. 21.

who took the goat out into the wilderness was declared unclean and had to go through a ceremony of purifying himself (v. 26), just as did those who took the sin offerings without the camp (v. 28). Such acts of purification, moreover, became necessary, not as though the wilderness were considered unclean (for it is never so called), or as though the sin offerings or the scape goat were superstitiously believed to be holy and possessed of some power to make those who contacted them "unclean" (!). Rather, the need for the men's purification arose from the fact that the sins of the people had been laid, even though only in symbol, upon these animals (v. 21).

One of the most striking features of Yom Kippur is the repetitiousness of its services. This observation applies, first of all, to the procedures that were executed throughout any given annual day of atonement. Moorehead has thus commented in reference to the actions of the high priest:

> He must offer first for his own sins before he could offer for the sins of the people (Lev. 9:8; Heb. 7:27). This fact indicates the inherent weakness of the Levitical priesthood itself, and points to the insufficiency of the whole system which could effect no more than symbolical atonement.[25]

Actually, the service of Israel's high priest constituted a type, which was designed to anticipate the work of the One who "needeth not, like those high priests, to offer up sacrifices, first for his own sins, and then for the sins of the people." The future antitype, in contrast, would be a high priest "holy, guileless, undefiled, separated from sinners, and made higher than the heavens" (Heb. 7:27, 28). Then secondly, one is struck by the necessity for the repetition, year after year, of the day of atonement rituals. Their very repetition, in fact, serves to underline the lack of intrinsic effectiveness that characterized the whole ceremony. So Zechariah, in the post-exilic period, looked forward to that newer testament, by means of which God would forever remove the iniquity of the land in one, unrepeated day (Zech. 3:9). The goal of true atonement would thus finally be achieved by Jesus Christ, whose infinite (divine) perfection eliminated the necessity —

> ". . . that He should offer Himself often, as the high priest entereth into the holy place year by year with blood not his own: but now once at the end of the ages hath He been manifested to put away sin by the sacrifice of Himself" (Heb. 9:25, 26).

No additions to the sacred calendar of Moses are known to have occurred throughout the course of the history of the Hebrew kingdoms. During the exile, however, there did arise four days of commemorative fasting. Their institution had not, apparently, been a

---

[25]Moorehead, *op. cit.,* pp. 186-187.

matter of divine revelation; but the prophet Zechariah records their historical observance and their associated symbolism as follows (Zech. 7:3, 5 and 8:19):

Month	Day	Event commemorated	Jer. ref.	II Kings ref.
4th	9th	Jerusalem captured, 586 B.C.	39:2, 52:6-7	25:3-4
5th	7th or 10th	Jerusalem burned, 586 B.C.	52:12-14	25:8-9
7th	3rd (by traditon)	The murder of Gedaliah, 586 B.C	41:1	25:25
10th	10th	Jerusalem siege begun, 588/7 B.C.	39:1, 52:4	25:1

When Zechariah was then asked whether Judah should continue to observe these fast days, now that the exile was over, he predicted that if his people would but turn their hearts to God in sincere moral repentance, the need for fasting would cease; instead, these four days would be converted into joyful feasts (8:15-19). The degree of the Jews' repentance is not known, but the fasts continued!

In the closing paragraphs of the post-exilic book of Esther, God ordained one additional festival for Israel, namely, the feast of Purim, one month before passover (Esther 9:21). Scripture explains this name as arising from the Babylonian "Pur," which means a "stone" or a "lot," and specifically, the lot that was cast before Haman in his attempt to destroy the Jews (3:7). The Lord, however, thwarted Haman; and this day, which might have dawned as one of sorrow, was turned into an occasion of feasting and gladness, of exchanging gifts, and of remembering those in need (9:22). Purim thus became the distinctively nationalistic holiday of later Israel; and it corresponds roughly to an American Independence Day, with certain elements of New Year's festivity included as well.

During the Jewish intertestamental period, on December of 165 B.C. (at what is now the Christmas season), Judas Maccabeus succeeded in driving back the forces of the tyrant Antiochus Epiphanes and was thus enabled to accomplish a cleansing of the Jerusalem temple, after three years of Greek profanation. This event came subsequently to be commemorated in the feast of "Hanukka," or dedication, also called "the feast of lights." The observance of Hanukka is mentioned historically in the New Testament (John 10:22), but the feast as such lacks divine authentication.

Out of the list of Israel's "sacred times," as these have been outlined above (cf. the summary in Appendix E), the Sabbath and the Passover have now become, respectively, the Lord's Day and the Lord's Supper; they have been explicitly continued in the New

Testament Church with moral, sacramental, and typical force.[26] Otherwise, however, the sacred seasons of the Hebrews, including the seventh day of the week for the observance of the sabbath, have been fulfilled in Christ and have been abrogated as far as their present observance is concerned. Vos properly evaluates them as —

> ". . . a cycle of feasts which is no longer in force now . . . From all this we have been released by the work of Christ, but not from the Sabbath as instituted at Creation. In this light we must interpret certain N.T. statements such as Rom. 14:5, 6; Gal. 4:10, 11; Col. 2:16, 17."[27]

The Holy Spirit accordingly, spoke through Paul and strictly admonished His church,

> "Let no man therefore judge you in meat, or in drink, or in respect of a feast day or a new moon or a sabbath day: which are a shadow of the things to come; but the body is Christ's" (Col. 2:16, 17).

The great moral principles that lay behind the feasts — of gratitude to God, of care for the poor, of commitment to His providence, and of joy in His service — all these heart characteristics retain their validity as elements of our permanently required response for inheritance under the testament; but the precise forms and times no longer possess relevance.

For Further Reading:

Hayyim Schauss, *The Jewish Festivals From Their Beginnings to Our Own Day.* Cincinnati, Ohio: Union of American Hebrew Congregations, 1938. Traces the feasts down to their present (perverted) observance in Judaism.

Robert G. North, *Sociology of the Biblical Jubilee.* Rome: Pontifical Biblical Institute, 1954. A Pontifical Biblical Institute publication. It constitutes a thorough study relative to the implications of the year of jubilee.

James Patterson Hutchinson, *Our Obligations to the Day of Rest and Worship.* Second edition; Colorado Springs, Colo.; James P. Hutchinson, 1916. A practical study on the application of the sabbath law, by a former secretary of the Lord's Day Alliance.

---

[26]It should be noted, however, that the typical force of the Lord's Supper in respect to Christ's future kingdom embodies some of the truths that were once conveyed by the feast of tabernacles and the year of jubilee, and that the moral and sacramental values of the other ancient feasts find a degree of correspondence in the practices of the Church, though not as divinely ordained parts of the church calendar. See Appendix E, pp. 524, 525, for a chart of the significance of sacred times in the Old Testament.

[27]*Op. cit.*, p. 159.

Part VII. The Inheritance: Reconciliation

"Nevertheless I am continually with Thee: Thou hast holden my right hand. Thou wilt guide me with Thy counsel, and afterward receive me to glory" (Ps. 73:23, 24).

29. Redeemed Life*

The goal of any given testament is that its heirs may receive their intended inheritance. Such a feature is no less characteristic of God's testament. The preceding parts of this study, moreover, have considered the four major, antecedent aspects of our Lord's testamentary arrangements:[1] the Testator, who is God Himself; the heir, the elect out of mankind; the means of effectuation, divine grace; and the condition that is required for men's inheritance, their commitment to God. This fourth aspect was then analyzed as including the basic elements of men's repentance and faith, together with conversion's practical demonstration through the medium of sincere obedience, both moral and ceremonial. As we come to consider, however, the fifth and final major aspect of the testament, we arrive at the ultimate purpose of God's whole redemptive activity in history, namely, "that they that have been called may receive the promise of the eternal inheritance" (Heb. 9:15).

In essence, the testamental inheritance consists of men's reconciliation with God. Mankind under the covenant of works had failed. They had failed inexcusably, miserably, and hopelessly. But God in His grace provided the redemptive testament, the goal of which is to bring about a corresponding restoration of men to Himself, even though such a testament should involve the death of His own beloved Son (v. 16).

God's gift of reconciliation, that constitutes the essential inheritance of the testament, is then summed up in the words of the basic testamentary promise, which is found from Genesis to Revelation, "I will be their God, and they shall be My people" (cf. Gen. 17:7; Rev. 21:3). The final accomplishments of this promise were to be eschato-

---

* BIBLE READING: Genesis 32; Psalm 23

Collateral Reading: Schultz, *Old Testament Theology,* II:79-86.
   Baab, *The Theology of the Old Testament,* pp. 156-173.
   T. C. Vriezen, *An Outline of Old Testament Theology,* pp. 301-314.

[1]See above, p. 87.

411

logical, either in the personal eschatology of life after death (topic 30) or in the general eschatology of (a) the new testament (topic 31) — for our present-day Church amounted to "eschatology" for the saints of the older dispensation — or (b) the testament of peace that is yet future (topic 32). Also, however, Jesus Christ promised to His disciples, "Whosoever believeth on Me *hath* everlasting life" (John 5:24); eternal life, in other words, begins right now! This promise, moreover, was just as true for the saints of the old testament as it is for us today. Anticipatory as their faith may have been, their Old Testament Scriptures yet abound with clear recognitions of, and joy in, a presently-experienced redeemed life with God. This appreciation is particularly characteristic of the poetic books of Psalms and Proverbs; but the precious law of Sinai insists with equal force, "See, I have set before thee *this day* life and good . . ." (Deut. 30:15).

A. GOD'S KINGDOM. The Davidic testament developed the concept of salvation as consisting of life in the Messiah's kingdom.[2] In a sense, this life was a future one (II Sam. 23:4); and yet it also possessed aspects that related to the present. David thus explained about his contemporary testament, "For this is all my salvation" (v. 5). His own victories then constituted an active, though external, demonstration of what it could mean in this present life to have God as one's king.[3] Centuries before David, however, Moses had revealed that God was, at that time, both king in general (Ex. 15:18), and ruler over Y'shūrūn (the "upright little people") in particular; and this latter phrase referred to the elect nation of the Hebrews whom He had visibly, just redeemed (Deut. 33:5; I Chron. 28:5). So Balaam could say of Israel, "Yahweh his God is with him, the shout of a king is among them" (Num. 23:21). This divine, ruling presence was the element that constituted the basis for Israel's day by day hope. Even when faced with calamity, God's chosen ones could yet speak with assurance, "Yahweh is my portion" (Lam. 3:24, 25); for He was their source of strength whatever might come to pass. David's chief musician thus summarized the confidence, both of himself and of his people, in the following affirmation: "Nevertheless I am continually with Thee" (Ps. 73:23).

When Israel was granted the inheritance of the testament and God became their king, it necessarily followed that they became also His servants. Possession, however, by God meant that individual

---

[2]See above, pp. 108, 109.
[3]Negative critics have questioned the historicity of David's victories as, in part, wishful thinking by his less effective successors. Thus Baab asserts, *The Theology of the Old Testament*, p. 158, "The authors of the [Biblical] legends, folk tales, and poems instinctively or deliberately reacted to national frustration by developing a myth of a golden age and by using this myth as the springboard for the projection of this golden age into a glorious future." Baab's very criticism, however, witnesses to the positive glory of David's life with God, as this is described in Scripture!

Israelites were correspondingly exempted from slavery to other persons (Lev. 25:42) and that the nation as a whole, as it continued subject to God, was enabled to live in freedom from bondage (26:13). As a result, even the wicked might share in the practical effects of the testamental blessings (cf. Gen. 18:26). The holding of citizenship in God's kingdom involved, it is true, a man's judgment in the case of his sin (I Sam. 8:7; cf. v. 18); but it also made possible a subsequent avenue for his gracious restoration. For example, David's attendant was struck down when he violated the ark of the testament; but, as this same throne of God's presence was later brought into Jerusalem, with the precise form of reverence that God had prescribed, David found that his sorrow was turned into joy and he exclaimed,

> "Lift up your heads, oh ye gates;
> And the King of glory will come in.
> Who is the King of glory?
> Yahweh strong and mighty, Yahweh mighty in battle!"
>   (Ps. 24:7, 8).

Indeed, these two principles of judgment and restoration come to dominate the entire thought of the testamental inheritance of God's kingship, particularly as this is developed in its eschatological aspects, see topics 31 and 32.

B. SPIRITUAL REDEMPTION. The experience of reconciliation with God and of entrance into His kingdom results, first of all, in a number of spiritual blessings that spring from a man's commitment by faith to Israel's heavenly king. For that matter, the very fact of the presence of this faith stands as evidence to an even prior activity on God's part, namely, to that act of regeneration by which He creates a clean heart within His own (Ps. 51:10).[4] From the time of Abraham and onward, the rite of circumcision had served as the outward sign and seal of spiritual rebirth;[5] see above, topic 18-B, on God's regenerating monergism. God's placing of His fear within men's hearts had thus constituted an essential part of the testament (cf. Jer. 32:40); and Jeremiah, accordingly, predicted that Israel's post-exilic restoration would be based upon Yahweh's having given "a heart to know Me" to Jehoiachin's "good figs" (24:7). The most fundamental factor in the blessed life is therefore that of God's favor (specifically through Christ, God's "Wisdom," (Prov. 8:35); in fact, God's favor is better than life itself (Ps. 63:3). For the Old Testament is by no means limited in its goals to matters of this world's material interests; and David's singers accordingly exclaim, "I had rather be a doorkeeper in the house of my God, than to dwell in the tents of wickedness" (Ps. 84:10). Isaiah, moreover, in the eighth century, came to per-

---

[4]Note the phrase, "renew a right spirit," indicative of God's former work, and cf. Vriezen, *An Outline of Old Testament Theology*, p. 311.
[5]See above, pp. 391-394.

ceive that worldly affliction may even serve as a necessary prerequisite to a man's gaining those God-given spiritual eyes which are so essential if he is to appreciate the Lord's eternal values (Isa. 30:20, 21). Many, even of Israel's leaders, did not have the understanding of divine regeneration that they should have had (John 3:5, 6). But this hardly justifies, for example, John Raven's following criticism of David's religious aspiration: "This was as noble an ambition as a man could have who had not received the gift of the Holy Spirit."[6] Criticisms such as these indicate actually a double misapprehension. 1) They confuse the indwelling presence of the Holy Spirit with His fulness; for the regenerating presence of the Spirit, David, like all born-again believers, enjoyed constantly (Ps. 143:10). 2) They minimize also the real, though confessedly temporary, fulness of the Spirit; for this charismatic blessing, men such as David are expressly declared to have possessed (cf. I Sam. 16:13).

Following upon a man's rebirth from above, the forgiveness of his sins becomes the next major spiritual result of testamental inheritance. Cain, in the primeval period, could not appreciate this truth of God's forgiveness and grasped only the fact of His punishment (Gen. 4:13); but divine reconciliation could have become a reality to him, if he had but committed his heart to God. From the Mosaic period and onward, non-presumptuous sins (Lev. 5:3) were specifically forgiven via the ritual law (v. 10; cf. Ps. 19:13)); and other, intentional violations were included as well (cf. Lev. 5:1, 4). The guilt, moreover, of even such serious transgressions as David's crimes in regard to Bath-sheba God promised to eradicate (II Sam. 12:13). In the last analysis, this blessing of divine forgiveness occurred, not because of men's acts of penitence, but "for His name's sake," that is, because of the grace of God's own essential nature (Ps. 25:11; 79:9). God is therefore described as sallāh, "forgiving" (86:5). The verbal root from which this adjective is derived may, on occasion indicate no more than a mild forbearance (cf. II Kings 5:18); but it normally describes the full and complete forgiveness of guilt (Jer. 33:8; 50:20).[7] Such remission was granted to the end "that Thou mayest be feared [reverenced]" (Ps. 130:4).

As the result, then, of divine grace, David's humble and sincere confession was, at that time, honored by God with the promised "covering" (forgiveness) of his sins (32:1, 5); and David could not cease to praise the God "who forgiveth all thine iniquities" (103:3; cf. 85:2). The sins of the Old Testament saints were thus perma-

---

[6]*The History of the Religion of Israel*, p. 231.
[7]Kohler's objection that Old Testament forgiveness applies predominantly to specific offences, rather than to God's general forgiveness of sin, serves only to underline the characteristic concreteness of the older revelation and hardly warrants his conclusion that these acts do not alter the relationship between God and His people, *Theology of the Old Testament*, pp. 217-218.

nently forgiven: "As far as the east is from the west, so far *hath* He removed our transgressions from us" (v. 12).[8] In the eighth century, therefore, God assured His people, "Though your sins be as scarlet they shall be as snow" (Isa. 1:18; cf. 44:22; Mic. 7:18); and at the time of the exile, He stated in respect to the repentant sinner, "None of his transgressions that he hath committed shall be remembered against him" (Ezek. 18:22). But though God's forgiveness was real and immediate, the Old Testament yet revealed that this action of divine grace had become possible only by anticipation of a still future, ultimate atonement that God would some day perform for His people (Zech. 3:9; Ps. 130:7, 8). Thus Micah concluded his prophecy with the as-yet-unfulfilled hope, "He *will* tread our iniquities under foot; and Thou *wilt* cast all their sins into the depths of the sea" (Mic. 7: 19). This very incompleteness, moreover, to the process of Old Testament forgiveness is what makes it such that "he that is but little in the kingdom" of Christ possesses today a blessed assurance which is far richer than that experienced by the most spiritual of the pre-Christian prophets (Matt. 11:11).

But God did, as it were, "on credit" restore to men their righteousness (Job 33:26): that is, the Old Testament, as surely the New, proclaims the blessing of justification, that follows upon a man's commitment to God in saving faith. Even in the earliest period of revelation, Scripture thus comments on God's grace toward Noah (Gen. 6:8) and then records the latter as a "righteous" individual (v. 9). This description of Noah does not mean that his actions always *were* righteous (cf. 9:21). The force of justification is rather this: that as he yielded his life to God he was *declared* to be righteous in the eyes of Yahweh, the heavenly Judge. So Proverbs 17:15 can speak of the possibility of "justifying the wicked"; and Moses provides a negative definition to justification, when he notes it as constituting the opposite of condemnation (Deut. 25:1). Isaiah as an heir of God's testament, could thus affirm with confidence, "He is near that justifieth me; who will condemn me?" (Isa. 50:8, 9; cf. Rom. 8:33). But it is axiomatic that God in His righteousness can only declare to be righteous those who possess a legitimate claim to righteousness (cf. I Kings 8:32); He will never justify the wicked (Ex. 23:7). The saved sinner can therefore be "justified" only on the grounds of the substituted righteousness of Jesus Christ, the sinless suffering servant (Isa. 53:11). As John Murray has expressed it:

> In God's justification of sinners there is no deviation from the rule that what is declared to be is presupposed to be. God's judgment is according to truth here as elsewhere. The peculiarity of God's action consists in this that he causes to be, the righteous state or relation which is declared to be . . . He constitutes the

---

[8]Vriezen thus speaks of the "inner peace" and relief from "alarm about guilt" that characterized the Old Testament saints, *op. cit.*, p. 306.

ungodly righteous, and consequently can declare them to be righteous. In the justification of sinners there is a constitutive act as
well as a declarative. Or, if we will, we may say that the declarative act of God in the justification of the ungodly is constitutive.
In this consists its incomparable character.[9]

Thus to Abraham, in the patriarchal period, there was reckoned
righteousness, through faith (Gen. 15:6; see above, topic 12-C);[10]
and Isaiah 45:24, 25 proclaims to God's people, "In Yahweh is
righteousness and strength . . . In Yahweh shall all the seed of Israel
be justified and shall glory." The principle which is involved is that
of Philippians 3:9, that we are found in God's Son, not having a righteousness of our own, but that which is through faith in Christ, the
righteousness which is from God by faith.

Justification then serves to introduce two further matters of revelation, both of which pertain to this same general subject of spiritual
redemption. The first of these is the blessing of divine adoption.
While it is true that the Old Testament contains no set formula for
the act of adopting a foster son, this deficiency by no means implies
that adoption as such was unknown among the Hebrews of Bible
times. Archaeological evidence from the Mesopotamian site of Nuzu
indicates, on the contrary, both that adoption was a common practice
in the ancient Near East and also that its functioning is reflected in
the very patriarchal narratives of the Old Testament. Thus the relationship of Eliezer of Damascus to his master Abraham (Gen. 15:2),
or of Jacob to his employer Laban (cf. 31:43), is best understood as
that of an adopted son to his foster father, by a specific, legal action.[11]
Men who had formerly been slaves or wanderers could thus become
testamentary heirs by means of "adoption." In the Mosaic period then,
Israel as a nation experienced just such a spiritual adoption under
the Sinaitic testament, whereby they became "sons of God" (Ex.
4:22; Deut. 32:6) or, as Romans 9:4 expresses it, "Israelites, whose is
the adoption, and the glory, and the testaments."[12] Divine adoption,
however, was never automatic: Human corruption could still cut off
from participation in the true kingdom of God such individuals as
were but nominal Israelites, with the result that God speaks of the
profane as "not His children" (Deut. 32:5; cf. v. 19). But when
saving faith did arise in the hearts of the people, then justification
gave to them the status of being "called by God's name" (Isa. 43:7);
they became His "sons" and His "daughters" (v. 6). In other words,
just as Eliezer long ago received adoption by Abraham, so now the
slave of sin may become, not only the seed of Abraham, but God's

---

[9]*Redemption—Accomplished and Applied*, p. 153.
[10]Pages 160, 161, and cf. p. 156, note 9, on Abraham.
[11]Cf. Cyrus H. Gordon, "Biblical Customs and the Nuzu Tablets," *The Biblical
Archaeologist* 3:1 (Feb., 1940), 1-12.
[12]See above, pp. 181, 182.

own redeemed child, whereby he cries, "Abba, Father" (Rom. 8:15; Gal. 3:29-4:7).[13] Murray therefore concludes,

> "Adoption is a distinct act carrying with it its own peculiar privileges . . . By adoption the redeemed become sons and daughters of the Lord God Almighty; they are introduced into and given the privileges of God's family."[14]

Stated in legal terminology, the designated heirs have, by grace, become "inner-family beneficiaries" of the testament (cf. Rom. 8:17).

The second corollary of justification consists of the blessing of divine sanctification. For though "holiness" may, with propriety, be treated under the aspect of one's commitment to the testament (signifying the sum total of men's response to God in volitional obedience)[15] sanctification may still, at the same time, be considered under the subject of one's inherited blessings from God. Both of these aspects constitute real elements in Christian experience.

> "Nothing shows this more clearly than the exhortation of the apostle: 'Work out your own salvation with fear and trembling; for it is God who works in you both to will and to do for his good pleasure'" (Phil. 2:12, 13).[16]

To this apostolic statement corresponds then the exhortation of the lawgiver: "Ye shall keep My statutes, and do them: for I am Yahweh who sanctifieth you" (Lev. 20:8). Sanctification in the Old Testament may, it is true, represent no more than the original (physical) idea of holiness, a holiness of separation which exists without necessary moral implications.[17] Exodus 29:27, for example, speaks of "sanctifying offerings." But sanctification may also describe that gracious, moral activity of God in the hearts of His own, by which he "cleanses you from all your iniquities" (Ezek. 36:33). Thus Isaiah 45:25, which was quoted in reference to justification — "In Yahweh shall Israel be justified" — goes beyond even the above-mentioned teaching on imputed righteousness. For the verb of the sentence, *sādhaq*, is here employed in its simple (qal) stem and means, literally, "In Yahweh shall all the seed of Israel *be righteous*." As Delitzsch sums up its full significance, the people of God are both "reconciled *and renewed*."[18]

With such spiritual blessings, the Old Testament saints were able to experience the fulness of the joy of God's redeemed (cf. Deut.

---

[13]The term *Abbā* is significant as pointing back to the Semitic (Aramaic), and specifically Old Testament, concepts of adoption. Cf. William H. Rossell "New Testament Adoption—Graeco-Roman or Semitic?" *Journal of Biblical Literature,* 71:4 (Dec. 1952), pp. 233-234.
[14]Murray, *op. cit.,* p. 165.
[15]See above, p. 297, and topics 25-28.
[16]Murray, *op. cit.,* p. 184.
[17]See above, topic 9-C.
[18]*Biblical Commentary on the Prophecies of Isaiah* (Trans. from the 3rd ed. by James Denney; London: Hodder and Stoughton, 1892), II, 186.

12:7; Ps. 51:12). David, though in the midst of severe persecution, could therefore sing, "Oh taste and see that Yahweh is good" (34:8); and even after his greatest crime, because of the God-given forgiveness and justification that followed upon his confession, he could witness,

> "Blessed is he whose transgression is forgiven,
>   Whose sin is covered.
> Blessed is the man unto whom Yahweh imputeth not iniquity,
>   And in whose spirit there is no guile" (32:1, 2).

Characteristic of this joyousness of Old Testament faith is the post-exilic stress upon thankfulness, upon gift-giving, and upon charity (Esther 9:22; cf. Ps. 126:2); and the injunction of Nehemiah constitutes a standing-order for the ransomed of the Lord: "Go your way, eat the fat, and drink the sweet, and send portions unto him for whom nothing is prepared; neither be ye grieved; for the joy of Yahweh is your strength" (Neh. 8:10).[19]

A final source of power for the Old Testament saints lay in their confidence of spiritual perseverance (cf. Ps. 55:22). Their assurance of salvation might, indeed, appear to be questioned by such passages as Ezekiel 18:24, 26, "When a righteous man turneth away from his righteousness . . ."; but these verses simply reiterate the well-known Biblical doctrine of our awareness of a man's character, and of his judgment, according to his known fruits (cf. Matt. 7:16). That those who seem to be righteous can, and sometimes do, turn away from God is an observable phenomenon; but such defection serves, in fact, only to demonstrate their actual lack of original commitment (Ezek. 18:30, 31). As I John 2:19 observes, "For if they had been of us, they would have continued with us." But, though believers may not possess final assurance in respect to their neighbor's salvation, both the Old and New Testament saints can be joyfully confident of their own spiritual security. The perseverance of the saints comes to definite expression in such Old Testament verses as Psalm 125:1, "They that trust in Yahweh are as mount Zion, which cannot be moved, but abideth for ever"; or as Isaiah 46:4, "Even to hoar hairs will I carry you: I have made, and I will bear you; yes, I will carry, and will deliver." Compare the familiar words of Psalm 1:3 about the man who delights in God's law, "Whose leaf also shall not wither" (cf. Ps. 92:4, 5; and Isa. 48:14). For salvation is by grace, and it is therefore as unfailing as the monergism of the Testator. The elect, moreover, of all the ages rejoice together in this same unchangeable experience of spiritual redemption. Thus the joyous standard of the anonymous 100th Psalm stands as timelessly relevant: "Serve Yahweh with gladness, come before His presence with singing" (Ps. 100:2;

---

[19]Note Vriezen's stress upon Old Testament piety as "a living, spiritual, personal, joyful thing," *op. cit.*, p. 302.

cf. Deut. 28:47; Rev. 15:3); and Schultz enthusiastically describes the heart-throb of the whole company of God's redeemed:

"The very thought of Him is dearer than all the fulness of earthly joy. He is the fountain of living water, the light which streams upon the saint. Like the light of the sun to the inhabitants of earth, the light of God's countenance shining graciously upon him is, to the saint, the highest ideal of joy."[20]

C. FULL SURRENDER. The experience of the patriarch Jacob at Peniel (Gen. 32) constitutes the outstanding Biblical example of that further work of grace in a man's heart, by which God causes one of His own to enter into the fulness of redeemed life with Himself. Jacob is known to have been a saved individual at least twenty years previously (1929 B.C.), when he is specifically said to have received God's testament, with its fundamental promise of reconciliation: "And, behold, I am with thee" (28:15). Jacob's life, however, had not exhibited a complete yieldedness to God; and his conduct with Laban had been far from exemplary. But at Peniel in Transjordan (1909 B.C.), when he was returning to Canaan, "a man" (the Angel of the testament, Christ, Hos. 12:4) wrestled with him throughout the whole of one night (Gen. 32:24) and brought him into a new and deeper experience of spiritual realities.

A valid appreciation of this event depends upon the answers that one gives to three basic questions of interpretation. 1) Was Jacob's wrestling with the Angel right or wrong? At first glance, one's analysis might seem to suggest the latter conclusion. For Jacob's wrestling is elsewhere compared with his grasping at the heel of his older brother Esau (Hos. 12:2, 3), and God ended by having to overcome the stubborn patriarch (Gen. 32:25). The point would then seem to be that God made no headway against Jacob's selfish unyieldedness, but that at the last He broke His impenitent opponent. Jacob's "prevailing" (v. 28) would then refer to his holding on to God after this unhappy defeat (v. 26). But the total context forbids one's thus treating the wrestling as inherently wrong. Jacob's striving in verse 28 is praised; and it must be the same striving as that which appears in verse 24, "not a reprehensible but a commendable thing."[21]

Concluding then that Jacob's wrestling was good, one must next ask, 2) Against what was it directed? The struggle cannot be that of the unsurrendered Jacob against God, for Jacob was the one who prevailed. Neither can it be, in essence, Jacob's regenerate nature together with God, struggling against Jacob's unsurrendered will; for his opponent was the divine Angel; and He fought against Jacob, the whole man. The presence of the Angel of Yahweh, however,

[20]*Old Testament Theology*, II:80, and note his copious proof-texts that accompany.
[21]Geerhardus Vos, *Biblical Theology*, p. 113.

suggests a reference to the concept of the testament, and particularly to the testamental conditions that are laid down by God, if one is to receive the inheritance of reconciliation with Himself. In this light, moreover, the wrestling may well be understood as that of Jacob against God's testamental requirements. Jacob met the divine requirements and won the victory.

But finally then, 3) What were these testamental requirements? The answer must be the same as that which is found throughout Scripture, namely, that "Thou shalt love Yahweh thy God with *all* thy heart, and with *all* thy soul, and with *all* thy might" (Deut. 6:5; cf. Matt. 22:37, 38). Jacob's victory accordingly meant, at the same time, his own final surrender of self. The two spiritual experiences took place simultaneously. But in addition, as occurs so frequently in the practical revelations of the older testament, the spiritual struggle (in prayer, Hos. 12:4) was given a corresponding, physical demonstration (in real wrestling). As a result, that which was simultaneous, spiritually, could only be demonstrated in succession, physically. So the practical enactment progressed through these successive stages: first, Jacob's unfaltering struggle (v. 24); then God's overpowering Jacob, by straining his thigh (v. 25) — for God's Person can never be overcome — and again Jacob's persistence (v. 26).

Such a victory, in the matter of full surrender, involves the same seeming paradox that appears in the experience of salvation itself, "For whosoever would save his life shall lose it: and whosoever shall lose his life for My sake shall find it" (Matt. 16:25). This principle then continues to be equally true in the redeemed life that arises subsequent to conversion. As it was with Jacob at Peniel, so also it was with Paul on his missionary journeys, when he concluded, "For when I am weak, then am I strong" (II Cor. 12:10). Because of self-surrender, the patriarch's name Jacob (*Ya'aqōv*, which means, "he grasps at the heel") was replaced by that of Israel (*Yisrā'ēl*, "he strives with God"); and, by yielding, he prevailed (Gen. 32:28). Jacob thus entered upon a new plane of victorious living, and never again did he become involved in the moral compromises that had marred his previous existence. Peniel, however, teaches that self-surrender comes at the price of struggle, of persistence, and of prayer. It is no easy matter to be filled with the Holy Spirit, "whom God hath given to them that obey Him" (Acts 5:32). Yet even this "second blessing" is basically a work of divine grace. It is part of the inheritance of the testament, for it was the Angel who graciously came and wrestled with Jacob, and not Jacob who sought out God (and cf. Luke 11:13).

The demand for full surrender, which is so simple and yet so profound, underlies the portrayal of the mature, redeemed life as this is found throughout the remainder of the Old Testament. Moses, for example, described God as the One who is found of those who seek Him with all their heart and soul (Deut. 4:29; cf. Jer. 29:13). Under the judges of the consolidation period, there confessedly took place a general spiritual retrogression; and those, indeed, who were filled with God's Spirit sometimes exhibited morals of a low order, even in their triumphs. Well-known is the case of the vindicativeness of Samson at his death, who prayed, "Oh God, that I may be avenged!" (Judg. 16:28). With his words, however, should be compared under similar circumstances, our Savior's prayer for the forgiveness of His persecutors (Luke 23:34). Such lapses as Samson's perhaps contribute to the explanation of the very periodic nature of their spiritual infilling (Judg. 13:25). David, in the next period, knew well that the true sacrifices of God consisted of a broken spirit (Ps. 51:17); and, after him, the wisest of all men insisted, "Trust in Yahweh with *all* thy heart . . . in *all* thy ways acknowledge Him," and then He will direct thy paths (Prov. 3:5, 6).

D. FELLOWSHIP WITH GOD, in proportion as a man was surrendered to Him, appears as the next blessed result of the testament (Ex. 24:11). Thus Schultz summarizes the inheritance of Old Testament believers as follows: "In a word, they enjoy, *in living communion with God*, the highest and truest happiness man can enjoy — a happiness greater and more needful far than any that earth can give."[22] The earliest primeval saints, before the human race had experienced the full effects of sin, actually walked with God (Gen. 5:22). As has been said in respect to the experience of the antediluvian Enoch: "This means more than that he led a pious life . . . 'To walk with God' points to supernatural intercourse with God"[23] (cf. Noah 6:9). Subsequent to the primeval period, however, these words appear only in Malachi 2:6, which refers back to Phinehas at the time of the Levitical testament (Mosaic period). Sin thus seems to have broken the intimacy of men's personal fellowship with the Lord, and the later saints are said simply to have walked "before Him" (Gen. 17:1). Solomon correspondingly prayed, "Oh Yahweh, Thou keepest the testament with Thy servants that walk *before* Thee with all their heart" (I Kings 8:23). The earliest indication of a group fellowship with God in collective worship is found in Genesis 4:26, "Then began men to call upon the name of Yahweh." This invocation does not imply that men at that time fully appreciated the testamental character of Yahweh, "the One who is present," as they came later to experience it (Ex. 6:3); but the phrase "to call upon the name of [deity]" does seem to convey the idea of some formal appeal to Him (cf. II Kings 5:11).

With Abraham and Isaac, in the patriarchal period, came the beginnings of the doctrine of prayer (Gen. 20:17; 25:21). Such fel-

---

[22]*Op. cit.*, II:80.
[23]Vos, *op. cit.*, p. 58.

lowship with God in prayer may well have existed previously, for example, in connection with the "blessings" of the patriarchs. For these blessings consist of divinely oriented wishes that are addressed to others and that would have constituted prayers, had they been addressed to God (cf. Noah's; Gen. 9:26, 27), though they are not actually so phrased in the Word. The early blessings did, however, serve as something of a last will or testament; and they constituted, by God's Spirit, inspired predictions of future benefits (cf. 27:27-29; 48:3-49:28, and the later blessings of Moses). Inspired curses were then characterized by a corresponding, though threatening, nature (cf. 49:7 and see below). Similarly related to prayer were Abraham's direct, conversational intercessions with Yahweh on behalf of Sodom (18:23-32). The first prayer actually to be recorded in Scripture is that of Abraham's servant as he sought a wife for Isaac (24:12-14, 42-44). In this passage, prayer is defined as a speaking with God (v. 15); but it takes place "in the heart" (v. 45). The urgent plea of Jacob, which was uttered just before he met Esau in 1909 B.C. (32:9-12), though brief, yet exists as an inspired pattern for the following basic elements of believing prayer: "I am not worthy" (confession); "Deliver me, I pray Thee" (petition); "and the mother with the children" (intercession); for "Thou hast showed *hésedh* [loyalty to the promises of the testament] unto Thy servant . . . and Thou saidst, I will surely do thee good" (thanksgiving).

The first prescribed or "set" prayers appear in the Mosaic legislation.[24] These consist of the following: Numbers 10:35, 36 (cf. Ps. 68:1), which records the two set invocations for the journeyings of the ark; Deuteronomy 21:7, 8, a prayer for community atonement; Deuteronomy 26:5-10, to be spoken at the offering of the firstfruits (". . . and now, behold, I have brought the first of the fruit of the ground, which Thou, oh Yahweh, hast given me") and 26:13-15, at the presentation of the third-year tithes.

Of the two classic Old Testament examples of individuals who were mighty in intercessory prayer (Jer. 15:1), the first concerns Moses (Ex. 32:32), who was willing to be blotted out of God's book of life for his people's sake. As the Word itself explains (Ps. 106:23), "He [God] said that He would destroy them, had not Moses His chosen stood before Him in the breach, to turn away His wrath." The second concerns Samuel in the consolation period, whose prayers for Israel are described in I Samuel 7:8; 12:19. Of similar import were the intercessions made by Amos in the eighth century (7:2, 5). But there came a point in Israel's sin against God when such prophetic intercession ceased to avail (Amos 7:8). Jeremiah, in the later prophetic period, was thus repeatedly warned not to pray

24Note, however, that Old Testament prayer remains predominantly unhampered by forms or prescriptions, Vriezen, *op. cit.*, pp. 304-305.

for his hopelessly apostate people (Jer. 7:16; 11:14; 14:11); and Ezekiel, in the exile, was informed that the prayers of God's greatest saints, past or contemporary, could accomplish their own deliverance, but not that of anyone else (Ezek. 14:14, 20).

Statements that are closely related to the Biblical prayers of intercession, though not themselves technically prayers, are the Mosaic blessings and curses. In fact, one of the most frequently repeated sections of all Scripture is that of the priestly blessing or benediction (Num. 6:24-26):

"Yahweh bless thee, and keep thee:
Yahweh make His face to shine upon thee, and be gracious unto thee:
Yahweh lift up His countenance upon thee, and give thee peace."

The pagans that surrounded Israel (and doubtless some Israelites too) entertained a superstitious belief in the inherent efficacy of blessings and curses, for example, in the magical power of the utterances of Balaam (Num. 22:6). A blessing or a curse could, indeed, serve as a valid prediction, if it were inspired by God's Spirit; and this actually turned out to be the case in the oracles of Balaam (23:12), at least in those that are preserved in Scripture. Compare also the long lists of Mosaic blessings and curses in Leviticus 26 and Deuteronomy 28. The Lord, in His concern for helpless women who might be falsely accused by their jealous husbands, did provide for one permanently valid curse, to be invoked in cases of suspected adultery (Num. 5:19, 27). But God, the free Testator, could not be bound to the whims of men who might invoke His ineffable name. Commandment III forbade the taking of His name in vain in the first place (Ex. 20:7); and the invalidity of flippant curses was expressly declared through Solomon (disruption period):

"As the sparrow in her wandering, as the swallow in her flying,
So the curse that is causeless alighteth not" (Prov. 26:2).

An intended blessing, moreover, if pronounced by the disobedient, might even be turned by Yahweh into a corresponding curse (Mal. 2:2).

Fellowship with God, however, carries with it the promise of answered prayer. An early prayer of uncertain background is that of Jabez (I Chron. 4:10), the record of which concludes with the statement, "And God granted him that which he requested." In particular, Yahweh answered His people's petitions for the birth of children (Gen. 25:21; cf. I Sam. 1:11). Yet when Israel drifted out of fellowship with God, they found that He refused to hearken to their pleas (Deut. 1:45). Even Moses' prayer that he might enter Canaan was rejected because of the great leader's sin (Deut. 3:25,

26). So Saul in the consolidation period, at the close of his checkered career, received no answer from God (I Sam. 28:6); and, in the next period, the child of David's sin died, despite all David's prayers on its behalf (II Sam. 12:16, 18). Solomon subsequently enunciated a basic divine truth when he explained, "The prayer of *the upright* is His delight" (Prov. 15:8). Thus Solomon's own pious prayer for wisdom to guide his people was answered in an unequaled measure (I Kings 3:9); Elijah by prayer raised the dead (17:20) and shut up heaven so that it rained not on the land for three years and six months (v. 1, cf. James 5:17); and Asa and Jehoshaphat were enabled to win victories against overwhelming odds when they sought the throne of grace, crying, for example, "Oh our God, we have no might against this great company that cometh against us; neither know we what to do: but our eyes are upon Thee!" (II Chron. 20:12; cf. 14:11).

The eighth century prophets repeatedly proclaimed the moral prerequisite for answered prayer. God thus spoke through Isaiah, "When ye make many prayers, I will not hear: your hands are full of blood" (Isa. 1:15; cf. 59:2); but on the other hand, "Loose the bonds of wickedness, and deal thy bread to the hungry . . . Then shalt thou call, and Yahweh will answer; thou shalt cry, and he will say, Here I am" (58:6, 7, 9). Because of his personal faithfulness, King Hezekiah's prayers for deliverance were answered, both from the armies of Sennacherib (II Kings 19:1, 15) and from the fatal disease which afflicted him in the middle of his reign (20:2, 3; cf. Job 8:5). In contrast to this latter situation, however, appears the Bible's notation in reference to King Asa's last years of sickness: "His disease was exceeding great: yet in his disease he sought not to Yahweh, but to the physicians" (II Chron. 16:12). God's Word is not here suggesting that we neglect the medical means that He has graciously placed at our disposal (cf. II Kings 20:7, and James 5:14), but our heavenly Father does desire and expect us to bring our every need to Him. If His children are in the right, and if their prayers are right, then this blessing that He has promised for the future kingdom may yet be anticipated today: "And it shall come to pass that, before they call, I will answer; and while they are yet speaking, I will hear" (Isa. 64:24).

Concerning the forms for offering up prayer, the Old Testament illustrates almost all of the bodily positions that might be assumed — whether standing, kneeling, or even prostrate. A distinctive feature, however, of Old Testament religion is that of the geographical direction of prayer. David established a precedent when he testified, "I cry unto Yahweh with my voice, and He answereth me out of His holy hill" (Ps. 3:4), that is, out of Mount Zion, where the ark of the divine presence rested in its tent. In the next period, with the construction of the Temple, Solomon assumed that Israel's prayers would henceforth be made toward this new and permanent sanctuary (I Kings 8:30, 35). So Jonah, in the eighth century, looked toward God's sacred house (2:4); and he went on to explain, "When my soul fainted within me, I remembered Yahweh; and my prayer came in unto Thee, into thy holy temple" (v. 7). Daniel too, in exile, knelt and prayed three times a day with his windows open toward Jerusalem (Dan. 6:10).

During the 430 years in Egypt (1876-1446 B.C.), Israel fell into idolatry and suffered a correspondingly broken fellowship with God (Josh. 24:14; Ezek. 23:8). But at their close, Moses appeared to his people and, in anticipation of the Sinaitic testament, proclaimed its promise of reconciliation: Israel has been adopted as God's own sons (Ex. 4:22). The truth of this national fatherhood of Yahweh over Israel is, then, the concept that underlies such passages as Jeremiah 3:4, "My Father, Thou art the guide of my [historical] youth." The people's appreciation of their divine sonship indeed constituted a marvelous heritage and a source of confident hope for the nation. It meant, for example, that Moses at the Red Sea could rely on "the Father" and assure his people, "The Egyptians whom ye have seen today, ye shall see them again no more forever!" (Ex. 14:13).

With David's closeness of fellowship, however, with Yahweh, there comes a more personal understanding of the doctrine of the fatherhood of God. It is true that the phrase, "My Father," does not yet appear in the frequency with which it would subsequently occur in the New Testament.[25] Indeed, the full Biblical appreciation of God's personal Fatherhood toward the elect arose only with the spoken teachings of Jesus and with His acted (incarnate) demonstration of God's paternal care; for, as He was later to explain, "He that hath seen Me hath seen the Father" (John 14:9). The predominant Old Testament understanding is rather that of God's Fatherhood in a collective sense. Thus the chief musician more often spoke of his divine sonship along with others in a group, "the generation of Thy children" (Ps. 73:15; cf. 103:13), than as an individual, "I am His child." Yet at the same time, the criticism of liberalism lacks validity when it asserts that the Old Testament nowhere comprehends God's individualistic fatherhood.[26] David's personal expressions of sonship — for example, "Thou art my Father, my God, and the rock of my salvation" (Ps. 89:26, by Ethan) — were well known to his contemporaries, and his own writings in the Word include such confessions of individualistic faith as Psalm 27:10, "When my father and my

---

[25]Cf. Baab's comment, "It is not as pronounced as it might have been had the baalism of the day contained no similar designation for its male deity (Jer. 2:27)," op. cit., p. 123.

[26]So even Schultz, op. cit., II:138, "Till God unveils Himself in the New Testament as the Father of the Son, nothing higher is said of Him than that He is Jahve . . . the trustworthy, faithful God."

mother forsake me, then Yahweh will take me up." He exclaimed,
"Sing unto God, the father of the fatherless" (Ps. 68:5); and Solomon,
in a similar but more sober vein, commented, "Whom Yahweh loveth
He reproveth, even as a father the son in whom he delighteth" (Prov.
3:12. David's statements, moreover, corresponded to his known, historical practice. For example, at one point "David was greatly distressed; for the people spake of stoning him . . . but [observe the
individualism:] David strengthened himself in Yahweh his God" (I
Sam. 30:6). The Psalms, in particular, abound in expressions that
are descriptive of the life of the redeemed individual with God.[27]
These writings of David are emotionally inspiring, as well as infallibly inspired; and, despite a certain collective use of the first person,
they yet constitute the greatest personal, devotional literature of all
time. Indeed, the most beloved chapter in the beloved Book is David's
individualistic 23rd Psalm:

> The LORD is *my* shepherd; I shall not want.
> He maketh *me* to lie down in green pastures,
> He restoreth *my* soul (vv. 1-3).

David, moreover, who was the man of the heart, was also (and
one might even say *necessarily*) the preeminent man of the Book.
For if an individual possesses a true love for God, he will surely
exhibit a corresponding love for His written special revelation, the
Bible. As an unknown psalmist expressed this fact:

> With my whole heart have I sought Thee [and therefore]:
> Oh let me not wander from thy commandments.
> Thy word have I hid in my heart,
> That I might not sin against Thee (Ps. 119:10, 11).

So David, with even the limited portion of Scripture that was extant
in his day (Genesis-Ruth), defined the ideal believer in terms of
God's Word:

> His delight is in the law of Yahweh,
> And on His law doth he meditate day and night (1:2).

These thoughts, moreover, constitute the fitting introduction to Book
I of the Psalter (Psalms 1-41), which David himself both composed
and compiled.[28] His praise of the Word, as this is then expressed
in Psalm 19:7-14, is subsequently exceeded in Scripture only by the
176 verses of the undated 119th Psalm. This latter composition goes
on to bear repeated testimony to the fact, which has been experienced
by the saints of all ages, that one of the greatest blessings of the
redeemed life under the testament occurs when God answers the
prayer, "Open Thou mine eyes, that I may behold wondrous things
out of Thy law" (119:18). For the Book is no magic thing: God's
Spirit must impress its truths into our thinking; and it must be read

---

[27]Cf. Vriezen's listing of particular psalms and verses, *op. cit.*, p. 303.
[28]Cf. Ps. 41:13, which was written by David and which he seems to have intentionally designed as a closing doxology for this collection of the Psalter.

REDEEMED LIFE 427

carefully, with understanding, to "get the sense" (Neh. 8:8). But when its content is received in faith, the written Word then becomes the spiritual medium through which all the other means of grace are subsequently revealed.

For David marks a high point in fellowship with God in yet a third way — that of individual devotion, through the Word, and finally through the sacraments and the various forms of public worship at Israel's central sanctuary. David's own experience and testimony, "I was glad when they said unto me, Let us go unto the house of Yahweh" (Ps. 122:1), must have encouraged a similar anticipation on the part of his associates. His Korahite singers thus expressed their eagerness for the public services:

As the hart panteth after the water brooks,
  So panteth my soul after Thee, oh God.
When shall I come and appear before God?
  I went with the throng and led them to the house of God
    (42:1, 2, 4).

For while private family worship continued to be conducted in godly homes (Ex. 12:26; Deut. 6:7), the nation's public worship came in David's day to be centered on Mount Zion.

Israel's collective devotion may then be analyzed under four major components. 1) Sacrifice; see above, topic 27-C. 2) Feasts; see above, topic 28-C. In fact, the verses in the above-quoted Psalm seem to refer to one of these annual convocations in the Mount Zion temple; compare similar references by David to musical processions and to joyful dancing (Ps. 68:25). This latter feature, of spontaneous dancing in praise to God, is first recorded in reference to Miriam and the women at the Red Sea (Mosaic period, Ex. 15:20). David had, himself, then danced with enthusiasm before the ark, when it was first conducted into Jerusalem (II Sam. 6:14); and such group activity became a natural expression of Israel's joyful faith in God.[29] Particularly would musical processions come to play their part each year in the three universally attended pilgrimage feasts (Deut. 16:16; cf. Isa. 30:29; Ps. 150:4). Thus the Psalms that are numbered 120-134, the "songs of degrees," though they may be simply psalms that are characterized by a "climactic" poetic form, may indeed have been, literally, "songs of ascents," that is, pilgrim songs that were sung on the way up to Jerusalem. Psalm 121:1, 2 seems particularly suitable in this regard:

I will lift up mine eyes unto the hills:
  From whence cometh my help?
My help cometh from Yahweh,
  Who made heaven and earth!

So too Psalm 118:25, 26 was appropriately voiced by the multitude, as Christ later ascended to Jerusalem on the first Palm Sunday:

---
[29]Vriezen thus speaks of Israel's worship as "exuberant" or even "tumultuous," *op. cit.,* p. 427.

"Hosanna! [Save now!] . . . Blessed is He that cometh in the name of Yahweh" (Mark 11:9).

3) Public praise of God, as a recognized part of Israel's worship service, likewise owed much to the sponsorship of David. Not only did the king personally compose the majority of the canonical Psalms; but he also organized the Levitical singers and appointed the chief musicians (I Chron. 16:4-6, 37, 41, 42; chap. 25), who were, in turn, responsible for the composition of many other selections and for the actual conduct of the sanctuary worship (II Chron. 5:12). Much of the leadership in singing was vested in the professional Levitical musicians, but the people too seem to have participated, at least in the responses. Examples of the latter include the refrain, "For His *hésedh* [testamental faithfulness] endureth for ever," which was repeated after each line of Psalm 136 (cf. Jer. 33:11), and the exclamations *Āmēn,* "Surely!" and *Hall'lū-Yāh,* "Praise Yah(weh)" (I Chron. 16:36). Even nature was called upon, in symbol, to praise the Lord (Ps. 96: 11, 12). Subjects for particular praise were the truths of God's creative acts (Ps. 104) and of His national redemption of Israel (e.g., 105). Continual worship (I Chron. 9;33) then included special night services (Ps. 134) and sabbath services (92).

Finally, 4) prayer constituted the form in which many of the Psalms were written; and the Psalter must have been extensively used as a guide to prayer in sanctuary worship, as well as in private. David wrote a number of special compositions for morning prayer (Ps. 3, 5, 63), for example:

My voice shalt Thou hear in the morning, oh Yahweh;
   In the morning will I direct my prayer unto Thee, and will
      look up (5:3).

He wrote likewise for the evening (4, 141); for example, this best-known of all children's prayers:

In peace will I both lay me down and sleep;
   For Thou, Yahweh, alone makest me dwell in safety (4:8).

The three set times of daily prayer that were observed by Daniel in exile (6:10) may likewise have arisen from a form of worship established by David (cf. Ps. 55:17; but see also I Chron. 23:30). An example of the formal or "long" prayer is Solomon's beautiful supplication, which was spoken at the dedication of the Temple, at the time of the feast of tabernacles, 958 B.C. (II Chron. 6:14-42).

Yet the fellowship of God's people with their divine Redeemer was not limited to the set occasions of prayer, Bible reading, and worship. David at all times relied on the presence of God's indwelling Spirit, and from his abiding communion with Yahweh came a constant flow of confidence and of joy: "Thy Spirit is good; lead me in the land of uprightness" (Ps. 143:10; cf. 90:15). Consistent gladness that originated in Yahweh was one of the particular themes of Solomon. He reiterated, "That every man should eat and drink, and enjoy good in all his labor, is the gift of God" (Eccl. 3:13; cf. I Kings 4:20); or again, "The hope of the righteous shall be gladness" (Prov. 10:28; cf. 15:13; 17:22; Eccl. 9:7-9). This positive stress on a full enjoyment of God and of His blessings[30] serves to explain the relative silence of the Old Testament in regard to fasting (cf. Deut. 14:1). The Bible never prescribes regular fasting, unless the "affliction of the soul" on the day of atonement be so interpreted (Lev. 16:29; cf. Num. 30:13; Isa. 58:3). Voluntary fasting was occasionally employed to reinforce prayer, in seasons of special need (I Sam. 7:6; Dan. 9:3; Esther 4:16) or sorrow (I Sam. 31:13). In such a way the four annual fasts of the exile seem to have arisen (Zech. 8:19) late in Israel's history; but they were observed, apparently, without divine authorization. The prophets specifically opposed such fastings as were limited to outward performances; and they rather proclaimed, "Is not this the fast that I have chosen: to loose the bonds of wickedness?" (Isa. 58:6; cf. Jer. 14:12). This was, in fact, characteristic of their attitude toward all externalized ceremonial. But the Old Testament's pervasive emphasis upon a life of positive wholesomeness in fellowship with God is perhaps most clearly expressed in Zechariah's wish that these four exilic fasts might become "to the house of Judah joy and gladness and cheerful feasts"; and he went on to summarize the Old Testament ideal by saying, "therefore love truth and shālōm" (8:19). The Hebrew noun shālōm means "peace," but shālōm is not simply the negative peace of an absence-of-strife. This term carries with it, positively, the rich implications of soundness and wholeness, of that full integration of life which becomes possible only for those who live in tune with the One who is the Master of all that a man may encounter (Isa. 26:3).

E. CONSECRATION. The redeemed life that is proffered by the Old Testament is one of activity and of purpose. David's charge to Solomon over the building of the Temple, "Arise and be doing, and Yahweh be with thee" (I Chron. 22:16), is characteristic of the emphasis of the older testament as a whole. The same words could be used for matters of much less pleasant but equally necessary execution (Ezra 10:4). Devotion to the duty at hand is the theme of the striking parable of I Kings 20:40 (disruption period); and the last major character in the post-exilic Old Testament history, Nehemiah, presents a masterful example of the overall consecration in which God takes delight. For this honored official was distinguished, both in respect to his attitude — "I am doing a great work, so that I cannot come down: why should the work cease, whilst I leave it, and come down to you?" (Neh. 6:3) — and in respect to his accomplishments: "So

---

[30]Cf. Kohler, *Old Testament Theology*, p. 151, "There is hardly a word so characteristic of the Old Testament as the word joy."

built we the wall; and all the wall was joined together; for the people
had a mind to work" (4:6).

Early in the history of revelation, however, there appear two
particular subjects of consecration that warrant special discussion in
relation to the inheritance of the older testament. Both were revealed
at the town of Bethel and at the same point in the career of the
patriarch Jacob. The first mentioned (Gen. 28:20) is that of the vow;
for Jacob expressed himself in this form: "If God will be with me . . .
then . . ." Vows may thus be defined as voluntary[31] obligations or
oaths made to God, generally on the condition of His bestowing
certain specified blessings.[32] So Jacob at Bethel asked of God protection and a safe return to his family; and he, in turn, promised to God
both sacrifices and certain property. Some interpreters have here
accused Jacob of practicing commercialistic bargaining. On the contrary, however, Jacob's vow appears actually as a sign of his (at least
partially) redeemed life: it shows his dependence upon God and
upon God's ultimate salvation. Vows then, though never prescribed,
are both explained and regulated in holy Scripture.

The two major types of vows that are found in Scripture are vows
of devotion and vows of abstinence. An object of voluntary devotion
might consist of a person, as the boy Samuel (I Sam. 1:11), or of an
animal, or of property (Lev. 27:9, 14, 16). Provision was also made
for the possible redemption of vowed articles, at a set monetary figure
(Lev. 27:2-27). The fundamental virtue of a vow, however, lies in
the sincerity of the one who makes it. As an unknown psalmist cautions, "I will pay Thee my vows, which my lips uttered . . . If I regard iniquity in my heart, the Lord will not hear" (Ps. 66:13, 14, 18).
These verses therefore constitute the condemnation of the very sort
of selfish casuistry that was later practiced by the Pharisees in their
"Corban" vows (Mark 7:11). A particular type of devotion vow was
the *hérem,* or "ban" (curse). The Hebrew word *hérem* comes from
the same root as "harem" and means a thing that is cut off from normal
life. No redemption, therefore, was possible for the *hérem* (Lev. 27:
28, 29). A prominent example of the *hérem* vow is that which was
uttered against the Canaanitish city of Jericho; for in 1406 B.C. Joshua
"devoted" this site to God (Josh. 6:17), which meant that it was cut
off from any other use (by being destroyed!).

The second major type of vow consists of the vows of abstinence.
These vows might concern a number of different kinds of self-imposed restrictions (Num. 30:13); or the person himself could become
nāzîr, "separated," to be a Nazarite (Num. 6:1-21). The Nazarite vow
involved one's separation to a priestly sort of life: it meant the avoid-

---

[31]Ps. 76:11, "Vow, and pay unto Yahweh your God," is not really a command to
vow, but rather to pay, once the vow has been made.
[32]Cf. John D. Davis, *A Dictionary of the Bible,* p. 805.

ing of wine and ceremonial defilement, especially from the dead, and the allowing of one's hair to grow (cf. Samson, Judg. 16:17). Untrimmed vines are, on this same basis, called *nāzîr*. The long hair seems to have served as a concrete symbol of unimpaired strength (Lev. 25:11), such as God granted in a special measure to Samson. Women could be Nazarites (Num. 6:2); and the Nazarite vows could be either temporary (for a stated time) or permanent, as in the cases of Samuel (I Sam. 1:11) and Samson (Judg. 13:7). God's gracious purpose in establishing the group of the Nazarites was to raise up within Israel a class of devoted spiritual leaders, similar to that of the prophets (Amos 2:11). For the vows of the Old Testament were always intended to contribute to the total blessedness of Israel's redeemed life with Yahweh.

In the regulation of vows, Moses made clear at the outset the strictly voluntary nature of these obligations: "If thou shalt forbear to vow it shall be no sin to thee" (Deut. 23:22). But once a vow was made, it became binding (v. 23; Num. 30:2). Vows of minors or of wives (because they might affect the welfare of a whole household) could be annulled by the man of the house, but not after he had once allowed them to stand (Num. 30:3-15). Allegiance to the binding nature of an oath or vow is illustrated by the decision of Israel (in the consolidation period) to spare the Canaanitish Gibeonites, after their elders had once sworn protection unto them by Yahweh (Josh. 9:18, 19). Whether Israel should actually have stood by their word in such a way, however, is another matter. Moses had furnished a procedure for release from oaths that were rashly undertaken (Lev. 5:4-6). The Gibeonites had gained protection for themselves under false pretenses; and God, who is the final authority, had demanded the utter destruction of all the Canaanites (Deut. 7:2). Obedience to Him should have come first, even at the expense of losing face. This latter principle is illustrated, for example, by the way in which Saul was forced (against his own will) to take back his oath against the life of his son Jonathan (I Sam. 14:45). An even more dreadful vow, which should surely have been abrogated but which was not, was Jephthah's; for it eventuated in his offering up of his daughter as a human sacrifice (Judg. 11:31, 39). Jephthah's inflexibility can only be understood as an evidence of the corrupting influence of Canaanitish theology. But the incident does serve this positive purpose in God's revelation; it underlines in an unforgettable fashion the truth later taught by Solomon, that "It is a snare to a man rashly to say, It is holy; and, after vows, to make inquiry" (Prov. 20:25; cf. Eccl. 5: 3-5). Solomon did, however, note the usefulness of oaths for enforcing justice, as they invoked divine intervention, should conflicting testimonies arise in court (I Kings 8:31).

In its later periods the Old Testament then proceeds to note two seemingly opposite, though equally necessary and practical, matters of consecration that develop out of the concept of the vow. The first of these is that of the believer's responsibility in respect to separation, in the precise religious connotation of this word. That is, there exist certain anti-Biblical features of the unbelieving world with which God's people simply cannot afford association and which should become the subject of a vow of abstinence on their part. Holiness had from the beginning required Israel's separation from evil; but as long as the people remained in control of their own destiny, God's directive concerning religious untruth was that the children of Israel were totally to destroy all such cases of false faith (whether Canaanitish, Deut. 7:2; or arising within their own nation, 17:5), rather than simply to withdraw from them. But when, in the eighth century, a major body out of Judah were first carried off to live as a minority in a pagan environment, namely, in the Assyria of Sennacherib (701 B.C.), Isaiah sharply warned them to maintain religious separation: "Depart ye, depart ye, go ye out from thence, touch no unclean thing; go ye out of the midst of her" (Isa. 52:11; cf. v. 4). Similar expressions by Jeremiah, in the later prophetic period, then appear in respect to Babylon (50:8; 51:6, 9, 45). These words are twice quoted, moreover, in the New Testament (II Cor. 6:17; Rev. 18:4) with this same admonition, that the saints are to keep themselves unspotted from the unbelieving world.

In spite of these specific teachings of the Word in respect to separation, some recent interpreters have claimed that the actual practices of the prophets tend to justify a more latitudinarian policy of toleration and of compromise within the organized church. They then regularly cite as evidence the continued acts of worship by the spiritual leaders of Judah in the corrupt Temple of their day (cf. Isa. 6:1; Jer. 26:2).[33] The example, however, is hardly an analogous one; for the Temple and its (albeit corrupt) priesthood served as special types of Jesus Christ, which could be repudiated only at the risk of salvation itself. Outside of the Temple, however, the Scriptural prophets felt obliged to extend no "right hand of fellowship" to any and all of the ministers of Yahweh who had come to exercise leadership in the established "church." Should the official prophets or priests deny God's Word, the true leaders would not simply ostracize them from association; they would also unhesitatingly denounce them as "lying spirits of Satan" (I Kings 22:23) and as "treacherous persons that have polluted the sanctuary" (Zeph. 3:4). Jeremiah summarized the Lord's own attitude by saying, "They are all of them unto Me as Sodom and Gomorrah" (Jer. 23:14). Separation, moreover, is both taught in theory and demonstrated in practice by the con-

---

[33]Cf. Edward J. Carnell, The Case for Orthodox Theology (Philadelphia, 1959), p. 134.

sistent refusal of the post-exilic Jews to grant religious recognition to the Samaritans (Ezra 4:3); for though the Samaritans boldly claimed the worship of the God of Jacob, they yet took willful exception to the law that He had revealed (II Kings 17:34). So today, in this present era of religious apostasy and compromise, loyalty to revealed Scripture impels consecrated evangelicals to maintain similar vows of separation. We must take care, for example, never to recognize as a legitimate minister of God's church any man who fails to meet the Biblical qualifications for the eldership, and especially that of "holding to the faithful word which is according to the teaching" (Titus 1:9). We must take with more seriousness, and search our hearts diligently before God, concerning these words of His Spirit: "Mark them that are causing the divisions and occasions of stumbling contrary to the doctrine which ye learned: and turn away from them" (Rom. 16:17; cf. II John 10, 11). But this precept also is designed for our good and constitutes a part of the inheritance of the redeemed life; for if "ye be separate, saith the Lord, . . . [then] I will receive you" (II Cor. 6:17).

Yet with the vow of separation comes, secondly, the equally stressed Biblical emphasis upon the responsibility of witnessing. An unknown psalmist was thus guided by the Holy Spirit to speak about vows as follows: "I will pay my vows unto Yahweh, yea, *in the presence of all His people*" (116:14). That is, the believer possesses not only the opportunity, but also the obligation, of giving testimony to his saving faith in the presence of other persons. David, for example, realized that the joy of God's forgiveness brought with it an individual, missionary responsibility; and he immediately added, "Then will I teach transgressors Thy ways; and sinners shall be converted unto Thee" (Ps. 51:13). Well-known is Solomon's proverb, in the next period, that "The fruit of the righteous is a tree of life; and he that winneth souls is wise" (Prov. 11:30). Witnessing too thus constitutes one of the blessings of the testamental heritage, for not simply does the spirit-filled life exist for the purpose of God's service — as Christ Himself said, "Ye shall receive power, when the Holy Spirit is come upon you: *and* ye shall be My witnesses" (Acts 1:8) — but this very service then constitutes a part of the privilege of the redeemed life; for "they that turn many to righteousness shall shine as the stars for ever and ever" (Dan. 12:3).

The second particular subject of consecration that appeared in connection with Jacob's experience at Bethel was that of tithing. Tithing, indeed, formed a major part of Jacob's vow, for His promise to Yahweh concluded with these words, "And of all that Thou shalt give me I will surely give the tenth to Thee" (Gen. 28:22). The tithe thus existed prior to the giving of the Sinaitic law; it was paid, in fact, by Jacob's grandfather Abraham, years before the vow at Bethel (14:

20). Both patriarchs, however, rendered this payment on their own initiative; and it received its external enforcement only in Leviticus 27:30: "All the tithe of the land, whether of the seed of the land, or of the fruit of the tree, is Yahweh's: it is holy unto Yahweh." Israel's tithe money was then specifically assigned to the Levites for their conduct of the religious activities of God's people (Num. 18:21); it would serve as the compensation for Levi's non-participation in the tribal distribution of the land of Canaan (v. 24). The Levites, in turn, were then expected to contribute a tithe of this tithe, for the support of Israel's priests (v. 26). The third-year tithe, which was prescribed in Deuteronomy 14:28, 29 (cf. 26:12), was a separate impost for charity (14:22-27 = part of Num. 18:21?). In the subsequent history of the tithe, it appears that Israel vascillated between two extremes: either the tithe could be overpaid and become a basis of false religious confidence, a heavenly bribe to "compensate" for a faithless life, (Amos 4:4); or, the more usual difficulty, it could be neglected altogether. The Levites would then have to take up secular employment and the worship of God would suffer accordingly. This latter event was what happened in the case of the Levite Jonathan (Judg. 17:8), only shortly after the death of Moses; and such failures continued down to the days of Nehemiah (Neh. 13:10), at the very close of the Old Testament.

The theory that underlies tithing is that of stewardship, and its specific principles are three-fold. 1) As David so aptly confessed to Yahweh, "All things come of Thee, and of Thine own have we given Thee" (I Chron. 29:14). For everything that exists comes from God, it belongs to God and it will some day revert to God (cf. I Cor. 4:7). 2) The relationship, therefore, of men to worldly property is that of temporary stewards, whose privilege is that of managing and of rendering back to God what is already His own. As I Chronicles 29:14 goes on to state: "But who am I, and what is my people, that we should be able to offer so willingly after this sort?" Thus even when we yield up all that we have to God, the act constitutes but our expected service (Rom. 6:12; 12:1); and it leaves us still as "unprofitable servants" (Luke 17:10). 3) In reference to our giving, however, God in His grace invokes only the principle of the firstfruits: He accepts, that is, a mere token offering (cf. Ex. 23:19; Deut. 18:4). This token then consists of a figure which He Himself specifies, which amounts to but a fraction of the whole to which He is entitled, and which He is yet pleased to treat as acceptable to Him. The figure which God has thus set is the tithe, 10 percent (Lev. 27:30). This tithe, moreover, is the only figure which God has ever revealed to men as genuinely acceptable. To receive men's tithes was His desire prior to the Sinaitic testament; it was His desire under it; and, as part of the changeless moral law, it seemingly continues to be His desire now, in the days that are subsequent to it. For men to attempt to withhold God's tithe constitutes the unthinkable act of robbing Yahweh (Mal. 2:8). But in faith to contribute it becomes a way for inheriting the manifold blessings of redeemed life under the testament; for He has promised,

"Bring ye the whole tithe into the store-house,[34] that there may be food in My house, and prove Me now herewith, saith, Yahweh of hosts, if I will not open you the windows of heaven, and pour you out a blessing, that there shall not be room enough to receive it" (3:10).

The consistent experience of Christian tithers down through the years, accordingly, has been this: that "you cannot out-give God"!

F. PROVIDENTIAL CARE. For a man to be reconciled with God and to be granted heirship under His testament places such a person in harmony with the One who, by His providence, sustains all the things that are in this world; see above, topic 10-A. Participation in the kingdom of God, therefore, brings him into a corresponding harmony with the natural environment, as well as with the spiritual. As Eliphaz so beautifully states it,

"Thou shalt be in league with the stones of the field;
And the beasts of the field shall be at peace with thee.
And thou shalt know that thy tent is in peace *shālōm* [which indicates a state of integration]" (Job 5:23, 24).

But the testament implies more than a simple harmony with the world. Even as it was originally, prior to man's fall (Gen. 1:28), so now, his reconciliation with God restores to man a position of dominion and of triumph over the world, through the active intervention of Yahweh, the God who is with us, in history. Yahweh's servant Moses thus promised to Israel, "Your enemies shall fall before you by the sword; and I will have respect unto you, and make you fruitful, and multiply you, and will establish My testament with you" (Lev. 26: 8, 9). Schultz therefore concludes, relative to the Old Testament believers,

"A firm confidence in their security and success, that agreed well with a humble reverence for this holy God, must have been the chief religious trait of the saints"[35] [cf. Ps. 145: 19, 20].

The whole course of Biblical history constitutes, then, an acted demonstration of the reality of God's providential care; and the following passages serve as but a representative selection of some of the

---

[34] With the transmutation of the Old Testament sanctuary into the New Testament Church (see above, p. 369), "store-house" giving comes, correspondingly, to designate such actions as are taken on behalf of the true Body of Christ.
[35] *Op. cit.*, II:79.

more significant of these acts. In the primeval period, (period A) God provided clothing to meet the very first physical needs of Adam and Eve (Gen. 3:21), who had fallen and who had yet become the initial heirs of God's testament of grace. Generations later, He preserved the life of Noah from the universal destruction of the Flood. In period B, He then kept the patriarchs to a "good old age" (15:15; 25:8); and He guided the career of Joseph, who stands as the supreme early example of the wonderful ways of divine providence (45:8; 50:20). In period C, when Israel fell into bondage in Egypt, "God heard their groanings, and [dispatched Moses because] God remembered His testament with Abraham, with Isaac, and with Jacob" (Ex. 2:24). Indeed, His very testamental name, *Yahweh*, "He is present [to deliver]" (3:14), constitutes a standing memorial to His basic promise of the testament, "I will be their God" (v. 15). He overruled Israel's enemy, Balaam (Deut. 23:5); and, to those who would be faithful to the conditions of the testament, He offered long life (Ex. 20:12; Deut. 4:40; cf. Ps. 91:16; Prov. 3:2), numerous children, success, and victory (Lev. 26:3-13; Deut. 28:1-14). To cite but two references, Moses advised his people,

> Remember Yahweh thy God, for it is He that giveth thee power to get wealth; that He may establish His testament which He sware unto thy fathers, as at this day (Deut. 8:18).

> The eternal God is thy dwelling-place,
> And underneath are the everlasting arms.
> Happy art thou, oh Israel:
> Who is like unto thee, a people saved by Yahweh! (33:27, 29).

In period D, in the consolidation period of King Saul, Israel experienced triumph over the Hagarites, "For they cried to God in the battle, and He was entreated of them, because they put their trust in Him . . . for the war was of God" (I Chron. 5:20, 22). The psalms of David and of his friends in period E then contain some of the most explicit elaborations of the Biblical theme — "He will ever be mindful of His testament" (Ps. 111:5). The following are classic examples:

> Cast thy burden upon Yahweh, and He will sustain thee:
> He will never suffer the righteous to be moved (55:22).
> I will instruct thee and teach thee in the way which thou shalt go:
> I will counsel thee with Mine eye upon thee (32:8).
> For Yahweh God is a sun and a shield:
> Yahweh will give grace and glory;
> No good thing will He withhold from them that walk uprightly (84:11).

As period F, Israel's disruption period, set in, Solomon yet assured his people, "In all thy ways acknowledge Him, and He will direct thy paths" (Prov. 3:6). In period G, Isaiah too could maintain a heart of confidence, despite the stresses of the eighth century, as he prophesied,

"But they that wait for Yahweh shall renew their strength; they shall mount up with wings as eagles" (Isa. 40:31). During period H, under the later prophets, when kingdoms were falling, God assured even Jeremiah's scribe, "Thy life will I give thee for a prey in all places whither thou goest"; though He cautioned the man to be satisfied therewith and not to seek great things for himself (Jer. 45:5). Even after Jerusalem had been taken and the exile was impending (period I), Jeremiah in faith could maintain,

> It is of Yahweh's *hésedhs* [faithful acts] that we are not consumed,
>> because His compassions fail not.
> They are new every morning; great is Thy faithfulness.
>> (Lam. 3:22, 23).

In period J, the post-exilic days, the dramatic history of Esther serves finally as Scripture's supreme later example of God's overruling, providential care (Esther 7:8; 4:14; cf. 5:2; 6:3, 13). What then can be the appeal of the world, in the light of assured redemption like that listed above!

God's providential care, however, does not guarantee us "flowery beds of ease"; life's reality may, in fact, seem to lie far from it. David's words are, in the long run, quite true:

> He will fulfill the desire of them that fear Him;
>> He also will hear their cry, and will save them.
> Yahweh preserveth all them that love Him;
>> But all the wicked will He destroy (Ps. 145:19, 20).

But for the present, the omniscient God may see fit to ordain suffering, even of a most serious nature, for the ultimate good of His chosen saints. It was to furnish them a guide, moreover, through days of such bitter experience that God first ordained the events of the life of Job (patriarchal period) and then inspired the inscripturation of the book that bears Job's name (early disruption period). The inspired answers that this work provides to the problem of suffering[36] are no less than five-fold. Each of these solutions may in turn be initially identified with one of the leading characters of the drama of Job. The discussion of the five answers may then be organized, each under three subheadings, as follows: (a) the definition that it provides to the nature of the suffering, (b) the response that it directs one make to it, and (c) the final solution that it reveals for the problem. Each general answer, moreover, as a part of God's inspired word, possesses permanent validity within its own frame of reference.[37]

1) The character of Satan may serve as a direct cause of trials for God's saints (Job 1-2). (a) This explanation is then defined under the category of temptation, of suffering, that is, because of evil that

---

[36]On the relation of evil to the power, justice, and goodness of God, see above, p. 200, on theodicy.
[37]On the normativeness of the various speakers in Job, see above, p. 337, note 53.

exists in the eternal, spiritual world (Job 2:3; I Pet. 5:8; Rev. 12:17).
(b) Man's required response in the face of Satan's temptation is to
become aware of the tempter's wiles, to be watchful, and to resist
him (I Pet. 5:9; James 4:7); or to quote the opposite of the words
of Job's wife, "Still hold fast thine integrity!" (Job 2:9; cf. v. 10).
(c) For the book of Job reveals God's contemporary solution to this
first category of suffering: the Lord *will* deliver the godly out of
temptation (42:10; cf. II Pet. 2:9; James 4:7). It remains true, however, that the ultimate solution, which concerns God's final destruction of Satan and his demonic hosts, became known only as a matter
of New Testament revelation (Rev. 20:10; II Pet. 2:4; though cf.
Zech. 3:2).

2) Job's three "friends," in their sections of the dialogue (Job
4-26), advance the explanation (a) that evil is to be accounted for on
the basis of retribution. It consists, in other words, of suffering because of one's own sin. As Bildad puts it, "Behold, God will not
cast away a perfect man, neither will He uphold the evil-doers" (8:
20). Retribution, moreover, receives confirmation as the consistent
teaching of Scripture, that "whatsoever a man soweth that shall he
also reap" (Gal. 6:7). Punishment thus came upon the first man
as a result of his initial violation of the covenant of works (Gen. 3:17;
cf. Ps. 1:6); and Jeremiah's admission of his people's guilt, while
lamenting their resultant woes (Lam. 3:39), witnesses to its continuing (temporal) validity in reference to the saints under the gracious
testament. Even after men have received divine forgiveness, crime
demands still its judicial punishment, "an eye for an eye and a tooth
for a tooth" (Ex. 21:23-25; cf. Prov. 26:27). Israel under Moses, for
example, were pardoned for their rebellion and were thus spared
from divine destruction; but the people were yet forced to wander
for forty years in the wilderness (Num. 14:20-23). David too was
forgiven his crime of adultery, and the penalty of his death was not
exacted (II Sam. 12:13); but, because his deed had "given great
occasion to the enemies of Yahweh to blaspheme," the child of sin
still had to die (v. 14) and David was himself punished by the same
sort of suffering that he had inflicted on others, the *lex talionis* (v.
11). So also in the apostate divided kingdoms, the subsequent repentance of their respective rulers (I Kings 21:29, ninth century, and
II Kings 22:20, seventh century) might bring about a postponement
of national punishment, but never its total countermanding. Elihu furnishes inspired validation to the principle of retribution (Job 34:11),
and its truth was admitted by Job himself (27:13, 14). Eliphaz of
course erred in his specific explanations of retribution in respect to
the sufferings of Job (22:9-11; cf. John 9:2); but the idea is in itself,
basically true (Isa. 59:2): God cannot "just forgive" men's misdeeds
(cf. Job 7:21) if He is to remain true to His own holy nature. Thus

even the severest of present day sufferings cannot serve as a sufficient penalty for the sins of mankind (11:6); and, for those who would
continue to live apart from God's saving testament, final equity must
be found in hell itself (18:14; Matt. 25:41). (b) The response which
man must therefore make to the threat of retribution is the act of
repentance. For Eliphaz rightly concluded:

> If thou return to the Almighty, thou shalt be built up,
> If thou put away unrighteousness far from thy tents,
>   (22:23; cf. Lam. 3:40; Luke 13:1-3).

As a result, even retributive punishment, when it leads men to repent,
may be seen as one of the blessings of the redeemed life under the
testament. (c) The ultimate solution to the problem of retribution
lies in the satisfaction of the justice of God, as His Son our Savior
offers up His divine life in willing substitution for the forfeited lives
of sinners (Job 33:24; I Pet. 2:24).

3) Elihu, the younger friend of Job (Job 32-37), not only composed an inspired analysis of the various explanations for suffering
that are presented by the other characters of the Book; but he also
presents his own explanation (a) namely, that evil serves to accomplish the chastening of mankind. Suffering, in other words, may occur
for one's own improvement. Elihu stated:

> Then God openeth the ears of men,
> And sealeth their instruction,
> That He may withdraw man from his purpose,
> And hide pride from man.
> He is chastened also with pain upon his bed,
> And with continual strife in his bones (33:16, 17, 19).

The historical reality of divine chastening had been first explicitly
revealed to Israel by Moses, in Deuteronomy 8:2-5, 16, 17: "He [God]
suffered thee to hunger, and fed thee with manna, that He might
make thee know that man doth not live by bread only, but by everything that proceedeth out of the mouth of Yahweh" (v. 3), "that He
might prove thee, to do thee good at thy latter end" (v. 16). So
throughout the course of the existence of the elect nation, Baab
explains,

> ". . . as they read the history of their people, they discov-
> ered that there was a history within a history, that within the
> changing forms of political and social life . . . there was a
> true history of God's eternal purpose for Israel, a history of
> the kingdom of God."[38]

This providential purpose centered, it is true, in God's preparation
for the coming of His Messiah and in the latter's accomplishing of
the testament; but God's purpose included, at the same time, a corrective discipline for each successive generation of the chosen people.

---

[38]*Op. cit.*, p. 164.

The nations that God left in Canaan after the conquest were thus providentially situated "to prove Israel, that the generations of the children of Israel might know, to teach them war" (Judg. 3:1, 2; cf. 2:20-22). So too for the Gentile Naaman of the disruption period, his awful leprosy proved to be the very crisis that finally led him to God (II Kings 5:15); though for Israel in the eighth century, the trials which were designed of God to bring them to repentance failed to succeed in their gracious purpose (Amos 4:7, 8). When, in the next period, Jeremiah was then faced by the desolation of Jerusalem, he confessed in faith, "It is good for a man that he bear the yoke in his youth" (Lam. 3:27); and the anonymous writer of Psalm 119 adds, "It is good for me that I have been afflicted; that I may learn thy statutes" (v. 71; cf. II Cor. 12:7). (b) The response to chastening, that God therefore expects of believers, is that they will receive it, in order to profit thereby. Indeed, not just are we to receive it, but we are to receive it with joy, as a blessing of the testament. So Eliphaz appropriately counsels:

> Behold, happy is the man whom God correcteth:
> Therefore despise not thou the chastening of the Almighty (5:17).

and Solomon goes on to explain:

> For whom Yahweh loveth he reproveth,
> Even as a father the son in whom he delighteth
> (Prov. 3:12; cf. v. 11; 17:3; Heb. 12:5, 6).

Job failed at first to grasp this truth, that his suffering could be of a chastening character. He felt rather that his trials required him to surrender his belief, either in God's justice, or in His sovereign power; and it was in respect to the former that he chose to express his doubt (Job 9:23). Later, however, he gained an at least temporary insight into the nature of chastening (23:10), and he ended his period of doubt in a genuine submission to God (42:6). The total response, however, of sincere joy while experiencing chastening was reserved for expression by Habakkuk in the later prophetic period (3:18; cf. II Cor. 12:9). (c) The solution that Scripture then presents to the problem of chastening is three-fold. Immediately, it serves to produce strength of character. As Job affirmed in the very course of his sufferings,

> But He knoweth the way that I take;
> When He hath tried me I shall come forth as gold
> (Job 23:10; cf. 1:21; I Pet. 5:10).

Hebrews 12:11, thus goes on to state, "It yieldeth peaceable fruit unto them that have been exercised thereby, even the fruit of righteousness." In time, moreover, chastening is followed by God-ordained restoration (Job 42:12; Hab. 3:19). Finally, in eternity, Yahweh's recognition of the faithfulness of His people results in a permanent crown of life (Job 14:14; Rev. 2:10).

4) Job himself, in his various speeches (especially Job 3, the

dialogues, and 27-31) most frequently attributes his troubles to (a) the fact of persecution. This fourth category may be then defined as the suffering which occurs because of the sins of others. Often such suffering may arise by reason of a general, undirected type of persecution. Job thus observed,

> From out of the populous city men groan,
> And the soul of the wounded crieth out (24:12; cf. Ex. 20:5).

Or again, persecution may be of an intensely personal nature, specifically directed against some righteous sufferer. This latter alternative seemingly accounts for Job's aggrieved words,

> If the scourge slay suddenly,
> He [God] will mock at the trial of the innocent (9:23).

Job's speech, moreover, suggests the possibility that God may be the One ultimately responsible for the persecution, a point that is confirmed by I Peter 3:17, "if the *will of God* should so will, that ye suffer for well doing. . . ." Job, admittedly, was at fault in accusing God of malicious persecution; but that this type of suffering does constitute a part of God's overall plan for His redeemed is indicated by the following prayer of faith, uttered by David when seized by the Philistines:

> Thou numberest my wanderings:
> Put Thou my tears into Thy bottle;
> Are they not in Thy book? (Ps. 56:8).

(b) But Job later went on to demonstrate the godly response to deeds of persecution, as well as the reality of such situations, when he affirmed,

> My friends scoff at me:
> But mine eye poureth out tears unto God (16:20).

A believer, that is, must preserve his faith in the God whose ways he may not, at times, be able to understand (cf. Hab. 2:4; I Pet. 3:14). The later prophets, therefore, took sharp issue against the unsubmissive attitude of the suffering captives of 597 B.C., who complained, "The fathers have eaten sour grapes, and the children's teeth are set on edge" (Jer. 31:29; Ezek. 18:2). For it was not true, as the exiles asserted, that "the way of the Lord was not equal" (v. 25). (c) God's ultimate solution was rather that of the vindication of the righteous. For example, the very Eliphaz who had told Job (correctly),

> Thou shalt be hid from the scourge of the tongue
> At destruction and dearth thou shalt laugh (5:21, 22),

and who had then gone on to administer to him just such a scourging, was himself, shortly thereafter, forced to bow in contrition before the man he had just persecuted but whom God had now vindicated (42:8)! Even when God's vindication remained uncertain, in the immediate context (cf. the case of the three friends of Daniel, before Nebuchadnezzar's furnace, 3:17), faith was yet to stand unwavering

(v. 18); for it would receive eventual justification. So Job, in a moment of assurance, could assert:

> But as for me I know that my *Gō'ēl* [Vindicator] liveth,
> And at least He will stand up upon the earth,
> Whom I, even I, shall see on my side (Job 19:25, 27; cf. Matt. 5:12).

5) God, the last speaker of the book of Job, suggests in its closing verses a final solution to the problem of human sorrow. (a) This solution consists of the truth of vicariousness, of one's suffering for the improvement of others. For when Job had once passed through the fires of suffering himself, he thereby attained to a position in which he could be of help to others. As God proceeded to explain to Eliphaz, "My servant Job shall pray for you; for him will I accept" (42:8). Moreover, it was only when Job did at length pray for his friends that God brought about his own restoration (v. 10). The long-range purpose, in other words, of Job's trials was that through him God might convey revelations about Himself and His ways, that would prove of blessing, not simply for Job's friends, but for all mankind. As James 5:11 now states, "Ye have heard of the patience of Job" (cf. John 9:3). So the great leaders of Israel consistently underwent vicarious suffering, to the end that God's gracious purposes in human history might be advanced and that His redemptive message might be made known to their fellows. Abraham the patriarch, with faith in God's promises for the future, stepped out into the immediate unknown (Gen. 12:1, 2). Joseph became a slave and a convict, that the lives of his family might be spared (45:5, 7). Moses refused to be called the son of Pharaoh's daughter, choosing rather to suffer ill treatment with the people of God, for the sake of Christ (Heb. 11:25, 26). David made open confession of his deepest sin, that God might be justified when He spoke and judged (Ps. 51:4). Isaiah was willing to experience a disgrace to himself, so that he might drive home his message to eighth century Judah (Isa. 20:2). Jeremiah, in the next period, accepted a career of sorrow, foregoing home life (Jer. 16:2) and suffering ostracism from his own family (11:21; cf. 1:19), that he might preach the testament under Josiah (11:6). Ezekiel in exile served obediently, to the point of defiling his priestly station (Ezek. 4:12-15) and of suppressing domestic tragedy, so as to carry out God's will (24:18). All these examples of vicariousness, however, were but preliminary to those supreme sufferings that were endured for others by God's righteous Servant; for "Yahweh hath laid on Him the iniquity of us all" (Isa. 53:6). (b) Today, moreover, it is not for the disciple to consider himself superior to the Master; and one's response to vicarious suffering must therefore be that of a willingness similarly to submit to it. We are admonished to "Have this mind in you, which was also in Christ Jesus, . . . who took the form of a servant" (Phil. 2:5, 7). (c) For the solution of a recompense

from God stands eternally sure. Christ Himself, "for the joy that was set before Him endured the cross, despising the shame" (Heb. 12:2; cf. Isa. 53:12). Moses likewise accounted "the reproach of Christ greater riches than the treasures of Egypt" (Heb. 11:26; cf. Mark 10:30; Rom. 8:17). Thus for us today, even though we may, like Job, be able to comprehend no more than the outskirts of God's ways (Job 26:14), still may we rest in the Spirit's assurance that "all things work together for good to them that love God, to them who are called according to His purpose" (Rom. 8:28).

For Further Reading:

James Freeman Rand, "Old Testament Fellowship with God, Parts III-IV," *Bibliotheca Sacra*, 108:432 (Oct.-Dec. 1951), pp. 423-433. On the benefits of the testament for the Old Testament saints.

John Wick Bowman, "Response in Fellowship," *Interpretation*, 6:3, (July 1952), pp. 279-289. A Neo-orthodox study of devotional life, centering in the prophets.

George A. E. Salstrand, *The Tithe, the Minimum Standard for Christian Giving.* Grand Rapids: Baker Book House, 1953. A practical study on the normativeness of the tithe in the present-day church.

30. Life After Death *

One of the five objective characteristics of the testament[1] is its feature of eternity. As early as the time of Abraham, God had expressly revealed, "I will establish My testament between Me and thee and thy seed after thee throughout their generations for an *everlasting* testament" (Gen. 17:7). This feature, moreover, involves eternity for the individual as well as eternal preservation for the family group. Indeed, the truth of a personal eternity follows directly from the facts of the testamentary situation: God is everlasting,[2] the promised inheritance under the testament consists of reconciliation to this eternal God, and it is therefore only to be expected that God's elect should continue to exist in fellowship with Him. Christ Himself employed this most basic of all arguments for man's life after death, when He adduced the necessity of human resurrection out of God's

---

* BIBLE READING: Psalms 49 and 73; Daniel 12

Collateral Reading: John D. Davis, "The Future Life in Hebrew Thought During the Pre-Persian Period," *The Princeton Theological Review*, 6,2 (April 1908), pp. 246-268.

Davidson, *The Theology of the Old Testament*, pp. 459-466, 477-495.

Burrows, *An Outline of Biblical Theology*, pp. 192-195.

---

[1]Monergism, the death of the testator, the promise of reconciliation, eternity, and the confirmatory sign; see above, pp. 88-90.

[2]See above, p. 152.

assurances to Moses at the burning bush. For these words of God were descriptive of His very testamental relationship: "I am the God of Abraham, the God of Isaac, and the God of Jacob" (Ex. 3:6). From the nature, then, of this relationship, arose the conclusion that He must be the God, not of the dead, but of the living (Mark 12:27). The redemptive situation of the Old Testament truly included Israel as a collectivity, "throughout their generations" (Gen. 17:7); but God is also concerned with each individual saint in the crises of his life. As the Korahite singers affirmed, "He will be our guide, even unto death" (Ps. 48:14). Nor does God's loving concern terminate with death. For death too exists as an object that is under His control (68:20; 90:3), and beyond it the Lord will continue to preserve His elect:

> My flesh and my heart faileth;
> But God is the strength of my heart and my portion for ever
> (73:26).

The high point in Job's solution to his bodily sufferings thus lay in that flash of inspired insight (19:26, 27) by which he related his vindication to a life which should arise after his present body's death:

> And after my skin, even this body, is destroyed,
> Yet in my flesh shall I see God;
> Whom I, even I, shall see on my side.

It is true that the facts of immortality were only progressively revealed and that, even in the later books, the Old Testament saints did not regularly integrate these God-given truths on life after death into a consistent solution to the problem of evil. It yet remained for Christ on that first Easter to tear the bars away, abolishing death, and bringing life and immortality to light through the Gospel (II Tim. 1:10). The facts, however, of God's eternal inheritance appear as validly present in the theology of the older testament: revelations of a hope for needy penitents that was as freely offered then as it is now; for,

> In the way of righteousness is life,
> And in the pathway thereof there is no death (Prov. 12:28).

PERIOD A, PRIMEVAL. Because of Adam's failure under the covenant of works, man not only forfeited the way to the tree of life, which might have confirmed him in an endless life (Gen. 3:22, 24), but he also became mortal, subject to physical death (v. 19).[3] No positive, verbal revelation of the hope of a life after death was as yet granted by God. But the eternal nature of the testamental relationship with Yahweh was given an active demonstration by the historical rapture of Enoch (Gen. 5:24); for Enoch was translated to heaven that he should not see death (Heb. 11:5). Unexplained as

---

[3]On the nature of man and the dissolution at death of the spirit from the body, see above, pp. 224, 225.

this event was, it yet served to provide even the primeval saints with a glimmering of the hope that was later expressed by the Davidic singers when they sang, "God will redeem my soul from the power of the grave, for He will receive me" (Ps. 49:15).

PERIOD B, PATRIARCHAL. When Jacob was informed of the supposed death of his son Joseph, he cried despairingly, "I will go down to sh'ōl to my son mourning" (Gen. 37:35). This Hebrew noun sh'ōl, "sheol," is presumably derived from the root, shā'al, which means to "ask." Its basic reference would thus be to the never satisfied grave (Prov. 30:16; cf. 1:12). Job 30:23, accordingly, speaks poetically of the grave as "the house appointed for all living"; and it is in regard to the inescapable grave that Scripture talks of the darkness and loss of order that follow upon death (10:21, 22). The Old Testament indeed possesses another word, qéver, for the physical grave; but "sheol," with its worms and corruption (Isa. 14:11), must likewise signify this final resting place of the dead body. Still a third parallel Hebrew term is bōr, "pit," which equals the grave, for example, in Psalm 28:1; 30:3. Of a similar import are verses such as Job's description of the wicked:

> They spend their days in prosperity,
> And in a moment they go down to sh'ōl (21:13).

Again, Sheol must refer to the grave. For the "downward" direction signifies a place, in preference to the abtract thought of death; and yet Sheol's meaning cannot be that of "hell," because in context what Job describes is something good.

But then, by a natural extension of meaning, the noun sh'ōl does come to identify death in the abstract (Ps. 18:5), or even hell (see Period C). In the speech, moreover, of Jacob in Genesis 37:35, he cannot have intended the root meaning of grave, even though he speaks of his "gray hairs" as being laid there (42:38; 44:29, 31). For Jacob expected to be found "with Joseph"; and Joseph he imagined to be devoured, or at best unburied. Sheol must therefore mean simply "death." But Jacob's words about being with his son in Sheol thus seem to indicate the patriarch's belief in a conscious reunion some day with Joseph. Likewise, the fact that God, in speaking with Isaac and Jacob, continued to call Himself the "God of Abraham," even though His words came subsequent to Abraham's physical death (26:24; 28:13), indicates the truth that this patriarch too must still have been preserved alive with God in spiritual immortality (see above on Ex. 3:6; Mark 12:27). So John Davis, after analyzing the circumstances of Abraham's earthly existence, concludes, "He had reason to cherish hope of a continuance of blessed association with God in the life beyond."[4] This belief is then born out by the New

[4]"The Future Life in Hebrew Thought During the Pre-Persian Period," *The Princeton Theological Review*, 6, 2 (April 1908), p. 253.

Testament revelation which specifically says of Abraham, "He looked for the city which hath foundations, whose builder and maker is God" (Heb. 11:10). God's Spirit further includes the conscious hopes of Isaac and Jacob; because He goes on to state, "*They* desire a better country, that is, a heavenly: wherefore God is not ashamed of them, to be called their God; for He hath prepared for them a city" (v. 16). On Abraham's particular faith for the resurrection of his son Isaac (Gen. 22:5; Heb. 11:19), see above, topic 24.[5]

PERIOD C, MOSAIC. Deuteronomy 32:39 teaches that God controls the processes of both life and of death (cf. I Sam. 2:6). But Moses' teaching went further. Specifically, in his first book he revealed that the patriarchs, after they had given up their spirits and died, were literally "gathered to their people" (Gen. 25:8). This "gathering" was an activity that preceded the act of their burial (v. 9; cf. 35:29; 49:33). These passages thus disprove the following explanation, which is sometimes advanced: namely, that with the accumulation of bodies in the family tombs, the older corpses (which had become reduced to skeletons) came eventually to be swept off the shelves, so as to make way for fresh corpses. As a result, in a corner bone pile, the former could be said to be "gathered to their people"(!).[6] But Abraham and Jacob were, in fact, "gathered" in lands that were located far from their ancestral tombs. This reunion of the family therefore becomes the Bible's first generalized revelation concerning the immortality of the soul.

But while he recognized the reality of life after death, Moses yet condemned all forms of attempted communication with the dead by spiritism or by witchcraft (Ex. 22:18; Deut. 18:10-12; cf. Isa. 8:19). The term *yidd'ōnī*, literally, a "knowing one," a "familiar spirit" (Deut. 18:12), was applied initially to the spirit of a dead man, and then by extension to the person of a spiritist, which testifies to a popular belief in Canaan that the dead did possess special knowledge. But, utterly apart from the impossibility of human communion with the dead (see below, period F), the very attempt on the part of men to seek out spirits tends to impair their single-hearted devotion to God. Spiritism accordingly is forbidden; and instead, "unto Him" God's people are to hearken (v. 15). Food offerings for the dead are likewise prohibited, because they develop out of the pagan idea that the dead remain in their graves and that they are still characterized by physical needs (26:14). This form of offering was, however, one of the sins into which Israel fell at Baal-peor (Ps. 106:28).

Through Moses, God for the first time applied the term "sheol" to the concept of hell (Num. 16:30). Hell is a place; for human spirits

---

[5]P. 306, and footnote 6.
[6]Cf. Jacob, *Theology of the Old Testament*, p. 303; but contrast Knight's more positive approach, *A Christian Theology of the Old Testament*, p. 335.

always occupy space definitively, and only the omnipresent God can be described as related to space repletively. There is therefore nothing incongruous about a "place" for the spirits of the departed. Scripture then consistently locates hell in the lowest part of the earth (Deut. 32:22; cf. Ps. 63:9; 86:13). Further, though God exercises His control over "lowest sheol" (Deut. 32:22), this awful place is yet described as the final abode for wicked men who have been cast out of God's presence. As Moses wrote, "The earth opened its mouth, and swallowed up all the men that appertained unto Korah. So they went down alive into hell: and the earth closed upon them" (Num. 16:32, 33). When "sheol," however, is used in a local sense with reference to the righteous, its meaning is consistently that of "the grave."[7]

Concerning the fate of the godly, it was Balaam who prayed,

> Let me die the death of the righteous,
> And let my last end be like his (Num. 23:10).

This couplet shows not only the blessing that accompanies the elect throughout their lifetime, but also the desirability of death for those who are among the saved.[8] Moses himself died, and the immediate context states that he was buried by God (Deut. 34:5, 6). Subsequently, however, Moses appeared in glory with Elijah (Luke 9:30, 31); and the enigmatic passage of Jude 9, which mentions Satan's dispute over his body, may indicate the later rapture or translation of this saint of God.[9]

PERIOD D, CONSOLIDATION. The song of Hannah contains the general statement, "Yahweh bringeth down to sheol" (I Sam. 2:6). These words thus illustrate how the term "sheol," meaning "the grave," may be used in reference to the good and bad, without distinction. Of identical, local significance is I Kings 2:6, 9, where the hoar heads of Abner and Shimei are said to "go down to sheol."

A unique incident in this period is the appearance of Samuel, who had recently died, to Saul, on the eve of his final battle (I Sam. 28). Saul, in desperate need of counsel, had asked for a woman with "a familiar spirit"; and despite his interdict against all witches (v. 3), one had promptly been found at En-dor (v. 7). Her very availability thus demonstrates Israel's general belief, not only in the truth of life after death, but also in the error of spiritism. The witch herself, however, was totally unprepared for the events that subsequently transpired (v. 12), which goes to prove the normally fraudu-

---

[7]Vs. Gustav F. Oehler, *Theology of the Old Testament*, p. 170.
[8]Again vs. Oehler; *ibid.,* p. 173. Note, however, that Moses's desire for death, as expressed in Numbers 11:15, arose simply because of his overwhelming burden of work (cf. Job 3:11, 12 and Eccl. 4:2, 3).
[9]The phrase in Deut. 32:39, "I kill and make alive," is not here relevant; for it possesses a more general reference.

lent character of her profession, both here and elsewhere.[10] But on this occasion Samuel was actually present, by Scriptural statement (v. 15), and consciously operative. He is described as being like the Samuel who had once lived — an old man, with a robe — and yet the woman called him *elōhīm*, "deity" (v. 13). There must therefore have been something supernatural about his appearance — it was not like the more normal-looking form of the body at resurrection (cf. John 20:14, 15).[11] The fact that Saul does not seem to have been able, initially, to see Samuel requires but little comment: it may have been simply because of an interval that had been set between himself and the woman (cf. v. 21), or because of his own physical and psychological condition, which was bordering upon collapse (v. 20). Samuel then proceeds to inform Saul of God's inspired truth (v. 19). Personally, moreover, he states that he would have preferred to remain at ease in glory (v. 15), rather than to have made even this brief return to the earth with its woes. Two other factors that are to be noted are these: 1) The witch's question, "Whom shall I bring up?" (v. 11), bears witness to the Canaanitish superstition that a man's spirit, like his body, was supposed to be found in the ground. God did, however, on this occasion specifically "bring up" Samuel,[12] presumably because of the material elements that were involved in the unique appearing form of the prophet. His soul, in contrast, need normally have possessed no such subterranean abode. 2) Samuel's final message to Saul was this: "Tomorrow shalt thou and thy sons be with me" (v. 19). His prophecy may constitute nothing more than a poetic expression of the fact that they, like Samuel, would soon be dead; though the literal sense, that they would before long be with him in heaven, is not devoid of possibility.

PERIOD E, DAVIDIC. Raven has observed, "The literature of David's time shows a considerable advance beyond the earlier conceptions of the future life";[13] and the Davidic period, in respect to this doctrine of life after death, is indeed the most significant of all those through which God chose to reveal the theology of His older testament. Older truths do continue to appear — for example, that David would rejoin his deceased son after death (II Sam. 12:23). Also, by way of a new definition for an old concept, the spirits of the dead are for the first time assigned a specific name: the *r'fā'îm*, or "shades" (Ps. 88:10). The title is identical with that of the Rephaim, the van-

---

[10]Divine intervention is, however, possible in special cases. Cf. Ezek. 14:4, "Every man of the house of Israel that taketh his idols into his heart . . . I Yahweh will answer him therein"; nor is demonism in the practices of spiritists totally to be discounted.

[11]Job 4:12-17 seems to refer to a theophany, and not to the coming of a spirit.

[12]Cf. I Sam. 2:6, "He bringeth down to the grave and bringeth up." The significance, however, of this phrase is a general one and means simply to bring back from the verge of death.

[13]*The History of the Religion of Israel*, p. 245.

ishing and, by David's time, almost extinct ancient inhabitants of Canaan (cf. Gen. 14:5). But at this point God saw fit to make known to mankind two new and highly significant revelations. Their importance is indicated by the very introduction that the Korahites prefixed to one of the passages that is the most concerned, Psalm 49:

> Hear this, all ye peoples;
>   Give ear, all ye inhabitants of the world,
> Both low and high,
> Rich and poor together.
> My mouth shall speak wisdom (vv. 1-3).

1) On the threatening side, God then for the first time revealed that hell was to be the destiny of all the wicked, and that it was designed for their punishment. He thus led the Korahites to write, in reference to the ungodly,

> They are appointed as a flock for hell (sheol);
>   And the upright [in contrast] shall have dominion over them in
>   the morning (v. 14).

As David's wise man Heman went on to explain, when the wicked die they are cut off from the sustaining care of the Lord. God no longer remembers them (Ps. 88:5), and He shows them no more wonders (v. 10).[14] David had indeed emphasized that the omnipresent God was there, even in hell (139:8; Job 26:6). But Asaph adds that while God controls their ultimate fate, He actually despises them (73:20) and causes them to be consumed with terrors (v. 19). Liberalism may blandly assert that "early Hebrew religion had no conception of judgment or salvation after death."[15] But the Old Testament of David's day sharply distinguishes between the fate of the wicked and of the righteous at death, saying of the former, "They shall never see the light" (49:19).[16]

2) Through the men of David, moreover, God went on to reveal the corresponding blessed truth that hell can never be the portion of the righteous: they, on the contrary, will enter at death into the glories of heaven itself. Psalm 49:19 had implied that, the godly as opposed to the wicked, *would* "see the light." The Psalm, however, carries this thought further; and, after its description in verse 14 of the appointment of the wicked for hell, it makes their distinction from the righteous explicit by stating,

> But God will redeem my soul from the power of hell (sheol);
>   For He will receive me (v. 15).

---

[14]These words do not have reference to the saved, Heman's inclusion of himself being due to the fact that he thought of himself, at this point, as being under God's wrath (v. 7).

[15]Burrows, *An Outline of Biblical Theology*, p. 192.

[16]In certain well-known passages, however, as for example in the line, "The wicked shall be turned into hell" (Ps. 9:17), the word "sheol" may mean, not "hell," but simply "the grave."

Similarly, David contrasts the fate of the lost with his own expectation of future life, by saying,

> As for me, I shall behold Thy face in righteousness;
> I shall be satisfied, when I awake, with beholding Thy form
>   (17:15).

This "awakening" cannot refer simply to his rousing up from a night's sleep; for it is presented in opposition to the status of the wicked, "whose portion is in this life" (v. 14).[17] Such a symbol for eternal life thus corresponds to that which was found in the Korahite Psalm already quoted, "And the upright shall have dominion over them *in the morning*" (49:14), that is, in the morning of immortality. After death, therefore, the separation of the elect from the lost is complete. When Biblical interpreters, moreover, seek to make assertions to the contrary, they not infrequently end up condemning themselves by the very evidence that they present. This appears, for example, in the following summary statement by Raven:

> These complementary ideas, that God would save the righteous from Sheol and that He would bring the wicked to Sheol, while not indicating any distinction between the condition of the righteous and the wicked after death, nevertheless prepared for this doctrine [!].[18]

The basis for David's heavenly hope, finally, is seen to lie in the fact of Israel's fundamental inheritance of reconciliation with God under the testament. As Davis concludes, "To those to whom fellowship with God had become a passion of the soul . . . it was natural both to see and to seize the truth of continued blessed fellowship with God in the world to come."[19] Thus the anonymous 102nd Psalm proceeds to link the status of Christ (which is everlasting) with that of His people (which must be similarly so), as follows:

> But Thou art the same,
>   And Thy years shall have no end.
> The children of Thy servants shall continue,
>   And their seed shall be established before Thee
>   (vv. 27, 28; cf. Isa. 51:6, 8).

Indeed, it is primarily because Asaph knew himself to be continually with God (Ps. 73:23) that he could state with confidence,

> Thou wilt guide me with thy counsel,
>   And afterward receive me to glory (v. 24; cf. v. 26).

Only the basic failure of liberal theology to appreciate the true nature of the testament — plus its dogmatically reached conviction that Israel's religion must be rationally derived from the concepts of surrounding pagan peoples — could lead its representative to assert with such unanimity that in Israel "the future life was supposed to be

---

[17]On the application in Psalms of the doctrine of immortality to the problem of theodicy, see above, p. 204.
[18]*Op. cit.*, pp. 246-247.
[19]Davis, *op. cit.*, p. 262.

merely a reduced, weakened, undesirable kind of existence to which all alike must come eventually."[20] Even Romanist and dispensationalist writers have been led to adopt similar positions.[21] Particularly, however, it was the revelation in this period of the Davidic testament, with its promise of life in God's kingdom, under the Messianic son of David, that seems to have become responsible for the contemporary stress upon the glorious life that lay in store for God's redeemed. Specifically, since the Messiah's soul would not be left to death (Sheol) nor His person allowed to see corruption (Ps. 16:10), it followed naturally that those who shared with Him in the Davidic testamental relationship should likewise participate in His triumph. So David himself exulted,

> My flesh also shall dwell in safety.
> Thou wilt show me the path of life:
> In Thy presence is fulness of joy;
> In Thy right hand there are pleasures for evermore (vv. 9, 11).

Further revelations, to give details about the nature of heaven, were as yet unnecessary. Simply to be with Him was eternal life! (Cf. Phil. 1:23).

However, in analyzing the future hope as it was understood in the Davidic period, one must keep in mind at least four major cautions. 1) Some of David's references to "deliverance" may refer, not to the afterlife as such, but to a preliminary (present) rescue from having to undergo death. An example appears in the verse which David spoke at the termination of the pestilence which followed upon the king's sinful census:

> Oh Yahweh, Thou hast brought up my soul from the grave (sheol);
> Thou hast kept me alive, that I should not go down to the pit
> (Ps. 30:3; cf. 86:13).

2) Other references, such as Psalm 85:6, "Revive us again," may best be taken as figurative expressions and prayers for national prosperity. 3) Moreover, there existed in the Israel of 1000 B.C. a real fear of death (II Sam. 22:6, 7); and Burrows has properly comprehended the Old Testament attitude toward the grave, as something that was "to be avoided as long as possible."[22] At least three reasons arise to explain this ancient fear. (a) Some of the Biblical forebodings are due to the physical agony that so often becomes a part of the experience of death. The sufferer would thus later recount,

> The cords of death compassed me,
> And the pains of death [sheol] gat hold upon me:
> I found trouble and sorrow (Ps. 116:3).

(b) Others of these qualms were doubtless due to the limited revelations that Israel had so far received concerning death. David pos-

[20]Burrows, *op. cit.*, p. 192.
[21]See Appendix G for an outline of Christendom's historical positions on the nature of man's life, after death and before the final resurrection.
[22]Burrows, *loc. cit.*

sessed, indeed, the promise of the testament to comfort him when death, for example, struck his loved ones:

Yea, though I walk through the valley of the shadow of death,[23]
I will fear no evil; for Thou art with me (23:4);

but he yet lacked the climactic Biblical revelation of Easter's empty tomb. (c) Finally, some of the anxiety of the Old Testament saints is due to the very nature of death, in whatever dispensation it may occur. As Davis remarks, after noting — appropriately — the apprehension with which believers even now face the mystery of the next world: "The creed did not dispel the gloom of sheol from the mind of every man. There were men of keen spiritual vision who yet felt dismay at the appearance of death."[24] The Old Testament, accordingly, presents almost no instance of suicide. Actually, only three such cases appear: the suicide of Saul and his armor bearer (I Sam. 31:4, 5), the case of Ahithophel (II Sam. 17:23), and the suicide of Zimri (I Kings 16:18). Each of these self-imposed deaths, moreover, took place under desperate straits. Commandment VI of the Decalogue had explicitly prohibited all murder, and this includes that of oneself. When God gives life, it is not for man to take it upon himself to defy the divine decree. Job's attitude in this regard was therefore most reprehensible (cf. Job 3:11, 12). Yet death did come to be accepted by the very old (II Sam. 19:37), though sometimes it would appear more through disinterest in life's present routine than because of an active anticipation of what lay ahead. Finally 4) there exist numerous Old Testament references to the separation of the dead from the living. The former can no longer witness to others of the reality of God's grace (Ps. 6:5; 30:9); and in this respect they are silent (115:17); they become forgotten (88:12). The dead, moreover, can never be brought back to this present life (II Sam. 12:23): "For we must needs die, and are as water spilt on the ground, which cannot be gathered up again" (14:14).

PERIOD F, DISRUPTION. Some of the statements on death that appear in Solomon's wisdom literature concern nothing more than its avoidance, for example, Proverbs 14:27,

The fear of Yahweh is a fountain of life,
That one may depart from the snares of death.

But though much of Solomon's writing is indeed characterized by a "this worldly" emphasis (cf. 11:31), his works yet contain a number of significant revelations on the life that is still to come. Death, in the first place, is described as inescapable. Each generation passes (Eccl.

---

[23]This traditional translation for *salmāweth* is validated by the New Testament analogy (cf. Matt. 4:16; Luke 1:79).
[24]*Op. cit.*, p. 267.

1:4); and the expectation of even the most righteous was stated to Job in the following terms:

> Thou shalt come to thy grave in a full age,
> Like a shock of grain cometh in its season (Job 5:26, apparently revealed to Israel in the days of Solomon).

Such an anticipation represents, of course, a marked contrast to the spirit of the New Testament, which admonishes us to be "looking for that blessed hope and the glorious appearing of the great God and our Savior Jesus Christ" (Titus 2:13), when "we that are alive, that are left, shall together with them be caught up in the clouds, to meet the Lord in the air" (I Thess. 4:17). But in all ages, life is uncertain — a fleeting shadow (Job 14:2; Eccl. 6:12; cf. James 4:14); and we know not when our end may come (Eccl. 9:12). For the saints who lived before Christ, there was thus no power over the day of death (8:8), which lay in the hands of the Almighty (Job 14:5, 20; 30:23; cf. 2:6). Strong and weak (21:26), wise and otherwise (Eccl. 2:14, 15), righteous and wicked (9:2),[25] man and beast (3:19) — "do not all go to one place?" (6:6). The inclusiveness of the grave was universal.

But then beyond the grave lay immortality. Near the beginning of his book of Ecclesiastes, Solomon asked his readers, "Who knoweth the spirit of man, whether it goeth upward and the spirit of the beast, whether it goeth downward to the earth?" (3:21). But later he provided the answer to his own question by affirming, "The dust returneth to the earth as it was, and the spirit returneth unto God who gave it" (12:7). This latter verse is no mere description of how a man "gives up the ghost" (8:8) and so ends it all. For the specified "return" of his spirit to God stands in contrast to the stated downward termination of the life of the beast, as this was expressed in the former verse. Job too then asks the fundamental question, "Man dieth and is laid low: yea, man expireth, and where is he?" (Job 14:10). The questioner was well aware that man's body lies down in the dust (7:21), that it is held by "the bars of sheol [the grave]" (17:16; cf. v. 14). In fact, it is Job's very knowledge of the nature of the coffin that serves to explain his description of death as "the land of darkness" (10:21), as the state which is "without any order" (v. 22). But the inspired Elihu went on to reply to Job with the same answer that is found in Ecclesiastes, namely, that when a man's body perishes, God "gathers unto Himself his spirit" (34:14, 15). Job thus concludes, "Man passeth, Thou changest his countenance and sendest him away [from earth]" (14:20).

Change, however, is neither annihilation, nor is it necessarily condemnation; for the wisdom writings then proceed to repeat the Davidic hope of the deliverance of the godly from hell. Character-

---

[25]The righteous may even go first (Eccl. 7:15), though generally this is not the case (7:17; 8:13).

istic of the book of Proverbs is its doctrine of the "two ways."[26] The book, for example, describes the findings of Wisdom (Christ) as life; while in contrast with this good way is the statement that to hate Him is to love death, the evil way (8:35-36; cf. 11:19). Righteousness thus results in *al-māweth*, "not death" (12:28); and the thought of this phrase is not simply that of a bare immortality, but of a positive life that is yet to be experienced: "The righteous hath hope in his death" (14:32). Solomon then states the direction of this better "way," when he writes,

> To the wise the way of life goeth upward,
>   That he may depart from hell (sheol) beneath (15:24).

"Upward," which is the opposite of hell, must therefore be heaven (Job 11:8); but the location of the heavenly abode of the redeemed, though it is real, is not further defined at this point. Its state, however, receives in the Solomonic period its first detailed Biblical elaboration. Negatively speaking, the state of the righteous dead is described as better than that of the sorrows of humanity's present life (Eccl. 4:2). Job 3:17-19, accordingly, contains the beautiful word-picture:

> There the wicked cease from troubling;
>   And there the weary are at rest.
> There the prisoners are at ease together;
>   They hear not the voice of the taskmaster.
> The small and the great are there:
>   And the servant is free from his master (cf. v. 13).

The social distinctions of this world have thus been replaced by a more valid standard of judgment. For, positively, Solomon describes the life that lies beyond by saying, "Man goeth to his everlasting home" (Eccl. 12:5), to the same celestial city, that is, which had been sought by Abraham ages before (Heb. 11:16). There blessings abound. For man's inheritance of the testament depends wholly upon the decision of God; and it is at the point when man's soul comes home that, as Job said to God, "Thou wilt have a desire to the work of Thy hands" (Job 14:15). God's fundamental blessing, moreover, is that of personal reconciliation with Himself; and Job had therefore grasped the essence of heaven when he affirmed with confidence, "After my skin, even this body, is destroyed . . . I shall see God, and not as a stranger. My heart is consumed within me!" (19:26, 27).

But the doctrine of the two ways possesses another, darker side:

> When a wicked man dieth, his expectation shall perish;
>   And the hope of iniquity perisheth (Prov. 11:7).

Thus, even as the promised hope of *al-māweth* (the lack of death) meant more in the way of blessing for the righteous than the simple fact of an unadorned immortality (12:28; 14:32), so the "perishing of the hope" of the wicked suggests something more serious for the

---

[26]See above, p. 344.

ungodly than the mere cessation of this existence. For opposite heaven there lies hell (Job 11:8). The subterranean character of hell, which has been noted previously,[27] is further defined in this period by the words of Yahweh Himself, which serve to locate "the gates of death . . . in the recesses of the deep" (38:16, 17). As Job had just revealed (26:5), "They that are deceased tremble beneath the waters." The wicked dead, in other words, are still alive; but they are held behind infernal gates as in a prison, and they tremble. Scripture indeed designates their darkened home as *avaddōn*, "destruction" (26:6; Prov. 15:11);[28] but hell is a place where they nonetheless continue to exist and where they lie eternally subject to the Satanic "king of terrors" (Job 18:14).[29] In the New Testament, "Abaddon" has thus become a name for "the angel of the abyss" himself (Rev. 9:11).

The specific horror of *avaddōn* springs from its association with the fire of the Lord's punishment. God's "flaming" retribution begins, in a sense, even on this present earth (Job 31:12); and an idea of its final, literal fearsomeness appears from the words of Song of Solomon 8:6, where hell (sheol) is described as cruel, in parallelism with "flashes of fire" and "the flame of Yah(weh)." Psychologically, however, hell is defined in terms that are even more terrifying. The best known description of its hopeless fixity appears in Ecclesiastes 9:4-6. These significant verses have indeed become a subject of consistent abuse, both by liberal writers and by various cultists; for both of these groups fail to appreciate that they describe, not the state of the saved, but rather the destiny of those whose hearts are "full of evil" (v. 3). As John Davis long ago cautioned,

> "The wicked . . . and the skeptics . . . [as well as] the spiritual: these different classes of men . . . must be duly considered in connection with every utterance concerning the future world, else the would-be interpreter will surely go astray."[30]

Verse 5 thus states, "The living know that they shall die; but the [lost] dead know not anything, neither have they any reward." The point is not that the damned have lost consciousness, but only that they no longer possess a hope toward which they can look forward. The living, that is, can always anticipate death; but for the unsaved dead there is no more any possibility of a reward, of a change in status, once the body enters its tomb. Verse 10 therefore reads, "Whatsoever thy hand findeth to do, do it with thy might: for there

---

[27]See above, p. 447.

[28]Like "sheol," Abaddon refers in the first instance to the grave, the place of the destruction of the body (Job 28:22, Ps. 88:11; Prov. 27:20). But it comes to have particular reference to the place of the punishment of the souls of the wicked; cf. the above passages from Job 26.

[29]See above, p. 293.

[30]*Op. cit.*, pp. 267-268.

is no work, no device, nor knowledge, nor wisdom in the grave."
This factor of unchangeableness is indeed the very thing that makes
death so ultimately serious, so utterly hopeless, for those who are
apart from Christ. For God declares in this passage that a man's
eternal destiny is settled at the point when he departs from this
world. As a result, enlightened piety disallows all prayers for the
dead.[31] Romanism, with its endless intercessions for the departed,
may continue to flout God's eternal decree, just as it correspondingly
fabricates its comforting never-land of purgatory. But these Romanist doctrines are simply man-made and Apocryphal (II Macc. 12:
43-45), not Biblical. Scripture, by contrast, insists that even for history's greatest men — now and only now — is the day of salvation:
"For to him that is joined with all the living there is hope; for a
living dog is better than a dead lion" (Eccl. 9:4).

A closely related topic, in reference to which the wisdom literature makes a unique contribution to Biblical theology as a whole, is
that of the relationship of the dead to the living. In the first place,
the Solomonic writings teach that the goods and the affairs of this
present life cannot be carried into the life that is to come (Job 1:21;
Eccl. 5:15; cf. 2:18-21; I Tim. 6:7). "You can't take it with you!"
Again, the wisdom writings serve to underline how rapidly one's lifetime accomplishments tend to fade away in this world too, when once
one moves on to the next. As Solomon sums it up, "In the days to
come all will have been long forgotten" (Eccl. 2:16; cf. 1:11). More
significantly, this section of Scripture then teaches that the dead are
able to sustain no active influence, however slight, over the affairs of
this world: "As well their love, as their hatred and their envy, is perished long ago; neither have they any more a portion for ever in anything that is done under the sun" (9:6). Indeed, they fail even to
possess knowledge of what goes on among the living. Job thus reveals
concerning the dead:

> His sons come to honor, and he knoweth it not;
> And they are brought low, but he perceiveth it not of them
>   (Job 14:21, cf. Eccl. 3:22).

Finally, moreover, they do not care (Job 21:21)! This seeming ruth-
lessness in attitude, however, will, upon reflection, be found to constitute a blessing of the first magnitude. For the living, it immediately
obviates any lurking fears of "ghosts" or baneful spirits. At the same
time it relieves the living from concern about the feelings of the

----

[31]Thus the approach of Scofield dispensationalism, which relegates Ecclesiastes to
"the best man can do . . . the reasonings of man apart from divine revelation,"
(C. I. Scofield, *Reference Bible*, pp. 697, 702), constitutes a most serious departure,
not only because it introduces a concept of partial inspiration into the Word, but
also because it discounts the crucial doctrine that is the subject of this particular
passage. Ecclesiastes is confessedly incomplete in its eschatology, but it is not
sub-standard. What it does say is the equivalent of God's words, and is both
accurate and needful.

departed, in reference to their involvement with the calamities, sorrows, and failures that constitute an inevitable part of this earthly existence. Then too for the dead, while it does require their separation for a time from a knowledge of the affairs of their loved ones on earth, God has yet granted to all of us ample time (eternity) for "catching up" on associations, after our blessed reunion which will take place on that fairer shore. More important, if living men go wrong, if a certain loved one, for example, rejects Christ and is thereby rejected from glory, it means that earth and hell will never be able to sabotage heaven by pulling on heart-strings or causing tears among the sainted dead.

A final problem, which was first to be taken up in Scripture by the Solomonic wisdom literature, concerns the matter of the ultimate return of the dead to the earth — the question, in other words, of men's resurrection. The resurrection had been a subject of personal belief ever since the time of the patriarch Abraham (Gen. 22:5). It had been implied, moreover, in the fact of the testamental relationship, when Yahweh had declared to Moses, "I am the God of Abraham" (Ex. 3:6). It might, indeed, have been elaborated by David (Ps. 16:9; cf. Acts 2:31). But the resurrection of man is, in fact, first seriously discussed only in the Solomonic book of Job. As a necessary prerequisite to this doctrine, the Old Testament had already presented the fact of the dichotomy of the human nature: a body, that returns to dust, and of the soul or spirit that at death returns to God. But at the same time, the Old Testament also teaches the unity of man's whole person,[32] and it was by means of this latter truth that God seems to have led the thinking of His people toward an appreciation of an eventual restoration of the entire man, body and spirit reunited. Thus the Holy Spirit guided Job in his inspired pondering:

> For there is hope of a tree,
>   If it be cut down, that it will sprout again.
> If a man die, shall he live again? (Job 14:7, 14).

On the one hand, Job well knew, as has been noted above,[33] that there could be no return of the dead to the present daily life:

> He that goeth down to the grave shall come up no more.
> He shall return no more to his house,
>   Neither shall his place know him any more (7:9, 10; cf. 10:21, 16:22).

But on the other hand, as A. B. Davidson has paraphrased Job's thought,

> The very extremity of the misery of man, so awfully realized in himself, forces into his mind the thought that there might be another life; that when God's anger was passed, which now con-

---

[32]See above, pp. 224, 225.
[33]See above, p. 452.

sumed him, He might remember His creature and awake him to
life and blessedness: "Oh that Thou wouldst hide me in Sheol
[the grave]; that Thou wouldst appoint me a set time and remember me (xiv. 13). . . . The phantom, for he will not believe it
to be quite a phantom, is too glorious to lose sight of, and he will,
in spite of reason and experience pursue it — 'All the days of my
appointed time would I wait till my change came.' "34

The resurrection hope, however, did not long remain a "phantom" in
the mind of this ancient seeker. The significance of chapter 19: 26,
27 as a demonstration of Job's belief in immortality has been discussed already.35 But these verses go further and present another
expectation as well:

> But as for me, I know that my Redeemer liveth,
>   And at last He will stand up upon the earth:
> And after my skin, even this body, is destroyed,
>   Then *in my flesh* shall I see God (vv. 25, 26).

That is to say, not simply would Job's spirit rise at death to live
with God in heaven; but the testamental promise would experience
an even greater accomplishment: and when the Messiah should
come to set up His future kingdom, Job's body would rise to live with
Him on earth. Liberalism generally refuses to have any part in this
revealed truth. It must be recognized, moreover, that in the last line,
the preposition which introduces the phrase "my flesh" is the Hebrew
word *min*, which means literally, "from." This preposition may then
be taken, either as a *min* of source, "from (being) in my flesh," or as
a *min* of separation, "(being) away from my flesh." Evolutionary religion, as might be expected, supports the latter alternative as being
the more natural (less supernatural); but evangelical religion adopts
the former rendering, as being the intention of God, on the basis of
the known analogy of subsequent Scriptures. Two corollary points
then remain to be recognized as they emerge from this passage. 1)
The outcome of man's bodily resurrection, involves, for Job, vindication: "I shall see God on my side" (v. 27). But to his friends, he
cautions, "Be ye afraid; know there is a judgment" (v. 29). 2) The
time of Job's resurrection is then defined as taking place when God
comes to stand upon the earth (v. 25). This time factor, moreover,
serves as an important element in Biblical harmonization, for the Old
Testament saint, as previously stated, could never have returned to
the world as he knew it. But a clue that is suggestive of that point
in history when mankind's general resurrection could occur, lies
recorded in the poetic but inspired phraseology of Job 14:12:

> So man lieth down and riseth not:
>   *Till the heavens be no more*, they [men's bodies] shall not awake,
> Nor be roused out of their sleep.

So in Revelation 20:11, 12, which is depicted as an event subsequent

---

34*The Theology of the Old Testament*, p. 483.
35See above, p. 454.

to our Lord's return to earth, John states, "The earth and the heaven fled away; *and* I saw the dead, the great and the small, standing before the throne."

Near the end of the disruption period, a series of miracles that were wrought through Israel's reforming prophets brought back to life three different people who had died (I Kings 17:21, 22; II Kings 4:34; 13:21). These instances do not, however, concern the ultimate resurrection of the persons involved: their souls simply came back into the bodies, their former lives were resumed, and the people themselves seem eventually to have died, in normal ways, a second time. Elijah's bodily rapture to heaven, however (II Kings 2:11; cf. his visible appearance with Christ 900 years later, Matt. 17:3), must have served to hasten Israel's popular readiness for God's more complete revelation of the doctrine of the resurrection, which followed in the next period.

PERIOD G, EIGHTH CENTURY PROPHETS. The prophet Isaiah spoke of the relative desirability of death for the elect, as he anticipated the calamitous results of the apostasy that was then arising under Manasseh: "The righteous perisheth and merciful men are taken away, none considering that the righteous is taken away from the evil to come. He shall enter into peace" (Isa. 57:1, 2). He also commented on the fact that a lack of burial, while it was a serious disgrace (14:18-20; cf. Eccl. 6:3), could still not affect the movement of a man's soul into its life beyond (Isa. 14:15). Isaiah then went on to reveal how the lost in hell would know it when a wicked king should come to join them (vv. 16, 17). His previous oracle to this king had stated, moreover, "Thou shalt be brought down to hell [sheol], *to the uttermost parts* of the pit" (v. 15). These words thus seem to constitute the first Biblical indication of the existence of degrees of punishment in hell, if we are to assume that in its lowest section God's punishments are indeed the most severe.[36] The prophet Amos once again stresses the reality of the Lord's control over hell (Amos 9:2). Hezekiah's prayer, after his illness, then re-emphasizes the truth that only in this present life does a man possess the opportunity of salvation and of witnessing to his Savior:

> For death (sheol) cannot praise Thee, death cannot celebrate Thee:
> They that go down into the pit cannot hope for Thy truth.
> The living, the living, he shall praise Thee, as I do this day:
> The father to the children shall make known Thy truth (Isa: 38:18, 19).

It is the last line of these verses that constitutes the real key to the passage: for the dead saints do praise God (cf. Rev. 6:10), but not to their children on earth.

---

[36]So Oehler, *op. cit.*, p. 173.

Considerable revelation relative to the doctrine of the resurrection occurs in the eighth century period. First of all, the basis for our resurrection hope lies in the initial resurrection of our Lord Jesus Christ, God's suffering Servant. For the Servant, after having passed through death, "shall prolong His days" and thus accomplish the redemptive pleasure of Yahweh (Isa. 53:10). Then, some day, death itself will be overcome in the resurrection of all of His redeemed saints. As Hosea predicts,

> I will ransom them from the power of the grave (sheol);
> I will redeem them from death:
> Oh death, where are thy plagues?
> Oh grave, where is thy destruction? (Hos. 13:14; cf. Isa. 25:8;
> I Cor. 15:55).

This later victory, however, is dependent upon Christ's previously having Himself risen from the dead on the third day; for the saints are resurrected only as they are identified with Him and with His experience: "After two days will He revive us: on the third day He will raise us up, and we shall live before Him" (Hos. 6:2; cf. I Cor. 15:4). Here again appears the fundamental truth of testamental thought that a man's hope for future life depends upon his reconciled relationship with Jesus Christ. The application of these two references from Hosea is indeed often limited by liberal writers to the idea of a figurative, national resurrection — to a revival, that is, of Israel's political body in ancient history.[37] But the analogy of I Corinthians 15 insures their individualistic meaning, provided one is willing to accept the New Testament authority. Certain other references, however, such as Jonah 2:6, "Yet hast Thou brought up my life from the pit" (cf. v. 2C in the anonymous 71st Psalm), refer only to one's deliverance from a threatened death even though the rescue be described poetically in terms of bodily resurrection.

One of the clearest Old Testament passages on the resurrection occurs in Isaiah 26:19, "Thy dead shall live; My dead bodies shall arise. Awake and sing, ye that dwell in the dust; for thy dew is as the dew of herbs, and the earth shall cast forth the dead." It should be noted, however, that in its context this reference does not apply to the general resurrection of the dead, but only to that of God's elect, "My dead." But such a limitation by no means implies that Isaiah questioned the eventual resurrection of all of mankind; for Isaiah 24:22 includes the (unsaved) kings of the earth and predicts: "They shall be gathered together, as prisoners are gathered in the pit (hell), and shall be shut up in the prison; and after many days shall they be visited." Their visitation will then indeed be one of resurrection, but only that they may suffer the final judgment and never-ending punishment of the lost. For Isaiah concludes the last chapter of his

---

[37]So Jacob, *Theology of the Old Testament*, p. 310.

prophecy with the dire prediction that the saved "shall go forth and look upon the dead bodies of the men that have transgressed against Me: For their worm shall not die, neither shall their fire be quenched; and they shall be an abhorring unto all flesh" (66:24).

PERIOD H, LATER PROPHETIC. The Bible's classic illustration of the future state of the lost received its best-known (but unintentional) embodiment when Josiah in 621 B.C. defiled *Gē Ven-Hinnōm,* "the valley of the son of Hinnom" (II Kings 23:10). This valley, which bordered Jerusalem under its southern walls, was named after a man who had actually lived centuries before (cf. Josh. 15:8). The valley of Hinnom, however, had served as the scene of numerous idolatrous rites, including even that of child sacrifice, as it was practiced by the apostate rulers of Judah, Ahaz (II Chron. 28:3) and Manasseh (33:6; Jer. 7:31). Josiah, then, in the execution of his great reform, seems to have brought Hinnom's "holy" standing to a permanent end by means of converting it into a city dump. Though without significance for Biblical religion during the days of the Old Testament, the name *Gē Hinnōm* (Greek, *geenna,* "gehenna") came thus to be adopted in the New Testament as an appropriate description of "hell; where their worm dieth not, and the fire is not quenched" (Mark 9:47, 48).

PERIODS I-J. EXILIC AND POST-EXILIC. Ezekiel in the exile reproduces and further extends Isaiah's picture of hell. Like his prophetic predecessor, he indicates how the damned of earlier periods are able to communicate with the fallen Egyptians who have come to join their number (Ezek. 32:21); and he too describes hell in terms of degrees, referring specifically to its "uttermost parts" (v. 23). Ezekiel locates hell deep in the interior of the earth; and he designates it by the Hebrew term *bōr,* "pit" (v. 18). The prophet furthermore depicts the inhabitants of hell as organized on the basis of their national groups (cf. v. 26); and each nation is then described as if composed of a group of graves (vv. 22, 26): "They are gone down to hell [sheol] with their weapons of war, and have laid their swords under their heads" (v. 27). The picture thus seems to be that of a world-sized sepulcher (cf. "their bones," v. 27), and it may be only to this material comparison that Ezekiel's details should be made to refer. The description of the resurrection of the dry bones in Ezekiel 37 is purely symbolical and is explicitly defined as a vision that refers to the restoration of Israel to Palestine after the Babylonian exile (vv. 11, 12).

The last important revelation on life after death that occurs in the Old Testament is that of Daniel 12, in 536 B.C., after the Jews had begun their post-exilic return. Here then the Lord made known the final truth of a sequence of two major stages within the future resurrection. Daniel 12:2 commences by predicting that "Many of them that sleep in the dust of the earth shall awake"; and liberal interpreters generally seek to take advantage of the adjective "many," thereby to deny to Daniel a belief in total resurrection: only those who were particularly good or bad, that is, could be expected to arise.[38] S. P. Tregelles has, however, proposed the following translation and paraphrase, which seems most adequately to meet the demands, not only of the Hebrew words that are involved and of the immediate context, but also of the overall analogy of Scripture:

> "And many from among the sleepers of the dust of the earth shall awake; these shall be unto everlasting life; but those the rest of the sleepers, those who do not awake at this time, shall be unto shame and everlasting contempt."[39]

The first resurrection then consists of "every one that shall be found written in the book" (v. 1), that is, of the elect inheritors of the testament. God further identifies them for Daniel as "thy people," that is, Israel, in the sense of the true. Church of all ages (cf. Rev. 20:4, 5). Daniel himself would stand in his lot among this first group (v. 13). God's monergistic grace will thus not rest until His testamental promise of reconciliation has become effective in the restoration of all His saints, made glorious both in soul and in body. As John Murray has summarized it:

> Glorification is the final phase of the application of redemption. It is that which brings to completion the process which begins in effectual calling . . . It is the redemption of the whole person when in the integrity of body and spirit the people of God will be conformed to the image of the risen, exalted, and glorified Redeemer (cf. Phil. 3:21).[40]

The apostle Paul accordingly penned the following as an "ordo salutis": "Whom He called, them He also justified: and whom He justified, them He also glorified" (Rom. 8:30).

But, as occurs with such consistency within testamental thought, together with restoration there goes judgment. Those who will not humble themselves to accept the grace of the testament must stand before God on the basis of His original covenant of works; and by the works of the law shall no flesh be justified in His sight (Rom. 3:20). Those in this second resurrection are forthwith condemned "unto shame and everlasting contempt" (Dan. 12:2), "cast into the lake of fire. This is the second death" (Rev. 20:14).

For Further Reading:

Loraine Boettner, *Immortality*. Grand Rapids: Wm. B. Eerdmans Publishing Co., 1956. A well written, scholarly, and orthodox presentation of the Biblical doctrine of the future life.

---

[38]Burrows, *op. cit.*, p. 205.
[39]*Remarks on the Prophetic Visions in the Book of Daniel* (London: Bagsters, 1864), pp. 162 ff.; Cf. the entire discussion in Robert D. Culver, *Daniel and the Latter Days* (Westwood, N. J.: Fleming H. Revell Co., c. 1954), pp. 172-176.
[40]*Redemption—Accomplished and Applied*, pp. 217-218.

Edmund F. Sutcliffe, *The Old Testament and the Future Life.* 2nd edition; Westminster, Md.: The Newman Bookshop, 1947. Romanist, and making serious concessions to the liberal position.

Sidney Zandstra, "Sheol and Pit in the Old Testament," *The Princeton Theological Review,* 5,4 (October 1907), pp. 631-641. He concludes that the two terms are identical and serve as abstractions for "death" or "grave."

31. The New Testament*

The testamental inheritance constitutes both the basis and the theme of Old Testament eschatology. The promise of the testament, "I will be their God," was what made possible the anticipation of a future relationship with God in the first place. Furthermore, it was the specific nature of this reconciliation that determined the form in which the eschatological kingdom of God came actually to be expressed, in the concrete predictions of the Old Testament. For, though the Old Testament possesses a genuine interest in the future significance of the testament for the individual (cf. the preceding topic, on the immortality of the soul and the resurrection of the body), its primary concern lies in the area of general eschatology — that is, in the outworkings of divine redemption in the history of the world.[1] For the salvation of the individual in his resurrection body depends, after all, upon the triumph of God's will in that future world where the saint will take up his glorified abode (topic 32, the testament of peace); even as the salvation of his immortal soul depends upon the historical accomplishment of the death of the Messiah, which has to be brought out (Heb. 9:16, 17) so that the testament may be of force. In reference then to this latter expectation, Jeremiah predicted God's establishing of the new testament as the immediate hope and the goal of His people Israel (Jer. 31:31-34), a prophecy which is fulfilled in Christ's first coming and in the Christian Church.[2] This

---

*BIBLE READING: Zechariah 11; Joel 2

Collateral Reading: Oswald T. Allis, *Prophecy and the Church,* pp. 134-159.
  Charles Caldwell Ryrie, *The Basis of the Premillennial Faith,* pp. 126-138.
  J. B. Payne, "Hosea's Family Prophecies and the Kingdom," Evangelical Theological Society, *1954 Papers,* pp. 11-21.

---

[1]Cf. Geerhardus Vos, "The eschatological element in the religion of the Old Testament is but the supreme expression of its character as a religion of God's free historical self-assertion, a religion, not of nature processes, but of redemption and revelation," in "The Eschatological Aspect of the Pauline Conception of the Spirit," Princeton Theological Seminary, *Biblical and Theological Studies* (New York: Charles Scribners' Sons, 1912), p. 217. Cf. Vriezen's insistence upon the lordship of Yahweh as the heart of the Old Testament eschatology, *An Outline of Old Testament Theology,* pp. 370-372.
[2]See above, pp. 75-78.

fulfillment constitutes, indeed, the most crucial part of the inheritance that God promised under the older testament; and it occupies a major place in what was, to the Old Testament saints, "last things."

A. THE DAY OF YAHWEH. The comprehensive phrase, by which the Old Testament describes God's intervention in human history for the accomplishment of His testament is *yōm Yahwe*, "the day of Yahweh." Its first specific Biblical citation appears in the mouths of certain of the contemporaries of Amos, about 760 B.C. These Israelites, confident of their position as members of God's elect people, were eager for the "day" to put in its appearance, that they might inherit the earthly blessings that had been foretold by Moses and others. They may have had in mind such an occurrence as "the 'day' of Midian" (Isa. 9:4) half a millennium previously, when God had granted Israel a great victory and rich plunder from their Midianitish enemies. Amos, however, analyzed the situation differently. By their blatant disregard for the fundamentals of social justice, his contemporaries had failed to meet the condition of moral obedience that God required for inheritance under His testament. They had thus forfeited their potential standing; and "the day" could involve them only in judgment, not blessing. Amos therefore cried out words of doom: "Woe unto you that desire the day of Yahweh! Wherefore would ye have the day of Yahweh? It is darkness and not light!" (Amos 5:18; cf. Joel 1:15; 2:1). Isaiah too, with a characteristic stress upon the freedom of the divine Testator, reminded his people that God does all things, not according to man's will, but according to His own. He proclaimed: "The loftiness of man shall be bowed down, and the haughtiness of men shall be brought low; and Yahweh alone shall be exalted in that day" (Isa. 2:17; cf. 3:18). The classic statement of this woeful aspect of the day of Yahweh comes to expression in the next period, in Zephaniah's presentiments of impending distress and desolation (Zeph. 1:15), from which has come the great Latin hymn, *Dies irae, dies illa*: "A day of wrath is that day." Yet Zephaniah then concludes his prophecy by coming back and affirming the ultimate truth of the older, popular optimism in reference to the day of the Lord: "Yahweh thy God is in the midst of thee [the promise of the testament], a mighty one who will save; He will rejoice over thee with joy" (3:17). This same pattern, moreover, appears consistently in the other prophets, even in Amos (cf. 9:14). Vos therefore proposes that "The two topics with which we have to deal may be called the doctrine of judgment and that of restoration."[3]

The basis for this two-fold development in the day of Yahweh lies in the quality of *qōdhesh*, or "holiness" (literally, *separateness*),

[3]Geerhardus Vos, *Biblical Theology*, p. 311.

that constitutes both the immediate essence and the ultimate purpose of Israel's adoption under the testament (Ex. 19:6). If Israel would not maintain "separation" from sin and the world, then she would have to be purged and resanctified before God could accomplish His further work through her. If, however, Israel *were* living in a way sufficiently separate, and if certain pagan nations from the outside should threaten to overwhelm God's people, then He would see to it that these Gentiles should be divinely "purged" (punished). As Isaiah assured his people against the threats of the Assyrian, "And the light of Israel [God] will be for a fire, and it will burn and devour his thorns and his briers in one day" (Isa. 10:17). This particular prediction seems then to have been fulfilled in the heavenly-sent destruction of Sennacherib's host, 701 B.C. (37:36). The "day" is thus characterized by an observable accomplishment of the general aims of divine providence. It refers to that point in history at which the sovereign God lays bare His holy arm on the behalf of His testament and of its heirs, whether in a way that is specifically miraculous, or not.

Furthermore, a survey conducted even casually of the Biblical usage of "day of Yahweh" makes it clear that in defining this term chronological aspects cannot be considered relevant. In Joel 1:15, the "day of Yahweh" consists of a contemporary locust plague, datable to about 735 B.C. In Zephaniah 1:7, it relates to the destruction of Jerusalem in 586 B.C. In Isaiah 13:7, 13, it concerns the capture of Babylon by the Medes and Persians in 539-538 B.C. Its point of specification thus advances down through the entire course of history and reaches its climax in passages such as Malachi 4:1, where "Behold, the day cometh" refers to God's final judgment at the end of the world. The "day," moreover, may entail either a blessing or a curse. It may concern God's elect people Israel, or it may apply to the nations of the pagan world. It may produce effects that are catacylsmic and cosmic, or it may come to pass in a way that is quietly providential and localized. The one feature common to all of these passages is this: that the day of Yahweh does concern the action of God in human history for the progressive accomplishment of His redemptive testament. Perhaps the most adequate, inclusive definition of the day of Yahweh is Vos' martially phrased suggestion: "The day monopolized by Jehovah as His day of victory."[5]

In interpreting the Biblical passages on the day of Yahweh, one must therefore guard himself against imposing upon them certain preconceived chronological restrictions, such as the following dog-

---

[4]Cf. L. Kohler, "Judgment is restoration of the honor and holiness of God," *Old Testament Theology*, p. 218.
[5]*Op. cit.*, p. 313. Cf. Edmond Jacob, *Theology of the Old Testament*, p. 319. Vos subsequently expresses preference for the idea of "the contrast between darkness and light [purging and conversion]," though both of these elements may be adequately subsumed under the above cited concept of "victory."

matic limitations, against both of which objections must be raised.
1) Vs. liberalism — The Old Testament's teaching on Christ, on the
Church, or on the future kingdom (e.g., Dan. 2:44; Zeph. 1:2, 3)
must not be forced back into pre-Christian settings. A. B. Davidson,
for example, seeks to restrict prophecy to matters that were consistently immediate in their intended fulfillment:

> As one in the darkness thinks he hears the approach of an evil
> which he dreads, these prophets, when the sound of Jehovah's go-
> ings was more distinctly heard than usual, deemed that what they
> heard was the warning of His coming to shake terribly the earth
> . . . His final appearance was closely connected with these mani-
> festations.[6]

But the primary author of Scripture, let it be said, is God, who is not
"in the dark," but who knows the end from the beginning. The prophetic speaking conveyed through the secondary authors must not
be limited to such subjects as were contained within their own contemporary environments. Isaiah 45:1 (on Cyrus) and Daniel 11 (on
the Seleucids) are among the outstanding examples of the supernaturalistic projection of Biblical prophecy into what was, at the time of
utterance, a distant future. In particular, the possibility of "prophetic
telescoping," which refers to the joining together in one context of
events that are widely separated in their temporal accomplishments,
must ever be kept in mind.[7]

2) Vs. dispensationalism — The Old Testament's teachings on ancient Israel, whether in Old Testament or New Testament times, must
not be pushed forward into dates that are still future. The following
three types of materials are among those that are the most frequently forced into such unwarrantedly futuristic settings by dispensationalist writers.[8] (a) Statements that are applicable to contemporary Old Testament situations. Representative subjects that have
been so abused are these: In Jeremiah 30:7, "the time of Jacob's
trouble" is a theme which need refer only to the events of 586 B.C.
(v. 5; cf. Isa. 26:20, which speaks of "entering one's chambers until
the indignation be past"). Again, Ezekiel 37:1-14, on the "dry bones,"
far from possessing any future significance, appears to relate wholly
to that return of the Jews to Palestine which began in 538 B.C. Chapters 40-46 Ezekiel seem likewise to center about instructions for a
temple that was to be rebuilt in this same sixth century B.C. More-

---

[6]*The Theology of the Old Testament*, p. 380.
[7]See above, p. 59, footnote 38, on basic principles for a Bible-believer's interpretation of predictive passages. Cf. also the listing of such hermeneutical principles
in Payne, "Hosea's Family Prophecies and the Kingdom," pp. 11-12; and "The
Church and Zionism in the Predictive Cycles of Zechariah 9-14," Evangelical
Theological Society, *1956 Papers*, pp. 55-57.
[8]Cf. the writer's discussion in, "The Imminent Appearing of Christ," *Bulletin of
the Evangelical Theological Society*, II:3 (Summer, 1959), pp. 10-11, and his
book by the same title (Grand Rapids: Eerdman's, 1962).

over, even as the phrase "day of Yahweh" often displays no point of
reference beyond the immediate times of the Old Testament, so also
its related expressions, such as *aharīth hay-yāmim,* "the latter (part
of the) days," labor under no necessity of exhibiting consistent applications to yet future periods. For example, the prediction in which
this phrase was first employed (Gen. 49:1) experienced most of its
fulfillment by the time of Joshua; or, as it was used in Deuteronomy
31:29, its threats were accomplished in the captivities of 722 and
586 B.C. and need have no reference to a great tribulation yet in store
for modern Zionists. (b) Statements that are fulfilled in Christ's ministry. For example, Malachi 4:5 on the coming of Elijah was adequately carried out in the person and ministry of John the Baptist;
and no future fulfillment has still to be expected. (c) Statements that
are applied to the Church. Dispensationalist theory asserts on dogmatic grounds that "the Church was not foreseen in the Old Testament" but that it constitutes an unknown "parenthesis" in God's
redemptive program.[9] The weight of the Biblical evidence, however,
renders such a hypothesis untenable. For if "the great parenthesis"
begin, as most claim, with Palm Sunday, then one is immediately
faced with numerous Old Testament predictions of passion week; and
the cross itself becomes but an afterthought in the plan of God.[10]
Or even if the parenthesis be limited to those materials that are concerned strictly with the apostolic church and its subsequent development up to the present, there still remains an embarrassingly extensive
amount of prophecy that is directly applied in the New Testament
to the Christian Church:[11] e.g., Joel 2:28, 29 = Pentecost; Jeremiah
31:31-34 = the new testament of Hebrews 8; and Christ Himself spoke
twice in the Old Testament predicting His Church and in fact calling
it by the equivalent of its very New Testament name, *Ekklesia* (Ps.
22:22; Isa. 8:18; cf. Heb. 2:12).[12] Allis is therefore entirely justified
in his criticism that —

> "In insisting that prophecy does not have reference to the
> Christian Church, Dispensationalists 'rob' the Church of many
> of the exceeding precious promises contained in the Old Tes-
> tament which she is fully entitled to claim and possess."[13]

More serious, however, than its misapplication of particular
prophecies, is what amounts to dispensationalism's repudiation of the
whole, unified redemptive plan of God in human history. Indeed,

---

[9]Ryrie, *The Basis of the Premillennial Faith,* pp. 130-131, 134. See above, p. 75.
[10]Cf. Allis, *Prophecy and the Church,* pp. 234-235.
[11]*Ibid.,* chap. VIII. G. Douglas Young's conclusion over Isa. 54:1 is to the same
effect: "Paul states that Isaiah is speaking by prophecy of the age in which we
live and he implies that Isaiah in that period sees the situation present to Paul's
day, the present age," in "Old Testament Theology—a Method and a Conclusion,"
Evangelical Theological Society, *1955 Papers,* p. 80.
[12]See above, pp. 76, 188.
[13]*Op. cit.,* p. 133.

the normative truthfulness of the older testament of the past is dependent upon its essential identity with, and fulfillment in, the newer testament of the present and the future. Correspondingly, the full blessing for the modern Church, as this is contained in the Old Testament, can be appropriated by today's saints only when they accept their own equation, as the Israel of God, with that ancient Israel to whom God extended His testamental promises. It thus becomes apparent that a comprehensive understanding of God's gracious purpose — which has been one and the same from Genesis 3:15, right on through to the closing chapters of Revelation — lies contingent upon the Christian's recognition of one cross, one testament, one faith, and one Church throughout all history. The apostolic preaching of Peter leaves no doubt in this regard:

> Yea and all the prophets from Samuel and them that followed after, as many as have spoken, they also told of these days. Ye are the sons of the prophets, and of the testament which God made with your fathers, saying unto Abraham, And in thy seed shall all the families of the earth be blessed (Acts 3:24, 25).

Allis has therefore concluded:

> This received interpretation is the interpretation placed by the writers of the New Testament themselves on Old Testament prophecy. To reject it is to reject the authoritative statements of the inspired writers of the New Testament. For they clearly believed that the New Testament Church was foretold in the Old Testament; and they appealed to it to establish their claiming that in preaching the gospel of the grace of God to Jew and to Gentile they were announcing the fulfillment of the ancient covenant and declaring none other things than those which the prophets and Moses did say should come.[14]

B. THE DAY, AS JUDGMENT, PRESENTLY FULFILLED. Although specific reference to the day of Yahweh appears only with the eighth century prophets, the reality of its major aspects, both of judgment and of restoration, became known at much earlier points in the history of redemption. In particular, God's sentences of judgment against Israel, as well as the reasons for these judgments, were revealed within a year or two of the very time of Moses' founding of the Hebrew nation. For while they were still in the wilderness, God's people were humbled and even starved by Yahweh that they might come to realize their dependence upon Him (Deut. 8:2, 3; cf. 13:3). They were warned, furthermore, that their breaking of the testament could only bring about terror and disaster (Lev. 26:15, 16): "the vengeance of the testament" (v. 25), or "the curses of the testament" (Deut. 29:21; cf. Isa. 24:5; Jer. 11:8). In fact, almost the entire 800 year course

---

[14]*Ibid.*, p. 159. It should be noted that the recognition of the validity of Allis' conclusion need have no necessary effect upon one's position in respect to the millennial question, a caution that becomes necessary in the light of Ryrie's claim that the truth of millennialism is "inseparably linked" to his Plymouth Brethren ecclesiology, *op. cit.*, p. 126.

of Israel's existence as an independent nation in Canaan was marked by God's continuous and increasingly severe judgments, a course that terminated only with the final destruction of the remaining Hebrew state of southern Judah in 586 B.C. (see above, topic 10-A, on providence).[15]

The exile of the ancient Israelites from Palestine had been predicted even before their entrance into the land, for God had warned them through His servant Moses, "You will I scatter among the nations, and I will draw out the sword after you: and your land shall be a desolation, and your cities shall be a waste" (Lev. 26:33; cf. also vv. 34-39; Deut. 28:25, 36, 63-68; 32:26). With such Mosaic precedents, Hosea and Amos then confronted northern Israel with their announcement of the imminent, the woeful day of Yahweh (Amos 5:18). Preliminary chastenings and afflictions had been suffered by the people, "yet have ye not returned unto Me, saith Yahweh" (4:8). In a series of visions, Amos even beheld how God twice turned back from inflicting final judgment, because of the prophet's own gracious intercessions (7:3, 6). But on the third such occasion he was flatly told that punishment must inevitably take place (vv. 8, 9). Israel would have to be carried off from Canaan (Hos. 5:14; 9:17) and go into captivity "beyond Damascus" (Amos 5:27). This particular judgment day of Yahweh was then carried out by the Assyrian destructions that climaxed in 722 B.C. But these awful events did fulfill at least one long-range, positive purpose. For Hosea had limited the duration of Israel's judgment in captivity "till they acknowledge their offence, and seek My face: in their affliction they will seek Me earnestly" (Hos. 5:15).

God also directed a somewhat similar series of warnings against the southern kingdom of Judah. Even in the same eighth century, the prophet Micah had threatened them by predicting, "Thou shalt go forth out of the city, and shalt come even unto Babylon" (4:10); and in the seventh century, Zephaniah spoke passionately concerning this impending "day of Yahweh's wrath" (Zeph. 1:18). Particularly would God's judgment descend upon His once beautiful Temple in Jerusalem (Mic. 3:12; Jer. 7:14; Ezek. 9:7). For the Hebrews had come to trust upon this building, as the visible guarantee of Yahweh's testamental presence and of their own status as His chosen people. Actually, of course, the disobedience of both Israel and Judah had already made them lō ammi, "not My people" (cf. Hos. 1:9); and the need for God's removal of Judah's testamentary sign, which was the Temple, thus became imperative as a demonstration of their forfeited status. God's purpose in this act, however, just as it had been in the destruction of Israel in Hosea's day, was a corrective one: "I have scattered thee, but I will not make a full end of thee; but I will correct

---

[15]Especially pp. 130-132 above.

thee in measure" (Jer. 30:11; cf. 10:24). North and south would at
length be able to unite in a return to Palestine, once the exile had
served to "take away the names of the Baalim out of their mouth"
(Hos. 2:17).

Moving beyond the immediate circle of Israel, however, the
prophets proclaimed, "The day of Yahweh is near upon all the nations" (Obad. 15; cf. Jer. 25:29; Ezek. 30:3). In the case of these
pagans, God's judgment would not be limited to one of paternal
correction: "For I will make a full end of the nations whither I have
scattered thee" (Jer. 30:11). Major sections within the books of
the prophets then concern the outworkings of divine judgment upon
the various ancient empires: Isaiah 13-23 (eighth century), Jeremiah
46-51 (later prophetic), and Ezekiel 25-32 (exilic). The reason for
their respective punishments rests, first of all, upon what they have
done to God's people (Amos 1:3; Zeph. 3:19); for, even when appointed as providential instruments of correction against Israel, the
nations became guilty of a ruthless overstepping of their commis-
sions (Isa. 10:7, 12; 47:6). God thus appropriately chose Israel itself,
under the Maccabees, to take its own vengeance on both Edom
(Obad. 18; Ezek. 25:14) and the Greeks (Zech. 9:13). But divine
punishment also comes down upon the pagans because of what they
do to each other (Amos 2:1; Nah. 3:19). For God's justice must be
maintained (Isa. 5:16); the sin of the nations must be punished
(59:18; Jer. 25:31); and, in the long run, whether their sin happens
to be against Israel or against some other nation makes no essential
difference.[16]

Israel's post-exilic return to Palestine did not, however, terminate
the day of Yahweh in its aspect of judgment upon God's elect. For
after predicting the rescue of the Hebrew people from Babylon (Mic.
4:10), Scripture goes on to reveal, "Now also many nations are assembled against thee" (v. 11). Israel thus suffered the persecutions of
Antiochus Epiphanes, which Daniel later defined as an element of
God's judgment because of their own transgressions (Dan. 8:12).
Then, even though Israel did win a brief period of independence from
143 to 63 B.C. (Dan. 11:34; Mic. 4:13; Zech. 10:4-7), they next became subject to the power of Rome; and the prophecy was fulfilled
which Micah had gone on to utter, "Therefore will He give them up,
until the time that she who travaileth hath brought forth" (5:3).

This last verse does not mean that God's judgment upon the

---

[16]Dispensationalist writers are thus seen to be in error when they seek to distinguish men's crimes against the Jews, even the modern *unbelieving* Jew's, as
peculiarly subject to God's wrath. For example, Matt. 25:40, 45, is often quoted
as if it taught that Adolf Hitler's downfall was due to his acts of anti-semitism.
But Christ was speaking in Matt. 25 of His "brethren," which the Jews no longer
are (cf. 12:48-50); and, if a particular reason were to be sought for the fall of
Hitler's reich, it would be due rather to his persecutions of Christian brethren in
the Church, the true Israel!

people was to cease with the birth of Jesus, but only that it was to be transferred. For Christ embodies the ultimate stage in the doctrine of the remnant of Israel (see above, topic 14-C).[17] He became the representative Son of Man, against whom the powers of evil were allowed to prevail (Dan. 7:21); He humbled Himself as the Suffering Servant, who by oppression and judgment was taken away (Isa. 53:8 ASV). As Isaiah foresaw so clearly, "He was wounded for our transgressions, He was bruised for our iniquities; the chastisement of our peace was upon Him; and with His stripes we are healed" (v. 5). Daniel thus summarizes the climax of redemptive history, when he foretells how the Messiah would be cut off to confirm God's testament (Dan. 9:26, 27). But though Christ did endure judgment, His work yet constitutes a triumph. By His very acceptance 'of Israel's punishment, He fulfilled the typical institutions of the older testament and caused the Mosaic sacrifices to cease (v. 27). Simultaneously, then, He ushered in that new testament of Jeremiah, which no longer emphasizes anticipatory ceremonial, but which proclaims that God has placed His law directly in men's consciousness "and in their heart will I write it" (Jer. 31:33). For it was only by the substitutionary judgment and condemnation of Christ that such a testament could be made to avail. It was through Him that the way into the holy place was made manifest (Heb. 9:15, 8), that God's elect might "all know Me [not just the priests, who served in their ceremonies as types of Christ, but] from the least of them unto the greatest" (Jer. 31:34).

Messiah's confirmation of the testament is subject, however, to a significant limitation. For Daniel's prophecy reveals that, "with many," it is to be confirmed only until the end of the latter half of the last of his seven-year "weeks,"[18] namely, until the conclusion of the period of about 3½ years that followed upon our Lord's crucifixion in A.D. 30 (Dan. 9:24). The seer's point is this: that the larger part of the Jewish nation is hereby warned that subsequent to the 70 weeks they would experience their most serious judgment of all, by being suspended from further participation in God's testament. Daniel's vision does not supply the reason for their abandonment. But the basis for such a judgment had been stated repeatedly by prophets before him and was yet further to be revealed by others after his time. In the eighth century God had, for example, explained: "Yet shall the land be desolate because of them that dwell therein, for the fruit of their doings" (Mic. 7:13), or again in a post-exilic context, "If ye will not hear, to give glory unto My name, then will I send the curse upon you, and behold I will rebuke your seed" (Mal. 2:2, 3). The most detailed predictive explanation, that of Zechariah 11,[19]

[17]Cf. also Knight, on Christ as the final remnant, *A Christian Theology of the Old Testament*, pp. 347-48.
[18]For the interpretation of Daniel's 70 weeks, see above, pp. 277, 278.
[19]Compare the chart presented here on pp. 530, 531 in Appendix I.

discloses how the Good Shepherd, the Messiah whom God should send to redeem Israel (Zech. 11:7), would meet with loathing on the part of the very people He had come to save (v. 8; cf. John 1:11). They would "prize" Him at thirty pieces of silver (vv. 12, 13; cf. Matt. 27:3-10) and would end by piercing (on a cross) the One who was none other than God Himself (Zech. 12:10; Acts 3:14, 15). The greatest blessing of Yahweh's entire predetermined counsel was thus to be accomplished by means of the lawless hands of the Jews in the greatest crime of human history (Acts 2:23). Yet even to men such as these, God in His patience and love saw fit to confirm His glorious new testament for a full 3½ years (vv. 38-40; 3:17; 4:12; 6:8; cf. Rev. 12:6, 14)!

At length, however, the Jews irrevocably committed themselves to the rejection of the Gospel by their stoning of Stephen, the same man, "full of grace and power, [who had] wrought great wonders and signs among the people" (6:8). For all manner of sin and blasphemy against the Son of Man could be forgiven, but not this crime against the Spirit (v. 10; cf. Matt. 12:32); for by denying the voice of God they deliberately cut themselves off from contact with their only source of hope (cf. v. 24). The Lord therefore broke asunder His testament (which had been symbolized in Zechariah 11:10 by the staff named "Beauty") and departed from the Jewish nation. This rupture also entailed God's terminating of the covenant by which He had previously restrained the other nations from accomplishing their cruel pleasure against Jerusalem (v. 10). As a result of their having rejected the Good Shepherd, Zechariah predicted that God would deliver over the apostate nation to a foolish shepherd, who would eat their flesh (v. 16). The afflictions that Rome would accomplish against the Semitic Near East had, indeed, been predicted by Balaam almost a millennium and a half in advance of their historic fulfillment (Num. 24:24); and Zechariah, accordingly, went on to anticipate the eventual overthrow of Jerusalem by the Romans in A.D. 70 (Zech. 9:10), with its accompanying slaughter of two-thirds of the people (13:8). Scripture furthermore revealed that God's elect would have to continue without a specific political organization, at least until the return of the Messiah. As Ezekiel had warned, "I will overturn, overturn, overturn it: this also shall be no more, until He come whose right it is; and I will give it to Him" (Ezek. 21:27).

There remain three other specific aspects of judgment, presently fulfilled, that were predicted in the Old Testament as characteristic of our Christian Church age. 1) The arm of the worthless Roman shepherd God would some day (A.D. 476?) cause to be dried up (Zech. 11:17) and bring to destruction (Num. 24:24). This empire would then be succeeded by an unstable balance of power of uncertain duration: the ten toes and ten horns of Daniel's visions (2:42;

7:8, 20; cf. Rev. 17:15, 16, 18). 2) The Church, as the true continuing remnant of Israel (see below, next section), would themselves be scattered after the Good Shepherd had been smitten (Zech. 13:7; Matt. 26:32). Their scattering, however, would have a positive and redemptive purpose; for God promised, "I will sow them among the peoples; and they shall remember Me in far countries; and they shall live with their children" (10:9; cf. Acts 8:1, 4). 3) The Jewish nation, while it is no longer God's testamental people (cf. Rev. 2:9) and is therefore but rarely mentioned, is still distinguishable in a few Old Testament passages where the exiled, unconverted, condition of the Jews marks them off from the members of God's redeemed Church. Included in such passages might be the following: a limited number of allusions to "My dispersed" (e.g., Zeph. 3:10); Hosea's description of Israel's abiding many days without a king, without sacrifice,. and yet without idolatry either (Hos. 3:4); and Zechariah's reference to their being brought through the fire, to be tried and refined like silver (Zech. 13:9; cf. Mic. 5:12). For God had long before promised that He would not forget the testament of their fathers, which He sware unto them (Deut. 4:31); He would not break His testament, so as to destroy them utterly (Lev. 26:44).

C. THE DAY, AS RESTORATION, PRESENTLY FULFILLED. Scripture reveals that God's judgments upon His servants, starting with the chastening dry weather of Amos' time (Amos 4:7) and culminating in the ultimate sacrifice of Jesus Christ on the cross, were all designed to serve constructive ends. God's love changes not; Israel, correspondingly, could not be wholly consumed (Hos. 11:8, 9; Isa. 49:15; Mal. 3:6); and, after His anger, Yahweh pardons the iniquity of the purer national remnants that remain (Mic. 7:18-20; cf. Ex. 34:6; Ps. 66:12). So in 538 B.C., after the Babylonian exile had at length served its purpose of sifting the idolators out of Israel (Hos. 2:17), God brought back to Palestine the faithful survivors of both North and South (Isa. 6:13; Ezek. 37:19), through the providentially arranged decree of Cyrus the Persian. Indeed, at the very founding of the Hebrew nation, God had promised tangible restoration upon genuine repentance: "If then in the land of their enemies their uncircumcised heart be humbled, and they confess their iniquity, then will I remember My testament with Jacob; and I will remember the land" (Lev. 26:40-42; cf. Ezek. 33:10, 11). First of all, therefore, God graciously protected Israel during its exile (Amos 9:9), for the sake of the faithful remnant that was contained therein (Isa. 65:8). Next, just as Jeremiah had predicted, God, in His love restored chastened Israel into the testamental status of being "His people" (Jer. 31: 3, 1). It was then only a matter of time until the nation was restored geographically, rebuilt (v. 4) and multiplied (Isa. 49:20, 21; Ezek. 36:10, 11). Looking back on it, God spoke through

Zechariah, "Because of the blood of thy testament I have set free thy prisoners" (Zech. 9:11). In the sweep of history, God moreover continued to guard His people against the marching armies of Alexander and the Diadochi (v. 8); He restored them after the depredations of Antiochus Epiphanes (vv. 16, 17; Dan. 8:25; 12:12); and He even brought about the second century B.C. incorporation of Philistia into the territory of Israel (Zech. 9:7).

The greatest "restoration day of Yahweh," however, occurred in the period of Daniel's fourth kingdom, which we identify as the Roman Empire. For in those days, "the God of heaven set up a kingdom which shall never be destroyed" (Dan. 2:44). As Amos had predicted, He "raised up the tabernacle of David that was fallen" (Amos 9:11), in the specific person of Jesus Christ, who is God's chosen heir to the throne of David (Luke 1:32). Israel's King came humbly (Zech. 9:9), preaching the Gospel, in the Spirit (Isa. 61:1, 2a); but He was, at the same time, the divine Angel of the testament, God Himself (Mal. 3:1; Zech. 2:10), who by His death removed sin in one day (Zech. 3:9). He thus accomplished the fundamental restoration for which mankind had been longing ever since the disaster of Eden — He put enmity between Satan and the seed of the woman; He brought into being that reconciliation with God which constitutes the essential inheritance of the testament; and He betrothed Israel to Himself as His bride forever (Hos. 2:19), truly to "know" Yahweh (v. 20).[20] Jesus Christ thus achieved the ultimate fulfillment of Moses' ancient promise to his people "Yahweh thy God will circumcise thy heart, and the heart of thy seed, to love Yahweh thy God with all thy heart, and with all thy soul, that thou mayest live" (Deut. 30:6). This was the same redemptive truth that Jeremiah later developed into the concept of the new testament, for the explicit forgiveness that he foresaw as one of its chief characteristics (Jer. 31:34) was made possible by Christ's open victory over sin, once and for all accomplished on the cross (Heb. 9:28).

Another of the leading features that the Old Testament prophesies in reference to the day of Yahweh is that of God's outpouring of the Holy Spirit (Isa. 44:3). This future, spiritual infilling would no longer be periodic in character; but it would be a permanent endowment of power from on high, available for all of God's people (Joel 2:28, 29). The fulfillment of this wonderful promise on Pentecost (Acts 2:16) is what makes possible Protestantism's commitment to the priesthood of all believers under Christ. It was this same Pentecostal outpouring, moreover, that brought into realization the other two distinctive characteristics of Jeremiah's new testament. For God had inspired the prophet to describe it as internal, "In their heart will I

---

[20]See below, Appendix H, with its outline on Hosea 1-3 and God's kingdom, p. 529; cf. also Payne, "Hosea's Family Prophecies," p. 15.

write it" (Jer. 31:33) and as marked by a direct personal faith, "They shall all know Me" (v. 34). By the coming to pass of these features, the old Israel was thus transformed into the New Testament Israel that constitutes the distinctively Christian phase of God's Church.[21] The externalities of the Old Testament, anticipatory of atonement, had now fulfilled their function; and, as Jeremiah had predicted of the templeless Church age,

> "It shall come to pass, when ye are multiplied and increased in the land, in those days [in the day of Yahweh] they shall say no more, The ark of the testament of Yahweh; neither shall it come to mind; neither shall they remember it; neither shall they miss it" (3:16).

Finally, this factor, which has just been quoted, of Israel's "multiplication and increase" constitutes perhaps the most obvious single feature of the day of Yahweh in the sense of restoration, presently fulfilled. To the patriarch Abram, at the very beginning, God had said, "I will make My testament between Me and thee, *and* will multiply thee exceedingly" (Gen. 17:2). He then confirmed the latter promise by changing Abram's name to Abraham, *av-rāhām*, with the meaning, "father of a multitude" (v. 5). The post-exilic writing of Zechariah 10:8 specifically noted that after God's new testament redemption, would come increase; and in Micah 5:3, after the prediction of our Lord's virgin birth, this earlier prophet declared, "Then the residue of His brethren shall return unto the children of Israel." As Jesus Himself explained (John 10:16), "And other sheep I have, which are not of this fold." These "other brethren" and "other sheep" who are so greatly to augment Israel suggest to us none other then the long-rejected Gentiles.

As far as the nation of the Jews was concerned, the coming of the Messiah tended, if anything, to reduce the observable size of God's Israel. Those who possessed a sincere faith in the older testament and whose names had thus already been written in heaven prior to Christ's atoning death, (Luke 10:20) naturally accepted Him as the fulfillment of all that it had predicted (cf. 2:25, 38). They continued to enjoy God's favor as true Israelites, though with all the additional blessings of the new testament (19:9; John 1:47; 10:42). Others, however, despite high national positions and a vaunted pride in their physical descent from Abraham, were shown up to be veritable sons of the devil (John 8:39, 44). They rejected Jesus and by so doing demonstrated that they were not really members of the true Israel, which is the Church, at all. In Paul's figure of Israel as an olive tree, they are to be identified with the branches of the tree that are broken off (Rom. 11:17). Indeed as God had long before revealed,

---

[21]For the general nature of the New Testament, see above, p. 115.

it was only "the poor of the flock that gave heed unto Me" (Zech. 11:11), "the little ones" (13:7).

But the goal of the testament had from the first been one of universal proclamation (see above, topic 14-D). Christ came "for a testament of the people, [but then also] for a light of the Gentiles" (Isa. 42:6); and it was through the augmentation of this latter group that God now "turned His hand in the behalf of the little ones" (Zech. 13:7). It was thus no accident that the outrage of Stephen's martyrdom, by which the confirmation of the testament to the nation of Israel was terminated, became the very psychological means, as it appears, through which Paul was conditioned to receive his call in A.D. 33 or 34 (?) to become the Apostle to the Gentiles (Acts 9:15). Shortly before this event, Philip had baptized the Ethiopian eunuch (8:27f.; cf. the prophecy Ps. 68:31 that "Ethiopia shall haste to stretch out her hands unto God"); and soon thereafter Peter baptized the uncircumcised Cornelius (Acts 10:48). The great ingrafting of "wild branches" into the olive tree of Israel was on!

The predictions of the Old Testament exhibit three stages of appreciation in respect to the presence of Gentiles within Israel, apart from their becoming actual proselytes to Judaism, as did Ruth or Namaan. 1) The Gentiles may be foreseen as fellow inheritors of the testament, heirs along with Israel of God's promise of reconciliation. To this category belong such prophecies as the following: "Many nations shall join themselves to Yahweh in that day [the day of Yahweh], and shall be My people" (Zech. 2:11); or "The strangers . . . shall have inheritance with you among the tribes of Israel" (Ezek. 47:22). Another oracle that seems to belong to this first stage of prophetic appreciation is the much disputed passage of Amos 9:12.[22] This verse is then repeated in Acts 15:15-18, the latter context being that of the Jerusalem council of the early Church. The council had been called to decide whether Gentile converts should be admitted to the fellowship of the Church or whether first they would have to become proselytes to Judaism and undergo circumcision in order to be saved (v. 1). Amos 9:12, however, speaks of the Gentile nations as being acceptable to Yahweh; and James, the brother of the Lord, by quoting its words and admonishing the council, "Wherefore trouble not them that from the Gentiles turn to God" (v. 19), forthwith ended the debate. Furthermore, though dispensationalist commentators have exhausted their ingenuity in attempts to explain away James' citation of this Old Testament prophecy in reference to the New Testament Church,[23] Allis' conclusion seems well established, that —

[22]Cf. Allis, op. cit., pp. 145-150, and Ryrie, op. cit., pp. 101-103.
[23]The dispensational claim that because Gentiles will have God's name called over them and will seek God in the millennium, and that therefore by analogy the apostolic Church could receive uncircumcised members, is a non-sequitur that James's Pharisaic opponents would have been quick to recognize and point out.

All of the difficulties involved in the Dispensational interpretation of this important passage in Acts are avoided, if it is simply recognized that the words quoted by James apply directly and definitely to the situation under discussion, the status of Gentiles in the Church, and that this is the reason that James appealed to them.[24]

Specifically, the context of Amos 9 (v. 10) had described God's exilic judgments upon Israel, which James summarizes in the phrase, "After these things" (Acts 15:16). Verse 11 had next spoken of the raising up of the tabernacle of David which was fallen, which James associates with Christ's having come and set up His kingdom. Scripture does, of course, teach a future consummation to this kingship; but the reality of Christ's present reign in His Church is not thereby to be denied (Luke 17:21). Verse 12 in the Masoretic Hebrew text then reads, "that they may possess the remnant of Edom, and all the nations that are called by My name." The Church of today, however, is hardly possessing Edom; and, following the minor textual corrections that have been cogently presented by Allan MacRae,[25] the verse may be more satisfactorily rendered, "that the remnant of mankind may seek (Yahweh), even all the nations that are called by My name." With this latter reading agrees the New Testament quotation as it is found in Acts 15:17, the accuracy of which is evinced by its acceptance by the whole Jerusalem council, some of whose members would have been only too eager to call into question the thought that is here involved. For it teaches the full participation of uncircumcised Gentiles in the kingdom of David.

2) In the next stage of Old Testament revelation, the Gentiles are foreseen as in some way related to the Israelites. An illustration of this sort of prophecy appears in the following words of Isaiah: "Nations shall come to thy light, and kings to the brightness of thy rising. They come to thee; *thy sons* shall come from far, and *thy daughters* (Isa. 60:3, 4),[26] cf. Ezekiel 16:61, "Thou shalt receive thy sisters . . . I will give them unto thee for daughters."

Finally, 3) believing Gentiles may be identified simply as Israelites, inseparable from God's people (56:3). For example, "One shall say, I am Yahweh's; and another shall subscribe with his hand unto Yahweh, and surname himself by the name of Israel" (44:5). With this third stage of appreciation go two passages that appear in the opening pages of Hosea: "The number of the children of Israel shall be as the sand of the sea; and it shall come to pass that, in the place where it was said unto them, Ye are not My people, it shall be said unto them, Ye are the sons of the living God" (1:10); and compare

---

[24]Allis, *op. cit.*, p. 149.
[25]"The Scientific Approach to the Old Testament," *Bibliotheca Sacra*, 110:440 (Oct. 1953), 313-316.
[26]An alternate rendering is that the "they" are not the Gentile kings, but Christians (Israelites) brought by the kings (cf. 66:20).

a statement of similar import at the end of the chapter 2 (v. 23). The New Testament analogy (Rom. 9:24-26) specifies that these verses refer to God's present, largely non-Jewish kingdom of the Church, as opposed to national Israel.[27] It is a fact, moreover, that prior to the revelation of the newer testament, the Gentiles were indeed more truly *lō-ammī*, "not My people" (outside God's testament), than even the basest of the national Israelites. But now, "if ye are Christ's, then are ye Abraham's seed, heirs according to promise" (Gal. 3:29), "the Israel of God" (6:16). "For we are the circumcision, who worship by the Spirit of God, and glory in Christ Jesus, and have no confidence in the flesh" (Phil. 3:2; cf. Rom. 2:29).

Therefore, even though the battle bow was cut off from Jerusalem in A.D. 70 (Zech. 9:10) and though only a remnant of the Jews believed (Rom. 9:27-29; 11:5), yet "more are the children of the desolate [the Jerusalem that is the Church, Gal. 4:26-28] than the children of the married wife [the old Hebrew nation]" (Isa. 54:1). As a result, the Israel of the new testament speaks peace to the nations (Zech. 9:10) to an extent that the Israel of the older testament was never able to do. In this respect also, the Church thus constitutes the goal of the older testament; and the last of Judah's prophets anticipated that day of the Church's missionary evangelism, now being fulfilled, when "from the rising of the sun even unto the going down of the same My name shall be great among the Gentiles" (Mal. 1:11).

For Further Reading:

H. H. Rowley, *Darius the Mede and the Four World Empires in the Book of Daniel.* Cardiff, Wales: University Press, 1935. A thorough, though liberal, study on the fulfillment of this important aspect of the day of Yahweh.

John C. Whitcomb, Jr., *Darius the Mede* (Evangelical Theological Society Monograph Series No. 3). Grand Rapids: Eerdmans Publishing Co., 1959. A scholarly, evangelical answer to Rowley's work.

Roderick Campbell, *Israel and the New Testament.* Philadelphia: The Presbyterian and Reformed Publishing Co., 1955. A recent work in the traditional, orthodox understanding.

H. A. Ironside, *The Great Parenthesis.* Grand Rapids: Zondervan Publishing House, 1943. A so-called exhaustive presentation of the dispensational view of Israel and the Church.

[27]See Appendix H, p. 529, for chart showing the application of Hosea's "family prophecies" to God's kingdom(s).

32. The Testament of Peace*

Glorious as is our contemporary experience of redemption under the new testament — with its internal character, accomplished reconciliation, direct faith, and explicit forgiveness — Scripture yet foresees a day, not in which these features will be transcended, but in which they will be expanded, brought to fulfillment, and rendered determinative for life throughout the entire world. Under this climactic testament of peace (Ezek. 37:24-28), which as yet lies still in the future, men's internal religion will become productive of a totally consistent external pattern of conduct (v. 24); their reconciliation with God, expressed at all points in history by the Biblical promise, "I will be their God, and they shall be My people" (v. 27), will then eventuate into the fullness of divine fellowship; the Christian's present blessing of direct faith will become that of direct sight (v. 26); and the explicit forgiveness that is now granted to the saints will be recognized and honored by the whole creation together (v. 28).[1] Humanly speaking, the kingdom of God's testament of peace may appear as an impossible utopian dream. In respect, however, to the potentialities of divine supernaturalism the picture finds itself to be totally congruous; and in the theology of the older testament it is this kingdom that constitutes the ultimate development that Scripture foresees as the inheritance of our reconciliation with God. In a remonstrance, the plausibility which would be difficult to question, "Thus saith Yahweh of hosts: If it be marvelous in the eyes of the remnant of this people in those days [the yet future day of Yahweh], should it also be marvelous in Mine eyes?" (Zech. 8:6).

A. THE DAY OF YAHWEH, AS FUTURE JUDGMENT. Modern commentators are united in acknowledging that Scripture speaks of —

". . . unprecedented calamities, just before the advent of the Messiah and the divine deliverance. This conception of the 'Messianic woes' corresponds psychologically to the general feeling that the darkest hour is just before the dawn."[2]

---

*BIBLE READING: Ezekiel 34:11-31; Malachi 3:13-4:6
Collateral Reading: Oehler, Theology of the Old Testament, pp. 494-521.
  J. B. Payne, "The Predictive Cycles of Zechariah 9-14," Evangelical Theological Society, 1956 Papers, pp. 55-68.
  George N. H. Peters, The Theocratic Kingdom of Our Lord Jesus, the Christ (Grand Rapids: Kregel Publications, 1948), I:396-400; III:83-91, 460-466.

---

[1]See above, pp. 116, 117.
[2]Millar Burrows, An Outline of Biblical Theology, p. 195.

The explanation that Oehler proposes for these Messianic woes is as follows:

> Prophecy starts from the state of contradiction to its Divine election into which Israel fell by apostasy. Sinful Israel belied its blessed vocation. God's holiness obliges Him to do away with this contradiction. The means by which He effects this end is the infliction of judgment. He expels His revolted people from their home, and delivers them up to the heathen powers. Thus, however, a fresh contradiction arises: Israel was chosen to realize the divine purpose of redemption even among the heathen; but now that judgment has fallen upon Israel, the heathen powers triumph over the people of Jehovah, and therefore, as they suppose, over Jehovah Himself. This contradiction must be done away with; and this is effected by the judgments inflicted upon the heathen powers for their self-exaltation.[3]

An illustration that appears in Old Testament times is that of Assyria, which constituted "the rod of God's anger" against Israel (Isa. 10:5); but Assyria in turn then had to be punished because of its God-defying insolence (vv. 15, 16). A similar example, though at the end of the age, is that of the international balance of power that has succeeded upon the once-unified Roman Empire — the "ten kings" that have arisen out of Daniel's fourth monarchy (7:24). This balance is said to be partially overthrown and assimilated by a "little horn";[4] and the little horn proceeds to go forth to "wear out the saints of the Most High." He even speaks words against Yahweh Himself for an indefinite period of "times" (v. 25), the "great tribulation" of Revelation 7:14 (cf. Dan. 12:1; Matt. 24:29).[5] But it is at this point that the Lord comes and intervenes in judgment on behalf of His own (vv. 26, 27) in "the day of vengeance of our God, to comfort all that mourn" (Isa. 61:2b). In the New Testament, one may specifically identify this evil figure of Daniel with the final Antichrist: he may also be equated with the "man of sin" (II Thess. 2:3) and with the "lawless one" who occupies the throne of "the beast" (world political power; see below, Appendix J, p. 534; Rev. 16:10; 19:19). But whether or not he corresponds to some present-day (Communist?) political leader can only be known *after* Christ returns to this earth and accomplishes his overthrow.[6] For those who have committed themselves to advance identifications, such as to one of the popes, to Napoleon, or to Mussolini, have so far achieved nothing but embarrassment, both for themselves and for the cause of Bible-believing prophetic interpretation. The precise time of the end is something we neither know

---

[3]Oehler, *Theology of the Old Testament*, pp. 494-495.

[4]This is not to be confused with the somewhat parallel description of Antiochus Epiphanes in Dan. 8:9.

[5]The "great tribulation," which is humanly caused and thus conceivably under way at present, must be carefully distinguished from the time of God's supernatural wrath that follows (Matt. 24:29), cf. Payne, *The Imminent Appearing of Christ* (Grand Rapids: Wm. B. Eerdmans Publishing Co., 1962), Chap. 4:A-2.

[6]*Ibid.*

nor are supposed to know (Mark 13:32), but only the reality of God's future judgment.

Scripture describes terrible natural phenomena as heralding this "judgment day of Yahweh." During the eighth century B.C. the prophet Joel had predicted a contemporary locust plague as darkening the very sun (Joel 2:2, 3); but he went on, by inspiration, to apply his description of the locusts to the yet future day of Yahweh's victory:

"And I will show wonders in the heavens and in the earth: blood, and fire, and pillars of smoke. The sun shall be turned into darkness, and the moon into blood, before the great and terrible day of Yahweh cometh" (vv. 30, 31).

Joel's picture of "the wrath of God" (cf. Rev. 14:19; 15:1) was almost immediately taken up by others of the inspired prophets (cf. Isa. 13:10, 11; 34:4), who added that this darkness would then be followed by a greater (redemptive) light than ever before (Zech. 14:6, 7; Isa. 30:26). Such overwhelming phenomena are designed of God to humble rebellious mankind, forcing even the proud to hide in caves (Isa. 2:17, 19); for "Who can abide the day of His coming?" (Mal. 3:2). No time span is given for these events. That the sun itself is to be darkened suggests that the duration should not be too great, perhaps a matter of minutes. The Church's hope in the imminency of God's intervention is thereby guarded against any calculable interval of deferment, such as the seven years that dispensationalists insist must elapse before Christ can be revealed[7] (see below, Appendix J, p. 533).

The natural phenomena, however, are but introductory to God's primary medium of future judgment, which is that of a world-embracing theophany. It was King David who first revealed, "For He [Yahweh] cometh, For He cometh to judge the earth" (Ps. 96:13;[8] cf. 98:9; 46:10). This awesome thought was then subsequently developed by the eighth century prophets: "Behold, your God will come with vengeance, with the recompense of God; He will come and save you" (Isa. 35:4; cf. 40:10; 52:12; Ezek. 34:11). Hosea's revelation, furthermore, includes both "Yahweh their God, and David their king" (3:5, and so Jer. 30:9); and Geerhardus Vos observes that the "activity

---

[7]The dispensational interpretation of the 70 weeks of Daniel not only repudiates its chronological significance, by separating the 70th week from the rest; but by making the 70th week still future and yet prior to Christ's Second Coming, it also extends the "great tribulation" period into seven years that are as yet unaccomplished, so that the imminency of the Lord's visible return is denied and the Church's blessed hope, "the glorious appearing of our great God and Saviour Jesus Christ" (Titus 2:13), becomes impossible of an hour by hour expectancy. Its anticipation must then be replaced by the un-Biblical theory of a secret rapture, far separated from Christ's appearing. Cf. the similar denial of imminent hope on the part of those who may oppose dispensationalism, but who yet follow its futuristic exegesis, e.g., George E. Ladd, The Blessed Hope (Grand Rapids, 1956), pp. 110-111.

[8]Known to be David's words from I Chron. 16:33.

THE THEOLOGY OF THE OLDER TESTAMENT

of the Messiah in the judgment drama of Isaiah and Micah (Isa. 9 and 11; Mic. 5:2ff)"[9] is even more pronounced. Ezekiel in the exile was the first to suggest the actual identity of the person of the God-who-comes with that of the Messiah; for he spoke in the name of Yahweh, saying both, "I Myself will search for My sheep as a shepherd" (34:11, 12); and yet, "My servant David, he shall feed them and he shall be their shepherd" (v. 23). Ezekiel's contemporary, Daniel, then made the equation more explicit in his figure of the Son of Man (7:13, 14), who was human, the ultimate figure in the remnant doctrine (as He represented the saints of the Most High), and yet at the same time divine.[10] In post-exilic days, Zechariah added that He would come with the divine retinue of angels (14:5) on a day known only to Yahweh (v. 7). The identification of the coming God with the coming Christ is then completed when one of the last prophecies of the older testament states, "The Lord, whom ye seek, will suddenly come to his temple, even the Angel of the testament, whom ye desire" (Mal. 3:1). Warfield, as a result, has observed:

> The New Testament writers throughout proceed on the assumption that all those Old Testament passages in which the Advent of Jehovah is spoken of refer to the coming of the Messiah [cf. Luke 1:16-17].[11]

The details of this Second Coming of Christ, of His coming in judgment, are as follows. He shall descend from heaven, and His feet stand upon the Mount of Olives, east of Jerusalem (Zech. 14:4). He comes, that is, in like manner as He ascended (Acts 1:11). At His appearing, however, the world will be no more disposed to receive Him than they were at the time of His first coming; the united nations will, in fact, rouse themselves to repel this threat to their sovereignty. But actually, their futile actions will serve only to accomplish a series of events that God has designed for His own purposes. Even as Micah had predicted about the forces of Antiochus Epiphanes, "They understand not the counsel of Yahweh; for He hath gathered them as sheaves to the threshing floor" (4:12).

The military engagements that are precipitated by Christ's Second Coming appear to be two-fold. 1) The forces of the universal antichristian opposition will effectuate an immediate attack upon Jerusalem (Zech. 12:2), capturing half of the city and working great destruction (14:2). The rapidity of their movement, it should be noted, becomes increasingly comprehensible in the light of modern military progress. The sufferers in the city will include a number of Jews (cf. 14:5). For though culturally they are identified as Israelites (Zechariah's own people), spiritually they appear to have been

[9]Geerhardus Vos, *Biblical Theology*, pp. 314-315.
[10]See above, pp. 264, 265.
[11]B. B. Warfield, *Biblical and Theological Studies*, p. 103.

as yet unconverted at the time of the Lord's appearing; for they have not been raptured from earth, along with the true Church, so as to meet the Lord in the air and to be joined to His heavenly train as it descends to Olivet (see below, next section). This is, therefore, one of the few still-future passages of the Bible where "Israel" cannot mean the Church. It also indicates that at least some Jews will be present in Palestine on the day of Christ's Second Coming.

The attack, however, that is made by the wicked upon Jerusalem, though culpable, yet constitutes an aspect of God's purposeful judgment. For the distress that it occasions is described not only as a time of unprecedented trouble (Dan. 12:1) but also as "like a refiner's fire" (Mal. 3:2), through which God shall witness against the ungodly in the Jewish nation (v. 5). It works to accomplish the purging of the blood of Jerusalem by the spirit of judgment and burning (Isa. 4:4). This attack therefore serves as a particular illustration of Oehler's principle that:

> "The judgment of Israel in point of time precedes; that of the nations of the world follows—the deliverance of the covenant people being effected by means of the latter. 'You only have I known,' it is said, Amos iii.2, 'of all the families of the earth: therefore will I punish you for your iniquities.'"[12]

But the Jews, half of them at least, are delivered by fleeing eastward into a supernaturally prepared valley, through which they succeed in reaching Christ and His saints on the Mount of Olives (Zech. 14:5). Their deliverance is then sealed by the Lord's judgment upon their attackers. For militarism, with its "plowshares beaten into swords" (Joel 3:9, 10), can be of no avail against the hosts of Jesus Christ and of the archangel Michael standing up for his people (Dan. 12:1). The enemy is forthwith shattered and destroyed in the nearby Valley of Jehoshaphat (Joel 3:2, 12, 13), which is appropriately designated "the valley of decision" (v. 14).

2) But the greater and more decisive battle is yet to follow. The anti-Christian leader in this all-out campaign is the "little horn" of Daniel; but neither he nor his forces can be clearly identified from Scripture, except that they seem to advance from the north of Palestine and to have overcome a more southerly power (Dan. 11:40).[13] In connection with the Antichrist's approach, Yahweh causes certain bodies of water to dry up, notably the Red Sea and the Euphrates River (Isa. 11:15; Zech. 10:11; cf. Rev. 16:12), though, in parallel with the ancient deliverances of Israel, these dry beds are intended ultimately to serve as "a highway for the remnant of His people" (Isa. 11:16). For Scripture leaves no doubt as to the outcome of this

[12]Oehler, op. cit., p. 500.
[13]This assumes that the prediction of Antiochus terminates at v. 39, for Antiochus' known career fails to correspond to what is thereafter described.

momentous conflict. From the day of Moses, Balaam's oracle had predicted that the Messiah would some day destroy all the sons of *shēth*, "tumult" (Num. 24:17). David had anticipated that his Lord would rule in the midst of His enemies (Ps. 110:2) and that He would "break them with a rod of iron" and "dash them in pieces like a potter's vessel" (2:9). Daniel in exile then spoke forth the specific doom of the little horn: "The judgment shall be set, and they shall take away his dominion, to consume and to destroy it unto the end" (Dan. 7:26).

The Old Testament delimits the site for the final battle only to the general area of western Canaan, "between the sea and the glorious holy mountain" (11:45), though the New Testament specifies its location at the mount of Megiddo, "Armageddon" (Rev. 16:16). Micah 5:5 indeed notes several subordinate military leaders who will carry on operations, particularly in the upper Tigris-Euphrates Valley; but the glorified army of the saints will press the main Palestinian battle at Christ's own side, "like flaming torches among sheaves" (Zech. 12:6). Completely overwhelmed by the power of God, the Antichrist "shall come to his end; and none shall help him" (Dan. 11:45). His fate had actually been sealed back in the days of the ancient Roman Empire, when the God of heaven set up a kingdom of divine righteousness (Dan. 2:44): the rule of the Suffering Servant, of the new testament, and of the Lamb that taketh away the sin of the world (John 1:29). For this seemingly insignificant Galilean fellowship was coupled to the Lord of all history and thereby inaugurated "a kingdom which shall never be destroyed"; and at the last, through the divinely-directed campaign of Armageddon, "It shall break in pieces and consume all these [other] kingdoms." In that day of Yahweh, the unrighteous shall hide themselves from "the wrath of the Lamb" (Rev. 6:16). For the King of salvation, by claiming His Davidic throne as the "Lion of the tribe of Judah" (5:5), will have brought to pass the testament of peace, in which "all that is proud and haughty shall be brought low" (Isa. 2:12).

B. THE DAY OF YAHWEH, AS FUTURE RESTORATION. In the very years when Moses was founding the elect nation, God revealed through him that a joyful future restoration would be associated with the above-outlined future judgment, and he proclaimed, "Rejoice, oh ye nations, with His people: for He will avenge the blood of His servants" (Deut. 32:43). The earliest of its aspects that was specifically to be defined was that of a restoration to the land of Palestine. Even some six and a half centuries prior to the Exodus, God had assured the patriarch Abraham, as a corollary to the basic testamental inheritance of reconciliation with God, that his believing seed should everlastingly possess the promised land of Canaan (Gen. 17:8). Israel's post-exilic restoration had thus commenced with a return to Palestine; and the prophets, as early as the eighth century B.C., described the restoration that is still future in corresponding terms: "The Lord will set His hand again the second time to recover the remnant of His people that shall remain" (Isa. 11:11), or, "Yahweh will roar like a lion; for He will roar, and the children shall come trembling from the west" (Hos. 11:10), or again, "In that day [of Yahweh] a great trumpet shall be blown; and they shall come that were ready to perish in the land of Assyria . . . and they shall worship Yahweh in the holy mountain at Jerusalem" (Isa. 27:13; cf. Zech. 8:7; 10:9, 10).

The Old Testament describes this gathering of God's own, to be with Him in the Holy Land, in the three stages. 1) There will occur the resurrection of the Church triumphant: "The dead in Christ shall rise first" (I Thess. 4:16). For the Lord Himself had proclaimed through Hosea, "I will ransom them from the power of the grave (sheol); I will redeem them from death: oh death, where are thy plagues? oh grave, where is thy destruction?" (Hos. 13:14; see above, topic 31). As had been recorded in the time of David, the believer could state with confidence, "Nevertheless I am continually with Thee" (Ps. 73:23); and it thus follows that when Christ returns to this physical earth, His saints will come bodily with Him. 2) Scripture also reveals that the Church militant, which has been sown among the peoples in far countries, shall return to appear in His presence at His Second Advent (Zech. 10:9). This fact too follows as a necessary inference from the promise that "My servant David shall be *among them*" (Ezek. 34:24). The particular statement in Zechariah 14:5, "My God shall come, and all the holy ones with Thee," seems further to suggest that the Church will meet Christ in the air during His very descent, and so return to earth with Him (cf. I Thess. 4:17), though the term "holy ones" does also signify the holy angels. Most of the Old Testament statements on the yet future regathering of Israel thus apply specifically to this rapture of the believing Church. 3) A limited number of passages, however, suggest a third group, those from among Israel after the flesh who experience restoration at the Messiah's return. As Vos has observed, "Israel in its *racial* capacity will again in the future be visited by the saving grace of God" (Rom. 11:2, 12, 25).[14]

The Old Testament contexts furnish a number of internal evidences, on the basis of which one may distinguish the passages that refer to the redemptive restoration of modern-day Jews. Here, in the first place, are to be included those verses that speak of Israelites who

---

[14]*Op. cit.*, p. 93; and cf. Warfield, who understands Rom. 11:26 as teaching the future salvation of the Jews. He also notes as an alternative interpretation (but which still includes the Jews), *op. cit.*, p. 486, "If Rom. 11:25 means 'those Gentiles who go toward filling up the kingdom,' then 'all Israel' of verse 26 must of necessity be the spiritual Israel, distinguished from the Israel of verse 25, by the inclusive 'all.' Then the sense would be that 'hardening has befallen Israel' temporarily—viz. until the Gentile contingent comes in—and thus ('in this way') all Israel shall be saved;—not part only, but all."

experience a regathering to Christ by means that are other than the Church's rapture (cf. Isa. 14:2; 49:22; 60:9; 66:20; Zeph. 3:10). Again, there exist certain contexts that describe "Israel" as exhibiting spiritual characteristics that are remote from application to the believing Church. Zechariah, chapter 12, is particularly significant in this regard; see the more detailed outline given below.[15] Verse 7 speaks of two groups: "Yahweh shall save the tents of Judah first, that the glory of the house of David and the glory of the inhabitants of Jerusalem be not magnified above Judah." The latter group, that includes the inhabitants of Jerusalem, is noted in 14:2 as consisting of non-raptured Jews, that must therefore be presently unconverted. So too in chapter 12, Jerusalem's inhabitants appear to be of similar character. For verse 10 says that at Christ's return they shall "look unto Me whom they have pierced; and they shall mourn"; and the next paragraph predicts, "In that day there shall be a fountain opened for them for sin" (13:1). But it is the unbelieving Jews (not the Church) who were guilty of piercing Christ, who will mourn at His appearing (Rev. 1:7), and who will then for the first time receive the atonement of His cleansing blood.

The day of Yahweh as future restoration thus involves the assimilation of a considerable group of Jews into God's kingdom. Paul, for example, describes their restoration in terms of a reingrafting of natural branches back into the olive tree of the true Church (cf. Rom. 11:15): "For if the casting away of them is the reconciling of the world, what shall the receiving of them be but life from the dead?" Similarly Zechariah 13:9 speaks of unconverted Israel, first as passing through fire, which is to arise because of their having smitten the Good Shepherd, but then also as entering again into the promise of the testament and confessing, "Yahweh is my God." Hosea 3:5 likewise predicts that the Jews, who now have no idols but who have no way of atonement either, will in the latter days seek "David their king" (cf. 1:11); and 14:4 notes how God will finally heal their backsliding. As Paul went on to say, "There shall come out of Zion the Deliverer; He shall turn away ungodliness from Jacob; and so all Israel shall be saved" (Rom. 11:26). This suggests that at least a large proportion of the Jews will experience salvation in that day. The number would seem to include all of those who retain the orthodox Jewish hope in the coming of their long awaited Messiah, along with such others as will be sincere enough to "turn from transgression" (Isa. 59:20), when they see Him coming with the clouds of heaven (Dan. 7:13). The seed of Israel *as a nation* does have eternal significance in God's eyes (Jer. 31:36).

Zechariah 12:7, however, speaks of a former group, "Judah," whom Yahweh will save first, and which therefore appears to indicate

---

[15]See Appendix I, pp. 530, 531, for chart of Zechariah's latter chapters.

the Church, those who already believe.[16] Verse 5 states further that
at Christ's appearing, "The chieftains of Judah [the Church] shall
say in their heart, The inhabitants of Jerusalem [the Jews] are my
strength in Yahweh of hosts their God." These words are significant in
two ways. On the one hand, they show that there will be unbelieving
Jews exercising power in the leading cities of Palestine when Christ
comes back. But the existence of such, at least to some extent, has
been true ever since the days of Rome; and no Scripture is evident
which requires the presence of a full-fledged Zionist state, as if this
were prerequisite to our Lord's return. On the other hand, it shows
that when the Jews are finally converted, they will then join in with
the Church as the means by which to resume their ancient status
within true Israel. For the "middle wall of partition" has been broken
down by Christ once and for all (Eph. 2:14). It will not be "rebuilt"
in the future; neither will there be two grades of believing citizens
in God's kingdom.[17] Such total equality is suggested as early as the
prophecy of Joel: "For in mount Zion shall be those that escape, and
among the remnant [Jews] those whom Yahweh doth call [other be-
lievers]" (Joel 2:32).

The next major event in the day of Yahweh as future restoration
consists of the formal celebration of the union of Christ with His
people. In New Testament terminology this is styled "the marriage
supper of the Lamb" (cf. Rev. 19:7); but the concept is much older.
At Sinai God had first espoused Israel to Himself as His Bride, His
wedded wife. Furthermore, though Israel proved consistently unfaith-
ful, God loved her and sought her still (Hos. 3:1). At His first coming Christ purchased back the Bride with His own blood (Eph. 5:
25-27), at the prophesied price of thirty pieces of silver (or its equivalent, in Hos. 3:2). But the marriage has not yet been consummated
(v. 3). Spiritually, Christ resides in our hearts under the new testament; but the full marriage will be formalized only under the testament of peace, when He will dwell among us visibly as well (Ezek.
34:24).

Such a union with the heavenly Bridegroom, however, demands
as a prerequisite the purification of His chosen Bride: "He that is left
in Zion shall be called holy, even every one that is written among

---

[16]This identification of Judah with the Church and Jerusalem with the Jews has
been defended by August Ebrard and by Theodor Kliefoth, continental theologians of the last century.
[17]Or, as George N. H. Peters has put it in *The Theocratic Kingdom of Our Lord
Jesus, the Christ* (Grand Rapids: Kregel Publications, 1948) I:400, "Being thus
incorporated with 'the commonwealth of Israel'—the Israel to whom pertain the
covenants—they [the Gentiles] *virtually* become Jews, and the distinctive title by
which the believing line of Jews is favored, *rightfully* also belongs to them. The
very name 'Israel' is a reminder to us of such an adoption and election." For
further data on the status of the as-yet-unconverted Jew in the future restoration,
and on his incorporation into the Church, see Payne, "The Predictive Cycles of
Zechariah 9-14," *Evangelical Theological Society, 1956 Papers,* pp. 62-65.

the living in Jerusalem" (Isa. 4:3). The resurrected dead had of course already been made perfect in heaven (cf. Heb. 12:23), but the raptured Church and converted Jews are led to expect a corresponding change of resurrection in their own lives (cf. I Cor. 15:51). For not only will the proud and haughty have been removed; but Christ's coming will also involve the sanctification to God of a chastened people, that take refuge in the name of Yahweh: "The remnant of Israel shall not do iniquity" (Zeph. 3:11-13); or, as expressed elsewhere, "Thy people shall be all righteous" (Isa. 60:21).

The union of Christ with His saints attains its formalization in the marriage feast. Christ Himself uttered the first words that predicted this festive aspect to the future restoration. As He spoke through David in the 22nd Psalm, "The meek shall eat and be satisfied; they shall praise Yahweh that seek after Him" (Ps. 22:26). Isaiah in the eighth century then developed the joyful hope by declaring, "In this mountain will Yahweh of hosts make unto all peoples a feast of fat things, a feast of wines on the lees" (25:6). In Christ's day, therefore, it was but natural for the pious Israelite to exclaim with anticipation, "Blessed is he that shall eat bread in the kingdom of God!" (Luke 14:15). For the marriage will result in unsurpassed joy for God's people. A beautiful example are the six brief verses of Isaiah chapter 12, which promises: "In that day [of Yahweh] thou shalt say, I will give thanks unto Thee, oh Yahweh . . . for Yahweh is my strength and song . . . therefore with joy shall ye draw water out of the wells of salvation" (vv. 1-3).

A feature of God's future restoration that so far has been assumed without detailed comment is that of its earthward orientation. When the Church is raptured to be with Christ, for example, Zechariah describes how He will "bring them into the land of Gilead and Lebanon" (Zech. 10:10); and Isaiah proceeds to locate the Marriage Supper of the Lamb "in this mountain," namely, Mount Zion. Concerning this point, however, sincere Bible-believing Christians exhibit a marked difference in interpretation. Some are convinced that Christ's advent will inaugurate a literal, earthly kingdom of God, prior to the final judgment and the final restoration which consists of the new heavens and the new earth; while others insist that the Second Coming of Christ will immediately usher in the final state. These are the positions respectively of millennialism (an earthly kingdom) and of amillennialism (no earthly kingdom). The basis for their disagreement lies in the hermeneutical method that each party applies to Biblical prophecy. Evangelicals in both of these positions are committed to the inerrancy of Scripture. But those who interpret its prophetic truths literally discover as a result the description of an earthly, millennial kingdom; while those who interpret them figuratively find, instead, a series of types that picture the spiritual Church and the heavenly Jerusalem. An exclusively figurative interpretation of the earthly elements in the prophecies of the eschatological kingdom thus leads one to a correspondingly amillennial position.

In support of the figurative hermeneutical approach, E. J. Young has contended:

> Since the revelation granted to the prophets was less clear than that given to Moses [Num. 12:6-8]; indeed, since it contained elements of obscurity, we must take these facts into consideration when interpretating prophecy. We must therefore abandon once and for all the erroneous and non-Scriptural rule of "literal if possible." The prophetic language belonged to the Mosaic economy and hence, was typical. Only in the light of the New Testament fulfillment can it properly be interpreted.[18]

But while recognizing both the elements of obscurity that appear within the prophetic oracles[19] and the basic function that prophecy executes as supplementary to the law,[20] one cannot but question whether these facts justify an *exclusively* typical application of the earthly predictions of the Old Testament to our own spiritual Church.

In the first place, the very use of the term "typical" is improper. For Biblical typology concerns contemporaneously existing objects and actions that were, at the same time, symbolic of the future; but it does not apply to verbal statements. Years ago Milton S. Terry exposed this logical fallacy, which is still so widely held. He stated that just —

> . . . as many persons and events of the Old Testament were types of greater ones to come, so the language respecting them is supposed to be capable of a double sense . . . But it should be seen that in the case of types the language of Scripture has no double sense . . . The types themselves are such because they prefigure things to come, and this fact must be kept distinct from the question of the sense of language used in any particular passage.[21]

The typical nature of some of the Mosaic *institutions* does not, therefore, automatically limit the Mosaic *predictions* to a figurative fulfillment.

In the second place, when the light of New Testament interpretation is brought to bear upon the matter of the Old Testament's prophetic fulfillment, the apostolic analogy is *not* found to support the claim that the earthly situations therein predicted are assigned only a spiritualized accomplishment. As Ramm has cautiously summarized the evidence,

> "Sometimes it [the Old Testament] is cited as being *literally fulfilled* . . . sometimes the New Testament cites the

---

[18]*My Servants the Prophets*, p. 215.
[19]The literary features of predictive prophecy, such as symbolism, poetic license, ambiguity, and generalization, prohibits its uncritical reading as mere "history written in advance." At such points the honest expositor must always be willing to confess ignorance or uncertainty.
[20]See above, pp. 49, 50.
[21]*Biblical Hermeneutics*, p. 494.

Old Testament *in an expanded typological sense* . . . An extreme literalism or an extreme typological approach is equally contrary to the method by which the New Testament interprets the Old."[22]

Furthermore, once the legitimacy of literal interpretation be granted, an objective exegesis would seem to forbid the exclusion of a clear, literal meaning and the substitution of a figurative interpretation, unless there be actual justification for each such instance. Ramm thus goes on to reason:

> "In keeping with the system of hermeneutics . . . we make the literal the control over the typological. Therefore, *interpret prophecy literally unless the implicit or explicit teaching of the New Testament suggests typological interpretation.*"[23]

Ultimately, the most satisfactory method of interpretation appears to lie in a synthesis that combines, wherever possible, the belief in a literal future accomplishment with the conviction of its universal applicability to the spiritual people of God. One may thereby maintain both the reality of the coming kingdom of Israel upon earth and, at the same time, the confidence that its saved citizenry will consist of our own New Testament Church. The amillennialists who deny the one and the dispensational premillennialists who deny the other seem to be equally subject to criticism.

In the particular matter of the earthly kingdom, Peters has thus stated, quite forcibly,

> While a purely material, naturalistic Kingdom, without spirituality, is unscriptural, so likewise an entire spiritual kingdom, without the sanctified union of the material or natural, is utterly opposed to the Word of God . . . We insist, in strict accordance with the Scriptures, that this spirituality is manifested, *not* in the third heaven, *not* outside this world, but *in* the world, *upon* this earth.[23a]

In the significant passage of Isaiah 49, for example, where Messianic prophecy reaches its climax in the equation of Christ with the divine testament, the ultimate relevance of our Lord's redemption is viewed as affecting the physical earth: "I will give Thee for a testament of the people, to raise up the land, to make them inherit the desolate heritages" (Isa. 49:8). The Old Testament is in fact filled with pre-

---

[22]*Protestant Biblical Interpretation*, pp. 243, 247. His analysis is as follows, "The amillennialist makes the greatest divorce between the form and the fulfillment of prophecy and that is why the more literal-minded postmillennarians and premillennarians are restive with it. The dispensationalists judge that the distinction between the form and the idea of prophecy is spurious, and therefore they look for the fulfillment of prophecy to be very similar to the precise form in which it was given in the Old Testament." But he concludes, "*Some change in the form of fulfillment* must be expected," p. 241.
[23]*Ibid.*, p. 247.
[23a]*Op. cit.*, III:460, 465.

dictions of Christ's reign on the earth; the kingdom concerns temporal peoples, among whom the King is literally to be present (Zeph. 3:15, 17; Obad. 21; Zech. 14:9, 21); and "the meek shall inherit the land" (Ps. 37:11). The force of this evidence cannot be gainsaid. As an illustration, Geerhardus Vos was a theologian who personally questioned the existence of a future, earthly kingdom; but, when he was then faced with the problem of the non-fulfillment and, for the amillennialist, the seeming impossibility of any future fulfillment of a number of Biblical prophecies which speak directly of events upon this earth, he conceded, "The adoption of premillennarianism would greatly limit the field of the impossible in this respect."[24] Indeed, there arise a number of points in Scripture in which prophecies of judgment, literally fulfilled, are balanced contextually by prophecies of restoration, that would seem to necessitate a correspondingly literal fulfillment. God spoke through Jeremiah, for example, saying, "Like as I have brought all this great evil upon this people, so will I bring upon them all the good that I have promised them" (Jer. 32:42, and cf. 31:28).

As a result, most theologians today admit the literal intent of the Old Testament prophets. Thus Oehler, even though joining with those who doubt the reality of the future, earthly kingdom, yet grants: "Generally speaking, the prophets when beholding the future state of God's kingdom in the Old Testament form, mean just what they say."[25] He then proceeds, however, to distinguish the thought of the Holy Spirit from that of the prophets. A. B. Davidson is even more explicit in this regard:

> When the prophets predict restoration of Israel to Zion and restitution to their own land, these things are literal in *their* mind at least. They are not dealing with ideals merely, but with concrete things, with literal people and with a literal land. This principle must be held firmly, or else no account can be given of the manner in which they speak.[26]

But while recognizing the literal sense as constituting the original meaning of Scripture, Davidson goes on to posit a shift in the divine intention, with the coming of New Testament times:

> Now, of course, the conditions of God's treatment of His Church might change. The time might come when He desired to throw them more directly upon the spirituality of His favor, and therefore withdrew from them the outward token of it, namely, the possession of Canaan . . . We believe such a change has come.[27]

---

[24]*Op. cit.*, p. 232.
[25]Oehler, *op. cit.*, p. 491. Knight too admits the "earthly" hope, though he concludes that these are "pictorial" terms, *A Christian Theology of the Old Testament*, pp. 341-43; compare his non-literal treatment of the new heaven, *op. cit.*, pp. 344-45.
[26]*Old Testament Prophecy* (Edinburgh: T. and T. Clark, 1904), p. 490.
[27]*Ibid.*, p. 491.

The present writer, however, experiences difficulty in justifying a belief in a temporal change, of such radical proportions, in the redemptive program to which the omniscient God had repeatedly committed Himself. The effect of ancient culture upon phraseology is of course admitted, but not a shift in the actual truths that are conveyed by the Biblical words. For example, Micah 5:6 predicts that at the time of Christ's reign, "They shall waste the land of Assyria with a sword." But while swords may be discarded as the actual weapons employed, the fact of such a military operation in such a general location should not, it seems, be dismissed. It is true that orthodox Christians have interpreted these oracles as figurative descriptions of the present Church, of heaven, or of the final new Jerusalem; or they have eliminated them as being conditional prophecies that have long since ceased to be subject to any fulfillment at all. The following reconstruction, however, is yet presented as a possible Biblical synthesis of the evidence that relates to the future restoration as this is pictured in the Old Testament, based on the conviction that what Scripture says must some day truly come to pass on this earth.

While the Israelites were still encamped at Sinai, God spoke through Moses and gave them His first general promises about the inheritance that would come upon the chosen people if they continued obedient to Himself. He said in summary, "I will establish My testament with you . . . and will set My tabernacle among you" (Lev. 26:9, 11). This latter declaration referred to something other than the anticipatory, ceremonial Tabernacle, that Israel was already enjoying; it pointed rather to the fulfillment of the blessings that their contemporary Tabernacle was designed to portray, as these would be experienced when God would visibly "tabernacle" with them in the ultimate testament of peace. For the Mosaic context goes on to describe a supernatural fertility of the land (Lev. 26:5; cf. God's earlier promise to the patriarchs, Gen. 49:11, 12), the elimination of evil beasts and war (v. 6), and a domination by God's people over all their enemies (v. 8; cf. Deut. 26:19; 28:1, 10). The basis of Israel's future peace would thus lie in their testamental relationship with Yahweh. As God expresses it throughout the whole of Scripture, "And I will walk among you, and will be your God, and ye shall be My people" (Lev. 26:12).

The Davidic testament pointed forward to the day when the Messianic seed of David would rule over His enemies from His throne on Zion (Ps. 110:2) and would judge all of the world's peoples with equity (96:10). Solomon in the next period composed Psalm 72, which combines the concept of the Mosaic blessings with that of the Davidic Messianic triumph. Christ's kingdom, he stated, would be universal, commencing at the point where his own great realm left off: "He shall have dominion from sea to sea, and from the River [Euphrates] to the ends of the earth" (v. 8). Christ's reign would then mean peace (v. 7), an abundance of food (v. 16), and deliverance for the needy (vv. 12-14).

From the eighth century and onwards, the prophets, in their attempts to motivate Israel's obedience to God's testament in the present, provide us with our most detailed descriptions of His testament for the future. They promised that the future testament would introduce a time of unmatched agricultural fertility; and they prophesied, "Behold the days come that the plowman shall overtake the reaper . . . and the mountains shall drop sweet wine" (Amos 9:13). In the Lord's kingdom "There shall grow every tree for food, whose leaf shall not wither, neither shall the fruit thereof fail: it shall bring forth new fruit every month, and the fruit thereof shall be for food, and the leaf thereof for healing" (Ezek. 47:12, exilic). This last prophecy, it may be added, was later expanded by the New Testament into the beautiful picture of "the tree of life" that grows in the final new Jerusalem (Rev. 22:2).

The explanation that lies behind these ideal agricultural conditions is that of the removal of the curse from nature and of the restoration of that good state which had once existed in Eden prior to man's fall.[28] For when Adam failed under the covenant of works, the very ground passed under condemnation for his sake (Gen. 3:17); but Christ, by satisfying the same covenant of works (Matt. 3:15), establishes the basis for a restoration that will some day include the now-cursed ground. By means of the testament, mankind may thus become identified with the Last Adam and with His world-shaping accomplishments. The effect of even the early Noachian testament is therefore defined as achieving a reconciliation "between God and every living creature of all flesh that is upon the earth" (Gen. 9:16). Similarly Hosea 2:18, which constitutes the first revelation of the future testament, commences: "In that day [of Yahweh] will I make a testament for them with the beasts of the field, and with the birds of the heavens, and with the creeping things of the ground"; and this theme is then progressively elaborated until it receives its detailed treatment under Ezekiel's testament of peace (34:25-27). The cause for the future harmony within nature is therefore expressly revealed as theocratic: it is not without significance, for example, that the restoring fountain from which the earth-healing waters flow (Joel 3:18; Ezek. 47:7-12) is said to be located in Jerusalem, the seat of government of the Messianic Testator.

The best known Biblical picture of the eschatological removal

[28]Allan MacRae lists as the four outstanding features of the future kingdom its earthly character, its external peace and safety, its universality, and its blessedness because of the removal of the curse, *The Millennial Kingdom of Christ* (Wilmington, Del.: Faith Theological Seminary, n.d.), pp. 4-7.

of the curse is that of Isaiah 11:6-8, "The wolf shall dwell with the lamb; and a little child shall lead them. And the cow and the bear shall feed; and the lion shall eat straw like the ox." It is noteworthy, however, that Scripture limits this curbed conduct of the wild beasts to their relations with men and with the domesticated animals of mankind. The Word says only that "They shall not hurt nor destroy *in all My holy mountain*" (65:25). Elsewhere, it would appear that lions are to be no less carnivorous than they seem to have been prior to or outside of Eden. Mankind, moreover — meaning that non-resurrected portion of the human race that manages to survive the judgments of the day of Yahweh (cf. Zech. 14:16) — are described as experiencing long life, though also death; and success, though on the basis of labor — "For the child shall die a hundred years old; and they shall plant vineyards and eat the fruit of them" (Isa. 65:20, 21).[29] Physical infirmities shall be overcome (35:5, 6); and "There shall yet old men and old women dwell in Jerusalem, and the streets of the city shall be full of boys and girls playing" (Zech. 8:4, 5).

The very name "testament of peace" arose out of God's promise, "I will break the sword and the battle out of the land and will make them to lie down safely" (Hos. 2:18; cf. Ezek. 34:25, 28; Isa. 60:18). Indeed, one of the chief goals of the preceding future judgments had been that violence might be cut off from human society (Mic. 5:9). The termination of the threat of ravenous beasts (Isa. 35:9) serves also as an evidence of world peace, for their savage increase is known often to have come about as a result of the devastations of sin and war (26:22; II Kings 17:25, 26; Ezek. 5:17). One of the most loved descriptions of the entire future kingdom is that which appears in Isaiah 2:4 (Mic. 4:3), "They shall beat their swords into plowshares, and their spears into pruning-hooks; nation shall not lift up sword against nation, neither shall they learn war any more." This worldwide and lasting peace is made possible, however, only because of the divine Prince of Peace, who has become earth's all-controlling king (Isa. 9:6). "He will judge between the nations" (2:4). But then, due to His personal rule (11:10), justice will flourish (9:7; 11:4, 5); and, "The work of righteousness shall be peace" (32:17). Because of Him, "The ransomed of Yahweh shall come with singing unto Zion, everlasting joy shall be upon their heads, and sorrow and sighing shall flee away" (35:10).

This last verse points up the significant place that is occupied by Jerusalem in God's program of future restoration. In the time of David, Yahweh had first chosen Zion, saying, "This is My resting

---

[29]Cf. D. K. Kromminga's valid (though overdone) emphasis upon "the maximum of continuity between the present age and that of the kingdom," *The Millennium* (Grand Rapids: Wm. B. Eerdmans Publishing Co.), p. 115.

place for ever" (Ps. 132:14). The eighth century prophets are analyzed by Vos as exhibiting a variety of geographic emphases:

> "Isaiah delights in depicting the era after the judgment as a supreme revelation of Jehovah's glory. His vision of it centers in the sanctuary and the city, whereas to Amos and Hosea, and even Micah, it rested upon the land."[30]

Isaiah, for example, predicts, "Behold, I create Jerusalem a rejoicing, and her people a joy" (65:18). The later prophets then carry on this Isaianic stress and actually specify particular local areas of Jerusalem as "holy unto Yahweh" (Jer. 31:40; cf. Zech. 14:20, 21). It is possible that certain geological changes may even alter the city's elevation (Isa. 2:2; Zech. 14:10). The climactic element, however, within the entire reconciling inheritance of the future testament of peace consists of the presence of "God, dwelling in Zion My holy mountain" (Joel 3:17); "and many peoples shall go and say, Come ye and let us go up to the mountain of Yahweh, to the house of the God of Jacob; and He will teach us of His ways, and we will walk in His paths: for out of Zion shall go forth the law, and the word of Yahweh from Jerusalem" (Isa. 2:3; cf. Jer. 31:6). For while psychologically it is through a universalized submission of mankind to God's Word that the basic peace of the testament will be maintained; still, in order to stimulate among the rest of the world this desire for peace, a certain degree of particularism and of localized leadership will be required, even in the future, earthly kingdom. As Oehler explains:

> The coming of this kingdom of God which embraces all nations is, however, as is evident from the passages quoted, combined, according to prophetic intuition, with the fact *that Israel is to remain the mediatory nation at the head of the nations,* and Jerusalem with its temple to form the central point of the kingdom to which the nations are to journey.[31]

The particularism that characterizes God's future restoration becomes most apparent from the Old Testament's teaching about the existence of a temple, a house of Yahweh, in Jerusalem. Its presence will not be characteristic of the final restoration, in the new heavens and the new earth (Rev. 21:22), because these latter will truly embody perfect holiness (v. 27). But in the future millennial restoration, the continuing presence of subdued but still unregenerate men will require a certain degree of sacramentalism, of outward signs and seals of truths that will be visible enough, but that will not have been wholly integrated into all of the elements of society. There will indeed exist no ark of the testament (Jer. 3:16); for Christ will be personally present, accomplishing the theophanic truth it once typified. But the annual feast of tabernacles will still have to be observed,

---

[30]Vos, *op. cit.,* p. 316.
[31]Oehler, *op. cit.,* p. 518.

as an educational device toward an increase in human holiness (Zech. 14:16-21),[32] and presumably also the new moons and sabbaths, whose permanent validity appears from their inclusion within the final restoration as well (Isa. 66:23).

Scripture then goes on to assert, "Neither shall the priests the Levites lack a man before Me to do sacrifice continually" (Jer. 33:18). Against this last point, however, even Peters, among others, has registered resistance:

> In the earthly Jerusalem a temple will be rebuilt in order to manifest in a public manner the worship of God, yet much confusion of ideas is found in not noticing, that the way in which the word is employed fully shows, that it does *not necessarily involve* the notion of a restoration of sacrifices. The temple can exist without the introduction of the Mosaic ritual.[33]

It should be carefully observed, however, that the presence of a millennial priesthood need suggest no spiritual retrogression to Mosaism. Christ has made the atonement for sin once and for all (Heb. 9:12, 28; 10:12), and there will be no more atoning sacrifices. Furthermore, with the possible exception of the burnt offerings mentioned in Jeremiah 17:26 and 33:18, the emphasis of the Old Testament centers upon how these future sacrifices are to "come up with acceptance on Mine altar" for the sole purpose of "proclaiming the praises of Yahweh" (Isa. 60:6, 7). They are "sacrifices of thanksgiving" (Jer. 17:26). The existence of the sacrificial ritual does not, therefore, demonstrate a reversion to the theological inferiority of Moses' typical atonement. It is rather but a realistic outworking of New Testament worship, a thankful memorial to the finished work of Christ (cf. Heb. 13:15).

Such sacrifice furnishes us, in fact, with one more positive example of the way in which the internal features of the new testament are raised to external realization in the more comprehensive testament of peace. Its observance by no means constitutes a return to the outer husks of Judaism; and the statement that Peters does make, that "This Kingdom is then an essentially Jewish Kingdom,"[34] is hardly a commendable one. His assertion may only be admitted as valid when we recognize that by it he means not a regression but a fulfillment. For one of the central truths of the present new testament for us, former Gentiles, is that "Ye are no more strangers and sojourners, but ye are fellow citizens with the [Jewish] saints" (Eph. 2:19). Thus, in the future kingdom, the fullest blessings ever enjoyed by Jews will become ours. Indeed, in that day those who were not originally Jewish may become even more than fellow citizens; for, as Isaiah 66:21 suggests, "Of them also will I take for priests and for Levites" (cf. Matt. 19:28). It is of the once-Gentile peoples, moreover, that

---

[32]See above, p. 405, on its particularly future significance.
[33]*Op. cit.*, III:90.
[34]*Ibid.*, I:24.

God "will send unto the nations, to the isles afar off that have not heard of My fame; and they shall declare My glory among the nations" (Isa. 66:19).

For the particularism of the testament of peace involves also world instruction and world domination. "Yahweh will punish the kings of the earth upon the earth, and . . . Yahweh of hosts will reign in mount Zion" (24:21, 23). Material treasures are predicted as pouring into Jerusalem from other nations (Isa. 23:18; 45:14; 61:6). The prophet Jeremiah speaks of the "shepherds," or administrators, that God will appoint to rule in righteousness (3:15; 23:4; cf. Isa. 1:26); and Daniel in the exile visualizes the saints of the Most High as succeeding to the rule of the empires of this world (7:27; cf. Mic. 7:17).[35] This particularism, however, is designed for the purpose of effectuating the universal proclamation of the Gospel: "And nations shall come to thy light and kings to the brightness of thy rising" (Isa. 60:3). As Oehler elaborates the overall situation:

> The opposition of the heathen world to the divinely purposed kingdom of God, is subdued by the destructive judgment inflicted upon it. But this judgment is to have also a positive result. When it is over, says Zeph. iii. 9, "I will turn to the people clean lips" (for their lips had been hitherto polluted by the invocation of idols), "that they may all call upon the name of the Lord, to serve Him with one shoulder" (i.e. bear the same yoke). As, however, Israel is to be restored only in a sifted remnant, so also it is only the *remnant* of the heathen rescued from judgment who do homage to the Lord.[36]

Micah in the eighth century thus explains that as a result of Yahweh's awesome intervention "The nations shall see and shall be ashamed of their might" (Mic. 7:16).

The focal point of this world-wide evangelistic ministry is found in the person of the Messiah: "He will not fail nor be discouraged, till He have set justice in the earth; and the isles shall wait for His law" (Isa. 42:4). At the same time, however, Isaiah 11:10 adds that "unto Him shall the nations seek." For though the saved of the kingdom consist only of "those whom Yahweh doth call," still, the ones whom God has indeed called can be determined, humanly speaking, only by the response that people make. From man's viewpoint it is true now, even as it will be then, that "Whosoever shall call on the name of Yahweh shall be delivered" (Joel 2:32; Acts 2:21). Thus, upon their own volition, strangers will be joined with Israel (Isa. 14:1); and many shall find the salvation that is offered in the Christ of Scripture: "In that day [of Yahweh] shall the deaf hear the words of the Book" (29:18; cf. v. 11 and 32:3). Even the most stubborn of

---

[35]The newly converted "house of David," appear to continue, however, as the leaders of the inhabitants of Jerusalem (Zech. 12:8).
[36]Oehler, *op. cit.*, p. 516.

the nations shall give up their idols and their sinful pride (Zeph. 2:11; Jer. 3:17; 16:19);

> "And it shall come to pass, if they will diligently learn the ways of My people, to swear by My name, As Yahweh liveth; then shall they be built up in the midst of My people" (Jer. 12:16).

Ezekiel in exile adds his caution that the testament is not directed to the Gentiles; it is Israel's testament (16:61). But in the shade of Israel's Messiah shall all yet live (17:23). Finally Zechariah, in postexilic days, anticipates the time when ten Gentiles shall take hold of one Christian (="Jew") so as to come to God (8:23); when there shall exist no more false prophets (13:2); and when monotheism shall everywhere prevail: "In that day shall Yahweh be one, and His name one" (14:9).

The restoration accomplished by Christ's future kingdom will thus be one of world-wide scope: "The earth shall be full of the knowledge of Yahweh, as the waters cover the sea" (Isa. 11:9). Isaiah had observed that God's historical humiliation of Egypt had been designed to lead these foreigners to Himself, "smiting and healing" (19:22); and similarly he describes how, in the future kingdom, the converted of Egypt, of Assyria, and of Israel will unite from earth's various quarters to serve together and to stand equally as God's people (v. 25). Jeremiah furnishes explicit hope for Elam (Jer. 49:39), and even for Moab (48:47) and Ammon (49:6), though the original nations would first have to be destroyed (48:42; cf. Deut. 23:3). As God had long before announced: "By Myself have I sworn, the word is gone forth from My mouth in righteousness, and shall not return, that unto Me every knee shall bow, every tongue shall swear" (Isa. 45:23). In this "word," moreover, lies revealed the ultimate purpose of the future earthly kingdom: the vindication of Yahweh, in the same arena of earthly history in which men have so often flouted His holy will and His love.[37]

C. THE DAY OF YAHWEH, AS FINAL JUDGMENT. Scripture repeatedly designates God's future kingdom as eternal. For example, "Yahweh will reign over them in mount Zion from henceforth, even for ever" (Mic. 4:7; cf. Amos 9:15; Isa. 9:6). His Bride, Israel, is described as betrothed to Him in perpetuity (Hos. 2:19); and His kingdom is one that shall never be destroyed (Dan. 2:44). But the fact that God's kingdom is eternal need not require that it be uneventful, or without development. Evangelicals who are committed to the concept of a limited, earthly kingdom recognize this future restoration as but the first stage of the kingdom that is truly endless, when viewed in its entirety. Furthermore, even though the duration

---

[37]Cf. the analysis by Kromminga, *op. cit.*, chap. 2, esp. pp. 46, 53.

of this initial portion is revealed within the Old Testament in only general terms, as "a season" (Dan. 7:12; cf. the 1000 years of Rev. 20:6), the subsequent transformation of its major features is described in some detail. For example, the Jerusalem of the millenium is "a tent that shall not be removed" (Isa. 33:20; cf. Joel 3:20); but God will some day "lay its foundations with sapphires" (Isa. 54:11), as after the thousand years it becomes the "new Jerusalem" of God (Isa. 65:17, 18; Rev. 21:2; cf. v. 19). Again, though Ezekiel 37:25 prophesies of the Lord's people, "They shall dwell in the land forever," chapter 38 proceeds to describe a desolating attack on the blessed land by a certain Gog, who comes from the region of Magog (v. 1). Isaiah 65:17 goes on to predict a thorough transformation of the whole universe: "For, behold, I create new heavens and a new earth." The crisis, then, which marks this transition within the eternal blessedness of Jerusalem and of the earth itself is that of the final judgment. All evangelicals unite in affirming the crucial reality of this greatest of all court scenes; for those who question the validity of the concept of the future earthly kingdom still accept the historical reality of the events which are about to be described, while treating them as occurring directly upon Christ's Second Advent.

The final judgment, according to Scripture, is precipitated by a final demonstration of human sinfulness. For the natural man is totally depraved (see above, topic 15-D). He is not subject to the law of God, and neither indeed can be (Jer. 13:23; Rom. 8:17). The ultimate demonstration of man's depravity, however, consists of that concluding rebellion against the Lord, which takes place, even after they have visibly experienced the presence of God in Christ, the Messiah, subsequent to His return in glory to this earth. Every knee may then indeed bow, but the natural heart is unyielded still. Micah 4, for instance, describes how the word of Yahweh will some day go forth from Jerusalem (v. 2), how God will terminate the study of war (v. 3), and how men in general will thus live in peace and plenty (v. 4). Yet Micah's paragraph concludes, resignedly, "All the peoples will walk every one in the name of his god, but we will walk in the name of Yahweh our God for ever and ever" (v. 5). For God's way is not permanently to force any man to remain in His kingdom.

The means by which God will provide living men with the opportunity for deciding in which way to cast their final lot are described in Isaiah 24:22. The preceding verse had depicted God's removal of Satan and of his demonic hosts from the earth during the time of His future kingdom.[38] The passage then goes on to say: "And they shall be gathered together, as prisoners are gathered in the pit, and shall be shut up in the prison; and after many days shall they be visited" (cf. Rev. 20: 2, 3). The Old Testament does not at this point describe

---

[38]See above, p. 291.

the nature of that divine visitation; but it seems impossible to avoid recalling the analogy of the New Testament, which states:

"And when the thousand years are finished, Satan shall be loosed out of his prison, and shall come forth to deceive the nations which are in the four corners of the earth, Gog and Magog, to gather them together to the war" (Rev. 20:7, 8).

The apocalyptic figures of Gog and his land of Magog (a region north of Assyria?), form the subject matter of Ezekiel 38-39. The evil prince Gog is there foretold as gathering a confederacy to attack the peacefully restored city of Jerusalem; and, human nature being as it is, "many people, hordes" flock to his standard (38:9). Pride, in other words, leads men to choose self-determination in hell, rather than submission to Christ in the kingdom of God! But this final human attempt at self-expression, which is actually Satan-expression, is already doomed by the prophetic Word. Gog is predicted as having to face civil revolt among his followers (for sin is self-destructive, v. 21); Jerusalem "shall not be plucked up, nor thrown down any more for ever" (Jer. 31:40); and the Lord "will send a fire on Magog, and on them that dwell securely in the isles; and they shall know that I am Yahweh" (Ezek. 39:6; cf. Rev. 20:9).

In connection with the overthrow of Gog and Magog, we come to the termination of earthly history and to the final destruction of this planet; for, "All that are upon the face of the earth shall shake at My presence, and the mountains shall be thrown down, and the steep places shall fall, and every wall shall fall to the ground" (Ezek. 38:20; cf. Rev. 20:11). In primeval days, near the beginnings of human history, God had stated to Noah, "Neither shall all flesh be cut off any more *by the waters of the flood*" (Gen. 9:11). This declaration had indeed ruled out any repetition of the watery deluge; but it had left open the possibility of earth's future destruction through some other medium (cf. II Peter 3:5, 6).[39] Detailed accounts of the end of the world were then first revealed through the eighth century prophets. God, for example, spoke through Isaiah: "I will make the heavens to tremble, and the earth shall be shaken out of its place, in the wrath of Yahweh of hosts, in the day of His fierce anger" (Isa. 13:13). So also Zephaniah, in the next period, spoke of God's utterly consuming men and all things off the face of the earth. In this way, then, the final vindication of God's moral nature would be accomplished, by the removal of all wickedness from His creation (Zeph. 1:2, 3). As the Lord added through Haggai, "Yet once, it is a little while, and I will shake the heavens, and the earth, and the sea, and the dry land" (Hag. 2:6; cf. v. 21; Heb. 12:26).

Yet for unregenerate man, these natural phenomena constitute

---

[39]Cf. Vos, *op. cit.*, p. 63.

but the beginning of sorrows, for they serve to introduce God's final judgment. For example, following Isaiah's description of a universal destruction (Isa. 25:7), he revealed to his eighth century audience, "He hath swallowed up death for ever" (v. 8); for at this time the rest of the dead, who have not been raised with the blessed elect at Christ's coming, will still join in a final resurrection (Dan. 12:2). But for this later group[40] the resurrection can only be one "to shame and everlasting contempt," as divine retribution is finally meted out. The Spirit of inspiration had first revealed through Moses that God possesses a "book," in which are written the names of those who are to receive the inheritance of the testament (Ex. 32:32). David further identified this volume as the "book of life," in which the wicked are "not written with the righteous" (Ps. 69:28). The final judgment therefore, involves first of all, a separation of the saved from the lost, of "the sheep from the goats" (Matt. 25:33). As David described the condemnation of the latter, "Therefore the wicked shall not stand in the judgment" (Ps. 1:5). The Psalms had long foretold: "He will judge the world with righteousness, and the peoples with equity" (98:9; cf. 96:13). But it is this very fact of justice that makes faith in Christ and in His gracious salvation so ultimately crucial. For equity saves no man (cf. Job 11:6); only mercy and grace can open the way to heaven (Ps. 51:1).

A second major element involved in the Lord's final judgment was revealed in the next period, when Solomon warned his people, "God will bring every work into judgment, with every hidden thing, whether it be good or whether it be evil" (Eccl. 12:14; cf. 11:9). What he was saying is this: that within the categories, both of the saved and of the lost, God will then measure out rewards or punishments according to every man's desert, though in reference to the lost there can, of course, be no possibility of a positive reward. Job, on the other hand, had affirmed, "As for me I know that my *Gō'ēl* ['Vindicator'] liveth . . . whom I shall see on my side" (Job 19:25, 27). But he had then warned his friends, "If ye say, How we will persecute him! be ye afraid of the sword: for wrath bringeth the punishments of the sword, that ye may know there is a judgment" (vv. 28, 29).

The inspired prophets then further developed the theme of God's final judgment book, identifying the saved by expressions such as: "written among the living" (Isa. 4:3; eighth century) or, "written in the writing of the house of Israel" (Ezek. 13:9, exilic). Thus to Daniel God stated, "Thy people shall be delivered, every one that shall be found written in the book" (Dan. 12:1). Daniel, however, in this last passage, indicates two additional matters of eschatological significance. 1) The judgment that distinguishes the saved from the lost

---

[40]See above, p. 462.

(Dan. 12:2) and the judgment that assigns the different rewards for the saved (v. 3) seem to be united in a single great assize, in one final judgment that climaxes all of human history.[41] This same thought had been implicit in the wording of Psalm 1:5, with its suggestion that at the same time when the wicked shall be unable to maintain their stand in the final judgment, the righteous shall stand up through it. 2) The rewards granted by God to the saved are then based in particular upon the uprightness of character of each believer and upon his activity in personal soul-winning; for, "They that are wise shall shine as the brightness of the firmament; and they that turn many to righteousness as the stars for ever and ever" (v. 3). The final judgment may thus be summarized as follows: The one condition for receiving the testamental inheritance is a man's faith in God's plan of salvation. The sincerity of one's faith is then demonstrated by his obedience. Gratitude for justification should therefore produce in God's own people, first, a conformity to the character of the Savior and second, a telling of others about Him; and each man's reward will be determined accordingly.

D. THE DAY OF YAHWEH, AS FINAL RESTORATION. The testament of peace, however, remains essentially unaffected, even by the great transition drama of the final judgment and its related events: "For the mountains may depart, and the hills be removed; but My *hésedh* [faithfulness to the testament] shall not depart from thee, neither shall My testament of peace be removed" (Isa. 54:10). The final judgment does, however, affect in two primary ways that final state of restoration into which the earlier millennial stage will eventuate. First, the intervening assize does serve to remove the non-elect from further participation in God's future kingdom. David had stated that as a result of the judgment the way of the ungodly should perish (Ps. 1:6; cf. Mal. 4:1, "burned"). This assertion, however, does not thereby teach the annihilation of the ungodly themselves. On the contrary, the bodies of them that slept in the dust are seen to have awakened and to have come forth in the final resurrection: Their judgment, moreover, involved not only shame but also a suffering of contempt that is characterized as endless (Dan. 12:2; exilic). Isaiah thus paints a fearsome picture of the living death of those who reject the grace of the testament: "For their worm shall not die, neither shall their fire be quenched; and they shall be an abhorring unto all flesh"

---

[41]There appears to be little Biblical basis for the distinction made by dispensationalist interpreters, who treat "the judgment seat of Christ" (II Cor. 5:10) as a separate act of judgment in reference to the saved at the start of the millennium, as distinguished from the later "great white throne judgment" (Rev. 20:11), in which the saint is asserted to have no part. Cf. in this regard the presence of the saved and the lost, both of them together, in the final judgment as described in Matt. 25:31-46 and in Rev. 20:12-15.

(Isa. 66:24; eighth century). The eternity to which the Christless are doomed consists of the indescribable fire of "gehenna"[42] (cf. Mal. 4:3).

But this very judgment of removal produces, in the second place, that purified situation by which God's final restoration is specifically distinguished:

"For, behold, I create new heavens and a new earth; and the former things shall not be remembered nor come into mind. Be ye glad and rejoice for ever in that which I create; for, behold, I create Jerusalem a rejoicing, and her people a joy" (Isa. 65:17, 18; cf. 66:22).

The point is this: that by His having shaken the heavens and the earth (Hag. 2:6), God thereby removed from history all that was wicked (Zeph. 1:3). The positive side of this discriminatory judgment, however, was "that those things which are not shaken may remain" (Heb. 12:27). For Scripture reveals that there will yet exist a basic continuation of heaven, and of earth, and even of Jerusalem. As a result, the characteristics of the future earthly restoration (as listed above, section B) are found to possess an eternal validity, so that they are carried over bodily into the Bible's description of the new, final earth. The fact is that it is well nigh impossible in the contexts of the Old Testament to distinguish the two, except at those points where the New Testament analogy of Revelation 21-22 makes it possible to discern certain features, as pertaining in particular to the final state of restoration. The only exception to this carry-over is that such of the aspects of the first stage of the eternal kingdom as may have been due to the presence of the unregenerate will, per force, reach their termination. After the final resurrection, for example, there will be no more death; "and the Lord Yahweh will wipe away tears from off all faces" (Isa. 25:8).

The fundamental feature of the final restoration lies then in the unique presence of God with His own. For it is the unqualified acceptance of men into God's fellowship that constitutes the ultimate accomplishment of the testamental reconciliation. Scripture therefore, describes this climactic day of Yahweh in glorious passages of restored personal harmony such as the following: "They shall be Mine own possession [Authorized Version: 'when I make up My jewels']" (Mal. 3:17):

"The sun shall be no more thy light by day: but Yahweh will be unto thee an everlasting light, and thy God thy glory. Thy sun shall no more go down, and the days of thy mourning shall be ended" (Isa. 60:19, 20; cf. 24:23).

"Unto you that fear My name shall the sun of righteousness [=salvation; see above, topic 12-C] arise with healing in its

---

[42]See above, p. 461.

wings; and ye shall go forth, and gambol as calves of the stall" (Mal. 4:2).

Such a situation, with God present and with evil absent, exhibits then a number of parallels to that which was found in Eden prior to man's fall; and this correspondence serves, in turn, to explain why "the prophet describes the future state as the restored paradise of the days of creation."[43] The following features, for example, suggest something of the degree of this parallelism.

The New Jerusalem:	Primeval Eden:
Precious stones (Isa. 54:12) and the precious things of all nations (Hag. 2:7; Rev. 21:24, 26)	cf. Gen. 2:11, 12
Weekly sabbath observance and new moons (Isa. 66:23)	cf. Gen. 2:3
Great peace [shālōm, "integration"] (Isa. 54:13)	cf. Gen. 1:31
Universal teaching by Yahweh (Isa. 54:13)	cf. Gen. 1:28-30

But in each such instance, the quality of the new earth stands forth as superior to that of the primeval. For in the course of history that has intervened, Jesus Christ, as the last Adam, has fully executed God's requirements under the covenant of works, an accomplishment which for the first Adam had never existed as more than a potentiality.[44] Then, by His testament of grace Christ has proceeded to bequeath this inheritance to His elect people. In their final restoration, accordingly, which is the new earth, the complete goal of the testament is at last attained. Such a reconciliation, the God of history had indeed long before typified in the sanctuary of His ancient people. It was therefore with an inspired appreciation for the theology of the older testament that the apostle John terminated the first half of his book of Revelation by referring back to the central object of Israel's sanctuary on Mount Zion. For, at the close of this comprehensive sweep of redemptive history, he depicts the essence of the post-judgment eternity in these words: "And there was opened the temple of God that is in heaven; and there was seen in His temple the ark of His testament" (Rev. 11:19).

For Further Reading:

A. B. Davidson, *Old Testament Prophecy*. Edinburgh: Charles Scribner's Sons, 1904. A comprehensive study of the subject, amillennial in its final conclusions respecting the earthly kingdom.

D. H. Kromminga, *The Millennium: Its Nature, Function, and Relation to the Consummation of the World*. Grand Rapids: Eerdmans Publishing Co., 1948. A study in the Reformed tradition, describing the philosophy of premillennialism, and advocating it.

Charles Lee Feinberg, *Premillennialism or Amillennialism?* 2nd ed.; Wheaton, Ill.: Van Kampen Press, 1954. A polemic work which equates premillennialism with Darbyite dispensationalism.

---

[43]Vos, *op. cit.*, p. 316. Cf. Jacob, *Theology of the Old Testament*, p. 325.
[44]In the long run, redemption from sin serves a grander purpose, as Knight points out, than if the world had remained good, *op. cit.*, p. 199.

APPENDIX

Appendix A. Basis for Belief in Inspiration

The foregoing study on the doctrine of inspiration (see above, Topic 4 pp. 63-70) has surveyed the teaching that the Old Testament presents in respect to sacred books, namely, in respect to its own contents. The question, however, still arises for modern man, "Should I believe the claims that the Bible makes for itself?" On the one hand, the advantages of holding to this high Scriptural view of verbal, plenary inspiration are obvious.

A. *Historically,* it places one in harmony with the position that has been held by the Church down through the ages (see Sec. III in outline that follows).

B. *Philosophically,* the belief in inspiration provides a man with even greater advantages. 1) It furnishes him with certainty. The Bible gives him final, absolute answers for most of the questions of theology[1] and even for certain questions (including some of the most fundamental) of science and history, wherever it happens to speak. 2) Such a belief is marked also by consistency with the teachings of Scripture itself. This quality contrasts sharply with the arbitrariness of neo-orthodoxy, which often finds that its negatively critical views are in conflict with the very Biblical authority that it claims to honor.[2] As Edward J. Young has summarized the logic of evangelicalism, "We hold to a high view of inspiration for the simple reason that the Bible teaches a high view."[3] The modern religious mood may indeed seek to find value in the Bible; but, as Young goes on to ask, "If it is not to be depended on when it speaks of itself, how do we know that it is to be trusted when it speaks about anything else?"[4] Only a position of thorough-going belief in Scripture can meet the test of plausibility in the light of Scripture. 3) The high view of inspiration is alone fully congruous with a high view of God and of the supernatural. The idea of the miraculously inerrant Book corresponds not only to the Biblical picture of the infallible God who directs history, but also to the consciously supernaturalistic type of religion that is needed by modern man, who would otherwise be faced

---

[1]The writer is very much aware of the advantage that this has given in the preceding studies, for when the Bible speaks, the question is settled. Contrast the frustrations that are involved in the necessary tentativeness of liberalism's conclusions; cf. Burrows' frank admission of his own lack of authority, *An Outline of Biblical Theology* (Philadelphia: The Westminster Press, c. 1946), pp. 41-42, 50.
[2]Note Burrows' further admission, p. 49, of the necessity he faces of continually having to "pick and choose" in the Bible.
[3]*Thy Word Is Truth* (Grand Rapids: 1, 1957), p. 31.
[4]*Ibid.,* p. 29.

with the despair of inevitable death and oblivion, by all the standards of nature.[5]

C. *Practically*, when a man holds to plenary inspiration, this very commitment gives him an assurance and a power, both in his personal devotions and in the public ministry, that neo-orthodoxy, all its protestations to the contrary, notwithstanding, has yet been unable to achieve. A funeral sermon, for example, by a preacher who questions the Bible is a sorry spectacle indeed.

But on the other hand, the disadvantages that are involved in holding to a high view of verbal inspiration must not be underestimated, at least as these are seen from unregenerate eyes.

A. Contemporaneously, it places the believer in opposition to the dominant church organizations and schools of thought, as these are found in modern Christendom. Because of loyalty to the Word of Christ, He will have to "go forth therefore unto Him without the camp, bearing His reproach" (Heb. 13:13). He must, in other words, endure the social and intellectual stigma of identification as a "fundamentalist."

B. Philosophically, moreover, adherence to plenary inspiration demands that the believer yield up his own independent authority in the same three areas that have just been noted. 1) The fact of Biblical certainty condemns all temptations to rationalistic skepticism, for it disallows the legitimacy of doubting God's Word. A man must be willing to humble himself and to hold his own judgments in abeyance, maintaining the truth of the propositions of the Bible, even though he may not have answers for all of the so-called difficulties (see below, sec. IV-A). 2) The standard of consistency with Scripture requires that a man commit himself to the doctrinal and moral positions of the Bible, even though he finds them personally disadvantageous or expressly contrary to his own pattern of life. 3) The attainment of the objectively supernatural involves the rejection of fallen mankind's inevitable longing to deify himself. When the Bible comes, pride must go. As a result, until God's Holy Spirit regenerates a man's heart, he simply will not, he indeed cannot, submit to God's revealed truth (Rom. 8:7). He would rather be an autonomous outcast in hell than a subservient son in heaven. The fundamental basis for believing in inspiration consists therefore of conviction by the Lord Himself.[6] Thus, even as a man comes initially to believe on Christ because the Spirit has touched his heart (Acts 11:18; Romans 9:16), so he comes subsequently to accept the Bible as the criterion for all truth (I John 2:20, 27) because of the Spirit's anointing that abideth in him. The validity of God's Word lies beyond man's ability to demonstrate (Isa. 55:9); it is the Spirit of Christ who must teach (I Cor. 2:13).[7]

---

[5]Liberals do well to ponder the inexorable logic, for all but Bible-believing evangelicals, of Corless Lamont's, *The Illusion of Immortality* (New York: 1936).

[6]Cf. Westminster Confession of Faith, I, I.

[7]Cf. Young's conclusion, *op. cit.*, p. 34, "The Christian is persuaded and assured of both the infallible truth and the divine authority of the Bible by the inward work of the Spirit within his heart."

When we inquire then as to the method by which the Holy Spirit teaches Christians that the Bible is in fact God's words, we find that He does not do so through direct, rational proofs. Even as liberalism's attacks upon Scripture through this means may be dismissed as incompatible with the nature of the subject (see Sec. IV-A-1-b), so it is not God's way to appeal to the believer by this method either (I Cor. 1:19; 2:1). In making such an assertion, we do not deny that the Bible contains within itself what Young called "the marks of divinity which God has placed therein."[8] When Scripture, for example, is compared with the polytheism and mythology that dominated the best of human thought at the time of the Old Testament's appearance, the Bible is seen to belong in a class by itself. Furthermore, the errors that were once alleged to exist in Scripture have demonstrated a remarkable tendency to eliminate themselves with the increase of scholarly knowledge! Archaeology, history, and the fact of fulfilled prophecies have generally served to vindicate the Bible as historically accurate, and liberalism has been forced to retreat, time after time.[9] In theory, indeed, all men ought to recognize these "marks of divinity." But in practice, as Young has stated,

> "Despite their clarity, not all men are willing to accept these evidences . . . The reason, however, why men do not perceive the force of these evidences is that their understanding has been darkened by sin."[10]

Moreover, regenerate Christians in this sin-blighted world must admit that they too do not always and at all points apprehend the Bible as indelibly stamped by divine authorship. Finally, even the quality of apprehensible accuracy does not necessarily prove the Bible's inspiration. One apparent discrepancy can actually outweigh the apologetic value of ninety-nine confirmations. We thus conclude that if a man depends upon human proofs for his belief in Biblical inerrancy, his foundation is most insecure. For when he meets problems that he cannot explain — and this is bound to occur — then either (a) he will be forced to abandon his faith;[11] or (b) he will become a hypocrite, defending a position the objections against which he knows he cannot adequately answer.

The real method by which the Spirit builds faith in Scripture must instead be one that is essentially authoritarian, through the testimony of One who possesses the requisite supernatural insight. Specifically, it is only God the Son, Jesus Christ, who is in the position to validate for us what constitutes the true teachings of God (John 1:18).[12] Our belief in inspiration may thus be outlined as follows:

---

[8]*Ibid.*, p. 33.
[9]Cf. Payne, "The Uneasy Conscience of Modern Liberal Exegesis," *Bulletin of the Evangelical Theological Society*, I:1 (Winter, 1958), pp. 14-18.
[10]Young, *op. cit.*, pp. 33-34.
[11]Cf. Burrows' charge, *op. cit.*, p. 44.
[12]This is confirmed experientially: men become Bible-believers because they are Christians, seldom vice versa. Cf. Laird Harris' conclusion, *Inspiration and Canonicity of the Bible* (Grand Rapids: Zondervan Publishing House, 1957), that the basis for belief is found "simply in the teaching of the Lord Jesus Christ," p. 45.

I. THE BASIS OF FAITH

A. The foundation of all our faith is our personal knowledge of the divine and living person of Christ (I Cor. 3:11; I Pet. 2:6; Isa. 28:16).

B. Such knowledge comes on the one hand from the historical fact of His resurrection (Rom. 1:4) and on the other hand from our experience of salvation (II Tim. 1:12). This latter is dependent upon the former (John 16:9-11; I Cor. 15:14). Subjectivism alone would be without content or certainty; objectivism alone would be without living faith.

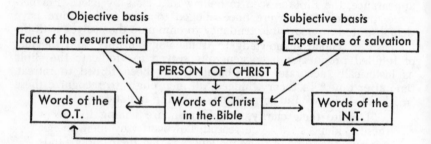

C. The absolute authority of the person of Christ takes shape in the words He spoke (Matt. 24:35; Mark 13:31; Luke 21:33), the reception of which is the great mark of discipleship (John 15:7). That His words as recorded in the original Biblical documents should correspond to His actual words was the promise of Christ (John 14:26; 16:13), and His statements which concern the verbal authority of the O.T. may be traced to the earliest sources underlying the Gospels.[13] Then textual criticism has made the reconstruction of the original documents almost certain.

Seen negatively, since the Biblical words constitute practically the only objective evidence to Christ, to pick and choose among them, to believe some and disbelieve others, amounts to "making Christ in our own image." In effect, to reconstruct "the historical Jesus" on our subjective standard is to lapse into idolatry.

D. Once the Biblical Christ be accepted as normative there must follow the plenary acceptance of the words of Scripture.
1. His specific statements:
   a. Matt. 5:18: "One jot or one tittle shall in no wise pass away from the law, till all things be accomplished." A liberal critic concedes, "Commentators have exhausted their ingenuity in attempting to explain away this passage, but its meaning is too clear to be misunderstood. Christ is here represented as speaking in the spirit of Alexandrine and

---

[13]B. B. Warfield, *The Inspiration and Authority of the Bible* (Philadelphia: The Presbyterian and Reformed Publishing Co., 1948), p. 144; and cf. Harris, *op. cit.*, p. 47 and note 2.

Rabinnical Judaism,"[14] that is, accepting Scripture absolutely.

b. Luke 16:16, 17: "The law and the prophets were until John: since that time the gospel of the kingdom of God is preached . . . but it is easier for heaven and earth to pass away, than for one tittle of the law to fall."

c. Luke 18:31: "All the things that are written through the prophets shall be accomplished unto the Son of man."

d. Luke 24:25: He condemned those who refused to believe *all* that the prophets had spoken.

e. Luke 24:44: "All things must needs be fulfilled, which are written in the law of Moses, and the prophets, and the psalms, concerning Me."

f. John 10:35: "And the Scripture cannot be broken." Liberalism can only admit, "Verbal inspiration of the sacred books was taught by the Rabbinical schools . . . the belief emerges distinctively in the Fourth Gospel, the evangelist ascribing this conviction to Jesus Himself. We may recall here some Synoptic passages which show that the belief that 'the Scripture cannot be broken' was shared by Matthew, Mark and Luke and that all three speak of it as having the authority of their Master."[15]

2. His attitude: (Note: The neo-orthodox have attempted to escape the force of Christ's specific statements with ingenious interpretations, but the following indirect evidence is conclusive as to the mind of Christ on inspiration.)

a. Matt. 4:4: "It is written (in Scripture)" terminated the temptations; Mark 9:12, it answered questions.

b. Matt. 4:14; 21:5; 26:31 (Mark 14:27); 26:54; Mark 14:49; Luke 22:37; John 12:14; 13:18; 17:12; 19:28; and 19:37: Specific instances in His life were to fulfill detailed verses, as well as His ministry to fulfill the whole O.T. (Luke 4:21; 24:27; and John 5:39).

c. Matt. 19:5, 6: For Him, Genesis 2:24 settled the divorce question.

d. Matt. 21:42 (Mark 12:10): He justified His own teaching on the basis of the O.T., "Have ye not read . . ." (Luke 4:21; Matt. 21:16).

e. Luke 16:31: He equated the authority of Moses and the prophets with that of one raised by God from the dead.

f. In His teaching, Christ authenticated O.T. historical statements about Adam, Abel, Noah, Moses, Elijah, Elisha, Jonah, Daniel.[16]

---

[14]W. C. Allen, *A Critical and Exegetical Commentary on the Gospel According to St. Matthew* (New York: Charles Scribner's Sons, 1907), p. 45.
[15]J. H. Bernard, *A Critical and Exegetical Commentary on the Gospel According to St. John* (New York: Charles Scribner's Sons, 1929), I:clii.
[16]Cf. Robert Dick Wilson, "Jesus and the Old Testament," *Princeton Theological Review*, 24:4 (Oct., 1926), 632-661.

    g. He accepted the statements of Scripture about its own human authorship, and at points that are most under attack today, for example: "The belief in the Davidic authorship of the Psalms, accepted by Jesus (Mark 12:36 ff.), shown by modern scholarship to be erroneous, and the Mosaic authorship of the Pentateuch (Mark 10:3; 12:26)."[17]

3. His use of Scripture:

    a. Matt. 22:32: He bases His proof of immortality on, not even a word, but simply the rules of Hebrew syntax which make, "I (am) the God of Abraham" a present tense. Cf. Mark 12:26; Luke 20:37 (see Ex. 3:6).

    b. Matt. 22:44: His argument turns on the 1st person singular suffix in "My Lord," in Hebrew one letter, the yodh, which is the smallest. Cf. Mark 12:36; Luke 20:42 (see Ps. 110:1).

    c. John 10:34: The force of the passage depends on the meaning of one Hebrew word (Ps. 82:6).

    d. These were not "ad hominem" arguments (meeting a man on his own suppositions); the parenthesis of John 10:35 is representative of His repeated statements, not an isolated argument.

    e. Liberalism admits, "When deductions have been made . . . there still remains evidence enough that our Lord while on earth did use the common language of His contemporaries in regard to the O.T."[18]

    f. Christ's doctrine of inspiration was verbal.

E. The New Testament claimed to be on the level of authority of the O.T. (II Peter 3:16).[19] Christ had promised the disciples the Spirit to guide them into all the truth (John 16:12, 13; Matt. 10:20; Mark 13:11; Luke 12:12); and the commandments of the Lord did come through the apostles (II Peter 3:2). Hence comes this further testimony:

1. Specific statements.

    a. About the N.T. itself:

        (1) I Cor. 14:37: "The things which I write unto you are the commandment of the Lord" (cf. I Cor. 2:4, 13).

        (2) II Cor. 13:3: "Christ speaketh in me."

        (3) I Thess. 2:13: "Not the word of men, but as it is in truth the word of God."

        (4) Rev. 22:18, 19: No *words* are to be changed.

---

[17]H. A. Guy, *The New Testament Doctrine of the Last Things* (London: 1948), p. 84.
[18]William Sanday, *Inspiration* (London: 1893), p. 393 ff. Some have indeed attempted to stigmatize the doctrine of Biblical infallibility as "sub-Christian," as Aaron Ungersma, *Handbook for Christian Believers* (Indianapolis: c. 1953), pp. 80-81; but such efforts stand self-condemned.
[19]For the Old Testament's testimony to its own inspiration, see above, topic 4. William Evans, *The Great Doctrines of the Bible* (Chicago: c. 1939), p. 203, has remarked that "The Lord said" or its equivalent appears 3,808 times in the Old Testament.

b. About the O.T.:
    (1) Rom. 3:2: To the Jews were intrusted the oracles of of God.
    (2) II Tim. 3:16: "All (plenary) Scripture (*hē graphē*) = O.T.),[20] is given by inspiration of God."
    (3) II Pet. 1:21: "No prophecy ever came by the will of man," (RV).

2. Use of Scripture. In general, "The historical setting of the O.T. is everywhere accepted as authentic."[21]
    a. Rom. 9:15-17; Gal. 3:8: "The Scripture saith" equals "God saith."
    b. Rom. 3:10: Paul's point depends on the absolute exclusion involved in the word "none" (Ps. 14:1).
    c. Rom. 10:13: And here on "whosoever" (Joel 2:32) being taken literally.
    d. Gal. 3:16: The singular form of the word "seed" (Gen. 13:15; 17:8; 22:18) is the basis of the argument.
    e. Heb. 12:5: Here the problem of sonship develops wholly from the one Hebrew word, "my son" (Prov. 3:11 ff.).
    f. Heb. 12:26: Christian eschatology is built upon the implications of the phrase, "yet once more" (Hag. 2:6).
    g. And so through the book of Hebrews,[22] "The written word was itself treated as the inspired and authoritative form in which the content of divine revelation had been expressed and handed down."[23]

F. The objective and subjective bases of faith further substantiate the words of Scripture, for increased knowledge has verified many Biblical statements (Isa. 48:3-8; I Cor. 15:4), and only from Scripture does the experience of salvation arise (John 15:3; Rom. 10:17).

    Our basis of faith is thus well summed up in Eph. 2:20, "Built upon the foundation of the apostles and prophets, Jesus Christ Himself being the chief corner stone."

II. THE NATURE OF INSPIRATION BY SCRIPTURAL TESTIMONY

A. Scripture is God-breathed, II Tim. 3:16, "all" Scripture (cf. Acts 24:14) requiring inspiration, plenary in extent and verbal so far as concerns God's guaranteeing the words: "If there is inspiration at all, it must penetrate words as well as thought, must mold the

---

[20]Joseph H. Thayer, *A Greek-English Lexicon of the New Testament* (Corrected edition; New York: American Book Co., c. 1889), p. 121.
[21]Francis Davidson, editor, *The New Bible Commentary* (Grand Rapids: 1, 1953), p. 16.
[22]L. Gaussen, *Theopneustia, the Plenary Inspiration of the Holy Scriptures* (Chicago: The Bible Institute Colportage Ass'n., [n.d.]), pp. 90-91.
[23]Davidson, *loc. cit.*

expression, and make the language employed the living medium of the idea to be conveyed."[24]

1. Inspiration is of divine, as opposed to human, source.
    a. Mark 7:13: The word of God (Ex. 20:12) is contrasted with human traditions.
    b. Num. 22:35; II Pet. 1:20, 21: The men spoke only as moved by the Holy Spirit, not on individual impulse, no extraneous matter being added. The Bible does not simply *contain* the word of God; it *is* the word of God.
    c. Acts 7:53; Gal. 3:19; Heb. 2:2: The O.T. was also received via angels.
2. But there is a human instrumentality.
    a. I Pet. 1:11; Acts 28:25: The Spirit of Christ testified in the hearts of the prophets and (Acts 1:16) of David.
    b. Ex. 34:27: This guidance was occasionally pure dictation.
    c. Acts 1:1: Normally, the author, while insured against error, had literary freedom.

"Inspiration is that extraordinary, supernatural influence (or, passively, the result of it) exerted by the Holy Ghost on the writers of our Sacred Books, by which their words were rendered also the words of God, and, therefore, perfectly infallible."[25] "It is the strong, conscious inbreathing of God into men, qualifying them to give utterance to the truth. It is God speaking through men, and the Old Testament is therefore just as much the Word of God as though God spoke every single word of it with His own lips."[26]

B. Inspiration compared with related but not identical matters, with which it is often confused.
    1. The relationship of revelation to inspiration.
        a. The content of some parts of the Bible could have come only by direct revelation (Gen. 1).
        b. Other sections apparently arose from observation or secondary sources, but not direct revelation (II Sam. 1:17; Acts 27), though the whole Bible, as approved by God, is necessarily revelation.
            Revelation makes truth known; inspiration guarantees and preserves truth.
    2. The relationship of the writers' illumination to inspiration.
        a. The words of the Biblical writers were often the result of careful investigation by human methods (Luke 1:1-4), understood but not recognized by them as divine.

---

[24]James Orr, *Revelation and Inspiration* (New York: Charles Scribner's Sons, 1910), p. 209. This is not to deny that words are but symbols of thoughts, and imperfect ones at that. The words of the human, secondary authors of Scripture were incapable of conveying all the infinite treasures of the mind of God. But it must be insisted that such limited truths as the words do convey are infallibly true; God's Holy Spirit so superintended the choice of words, even if from primarily a negative standpoint, that no false symbol of His truth was allowed to remain.

[25]Warfield, *op. cit.*, p. 420.

[26]Evans, *op. cit.*, pp. 194-195.

    b. The men both understood and were conscious frequently of their divinely inspired words (I Thess. 2:13), recognizing them as coming from God's wisdom, not man's (I Cor. 2:13).

    c. Sometimes the men did not know the import of their own words (Dan. 12:8; I Pet. 1:11), recognizing them as divine but not understanding them.

    d. Occasionally the human source of inspired words neither understood them nor recognized them as divine (John 11: 49-52; Ps. 69:21 [?]).

      Yet all four of the above are by inspiration. It is the words and not primarily the men that are inspired. Further, men have degrees of illumination; the Bible words do not have "degrees" of inspired truthfulness.

3. The relationship of the readers' feelings to inspiration.

    a. Scripture has various purposes (II Tim. 3:16), not all its truth being inspirational.

    b. It need not be inspiring to be inspired.

4. The relationship of the readers' activity to inspiration.

    a. Scripture may non-committally quote exhortations to evil (Job 1:9), human misstatements (John 1:21; cf. Matt. 11: 14; 17:12, 13); or laws since abrogated (Col. 2:16, 17).

    b. Only accuracy against misrepresentation is to be maintained.

    c. Statements by the human authors of Scripture in their writings are, however, divinely normative, not opinions (e.g., O.T. prophets and psalmists).

III. THE CHURCH'S HISTORIC ACCEPTANCE OF SCRIPTURE

A. The church in the past.[27]

1. The early fathers held verbal inspiration from the first, often even mechanical dictation.

    Irenaeus, "The Scriptures are perfect, seeing that they are spoken by God's Word and His Spirit." *Against Heresies*. Augustine, "I firmly believe that no one of their authors has erred in anything in writing." *Epistulae* (ad Hier.) lxxxii 1, 3.

2. The reformers.

    Luther adopted the above of Augustine, adding that since the whole of Scriptures are to be assigned to the Holy Spirit, they cannot err. *Works* (St. Louis ed.) xix, 305.

    Calvin, "For our wisdom ought to consist in embracing with gentle docility, and without any exception, all that is delivered in the sacred Scriptures. *Institutes*, I, 18, 4.

B. Credal testimonies.

1. Lutheran, We must not "hold anything contrary to the Canonical Scriptures of God." (Augsburg Confession, XXVIII)

---

[27]See also, Evangelical Theological Society, John F. Walvoord, editor, *Inspiration and Interpretation* (Grand Rapids: Wm. B. Eerdmans Publishing Co., 1957), chapters I-V; and Warfield, *op. cit.*, pp. 106-109.

2. Reformed, "The Old and New Testaments . . . against which nothing can be alleged . . . We receive all these books . . . believing without any doubt all things contained in them." (Dort, IV-V)

3. Presbyterian, "A Christian believeth to be true whatever is revealed in the Word, for the authority of God Himself speaketh therein." (Westminster Conf., XIV:2) The same is Congregational (Savoy Declaration) and S. Baptist (Philadelphia Conf.)

4. Episcopalian, "It is not lawful for the Church to ordain anything that is contrary to God's Word written." (39 Articles, XX)

5. Methodist, Let "nothing be ordained against God's Word." (Articles of Relig., XXII; equals 39 Articles, XXXIV)

6. Baptist, N., "We believe that the Holy Bible . . . has God for its author, salvation for its end, and truth without any mixture of error for its matter." (New Hampshire Conf., I)

C. The modern Church, often apostate, yet:

1. Belief in plenary inspiration is still justified by the results:

   a. Men with the greatest evangelistic ministry, as Charles Fuller and Billy Graham, accept the Bible as verbally inspired and so use it.

   b. Foreign missionaries generally must, because of their work, give Scripture the highest position.

   c. America's most powerful youth leaders, as Jack Wyrtzen and Bob Cook, are characterized by unwavering loyalty to the inspired Word.

2. Complete infilling by the Holy Spirit depends upon it.

   a. Rom. 8:13; 12:1, 2: Consecration is a matter of surrender and yielding to the Spirit in order to be filled and used.

   b. Phil. 2:5: At the very foundation lies mental yielding to Christ, the mind of whom, on Scripture, is clear; this will ultimately determine all else: "As a man thinketh in his heart, so is he" (Prov. 23:7).

IV. MODERN ATTACKS AGAINST SCRIPTURE

A. Man's resistance to plenary inspiration.

1. Cautioning principles:

   a. Anti-supernaturalism must disprove inspiration if it is to exist, and therefore it cannot be open-minded. Historically, criticism has varied inversely with the personal faith of the critic.

   b. To say, "Let the Bible speak for itself; natural, scientific investigation will only vindicate its truth" is false. The scientific method applies only to the subjects a man is capable of analyzing, but God and eternity are outside man's range of experience. A man who insists on acting as an "impartial" judge of Scripture has already assumed his own ability

to judge it and therefore denied in advance the possibility
of a divinely given book.
   (1) The "natural," human mind is biased by sin from what
       it would otherwise understand; Satan blinds (II Cor.
       4:3, 4; Eph. 4:17, 18).
   (2) Even if this were not so, God's Word could not be
       made subject to human standards.
   (3) On the contrary, the proof of a book's being from God
       is the statement of God Himself. The man who would
       know must therefore first yield his thought to Christ's
       direction (John 1:18).
   (4) Then divine work must be Spiritually discerned (I
       Cor. 2:14).
       Only a spirit-filled Christian can be a true scholar
       of the Word.
2. Objections on the grounds of internal evidence:
   a. Historico-critical studies are legitimate and desirable as long
      as they do not run counter to the claims of Scripture itself.
      (1) Consecrated study will only vindicate these claims.
      (2) To oppose the testimony of Scripture with one's own
          scientific insight is to replace God by non-authorita-
          tive human rationalism.
      (3) Always see what Scripture says first, e.g., how much
          of the Pentateuch it claims to have been written by
          Moses.
   b. For supposed contradictions in Scripture, the following prin-
      ciples should be kept in mind:
      (1) Variations of statement are not contradictions when
          they arise, either from recording different parts of some
          common event, or from assigning a different emphasis
          or importance to the same parts.
      (2) Separate transactions are not to be identified with each
          other because of a parallelism between some circum-
          stances of an event or some portions of a discourse.[28]
      (3) Discrepancies between quotations are not contradictions
          when fair translations of an original statement in an-
          other language.
3. Objections on the grounds of external evidence:
   a. Conflicts with science.
      (1) Most disappear if science be limited to its proven facts
          and Scripture be carefully exegeted.
      (2) But to say, "The Bible is not intended to be a textbook
          in science" is a dangerous half-truth. Its statements,
          though not detailed, are accurate and were accepted
          by Christ and the apostles.

---

[28]Francis Patton, *The Inspiration of the Scriptures* (Philadelphia: Presbyterian
Board of Publication, 1869), pp. 99-104.

b. Conflicts with history.
   (1) These are few and are being increasingly disproved. Wellhausen, for example, is outmoded.[29]
   (2) Archaeology is particularly significant. Millar Burrows has asserted (1941) that some evidence specifically contradicts Scripture,[30] but he admits his liberal bias[31] and his claims seem untrustworthy. Cf. George L. Robinson (1941), "No explicit contradiction of Scripture of any moment has ever been found."[32]

4. The Christian's attitude toward unresolved difficulties.
   a. We must not sidestep issues, but rather seek solutions.
   b. If in a problem we discover only weak answers, or no answer, we must be honest and admit the fact; or we lose the faith we seek to defend.
   c. But such cases constitute a small percentage as compared to the perfections of the Word. God has the solution; do not limit Him to our capacities.
      "It being a settled logical principle that so long as the proper evidence by which a proposition is established remains unrefuted, all so-called objections brought against it pass out of the category of objections to its truth into the category of difficulties to be adjusted to it."[33]

B. The alternative proposed by neo-orthodoxy, the only other presently serious contender for the Christian's allegiance.
   1. This new approach stresses revelation as an experience with Christ, Scripture being merely the channel through which God may encounter the individual today. As Karl Barth teaches, Scripture is not the word of God, but it may become the word of God at any time.[34]
      a. This emphasizes the needed truth that revelation must be received by the individual, applied to the heart by the Holy Spirit, before God's message has really "gotten through." For many, the Bible never does become God's Word to them.
      b. But neo-orthodoxy goes further and denies that revelation is a matter of propositional truths at all. God is felt to be so "wholly other" that He can never be an object for study, only a subject who confronts a man. Such an emphasis is one-sided: there must first be a word of God from Him, and then it must be received to become God's word to the

---

[29]Henry S. Gehman, reviser, *The Westminster Dictionary of the Bible* (Philadelphia: The Westminster Press, 1944), p. 469.
[30]*What Means These Stones?* (New Haven: American Schools of Oriental Research, 1941; copyright 1956 by Millar Burrows; Living Ace Books Edition published 1957 by Meridian Books), p. 276.
[31]*Ibid.*, p. xi.
[32]*The Bearing of Archaeology on the Old Testament* (New York: American Tract Society, c. 1941), p. 12.
[33]Warfield, *op. cit.*, p. 174.
[34]*The Doctrine of the Word of God* (New York: Philosophical Library, 1936), pp. 124-125.

individual. In theory, Barth's approach becomes agnosticism, the impossibility of knowing anything about God.

c. So in pracitce, neo-orthodoxy means partial inspiration, accepting those parts of Scripture through which God "speaks to me," namely, some (but not all) of the doctrinal teachings. As far as the truth of the facts recorded is concerned, the Bible is just another human book.

2. The great appeal of neo-orthodoxy, or any other view of partial inspiration, is that it claims to be able to accept the destructive criticism of the Bible and yet maintain the central evangelical doctrines of God's sovereignty, man's sin, and salvation in Christ. Thus Emil Brunner states that today's theology is to be built "on the ruins of Scripture."

3. But it is impossible to cut loose from the foundation of Scripture and yet hold the essentials of Christianity.

a. Partial inspiration is inconsistent with Scripture's own attitiude toward itself; see the warnings in Deut. 4:2; 12:32; Rev. 22:18, 19, that the words of Scripture are not to be changed. That the inspiration of Scripture extends beyond doctrine to the truth of its historical references is one of the Bible's clear doctrines!

As Warfield said, "The real conflict is no longer with 'the traditional theory of inspiration,' but with the credibility of the Bible."[35]

b. Partial inspiration is inconsistent with the authority and deity of Christ. It is true, as the neo-orthodox say, that Christ's Spirit does "encounter" and speak to me today, but ideas of human and even demonic origin also encounter me today (I John 4:1). Such mystical experience demands authentication, and the test is conformity to the Jesus who came in the flesh (I John 4:2; John 16:13, 14; 15:26). But the historical Jesus accepted the full authority of Scripture (see above, Sec. I, D). The honest Barthian must admit that he is contrary to the mind of Christ.

c. Partial inspiration is inconsistent with true religion.

(1) Though apparently without evil results at first, loss of the evangel destroys evangelism and, in time, faith. Man on his own will go his own way. One of the greatest critics admitted, "Biblical criticism is at the bottom of the reconstruction that is going on throughout the Church . . . the demand for the revision of creeds and change in methods of worship and Christian work."[36]

(2) Biblical fact and Christian faith are inseparable. Burrows claims, "Religious truth is one thing; historical fact is another. Neither necessarily presupposes or ac-

---

[35]*Ibid.*, p. 175.
[36]Charles Augustus Briggs, "The Higher Criticism," *Public Opinion* 10 (1891), p. 576.

companies the other."[37] For example, may one not
claim that Gen. 6-8 teach the divine punishment of
sin, irrespective of the historical reality of such a flood
as the Bible describes? But 1) to deny Noah and the
Flood makes the doctrine merely a theory, not a reality
proven by history. And 2) when the doctrine is based
on a claimed event, but when the record is actually
false and the real event is just the opposite, then the
probability is that the doctrine is false too. As the N.T.
asserts, "If Christ hath not been raised, your faith is
vain; ye are yet in your sins" (I Cor. 15:17). As Augustine said 1500 years ago:

"Now faith will totter if the authority of Scripture
begin to shake. And then, if faith totter, love itself
will grow cold. For if a man has fallen from faith, he
must necessarily also fall from love; for he cannot love
what he does not believe to exist."[38]

(3) In reality, neo-orthodoxy is but another form of man-
made religion. As Berkhof has pointed out, "Among
those who adopt a partial inspiration of Scripture there
is no unanimity whatever. Some would limit the inspiration to doctrinal matters, others to the N.T., others
to the words of Jesus, and still others to the Sermon on
the Mount. This shows as clearly as anything can
that the theory is purely subjective and lacks all objective basis. The moment one accepts it in any one of its
many forms, one has virtually lost one's Bible."[39]

"Surely the people is grass. The grass withereth, the flower fadeth;
but the word of our God shall stand forever" (Isa. 40:7, 8).

RECOMMENDED READING BIBLIOGRAPHY ON INSPIRATION

Berkhof, Louis, *Introductory Volume to Systematic Theology*, rev. ed. Grand
    Rapids: Eerdmans Publishing Co., c. 1932, pp. 144-169. The best single
    study: inclusive but concise, scholarly, thoroughly trustworthy, and up-to-date.
Boettner, Loraine, *The Inspiration of the Scriptures*, 2nd ed. Grand Rapids: Eerd-
    mans Publishing Co., 1940. A splendid survey of the problem. Good to put
    into the hands of students and all serious enquirers.
Engelder, Theodore, *Scripture Cannot Be Broken*. St. Louis: Concordia, 1944.
    The objections to a high view of Scripture thoroughly analyzed and answered.
    Well documented.
Gaussen, L., *Theopneustia, the Plenary Inspiration of the Holy Scriptures*. Chi-
    cago: The Biblical Institute Colportage Ass'n., n.d. The old classic, translated
    from the French. Wordy and polemical, but a mine of texts and logic.
Harris, R. Laird, *Inspiration and Canonicity of the Bible*. Grand Rapids: Zonder-
    van Publishing House, 1957. Winner of the Zondervan 1956 prize contest.
    An excellent, up-to-date study.

---

[37]*Op. cit.*, p. 4. So also the entire school of R. Bultmann, the "demythologizing"
methods of which amount simply to the removal of God from any objective effect
upon history.
[38]*De Doctrina Christiana*, I:37, Philip Schaff, ed., *A Select Library of the Nicene
and Post-Nicene Fathers* (Buffalo: The Christian Literature Co.), Vol. II.
[39]*Introductory Volume to Systematic Theology* (Revised edition; Grand Rapids:
Wm. B. Eerdmans Publishing Co., 1932), p. 154.

Packer, J. I., *"Fundamentalism" and the Word of God*. London: Inter-Varsity Fellowship, 1958. A recent British study, generally acceptable in defending the authority of Scripture.

Patton, Francis, *The Inspiration of the Scriptures*. Philadelphia: Presbyterian Board of Publication and Sabbath-school Work, c. 1869. A semi-popular presentation. Exegetical and philosophical.

Warfield, B. B., *The Inspiration and Authority of the Bible*. The Presbyterian and Reformed Publishing Co., 1948. A thorough and detailed presentation of verbal inspiration, particularly in the light of history and modern attack.

Young, Edward J., *Thy Word Is Truth*. Grand Rapids: Eerdmans Publishing Co., 1957. The most recent evangelical study. Significant for its appreciation of neo-orthodoxy and modern Biblical criticism.

Appendix B. Messianic Psalms

The following outline summarizes those passages within the Psalter that may be considered legitimate sources for Messianic teaching (see topics 20-21, pp. 257-284). *Other psalms may indeed possess a N.T. relationship, yet are not to be classified as properly Messianic because they:

A. Were fulfilled in David (the N.T. truth may be similar, but there exists no real identity):

Ps. 18 (v. 43; cf. Eph. 2:11, 12)   Ps. 21 (v. 4; cf. Heb. 7:24)
Ps. 24 (vv. 7-10; cf. Matt.   Ps. 61 (v. 7; cf. Heb. 7:24)
   21:8-11)

B. Are confused with other O.T. passages having true Messianic fulfillment:

Ps. 34 (v. 20. But John 19:36 relates to Ex. 12:46 and Num. 9:12)
Ps. 35 (v. 19. But John 15:25 relates to Ps. 69:4)
Ps. 55 (v. 13. But John 13:18 relates to Ps. 41:9)
Ps. 97 (v. 7.   But Heb. 1:6 relates to Deut. 32:43, LXX)

C. Were fulfilled in God's theocratic reign, but possess no particularly Messianic note:

Ps. 9 (v. 8, cf. Luke 23:46)   Also Ps. 50, 96, 98, etc.

D. Contain principles of universal application, or appropriate phraseology, only:

Ps. 31 (v. 15; cf. Luke 23:46)   Ps. 38 (v. 11; cf. Luke 23:49)
Ps. 42 (vv. 5, 11; cf. Matt. 26:38) Ps. 88 (v. 8; cf. Luke 23:49)
Ps. 44 (v. 22; cf. Rom. 8:36)   Ps. 116 (v. 10; cf. II Cor. 4:13)

These psalms, however, remain distinctly Messianic:

A. Christ spoken of in the 3rd person:

Ps.	Subject	Messianic vv. (Eng.)	N.T. proof	O.T. clue to exclusively Messianic meaning
8	Humiliation and glory	4b-8	Heb. 2:5-10 I Cor. 15:27	v. 6, all things are under His feet, which cannot apply to man.
72	Rule	6-17	......	v. 5 is transition to future; 7, His reign is forever; 8, territory; 9-11, all worship Him.
89	To come of David	3-4, 28-29, 34-36	Acts 2:30	vv. 4, 29, 36-37, the seed is eternal.
109	Judas cursed	6-19	Acts 1:16-20	Adversaries (plu.) in 4-5; shift in v. 6 to one preeminent betrayer. Plural resumed in v. 20.
118	Rejection (The O.T. indication of this thought is weak)	22	Matt. 21:42-44, etc.; Acts 4:11; I Pet. 2:7	Christ's rejection, the means of salvation, is greater than Israel's, that required it, for only He became "head," "Thou my salvation" (v. 21).
132	To come of David		Acts 2:30	v. 12, the seed is eternal.

B. Christ addressed in the 2nd person:

45	Throne ever	6-7	Heb. 1:8, 9	v. 6, He is deity; yet (v. 7) not the Father.
68	Ascension (Weak)	18	Eph. 4:8-10	v. 18 shifts abruptly to 2nd person and the One addressed is distinguished from Yah-Elohim. A historical ascension is only Christ's.
102	Eternity (Weak)	25-27	Heb. 1:10-12	1-22 addressed to Yahweh, v. 24, to El, a change. Christ is the true Redeemer of Israel.
110	Ascension & priesthood	All	Matt. 22:43-45; Acts 2:33-35 Heb. 1:13; 5:6-10; 6:20; 7:24	v. 1, He is David's Lord; v. 4, eternal priest.

C. Christ speaks in the 1st person:

2	Kiss the Son	All	Acts 4:25-28; 13:33 Heb. 1:5; 5:5	v. 7, the speaker is God's begotten Son; v. 8, He possesses more than David, all the earth.
16	Incorruption	10	Acts 2:24-31; 13:35-37	Not seeing corruption cannot apply to David.
22	Passion	All	Matt. 27:35-46; John 19:23-25; Heb. 2:12	v. 16, His pierced hands and feet and v. 18, lots cast on His garments, not true of David.
40	Incarnation (Weak)	6-8	Heb. 10:5-10	Praises in vv. 1-5, 9ff., are interrupted by a descriptive section. David (v. 12) did not always "delight to do His will"; but Christ did.
41	Judas' betrayal (Weak)	9b-c	John 13:8	9a applies to Ahithophel, but cannot to the untrusted Judas (John 2:24-25); 9b-c is not known to apply to Ahithophel, but to Judas (John 12: 26).
69	Passion	4, 21, 25	John 15:25; 19:28-30; Acts 1:16-20	v. 4, speaker hated without cause; but (v. 5) David confesses sin. v. 21 gall and vinegar not David's food
78	Parables (Weak)	2	Matt. 13:35	Asaph does not here use "dark sayings"; Psalm is not problematic or obscure (as 49:4; Ezek. 17:2). He is prophetic of Christ (Matt. 13:35).

°For further explanation, see Payne, "So-called Dual Fulfillment in Messianic Psalms," Evangelical Theological Society, 1953 Papers, pp. 62-72.

Appendix C

The following outline surveys the point by point conclusions of the four schools of interpretation of Daniel 9,° as they are elaborated in the following representative studies: LIBERAL, James A. Montgomery (*A Critical and Exegetical Commentary on the Book of Daniel*, New York: Charles Scribner's Sons, 1927; TRADITIONAL, E. B. Pusey (*Daniel the Prophet*, New York: Funk and Wagnalls, 1891); DISPENSATIONAL, Joseph A. Seiss (*Voices from Babylon or, the Records of Daniel the Prophet*, Philadelphia: Muhlenberg Press, c. 1879), with supplementation from A. C. Gaebelein (*The Prophet Daniel*, New York: "Our Hope" Publishing Co., c. 1911) and SYMBOLICAL, H. C. Leupold (*Exposition of Daniel*, Columbus, Ohio: Wartburg Press, c. 1949). The page numbers in each column then refer to these respective books.

°Cf. the interpretation suggested above, pp. 276-278.

Subject	Liberal	Traditional	Dispensational	Symbolical
9:24 Thy people	Israel past, p. 393.	Israel & church past, p. 185	Israel past & future, p. 240	Israel & church past & fut., 411
Weeks = periods of	7 years, 373	7 years, 186	7 x 360 days, Gaebelein, p. 140	Perfecting, 409
Make an end of sins and bring in right-eousness	Maccabean utopian dreams, 375	Atonement on Calvary, 194	All promises to Israel fulfilled, 242	The new heaven and earth, 411
Anoint the most holy	Altar cleansed in 165 B.C. 375	Christ anointed by Holy Spirit, 196	Consecration of millennial Jews, 241	Consummation of God with man (Rev. 21: 3), 416
9:25 Command to rebuild Jerusalem	Jeremiah's word at Jerusalem's fall, 586 B.C., 392	Artaxerxes I's decree to Ezra, 458 B.C., 189	Artaxerxes I to Nehemiah, 444 B.C., 246	Cyrus' decree of return, 538 B.C., 418
End of 7 weeks	The return in 437 B.C., 379	Through the reforms of Nehemiah, 409 B.C., 191	Jerusalem's restoration, 396 B.C. (?), Gaebelein, 136	Christ's incar-nation, 421
7 & 62 joined?	No, 392	Yes, 189	Yes, 242	No, 417
Anointed one	Jeshua, 379	Christ, anointed at baptism, 189	Christ, at His triumphal entry, 243	Christ, birth, 422
End of 62 weeks (total of 69)	171 B.C., 394	A.D. 26, 189	A.D. 30, 247	End of expan-sion of church, 424
9:26 "After" 62	Immediately after, 394	Later, midway in next 7 yrs., 201	Later, by five days, 248	Immediately after, 427
Messiah cut off	Onias III murdered, 381	Christ cruci-fied, 198	Christ cruci-fied, 249	Church prog-ress ends, 427
Nothing for Him	Has no guilt, 381	Rejected by Jews, 197	Rejected by Jews, 250	Has no in-fluence, 427
Prince that shall come	Antiochus IV in 168 B.C., 383	Christ (see above, p. 257, note 1), or Titus in A.D. 70, 200	Titus in A.D. 70, 251	Antichrist in the future, 428
Unto the end thereof shall be war	To his death in 164 B.C., 384	To its (Jeru-salem's) fall in A.D. 70, 201	To its (Israel's) restoration 7 yrs. before Christ's appear-ing, 250	To his death at Christ's appear-ing, 429

9:27 "And"; subsequent events?	No, v. 27 elaborates v. 26, 384	No, v. 27 elaborates v. 26, 192	Yes, different matters, 251	No, v. 27 elaborates v. 26, 431
Firm covenant	Antiochus allied with Hellenizers 385	Christ's new testament with the saved, 193	Antichrist allied with regathered infidel Jews, 252	Antichrist enslaves the masses, 432
Beginning of 70th week	Follows 69th, 386	Follows 69th, 192	Parenthesis between 69 & 70, 251	Follows 69th, 428
In midst of week	For 3½ yrs., 168-165 B.C., 386	After 3½ yrs., in A.D. 30, 192	After 3½ yrs., in middle of tribulation; and for its latter ½; 252	After ½ his period, 432; and for the latter ½, 433
Sacrifice cease	Altar polluted, 386	O.T. system ended, 192	Altar polluted, 253	No church worship, 433
End of 70th week	Maccabean victory, 386	Stephen stoned, Jews reject new testament, Paul called, A.D. 33, 193	God's judgment, 251	God's judgment, 436
Upon the wing of abominations, a desolator	On a peak of the Temple, Greek idolatry, 388	Against the Temple with its Jewish sins, Titus; 199	On a peak of the Temple, an idol, 253	By means of idolatry, Antichrist, 433
Until an end shall pour on a desolate (-or)	Until Antiochus' death, 389	Until the end of desolate Jerusalem, 200	To the "consummation" and Antichrist's death, 255	Until his death, 436

Appendix D

THE SONG OF SOLOMON*
(A Semi-dramatic Pastoral)

Act I. ABISHAG'S PLIGHT (1-3:5). Setting: "The city" (Jerusalem, 3:3), the palace chambers (1:4; 2:9).

Scene 1 (1-2:7).

Daughters of Jerusalem: (2-4) Rightly do we all love Solomon.
Abishag: (5-7) describes herself, But I love a shepherd.
Dau: (8) You can have him! (enter Solomon).
Solomon: (9-11) praises her.
Abi: (12-14) But I have a spice plant in my bosom reminding me of Shepherd
Sol: (15) praise.
Abi: (16-2:1) My beloved is the fair one; I'm a country flower.
Sol: (2) You're a lily among thorns (reflects on the harem).
Abi: (3-7) Shepherd's banner over me was love (5, *overcome with love,*
        not sick of it). Refrain: the charge, Don't force love.

Scene 2 (2:8-3:5), reveries.

Abi: (8-9) I can hear him saying:
Shepherd: (10-14) Come to me (a high-point in poetic expression).
Abi: (15-17) Stop the foxes first? But why worry, it's love!
        (3:1-5) second reverie, finding him and marriage. The charge.

Act II. ABISHAG'S STEADFASTNESS (3:6-8:4). Setting: Lebanon (4:8), in a royal dwelling (5:4); with a view (3:6).

Scene 1 (3:6-5:1).

Dau #1: (6) What comes?
Dau #2: (7-11) Solomon in chariot, ready for his wedding, all turn out!
Sol: (4:1-5) praises Abishag.
Abi: (6) I would rather be home.
Sol: (7-15) Come with me, my heart is ravished.
Abi: (16) May I be worthy of my Shepherd, whose I am.
Sol: (5:1) But here I am, let's drink.

Scene 2 (5:2-6:3), dream told the daughters.

Abi: (2-8) I dreamed I missed him; if you see him tell him I'm true.
Dau: (9) Who is this man, anyhow?
Abi: (10-16) He's the fairest of 10,000, altogether lovely.
Dau: (6:1) We become interested.
Abi: (2-3) Oh no, I am his and he is mine.

Scene 3 (6:4-8:4).

Sol: (4-9) You dismay me, better than 60 queens and 80 concubines.
Dau: (10) (insulted), What are you saying!
Abi: (11-12) I was summoned to court; I came not by my own will.
Dau: (13a) Good, let us see thee.
Abi: (13b) I'm no public dancer.
Sol: (7:1-9a) praise; ends, "Thy mouth is like the best wine—"
        He may have been building up to a kiss and she breaks in,
Abi: (9b-8:4) "—reserved for my Shepherd. I am his." She calls for Shepherd
        to come and get her (Solomon agrees?) The charge.

ACT III. ABISHAG'S REWARD (8:5-14). Setting: Abishag's home in Shunem. Only scene.

Brothers: (5a) Who comes with her beloved?
Shep: (5b) points out "old apple tree" where we fell in love; and her cottage.
Abi: (6-7; the climactic statement), Love conquers all, a very flame of God.
Bro #1: (8) When she was young, what did we warn her?
Bro #2: (9) A firm, chaste wall, rewarded; a yielding door, no.
Abi: (10-12) I proved a wall before Solomon. He can have his wealth: I have
        my "vineyard."
Shep: (13) Say that to me.
Abi: (14) Make haste, my beloved (how does the scene end?).

---

*Compare also W. Tyman Williams, "The Song of Solomon" *Moody Monthly,* Feb. 1947, 398-400, 422-423, and the applications made above, p. 344.

Appendix E

THE SIGNIFICANCE OF THE SACRED TIMES OF THE OLD TESTAMENT*

	Moral Obligation		Historic Symbolism		Spiritual & Sacramental Symbolism		Typology	
	O.T.	Present form	O.T.	Present	O.T.	Present form	O.T.	Present form
Sabbath (weekly, & 7 convocation)	Rest (Ex. 23:12; cf. creation, 20:11)	Rest (Sunday, changeless moral duty; Rom. 13:10)	Israel's rest from Egypt (Deut.5:15)	—	God's sanctifying of Israel (Ex. 31:13)	Sunday preaching & sacraments (Acts 20:7)	Rest in Christ (Matt. 11:28) Heavenly rest (Isa. 66:23)	Sunday worship of Christ (Rev. 1:10) Sunday, type of heaven (Heb. 4:11)
New Moons	—	—	—	—	God to remember Israel (Num. 10:10)	Regular intercessory prayer (?)	—	—
Sabbatic Year	Charity (Ex. 23:11; Deut. 15:2)	Relief offerings (Gal. 2:10)	—	—	God's control of land (Lev. 25:2)	Stewardship of property (?)	—	—
Year of Jubilee	Liberty and property rights (Lev. 25:10)	Individual rights under God (?)	—	—	Same (Lev. 25:23)	Same	Eschatological blessing (Isa. 61:2-4)	Lord's Supper, type of future kingdom (I Cor. 11:26)
Passover	—(it was exclusivistic (Ex. 12:43-44)	—	The Exodus (Ex. 12:14)	—	Redemption (Ex. 13:15) in common (12:22)	Lord's Supper, sacramental communion (I Cor. 10:16)	Christ's substitutionary death (I Cor. 5:7)	Lord's Supper, memorial of past atonement (I Cor. 11:24)

*See above, chapter 28.

	Moral Obligation		Historic Symbolism		Spiritual & Sacramental Symbolism		Typology	
	O.T.	Present form	O.T.	Present	O.T.	Present form	O.T.	Present form
Pentecost	Social sharing (Deut. 16:11)	Christian compassion (?)	Hasty departure (12:34)	—	Unleavened purity (Ex. 23:18) First sheaf is God's (Lev. 23:11)	Sincerity & truth (I Cor. 5:8) Church offerings (?)	—	—
Tabernacles	Same (Deut. 16:14)	Same	Wilderness camping (Lev. 23:43)	—	Loaves dedicated to God (Lev. 23:17)	Grace at meals (?)	Eschatological ingathering (Zech. 14:16)	Lord's Supper, type of future kingdom (I Cor. 11:26)
					Harvest is from God (Lev. 23:39)	Thanksgiving (?)		
Trumpets	—	—	Former New Year? (Ex. 12:2; 23:16)	—	Same as New Moon (Lev. 23:24)	New Year's	—	—
Day of Atonement	Humble confession (Lev. 16:28)	Times of penitence (?)	—	—	Cleansing from sin (Lev. 16:30)	Baptism (Acts 22:16)	Christ's redemption (Heb. 9:12)	Good Friday and Easter services (?)
4 annual fasts	—	—	Fall of Jerusalem (Zech. 7:3)	—	Seeking God's favor (Zech. 8:21)	Intercessory prayer (?)	—	—
Purim	Gift giving (Esther 9: 22)	Christmas (?)	Haman foiled (Esther 9:17)	—	Joy for deliverance (Esther 9:19)	Independence Day (?)	—	—

Appendix F

THE OLD TESTAMENT OFFERINGS*

Name	Translation	Major references	Distinctiveness	Symbolism	Typology
"Sweet Savor" Offerings:					
Olā	Burnt offering	Lev. 1; 6:8-13	Wholly burnt on the altar (Lev. 1:19)	1. Placating the wrath of God by substituting a victim in death (Gen. 8:20; Lev. 1:4) 2. Complete consecration (cf. Lev. 6:13, a continual offering)	1. Christ's vicarious death for the redemption of sinners (II Cor. 5:21) 2. His entire self-surrender (Ps. 40:8; cf. Luke 2:49; Matt. 26:39)
Minhā	Meal offering	Lev. 2; 6:14-23	Non-bloody products, accompanying other bloody offerings (Lev. 2:1; cf. 23:18)	Consecration of one's life and substance (Lev. 2:14)	His righteous fulfilling of the law (Matt. 3:15)
Sh'lāmim	Peace offering	Lev. 3; 7:11-34	Most parts eaten before God by the sacrificer (Lev. 7:15)	1. Placating God's wrath (as above, cf. Lev. 3:2) 2. A thanksgiving meal of reconciliation with God (Lev. 7:12)	1. Vicarious redemption (as above) 2. Communion in Christ, now (John 6:51) and in the future kingdom (Rev. 19:6-10)
Guilt Offerings:					
Hattāth	Sin offering	Lev. 4-5:13; 6:24-30	For a specific sin (Lev. 5:1-4) Some victims' bodies burned outside the camp (Lev. 4:12)	1. Placating God's wrath (as above, cf. 4:4) 2. Confession (5:5), with transference of the guilt to the animal (4:21)	1. Vicarious redemption (as above) 2. Christ's suffering "without the camp" (Heb. 13:12), the passive bearing of the penalties of men's sins (Isa. 53:6)
Āshām	Trespass offering	Lev. 5:14-6:7; 7:1-10	Same as the hattāth, plus repayment to the wronged party (Lev. 5:15)	1. Placating God's wrath (as above, cf. 5:18) 2. Confession with transferred guilt (as above 7:7) 3. Social restitution for wrong (5:16)	1-2. Same as above (Isa. 53:10), plus 3. His active redressing of every legal claim of God (Gal. 4:4)

*See above, pp. 385-388.

Appendix G

LIFE AFTER DEATH*

The historical positions on man's life, after death and before the final resurrection, may be outlined as follows:

Romanist: 1) The wicked descend to hell fire (Mark 9:47, 48), *haidēs* (Matt. 11:23). 2) a. The O.T. righteous went to the *"limbus* (fringe of hell) *patrum,"* but were released and taken to heaven at Christ's descent into hell. This is based upon the Medieval doctrine that heaven was not opened up until Christ had made His propitiation. b. The N.T. righteous and the martyrs go directly to heaven, if their lives are free from the stain of sin. c. Purgatory exists for the saved, but who must yet be purged from the guilt of venial sins (II Macc. 12:45; Mal. 3:2).

Traditional Protestant: 1) Hell is real (Luke 16:23; Num. 16:30; Amos 9:2). 2) O.T. believers at death went direct to God and to glory (Eccl. 12:7; Ps. 73:24), and N.T. believers have the identical hope (II Cor. 5:8; Phil. 1:23).

Liberal: Those of this persuasion hold no common belief, but the Biblical teaching is represented as follows: 1) The Hebrews borrowed the pagan concept of *sh'ōl,* which means "asking" or "hollow." Sheol is: a. An underground space (Prov. 7:27); b. For good and bad (Job 30:23); c. Dreary, with no rewards (Eccl. 9:10); but d. Jews may escape (?) (Isa. 26:19). 2) The N.T. then adopted the intertesta-mental developments on rewards and punishments after death.

Dispensational: 1) This follows the liberal view, that all go to Hades (Sheol), "the place of spirits." Scofield includes N.T. saints here too (*Reference Bible,* p. 1098). 2) It follows the Romanist view of compartments: hades (hell) proper for the lost, and paradise or Abraham's bosom, "the part reserved for the blessed," Chafer, *Systematic Theology* (Dallas: 1947), VII: 247, (cf. Luke 16:19-31). 3) "Paradise is now, since the resurrection of Christ, removed from hades and located [in] the 3rd heaven," *loc. cit.,* (cf. II Cor. 12:1-4 compared with Eph. 4:8-10, Scofield does not use I Pet. 3:19 in this connection).

These four positions may then be evaluated, in outline, as follows: *The Romanists* resort to Papal tradition and to a questionable exegesis of "descent into hell" passages (Acts 2:27; Eph. 4:8; I Peter 3:19; 4:6). Other passages on limbo and purgatory are either twisted or non-canonical.

The Liberals do not accept the Bible as God's words; it is but human guesses. 1) So their exegesis, though to be studied, is hope-lessly biased. a. There is no regard for contradictions that may be produced: the principle of the "Analogia Scripturae" is rejected; and clear vv. in either O.T. or N.T. (as, for example, on the fact that sin is punished after death) are not considered to be determinative. b. The O.T. is thus made to conform to the contemporary thought pat-

---

*Cf. discussion of chapter 30.

terns of the pagan world and to an assumed evolutionary progress. It contains actually no valid revelation on life after death. As Kohler candidly admits, it is "not theology" (*Old Testament Theology*, p. 155). 2) Specifically, however, the liberal theory of the "abode of shades" fails to account for: a. The fact of punishment in sheol. As some liberals admit: "abaddon" (Prov. 15:11) is "The place of ruin in Sheol for the lost or ruined dead, as a development of an earlier distinction of condition in Sheol," (Brown, Driver, and Briggs, *A Hebrew and English Lexicon of the Old Testament*, p. 2; cf. Rev. 9:11). b. The fact that sheol is held up as a warning to the wicked (Ps. 49:14; 55:15). c. The hope of the righteous in death (Prov. 14: 32), to be delivered from Sheol and received by God (Ps. 49:15; cf. Heb. 11:6).

Traditional Protestantism maintains the validity of all the O.T. statements on Sheol and at the same time the unity of the Biblical revelation on life after death in both the O.T. and N.T. This position necessitates a recognition of different uses of the term "sheol." (Note: such a distinction appears legitimate, not forced. From the basic meaning of "place of the dead" [grave], comes the abstract meaning "death," cf. English, "the grave"; and, from its sorrow, it becomes the term to describe the fate of the lost, cf. English "death" as a euphemism for hell). The O.T. mentions Sheol 65 times. 1) The local meaning, "GRAVE," occurs 20 times. For example: Job 17:13, 14, parallel to the place of the worm, corrupt; Ps. 88:3, parallel to one's going down into the pit; Ps. 49:14; where the form is consumed (cf. Gen. 42:38; I Sam. 2:6; I Kings 2:6). The "grave" concept thus explains all passages in which the righteous are said to "go *down*" into sheol (local) though such meaning is denied by both liberals and dispensationalists. 2) The local meaning, "HELL" (Ps. 55:15) occurs 24 times. Cf. Num. 16:30, "to go down alive into hell"; Prov. 15:11, sheol-abaddon; Prov. 15:24, what the righteous man escapes. This sense is applied to the saved only in Ps. 86:13 and Prov. 15:24, and then as escape from it. 3) The abstract meaning, "DEATH" occurs 21 times. Ps. 89:48, parallel to death; so Ps. 16:10 (Acts 2:27). All men, good and bad, suffer this "sheol." It should be noted, however, that many Hebrews did have the pagan concept, cf. I Sam. 28:11, "Bring him up."

Dispensational theory accommodates to liberal attack and leaves the O.T. as substandard. 1) But Luke 16:23 contrasts sheol-hades (torture) with the abode of the O.T. saved. 2) Eph. 4:8 is abstract in its terminology ("captivity") and can at the most refer only to God's enemies, not to O.T. saints brought up from Hades. 3) Paradise (Luke 23:43)— and Abraham's bosom? — is heaven (II Cor. 12:3). To claim that, before II Cor. 12, it was part of the hades and was then moved is highly . . . arbitrary. 28 of the 65 . . . O.T. sheol references, include the saved, but these references never apply locally, except for the idea of the "grave." 4) Contrariwise, the O.T. states its own hope to be this: "Thou wilt receive me to glory" (Ps. 73:24).

Conclusion: The traditional Protestant position is to be maintained as: 1) The most simple, in holding to the hope stated in the O.T. and

N.T. (and nowhere denied) of a carrying to heaven immediately upon death for all believers. 2) The most Scriptural, in recognizing the paucity of revelation on O.T. life after death and in rejecting hypothetical infernal migrations. 3) The most consistent, in refusing the poor "hades" concepts of paganism and in maintaining the divine normativeness of the O.T. Scriptures.

Appendix H

The application of Hosea's "family prophecies"* to God's kingdom(s) may be pictured in tabular form as follows:

	Hosea 1-2:1 Extent of the kingdom	Hosea 2:2-23 Character of the kingdom		Hosea 3 Process of the kingdom
Pre-deportation sin (cf. II Kings 15:8-12)	1-4b Whoredom from God; Vengeance on Jehu's dynasty	2 Whoredom to be put away	8 Gifts used for Baal	1 God loves Israel despite their other gods
Assyrian punishment (cf. II Kings 17:16-18)	4c-9 Israel to cease; Judah saved, 701 B.C.	3-5 Slay her with thirst	9-13 Her mirth to cease	
Exilic repentance (cf. Ezek. 18:30-32)		6-7 Her way hedged, so a return to her Husband	14-17 Baal taken away	
Present kingdom (cf. Rom. 9:24-26)	10 Numerous children; Sons of God	The B'rith: 18 Break the sword | 19-20 Thou shalt know God	23b-c Be My people	2-4 I bought her; Israel kingless
Future kingdom (cf. Rom. 11:25-27)	1:11-2:1 Judah with Israel, Under One Head	21-23a Grain & wine		5 Israel's return to David their king

*Cf. references above, pp. 474, 478.

Appendix 1

The latter chapters of Zechariah* may be organized into four cycles of inspired predictions, each of which moves from ancient time to Christ's eschatological kingdom, as follows:

BEFORE THE NEW TESTAMENT

Alexander the Great and after

1st Cycle	9:1	Damascus falls to the Greeks
9:1-10	4	Island of Tyre taken, 332 B.C.
	5	Alexander storms Gaza, 332.
2nd	9:12	The Jews, prisoners to Persia and then to Alexander and the Diaochi
9:11– ch. 10		
3rd	11:5	Jews slain by their possessors,
11-13:6	6	Diadochi strive over the earth
4th, 13:7– ch. 14		

Maccabean revolt and after

9:7	The Philistine remnant incorporated into Judah, 148-146 B.C.
9:13	Maccabean victories over the Greeks
10:3	Seleucid shepherds to be punished by Jewish rulers; 10:7, joy results
4	
11:8a	3 native shepherds (cf. v. 5) to fall, corrupt Hellenistic high-priests (?)

THE NEW TESTAMENT WORLD

Jesus Christ

CHRIST'S FIRST COMING:

1st	9:9	The King comes humbly (Matt. 21:5)
2nd	10:8b	Redemption of Israel's children
3rd	11:8b	Hebrews loath God, prizing the
	12	Good Shepherd at 30 pieces of silver (Matt. 26:15), which are
	13	thrown to the potter (27:7)
	12:10	They pierce God (John 19:37)
4th	13:7a	The Shepherd who is God's equal is smitten (Matt. 26:31)

Ancient Roman Empire

9:10a	Jerusalem's battle-bow broken, A.D. 70
11:3	Native shepherds (Sadducees?) wail for the wasted land (opening summary)
16	An evil shepherd plunders, A.D. 70
17	But he (Rome) will fall in turn, A.D. 476 (cf. Rev. 17:15-16, 18)
13:7b	Faithless Hebrews are scattered
8a	⅔ of those in Palestine die, A.D. 70

THE PRESENT:

The church, Jew & Gentile

1st	9:10b	Peace to the heathen
2nd	10:8a	A 2nd gathering (9:11 was 1st) and increase (Isa. 54:1 & Gal. 4:25-8)
	8c	
3rd	11:11	The poor of the flock (remnant) heed Christ
4th	13:7c	God's hand turned for (not against) the little ones (the remnant)

World-wide church

10:9a	Sown afar they
9b	believe, & they
9c	& their children live
13:7b	Faithful scattered (Galilee, Matt. 26:32) (& world, Acts 8:1, 4)

Hebrews cut off

12:10	Hebrew inhabitants are in Jerusalem
13:8b	⅓ of Hebrews left.
9a	God will bring them into fire & try them

CHRIST'S SECOND COMING:

	Tribulation-appearing	Rapture of church	Opposition	Hebrews reingrafted
1st	—			—
2nd	10:11a He comes, affliction. 11b Rivers dry up (Rev. 16:12)	10:9b Believers return 10 to Him in Palestine	10:11b Pride and scepters brought down	—
3rd	12:10 The One pierced appears	12:7 The tents of Judah (Rom. 2:28, 29) saved before the Jerus. Hebrews	12:2 Siege of Jerusalem 3 by all 9 They fall to Christ	13:1 A fountain is opened for Jerusalem's sin 12:10 Prayer to the pierced One 12:5 The church recognizes the Hebrews as allies
4th	14:4 His feet on Olivet 5 Mountains moved 6 Heaven dark	14:5b God comes with holy ones (angels, and also the church?)	14:2 Jerus. taken ½ captive 13 Dissension in enemy 7 Evening victory	13:9b Hebrews call on God 14:5a Flee Jerus. by a valley 5b Join the saints on Olivet 14 Church assists in the relief of Jerusalem

THE FINAL ESCHATOLOGICAL KINGDOM

1st 9:10c Christ's world dominion (Ps. 72:8; Rev. 20:3)

2nd 10:12 Believer's walk secure in His authority.

3rd 12:6b Jerusalem restored; 13:2–3, the unclean spirit and deceptive prophets gone

4th 14:8 Living waters flow from Jerusalem; 14:9, Yahweh is king over all the earth

14:16 The remnant of the nations worship at Jerusalem

Appendix J. The Day of Yahweh in The Revelation

The most detailed single source for the Bible's eschatology consists of its last book, the Revelation. As a basis, therefore, for appreciating the many disconnected "Day of Yahweh" prophecies of the Old Testament (see topics 31-32, pp. 464-504), the writer would propose the following analysis for the New Testament Apocalypse.

GOVERNING PRINCIPLES

Method of Approach. 1) The events of Revelation are historical, though with some symbolic description. 2) If an event has been adequately fulfilled in the past or present, nothing further need be sought; if it has not, it shall be fulfilled in the future. 3) The analogy of other Scripture passages is basic for interpretation.

Resulting Conclusions. 1) The book of Revelation is generally chronological in two main cycles. 2) Particular sections may, however, follow logically rather than chronologically. 3) "Prophetic telescoping" may cause the inspired text to move from one event to another without notice of intervening events.

A SUGGESTED OUTLINE

Prologue (1:1-8)
  Preface (1:1-3) This prophecy is revealed to John from Christ via an angel. It must be carried out soon. Blessings on those giving attention.
  Summary (1:4-8) Greetings to the seven churches in Christ our Savior. He is the focus of history and is coming back to the earth.
  Introduction (1:9-20) John's vision of Christ in heaven. By His death, Christ controls death. John is commissioned to write.

I. The first Cycle (Chapters 2-11)
  A. Exhortation for John's time, about A.D. 65 (?) (Chapters 2-3)[1]
    The letters to the seven churches of western Asia Minor
  B. General matters continuing today (4-6:11)[2]
    God's glory in heaven (4). Christ, the sacrificed Lamb, receives the roll of the elect, cf. 13:8 (5). Successive scenes appear as Christ breaks the roll's seals, before its reading at the last judgment, cf. 20:12 (6:1-11)
    Seals 1-5: aggression, war, famine, death, and martyrdom
  C. God's wrath immediately preceding Christ's coming (6:12-ch. 7)
    Seal 6: physical phenomena as Christ is about to appear (6:

---

[1]1:4, 9 set chapters 1-3 as referring to John's time. The messages to the churches exhibit eternally valid principles, but they give no indication of being predictions of any other periods.
[2]4:1 commences the section after John's time, but 5:10 shows that the kingdom on earth has not yet been set up (so AV and RSV; manuscript differences provide the less likely RV reading). 6:11, on the saints' souls in heaven, still applies at present, the climax of persecution being called "the great tribulation" 7:14.
[3]Cf. Matt. 24:29-31. Seal 6 is just before Christ's return, the same day, 6:17.

12-17)[3] Just previously, certain of the Israel of God are placed under special protection (7:1-8)[4]

[Reversion to seal 5; cf. 6:11: the saints triumph, though killed in the great tribulation that immediately precedes God's wrath, cf. Matt. 24:29 (7:9-11)]

D. God's wrath immediately following Christ's coming (8:11:15), the "Three Woes"

Seal 7, at Christ's appearing, suspends the wrath for ½ hour (8:1)

[Reversion to the events of seal 6: the physical phenomena are elaborated as 4 angels sound the first four trumpets (8:2-13)][5]

Woes 1-2, the 5th and 6th trumpet angels, terrible war preparations and mobilization via the Euphrates River (9)[6]

---

[4] 7:3-4; the 144,000 appear to be identical with the same number in 14:1-5, a chosen youth group of the Church, the Israel of God, Gal. 6:16. Their sealing, as firstfruits (14:4) is symbolical of the protection for believers from the coming wrath of God (Luke 21:36). It must precede the wrath of the 6th seal, which answers the prayers of the saints in the 5th seal (6:10), hence the reversion to describe the saints killed in the great tribulation.

[5] 8-11, cf. 15, 16, the trumpets and bowls correspond to the 6th seal and following:

Seal	Trumpet	Bowl	Nature	Reference	Time
1			Conquests	Rev. 6:2	
2			War	6:4	The
3			Famine	6:6	present
4			Death	6:8	age
5			Souls in heaven		
A great earthquake				6:12, 8:5	
	1	1	Thunder and hail	6:14, 8:7	
			Sores on men (bowl)	16:2	5 minutes*(?)
	2	2	The sea of blood	8:8, 16:3	5 minutes
6	3	3	Waters poisoned	6:13, 8:10, 16:4	(with #2?)*
	4	4	The sun affected	6:12, 8:12, 16:8	5 minutes
		Total time of God's wrath so far,			15 minutes(?)
The appearing of Christ				6:17, 14:14, 19:11	
7			Silence in heaven	8:1	½ hour
			Flying woe-angel	8:13	5 minutes(?)
	5	5	Pain and war	9:3, 16:10	5 months
		6	Euphrates dried up	9:14, 16:12	
	6	7	Earthquake and battle of Jerusalem	11:13, 14:20, 16:18	
7					
The Battle of Armageddon				11:15, 19:19	

*with reactions continuing into the 5 months.

[6] The 5th and 6th trumpets, with war and preparations for Armageddon, presuppose Christ's visible presence as the One opposed. 9:5, 10: they extend five months into the millennium. 10:6, no more "delay": the 7th trumpet will finish world history as it is now known.

[A' John's ministry resumed (10-11:2)[7]
John is forbidden to reveal certain things; the end comes as prophesied (10:1-7). He is commissioned for further speaking (10:8-11). Jerusalem shall fall after 3½ yrs. destruction, A.D. 66-70(?) (11:1-2)]

[B' Matters continuing today resumed: the law and the prophets in the witnessing church are condemned by the world, with martyrdoms (11:3-10)][8]

The church will be resurrected and raptured (11:11, 12)[9]
Jerusalem will be punished and repent at Christ's appearing (11:13, 14)[10]
Woe 3, the 7th trumpet angel, Christ's conquest of the world at Armageddon (11:15)[11]

E. Christ's reign on earth, the final judgment, and the New Jerusalem (11:16-19)[12]

II. The Second Cycle (Chapters 12-22:7)

A. Events of John's period (12-13)
Israel produces Christ, who conquers Satan and casts him to the earth (12).[13] Political power (here Rome) comes from across the sea, apparently unphased by Christ's triumph, with emperor worship and persecution, aided by native religions of the land (13)[14]

---

[7]These verses seem to return to John's time: take courage from what has so far been revealed! 10:11 shows John's immediate responsibility. 11:1 suggests that Revelation was written before Jerusalem's fall in A.D. 70, with v. 2 referring to the impending Jewish war and sieges.
[8]Present day preaching: the two witnesses, described in terms of Moses and Zerubbabel (governing) and Elijah and Jeshua (religious, cf. Zech. 4), seem to signify the law and the prophets, as proclaimed by the Church. 11:3, the 1260 days are simply Elijah's 3½ yrs., I Kings 17:1; Luke 4:25; James 5:17; 11:7, the martyrdoms seem to correspond to those of 6:9. 11:8-9, cf. Stephen's death at Jerusalem, Acts 7:58, and exposed body, 8:2, though the 3½ days may be merely to contrast short (days) defeat with long (years) ministry.
[9]See below, on 19:7.
[10]This earthquake, 11:13, may equal Zech. 14:4, the means of delivering Jerusalem, under immediate attack by those opposing Christ, who has returned to the Mount of Olives. On the conversion of the Jews, cf. Zech. 12:10 and Rom. 11:25-27.
[11]The millennium follows the conquest of earth's kingdoms at Armageddon.
[12]11:19 looks on God's testament as fulfilled, Rev. 21:3; and the first cycle of the book is finished.
[13]12:5 dates this section to Christ's birth and ministry. The second cycle therefore starts even before the first. 12:6, 14, may be associated with Dan. 9:27, the rest of the "70th week," that is, from the Crucifixion to the stoning of Stephen, when Christians (the woman, the true Israel, God's people) prospered among the Jews (the desert).
[14]13:1, the beast, is explained in 17:9-16 as supporting and yet surviving the ancient Roman Empire; so it seems to equal world political power in general. 13:5 refers to some aspect of Roman rule, probably the 3½ yr. Jewish wars, as 11:2. 13:12-16, the beast may be equated with one head (a king, or kingdom, 17:10), or even as 8th head (17:11); so his mark may equal some specific Roman persecution.

B. The present is marked by Satan's continued persecution of the true Israel, the Church (12:17)[15]

C. God's wrath immediately preceding Christ's coming (15-16:9)[16] Vials (bowls) 1-4 review and intensify the pre-appearing physical phenomena

D. God's wrath immediately following Christ's coming (14, 16:10-chap. 19)

The true Israel, cf. 7:1-8, will be raptured to be with Him on Mount Zion (14:1-7)

[A' Exhortations to John's time for patience, because of victory over Rome (14:8-13)][17]

Christ returns with the clouds to reap His harvest (the rapture); wrath is executed at Jerusalem (14:14-20).

Vials (bowls) 5-7: men gather to Armageddon to oppose Christ 16:10-21)[18]

[A' John's ministry resumed (17-19:5)[19]

He is to encourage Christian's with Rome's overthrow by other nations (17). Christians escape, pagans mourn, and heaven rejoices (18-19:5)]

The whole Church will be raptured (along with the "firstfruits" of 14:1-7) to meet Christ in the air and then celebrate the "marriage supper" on earth (19:6-10)[20]

---

[15]"The rest of her seed" (Christ is the first) must be the Church, both Gentile and Jewish.

[16]14:14—chap. 16 describes Christ's appearing and what follows, though 15:1 backtracks with the 7 vials, the first 4 of which precede His coming (see chart above). 15:4 shows that some things leading to the world's submission have already taken place. Except for the 1st and 7th, the vials equal the trumpets, but more intense. 16:2, the "mark of the beast," submitting to power other than God's, continues to be a factor beyond the fall of Rome; so 19:20.

[17]14:1-7 moves to immediately after the appearing of Christ, though 14:9-13 is a parenthetical application to John's time. Verse 12 gives a general, timeless principle. 14:8, Babylon the Great (Rome), anticipates 17:5, 6, 18.

[18]16:19a: on the Jerusalem attack, see above, 11:13. 16:19b: the fall of cities leads logically to a description of the now historic fall of Rome.

[19]On the Roman Empire, contemporary with John: note references assuming his own time, 17:8-11, and particularly v. 12, the 10 kings of the "balance of power," as Dan. 2:42, which has been the world situation ever since the fall of ancient Rome. 17:3, the woman must be Rome: makes martyrs (v. 6), sits on the seven hills (9), has universal rule (15), and is a great city (18). 17:3, the beast, having survived the blow by Christ's incarnation into history (v. 8), is separate and bears both the woman and the 10 (16). It seems to signify pagan political power, and particularly its 8th (11) and final (19:19, Antichrist) embodiment. 17:3, the 10 horns were not contemporary with John, v. 12, but succeeded the woman. Revelation suggests no place for a revived Rome in prophecies still future.

[20]19:6 onward applies to the future, with Christ reigning on earth. 19:7, the Marriage Supper of the Lamb (Luke 14:15; 22:16), is the immediate result of the rapture of the Church (I Thess. 4:17), the Bride of Christ (II Cor. 11:2; Eph. 5:25-27). The rapture cannot take place before this point: for it is preceded by the resurrection of the dead saints (I Thess. 4:15, 16), which is at this time, 20:6. Note also: I Cor. 15:51-52, the resurrection precedes the rapture. Matt. 24:29-31, Mark 13:24-27, the Biblical order is always tribulation, appearing, rapture (Matt. 24:31 cannot come after the rapture of the Church for this verse mentions the trumpet, and the rapture trumpet, I Cor. 15:51, is the last). I Thess. 3:13, we are on earth when He comes with the saints from heaven. II Thess. 1: 7-10, our rest is only when Christ rules.

Christ destroys worldly political power at Armageddon (19: 11, 21)[21]

E. Christ's millennial reign, the final judgment, and the New Jerusalem (20-22:5)[22]
Satan is bound and the resurrected Christian dead reign with Christ on earth 1000 years (20:1-6). Satan's final revolt and defeat, cf. 11:18a (20:7-9). The final judgment (20:10-15).[23]

The new heaven and earth: New Jerusalem (21-22:5)[24]

Conclusion (22:6-19). This is factual and soon (rapid). Let the faithful rejoice and sinners die or come to Christ, who is the focus of history and of God's unchangeable Book

Epilogue (22:20-21) *Come, Lord Jesus!*

---

[21] 19:20, the future false prophets (liberalism? Romanism?) is similar to the ancient beast from the earth, 13:10-16: false religion aiding false politics.
[22] 20:4, all the saints are included in the millennial reign, not just martyrs, cf. I Cor. 15:21; I Thess. 4:14.
[23] The second resurrection and the second death are for all who are not Christ's.
[24] A new (the old, purified, Heb. 12:27) and wonderful existence for Christ's own.

BIBLIOGRAPHY
of works cited

Albright, William F. *From the Stone Age to Christianity*. Baltimore: The Johns Hopkins Press, 1946.

Alexander, J. A. *Isaiah*. Grand Rapids: Zondervan Publishing House, reprint 1953.

Alford, Henry. *The Greek Testament*. 7th ed.; London: Rivingtons, 1874-1875.

Allen, W. C. *A Critical and Exegetical Commentary of the Gospel According to St. Matthew*. New York: Charles Scribner's Sons, 1907.

Allis, Oswald T. *Prophecy and the Church*. Philadelphia: The Presbyterian and Reformed Publishing Co., 1945.

————. "The Transcendence of Jehovah, God of Israel." Princeton Theological Seminary, *Biblical and Theological Studies*. Princeton: 1912.

Augustine, Saint. *De Doctrina Christiana*. Philip Schaff, ed., *A Select Library of the Nicene and Post-Nicene Fathers*. Vol. II. Buffalo: The Christian Literature Co., 1890.

Baab, Otto. *The Theology of the Old Testament*. Nashville, Tenn: Abingdon-Cokesbury Press, 1949.

Baillie, John. *The Idea of Revelation in Recent Thought*. New York: Columbia University Press, 1956.

Barth, Karl. *Dogmatics in Outline*. Trans. by G. T. Thompson. New York: Philosophical Library, 1949.

————. *The Doctrine of the Word of God*. Trans. by G. T. Thompson. New York: Charles Scribner's Sons, 1936.

Barton, George A. *Archaeology and the Bible*. Seventh Edition. Philadelphia: American Sunday School Union, 1937.

Berkhof, Louis. *Introductory Volume to Systematic Theology*. Grand Rapids: Wm. B. Eerdmans Publishing Co., 1932.

————. *Principles of Biblical Interpretation*. Grand Rapids: Wm. B. Eerdmans Publishing Co., 1950.

————. *Systematic Theology*. Grand Rapids: Wm. B. Eerdmans Publishing Co., 1941.

————. *Textual Aid to Systematic Theology*. Grand Rapids: Wm. B. Eerdmans Publishing Co., 1942.

Bernard, J. H. *A Critical and Exegetical Commentary on the Gospel According to St. John*. (*The International Critical Commentary.*) New York: Charles Scribner's Sons, 1929.

Briggs, Charles Augustus. *A Critical and Exegetical Commentary on the Book of Psalms* (*The International Critical Commentary*). Edinburgh: T. and T. Clark, 1907.

————. "The Higher Criticism," *Public Opinion 10*. (March 21, 1891), p. 576.

Brown, Driver, and Briggs. *A Hebrew and English Lexicon of the Old Testament*. Oxford: The Clarendon Press, 1939.

Bruce, F. F. *Biblical Exegesis in the Qumran Texts*. Grand Rapids: Wm. B. Eerdmans Publishing Co., 1959.

Brunner, Emil. *The Divine-Human Encounter*. Trans. by A. W. Loos. Philadelphia: The Westminster Press, 1943.

————. *Revelation and Reason*. Trans. by Olive Wyon. Philadelphia: The Westminster Press, 1946.

Burrows, Millar. *An Outline of Biblical Theology*. Philadelphia: The Westminster Press, 1946.

————. *More Light on the Dead Sea Scrolls*. New York: Viking Press, 1958.

————. *What Mean These Stones?* New Haven: American Schools of Oriental Research, 1941; copyright 1956 by Millar Burrows; Living Age Book Edition copyright 1957 by Meridian Books.

Calvin, John. *Commentary on the Book of the Prophet Jeremiah and the Lamentations*. Trans. by John Owen. Grand Rapids: Wm. B. Eerdmans Publishing Co., 1950.

————. *Commentaries on the Four Last Books of Moses Arranged in the Form of a Harmony*. Grand Rapids: Wm. B. Eerdmans Publishing Co., 1950.

————. *Institutes of the Christian Religion*. Trans. by John Allen. Seventh American Edition. Philadelphia: Presbyterian Board of Christian Education, n.d.

Chafer, Lewis. *Systematic Theology*. Dallas: Dallas Seminary Press, 1948.

Coppens, J. *The Old Testament and the Critics*. Trans. by Edward A. Ryan, Edward W. Tribbs. Patterson, New Jersey: St. Anthony Guild Press, 1942.

Davidson, A. B. *The Book of Job*. (*The Cambridge Bible for Schools and Colleges*). Cambridge: The University Press, 1908.

————. *Old Testament Prophecy*. Edinburgh: T. and T. Clark, 1904.

————. *The Theology of the Old Testament*. Edinburgh: T. and T. Clark, 1925.

Davidson, Francis (ed.). *The New Bible Commentary*. Grand Rapids: Wm. B. Eerdmans Publishing Co., 1953.

Delitzsch, Franz. *Biblical Commentary on the Book of Job*. Trans. by Francis Bolton. Edinburgh: T. and T. Clark, 1876.

————. *Commentary on the Epistle to the Hebrews*. Edinburgh: T. and T. Clark, 1871.

————. *Biblical Commentary on the Prophecies of Isaiah*. Trans. from the 3rd edition by James Denney. London: Hodder and Stoughton, 1892.

Dentan, Robert C. *Preface to Old Testament Theology*. New Haven: Yale University Press, 1950.

Dodd, C. H. *The Epistle of Paul to the Romans*. (*Moffatt Commentary.*) New York: R. Long & R. R. Smith, Inc. n.d.

Eichrodt, Walther. *Theology of the Old Testament*. Trans. by J. A. Baker. Philadelphia: Westminster Press, 1961.

Evans, William. *The Great Doctrines of the Bible*. Chicago: The Moody Press, 1939.

Fairbairn, Patrick. *The Typology of Scripture*. Grand Rapids: Zondervan Publishing House, 1952.

Fritsch, Charles T., *The Qumran Community: Its History and Scrolls*. New York: The Macmillan Co., 1956.

Gaussen, L. *Theopneustia, the Plenary Inspiration of the Holy Scriptures*. Chicago: The Bible Institute Colportage Assn., n.d.

Gehman, Henry S. (revisor). *The Westminster Dictionary of the Bible*. Philadelphia: The Westminster Press. 1944.

Gesenius-Buhl. *Hebräisches und aramäisches handwörterbuch über das Alte Testament*. Leipzig: C. W. Vogel, 1915.

537

Girdlestone, Robert. *Old Testament Theology and Modern Ideas*. London: Longmans, Green and Co., 1909.

Guy, H. A. *The New Testament Doctrine of the Last Things*. London: Oxford University Press, 1948.

Harris, R. Laird. *Inspiration and Canonicity of the Bible*. Grand Rapids: Zondervan Publishing House, 1957.

Hastings, James, ed. *A Dictionary of the Bible*. New York: Charles Scribner's Sons, 1927.

Heinisch, Paul. *Theology of the Old Testament*. Trans. by Wm. G. Heidt. Collegeville, Minnesota: The Order of St. Benedict, Inc., 1955.

Hengstenberg, E. W. *Christology of the Old Testament*. Trans. by Theodore Meyer and James Martin. Grand Rapids: Kregel Publications, 1956.

Henry, Carl F. H. *Contemporary Evangelical Thought*. Great Neck, New York: Channel Press, 1957.

Herodotus. *History*. London: J. M. Dent, 1949.

Hodge, Charles. *Commentary on the Epistle to the Romans*. Grand Rapids: Wm. B. Eerdmans Publishing Co., 1950.

Hopkins, Vincent D., ed. *The Catholic Encyclopedia*. New York: Robert Appleton Co., 1950.

Irenaeus. *Against Heresies*. Alexander Roberts and James Donaldson, eds., *The Ante-Nicene Fathers*. New York: The Christian Literature Co., 1896. Vol. I.

Jacob, Edmond. *The Theology of the Old Testament*. Trans. by A. W. Heathcote and Philip J. Allcock. New York: Harper and Brothers, 1958.

Jamieson, Fausset and Brown. *A Commentary, Critical, Experimental and Practical on the Old and New Testaments*. VI. Philadelphia: n.d.

Johnson, Aubrey. *The Cultic Prophet in Ancient Israel*. Cardiff, Wales: University of Wales, 1944.

Josephus, Flavius. *Antiquities. The Jewish War; in The Life and Works of Flavius Josephus*. Philadelphia: John C. Winston Co., 1936.

Kaufmann, Yehezkel. *Religion of Israel*. Trans. by Moshe Greenberg. Chicago: University of Chicago Press, 1960.

Keil, C. F., and Delitzsch, Franz. *Biblical Commentary on the Old Testament, the Twelve Minor Prophets*. Edinburgh: T. and T. Clark, 1889.

————. *Biblical Commentary on the Old Testament: The Prophecies of Jeremiah*. Trans. by James Kennedy. Edinburgh: T. and T. Clark, 1874.

————. *Biblical Commentary on the Old Testament: The Pentateuch*. Trans. by James Martin. Grand Rapids: Wm. B. Eerdmans Publishing Co., 1949.

Kirkpatrick, A. F. *The Book of Psalms*. (*The Cambridge Bible for Schools and Colleges*.) Cambridge: The University Press, 1914.

Knight, George A. F. *A Christian Theology of the Old Testament*. Richmond: John Knox Press, 1959.

Koehler, Ludwig. *Lexicon in Veteris Testamente Libros*. Leiden: E. J. Brill, 1953.

————. *Old Testament Theology*. Trans. by A. S. Todd. Philadelphia: The Westminster Press, 1957.

Kromminga, D. H. *The Millennium: Its Nature, Function, and Relation to the Consummation of the World*. Grand Rapids: Wm. B. Eerdmans Publishing Co., 1949.

Ladd, George E. *The Blessed Hope*. Grand Rapids: Wm. B. Eerdmans Publishing Co., 1956.

Laetsch, Theodore, *Bible Commentary, Jeremiah*. St. Louis: Concordia Publishing House, 1952.

Lanchester, H. C. O., *The Books of Nahum, Habakkuk, and Zephaniah*. (*The Cambridge Bible for Schools and Colleges*). Cambridge: The University Press, 1920.

Leupold, H. C. *Exposition of Genesis*. Columbus, Ohio: The Wartburg Press, 1942.

Liddell, Henry George and Scott, Robert. *A Greek-English Lexicon*. Eighth Edition. Oxford: The Clarendon Press, 1901.

MacRae, Allan. *The Millennial Kingdom of Christ*. Wilmington, Delaware: Faith Theological Seminary, n.d.

Mayor, J. B. *The General Epistle of Jude*. (*The Expositor's Greek Testament*, ed. W. Robertson Nicoll.) Grand Rapids: Wm. B. Eerdmans Publishing Co., n.d.

McKenzie, John L. *The Two-Edged Sword: An Interpretation of the Old Testament*. Milwaukee: Bruce Publishing Co., 1956.

Meek, Theophile J. *Hebrew Origins*. Revised Edition. New York: Harper & Brothers, 1950.

Mendenhall, George E. *Law and Covenant in Israel and the Ancient Near East*. Pittsburgh: Biblical Colloquium, 1955.

Moorehead, W. G. *Studies in the Mosaic Institutions*. New York: Fleming H. Revell, Co., c. 1895.

Morris, Leon. *The Apostolic Preaching of the Cross*. Grand Rapids: Wm. B. Eerdmans Publishing Co., 1955.

Mowinckel, Sigmund. *He That Cometh*. Trans. by G. W. Anderson. Nashville: Abingdon Press, 1956.

Murray, John. *Christian Baptism*. Philadelphia: The Presbyterian and Reformed Publishing Co., 1952.

————. *The Covenant of Grace*. London: Tyndale Press, 1953.

————. *Principles of Conduct*. Grand Rapids: Wm. B. Eerdmans Publishing Co., 1957.

————. *Redemption — Accomplished and Applied*. Grand Rapids: Wm. B. Eerdmans Publishing Co., 1955.

Nelson, Byron. *Before Abraham*. Minneapolis: Augsburg Publishing House, 1948.

Nicoll, W. Robertson. *The Expositor's Greek Testament*. Grand Rapids: Wm. B. Eerdmans Publishing Co., n.d.

Nygren, Anders. *Agape and Eros*. Trans. by Philip S. Watson. Philadelphia: The Westminster Press, 1953.

Oehler, Gustav F. *Theology of the Old Testament*. Grand Rapids: Zondervan Publishing House, n.d.

Oesterley, W. O. E., and Robinson, T. H. *Hebrew Religion: Its Origin and Development*. Second Edition. New York: The Macmillan Co., 1937.

Orr, James, ed. *International Standard Bible Encyclopedia*. Grand Rapids: Wm. B. Eerdmans Publishing Co., 1939.

————. *Revelation and Inspiration*. New York: Charles Scribner's Sons, 1910.

Patterson, Charles H. *The Philosophy of the Old Testament*. New York: The Ronald Press Co., 1953.

Patton, Francis. *The Inspiration of the Scriptures*. Philadelphia: Presbyterian Board of Publication, 1869.

Payne, J. B. *An Outline of Hebrew History*. Grand Rapids: Wm. B. Eerdmans Publishing Co., 1954.

Peake, A. S. *Hebrews*. (*The Century Bible*.) Edinburgh: T. C. and E. C. Jack, n.d.

Pedersen, Johannes. *Israel, Its Life and Culture*. Vol. I. translated by Mrs. Aslaug Moller; Vol. II translated by Annie I. Fausboll. London: Oxford University Press, 1926-1940.

Peters, George N. H. *The Theocratic Kingdom of Our Lord Jesus, the Christ.* Grand Rapids: Kregel Publications, 1948.

Pfeiffer, Charles F. *Introduction to the Old Testament.* New York: Harper and Brothers, 1941.

Piper, Otto. *God in History.* New York: The Macmillan Co., 1939.

Porteous, Norman W. "Old Testament Theology." *(The Old Testament and Modern Study,* ed. H. H. Rowley.) Oxford: Clarendon Press, 1951.

Pusey, E. B. *The Minor Prophets.* New York: Funk and Wagnalls, 1885.

Ramm, Bernard. *The Christian View of Science and Scripture.* Grand Rapids: Wm. B. Eerdmans Publishing Co., 1954.

————. *Protestant Biblical Interpretation.* Revised edition. Boston: W. A. Wilde Co., 1950.

Raven, John. *The History of the Religion of Israel.* New Brunswick: New Brunswick Theological Seminary, 1933.

Ringgren, Helmer. *The Messiah in the Old Testament.* (*Studies in Biblical Theology* No. 18). London: Student Christian Movement Press, 1956. U.S. distributor, Allenson, Naperville, Ill.

Robinson, H. Wheeler. *The Religious Ideas of the Old Testament.* London: Duckworth, 1944.

Rowley, H. H. *The Biblical Doctrine of Election.* London: Lutterworth Press, 1953. U.S. distributor, Allenson, Naperville, Ill.

————. *The Faith of Israel.* Philadelphia: The Westminster Press, 1956.

————. *The Re-discovery of the Old Testament.* Philadelphia: The Westminster Press, 1946.

————. *The Relevance of Apocalyptic.* Second edition. London: Lutterworth Press, 1952.

————. *The Old Testament and Modern Study.* Oxford: Clarendon Press, 1951.

————. *The Unity of the Bible.* Philadelphia: Westminster Press, 1953.

Ryrie, Charles C. *The Basis of Premillennial Faith.* New York: Loizeaux Brothers, 1953.

Sanday, William. *Inspiration.* London: Longman, Green, & Co., 1893.

Sanday, William and Headlam, Arthur C. *A Critical and Exegetical Commentary on the Epistle to the Romans.* (*The International Critical Commentary*). New York: Charles Scribner's Sons, 1911.

Sauer, Erich. *The Dawn of World Redemption.* Trans. by C. H. Lang. Grand Rapids: Wm. B. Eerdmans Publishing Co., 1952.

Schultz, Hermann. *Old Testament Theology.* Second edition. Trans. by J. A. Paterson. Edinburgh: T. and T. Clark, 1898.

Scofield, C. I., (ed.). *The Holy Bible.* New York: Oxford University Press, 1917.

Shedd, Russel P. *Man in Community.* London: The Epworth Press, 1958.

Smith, Wilbur. *Therefore Stand.* Boston: W. A. Wilde Co., 1945.

Snaith, Norman H. *The Distinctive Ideas of the Old Testament.* Philadelphia: The Westminster Press, 1946.

————. *Mercy and Sacrifice: a Study of the Book of Hosea.* London: Student Christian Movement Press, 1953. U.S. Distributor, Allenson, Naperville, Ill.

Spier, J. M. *Christianity and Existentialism.* Trans. by David H. Freeman, Philadelphia: Presbyterian & Reformed Publishing Co., 1953.

Sutcliffe, Edmund F. *The Old Testament and the Future Life.* Second edition. Westmin-

ster, Maryland: The Newman Bookshop, 1947.

Terry, Milton S., *Biblical Hermeneutics.* Revised edition. New York: Phillips and Hunt, 1890.

Thayer, Joseph H. *A Greek-English Lexicon of the New Testament.* Corrected edition. New York: American Book Company, 1889.

Thomson, J. G. S. S. *The Old Testament View of Revelation.* Grand Rapids: Wm. B. Eerdmans Publishing Co., 1960.

Tregelles, S. P. *Remarks on the Prophetic Visions in the Book of Daniel.* London: Bagsters, 1864.

Unger, Merrill F. *Biblical Demonology.* Wheaton, Ill.: Van Kampen Press, 1952.

Ungersma, Aaron. *Handbook for Christian Believers.* Indianapolis: The Bobbs-Merrill Co., 1953.

Urquhart, John. *The Bible: Its Structure and Purpose.* New York: Gospel Publishing House, 1904.

Van Til, Cornelius. *The New Modernism.* Philadelphia: The Presbyterian and Reformed Publishing Co., 1946.

Vischer, Wilhelm. *The Witness of the Old Testament to Christ.* Trans. by A. B. Crabtree, London: Lutterworth Press, 1949.

Vos, Geerhardus. *Biblical Theology.* Grand Rapids: William B. Eerdmans Publishing Co., 1948.

————. "The Eschatological Aspect of the Pauline Conception of the Spirit." Princeton Theological Seminary, *Biblical and Theological Studies.* New York: Charles Scribner's Sons, 1912.

Vriezen, T. C. *An Outline of Old Testament Theology.* Trans. by S. Neuijen. Newton, Mass. Charles T. Branford Co., 1958.

Warfield, B. B. *Biblical and Theological Studies.* Philadelphia: The Presbyterian and Reformed Publishing Co., 1952.

————. *Biblical Doctrines.* New York: Oxford University Press, 1929.

————. *The Inspiration and Authority of the Bible.* Philadelphia: The Presbyterian and Reformed Publishing Co., 1948.

————. *The Plan of Salvation.* Grand Rapids: Wm. B. Eerdmans Publishing Co., 1942.

Westcott, Brooke Foss. *The Epistle to the Hebrews.* London: Macmillan and Co., 1889.

Willoughby, Harold R., ed. *The Study of the Bible Today and Tomorrow.* Chicago: University of Chicago Press, 1947.

Wright, G. Ernest. *The Old Testament Against Its Environment.* Chicago: H. Regnery Co., 1951.

————. *The Rule of God.* Garden City, New York: Doubleday, 1960.

Young, Edward J. *An Introduction to the Old Testament.* Grand Rapids: William B. Eerdmans Co., 1949.

————. *My Servants the Prophets.* Grand Rapids: Wm. B. Eerdmans Co., 1952.

————. *The Prophecy of Daniel, a Commentary.* Grand Rapids: Wm. B. Eerdmans Publishing Co., 1949.

————. *Studies in Isaiah.* Grand Rapids: Wm. B. Eerdmans Publishing Co., 1954.

————. *The Study of Old Testament Theology Today.* London: J. Clarke, 1958.

————. *Thy Word Is Truth.* Grand Rapids: Wm. B. Eerdmans Publishing Co., 1957.

MAGAZINE ARTICLES

Albright, William F. "What Were the Cherubim?" *The Biblical Archaeologist*, I, (February, 1938), 2.

Beegle, Dewey M. "Virgin or Young Woman?" *Asbury Seminarian*, VII (Fall-Winter, 1954), 34.

Clark, Gordon. "Can Moral Education Be Grounded on Naturalism?" *Bulletin of the Evangelical Theological Society*, I (Fall, 1958), 21-23.

Davis, John D. "The Future Life in Hebrew Thought During the Pre-Persian Period," *The Princeton Theological Review*, VI (April, 1908), 262, 267-268.

Freedman, David N. "The Name of the God of Moses," *Journal of Biblical Literature*, LXXIX (June, 1960), 151-156.

Fritsch, Charles T. "New Trends in Old Testament Theology," *Bibliotheca Sacra*, CIII (July-September, 1946), 294.

Huffman, Herbert F. "The Covenant Lawsuit in the Prophets," *Journal of Biblical Literature*, LXXVIII, 286-295.

Kline, Meredith. "Dynastic Covenant," *The Westminster Theological Journal*, XXIII (1960), 13, 15.

_____, "Two Tables of the Covenant," *The Westminster Theological Journal*, XXII (1960), 143-144.

MacRae, Allen. "The Principles of Interpreting Genesis 1 and 2," *Bulletin of the Evangelical Theological Society*, II (Fall, 1959), 1-2.

_____, "The Scientific Approach to the Old Testament," *Bibliotheca Sacra*, CX (October 1953), 313-316.

Mendenhall, George E. "Covenant Forms in Israelite Tradition," *Biblical Archaeologist*, XVII (1954), 60, 64-65.

Pfeiffer, Charles F. "Figures of Speech in Human Language," *Bulletin of the Evangelical Theological Society*, II (Fall, 1959), 20.

Speiser, E. A. " 'People' and 'Nation' of Israel," *Journal of Biblical Literature*, LXXIX (June, 1960).

Vos, Geerhardus. "Reviews of Recent Literature," *Princeton Theological Review*, IV (January 1906), 115-120.

Walvoord, John F. "A Review of 'Crucial Questions About the Kingdom of God,' " *Bibliotheca Sacra*, CX (January, 1953), 3.

Wilson, Robert Dick. "The Meaning of 'Alma' (A. V. 'Virgin') in Isaiah vii. 14," *Princeton Theological Review*, XXIV (April, 1926), 316.

_____, "Critical Note on Exodus vi. 3," *Princeton Theological Review*, XXII (January, 1924), 108.

Young, G. Douglas. "Old Testament Theology — a Method and a Conclusion," *Evangelical Theological Society*, *1955 Papers*, 80.

_____, "The Effects of Poetic and Literary Style on Interpretation of the Early Chapters of Genesis," *Bulletin of the Evangelical Theological Society*, II (Fall, 1959), 15-16.

READING BIBLIOGRAPHY

The following represents a bibliography in English on the general subject of Old Testament theology. For studies on particular subjects, see the collateral reading, the footnote citations, and the suggestions for further reading under the topics concerned.

Alexander, W. Lindsay, *System of Biblical Theology*. Edinburgh: 1888. A survey of both Old and New Testaments, but more systematics than Biblical theology.

Auberlen, Carl August, *Divine Revelation*. English translation by Rev. A. B. Paton; Edinburgh: T. & T. Clark, 1867. A survey of revelation in the Old Testament as well as in the New Testament, with a conservative apologetic.

Baab, Otto, *The Theology of the Old Testament*. New York: Abingdon-Cokesbury Press, c. 1949. The most complete example of American Neo-orthodoxy. Recognizes the deficiencies of historicism but clings to its negative Biblical criticism and so fails to provide much improvement.

Bennett, W. H., *The Theology of the Old Testament*. London: Hodder & Stoughton, 1896. A handbook which, although it lists the evangelical approach to the Old Testament books, ends by making broad concessions to destructive liberal criticism.

Burney, C. F., *Outlines of Old Testament Theology*. New York: Gorham, 1904. Brief, compact. Accepts the results of liberal criticism.

Burrows, Millar, *An Outline of Biblical Theology*. Philadelphia: Westminster, c. 1946. Sketchy, and includes the New Testament. A significant survey by left-wing American Neo-orthodoxy.

Davidson, A. B., *The Theology of the Old Testament*. Edinburgh: T. & T. Clark, 1925.

A post-humous collection of the author's manuscripts by S. D. F. Salmond. Of necessity, incomplete, and not thoroughly organized, but still the best Old Testament theology of England. Davidson capitulated to negative higher criticism, but he did not have time to integrate it into much of his theology.

Dentan, Robert C., *Preface to Old Testament Theology*. Yale Studies in Religion, Number XIV. New Haven: Yale University Press, 1950. A thesis condensation, defining Biblical theology according to Neo-orthodoxy, and tracing the history of Old Testament theology as a discipline.

Duff, Archibald, *Old Testament Theology*. London: 1891. A liberal history of the religion of Israel from 800 B. C. and hardly a theology.

Eichrodt, Walther, *Theology of the Old Testament, Volume I*. Trans. by J. A. Baker, Philadelphia: Westminster Press, 1961. The most important product of German neo-orthodoxy, now partially available in English. Stresses the centrality of the covenant as the organizing principle for Biblical theology, but still concedes too much Old Testament material to the influence of ancient pagan religion.

Ewald, Heinrich, *Old and New Testament Theology*. Translated by T. Goadby; Edinburgh: T. & T. Clark, 1888. A liberal philosophical and even mystical study, rather than an actual theology.

Fosdick, Harry Emerson, *A Guide to the Understanding of the Bible: the development of ideas within the Old and New Testaments.* New York: Harper & Brothers, 1938. A popular treatment of the religion of Israel evolutionarily conceived; dismissed by Eichrodt as already outmoded by the Neo-orthodox reaction.

Foster, Robert V., *Old Testament Studies, an Outline of Old Testament Theology.* New York: Fleming H. Revell, 1890. The first American theology of the Old Testament, and of somewhat inferior style and appearance. Brief, but valid Biblical theology, and thoroughly evangelical.

Fox, Arthur W., *The Ethics and Theology of the Old Testament.* London: Strand, 1918. Brief "notes" organized in seven chronological periods and designed to popularize pre-World War I liberal conclusions.

Girdlestone, R. B., *Old Testament Theology and Modern Ideas.* London: Longmans, Green and Co., 1909. A brief but comprehensive evangelical survey. A historical outline followed by discussion of basic doctrines.

Hanke, Howard A., *Christ and the Church in the Old Testament.* Grand Rapids: Zondervan Publishing House, 1957. An evangelical, non-dispensational study of redemption.

————————, *From Eden to Eternity.* Grand Rapids: Eerdmans Publishing Co., 1959. Stresses the unity of Christology and ecclesiology in the Old and New Testaments.

Heinisch, Paul, *Theology of the Old Testament.* Translated by William G. Heidt; Collegeville, Minn.: The Order of St. Benedict, c 1955. Roman Catholic, so includes apocrypha references along with Old Testament. A few concessions to negative higher criticism. Along with Oehler, perhaps the best all round complete Old Testament theology.

Hengstenberg, E. W., *History of the Kingdom of God under the Old Testament.* Trans. by Theodore Meyer and James Martin. Grand Rapids: Kregel Publications, 1956. 2 vols. A survey of the history of Israel from a thoroughly conservative point of view.

Jacob, Edmond, *Theology of the Old Testament.* Translated by A. W. Heathcote and P. J. Allcock. New York: Harper & Brothers, 1958. A French Protestant study, and the most recent example of continental Neo-orthodoxy. The Old Testament, when "brought to perfection," has a Christological theology; but as it stands much is yet false.

Kaufmann, Yehezkel, *Religion of Israel.* Translated by Moshe Greenberg; Chicago: Univ. of Chicago Press, 1960. The latest and most challenging, product of Israeli study, in the critical tradition.

Knight, George A. F., *A Christian Theology of the Old Testament.* Richmond, Va.: John Knox Press, 1959. The most recent example of English speaking Neo-orthodoxy, seeking Christian elements in the Old Testament but still rejecting Christ's own view as to its total inspiration and authority.

Knudson, Albert C., *The Religious Teaching of the Old Testament.* New York: The Abingdon Press, 1918. A 20th Century liberal history of religion that rarely attains to true theology.

Koehler, Ludwig, *Old Testament Theology.* Translated by A. S. Todd. Philadelphia: Westminster, 1957. The first translation into English of one of the chief studies that marked the Neo-orthodox revival of Biblical theology in Germany. God's lordship is chosen as the dominant theme of the Old Testament.

Kurtz, J. H., *History of the Old Covenant.* Translated, Vol. I., by Alfred Edersheim; Vols. II-III, by James Martin; Philadelphia: Lindsay & Blakeston, 1859. A thorough,

conservative study of Old Testament history, through the Pentateuch.

Meek, Theophile J., *Hebrew Origins.* Revised edition; New York: Harper & Brothers, 1950. The most up to date, and at the same time one of the most blasphemous, evolutionary antisupernaturalistic reconstructions of the religion of Israel.

Oehler, Gustav F., *Theology of the Old Testament.* Translated by George E. Day. Grand Rapids: Zondervan Publishing House, n.d. Old, and yet still perhaps, along with Heinisch, the best all round complete Old Testament theology. Generally evangelical with but occasional lapses into rationalism or non-normative history of religion.

Oesterley, W. O. E., and T. H. Robinson, *Hebrew Religion: Its Origin and Development.* New York: The Macmillan Co., 1937. Perhaps the most thorough modern English treatment of the history of the religion of Israel, as reconstructed by evolutionary presuppositions.

Patterson, Charles H., *The Philosophy of the Old Testament.* New York: The Ronald Press, c. 1953. A well-written work by a radical philosopher, who stepped outside his field. It was outmoded before its publication, a monument to a dead historicism.

Payne, J. Barton, *An Outline of Hebrew History.* Grand Rapids: Eerdmans Publishing Co., 1954. A survey of the doctrine of the testament, as it developed in Biblical and Near Eastern history.

Pederson, Johannes, *Israel, Its Life and Culture.* Vol. 1 translated by Mrs. Aslaug Moller, vol. 2, by Annie I. Fausboll; London: Oxford University Press, 1926-1940. The leading example of Scandinavian Neo-orthodoxy, stressing the sociological factors of ancient Israel and the cultic origin of much of the Old Testament.

Pfeiffer, Robert H., *Religion in the Old Testament.* Ed. by Chas. C. Forman; New York: Harper & Bros., 1961. Post-humous. Radically evolutionary and outdated. Good footnotes.

Piepenbring, Chas., *Theology of the Old Testament.* Translated by H. G. Mitchell. New York: Thomas Y. Crowell, c. 1893. An example of French liberalism attempting to save a degree of theological significance in the Old Testament.

Raven, John Howard, *The History of the Religion of Israel.* New Brunswick, N.J.: New Brunswick Theological Seminary, 1933. A true theology of the Old Testament, starting with God's revelation to Adam. Incomplete, terminating with the reign of Manasseh, where Raven placed Job.

Robinson, H. Wheeler, *The Religious Ideas of the Old Testament.* London: Duckworth, 1913. As indicated by the title, a liberal work, only little better than most such histories of Israel's religion.

Rowley, H. H., *The Faith of Israel.* Philadelphia: Westminster, 1956. An incomplete survey of Old Testament theology by the outstanding representative of Neo-orthodoxy in English Biblical study. Excellent coverage of the recent bibliography in copious footnotes.

————————, *The Relevance of the Bible.* London: 1941. The first work of the Neo-orthodox revival of Biblical theology in England.

Sauer, Erich, *The Dawn of World Redemption.* Translated by G. H. Lang; Grand Rapids: Eerdmans Publishing Co., 1952. An outline of the plan of redemption, and particularly of the doctrine of the Messiah, in the Old Testament. Mildly dispensational.

————————, *From Eternity to Eternity.* Translated by G. H. Lang. Grand Rapids: Eerdmans Publishing Co., 1954. An outline of God's overall purpose in history.

Schultz, Hermann, *Old Testament Theology.* 2nd English edition; translated by J. A. Paterson; Edinburgh: T. & T. Clark, 1898. 2 vols, the first being a chronological treatment of Old Testament theology; the 2nd, a topical. A thorough work, basically true Biblical theology, though with lapses into simply descriptive history of religion.

Vos, Geerhardus, *Biblical Theology.* Grand Rapids: Eerdmans Publishing Co., 1948. The best single study of Old Testament theology: scholarly and thoroughly evangelical. Suffers from its date, having been composed before the flood of Neo-orthodox Biblical theology, and from its incompleteness. Includes some of the first part of New Testament theology.

Vriezen, T. C., *An Outline of Old Testament Theology.* English translation by S. Neuijen; Newton, Mass.: Chas. T. Branford Co., 1958. The translation of a neo-orthodox study from Holland. Stress is laid upon the Christian approach, but much of the Old Testament is dismissed as sub-Christian.

Watts, J. Washington, *A Survey of Old Testament Teaching.* Nashville, Tenn.: Broadman Press, c. 1947. 2 vols. A conservative, Southern Baptist book-by-book treatment of the Old Testament. Written largely in outline form.

Wright, G. Ernest, *The Challenge of Israel's Faith.* Chicago: University of Chicago Press, 1944. The first work of the neo-orthodox revival of Biblical Theology in America.

—————————, "The Faith of Israel," G. A. Buttrick, ed., *The Interpreter's Bible.* Nashville, Tenn.: Abingdon-Cokesbury, 1952. I:349-389. A concentrated summary of the neo-orthodoxy understanding of Biblical faith, much of the O.T. being rejected as sub-standard.

—————————, *God Who Acts. Studies in Biblical Theology, No. 8.* Chicago: H. Regnery, 1952. A brief neo-orthodox interpretation of modern Heilsgeschichte, both Old Testament and New Testament.

—————————, *The Old Testament Against its Environment.* Chicago: H. Regnery Co., 1951. Studies in Biblical Theology, No. 2. A brief, neo-orthodox treatment of distinctives in the theology of Israel

—————————, *The Rule of God.* Garden City, N.Y.: Doubleday, 1960. A series of popular essays on God, man, and salvation in the O.T. Somewhat polemical, but good insights.

————————— and Reginald H. Fuller, *The Book of the Acts of God.* Garden City, New York: Doubleday, 1957. The Old Testament section, by Wright, combines introduction and Neo-orthodox Heilsgeschichte in a popularizing form.

Young, Edward J., *The Study of Old Testament Theology Today.* London: J. Clarke, 1958. An evangelical analysis of the nature of the discipline, its recent resurgence, and the inadequacy of its neo-orthodox formulations.

INDEX OF SUBJECTS

INDEX OF WRITERS AND PUBLICATIONS

553